A Bibliography of Joseph Conrad

Compiled by

Theodore G. Ehrsam, Ph. D.

Professor of English
New York University

The Scarecrow Press, Inc.

Metuchen, N. J.   1969

Table of Contents

Preface

This bibliography of Joseph Conrad has been compiled from a multitude of sources. It includes bibliographical, biographical, and critical articles, pamphlets, essays, and books in English and in other languages employing the Latin alphabet.

For each entry I have supplied full information: for books and pamphlets I have given place of publication, publisher, and date of publication, the number of pages, and the reviews of the item; for articles in periodicals I have cited the volume and the number of the periodical, precise and inclusive pagination, month, day, and year. The exact title is listed for all items.

I am grateful to the many libraries and librarians who helped me while I was gathering and checking these materials: in particular to the Harvard University Library and to Yale University Library, as well as to the Library of Congress, the library of Princeton University, and the New York Public Library. I owe special thanks to Mr. William R. Cagle of the Lilly Library, Indiana University.

In the final stages my research was aided by two grants from the Graduate School of Arts and Sciences, New York University. Throughout, I have been immeasurably assisted by the cheerful and resourceful labors of my wife, Wanda, without whose help this book would not have been completed.

May 15, 1968   Theodore G. Ehrsam

New York University

A

Joseph Conrad: A Chronology

1857 Born, December 3rd

1895 Almayer's Folly (London: Unwin, April 29; NY: Macmillan, c. May 3)

1896 An Outcast of the Islands (London: Unwin, March 4; NY: Appleton, c. Aug. 15)

1897 The Children of the Sea (NY: Dodd, Mead, November 30)

1897 The Nigger of the "Narcissus" (London: Heinemann, Dec. 2, but dated "1898")

1898 Tales of Unrest (NY: Scribner's, March 26; London: Unwin, April 4)

1900 Lord Jim (Edinburgh: Blackwood, October 9; NY: Doubleday, October 31)

1901 The Inheritors (NY: McClure, Phillips, c. June 8; London: Heinemann, June 26)

1902 Typhoon (NY: Putnam's, September 4)

1902 Youth: A Narrative and Two Other Stories (Edinburgh: Blackwood, November 13)

1903 Youth, and Two Other Stories (NY: McClure, Phillips, c. February 8)

1903 Typhoon, and Other Stories (London: Heinemann, c. April 22)

1903 Falk, Amy Foster, To-Morrow (NY: McClure, Phillips, c. September 25)

1903 Romance (London: Smith, Elder, c. October 21)

1904 Romance (NY: McClure, Phillips, March)

1904 Nostromo (London: Harper, October 14; NY: Harper, November 23)

1906 The Mirror of the Sea (London: Methuen, October 4; New York: Harper, October 4)

1907 The Secret Agent (London: Methuen, September 12; NY: Harper, September 12)

1908 Some Reminiscences (Serially in England, December, 1908 to June, 1909)

1908 A Set of Six (London: Methuen, August 6)

1908 The Point of Honor (NY: McClure, Phillips, c. October 2)

1911 Under Western Eyes (London: Methuen, October 5; NY: Harper, October 19)

1912 Some Reminiscences (London: Nash, c. January 23)
1912 A Personal Record (NY: Harper, January 19)
1912 'Twixt Land and Sea: Tales (London: Dent, October 14; NY: G. H. Doran, Dec. 3)
1914 Chance (London: Methuen, January 15; New York: Doubleday, Page, c. Jan. 30)
1915 A Set of Six (NY: Doubleday, Page, January 15)
1915 Victory (NY: Doubleday, Page, c. March 27; London: Methuen, September 24)
1915 Within the Tides (London: Dent, February 24)
1915 Wisdom and Beauty from Conrad (London: Melrose, c. December 20)
1916 Within the Tides (NY: Doubleday, Page, January 15)
1917 The Shadow-Line (London: Dent, March 19; NY: Doubleday, Page, April 27)
1919 The Arrow of Gold (NY: Doubleday, Page, April 12; London: Unwin, August 6)
1920 The Rescue (NY: Doubleday, Page, May 21; London: Dent, June 24)
1921 Notes on My Books (NY: Doubleday, Page, March 4; London: Heinemann, May 19)
1921 Notes on Life and Letters (London: Dent, March 25; NY: Doubleday, Page, Apr. 22)
1923 Conrad arrived in New York City (May 1st)
1923 Conrad left New York City (June 2nd)
1923 The Rover (NY: Doubleday, Page, December 1; London: Unwin, December 3)
1924 Died, August 3rd, at 8:30 a. m.
1924 Buried, August 7th, in Canterbury Cemetery, Canterbury, England
1924 The Nature of A Crime (London: Duckworth, Sept. 26; NY: Doubleday, Page, Sept. 26)
1924 Laughing Anne, and One Day More (London: Castle, c. October 21)
1924 Shorter Tales of Conrad (NY: Doubleday, Page, October 30)
1925 Tales of Hearsay (London: Unwin, Jan. 23; NY: Doubleday, Page, Jan. 23)
1925 Laughing Anne, and One Day More (NY: Doubleday, Page, May 8)
1925 Suspense (unfinished novel) (NY: Doubleday, Page, Sept. 15; London: Dent, Sept. 16)
1926 Last Essays (London: Dent, March 3; NY: Doubleday, Page, March 26)

Biographical and Critical Material

A. , C. E. [Conrad Aiken ?]
   Nostr'Omo. New Republic 39:391 Ag 27 '24   1
Abbott, Lawrence F.
   Joseph Conrad. Outlook (NY) 134:14-15 My 23 '23   2
Abbott, William M.
   Victory. Chapter notes and criticism. New York: Ameri-
      can RDM Corporation [c1965] p23-72   3
Adams, Elbridge Lapham
   In memory of Joseph Conrad. Nation (NY) 122:725 Je 30
      '26
   Joseph Conrad memorial. New York Herald Tribune Ap
      22 '26 p16
   Joseph Conrad - the man. Outlook (NY) 133:708-12 Ap 18
      '23; same. published separately: Joseph Conrad: the
      man. A burial in Kent, by John Sheridan Zelie, togeth-
      er with some bibliographical notes. New York: Rudge,
      1925. 3-72 p; portrait (485 copies, 450 for sale)
      (Adams' article is on pages 3-38; Zelie's is on pages
      41-52. "Bibliographical notes," p55-72)
      (Reviewed in Saturday Review of Literature (NY) 2:89
      Ag 29 '25; Bookman (NY) 62:350-1 N '25; New York
      Times Book Review Ag 9 '25 p13; Wiadomości Liter-
      ackie 2, no 50:2 D 13 '25)   4
Adams, J. Donald
   Introduction. In Lord Jim, by Joseph Conrad. New York:
      Modern Library [c1931] pv-vii
   Speaking of books. New York Times Book Review F 8 '48
      p2 (Thinks Conrad's reputation is once more on the
      rise. Refers to the Preface of The Nigger of the "Nar-
      cissus")
   Speaking of books. New York Times Jl 14 '63 Section VII
      p2 (Asks for a revival of interest in Conrad)   5
Adams, Richard P.
   The apprenticeship of William Faulkner. Tulane Studies in
      English 12:113-56 '62
      (Suggests influence of Conrad on Faulkner)   6
Adams, Robert M.
   Views of Conrad. Partisan Review 27, no 1:124-30 Ja-F
      '61   7

Airy, Osmund
    Mr. Conrad: a coincidence.   Athenaeum My 29 '15 p485
                                                8
Alden, William L.
    London literary letter. New York Times Saturday Review
        of Books & Art F 11 '99 p96; My 6 '99 p304
        (Conrad has "arrived." His novels have given him "a
        place among the most original writers of the day.")
    London literary letter. New York Times Saturday Review
        of Books & Art Ap 11 '03 p249
    Mr. Alden's views. New York Times Saturday Review of
        Books F 13 '04 p109
        (A note on T. P. O'Connor's sketch of Conrad's life) 9
Aldington, Richard
    Conrad and Hardy. Literary Review of the New York Eve-
        ning Post 5:8 S 6 '24; same. Literary Review of the
        Public Ledger (Philadelphia) S 7 '24 p8   10
Allen, Carleton Kemp
    Joseph Conrad. Contemporary Review 125:54-61 Ja '24
        (Calls Conrad's attitude stoic)   11
Allen, Jerry
    Afterword. In Great short works of Conrad. New York:
        Harper & Row [c1966] p369-75   12
    Conrad's river. Columbia University Forum 5, no. 1:29-
        35 Winter '62
    Joseph Conrad - boatman. Popular Boating (NY) 7, no
        3:137-41 Mr '60
    Lord Jim's line. Times Literary Supplement N 10 '66
        p1032; D 8 '66 p1149; D 15 '66 p1175
    The sea years of Joseph Conrad. Garden City, New York:
        Doubleday and Co. , Inc. , 1965. [vii]-xvi, 368p; bibli-
        ography, p[348]-360 (End paper maps of the voyages of
        Joseph Conrad in the Eastern seas, 1883-8)
        Also published in England: London: Methuen, 1967.
        366 p
        (Reviewed by Ian Watt in Virginia Quarterly Review 42:
        644-9 Autumn '66; Times Literary Supplement Je 15 '67
        p544; Times Literary Supplement N 3 '66 p1-2; Phoebe
        Adams in Atlantic Monthly 216:174 O'65; C. W. Mann,
        Jr. in Library Journal 90: 4762 N 1 '65; Library Jour-
        nal 90:5536 D 15'65)
    The thunder and the sunshine: a biography of Joseph Con-
        rad. New York: G. P. Putnam's sons [1958] [7]-256p;
        bibliography and acknowledgements, p241-8
        (Dated 1958 unless otherwise noted: Reviewed by De
        Lancey Ferguson in New York Times Book Review My
        4; M. D. Zabel in New York Herald Tribune Books Ag

Allen, Jerry (cont.)
   17, pl, 9; Phoebe Adams in Atlantic Monthly 202:86 Jl;
   Elektor in Zycie Literackie no 7:11 '59; Witold Ostrowski in Kieranki no 3:3 '59; Edward Wagenknecht in Chicago Sunday Tribune My 8 p4; Charles W. Mann, Jr.
   in Library Journal 83:2163-4 Ag; Ian Watt in Nineteenth-Century Fiction 13:258-9 D; Leonard Wibberley
   in Saturday Review (NY) 41:31-2 Ag 16; Marvin Mud-
   rick in Virginia Quarterly Review 34:630-3 Autumn) 12
Allen, Robert Trawick
   Alchemy and experience: the concept of alter ego in
   "Heart of Darkness" and Moby Dick. M. A. thesis,
   Cornell University, September, 1966. ii, 34f   12a
Allen, Vio
   Memories of Joseph Conrad. Review of English Literature
   8:77-90 Ap '67   13
Allen, Walter Ernest
   The English novel... New York: Dutton, 1954. p290-300
   Joseph Conrad. In Six great novelists. London: H. Ham-
   ilton, 1955. p154-82   14
Allott, Miriam
   Novelists on the novel. New York: Columbia university
   press, 1959. p28-31, 38-40, 117-18, 194-6   15
Altick, Richard Daniel
   The search for Sambir. In The scholar adventurers.
   New York: Macmillan, 1951. p289-97   16
Ames, Van Meter
   Aesthetics of the novel. Chicago: University of Chicago
   press [c1928] p179-81, 183-4   17
Anchorite [pseud.]
   Obituary. Joseph Conrad. Nautical Magazine 112:249-51
   S '24   18
Anderson, Gerald
   Symbolism in six works of Joseph Conrad. M. A. thesis,
   North Texas State College, 1950. 97p; abstract in North
   Texas State College, Graduate School Bulletin no 226:
   230-1 Je '51   19
Anderson, Johannes C.
   Jubilee history of South Canterbury. Christchurch (New
   Zealand) 1916   20
Anderson, Quentin
   Introduction. In Lord Jim, by Joseph Conrad. New York:
   Washington Square Press [1963] pvii-xiv   21
Andreach, Robert J.
   The two narrators of "Amy Foster." Studies in Short Fic-
   tion 2:262-9 Spring '65   22

12 A Bibliography of Joseph Conrad

Andreas, Osborn Stolz
Joseph Conrad: a study in non-conformity. New York:
Philosophical Library [1959]; [London:] Vision [1962,
c1959] 212p
(Reviewed by Robert D. Spector in Modern Language
Quarterly 21:275-6 S '60; Carl H. Ketcham in Arizona
Quarterly 16:192 Summer '60; Arthur Lerner in Books
Abroad 35:184 '61; Frederick L. Gwynn in College
English 21:235 Ja '60; Kellogg W. Hunt in English
Journal 48:556-7 D '59; Zdzisław Najder in Journal of
Aesthetics & Art Criticism 18:534-5 Je '60; William
Blackburn in South Atlantic Quarterly 59:122-3 Winter
'60; W. F. Wright in Nineteenth-Century Fiction 14:
278-80 D '59)   23
Andrews, Clarence A.
Introduction. In Heart of Darkness and The End of the
Tether, by Joseph Conrad. New York: Airmont Pub-
lishing Co., Inc. [c1966] p3-12   24
Andrzejewski, Jerzy
Trzykrotnie nad "Lordem Jimem." Twórczość 12, no 2:
147-59 F '56; same. In Joseph Conrad Korzeniowski,
by Róża Jabłkowska. Warsaw: Państwowe Zakłady
Wydawnictwo Szkolynch, 1964. p331-42   25
Anegdoty o Conradzie. Wiadomości (London) 4, nos 176-7:
5 Ag 21 '49   26
Anglin, Norman
Conrad: from life to literature. Manchester Quarterly
39:60-75 Ja '20; same. In Papers of the Manchester
Literary Club 46:60-75 '20   27
Another Conrad memento. Lookout (NY) Je '46 p 14
(A plaster cast of the figurehead of Joseph Conrad which
Bruce Rogers carved to adorn the bow of the ship,
Joseph Conrad)   27a
Anthony, Irvin
The illusion of Joseph Conrad. Bookman (NY) 74:648-53
Mr '32   28
The appreciation of Conrad. Manchester Guardian Ag 5
'24 p6   29
Arcangeli, Francesco
Per un racconto di Conrad. Paragone 1, No 4:[3]-12
Ap '50   30
Armitage, C. M.
The location of Lord Jim's Patusan. Notes & Queries
211:409-10 N '66 (In Northwest Sumatra)   31
Armstrong, Martin
Joseph Conrad. Bookman (London) 65:237-9 F '24; same.
Living Age 320:512-16 Mr 15 '24   32

Arnold, Fred
  Where Conrad held court. Telegraph (London) Ja 8 '58
    (In the Fleur-de-Lys Inn, Canterbury)   33
Aronsberg, E.
  Joseph Conrad. Literary Review Ag 16 '24 p974
    (On Under Western Eyes)   34
Ashton-Gwatkin, W. H. T.
  A Conrad memorial. Times Literary Supplement Mr 11
    '26 p182   35
Askins, Donald H.
  Isolation and solidarity in Conrad's works. M. A. Thesis,
    University of Virginia, 1962. 42f   36
Assmann, P. W.
  Joseph Conrad. Boekenschouw (Amsterdam) 21:211-
    18 '27   37
Atkinson, Brooks
  Books that hold the harsh salt of the sea. New York
    Times Book Review S 13 '42 p2   38
Atkinson, Mildred
  Conrad's Suspense. Times Literary Supplement F 25 '26
    p142; same. Saturday Review of Literature (NY) 2:
    666 Mr 27 '26
  (Asserts similarity between Suspense and Memoirs of the
    Countess de Boigne)   39
Atteridge, A. Hilliard
  Conrad the Catholic. Catholic Mind 23, no 4:78-80 F
    22 '25; same. Columbia '25   40
Attorp, Gösta
  Conrad across the Baltic. Everyman ns 1, no 2:25-6
    N '53
  (Noted in Wiadomości 9, no 29:6 Jl 18 '54 as "Conrad's
    last journey")   41
Aubry, Georges Jean-
  Conrad à Marseille. Les Nouvelles Littéraires 7, no
    311:7 S 29 '28
  C'etait à Borneo. Le Jour Ap 11 '37
  Un héros polonais de Conrad: "Le Prince Roman."
    Maestricht: A. A. M. Stols [1933] Translation, p7-[36];
    commentaries, p39-58; bibliographical note, p59; por-
    trait (415 copies only)
  The inner history of Conrad's Suspense. Bookman's
    Journal 13, no 49:3-10 O '25
  (Includes notes and extracts from letters)
  Introduction. In Falk... translated and with an introduc-
    tion by Georges Jean-Aubry. Paris: Gallimard
    [1934] p[9]-15
  Introduction. In Twenty letters to Joseph Conrad. An

Aubry, Georges Jean-(cont.)
    introduction and some notes.   [London: First Edition
    Club, Printed by the Curwen Press, 1926] 3-7p
    (220 copies only)
    (A separate pamphlet, one of twelve such published
    by this club)
    La jeunesse de Conrad. Revue De Paris 45 année, no
    5:92-107 My '47
    Joseph Conrad. Revue Hebdomadaire année 33, tome
    2:439-52 F 23 '24
    Joseph Conrad au Congo: d'après des documents inédits.
    Mercure de France année 36, tome 183:289-338 O 15
    '25; same. published separately: Paris: Extrait du
    Mercure de France, 1925. 54p; same. (entitled "Joseph
    Conrad in the Congo.") London: The Bookman's Jour-
    nal Office, 1926. 17-75p
    (470 copies only)
    (Noted in Notes & Queries 149:325 N 7 '25; noted in
    Wiadomości Literackie 4, no 14:3 Ap 3 '27; reviewed
    in Times Literary Supplement (London) Ag 26 '26
    p557)
    (Much of this material was later incorporated in Jean-
    Aubry's Joseph Conrad, Life and Letters, published
    in 1927)
    Joseph Conrad, ecrivain française. Candide 10, no 511:
    3-4 D 28 '33 (On "Heart of Darkness")
    Joseph Conrad et la France. Le Figaro no 211:1 Ap 21
    '23; same. (excerpt) Chronique des Lettres Fran-
    çaises 1:425 My-Je '23; Les Nouvelles Littéraires 7,
    no 278:7 F 11 '28
    Joseph Conrad et l'Amérique Latine. Revue de l'Amérique
    Latine année 2, volume 4:290-9 Ap '23; same. (en-
    titled: "Joseph Conrad and Latin America") Living Age
    317:350-5 My 12 '23
    Joseph Conrad in The Heart of Darkness. Bookman
    (NY) 63:429-35 Je '26
    (Later incorporated into Aubry's Joseph Conrad, Life
    and Letters)
    Joseph Conrad (6th December, 1857 - 3rd August, 1924).
    Fortnightly Review 122:303-13 S 1 '24
    Joseph Conrad, life and letters. London: Heinemann;
    Garden City, New York: Doubleday, Page, 1927.
    Volume I:[v-xi], 339p; Volume II: v-[ix], 376p; bibli-
    ography, volume II, p351-61; portrait.
    Included also as Volumes XXIII-XXIV of The Works of
    Joseph Conrad. . . 1928
    (Dated 1927 unless otherwise noted: Reviewed by John

Macy in Bookman (NY) 66:566-70 Ja '28; Times Literary Supplement O 27 p761; Edward Garnett in Nation-Athenaeum 42:280, 282 N 19; Robert Morss Lovett in New Republic 52:214-15 O 12; Joseph Anthony in Century 114:633-4 S; H. L. Mencken in Nation (NY) 125: 384, 386 O 12; Percy Hutchison in New York Times Book Review S 18 pl, 19, 22; Ford Madox Ford in New York Herald Tribune Books O 2 p2; Edward Shanks in Saturday Review (London) 144:622 N 5; Wilbur Cross in Yale Review ns 18:582-3 Mr '29; Richard Curle in New Statesman (Literary Supplement) 30:ix-x, xii N 5; Granville Hicks in Springfield Republican O 16 p7; H. M. Tomlinson in Saturday Review of Literature (NY) 4:191-2 O 15; same. In Designed for reading: an anthology drawn from the Saturday Review of Literature, 1924-1934... New York: Macmillan, 1934. p288-93; Karl Schriftgiesser in Boston Evening Transcript (Book Section) S 17 p4; Herbert Gorman in New York Evening Post S 24 p10; Annual Register... for the year 1927.   London: Longmans, Green, 1928. p18; John Shand in New Adelphi no 3:282-3 Mr '28; noted by John Farrar in Bookman (NY) 66:288 N; Harry Hansen in The World (Metropolitan Section) S 11 p7; Herschel Brickell in North American Review 224: advertising N; Edmund Blunden in London Mercury 17:179-86 D; R. L. Mégroz in Bookman (London) 73:237-8 Ja '28; Booklist 24:115-16 D; Richard Church in Spectator 139:829, 831 N 12; (Richard Curle) in Weekly Dispatch O 23 p19; (Richard Curle) in Daily Mail (London) O 27 p6; Richard Curle in New York Herald Tribune S 30 '28; H. J. Davis in Canadian Forum 8, no 90:574, 576 Mr '28; Jan Parandowski in Słowo Pol. no 89, 1929; A. Tretiak in Tęcza nos 9-10, 1928)
Joseph Conrad's confessions.   Fortnightly Review 115: 782-90 My '21
Józef Conrad a Polska.   Tygodnik Illustrowany nos 41-44: 815, 836, 854, 876 O 10 - O 31 '25
(Noted by W. F[ilochowski] in Gazetta Warszawska no 318, 1925)
More about The Nigger of the 'Narcissus.'   Bookman's Journal & Print Collector 11, no 37:7-10 O '24
La Pologne dans la vie et l'oeuvre de Joseph Conrad. Pologne Littéraire sixième année, no 68:2 My 15 '32; same.   Droga no 12:18-29 D '27 (in Polish)

(Reviewed by E. S. in Osteuropa 3:816 S '28)
Preface du traducteur.   In Joseph Conrad's Angoisse

Aubry, Georges Jean-(cont.)
(Suspense). Paris: Gallimard, 1956. p7-22
Le roman inacheve de Joseph Conrad. Climats F 28 '48
The Rover. In: George T. Keating. A Conrad memori-
    al library. Garden City, New York: Doubleday,
    Doran, 1929. p326-36
The sea dreamer: a definitive biography of Joseph Con-
    rad, translated by Helen Sebba. London: Allen & Un-
    win, 1957. 321p; bibl., p295-312
    (A translation of Aubry's Vie de Conrad, published in
    1947)
    (Dated 1957 unless otherwise noted. Reviewed by Ed-
    ward Wagenknecht in Chicago Sunday Tribune F 3 p3;
    Francis Russell in Christian Science Monitor Ja 31 p5;
    Edith Lenel in Library Journal 81:2947 D 15 '56;
    David W. Bone in Library Review 16:280 Winter;
    Bruce Harkness in Journal of English & Germanic
    Philology 57:157-8 '58; Hans J. Gottlieb in Victorian
    News Letter no 13:15-17 Spring '58; Eric Gillett in
    National & English Review 149:134S; noted in Nine-
    teenth-Century Fiction 12:173 S; Times Literary Sup-
    plement Jl 26 p454; C. B. Oldman in Times Literary
    Supplement Ag 2 p471; Listener 58:139 Jl 25; V. S.
    Pritchett in New Statesman 54:229 Ag 24; Jocelyn
    Baines in Spectator 199:139 Jl 26; Carlos Baker in New
    York Times Book Review F 3, pl, 24; David Daiches
    in New York Herald Tribune Books F 3 p5; Charles J.
    Rolo in Atlantic Monthly 199:81-3 Mr; J. W. Krutch in
    Saturday Review (NY) 40:12 F 9; Joseph L. Blotner in
    College English 20:54-5 O '58; Sir John Squire in Il-
    lustrated London News 231:264 Ag 17; Richard Curle
    in London Magazine 4, no 11:46-9 N; C. A. Brady in
    America 96:560 F 16; A. J. Guerard in Reporter 16:
    42-4 Mr 21; Newsweek 49:94 F 4; Time 69:96 F 4;
    Joseph Swastek in Polish American Studies 14, nos 3-
    4:126 Jl-D; Listener 58, no 1478: 139 Jl 25)
Souvenirs. La Nouvelle Revue Française 23:672-80 D '24
Stosunek J. Conrada do muzyki, by M. Gliński. Muzyka
    no 5, 1926
Sur le mort de Joseph Conrad. Revue de France année
    4, tome 5:616-22 O 1 '24
Suspense. In Keating, George T. A Conrad memorial
    library. Garden City, New York: Doubleday, Doran,
    1929. p351-7
Un récent entretien avec le grand romancier anglais. Les
    Nouvelles Littéraires année 3, no 95:1 Ag 9 '24
Un idylle de Conrad à l'Île Maurice. Le Figaro My 14

'32 p5
(New biographical material)
Vie de Conrad. Paris: Gallimard [1947] 7-[303]p; bibli-
ography, p[281]-299
(Reviewed in Times Literary Supplement N 29 '47
p614, 645; Francois Deltiel in La Croix Mr 28 '48;
Pierre Pascal in Paru no 36:70-1 N '47; Marcel
Thiébaut in Revue de Paris 54, no 10:167 O '47)
Vie de Conrad: premier commandement (1888). Gazette
des Lettres 3rd année, no 38:6-7 Je 14 '47
Życie Conrada. Translated by Maria Kornilowiczowna.
Warsaw: Państwowy Instytut Wydawniczy, 1958.
(Reviewed by S. Zieliński in Nowe Książki no 18:
1097-9 '58; Z. Dolecki in Kierunki no 4:6 '59; Litera-
tura Piekna, 1958. Warsaw: S. B. P. , 1960. p269-70;
W. Stowarzyszenie in Bibliotekarzy Polskich, 1960;
Bogdan Wojdowski in Trybuna Literacka no 35:3 '58;
Jarosław Iwaszkiewicz in Życie Warszawy no 233:4
'58; Wanda Leopold in Nowa Kultura no 38:2 '58; Kon-
rad Eberhardt in Życie Literackie no 42:8 '58; Bronis-
law Miazgowski in Tygodnik Morski no 12:4, 8 '58)
                                                        42
Aubry, Georges Jean- (editor)
Twenty letters to Joseph Conrad.   [London: The First
Edition Club, Printed by the Curwen Press, 1926] 12
volumes; in board portfolio
(220 copies of each volume)
(A collection of twelve pamphlets, each for a different
letter-writer, including Edward Garnett, Constance
Garnett, Rudyard Kipling, John Galsworthy, Stephen
Crane, Arnold Bennett, Henry James, E. V. Lucas,
J. G. Huneker, George Gissing, H. G. Wells, plus a
separate pamphlet for the introduction written by Jean-
Aubry)   43
Auernheimer, Raoul
Ein männlicher Erzähler.   Neue Freie Presse no 22468:
1-3 Ap 3 '27   44
Austin, Hugh P.
Joseph Conrad and the ironic attitude.   Fortnightly Re-
view 130:376-88 S 1 '28 (Compares Conrad and Ana-
tole France)   45
Austin, Mary
Joseph Conrad tells what women don't know about men.
Pictorial Review 24, no 12:17, 28, 30-31 S '23
Typhoon. In George T. Keating.   A Conrad memorial
library.   Garden City, New York: Doubleday, Doran,
1929. p103-10   46

Ay'ard, Joseph
  L'exotisme de Joseph Conrad à propos de Lord Jim.
    Journal des Débats année 134, no 320:3 N 18 '22
  Joseph Conrad.   Journal des Débats 31, pt 2:333-5 Ag
    22 '24
  Le roman du hasard par Joseph Conrad.   Journal des
    Débats année 126, no 128:1-2 My 9 '14   47
B., A. P.
  Conrad Korzeniowski.   Praca (Work) no 19, 1924   48
B., J.
  The burial of Conrad.   Manchester Guardian Weekly 11,
    no 7:ii (facing p133) Ag 15 '24   49
Baasner, Peter
  Stephen Crane and Joseph Conrad.   In Kleiner beiträge
    zur amerikanischen Literaturgeschichte, edited by Hans
    Galinsky and Hans-Joachim Lang.   Heidelberg: Winter,
    1961. p34-9   50
Babb, James T.
  Note.   Yale University Library Gazette 13:29 Jl '38   51
Bacewiczówna, Wanda
  Środa literacka.   Dziś i Jutro rok 2, no 5:7 F 3 '46 51a
Bache, William B.
  Nostromo and "The Snows of Kilimanjaro."   Modern Lan-
    guage Notes 72:32-4 Ja '57
  Othello and Conrad's Chance.   Notes & Queries 200:478-
    9 N '55   52
Bachrach, A. G. H.
  Joseph Conrad and the Dutch.   Review of English Literature
    8:9-30 O '67
  Joseph Conrad's western eye, I - II.   Neophilologus 37:
    157-67 Jl '53; 37:219-26 O '53; same.   (translated)
    Nieuwe Stem 8:641-53, 704-14 N-D '53   53
Baczkowska, Irena
  [Letter to the editor] Wiadomości 21. no 32:6 Ag 7 '66 53a
Bacon, Josephine Dodge
  The autobiography of a book.   New York: American Mer-
    chant Marine Library Association, 1926. 16p (From
    The Ammla, volume 1, no. 1, June, 1925)
    (On Lord Jim)   54
Baines, Jocelyn
  The affair in Marseilles.   London Magazine 4:41-6 N
    '57
  Afterword.   In Almayer's Folly and other stories, by
    Joseph Conrad.   New York: New American Library
    [c1965] p306-18
  Joseph Conrad: a critical biography.   London: Weiden-
    feld and Nicholson, 1959; New York: McGraw-Hill,

1960. 507p; bibliographies, p452-61. Excerpt (entitled: "Nostromo") In Conrad. A collection of critical essays, ed. by Marvin Mudrick. Englewood Cliffs, New Jersey: Prentice-Hall [1966] p83-101 (Dated 1960 unless otherwise noted. Reviewed by Leo Gurko in American Scholar 29:574 Autumn; Adam Gillon in Dalhousie Review 40:415-19 Fall; Jacques Vallette in Mercure de France 340:340-2; G. D. Klingopulos in Universities Quarterly 14:307-11 Je; Carlisle Moore in Comparative Literature 16:167-70 Spring'64; Pál Vámosi in Filológiai Közlöny 9:287-90 '63; Booklist 56:538 My 1; Edward Wagenknecht in Chicago Sunday Tribune My 15 p15; Christian Science Monitor Mr 31 p15 by D. E. McCoy; Douglas Hewitt in Guardian F 5 p6; C. W. Mann Jr. in Library Journal 85:1783-4 My 1; Thomas Moser in Nation 190:386 Ap 30; Kenneth Millar in San Francisco Chronicle My 29 p21; D. B. Bagg in Springfield Republican Ap 24 p14c; Times Literary Supplement F 5 p73-4, replied to by J. Baines in Times Literary Supplement F 19 p113; V. S. Pritchett in New Statesman 59:157-8 Ja 30; Frank Kermode in Spectator 204:189 F 5; W. W. Robson in London Magazine 7:75-8 Jl; Richard Rees in Twentieth Century 168:87-9 Jl; David Daiches in New York Times Book Review Ap 3 p5; A. M. Hollingsworth in Victorian Studies 4:65-7 S; Robert M. Adams in Partisan Review 28:124-30 Ja-F '61; Charles Poore in New York Times Ap 26 p35; Vincent Brome in Listener 63:273 F 11; Michael Straight in New Republic 142:15-17 Ap 18; A. West in New Yorker 6:137-41 My 28; R. Ellmann in Reporter 22:50-2 My 26; A. J. Guerard in New York Herald Tribune Books Ap 3 p4; Wiadomości 15, no 18:1 My 1)

Joseph Conrad - raw material into art. Kwartalnik Neofilologiczny 5:11-18 '58; same. In Joseph Conrad Korzeniowski. Essays and studies. Warsaw: Państwowe Wydawnictwo Naukowe, 1958.p[11]-18

The young Conrad in Marseilles. Times Literary Supplement D 6 '57 p 748   55

Baker, Cynthia Patricia

Realism and symbolism in the shorter works of Joseph Conrad. Radcliffe College Honors Thesis in English, 1949. 40f   56

Baker, Ernest Albert

Conrad, the teller of tales. Conrad, the novelist, with his next of kin. In The history of the English novel... Yesterday. London: Witherby [1939] Volume X, p11-

Baker, Ernest Albert (cont.)
   44, 45-104; bibliography, p394-5   57
Baker, Ernest Albert and Packman, James
   [List of Conrad's works arranged chronologically with
   brief comments on each] In A guide to the best fic-
   tion... London: Routledge, 1932. new and enlarged edi-
   tion, p110-12   58
Balderston, John L.
   Victory. From the novel by Joseph Conrad. Screen
   play by John L. Balderston. Final shooting script.
   May 1, 1940. 132f. Paramount Pictures, Inc.
   (A copy is in the Rare Book Room, Univ. of Southern
   California Library)   58a
Baliński, Ignacy
   Do redaktora "Wiadomości." Wiadomości 4, no 181:4 S
   18 '49   58b
Ballard, E. G.
   Principles of structure in Joseph Conrad's novels. Ph. D.
   Thesis, North Texas State Teachers College, Denton,
   1952   59
Bancroft, William Wallace
   Joseph Conrad: his philosophy of life. Philadelphia:
   University of Pennsylvania Press, 1931. [v], 94p; list
   of novels and tales, p93-4. A Ph. D. Thesis, Univ.
   of Pennsylvania, 1931.
   Also published: Boston: Stratford Co. [c1933]
   Reprinted: New York: Haskell House, 1964
   (Reviewed in New Republic 76:316 O 25 '33; Herbert J.
   Muller in Philosophical Review 43:542 S '34; E. B. G.
   in America 49:377 Jl 22 '33; T. V. Smith in Interna-
   tional Journal of Ethics 44:172 O '33; E. C. Beckwith
   in New York Times Book Review Je 4 '33 p9; Spring-
   field Republican Jl 5 '33 p8)   60
Bantock, Geoffrey Herman
   Conrad and politics. English Literary History 25:122-36
   Je '58
   The two "moralities" of Joseph Conrad. Essays in Criti-
   cism 3, no 2:125-42 Ap '53
   (Noted in Times Literary Supplement My 29 '53 p353)
          61
Baranowicki, Antoni
   Conradiana. Wiadomości 4, no 186:4 O 23 '49   61a
Barth, Emil
   Westen und osten. Ein roman der östlichen Welt. Mittag.
   (Düsseld.) Leben 250 '33   62
Barthlome, Mary
   Sources of the Latin element in the works of Joseph Con-

Beachcroft, T. O.
   James, Conrad, and the place of the narrator. In The
      English short story (II). [London:] Published for the
      British Council & the National Book League by Long-
      mans, Green & Co. [1964] p14-18   75
Bebee, M.
   The symbolic character of Joseph Conrad's novels. M. A.
      Thesis, University of Buffalo, 1932   75a
Becker, May Lamberton
   Read this one first. Joseph Conrad. Scholastic 31:22 O
      9 '37
   The reader's guide. Evening Post (NY) Book Review Je
      19 '20 p15   76
Becker, Robert J.
   Recurring themes in the fiction of Joseph Conrad. M. S.
      Thesis, Mankato State College, 1962. 44p   77
Beebe, Maurice
   Art as religion: the ivory tower tradition. In Ivory
      towers and sacred founts... New York: New York Uni-
      versity Press, 1964. p114-71
   Criticism of Joseph Conrad: a selected checklist. Modern
      Fiction Studies 10:81-106 Spring '64
   Criticism of Joseph Conrad: a selected checklist with an
      index to studies of separate works. Modern Fiction
      Studies 1:30-45 F '55
   The masks of Conrad. Bucknell Review 11, no 4:35-53
      D '63   78
Beer, Thomas
   Stephen Crane... with an introduction by Joseph Conrad.
      New York: Knopf, 1926. p239-40
      (Reviewed in Adelphi 2, no 6:546 N 24 '26)   79
Beerbohm, Max
   Caricature of Conrad. Bookman (London) 40, no 239:207
      Ag '11
   Diffidence. In Things new and old. London: William
      Heinemann, Ltd. , 1923. Plate 13 (Sir Arthur Pinero
      and Conrad)
   The Feast by Joseph Conrad. In A Christmas garland.
      New York: Dutton; London: Heinemann, 1912. p[123]-
      130; same. In Woolcott's second reader, edited by
      Alexander Woolcott. New York: Viking, 1927. p120-
      3; same. In Conrad. A collection of critical essays,
      edited by Marvin Mudrick. Englewood Cliffs, New
      Jersey: Prentice-Hall, Inc. [1966] p13-15
      (Reviewed by Richard Curle in Rhythm 2:xxix-xxx
      (literary supplement) Mr '13)
   Joseph Conrad. In Observations. London: William

Heinemann, 1925. p43; same. Atlantic Monthly 201:63
F '58
(A caricature of the young and the old Conrad)
Mr. Conrad's play. Saturday Review (London) 100, no
2593:48-9 Jl 8 '05; same. In Around theatres. New
York: Knopf, 1930. Volume II, p495-9
(A review of the 1905 production of Conrad's One Day
More)
A party in the parlour. In A survey. New York:
Doubleday, Page, 1921. Item 51
Somewhere in the Pacific. In A survey. New York:
Doubleday, Page, 1921. Frontispiece
(A caricature of Conrad, done in 1920)   80
Begun, Jean Elizabeth
Impressionism in the novel: Henry James, Joseph Con-
rad, and James Joyce. M. A. Thesis, Stanford Univer-
sity, 1954. iv, 60f   81
Beker, Miroslav
Virginia Woolf's appraisal of Joseph Conrad. Studia Ro-
manica et Anglica Zagrabiensia no 12:17-22 D '61 82
Belden, Albert D.
Joseph Conrad: an apostle of loyalty. Expository Times
(Edinburgh) 63:77-9 D '51   83
Bendz, Ernst (Paulus)
Joseph Conrad. Ett tioårsminne. In Studia Germanica,
tillägnade Ernst Albin Kock, den 6 December 1934.
(Lunder Germanistische Forschungen, herausgegeben
von Erik Rooth. 1.) Lund: Gleerup, 1934. p10-21
Joseph Conrad: an appreciation. Gothenburg: Gumpert,
1923. 7-117p
(500 copies only)
Also published: New York: H. W. Wilson Co. , 1923
(Reviewed in Times Literary Supplement Ap 26 '23
p284; Notes & Queries 12th series 12:280 Ap 7 '23;
Spectator 130:969-70 Je 9 '23; Delmar Gross Cooke in
Journal of English & Germanic Philology 22:586-8 O
'23; Walter F. Schirmer in Englische Studien 58, heft
2:286-8 '24; Publishers' Circular 118:295 Mr 17 '23)
Joseph Conrad, sexagenarian. Englische Studien 51, heft
3:391-406 Ja '18   84
Benkert, Irmalyn (Sister)
Conrad's use of the Casa Gould as motif and symbol in
Nostromo. M. A. Thesis, Catholic University of
America, 1964. 50f; bibliography, f49-50   85
Bennett, Arnold
Arnold Bennett to Joseph Conrad. [London: First Edition
Club, Curwen Press, 1926] Text of letter, p[1-2];

Bennett, Arnold (cont.)
  Editor's note, p[3].
  (220 copies only)
  (The letter from Bennett to Conrad is dated Nov. 22,
  1912)
  Books and persons. New Age ns 3:391 S 12 '08
  Confessions of a book-buyer. New Age ns 3:370 S 5 '08
  Joseph Conrad and the Athenaeum. New Age ns 3:33
  My 9 '08; same. In Books and persons... London:
  Chatto and Windus, 1911. p36-40.
  (On A Set of Six)
  The journal of Arnold Bennett. New York: Literary
  Guild, 1933. passim   86
Bennett, Carl Douglas
  A choice of nightmares; a study of Conrad's ethical vi-
  sion. Ph. D. Thesis, Emory University, 1962. 363f;
  bibliography, f[361]-363. Abstract in Dissertation Ab-
  stracts 24:293-4 '63   87
Bennett, Michael Isaiah
  Only a night, only a silence: a study of the dream in the
  fiction of Joseph Conrad. Honors Thesis, Harvard
  College, 1966. 33f   88
Bennewitz, Hildegard
  Die Charaktere in den Romanen Joseph Conrads. (Greifs-
  walder Beiträge sur Literatur-und-Stilforschung, 2)
  Greifswald: Dallmeyer, 1933. iii-v, 70p; bibliography,
  p67-70
  (Reviewed by Louis Cazamian in Beiblatt zur Anglia
  46:220-2 Jl '35)   89
Benson, Carl
  Conrad's two stories of initiation. Publications of the
  Modern Language Association of America 69:46-56 Mr
  '54   90
Benson, Donald R.
  'Heart of Darkness:" the grounds of civilization in an
  alien universe. Texas Studies in Language & Litera-
  ture 7:339-47 Winter '66   91
Bentley, Eric
  Note. In The modern theatre, Volume three, edited by
  Eric Bentley. Garden City, New York: Doubleday &
  Co. [1955] p305-6
  (On Conrad's One Day More)   92
Bentley, Thomas Roy
  Sources for Shakespeare's Hamlet, Shaw's Saint Joan,
  Conrad's 'Heart of Darkness," compiled by Thomas
  Roy Bentley. Agincourt [Ontario]: Book-Society of
  Canada [1966] 108p
                                                           93

Berend, Alice
    Innere und aussere Abentever. Reclams Universum (Leip-
        zig) 43, no 52:1353-4 S 22 '27   94
Bernaciack, Joel Joseph
    Microcosm versus macrocosm: a study of setting in the
    fiction of Joseph Conrad. Ph. D. Thesis, Univ. of
    Michigan, 1966. 233p.
    Abstract in Dissertation Abstracts 27:3034A Mr '67
                                             95
Bernard, Kenneth
    Marlow's lie. English Record 13, no 4:47-8 Ap '63
    (In "Heart of Darkness")   96
    The significance of the Roman parallel in Joseph Con-
    rad's "Heart of Darkness." Ball State Teachers Col-
    lege Forum 5, no 2:29-31 Spring '64   97
Berryman, John
    Stephen Crane. [New York:] William Sloane Associates
    [c1950] p200-2, 206-8, 238-9, 251-2   98
Bidou, Henry
    La vocation de Conrad. Journal des Débats 34, pt 1:
    615 Ap 15 '27   99
Bidwell, Alice Townsend and Rosenstiel, Isabelle Denison
    Joseph Conrad. In The places of English literature.
    Boston: Stratford co. [c1924] p184   100
Bieber, Hugo
    Joseph Conrad. Berliner Börsen Courant no 97, F '27
                                             101
Bielańska, Karolina
    Conrad o ks. Romanie Sangusze. Bluszcz nos 30-1, Jl
    25, Ag 1 '25   102
Bielawski, Jan
    Conrad. Gazeta Lwowska no 209, 1924   103
Bien, Horst
    Joseph Conrad und der Anarchismus. Zeitschrift für
    Anglistik und Amerikakunde 111:445-70 '55   104
Bier, Ruth Stutzman
    Reality of characterization in the novels of Joseph Con-
    rad. Master's Thesis, Univ. of Pittsburgh, 1931. 66f.
    Abstract in Abstracts of Masters' Theses. University
    of Pittsburgh Bulletin 28:329 D 30 '30   105
Bigongiari, Piero
    Conrad nei mari del Sud. Il Nuova Corriere 7:15, 16,
    17, 18 '56
    Joseph Conrad: un universo paramente spettacolare. In
    Il senso della lirica Italiana. Firenze: Sansoni, 1952.
    p262-9   106

Billy, André
 Un grand romancier presque oublié.   Figaro Littéraire
 S 6 '47   107
Binsse, Harry Lorin
 Polish picture.   Commonweal 42:43-5 Ap 27 '45
 (An evaluation of Conrad's A Personal Record)   108
Binz, Arthur Friedrich
 Joseph Conrad.   Orplid 4, nos 11-12:95-7 F-Mr '28
 Joseph Conrad.   Kölnische Stadtanzeitung Zeit My 22 '28
 Joseph Conrad. Rhein. Main Volkzeitung, Lit. Bl. 17,
 1930   109
Birkenmajer, Józef
 Dookala Conrad (Around Conrad).   Kurier Poznański
 (Poznan Courier) no 197, 1927   110
Birrell, Anthony
 The reticence of Joseph Conrad. Blackfriars 27:206-8
 Je '46   111
A bit of Mr. Joseph Conrad's "Copy" of "Youth." Bookman
 (London) 21:53 N '01   112
Björkman, Edwin August
 A Conrad from Armenia.   Public Ledger Literary Review
 (Philadelphia) S 14 '23 p3 (A review of Michael Arlen's
 The Green Hat)
 Joseph Conrad, master of literary color. Review of Re-
 views (NY) 45:557-60 My '12; same. In Voice of to-
 morrow... New York & London: Mitchell Kennerly,
 1913. p240-259 (entitled: "Graal knights of modern lit-
 erature. II. Joseph Conrad")   113
Blackburn, William
 Introduction. In Joseph Conrad. Letters to William
 Blackwood and David S. Meldrum, edited by William
 Blackburn. Durham, North Carolina: Duke University
 press, 1958. p[v]-xxxvii   114
Blaess, F. J. H.
 Handbook on Conrad. M. A. Thesis, Univ. of Adelaide,
 1943   115
Blose, Inez Canfield
 (A letter about Joseph Conrad in Percy Hammond's
 Column, "Oddments and Remainders"). New York
 Tribune My 21 '23 p 10   116
Bluefarb, Sam
 The sea - mirror and maker of character in fiction and
 drama. English Journal 48, no 9:501-10 D '59   117
Blunden, Edmund
 A Conrad repository. London Mercury 17:179-86
 D '27   118
Blunt, John [pseud.]

See: Curle, Richard 119
Blüth, Rafał Marceli
Conradiana. Wiersz na dzien chrztu Konrada. Ruch
Literacki 7, no 8:249-50 Ag '32
Dwie rodziny kresowe. Ateneum no 1, 1939, p1-24
Ewolucja heroizmu u Conrada. Ruch Literacki 7, no 8:
230-6 Ag '32
Joseph Conrad et Dostoievski: le problème du crime et
du châtiment. Vie Intellectuelle 12:320-39 My 10 '31
(Compares Lord Jim and Crime and Punishment)
O tragicznej decyzji krakowskiej Konrada Korzeniowskiego
(Conrad's tragic decision taken at Cracow). Verbum no
2, 1936; same. In Wspomnienia i studia o Conradzie,
edited by Barbara Kocówna. [Warsaw:] Państwowy
Instytut Wydawniczy [1963] p379-405
Pesymizm Conrada. (Conrad's pessimism). Polska
Zbrojna (Armed Poland) no 126, 1926
Ucieczka Conrada Korzeniowskiego (Conrad's flight).
Polska Zbrojna no 93, 1926 120
Blazek, Zygmunt
Jeszce o Polkości Conrada (More on Conrad's Polish
character). Tygodnik Powszechny 9, no 21:6-7 O 4
'53 121
Board, D. H.
Joseph Conrad. M. A. Thesis, Sheffield University,
1958 122
Boas, Ralph Philip
The study and appreciation of literature. New York:
Harcourt, Brace [c1931] passim 123
Bobkowski, Andrzej
Alma. In Conrad żywy, edited by Wit Tarnawski.
London: B. Świderski, 1957. p58-68 124
Bobrowski, Tadeusz
Pamiętniki. Lvov, 1900. 2 volumes 125
Boebel, Charles Edward
Irony and belief in Joseph Conrad. M. A. Thesis, Univ.
of Iowa, 1962. 148p 126
Boersch, Alfred H.
Ford Madox Ford: a study of his collaboration and its ef-
fect upon his novels with Joseph Conrad. M. A. Thesis,
Univ. of Minnesota, 1950 127
Bogdański, Jerzy
Z dziejów Conrada (From the history of Conrad). Gazeta
Ludowa (People's Gazette) no 220, 1946 128
Boger, Ruth Bolton
Joseph Conrad's treatment of nature. Master's Thesis,
University of Texas, 1941. iii-v, 93f 129

Boileau, Horace Tippin
Francis Brett Young and a glimpse of the Conradian
manner. In Italy in the post-Victorian novel. Phila-
delphia, 1931. p70-9; Ph. D. Thesis, Univ. of Pennsyl-
vania, 1931. 130
Bojarski, Edmund A.
Conrad in Cardiff: impressions 1885-1896. Anglo-Welsh
Review (Wales) 15, no 36:57-63 Summer '66
Conrad studies in American graduate schools. Polish
American Studies 22, no 2:117-18 Jl-D '65
Conrad's first Polish interview. Polish American Studies
17, nos 3-4:65-71 Jl-D '60
A conversation with Kipling on Conrad. Kipling Journal
34, no 162:12-15 Je '67
Joseph Conrad, alias "Polish Joe." English Studies in
Africa (Johannesburg) 5:59-60 Mr '62
Joseph Conrad: original ugliness. Polish American
Studies 23, no 1:8-11 Ja-Je '66
Joseph Conrad's Polish soul. Theoria 16:41-6 '61; same.
English Studies 44:431-7 D '63
Joseph Conrad's sentimental journey: a fiftieth anniver-
sary review. Texas Quarterly (Univ. of Texas) 7,
no 4:156-65 Winter '64
A stranger and afraid: Joseph Conrad. English Studies
in Africa 10, no 1:94-100 Mr '67
(Conrad's meeting with Jan Perlowski) 131
Bojarski, Edmund A. and Bojarski, Henry T.
Joseph Conrad, a bibliography of masters' theses and
doctoral dissertations. (Occasional Contributions, no
157) Lexington, Kentucky: Libraries of the University
of Kentucky, 1964. 33p 132
Bolander, Louis H.
Joseph Conrad's last ship. A model made of the Tor-
rens... New York Times Magazine Ap 17 '32 p15 133
Bolhoevener, R.
Joseph Conrad. Aus Fremden Zungen 12, no 9, 1902
(Noted in Das Literarische Echo 4:1477 Ag '02) 134
Bolles, Edwin Courtlandt
The literature of sea travel since the introduction of
steam, 1830-1930. Philadelphia, 1943. p36-7, 76-7,
84-5, 109-11, 118-19.
Ph. D. Thesis, University of Pennsylvania, 1943 135
Bol'shaia Sovetskaia Entsiklopediia (Moscow), 1927 edition:
xxiv, column 30; 1953 edition: xxxii, p309 136
Bone, David
Introduction. In: Joseph Conrad, Four Tales, edited by
David Bone. (World's Classics) London: Oxford Univer-

sity Press, 1950. p[vii]-[xv]
Memories of Conrad. Saturday Review of Literature 2:
286 N 7 '25
The Shadow-Line. In Keating, George T. A Conrad
memorial library. Garden City, New York: Doubleday,
Doran, 1929. p255-61 137
Bone, Muirhead
Introduction. In The Mirror of the Sea, by Joseph Con-
rad. (Memorial Edition) Garden City, New York:
Doubleday, Page, 1925. Volume XII, p vii-xiii
(In this volume A Personal Record precedes The Mir-
ror of the Sea and each work is separately paged)
The soul of Conrad. An artist's impression. Manchest-
er Guardian Weekly 11, no 6:124 Ag 1 '24; same.
Living Age 322:551-4 S 13 '24; same. (excerpt) Liter-
ary Digest 82:31 S 27 '24
Ulysses. Manchester Guardian Ag 26 '24 p5; same.
(excerpt) Literary Digest 82:31 S 27 '24 138
Books for the Conrad Memorial Library. Lookout 25, no
1:1-2, 11 Ja '34 139
Booth, Wayne C.
The rhetoric of fiction. [Chicago:] University of Chi-
cago press [c1961] p191 140
Borinski, Ludwig
Joseph Conrad. In Meister des modernen englischen
Romans. Heidelberg: Quelle & Meyer, 1963. p[127]-
157 141
Borko, Božidar
Joseph Conrad and the Poles. Jutro no 45, 1933 141a
Borowy, Wacław
Conrad krytykiem polskiego przekładu swojej noweli 'Il
Conde." Sprawozdania z Cyności i Posiedzeń Polskiej
Akademii Umiejetności no 7, 1947; same. Zeszyty
Wrocławski nos 3-4:36-47 '50; same. In Studia i
Rozprawy. Wrocław: Wydawnictwo Zakładu Narodo-
wego Iminia Ossolińskich, 1952. Volume II, p[61]-72;
same. In Joseph Conrad Korzeniowski, by Róża Jab-
łkowska. Warsaw: Państwowe Zakłady Wydawnictwo
Szkolynch, 1964. p250-63
(Reviewed by Wiktor Weintraub in Wiadomości 8, no
27:2 Jl 5 '53)
Czy Conrad przedstawił polskiego górala? (Did Conrad
depict a Polish mountaineer?) Wiadomości Literackie
11, no 38:8 S 16 '34
Fredro i Conrad. Z tajników sztuki pisarskiej. (Fredro
and Conrad. Secrets in the art of writing.) Tygodnik
Wileński no 16, 1925; same. In Wspomnienia i studia

30   A Bibliography of Joseph Conrad

Borowy, Waclaw (cont.)
    o Conradzie, edited by Barbara Kocówna. [Warsaw:]
    Państwowy Instytut Wydawniczy [1963] p246-52
    Hołd pamieci Conrads. Warszawianka no 8, 1925
    O Lordzie Jima. In Wspomnienia i studia o Conradzie,
    edited by Barbara Kocówna. [Warsaw:] Państwowy
    Instytut Wydawniczy [1963] p329-32
    Przekłády. Literatura angielska. In Rocznik Literacki
    za rok 1932. Warsaw: Instytut Literacki, 1933. p112-
    13
    Szaleństwo Almayera. Tygodnik Powszechny no 98, 1947;
    same. In Wspomnienia i studia o Conradzie, edited by
    Barbara Kocówna. [Warsaw:] Państwowy Instytut
    Wydawniczy [1963] p406-13   142
Bowen, Elizabeth
    Conrad. In Collected impressions. New York: Knopf,
    1950. p151-3   143
Bowen, Robert O.
    Loyalty and tradition in Conrad. Renascence 12:125-31
    Spring '60   144
Bowrou, Gayle Louise
    The Conradian hero. M. A. Thesis, Univ. of Alberta,
    1952. 88p   145
Boyd, Ernest
    [Joseph Conrad, the perfect example of the "romance" of
    the sea] In The ten dullest authors: a symposium.
    Vanity Fair 20:86 Ag '23
    Readers and writers. Independent 114, no 3894:76 Ja 17
    '25   146
Boyett, Annie Loucassia
    Joseph Conrad - raconteur. M. A. Thesis, Columbia
    Univ. , 1924. 50p   147
Boyle, Ted Eugene
    Marlow's 'Lie' in "Heart of Darkness." Studies in Short
    Fiction (Newberry College) 1:159-63 Winter '64
    Symbol and meaning in the writings of Joseph Conrad.
    Ph. D. Thesis, Univ. of Nebraska, 1962. 312p; ab-
    stract in Dissertation Abstracts 23:3894 '63
    Symbol and meaning in the fiction of Joseph Conrad.
    The Hague: Mouton, 1965. (Studies in English Litera-
    ture, Volume VI) 245p; bibliography, p[239]-245
    Also published: New York: Humanities Press, 1965.
    (Reviewed by Allen B. Brown in College English 28:
    262 D '66)   148
Boynton, Henry Walcott
    Joseph Conrad. Nation (NY) 98:395-7 Ap 9 '14   149
Boy-Żeleński, Tadeusz

Dusza Conrada. In Plotki, plotki... Warsaw: Biblioteka
   Polska [1928]; same. Kurjer Poranny no 163, 1927
                                                      150
Boz [pseud.]
   Suppose. Bookmark (London) 9, no 33:[29] Summer '33
                                                      150a
Bradbrook, Frank W.
   Samuel Richardson and Joseph Conrad. Notes & Queries
   203:119 Mr '58   151
Bradbrook, Muriel Clara
   Conrad and the tragic imagination. Kwartalnik Neofilol-
   ogiczny 5:7-10 '58; same. In Joseph Conrad Korzeni-
   owski. Essays and Studies. Warsaw: Państwowe
   Wydawnictwo Naukowe, 1958. p[7]-10
   Joseph Conrad... Poland's English genius. New York:
   Macmillan; Cambridge: Cambridge Univ. press, 1941.
   [80]p. "Books on Conrad, a select list," p[78]-79
   (Reviewed in Times Literary Supplement Ag 2 '41 p372;
   Notes & Queries 181:98 Ag 16 '41; Harold Hobson in
   Christian Science Monitor S 20 '41 p10; J. J. Reilly in
   Catholic World 154:242-3 N '41; Wilfred Gibson in Eng-
   lish 4:26-7 Spring '42; Dublin Review 211:188-90 O '42;
   Tablet 178:154 S 6 '41; J. R. Leavis in Scrutiny 10:181
   O '41; noted in New Republic 105:446 O 6 '41)   152
Braddy, Nella
   Introduction. In Youth and two other stories, by Joseph
   Conrad. Garden City, New York: Doubleday, Page,
   1925. pvii-viii   153
Bradford, Gamaliel
   The letters of Gamaliel Bradford, edited by Van Wyck
   Brooks. Boston: Houghton Mifflin, 1934. p113-14
   (A letter to George Herbert Clarke dated July 3,
   1922)   154
Brady, Charles Andrew
   Conrad: A Polish Palinurus. America 97:649-51 S 21
   '57   155
Brady, Elsie Gertrude
   The credibility of Joseph Conrad. M. A. Thesis, Boston
   College, 1943. iv, 62f; bibliography, f59-61   156
Brady, Emily Kuempel
   Conrad and Faulkner. In The literary Faulkner: his in-
   debtedness to Conrad, Lawrence, Hemingway, and other
   modern novelists. Ph. D. Thesis, Brown University,
   1962. f12-98. Abstract in Dissertation Abstracts 23:
   2131-2 '62   157
Brady, Marion B.
   Conrad's whited sepulcher. College English 24:24-9 O '62

Brady, Marion B. (cont.)
    (Also see pages 561-2, a rebuttal by Thomas C. Kish-
    ler, and pages 562-3, April, 1963, an answer by
    Marion B. Brady)   158
Braga, Dominique
    Deux romanciers anglais.   Crapouillot N 1 '23 p4-5
    (Conrad and George Moore)   159
Brashear, Jordan L.
    Joseph Conrad: social critic. Ph. D. Thesis, Univ. of
    California at Berkeley, 1955   160
Brashear, Minnie May
    The angle of narration in the fiction of Joseph Conrad.
    M. A. Thesis, Univ. of Missouri, 1922. 147p   161
Brashear, William R.
    'Tomorrow' and 'tomorrow:' Conrad and O'Neill.
    Renascence 20:18-21, 55 '67   161a
Brauch, Lillian Marie
    The hamartia in Conrad's heroes. M. A. Thesis, Ohio
    State University, 1925. 25p   162
Braybrooke, Patrick
    Joseph Conrad: an appreciation. Dublin Review 189:
    318-25 O '31
    Joseph Conrad: master novelist. In Some Victorian and
    Georgian Catholics, their art and outlook. London:
    Burns, Oates & Washbourne [1932] p137-68; portrait
    163
Bregenzer, Don
    Conrad after five years. New Republic 61:277 Ja 29 '30
    (A reply to an article by Granville Hicks)   164
Breinling, Roberta Jean Blanton
    Myth and moral criticism in Lord Jim. M. A. Thesis,
    Univ. of Virginia, 1967. 28f   165
Breit, Harvey
    A talk with Christopher Morley. New York Times Book
    Review Jl 31 '49 p13   166
Breiter, Emil
    Conrad-Korzeniowski. Głos Prawdy nos 257-8, 1928
    Nowy tom nowel Conrada. Wiadomości Literackie rok 9,
      no 431:3 Ap 3 '32
    Ostatni romantyk żeglarstwa. Wiadomości Literackie
      rok 12, no 612:4 Ag 11 '35
    Poeta siły i natchnienia. Wiadomości Literackie rok 1,
      no 33:3 Ag 17 '24
    Studjum o bohaterstwie. Wiadomości Literackie rok 11,
      no 10:3 Mr 11 '34   167
Brennan, Joseph X. and Seymour Gross
    The problem of moral values in Conrad and Faulkner.

Personalist 41:60-70 Winter '60   168
Brewster, Dorothy
East-West passage: a study in literary relationships.
    London: George Allen & Unwin, Ltd. [1954] p214-
    15   169
Brewster, Dorothy and Burrell, Angus
Conrad's Nostromo: thirty years after. In Modern fic-
    tion, by Dorothy Brewster and Angus Burrell. New
    York: Columbia Univ. press, 1934. p65-83; bibliog-
    raphy p328
Conrad's Nostromo: twenty years after. In Dead reckon-
    ings in fiction. New York: Longmans, Green, 1924.
    p101-28   170
Brians, Paul
Conrad's Under Western Eyes and Zola's Germinal: a
    comparison. M. A. Thesis, Indiana University, 1966.
    67f; bibliography f63-7   170a
Briarez, Ir.
Jean-Aubry w. Paryzu. Kuryer Poznański no 193, 1927
                                                               171
Brickell, Herschel
A Conrad library. New York Post My 17 '34 p10   172
Bridges, Horace James
The genius of Joseph Conrad. In The God of fundamental-
    ism and other studies. Chicago: Covici, 1925. p297-
    319
Joseph Conrad: a memorial tribute. Standard 11:75-82
    N '24   173
Briggs, Austin Eugene
The light of illusion in a world of darkness: a study of
    Conrad's volume "Youth." Honors Essay, Harvard Col-
    lege, March 15, 1954. 34f, plus a bibliography, 2f
                                                               174
Brighouse, Harold
Dukes' excursions. In Modern essays and sketches,
    edited by James William Marriott. London: Nelson
    [1935] p91-5 (from the Manchester Guardian)   175
Brinkley, Thomas Edwin
The search for human solidarity in Conrad's Victory and
    Lord Jim. Honors Essay, Department of English,
    University of North Carolina, May, 1963. 93f   176
Briscoe, John D'Auby; Shays, Robert Lathrop; Borish, Mur-
    ray Eugene
A mapbook of English literature. New York: Holt
    [c1936] maps vii, viii, xv   177
British acquire Conrad picture by American. New York
    Herald Tribune Mr 24 '33

British (cont.)
(The portrait of Conrad done by Walter Tittle)   178
Britten, Lew
Conrad. Reading and Collecting 2, no 1:15 D '37   179
Brock, H. I.
Gentlest of deep-sea skippers. New York Times Maga-
zine My 13 '23
Joseph Conrad, able seaman. New York Times Book Re-
view Ag 10 '24 pl, 18
Joseph Conrad, sculptor of words. New York Times
Book Review Je 10 '23 p1-2, 28 (illustrated)   180
Broderick, Lillian Negueloua
A study of Conrad's prose style. Ph. D. Thesis, Harvard
Univ., June 1964. 217f; bibliography, f214-17   181
Brody, Elizabeth C.
Lord Jim and the question of moral judgment. Honors
Thesis, (English) Radcliffe College, 1966. 40f   182
Broncel, Zdzisław
"Heart of Darkness." In Conrad żywy, edited by Wit Tar-
nawski. London: B. Świderski, 1957. p159-68
Jądro faszyzmu. Nowa kultura 1, no 1, 1958   183
Brooker, Bertram R.
Conrad's view of life. Canadian Forum 5, no 55:207-9
Ap '25   184
Brooks, Van Wyck
From a writer's notebook. London: Dent, 1958. p 68
(Noted in Wiadomości 16, no 46:5 N 12 '61)
The world of H. G. Wells. New York: Mitchell Kenner-
ley, 1915. p153-61   185
Brotman, Jordan Lloyd
Joseph Conrad, social critic. Ph. D. Thesis, Univ. of
California at Berkeley, 1955. 241p   186
Brown, Bob
Collector's luck... Coronet 3, no 3:95-8 Ja '38; same.
(excerpt) Literary Digest 125, no 6:15 F 5 '38 (en-
titled: "Conrad by Chance")
(Discusses the first edition, first issue of Chance) 187
Brown, Dorothy Snodgrass
The irony of Joseph Conrad. Ph. D. Thesis, Univ. of
Washington, 1956. 183p. Abstract in Dissertation Ab-
stracts 16:2148 '56   188
Brown, Douglas
Critical commentary. In The Nigger of the "Narcissus,"
by Joseph Conrad. (London University English Litera-
ture Series) London: Univ. of London Press | 1960| p9-34
From Heart of Darkness to Nostromo: an approach to
Conrad. In The modern age, edited by Boris Ford.

(The Pelican guide to English literature, vol. 7) London: Penguin books, 1961. p119-37
Introductory Essay. In Three tales from Conrad: with an introductory essay by Douglas Brown. London: Hutchinson, 1960. p1-26
(Reviewed in Use of English 13:140 Winter '61)
Towards a reading of Nostromo. Summer Highway May-Sept '52 p51-64   189
Brown, E. K.
James and Conrad. Yale Review ns 35, no 2:265-85 Winter '46   190
Brown, Emerson Lee
Joseph Conrad's last novels: The Shadow-Line, The Arrow of Gold, and The Rover. Master's Thesis, Syracuse Univ. 1958. 62f   191
Brown, Leonard Stanley
The expositional and moralizing substance in the novels of Joseph Conrad. M. A. Thesis, Univ. of Nebraska, 1925. 59p   192
Browne, Alex F.
[Two Conrad incidents] Sea Breezes ns 11:235 Mr '51
                                                             193
Brownrigg, (Rear Admiral) Douglas
Indiscretions of the naval censor. New York: George H. Doran [c1920] p78-9
(Reviewed in Land & Water no 3014:27 F 12 '20) 194
Bruccoli, Matthew J. and Charles A. Rheault, Jr.
Imposition figures and plate gangs in The Rescue. Studies in Bibliography (Univ. of Virginia) 14:258-62 '61   195
Bruecher, Werner
The concept of the "double" in Joseph Conrad. M. A. Thesis, Univ. of Arizona, 1962.   196
Bruffee, Kenneth A.
The lesser nightmare: Marlow's 'Lie' in "Heart of Darkness." Modern Language Quarterly ·25:322-9 S '64
                                                             197
Brzeska, W.
Francja anektuje K. Korzeniowskiego. Literatura i Sztuka no 15, 1928   198
Brzezinski, Roman
Milośc niewygasla... Zycie no 32, 1949   199
Brzozowski, Stanisław
Józef Conrad. In Głozy wśpód nocy... Lwów: Polniecki, 1912. p369-77
O znaczeniu wychowawczem literatury angielskiej. Widnokręgi (Lwów) nos 10-12 '10; same. In Glosy wśród

Brzozowski, Stanislaw (cont.)
    nocy... Lowów: Polniecki, 1912. p302-21
    Pamiętnik. Lowów: 1913. p157-9   200
Buck, Jule R.
    A study of some of the important characters of Joseph
    Conrad. Senior Essay in English, Wells College,
    1949. 50f   201
Buckler, William E. and Arnold B. Sklare
    A suggested interpretation [of "Youth"] In Stories from six
    authors, edited by William E. Buckler & Arnold B.
    Sklare. New York: McGraw-Hill, 1960. p509-11 202
Budrecki, Lech
    Nad Conradem (Reflections on Conrad). Kuźnica (Forge)
    no 16, 1948   203
Budziak, Lydia Martha
    Joseph Conrad as a novelist. M. A. Thesis, St. Louis
    Univ. 1930. 51f   204
Bullett, Gerard William
    Joseph Conrad. In Modern English fiction, a personal
    view. London: Jenkins, 1926. p54-69   205
Burgess, C. F.
    Conrad's pesky Russian. Nineteenth-Century Fiction 18,
    no 2:189-93 S '63
    (In "Heart of Darkness")   206
Burgess, O. N.
    Joseph Conrad: the old and the new criticism. Australi-
    an Quarterly 29:85-92 Mr '57   207
Burkhardt, Johanna
    Das Erlebnis der Wirklichkeit und seine künstlerische
    Gestaltung in Joseph Conrads Werk... Marburg: Bauer,
    1935. 108p. Dissertation, Marburg. "Literaturver-
    zeichnis," p[iii]-v   208
Burkhart, Charles
    Conrad the Victorian. English Literature in Transition 6,
    no 1:1-8 '63   209
Burner, Jarvis
    One source of Nostromo. Ph. D. Thesis, Coe College
    (Cedar Rapids, Iowa), 1952   210
Burt, H. T.
    Joseph Conrad: an appreciation. Hibbert Journal 23:141-
    57 O '24
    (Examines Conrad's heroes as Aristotelian, with tragic
    flaws)   211
Burt, Struthers
    Within the Tides. In Keating, George T. A Conrad me-
    morial library. Garden City, New York: Doubleday,
    Doran, 1929. p230-9   212

Burton, D. L.
    Teaching "The Secret Sharer" to high school students.
        English Journal 47:263-6 My '58   213
    A bust of Conrad.   Bookman (NY) 45:637 Ag '17   214
Busza, Andrzej
    Conrad's Polish literary background and some illustra-
        tions of the influence of Polish Literature on his work.
        Antemurale 10:109-255 '66.   Rome: Institutum His-
        toricum Polonicum, 1966.
        (Reviewed by Edmund A. Bojarski in English Litera-
        ture in Transition 10, no 3:163-6 '67; John Espey in
        Nineteenth-Century Fiction 22, no 3:311 D '67; H. B.
        Segel in Slavic & East European Journal 12, no 2:254-
        5 Summer '68)   215
Butcher, Fanny
    Death of Conrad recalls hard days of his struggle.   Chi-
        cago Daily Tribune Ag 9 '24 p 8
    [Note on Conrad's Polish origins]   Chicago Sunday Tribune
        F 7 '15 part 8 p4   215a
Buus, Barbara Douglass
    The significance of love and marriage in Joseph Conrad's
        fiction.   M. A. Thesis, Ohio State University, 1967.
        79f   215b
Butler, Lillian Louise
    The light and the dark; a study of Conrad's enigmatic
        imagery.   M. A. Thesis, Univ. of Toronto, 1963.
        131f   216

C. , C.
    L'aristocratisme slave de Conrad.   Le Figaro no 247:3
        D 29 '23; same.   (excerpt) Chronique des Lettres
        Françaises 2:412-14 My-Je '24   217
Cadby, Will
    Conrad's dislike of the camera and how it was conquered
        by Will Cadby.   Graphic 110:728 N 1 '24 (portraits)
                                                        218
Cadot, Raoul
    Conrad et le navire.   Revue de l'Enseignement des
        Langues Vivantes 49:390-6, 433-8 '32
    Les traits moraux de la mer dans l'oeuvre de Conrad.
        Revue de l'Enseignement des Langues Vivantes 50:399-
        407 N '33   219
Cagle, William R.
    The publication of Joseph Conrad's Chance.   Book Collec-
        tor 16, no 3:305-22 Autumn '67   220
Cambon, Glauco
    Giacobbe e l'angelo in Melville e Conrad.   Letteratura

Cambon, Glauco (cont.)
    4:53-69 My-Ag '56   221
Camerino, A.
    Centenario de Conrad.   Giornale del Mattino 12:31 '57
                                              222
Campbell, Malcolm
    Joseph Conrad.   Berliner Börs.   Courant 1924, p 369
                                              223
Canario, John W.
    The harlequin in "Heart of Darkness." Studies in Short
       Fiction 4, no 3:225-33 Spring '67   224
Canby, Henry Seidel
    Conrad and Melville.   Literary Review of the New York
       Evening Post F 4 '22 p393-4; same.   In Definitions...
       New York: Harcourt, Brace [c1922] p257-68; same.
       In Modern essays, selected by C. D. Morley. New
       York: Harcourt, Brace, 1924. 2nd series, p202-14
       Introduction.   In Within the Tides, by Joseph Conrad.
       (Memorial Edition) Garden City, New York: Doubleday,
       Page, 1925.   Volume XV, pvii-ix (In this volume,
       Tales of Unrest follows, separately paginated)
       Under Western Eyes.   In Keating, George T.   A Conrad
       memorial library.   Garden City, New York: Doubleday,
       Doran, 1929. p187-93   225
Candee, Marjorie Dent
    Joseph Conrad's last ship... Sea Breezes (The P. S. N. C.
       Magazine) 19:4-5, 7 D '34   226
Cândido, Antônio
    Tese e antítese.   S. Paulo: Cia.   Editôra Nacional,
       1964   227
Canning, Peter Crooke
    An examination of Nostromo.   Honors Thesis, Harvard
       College, 1959. 44f; bibl., f44   228
Captain Conrad.   Outlook (NY) 133:879-80 My 16 '23; New
    York Tribune My 3 '23 p12; same.   Book Leaf (NY)
    My 4 '23   229
Carey, Robert
    Joseph Conrad: self-recognition.   M. A. Thesis, Wesleyan
       Univ. 1961   230
Carlile, (Reverend) J. C.
    At Conrad's grave.   British Weekly 76:428 Ag 14 '24
                                              231
Carr, Thomas
    Joseph Conrad.   Spectator 141:581 O 27 '28   232
Carrington, N. T.
    Joseph Conrad: Typhoon and Youth.   (Notes on Chosen
       English Texts) London: James Brodie, 1964. 48p   232a

Carroll, Eleanor
Conrad's books hold his secrets. New York Evening
   Post My 8 '23 p16   233
Carroll, Sydney Wentworth
   Conrad and the critics. In some dramatic opinions.
   London: F. V. White & Co. [nd ? 1923] p171-4   234
Carroll, Wesley Barnett
   The fiction of Joseph Conrad. Ph. D. Thesis, Cornell
   Univ., 1934. 382p; bibl., p368-82. Abstract: Ithaca,
   New York: Sept. 1934. [4]p
   The novelist as artist. Modern Fiction Studies 1:2-8
   F '55   235
Carruthers, John [pseud.]
   See Grieg, J. Y. T.   236
Carving of Joseph Conrad in form of a ship's figurehead.
   New York Herald Tribune, Section VI, May 13 '34
   p8   237
Casey, Bill
   André Malraux's Heart of Darkness. Twentieth Century
   Literature 5, no 1:21-6 Ap '59
   (Malraux's The Royal Way resembles Conrad's "Heart
   of Darkness")   237a
Cassell, Richard A.
   Ford Madox Ford: a study of his novels. Baltimore:
   Johns Hopkins press [1961] p20-1, 32-3, 35-6, 43-72,
   206-7   238
Cazamian, Madeleine
   Joseph Conrad. In Le roman et les idées en Angleterre.
   (Strasbourg. Université. Faculté des Lettres. Fasci-
   cule 125) Paris: Les Belles Lettres, 1955. p128-69
                                                          239
Cecchi, Emilio
   Indiscrezioni su J. Conrad. In Scrittori inglesi e
   americani. Rome: G. Carabba [1935] p186-91
   Joseph Conrad. Il Convegno anno 5, no 8:375-94 Ag '24;
   same. In Scrittori inglesi e americani. Rome: G.
   Carabba [1935] p162-85
   (Noted in La Nouvelle Revue Française 23:805-6 D
   '24)   240
Cecil, David
   Joseph Conrad. London Magazine 1:54-71 S '54; same.
   In The fine art of reading and other literary studies.
   New York: Bobbs-Merrill, 1957. p177-215
   (Reviewed in Wiadomości 12, no 43:5 O 27 '57)   241
Centnerszwerowa, Róża
   Głos z za grobu "Książę Roman" Conrada; wielki pisarz o
   patrjotyzmie. Wiadomości Literackie rok 2, no

Centnerszwerowa, Róża (cont.)
 79:2 Jl 5 '25   242
Ch., Leon
 W domu Conrada Korzeniowskiego. Wizyta w Canterbury
 u wdowy po wielkim pisarzu. (At Conrad's home. A
 visit with the great writer's widow at Canterbury.)
 Polonia no 3302, 1933   243
Chadbourne, Marc
 Du nouveau sur la collaboration de Joseph Conrad avec
 Ford Madox Hueffer. Les Nouvelles Littéraires année
 4:5 Jl 18 '25   244
Chaikin, Milton
 Zola and Conrad's "The Idiots." Studies in Philology 52:
 502-7 Jl '55   245
Chałasiński, Józef
 "Mitologia i realizm," by J. Kott. Mysł Współczesna
 no 5:96-104 O '46   246
Chalko, Zbigniew
 [Poem to Joseph Conrad] In Conrad żywy, edited by Wit
 Tarnawski. London: B. Świderski, 1957. p36-8   247
Chandler, Arnold Edward
 "A tiny white speck in a darkened world:" a study of
 four Conrad heroes. Ph.D. Thesis, Univ. of Texas,
 1967. 202f; abstract in Dissertation Abstracts 28:
 2238A-2239A Dec. '67   247a
The characters of Suspense. Book Leaf (NY) Mr 24 '26
                                                                 248

Charbonneau, Louis H. Jr.
 The nature and significance of Joseph Conrad's morality.
 M.A. Thesis, Univ. of Detroit, 1949. 75p   249
Chatterjee, Sisir
 Joseph Conrad: the power of the written word. In Prob-
 lems in modern English fiction. Calcutta: Bookland
 Private Ltd. [1965] p112-22   250
Chevalley, Abel
 Joseph Conrad. In The modern English novel, translated
 from the French by Ben Ray Redman. New York:
 Knopf, 1925. p180-9   251
Chevrillon, André
 Conrad. La Nouvelle Revue Francaise 23:704-7 D 1 '24
                                                                 252
Chevrillon, Pierre
 L'homme dans le roman marin de Conrad. Revue Anglo-
 Américaine 5:316-30 Ap '28   253
Chew, Samuel Claggett
 Essay on Conrad's Suspense. Saturday Review of Litera-
 ture 2:289-90 N 14 '25   254

Childs, John Burgwin
Male-female relationships in Joseph Conrad's fiction.
M. A. Thesis, Trinity College (Hartford, Connecticut),
1967. 82f; bibl., f81-2   255
Chillag, Charles
The 'others' in Conrad's Lord Jim.   English Analyst
(Northwestern University) no 21, Feb '53   256
Chubb, Edwin Watts
Romance of Conrad. In Stories of authors, British and
American. New York: Macmillan, 1926. new edi-
tion, p393-400   257
Church, Hayden
Novelist jilts his sea muse. Detroit Free Press Jl 25
'20   258
Church, Richard
British authors. New York: Longmans, 1948. new edi-
tion, p28-31   259
Churchill, R. C.
Conrad in school. Journal of Education (London) 79:130,
132 Mr '47   260
Chwalewik, Witold Jerzy
Conrad a Polska i Anglia (Conrad and Poland and Eng-
land). Myśl Narodowa (Nationalist Thought) nos 10-11,
1926
Conrad a tradycja literacka. Kwartalnik Neofilologiczny
5, nos 1-2: 29-37 '58; same. Polska Akademia
Naukowych Sprawozdania Wydziału Nauk. Społecznych
1:74-7 '58; same. In Joseph Conrad Korzeniowski.
Essays and studies. Warsaw: Państwowe Wydawnictwo
Naukowe, 1958. p[29]-37; same. In Wspomnienia i
studia o Conradzie, edited by Barbara Kocówna.
[Warsaw:] Państwowy Instytut Wydawniczy [1963] p439-
56
Conrad i Stevenson jako pisarze katoliczy. Ruch Liter-
acki 2, no 6:169-74 Je '27
Czy Conrad jest pisarzem polskim? Myśl Narodowa 3,
nos 39-41:189-90, 208-9, 226-8 '26
Józef Conrad w Kardyfie. Ruch Literacki 7, no 8:225-9
Ag '32; same. In Wspomnienia i studia o Conradzie,
edited by Barbara Kocówna. [Warsaw:] Państwowy
Instytut Wydawniczy [1963] p61-9
O głównym motywie wczesnej twórczości Conrada. In
Wspomnienia i studia o Conradzie, edited by Barbara
Kocówna. [Warsaw:] Państwowy Instytut Wydawniczy
[1963] p427-38
Literatura angielska. Rocznik Literackie, 1962. [War-
saw:] Państwowy Instytut Wydawniczy [1963] p310-12

Chwalewik, Witold Jerzy (cont.)
  Paradoks Conrada-marynarza (The paradox of Conrad the
    sailor.)   Polska Literacka (Literary Poland) no 1,
    1930
  Przekłady.   Literatura angielska i anglo-amerykańska
    (Translations.   English and American literature).
    Rocznik Literacki, 1933.   Warsaw: Instytut Literacki,
    1934.   p137-41
  Przekłady.   Literatura angielska i anglo-amerykańska.
    Rocznik Literacki, 1934.   Warsaw: Instytut Literacki,
    1935.   p137-40
  Przekłady.   Literatura angielska.   In Rocznik Literacki,
    1935.   Warsaw: Instytut Literacki, 1936.   p121-7
  Skąd kult Conrada?   (Whence the Conrad cult?)   Myśl
    Narodowa no 37, 1925   261
Cichowicz, W.
  Nieznane dwa lista Conrada (Two unknown letters of Con-
    rad.)   Tęcza (Rainbow) no 18, 1929   262
Ciołek, Jerzy
  Pod obcą banderą (Under a foreign flag.)   Świat (World)
    no 35, 1949   263
Clark, Barrett H.
  Joseph Conrad explains his Victory.   The Sun Books &
    the Book World Je 30 '18 Section 6 p10
    ("The victory Conrad speaks of is the victory of the
    woman and her love," says Clark, and Conrad, in a
    letter to Clark dated May 4, 1918, agrees.)   264
Clark, Rupert Esmond
  Racial and national types in the works of Joseph Conrad.
    M.A. Thesis, Univ. of Texas, 1936. iii-vi, 147f 265
Clark, Winifred
  Conrad's man against the universe.   M.A. Thesis, Univ.
    of Tulsa, 1963   266
Clarke, David Waldo
  Modern English writers.   New York: Longmans, 1947.
    p18-24   267
Clarke, George Herbert
  Joseph Conrad and his art.   Sewanee Review 30:258-76
    Jl '22   268
Clarke, Joseph C.
  [Adventure in Conradese] Bookman (NY) 51:602 Jl'20;
    answer in Bookman (NY) 52:93 S '20 by G. G. F.   269
Clarke, Kenneth Wendell
  The treatment of race prejudice in Joseph Conrad.   M.A.
    Thesis, State College of Washington at Pullman, 1949.
    83p   270
Clarkson, Max

The short story in England in the later nineteenth century.
   M. A. Thesis, Univ. of Toronto, 1946. 114p   271
Clay, N. L.
   Typhoon and Youth, by Joseph Conrad, edited by N. L.
   Clay. San Francisco: Chandler Publishing Co. [1962?]
   vii-[xi], 148p.
   Commentary and questions on the works, p125-48; life
   of the author, pix-x   272
Clemens, Cyril
   A chat with Joseph Conrad. Hobbies 70:85 Ja '66   273
Clemens, Florence
   Conrad's favorite bedtime book. South Atlantic Quarterly
   38:302-15 Jl '39 (Examines Conrad's use of Alfred
   Wallace's The Malay Archipelago)
   Conrad's Malaysia. College English 2:338-46 Ja '41
   Conrad's Malaysian fiction: a new study in sources with
   an analysis of factual material involved. Ph. D. Thesis,
   Ohio State Univ., 1937. 284f. Abstract in Ohio State
   Univ. Abstracts of Dissertation ns, Spring Quarter, no
   24:43-52 '37
   Joseph Conrad as a geographer. Scientific Monthly 51:
   460-5 N '40 (bibliography)   274
Clifford, (Sir) Hugh
   Concerning Conrad and his work. Empire Review 47:
   287-94 My '28
   The genius of Mr. Joseph Conrad. North American Re-
   view 178:842-52 Je '04; same. Literary Digest 29,
   no 1:11-12 Jl 2 '04
   Introduction. In Lord Jim, by Joseph Conrad, with an
   introduction by Hugh Clifford. (Memorial Edition)
   Garden City: Doubleday, Page, 1925. Volume IV p vii-
   xii
   Joseph Conrad: some scattered memories. Bookman's
   Journal & Print Collector 11, no 37:3-6 O '24; noted.
   Manchester Guardian Weekly 11, no 16:333 O 17 '24
   An Outcast of the Islands. In Keating, George T. A
   Conrad memorial library. Garden City, New York:
   Doubleday, Doran, 1929. p14-21
   A sketch of Joseph Conrad. Harper's Weekly 49:59 Ja
   14 '05
   A talk on Joseph Conrad and his work. Colombo: Cave
   & Co., Feb. 1927. 16p. (A lecture delivered to the
   Ceylon branch of the English Association)
   (Reviewed in Times Literary Supplement Je 2 '27
   p394-5)   275
The clipper ship "Torrens." Blue Peter 3:241 S '23   276

The close of a unique literary career.   Publishers' Weekly
    106:500-1 Ag 9 '24   277
Clothier, Selma Vaughn
    A study of Joseph Conrad's interpretation of character.
    M. A. Thesis, Univ. of Southern California, 1935. ii,
    60p   278
Cobley, W. D.
    Joseph Conrad.   Papers of the Manchester Literary Club
    52:69-94 '26   279
Coburn, Alvin Langdon
    More men of mark.   New York: Knopf, 1922. Plate
    XXIV (A photo of Conrad)   280
Cocke, Leta Mae
    Joseph Conrad's portrayal of Malay characters.   M. A.
    Thesis, Univ. of Texas, 1938. vi, 90f   281
Cockerell, Sydney Carlyle
    Friends of a lifetime.   Letters to Sydney Carlyle Cocker-
    ell.   Edited by Viola Meynell.   London: Cape [1940]
    p324-5, 360-1 (Two letters from Conrad, dated Aug.
    19, 1919 and Nov. 21, 1923; also two letters by
    Thomas Edward Lawrence, dated Dec. 25, 1923 and
    Jan. 13, 1924 concerning Conrad's Rover)   282
Coe, Lloyd
    Conradia, a map locating the scenes of various books by
    Joseph Conrad.   Designed and drawn by Lloyd Coe.
    [New York:] The Phoenix Book Shop [?1927] 17.5
    x 26 inches   283
Coffey, Ada Opalene
    Joseph Conrad: a dictionary of characters.   M. A. Thesis,
    Univ. of Kansas, 1939. v, 327f   284
Colbron, Grace Isabel
    Joseph Conrad's women.   Bookman (NY) 38:476-9 Ja '14
                                                            285
Colby, Robert A.
    Joseph Conrad, voyager through strange seas.   Queens
    College, New York: Paul Klapper Library, 1958 286
Cole, (Captain) A. G.
    Another Conrad ship.   Sea Breezes ns 16:70-1 Jl '53
    (Refers to the Jeddah)   287
Coleman, Arthur Prudden
    Polonisms in the English of Conrad's Chance.   Modern
    Language Notes 46:463-8 N '31   288
Colenutt, Richard
    Joseph Conrad: personal side.   English Literary & Edu-
    cational Review for Continental Readers 6:8 '35
    Joseph Conrad - twelve years after.   Cornhill Magazine
    154:129-40 Ag '36; see also: Notes & Queries 171:

Conquest, Edwin Parker, Jr.
The abyss of unrest. Joseph Conrad's early tales. Ph. D.
Thesis, Princeton University, 1967. vi, 205f; bibliog-
raphy, f187-9 (On Tales of Unrest)					302a
Conrad, Alf Borys
A famous father and his son. New York Times Book Re-
view 62:7, 74 D 1 '57
As his son saw Conrad. New York Herald Tribune Maga-
zine Ag 24 '30 p11 (Portrait)
Joseph Conrad at home; memories of my father and some
of his contemporaries. Courier (London) 24, no 2:61-
8 F '55; same. (translated by Zdzisław Najder)
Twórczość 13, no 12:54-62 D '57
(Recollections of John Galsworthy, Hugh Walpole, Per-
ceval Gibbon, H. G. Wells, Rudyard Kipling, F. M.
Hueffer, and R. B. Cunningham Graham)					303
Conrad, Carl
Zum bilde Joseph Conrads. Gestalten und hintergründe.
Frankfurter Zeitung no 351:1-2 Jl 13 '38					304
Conrad, (Mrs.) Jessie (George)
A blessing in disguise. Bookman (NY) 59:533-4 Jl '24
Co Conrad zawdzięczał swemu wujowi Tadeuszowi. Il-
lustrowany Kurjer Codzienny no 138, 1930 (Translated
by Joli Fuchsówny)
Comment j'épousai Joseph Conrad. Translated by Mar-
guerite de Ginestet. Revue de Paris année 45, no 3:
631-48 F 1 '38
Conrad's share in The Nature of a Crime and his Congo
Diary. Bookman's Journal 12, no 46:135-6 Jl '25
Conrad's skill as an artist. Saturday Review of Litera-
ture 2:700-1 Ap 10 '26; same. (excerpt) Poland 7, no
8:frontispiece (facing p469) Ag '26
Dale i niedale naszych pierwszych lat małżeńskich.
(Translated by Joli Fuchsówny) Illustrowany Kurjer
Codzienny no 111, 1930
Did Joseph Conrad return as a spirit? With an introduc-
tion by Cyril Clemens. Webster Groves, Missouri:
International Mark Twain Society, 1932. 8p; portrait
Earlier and later days. Saturday Evening Post 197:12-13,
212-14 S 13 '24
Eine Reise mit Joseph Conrad. Berliner Börs. Courant
no 51, 1932
Ekspedycja Conrada do Congo. (Translated by Joli
Fuchsówny) Illustrowany Kurjer Codzienny no 131,
1930
In memoriam. Bookmark (London) 3, no 12:13 N '27
(Written to accompany the photograph of the panel

placed to the memory of Joseph Conrad; a supplement
to the Bookmark Christmas number, 1927)
Introduction. In A Personal Record, by Joseph Conrad.
(Memorial Edition) Garden City, New York: Doubleday,
Page, 1925. Volume XII, p v-vii
Joseph Conrad. Bookmark (London) 1, no 3:3-4 Autumn
'25 (Refers to early recollections and to A Personal
Record)
Joseph Conrad, an eccentric, but lovable genius. World
Today 53:582-4 My '29
Joseph Conrad: an intimate recollection. Bookmark
(London) 3, no 10:17 Je '27
(Discusses a photograph of Conrad taken outside Pent
Farm, 1901)
Joseph Conrad and his circle. London: Jarrolds; New
York: Dutton, 1935. 7-283p; portraits. Paris: Galli-
mard [1939] Translated by Marguerite de Ginestet.
[7]-274p; portrait
(Dated 1935 unless otherwise noted. Reviewed by Jean
Thomas in Annales Politiques et Littéraires 113:585-6
Je 10 '39; William McFee in American Mercury 37:
116-19 Ja '36 and in Sun (NY) S 25; Times Literary
Supplement Jl 18 p460; Graham Greene in Spectator
155:164 Jl 26; G. W. Stonier in Fortnightly Review 144:
378 S; Douglas Goldring in English Review 61:366-7 S;
Edward Garnett in London Mercury 32:385-7 Ag; Morton
D. Zabel in New Republic 85:180 D 18; Percy Hutchison
in New York Times Book Review S 29 p 4; Christopher
Morley in Book-of-the-Month Club News O, p 15; H. L.
Mencken in Nation (NY) 141:144 O 16; Booklist 32:62-3
N; Clara Gruening Stillman in New York Herald Tribune
Books S 22 p8; V. S. Pritchett in Christian Science
Monitor S 18 p11; Cleveland Open Shelf O, p19; John
Chamberlain in Current History 43:xii N; Saturday Re-
view (London) 159:951 Jl 27; David Garnett in New
Statesman & Nation ns 10:96 Jl 20; Saturday Review of
Literature 12:12 O 12; Springfield Republican S 18 p8;
R. Mirande in Annales Politique et Littéraires 106:368-
70 O 10; John O'London's Weekly 33:590 Jl 27; B. Ifor
Evans in Manchester Guardian Weekly 33, no 4:74 Jl
26; Alice McLarney in America 54:114-15 N 9; Isabel
Paterson in New York Herald Tribune S 16 p13)
Joseph Conrad and his circle. Port Washington, New
York: Kennikat Press, 1964. 2nd edition. 283p plus:
A Handlist... by Richard Curle, p1-23 appended, with
separate pagination
Joseph Conrad and the Congo. London Mercury 22:261-3

Conrad, (Mrs.) Jessie (George) (cont.)
Jl '30
Joseph Conrad as a ship's prow: Miss Dora Clarke's
wooden ship's figure-head.   T. P.'s & Cassell's Weekly
ns 8:271-2 Je 25 '27
Joseph Conrad as I knew him.   With an introduction by
Richard Curle.   London: Heinemann; Garden City,
New York: Doubleday, Page, 1926.   vii-xxi, 162p.
"Introduction," p vii-viii. $2
Serialized in Boston Evening Transcript in 1925, con-
cluding with the S 19 '25 number; excerpt.   Evening
World (NY) S 16 '26 p16; Literary Digest 91, no 5:50,
52 O 30 '26; World Today (London) 53:582-4 My '29
(Dated 1926 unless otherwise noted.   Reviewed in
Booklist 23:218 D; William McFee in New York Herald
Tribune Books N 21 p6; Grace Willard in Literary Re-
view of the New York Evening Post O 9 p5; Nation-
Athenaeum 40:90, 92 O 16; New York Times Book Re-
view S 26 p2, 14; Saturday Review (London) 142:289-
90 S 11; Saturday Review of Literature 3:394 D 4;
Spectator 137:387 S 11; Times Literary Supplement S
9 p594; Osbert Burdett in Bookman (NY) 75:55 Ap '32;
T. P.'s & Cassell's Weekly 4:852 O 17; Bookman (London) 71:23 O; J. P. O'R. in Irish Statesman 7, no 14:
334 D 11; Henry D. Davray in Mercure de France
année 38, tome 193:485-7 Ja 15 '27; John O'London's
Weekly 17:768 S 25; A. K. in English Review 43:736-7
D; Chartres Biron in London Mercury 15:106-7 N;
Punch 171:363-4 S 29; noted in New York Herald Trib-
une S 19 Section III p6; F. X. Talbot in America 36:
45 O 23; Cz. Znamierowski in Głos Prawdy no 125 '27)
Joseph Conrad's war service.   Blue Peter 11, no 110:
252-5 My '31
Journeys with Joseph Conrad: Poland in the Great War.
Chambers's Journal series 7, volume 21:497-500 Ag
'31
Józef Conrad.   Translated by Wanda Nałęcz-Korzeniowska.
Edited by Róża Jabłkowska.   Krakow: Wydawnictwo
Literackie [1959] 7-475p.   Notes and postscript by
Róża Jabłkowska, p417-[459]; "from the translator,"
p461-[464].   A translation of Joseph Conrad and His
Circle.
(Reviewed by Feliks Fornalczyk in Tydognik Morski no
11:6-7 '59; Antoni Gołubiew in Tygodnik Powszechny 13
no 19:5 My 10 '59; Joanna Guze in Nowa Kultura no
17:2 '59; Juliusz Kydryński in Życie Literackie no 37:
4-5 '59; J. Wilhelmin in Trybuna Literacka no 9 '59;

Nowe Książki no 8:481-3 '59; Literatura Piękna 1959
p205)
Listy wuja Tadeusza. (Translated by Joli Fuchsówny)
Illustrowany Kurjer Codzienny no 145, 1930
The manuscript of Almayer's Folly. Bookman's Journal
3rd series 18, no 13:1-3 '30
Memories of Joseph Conrad. Blue Peter 10:304-9, 347-
52 Je-Jl '30; Vossische Zeitung (Unt.-Bl.) 274, 1933;
Neue Zürcher Zeitung nos 2486, 2511, 2518, 2562 '29
Odwiedzając ojczyznę Conrada dostajemy się w wir wojny.
Illustrowany Kurjer Codzienny no 124, 1930 (Trans-
lated by Joli Fuchsówny)
Our visit to Poland in 1914. Blue Peter 5:209-13, 290-3
Ag-S '25
Personal recollections of Joseph Conrad. London: Pri-
vately printed [by Strangeways, Printers] 1924. 5-82p
(100 copies only)
(Later included in: Mrs. Conrad's Joseph Conrad As I
Knew Him. 1926)
Preface. In Joseph Conrad's letters to his wife. London:
Privately printed [by Neill & Co., Edinburgh] 1927.
p7-8
(220 copies only)
Preface. In Notes by Joseph Conrad, written in a set of
his first editions in the possession of Richard Curle,
with an introduction and explanatory comments... Lon-
don: Privately printed [by Strangeways, Printers]
1925. p[5]-7
(100 copies only)
Pure chance. New York World, editorial section, D 9
'23, p 6E (On Conrad's manuscripts)
Recollections of Stephen Crane. Bookman (NY) 63:134-7
Ap '26
Rękopisy Conrada. Wiadomości Literackie rok 1, no 23:
4 Je 8 '24
The romance of The Rescue. Bookman's Journal 12, no
43:19-20 Ap '25
Some Reminiscences. In Keating, George T. A Conrad
memorial library. Garden City, New York: Doubleday,
Doran, 1929. p196-9
Spotkanie Conrada z Rogerem Casementem. Illustrowany
Kurjer Codzienny no 158, 1930
Why lie? Bookman's Journal & Print Collector 10:7 Ap
'24
Wbitni przyjaciele i goscie Conrada (Translated by Joli
Fuchsówny). Illustrowany Kurier Codzienny no 117,
1930

Conrad, (Mrs.) Jessie (George) (cont.)
Z cyklu: moje wspomnienia o J. Conradzie: moje
pierwsze spotkanie z J. Conradem (translated by Joli
Fuchsówny). Illustrowany Kurier Codzienny no 105, 1930
Z J. Conradem-Korzeniowskim na Korsyce. Gazeta
Polska no 262, 1930 (Includes a letter by Conrad dated
Feb. 5, 1921) 305
Conrad, John
Joseph Conrad. Głos Anglii (Voice of England) (Cracow)
no 9 (1947)
Some reminiscences of my father. In Conrad żywy,
edited by Wit Tarnawski. London: B. Świderski, 1957.
p10-31; same. In Joseph Conrad Korzeniowski, by
Róża Jablkowska. Warsaw: Państwowe Zakłady Wy-
dawnictwo Szkolynch, 1964. p145-151
Z ocjem na morzu (translated from the English by Mariusz
Hrynkiewicz-Moczulski). Wiadomości 4, nos 176-7:1
Ag 21 '49 306
Conrad, (Mrs.) Joseph
See: Conrad, (Mrs.) Jessie (George) 307
Conrad. Publishers' Circular 119:311 S 15 '23; Manchester
Guardian Weekly 11, no 7:145 Ag 15 '24; Canadian
Forum 4:357 S '24; Bund (Bern) Kl. Bund. 11, F-Mr
'28; Neues Wiener Journal Ag 20 '24; same. Baltische
Presse no 222, 1924 308
Conrad a literatura polska. Wiadomości Literackie 1, no
33:4 Ag 17 '24 309
Conrad after 100 years. Saturday Review 40, no 6:13 F 9
'59 (Comments on 10 of Conrad's books) 310
Conrad and American literature. Wiadomości 13, no 35:1-2
Ag 31 '58
(Gives answers to four questions about Conrad's rank
in English letters from Paul D. Boles, Marc Brandel,
John Brooks, Van Wyck Brooks, B. J. Chute, Anne M.
Downes, Ralph Ellison, James T. Farrell, Howard
Fast, Bernard Glemser, Herbert Gold, John D. Gordan,
Albert J. Guerard, Mark Harris, Robert F. Haugh,
Fannie Hurst, David Karp, Robie Macauley, James A.
Michener, Henry Miller, Wright Morris, Frederic Mor-
ton, Thomas C. Moser, Robert Nathan, Robert Payne,
John Dos Passos, Robert Pick, Katherine Anne Porter,
Harrison Smith, John Steinbeck, William Styron, Glen-
don Swarthout, Robert P. Warren, Glenway Wescott,
Dan Wickenden, Thornton Wilder, Neal Woodruff, Jr.,
Herman Wouk, Morton D. Zabel) 310a
Conrad and character. New York Tribune Ap 30 '23 p 10
(an editorial) 311

Conrad for 'movies' but can't sell one.   New York Times
    My 8 '23   332
Conrad fought death to finish his book; author's widow tells
    of last vain efforts.   New York Times S 17 '25 p 8
                                                                 333
Conrad frequently despondent over reception of works.   New
    York Herald Tribune Ja 13 '28   334
[Conrad granted Civil List pension] Nation (NY) 93:24 Jl
    13 '11   335
Conrad honored.   New York Times Ja 5 '58 Section II
    p16   336
Conrad in Corsica.   Glasgow Evening News Ap 28 '21 p2
                                                                 337
Conrad in England.   Manchester Guardian Ag 4 '24 p6   338
Conrad in Poland.   Bookman (NY) 46:659 F '18   339
Conrad in sculpture.   Sphere 100:87 Ja 24 '25   340
Conrad in the city of New York.   New York Herald Tribune
    S 10 '28 p12 (editorial) (? By Richard Curle?)   341
Conrad Korzeniowski.   W 30-lecie śmierci (Conrad.   On the
    30th anniversary of his death) Radio i Świat no 31,
    1954   342
Conrad library opens at Seaman's Institute.   Christopher
    Morley recalls anecdotes of author.   New York Herald
    Tribune My 25 '34 p15   343
Conrad manuscript bought for $21,000.   New York Times
    My 9 '63 p29 (The manuscript of Victory)   344
A Conrad memorial.   John O'London's Weekly 14:46, 614
    Ap 10, Ag 21 '26 (By "Colophon")   345
Conrad memorial library drive for $1,000,000 opens.   New
    York Herald Tribune O 31 '26 p20   346
[Conrad moves from Pent Farm, Kent, to Bedfordshire]
    British Weekly 43:205 N 28 '07   347
Conrad o cenzurze.   Wiadomości Literackie 9, no 28:2 Jl
    3 '32   348
Conrad o Polsce.   Wiadomości Literackie rok 1, no 6:1
    F 10 '24 (By "J. M.")   349
Conrad o rosji.   Wiadomości 4, nos 176-7:5 Ag 21 '49 350
Conrad o swojej powieści.   Wiadomości Literackie 10, no
    523:11 D 3 '33   351
Conrad offered knighthood, but declined the offer.   New
    York Herald Tribune Jl 20 '27   352
Conrad of the uncritical mind.   Argonaut (San Francisco)
        '23; Publishers' Circular & Booksellers' Record
    119:67-8 Jl 28 '23   353
Conrad on his writings.   A tribute to Mr. Thomas Wise.
    Bookman's Journal & Print Collector 3:177 Ja 7 '21
                                                                 354

Conrad pays tribute to Mark Twain. Mentor 12, no 4:45
    My '24 (An interview with Conrad)   355
Conrad porch unveiled. New York Times O 20 '27 p 10
    (At Bishopsbourne)   356
The Conrad prow. Lookout 18, no 9:15 S '27   357
Conrad reading room. Newark Evening News no 13, 031:
    5-x N 21 '25   358
Conrad sea relic off for last port. New York Times Ag
    19 '49 (The wheel of the Otago)   358a
Conrad, sea writer, dies suddenly at 66. New York Eve-
    ning Post Ag 4 '24 p7   359
Conrad, sea writer, here for first time. New York
    Herald My 2 '23 p 24   360
Conrad, sea writer, here on first visit. New York
    Times My 2 '23 p21   361
Conrad ship's steering wheel on way home. Oxford Mail
    Ag 19 '49 p5 (The wheel of the Otago)   362
A Conrad sidelight. Toronto Globe O 8 '24; same.
    Canadian Bookman 6, no 10: 216 O 24 '24; same.
    Publishers' Circular & Booksellers' Record 121:671
    N 8 '24   363
Conrad supplement. Transatlantic Review 2, no 3:325-
    50 O '24   364
Conrad, the artist. In The Duel. A Military Tale, by
    Joseph Conrad. Garden City, New York: Garden
    City Publishing Co., 1923. p[120]   365
Conrad, the man. New York Evening Post Literary Re-
    view Ag 9 '24 p952 (By "G. W.")   366
Conrad, the new great figure in literature. New York
    American Ap 11 '03 p14; same. (excerpt) Academy
    64:405 Ap 25 '03   367
Conrad, the Pole famous in English letters. World Re-
    view 1:263 F 1 '26   368
Conrad, the writer: lecture for college club by Professor
    William L. Phelps. Springfield Republican O 22
    '14 p3   369
Conrad thoughtful of others to the last. New York Times
    Ag 7 '24 p3   370
Conrad visits Boston. New York Times My 21 '23 p15 371
Conradiana. Wiadomości Literackie 8, no 2:2 Ja 11
    '31; Wiadomości Literackie 2, no 50:2 D 13 '25;
    Wiadomości Literackie 8, no 2:2 Ja 11 '31   372
Conradiana. A new journal.
    (Noted in Victorian Studies 11, no 3:424 Mr '68) 372a
[Conrad's attempt at suicide] New York Times Ag 15
    '37   373
Conrad's birthday. Bookman (NY) 46:552 Ja '18 374

Conrad's estate valued at Ł 20,000. Sun (NY) N 15 '24 374a
Conrad's first ship [the Otago] Bookman (NY) 41:129-30
   Ap '15 (With a drawing by G. F. W. Hope) 375
Conrad's friend comes to rescue novelists here. New
   York Herald Tribune O 30 '26 p11
   (Refers to Ford Madox Ford) 376
Conrad's great episode. Book Leaf (NY) F 24 '28 377
Conrad's jungle drama inspired "Rhapsodie." Herald
   (NY) My 20 '23 ("Heart of Darkness" inspired John
   Powell's "Rhapsodie Negre") 377a
Conrad's Lord Jim. Sunday Times (London) Ag 3 '24 378
[Conrad's Napoleonic novel] Bookman (NY) 53:65-6 Mr
   '21 379
Conrad's old ship sent to bottom. New York Times Maga-
   zine Mr 10 '35 p22 (The Otago) 380
Conrad's place and rank in English letters. Wiadomości 4,
   no 28:3 Jl 10 '49
   (Paragraphs by Walter Allen, B. I. Evans, Robert
   Graves, Graham Greene, Robert Henriques, Christo-
   pher Hollis, F. T. Jesse, Robert Liddell, B. H. Lid-
   dell Hart, R. L. Mégroz, Raymond Mortimer, Irene
   Rathbone, Herbert Read, Robert Speaight, Freya Stark,
   L. A. G. Strong, Evelyn Waugh, Aldous Huxley, Rosa-
   mund Lehmann, Secretary to Noel Streatfeild) 381
Conrad's Poland. New York Tribune Ap 5 '20 p10 (an
   editorial) 382
[Conrad's Polish name] Literary World (Boston) 35:262
   S '04 383
[Conrad's reputation] Book Buyer 16:389-90 Je '98 384
[Conrad's return from Corsica] Daily Mail (London)
   Ap 16 '21 385
Conrad's spoken English betrayed his nativity. New York
   Herald Tribune N 4 '28 386
Conrad's Suspense. Saturday Review of Literature 1:833
   Je 20 '25 387
Conrad's Suspense; a competition. Publishers' Circular
   & Booksellers' Record 123:797 D 12 '25 388
Conrad's "The Lagoon." Explicator 9, item 7, 1951
   (by F. A. D.) 389
Conrad's treasure chest of experience. New York Times
   Book Review Ag 26 '23 p9, 22 390
Conrad's unfinished novel. World (NY) S 8 '25 (An
   editorial on Suspense) 391
Conrad's widow tells of genius. Evening World (NY) S
   16 '26 p17 392
Conrad's wife tells how she coddled him while he wrote.
   New York Herald Tribune S 19 '26 Sec. III p2 393

Conrad's words attributed to Ford.   Book Leaf (NY)
   F 23 '27   394
Conrad's writing bullet-proof.   Argonaut 94:73 F 2 '24   395
Conrad wciąz aktualny.   Dziś i Jutro rok 3, no 65:5
   F 23 '47   395a
Conrad w oczach syna.   Wiadomości 11, no 51:4 D 15
   '56   395b
Conrad w rodzinie.   Wiadomości (London) 4, nos 176-7:
   5 Ag 21 '49
   (Excerpts from Mrs. Conrad's Joseph Conrad As I
   Knew Him and Joseph Conrad and His Circle)   396
Constant Reader [pseud.]
   Looking backward: Joseph Conrad.   New York Evening
   Post Literary Review Ap 28 '23 p647   397
Cook, Albert Spaulding
   Conrad's void.   Nineteenth-Century Fiction 12:326-
   30 Mr '58
   Plot as discovery: Conrad, Dostoevsky, and Faulkner.
   In The meaning of fiction.   Detroit: Wayne State Uni-
   versity Press, 1960.   p202-8, 241   398
Cook, William J., Jr.
   A study of the light and dark imagery in the early works
   of Joseph Conrad: 1895-1900.   M. A. Thesis, Auburn
   University, 1964.   iv-vi, 149f; bibliography, f147-9
                                                           399
Coole, Albert
   Joseph Conrad, 1857-1924.   In The literary tradition of
   Canterbury from Chaucer to Conrad.   Cambridge:
   Cambridge University Press, 1930.   p[35]-39; portrait,
   p[34]   400
Cooper, Frederick George
   The story of Conrad's Lord Jim.   In The Annual Dog-
   Watch.   Victoria no 10:53-5 '53
   Joseph Conrad - an appreciation.   Blue Peter 9, no 84:
   128-32 Mr '29
   Joseph Conrad: a seaman's tribute.   Nautical Magazine
   (London) 105:4-9, 97-101, 199-204, 328-32 Ja-Ap
   '21; same.   In Yarns of the seven seas.   London:
   Heath Cranton, 1927.   p44-73
   (Reviewed in Blue Peter 7, no 63:155 Je '27
   Some aspects of Joseph Conrad.   Mariner's Mirror 26,
   no 1:61-78 Ja '40 (bibliography)   401
Cooper, Frederic Taber
   Representative English story tellers.   I. - Joseph Conrad.
   Bookman (NY) 35:61-70 Mr '12; same.   In Some
   English story tellers...   New York: Holt [c1912]
   p1-30   402

Cornelius, Samuel Robert
The sea as the core of Conrad. Ph. D. Dissertation,
Univ. of Pittsburgh, 1949. 175f; bibliography f151-75.
Abstract in Univ. of Pittsburgh Bulletin 46, no 6:
3-9 Je '50   403
Cornish, W. Lorne
Joseph Conrad: 'a dedicated soul.' London Quarterly
Review 165:75-7 Ja '40   404
Cournos, John and Sybil Norton [pseud.]
Novelists of character and environment. In Famous
British novelists. (Famous biographies for young
people) New York: Dodd, Mead, 1952. p[83]-91
(Miss Norton is Mrs. John Cournos)   405
Courtney, W. L.
Rosemary's letter book. (The wayfarer's library)
London: Dent [nd] p82, 88-9   406
Cowie, Alexander
The rise of the American novel. New York: American
book co., 1948. p164, 377, 392, 396-7, 703, 733   407
Cox, C. B.
Nostromo (Joseph Conrad). Oxford: B. Blackwell,
1964. 73p
(Notes on English Literature)
(Includes questions on the text and suggestions for
further reading.)   408
Cox, John Collingsworth
Gide and Conrad. In André Gide and his interest in
Blake, Conrad, Browning and Whitman. M. A.
Thesis, Univ. of Illinois, 1952. f10-29   409
Cox, Roger Lindsay
Conrad's Nostromo as boatswain. Modern Language
Notes 74:303-6 Ap '59
Master and man: a study of Conrad's Nostromo. Doctoral
Dissertation, Columbia Univ., 1961. 197p; abstract in
Dissertation Abstracts 22:255 '61   410
Cox, Sidney
Joseph Conrad: the teacher as artist. English Journal
(College Edition) 19:781-95 D '30   411
Coyle, G. C.
Joseph Conrad. John O'London's Weekly 11:561 Jl 19
'24   412
Craig, Robert.
Conrad and the Riversdale. Times Literary Supplement
(London) Jl 25 '68 p 788   412a
Cramblett, Mary Louise
Idea and theme in the fiction of Joseph Conrad. M. A.
Thesis, Univ. of Iowa, 1955. 114p   413

Cramer, Frances Isabel
  The irony of Joseph Conrad.   M. A.   Thesis,   Ohio State
    University, 1931.   102p; abstract in Ohio State Univer-
    sity Graduate School Abstracts of Masters' Essays,
    6:46-50 '31   414
Crämer, Tordis
  Der Stil im Frühwerk Joseph Conrads.   Dissertation,
    Hamburg, 1966.   204p   414a
Crane, Stephen
  Two letters from Stephen Crane to Joseph Conrad.
    [London: First Edition Club, Curwen Press, 1926]
    Letters, p[3-4]; preface, p[1-2]
    (220 copies only)
    Stephen Crane: letters, edited by R. W. Stallman and
    Lillian Gilkes.   With an introduction by R. W. Stall-
    man.   New York: New York University press, 1960.
    [passim]   415
Cranfield, Lionel
  Books in general.   New Statesman & Nation ns 31:28 Ja
    12 '46 (On Joseph Conrad's silences)   416
Crankshaw, Edward
  Joseph Conrad and to-day.   National & English Review
    128:224-30 Mr '47
  Joseph Conrad: some aspects of the art of the novel.
    London: Lane [1936] [iii]-v, 248p.   Reprinted: New
    York: Russell & Russell, 1963
    (Dated 1936 unless otherwise noted.   Reviewed in
    Times Literary Supplement Ap 18 p330; Elizabeth
    Bowen in Spectator 156:758 Ap 24; R. T. in Criterion
    16:188-9 O; Campbell Nairne in John O'London's Weekly
    35:185 My 9; B. Ifor Evans in Manchester Guardian
    Weekly 34, no 19:374 My 8; Edward Garnett in London
    Mercury 34:67-9 My; H. E. Bates in New Statesman &
    Nation ns 11:934 Je 13; M. L. Cazamian in Études
    Anglaises 1:257-9 My '37)
  Russia and the Russians.   London: Macmillan, 1947.
    p209-24   (Noted in Wiadomości 4, nos 178-9:3 S
    4 '49)   417
Craz, Albert G.
  Lord Jim, by Joseph Conrad, edited by Albert G. Craz.
    (Macmillan paperback) New York: Macmillan [1963]
    321p   418
Cresswell, Peter
  'That, too, is Romance...'   Listener 4, no 91:580
    O 8 '30   418a
Crews, Frederick
  The power of darkness.   Partisan Review 34, no 4:507-

Crews, Frederick (cont.)
    25 Fall '67 (On "Heart of Darkness")   418b
Croft-Cooke, Rupert
    Introduction. In Nostromo, a tale of the seaboard, by
        Joseph Conrad. San Francisco: Printed for the mem-
        bers of the Limited Editions Club by Taylor and Tay-
        lor, San Francisco, 1961. p[ix]-xvii
        (1500 copies only)   419
Cronin, Edward J.
    Joseph Conrad: a moral analysis. Ph. D. Thesis, Univ.
        of Minnesota, 1952.   420
Cross, D. C.
    Nostromo: further sources. Notes & Queries ns 12:265-
        6 Jl '65
    On many seas. Times Literary Supplement S 2 '65
        p761   421
Cross, Wilbur Lucius
    The illusions of Joseph Conrad. Yale Review ns 17:
        464-82 Ap '28
    Joseph Conrad. In Four contemporary novelists. New
        York: Macmillan, 1930. p7-60. "Reading list," p198
        (Reviewed by Alan R. Thompson in Bookman (NY) 72:
        435-6 D '30; Booklist 27:196 Ja '31; A. N. M. in Man-
        chester Guardian Weekly 23, no 21:432 N 28 '30; New
        York Times Book Review O 26 '30 p2; Outlook 156:347
        O 29 '30; Times Literary Supplement D 18 '30 p1090;
        New York Herald Tribune Books N 23 '30 p7)
    Some novels of 1920. Yale Review ns 10:402-3 Ja '21
                                                        422
Croston, A. K.
    Joseph Conrad, an introductory study. University College,
        Jamaica, West Indies, 1952   423
Crozier, G. L.
    The literary values in the novels of Joseph Conrad. M. A.
        Thesis, Univ. of Nebraska, 1922. 52p   424
Cruse, Amy
    After the Victorians. London: Allen & Unwin [1938]
        passim   425
Cullen, Countee P.
    A group of epitaphs. For Joseph Conrad; poem.
        Harper's Magazine 150:342 F '25   426
Cundy-Cooper, P.
    Conrad's ships. Sea Breezes ns 13:395 My '52   427
Cunliffe, John William
    Conrad and Galsworthy. New York Times F 6 '33
        p14
    Joseph Conrad (1857-1924). In English literature in the

twentieth century. New York: Macmillan, 1933. p125-
38; bibl. , p137-8
Late Victorian novelists. In Leaders of the Victorian
revolution. New York: Appleton-Century [c1934] p290-
5   428
Cunninghame Graham, Robert Bantine
Hudson's Far Away and Long Ago. Bookmark (London)
7:10-12 Christmas '31
Introduction. In Lord Jim, by Joseph Conrad. (Every-
man's Library) London: Dent, 1935. p i-ix
Introduction. In Tales of Hearsay, by Joseph Conrad.
(Memorial Edition) Garden City, New York: Doubleday,
Page, 1926. Volume XXIII, p vii-xv (In this volume,
Last Essays follows, separately paginated)
Inveni portum. Joseph Conrad. Saturday Review 138:
162-3 Ag 16 '24; same. La Nouvelle Revue Française 23:695-702 D '24 (translated into French by
Georges Jean-Aubry); same. In Selected modern Eng-
lish essays, edited by H. S. Milford. (World's clas-
sics, 280) London: Oxford University press [1925] p54-
60; same published separately: Cleveland, Ohio: [The
Merrymount Press for] The Rowfant Club, December,
1924. 15 pages (157 numbered copies on Whatman's
paper); same. In Redeemed and other sketches. Lon-
don: William Heinemann, Ltd. [1927] p161-71; same.
In Thirty tales and sketches, by R. B. Cunninghame
Graham, selected by Edward Garnett. New York:
Viking Press, 1929. p346-54
Preface. In Tales of hearsay, by Joseph Conrad... Lon-
don: T. Fisher Unwin [1925] p7-28; Garden City, New
York: Doubleday, Page, 1926. p vii-xv
Tales from the lips of others retold by Joseph Conrad.
New York Times Book Review Ja 4 '25 p2   429
Curle, Richard Henry Parnell
Account of Conrad's last illness and death; and obituary.
Daily Mail (London) Ag 4 '24
The Arrow of Gold. In Keating, George T. A Conrad
memorial library. Garden City, New York: Doubleday,
Doran, 1929. p273-7
The art of Joseph Conrad. Everyman 1, no 6:176 N 22
'12
The background of Nostromo. In Caravansary and conver-
sation... New York: Stokes, 1937. p207-21
Biographical and autobiographical. Novels and stories
[condensed from Curle's Joseph Conrad] In The Country
Life Press... Garden City, New York: Doubleday, Page,
1919. p105-15; same. In A set of six, by Joseph Con-

Curle, Richard Henry Parnell (cont.)
    rad. Garden City, New York: Doubleday, Page, 1916.
    11 unnumbered pages appended
Conrad and exploration.   New York Herald Tribune S 11
    '28 p20
Conrad and the younger generation.   Nineteenth Century
    107:103-12 Ja '30
Conrad at home. Daily Mail Ap 7 '22 p8
Conrad in the East.   Yale Review ns 12:497-508 Ap '23
    [Conrad's life, 1881-7, and the stories which grew
    out of these years]
Conrad's favourite novel.   Times Literary Supplement O
    14 '55 p605 [Conrad regarded Nostromo as his greatest
    creative effort]
Conrad's last novel [Suspense] Bookmark (London) 1, no 3:
    7-8 Autumn '25
Conrad's Suspense [a letter to the editor] Sun (NY) My 8
    '25 p18
Conrad's village unveils porch as memorial.   New York
    Herald Tribune section III, N 13 '27 p2
    [A portion of this was later included in Chapter X of
    Curle's The Last Twelve Years of Joseph Conrad]
Dispelling a legend: the first meeting of Galsworthy and
    Conrad. New York Herald Tribune F 3 '33 p14
La fin de Conrad [translated into French by Isabelle
    Rivière] La Nouvelle Revue Française 23:681-94 D 1
    '24
    [On Conrad's last days and death]
The history of Mr. Conrad's booĸs.   Times Literary Sup-
    plement Ag 30 '23 p570; same (excerpt).   New York
    Times Book Review Ag 26 '23 p9, 22; same published
    separately, entitled: Joseph Conrad: the history of
    his books. London: Dent, 1924. 8p; same. Joseph
    Conrad; including an approach to his writings... Garden
    City, New York: Doubleday, Page [c1926] p47-56 [A
    summary of plots]
The history of my Conrad collection.   Mermaid (Detroit)
    O '26; same. In The Richard Curle Conrad collection...
    New York: American Art Association [1927] p[1-3]
The history of The Nigger of the 'Narcissus,' human,
    literary, bibliographical. [n p] 1929. One hundred
    copies privately printed for Henry A. Colgate, 1929.
    14 leaves
    (Preface, page 1; text, p2-20, of revised page proofs)
    At the Baker Library, Dartmouth College
Introduction. In Conrad to a friend. 150 selected letters
    from Joseph Conrad to Richard Curle. Edited with an

introduction and notes by Richard Curle. London:
Sampson Low, Marston & Co. 1928. p vii-xi
Introduction. In a Conrad library. A catalogue of printed
books, manuscripts and autograph letters by Joseph
Conrad... collected by Thomas James Wise. London:
Printed for private circulation only (by the Dunedin
Press, Edinburgh) 1928. p xv-xvii
Introduction. In Joseph Conrad's diary of his journey up
the valley of the Congo in 1890. With an introduction
and notes by Richard Curle. Blue Peter 5, no 43:
319-21 O '25; same. Yale Review ns 15:254-59 Ja '26;
same published separately: London: Privately printed
by Strangeways, January, 1926. p[5]-13
Introduction. In Last essays, by Joseph Conrad. (Memorial Edition) Garden City, N. Y. : Doubleday, Page,
1926. Volume XXIII, p ix-xviii. Last Essays is pre-
ceded by Tales of Hearsay, separately paginated)
Introduction. In Nostromo, by Joseph Conrad. (Everyman's Library, 38) London: Dent [1957] p vii-xiii; bibl.
p xiv-xv
Introduction. In Nostromo, by Joseph Conrad. (Memorial Edition) Garden City, New York: Doubleday, Page,
1925. Volume VIII, p vii-x
Introduction. In Notes by Joseph Conrad, written in a
set of his first editions in the possession of Richard
Curle... London: Privately printed [by Strangeways,
printers] 1925. p[9]-13
(100 copies only)
Introduction. In Suspense, a Napoleonic novel, by Joseph
Conrad. (The Complete Works of Conrad. Kent Edi-
tion. Volume XXV) Garden City, New York: Double-
day, Page, 1926. p v-vii
Joseph Conrad. Rhythm 2, no 10:242, 245-51, 253-5 N
'12 (Largely about Nostromo)
Joseph Conrad and his characters: a study of six novels.
London: Heineman [1957]; Fair Lawn, New Jersey:
Essential Books, 1958. 254p
(Dated 1958 unless otherwise noted. Reviewed by Ed-
ward Wagenknecht in Chicago Sunday Tribune My 18 p4;
Charles Mann, Jr. in Library Journal 83:2163-4 Ag;
Nineteenth-Century Fiction 13:79 Je; John Baily in Na-
tional & English Review 150:72-3 F; Leonard Wibberley
in Saturday Review (NY) 41:31-2 Ag 16; Marvin Mud-
rick in Virginia Quarterly Review 34:630-3 Autumn;
Dorothy Van Ghent in Yale Review 48:155-6 Autumn;
Times Literary Supplement N 29 '57 p723; Listener 59:
210 Ja 30; John Baily in Spectator 199:840-1 D 13 '57;

Curle, Richard Henry Parnell (cont.)
  David Daiches in New York Times Book Review Ag 17
  p4, 18; M. D. Zabel in New York Herald Tribune Books
  Ag 17 pl, 9; Phoebe Adams in Atlantic Monthly 202:
  86 Jl; Wiadomości 12, nos 51-2:29 D 22-29 '57)
Joseph Conrad and the Daily Mail. Daily Mail Ag 14 '24
Joseph Conrad as a letter-writer. New York Herald
  Tribune Books S 30 '28 (portrait) pl, 6
Joseph Conrad as I remember him. Contemporary Re-
  view 196:25-31 Jl '59
Joseph Conrad: a study. Garden City, New York:
  Doubleday, Page; London: Kegan, Paul, 1914. vii-ix,
  245p; bibliography, p237-8; portrait
  (First appeared in Bookman (NY) 39:662-8 Ag '14; 40:
  99-104, 187-201 S-O '14)
  Reviews are dated 1914 unless otherwise noted
  (Reviewed in Athenaeum 1:885 Je 27; Spectator 113:
  300-1 Ag 29; Booklist 11:67-8 O; Calvin Winter in Bookman (NY) 40:566 Ja '15; Van Wyck Brooks in New Republic 1:26-7 D 26; Holbrook Jackson in T. P. 's Weekly
  25:251-2 Mr 13 '15; Standard (London) Ap; Times (London) Ap; [? Norman Douglas in] English Review 17:
  569-70 Jl; A. G. van Kranendonk in English Studies 2:1-
  8 F '20; noted in T. P. 's Weekly 23:828 Je 26; noted
  by R. H. C. in New Age ns 14: no 17:530-1 F 26; H. L.
  Mencken in Smart Set 44, no 3:151-2 N)
Joseph Conrad in the East. Blue Peter S-O '22; same
  published separately: London: Privately printed for the
  author, 1922. 7p
  (21 copies only, issued July, 1922)
Joseph Conrad: ten years after. Virginia Quarterly Review 10:420-35 Jl '34; same. Fortnightly Review 142:
  189-99 Ag '34
Joseph Conrad: the history of his books. See: The history of Mr. Conrad's books
Joseph Conrad's last day. John O'London's Weekly 11:
  813-14, 829, 848-9 S 20, 27 '24; same. Mentor 13,
  no 2:13-19 Mr '25; same. Johannesburg Star '25;
  same published separately: London: Privately printed
  (by Strangeways, printers) 1924. 5-34p
  (100 copies only)
  (Reviewed in Outlook (NY) 139:138 Ja 28 '25)
[The last hours of Conrad] Berliner Börs-Courant no 375,
  1928
The last of Conrad.
  See: Joseph Conrad's last day
The last twelve years of Joseph Conrad. London: Samp-

son, Low, Marston, 1928. vii-viii, 236p; portrait.
Garden City, New York: Doubleday, Doran, 1928 [ix],
212p
(Reviewed by A. G. Brocklehurst in Manchester Liter-
ary Club Papers 55:69-75 '29; George Sampson in
Bookman (London) 75:8-9 O '28; Times Literary Supple-
ment S 13 '28 p641; Nation-Athenaeum 44:449-50 D 22
'28; English Review 47:616 N '28; Wilbur Cross in
Yale Review ns 18:580-3 Spring '29; Mary Ellen Chase
in Commonweal 9:295 Ja 9 '29; Booklist 25:161 Ja '29;
Richard Church in Spectator 141:374, 376 S 22 '28;
A. Maurice in Bookman (NY) 68:594 Ja '29; New
Statesman 32:329-30 D 15 '28; William McFee in New
York Herald Tribune Books N 4 '28 p4; Percy Hutchi-
son in New York Times Book Review N 4 '28 p2, 10;
E. G. in Manchester Guardian Weekly 19, no 14:273
O 5 '28; noted in Canadian Forum 8, no 91:622 Ap '28)
My impressions of the Conrad centenary celebrations.
Kwartalnik Neofilologiczny 5:3-5 '58; same. In Joseph
Conrad Korzeniowski. Essays and studies. Warsaw:
Państwowe Wydawnictwo Naukowe, 1958. p[3]-5
Objection and reproof. New York Times Book Review My
9 '26 p25
[Discusses Conrad's birthplace and religion]
The personality of Joseph Conrad. Edinburgh Review 241:
126-38 Ja '25; same published separately: London:
[Privately printed, 1925] 15p (100 copies only)
[This essay was later included in Curle's The Last
Twelve Years of Joseph Conrad]
The real Conrad. New York Herald Tribune O 23 '26
p14
A remarkable friendship: Conrad and Galsworthy. In
Two essays on Conrad, by John Galsworthy, with The
story of a remarkable friendship, by Richard Curle.
Freelands; Privately printed [Cincinnati, Ebbert &
Richardson, printers] 1930. 83p (93 copies only) same.
In Caravansary and conversation... New York: Stokes,
1937. p153-63
Resolution: a moral from Joseph Conrad. Daily Mail Ag
5 '24 [Written under the pseudonym of John Blunt]
Sea captain and novelist: memories of Joseph Conrad.
Listener 32:102-3 Jl 27 '44
Some initimate recollections of Joseph Conrad. Blue
Peter 6:17-18 Ap '26
The story of Lord Jim. Times Literary Supplement S 13
'23 p604
Wanderings, a book of travel and reminiscences... London:

Curle, Richard Henry Parnell (cont.)
>   Kegan Paul, Trench, Trübner, 1920.   xii, 350p passim
>   (Dedicated to Joseph Conrad)
>   Warszawa pod kuministami (translated by Tymon Terlecki).
>   Wiadomości 14, no 4:2 Ja 25 '59
>   The world's great books in outline, Part VI, January 12,
>   1926 (A summary, with an introduction: "A Note on
>   Joseph Conrad")   430
Curley, Daniel
>   Legate of the ideal. In Conrad's "Secret Sharer" and the
>   critics, edited by Bruce Harkness. Belmont, Cali-
>   fornia: Wadsworth Publishing Co., Inc. [1962] p75-82;
>   same. In Conrad. A collection of critical essays,
>   edited by Marvin Mudrick. (A Spectrum Book) Engle-
>   wood Cliffs, New Jersey: Prentice-Hall, Inc. [1966]
>   p75-82
>   The writer and his use of material: the case of "The
>   Secret Sharer." Modern Fiction Studies 13, no 2:179-
>   94 Summer '67   431
Curran, Edward F.
>   A master of language. Catholic World 92:796-805 Mr
>   '11   432
Curran, Mary Veronica
>   A study of Joseph Conrad through his stories. M. A.
>   Thesis, State College, at Boston, Massachusetts,
>   1936.   433
Cushwa, Frank William
>   An introduction to Conrad. Garden City, New York:
>   Doubleday, Doran [c1933] v-xiv, 436p; maps on inside
>   cover pages. Chronological table of Conrad's life and
>   works, p ix-xiv; Table of references, p425-8; Glossary,
>   p429-36   434
Cutler, Frances Wentworth
>   Why Marlow? Sewanee Review 26:28-38 Ja '18   435
Czachowski, Kazimierz
>   Józefa Ujejskiego "O Konradzie Korzeniowskim." In
>   Pod piórem. Kraków: Ksiegarnia S. Kamińskiego,
>   1947.
>   Ojciec Conrada (Conrad's father). Wiadomości Literackie
>   4, no 36:2 S 4 '27
>   O Josephie Conradzie-Korzeniowskim: Polska książka o
>   Conradzie. In Pod piórem. Kraków: Ksiegarnia S.
>   Kamińskiego, 1947.   436
Czarnecki, Antoni
>   Jeden wieczór z Conradem (One evening with Conrad).
>   Ameryka-Echo (Ohio) Ag 31 '24; same. (excerpt) Prze-
>   glad Warszawski rok 4, tom 4, no 38:265-6 N '24;

same. Daily News (Chicago) Ja '19   437
Czekalski, Eustachy
Joseph Conrad w świetle listów pisanych do K. Wali-
szewskiego. Świat 22, no 12:16 Mr '27   438
Czosnowski, Stanislaw
Conradiana. Epoka (Cracow) no 136:8 My 19 '29; same.
In Wspomnienia i studia o Conradzie, edited by Barbara
Kocówna. [Warsaw:] Państwowy Instytut Wydawniczy
[1963] p85-8; same. Kurjer Poznanski no 312, 1929
439
Czubakowska, H.
The narrator in the structure of three novels by Joseph
Conrad: "Heart of Darkness," Lord Jim, and Chance.
M. A. Thesis, Jagiellonian University, 1958   440

D., F. A.
Conrad's "The Lagoon." Explicator 9, no 7,   question 7,
My '51   441
Dąbrowska, Marja (Szumska)
Conrad skandaliczny. Współczesność 1:80 '60
Conradowskie pojęcie wierności (Conrad's concept of
loyalty). Warszawa no 1, My 19, 1946; same. In
Szkice o Conradzie. [Warsaw:] Państwowy Instytut
Wydawniczy [1959] p148-[163]
1857-1957. Nowa Kultura 1957; same. In Szkice o Con-
radzie. [Warsaw:] Państwowy Instytut Wydawniczy
[1959] p112-[120]
Głębiej niż dno. Tygodnik Illustrowany 1925; same. In
Szkice o Conradzie. [Warsaw:] Państwowy Instytut
Wydawniczy [1959] p30-[35]
Kula w płot. Głos Prawdy 1926; same. In Szkice o Con-
radzie. [Warsaw:] Państwowy Instytut Wydawniczy
[1959] p138-[144]
Na drodze uczynków (On the road of deeds). Wiadomości
Literackie (Literary News) 3, nos 28-29:1 Jl 18 '26;
same. In Szkice o Conradzie. [Warsaw:] Państwowy
Instytut Wydawniczy [1959] p41-[46]
Notatka na marginesie artykulu J. Kotta. Warszawa,
1946; same. In Szkice o Conradzie. [Warsaw:] Pań-
stwowy Instytut Wydawniczy [1959] p164-[68]
Nowe przekłady Conrada. Bluszcz, 1924; same. In
Szkice o Conradzie. [Warsaw;] Państwowy Instytut
Wydawniczy [1959] p27-[29]
O "Smudze Cienia." Głos Prawdy, 1926; same. In Szkice
o Conradzie. [Warsaw:] Państwowy Instytut Wydawniczy
[1959] p36-[40]; same. In Joseph Conrad Korzeniowski,
by Róża Jabłkowska. Warsaw: Państwowe Zakłady

66   A Bibliography of Joseph Conrad

Dąbrowska, Marja (Szumska) (cont.)
    Wydawnictwo Szkolynch, 1964. p274-7
Pisane z przykrością. Życie Literackie 10:476 '61
Pożegnanie z Conradem. Nowa Kultura 10, no 21:1,
    6-7 My 24 '59; same. In Szkice o Conradzie.
    [Warsaw:] Państwowy Instytut Wydawniczy [1959] p171-
    [194]
Prawdziwa rzeczywistość Conrada. Wiadomości Literackie
    6, no 24:3-4 Je 16 '29; same. In Szkice o Conradzie.
    [Warsaw:] Państwowy Instytut Wydawniczy [1959] p55-
    [77]; same. In Wspomnienia i studia o Conradzie,
    edited by Barbara Kocówna. Warsaw: Państwowy
    Instytut Wydawniczy [1963] p270-89
Przypis szikicow o Conradzie. Nowa Kultura 1:510 '60
Rozmowa z J. Conradem (A talk with Conrad). Tygodnik
    Illustrowany no 16:308 Ap 18 '14; same. (translated by
    B. A. Jezierski) American Scholar 13, no 3:371-5 Jl
    '44; same. (excerpt) Poland no 4:27 Je '60 (entitled:
    "A Polish press interview with Joseph Conrad"); same.
    In Szkice O Conradzie. [Warsaw:] Państwowy Instytut
    Wydawniczy [1959] p17-23
Społeczne i religijne pierwiastki u Conrada. Wiadomości
    Literackie 9, no 7:1-2 F 14 '32; same. In Szkice
    o Conradzie. [Warsaw:] Państwowy Instytut Wydawn-
    iczy [1959] p78-[102]
Spotkanie z Conradem w podróży. Pion, 1934. same. In
    Szkice o Conradzie. [Warsaw:] Państwowy Instytut
    Wydawniczy [1959] p103-[110]
Szkice o Conradzie. [Warsaw:] Państwowy Instytut
    Wydawniczy [1959] 5-[195]p; excerpt In Wspomnienia i
    studia o Conradzie, edited by Barbara Kocówna. [War-
    saw:] Państwowy Instytut Wydawniczy [1963] p270-89;
    except In Joseph Conrad Korzeniowski, by Róża Jabł-
    kowska. Warsaw: Państwowe Zakłady Wydawnictwo
    Szkolynch, 1964. p277-91
    (Reviewed by Barbara Kocówna in Przegląd Human-
    istyczny 4, no 4:161-8 '60; noted by Ryszard Matusz-
    ewski in Rocznik Literacki for 1958-1960, p181; Zbig-
    niew Grabowski in Wiadomości 15, no 12:4 Mr 20 '60)
Tragizm Conrada. Wiadomości Literackie 2, no 11:2 Mr
    15 '25; same. In Smuga Cienia, by Joseph Conrad,
    translated by Jadwiga Sienkiewiczówna. Warsaw:
    Państwowy Instytut Wydawniczy, 1945; same. In Szkice
    o Conradzie. [Warsaw:] Państwowy Instytut Wydawniczy
    [1959] p123-[137]
Le vaisseau embrase de Lord Jim. Joseph Conrad et la
    Pologne. Pologne Littéraire 1, no 3:1 D 15 '26

W sprawie "demaskowania" Conrada. Wiadomości Literackie 11, no 530:3 Ja 21 '34; same. In Szkice o Conradzie. [Warsaw:] Państwowy Instytut Wydawniczy [1959] p145-[147]

"Zwycięstwo" J. Conrada. Świat Książki, 1928; same. In Szkice o Conradzie. [Warsaw:] Państwowy Instytut Wydawniczy [1959] p47-[51]   442

Dąbrowski, Jan P.
   Conrad and "The Big Three" of Russian literature. In Conrad żywy, edited by Wit Tarnawski. London: B. Świderski, 1957. p150-8 (Conrad and Dostoievsky, Tolstoi, and Turgenev)
   Conrad - na raty? Głos Prawdy no 78, 1927   443

Dabrowski, Marian
   Rozmowa z J. Conradem. Tygodnik Illustrowany no 16, Ap 18 '14; same. Polish American Studies 17, no 3-4: 66-71 Jl-D '60   443a

Dąbrowski, Wojciech
   Powrót Konrada. Rzeczpospolita no 203, Jl 26 '24   444

Daglish, Eric Fitch
   Foreword. In Mirror of the Sea, by Joseph Conrad. With foreword and two wood engravings by Eric Fitch Daglish. (Open Air Library) London: Dent, 1933. xvi, 244p   445

Dahlmanns, Hans
   Charakterdarstellung bei Conrad. Dissertation, 1950   446

Daiches, David
   Experience and the imagination: the background of "Heart of Darkness." In White men in the tropics: two moral tales. New York: Harcourt, Brace [c1962] college edition, p3-16
   Joseph Conrad. In The novel and the modern world. Chicago: University of Chicago press [c1939] p48-64   447

Dale, James
   'One of us': craft and caste in Lord Jim. English Record 15, no 4:5-7 Ap '65   448

Dale, Patricia
   Conrad: a borrowing from Hazlitt's father. Notes & Queries ns 10:146 Ap '63   449

Danchin, F. C.
   Songs of the sea. (Kipling and Conrad). Les Langues Modernes 26:314-24 Je '28   450

Daniel-Rops, Henry
   See: Rops, Daniel Henry   451

Danilewicz, Maria
   Polska młodość Conrada. Wiadomości 11, no 43:2 O 21

Danilewicz, Maria (cont.)
'56; same. In Pierścień z Herkulaneum i płaszcz
pokutnicy. London: B. Świderski, 1960. p292-310
Trwała wielkość Conrada. Wiadomości 17, no 28:4
Jl 15 '62   451a
Danner, Marguerite Fullerton
The interpretation of the common elements in the fiction
of Conrad and Dostoievski. M. A. Thesis, Ohio State
Univ. 1932. 35p. Abstract in Ohio State Univ. Gradu-
ate School Abstracts of Masters' Essays 9:37-8 '32
(On Lord Jim, Victory, and Crime and Punishment)
                                                                452
D'Arese, G.
Prefazione. In Il reietto delle isole, by Joseph Conrad,
translated by G. D'Arese. Torino: Slavia, 1932.
Volume I, p[7]-13   453
Dargan, Edward Preston
The voyages of Conrad. Dial 66:638-41 Je 28 '19   454
Dark, Sidney
Little portraits. Three writers and a politician. John
O'London's Weekly 8:853 Mr 17 '23   455
D'Arzo, Silvio
Joseph Conrad o dell' "umanità." Il Ponte 6, no 5:505-
10 My '50   456
Dataller, Roger
The plain man and the novel. (Discussion books) London:
Nelson [1940] p65, 121-31
(Reviewed in English 3, no 16:199 Spring '41)   457
Daulton, Patricia Anna
The contrast of illusion and reality in three novels by
Joseph Conrad: "Heart of Darkness," The Nigger of the
"Narcissus," and Nostromo. M. A. Thesis, Univ. of
Cincinnati, 1955. 176p   458
D'Avanzo, Mario Louis
Conrad's motley as an organizing metaphor in "Heart of
Darkness." College Language Association Journal
(Baltimore) 9:289-91 Mr '66
Conrad's use of Marlow as a character and device. M. A.
Thesis, Trinity College (Hartford, Conn.), 1954. 85f;
bibl., f83-5   459
David, Maurice
Joseph Conrad, l'homme et l'oeuvre... (Collection des
célébrités étrangères, I, 3) Paris: Editions de la
Nouvelle Revue Critique [1929] 80p; bibl., p77-80; por-
trait
(Reviewed by M. Kridl in Przegląd Wspolczesny no 96,
1930; W. St. in Prezgląd Humanistyczny 5, no 3, 1930;

Pierre Mille in Les Nouvelles Littéraires 8, no 368: 1 N 2 '29)

La psychologie et la morale de Conrad. Nouvelle Revue Critique 13:289-304 My '29

(Later included in David's Joseph Conrad...) 460

Davidson, Donald

Essay on Conrad's Suspense. Saturday Review of Literature 2:315, 326 N 21 '25

The inversive method of narration in the novels and short stories of Joseph Conrad. M. A. Thesis, Vanderbilt Univ. 1922. 117f; bibl., f115-17

Joseph Conrad's directed indirections. Sewanee Review 33:163-77 Ap '25 461

Davis, Edward

Lord Jim. In Readings in modern fiction. Cape Town: Simondium, Publishers, 1964. p190-204 461a

Davis, Harold Edmund

Conrad's revisions of The Secret Agent: a study in literary impressionism. Modern Language Quarterly 19: 244-54 S '58

Method and form in the novels of Joseph Conrad. Ph. D. Thesis, Louisiana State University, 1956. 252p. Abstract in Dissertation Abstracts 16:1682 '56

Symbolism in The Nigger of the 'Narcissus.' Twentieth Century Literature 2:26-9 Ap '56 462

Davis, Robert Gorham

Joseph Conrad. In Ten modern masters... New York: Harcourt, Brace [c1953] p150-2 463

Davray, Henry-D.

Joseph Conrad. Semaine Littéraire année 11, no 500: 361-3 Ag 1 '03

Joseph Conrad. Mercure de France (series moderne) 175:32-55 O 1 '24; same. (excerpt) Chronique des Lettres Françaises 3:57-61 Ja-F '25

Lettres Anglaises. Mercure de France (series moderne) 31:265-6 '99; 39:249 '01; 43:542 '02; 45:830-1 '03; 193:485-91 Ja 1 '27 464

[Dawson, Clarence H.]

A trying episode. Poland 8:664-5 N '27 465

Dawson, Ernest

Some recollections of Joseph Conrad. Fortnightly Review 130:203-12 Ag 1 '28; same. Living Age 335:132-5 O '28 466

Dawson, Francis Warrington

The crimson pall; a novel by Warrington Dawson with letters exchanged on "critical novelists" by Joseph Conrad and the author. Chicago: Bernard Publishing

Dawson, Francis Warrington (cont.)
    Co. [c1927] 266p (The Foreword contains an exchange
    of letters between Dawson and Conrad, two by Conrad,
    one by Dawson. Conrad's letters are on pages 9-11
    (undated but before Dec. 25, 1921) and on pages 22-4
    (July 29, 1923)).   467
Day, A. Grove
    Pattern in Lord Jim: one jump after another.   College
    English 13:396-7 Ap '52   468
Day, Esther
    Joseph Conrad's use of the double.   M. A. Thesis, Univ.
    of Houston, Texas, 1963. vi, 91p   469
Day, Robert A.
    The rebirth of Leggatt.   Literature and Psychology 13:74-
    81 Summer '63   470
Dean, Leonard Fellows
    Introduction [to Conrad's Victory] In A college omnibus,
    8th edition... New York: Harcourt, Brace [c1935]
    p597-600
    Tragic pattern in Conrad's "The Heart of Darkness."
    College English 6:100-4 N '44
    Heart of Darkness: backgrounds and criticisms, edited
    by Leonard F. Dean.   Englewood Cliffs, New Jersey:
    Prentice-Hall [c1960] iii-vii, 184p; preface, p iii-iv
    (Reviewed by Pál Vámosi in Filológiai Közlöny 9:472-
    4 '63)   471
DeArmas, Delia Wade
    A study of Joseph Conrad and "Heart of Darkness." M. A.
    Thesis, Stetson University, 1962. 62f   472
Death of Conrad widely mourned.   Newark Evening News
    no 12,631:4 Ag 4 '24   473
The death of Mr. Conrad.   Manchester Guardian Ag 4 '24
    p6; Graphic 110:198 Ag 9 '24; Morning Post (London)
    Ag 4 '24 p6   474
Death takes famous writer of the sea.   Daily News (Chicago)
    Ag 9 '24 Photogravure Section pl (The bust by Jo
    Davidson)   474a
Dębicki, Zdzisław
    "Filozof morza" (Philosopher of the sea.)   Kurier War-
    szawski (Warsaw Courier) no 234, 1924   475
De Chastellier, Alfred
    Conrad à la recherche de l'amour.   Avignon: Aubanel,
    1957. 141p (Reviewed by Alphonse V. Roche in Books
    Abroad 32:36 Winter '58)   476
[Dedication of porch and tablet to Conrad at Bishopsbourne]
    Wiadomości Literackie 4, no 49:4 D 11 '27   477
Dees, Mary Cone

Joseph Conrad's dominant tone of sobriety as revealed by
an analysis of his works.   M. A. Thesis, Univ. of
Texas, 1940. iii-viii, 84f.   478
Deffge, Francis (Sister)
    The use of myth in Conrad's "Falk." M. A. Thesis, Catho-
        lic Univ. of America, 1960. iii, 46f; bibl. , f42-6   479
De la Mare, Walter
    Conrad's Victory. In Private view. London: Faber &
        Faber, 1953. p19-22   480
De Lano, Agnes
    A canon for critics. Freeman 1:184-5 My 5 '20   481
De Lanux, Pierre
    [Conrad's popularity in France] Bookman (NY) 61:245-6
        Ap '25   482
De Laura, David J.
    Echoes of Butler, Browning, Conrad, and Pater in the
        poetry of T. S. Eliot. English Language Notes (Univ.
        of Colorado) 3:211-21 Mr '66   483
Demeure, Fernand
    Joseph Conrad, ou le misogyne passionné. Revue Mon-
        diale 25th année, volume 162:291-6 D 1 '24   484
J. M. Dent and Sons, London
    Joseph Conrad. A prospectus of the Uniform Edition of
        Joseph Conrad's works. London: J. M. Dent and Sons
        [nd ?1923] 11p
        (Contents: Conrad's place in literature, p3-4; The Uni-
        form Edition of Joseph Conrad's Complete Works, p5;
        A Bibliographical List of the Works of Joseph Conrad
        Included in the Uniform Edition, p6-7; A Biographical
        Note. Joseph Conrad, p8-10)
    Joseph Conrad Centenary, 3rd December 1857-1957.
        Letchworth, Herts: Printed at the Aldine Press [1957]
        8p
        (Contents: Portrait, p2; Biographical Notes, p3-5;
        Joseph Conrad's Collected Works, p6-8)   484a
De Robertis, Domenico
    Conrad. Paragone 2:78-80 F '51   485
De Smet, Joseph
    See: Smet, Joseph De   486
Desmond, John Francis
    Joseph Conrad, the man and the artist. M. Ed. Thesis,
        Teachers College of the City of Boston (now State Col-
        lege at Boston), 1940. xix, 55f   487
De Ternant, Andrew
    An unknown episode of Conrad's life. New Statesman 31:
        511 Jl 28 '38   488

Deutsch, Helene
    Lord Jim and depression. In Neuroses and character...
    New York: International Universities Press, 1965.
    p353-7
    (A paper which was read April 14, 1959 at the Boston
    Medical Library)   489
Dewitt, Robert Henry
    Joseph Conrad's view of life as shown principally by his
    descriptions. M. S. Thesis, Kansas State College of
    Pittsburg, 1938. 44p   490
Diakonowa, N.
    Predislovie Joseph Conrad: Lord Jim. Moscow: 1959.
                                                                   491
Dickinson, Asa Don
    Joseph Conrad. In The best books of our time, 1901-
    1925... New York: Wilson, 1931. p69-75   492
Dickinson, Maude Antoinette
    The continuing characters in the stories of Joseph Conrad.
    M. A. Thesis, Ohio State University, 1925. 51p   493
Dierlamm, G.
    Joseph Conrad. Zeitschrift für Französischen und Eng-
    lischen Unterricht 28, heft 2:93-102 '29   494
Digby, Kenelm
    The literary lobby. Literary Review of the New York
    Evening Post My 5 '23 p672   495
Diggs, Della A.
    Literary citation in the works of Joseph Conrad. M. A.
    Thesis, University of Arizona, 1938. Abstract in the
    Arizona University Record 32:19-20 F '39   496
Dike, Donald A.
    The tempest of Axel Heyst. Nineteenth-Century Fiction
    17:95-113 S '62   497
Dillon, Martin
    The meaning of time in the development of Conrad's fic-
    tion. Ph. D. Thesis, State University of New York at
    Buffalo, 1967. 276p; abstract in Dissertation Abstracts
    28:673A '67   498
Dobraczyński, Jan
    Conrad, Przybyszewski i Morze. Dziś i Jutro 2, no 27:
    4-5; 31:4-5 Jl 14, Ag 11 '46
    Tragedia Lorda Jima. Tygodnik Powszechny no 24, 1945
    Wina i morze (Guilt and the sea). Wiatr od Morze no 1,
    1946   499
Dodd, Lee Wilson
    One of the masters. Saturday Review of Literature 1:27
    Ag 9 '24   500
Dodge, Norman L.

And bedside books of Conrad. The Month at Goodspeed's
(Boston) volume 7, no 6:187-90 F '36
(A list of books read by Conrad, the collection for
sale at $100)   501
Donlin, George Bernard
The art of Joseph Conrad. Dial 61:172-4 S 21 '16   502
Donoghue, Denis
Conrad's facts. New Statesman 72:291 Ag 26 '66   503
Doorn, W. van
Joseph Conrad. Amsterdamer Weekbladt Ag 9 '24   504
Doran, George Henry
Chronicles of Barabbas, 1884-1934. New York: Rine-
hart [1952] passim   505
Doubleday, Florence (Mrs. Frank N. Doubleday)
Episodes in the life of a publisher's wife. New York:
[Privately printed] December, 1937. p67-86
(100 copies only)
(Reminiscences of Conrad's trip to America in 1923
and Mrs. Doubleday's acquaintanceship with him)   506
Doubleday, Frank N.
Introduction. In The Rescue, by Joseph Conrad. (Me-
morial Edition) Garden City, Long Island, New York:
Doubleday, Page, 1925. Volume XVIII, p vii-x
Joseph Conrad as a friend. World Today (London) 52:
145-7 Jl '28   507
Doubleday, Doran and Company, Inc., New York
Publishers note [on Conrad] In A book of great autobiog-
raphy. Garden City, New York: Doubleday, Doran &
Co. 1934. 2p, unnumbered, but prefatory to Conrad's
A Personal Record   508

Doubleday, Page and Company, New York
The approach to Joseph Conrad. Twenty famous critics
tell those who are interested in Conrad how to begin
reading his works, so as to obtain the greatest enjoy-
ment from them. Garden City, New York: Doubleday,
Page [nd/?1925] 9p; same. Book Dial 2, no 4:7-14
Spring '25
(Letters from Wilson Follett, William McFee, Burton
Rascoe, Lee W. Dodd, Simeon Strunsky, W. R. Benét,
Isabel Paterson, Gene Markey)
Joseph Conrad. [Garden City, New York: Doubleday, Page]
[191-?] 20p; map on inside cover pages
Joseph Conrad. [Garden City, New York:] Doubleday,
Page & Co. [nd ?1914] [24]p; map on inside cover pages
(Contents: Joseph Conrad, a pen portrait, by James
Huneker, p[2]; The romantic story of Joseph Conrad,

Doubleday, Page and Co., NY (cont.)
     by E. F. Saxton, p[3-6]; Biographical and critical [con-
     densed from Richard Curle's Joseph Conrad] p[6, 9-13];
     Novels and stories [condensed from Curle's Joseph
     Conrad], p[13-16, 19-20]; Books by Joseph Conrad,
     p[21]; What is said of Joseph Conrad and his work,
     p[22-24]; Portraits, p[8, 18])
Joseph Conrad. Garden City, New York: Doubleday, Page
     & Co. [nd ? 1913] 24p; portraits are dated "September,
     1913"
     (Contents: Joseph Conrad, a pen portrait, by James
     Huneker, pl from New York Times Magazine Section N
     17 '12 p4; Joseph Conrad, the romance of his life and
     books, by Alfred A. Knopf, p3-6, 9-19; Bibliography,
     p19-23)
     (Noted in Bookman (NY) 38:352-4 D '13)
Joseph Conrad: a brief chronicle. Garden City, New
     York: Doubleday, Page [1923] 21p; caricature
Joseph Conrad, a sketch, with a bibliography, illustrated
     with many drawings by Edward A. Wilson. Garden
     City, New York: Doubleday, Page [c1924] 5-45p; bibli-
     ography, p39-45
Joseph Conrad: including an approach to his writings, a
     biographical sketch, a brief survey of his works, and a
     bibliography. Garden City, New York: Doubleday, Page
     [c1926] [60]p; portrait
     (Contents: Introduction, p[1-2]; The Approach to Joseph
     Conrad, p[3-14]; Joseph Conrad, A Sketch, p[15-46];
     The History of Joseph Conrad's Books, by Richard
     Curle, p [47-56]; Joseph Conrad, A Bibliography, p
     [57-60])   509
Douglas, Norman
     Looking back: an autobiographical excursion. New York:
     Harcourt, Brace [c1933] p340   510
Douglas, Robin
     My boyhood with Conrad. Cornhill Magazine ns 66:20-8
     Ja '29   511
Dowd, C. R.
     The world of Conrad. M. A. Thesis, Boston University,
     1924. 41p   512
Dowden, Wilfred S.
     Almayer's Folly and Lord Jim: a study in the development
     of Conrad's imagery. Rice University Studies 51, no
     1:13-27 Winter '65
     The "illuminating quality:" imagery and theme in The
     Secret Agent. Rice Institute Pamphlets 47, no 3:17-
     33 O '60

The light and the dark: imagery and thematic develop-
ment in Conrad's "Heart of Darkness." " Rice Institute
Pamphlets 44:33-51 Ap '57   513
Downarowicz, Janusz
Romantyzm Conrada (Conrad's romanticism). Dziś i
Jutro (Today and Tomorrow) 10, no 32:3 Ag 8 '54   514
Downing, Francis
The meaning of victory in Joseph Conrad. Commonweal
55:613-14 Mr 28 '52   515
Drew, Elizabeth A.
Joseph Conrad. In The modern novel; some aspects of
contemporary fiction. New York: Harcourt, Brace
[c1926] p223-40
(Reviewed by Edwin Muir in Nation & Athenaeum 39:
448 Jl 17 '26)
Joseph Conrad: Lord Jim. In The novel: a modern
guide to fifteen English masterpieces. New York:
W. W. Norton, 1963. p156-72   516
Drinkwater, John
Joseph Conrad. In The outline of literature... New York:
Putnam's, 1924. volume III, p1105-8   517
Droz, Juliette
A propos d'un livre de M. Joseph Conrad. Revue Heb-
domadaire année 27: tome 9:322-37 S 21 '18
(On Lord Jim)   518
Drucker, Rebecca
Recent letters of Conrad reveal his real literary ideals.
Tribune (NY) My 17 '19 p8   518a
Drzewiecki, Jerzy
W obronic Conrada (In defense of Conrad). Dziennik
Baltyki (Baltic Daily) no 134, 1945   519
Dudley, Edward Joseph
Patterns of imagery in Conrad's early fiction. M. A.
Thesis, Univ. of Minnesota, 1951
Three patterns of imagery in Conrad's "Heart of Dark-
ness." Revue des Langues Vivantes (Brussels) 31:
568-78 '65   520
Dudzinski, Bolesław
Conradiana. Wiadomości Literackie 12, no 586:7 F 10
'35   521
Duffin, Henry Charles
Conrad: a centenary survey. Contemporary Review 192:
319-23 D '57   522
Duggan, Sister Mary Rosary
The function of landscape description in Joseph Conrad's
Nostromo. M. A. Thesis, Catholic Univ. of America,
1963. 48p   523

Dukes, T. Arch.
Memories of Joseph Conrad.   Spectator 141:526 O 20 '28
                                                                                524
Duncan-Jones, E. E.
Mrs. Gould and Fairy Blackstick.   Notes & Queries ns
   14:245 Jl '67 (On Nostromo)   525
Dunn, Frederick Demarest
The dark powers: a study of Joseph Conrad. M. A.
   Thesis, Wesleyan University, 1960.   526
Dürr, Jan
Józef Conrad na drodze do Polski.   Ruch Literacki 7,
   no 8:236-43 Ag '32   527
Duvignaud, Jean
A new look at Conrad.   Express (London) Jl 14 '60;
   same.   Wiadomości 15, no 32:4 Ag 7 '60   527a
Dwa listy o Conradzie.   Wiadomości 7, no 26:3 Je 29 '52
   (Two letters from Mrs. Conrad to Gladys Langham)
                                                                                527b
Dyboski, Roman
A Conrad memorial (in Cracow).   Times Literary Supple-
   ment Mr 25 '26 p 236; same.   Poland 7, no 8:469-70
   Ag '26
Joseph Conrad.   In Great men and women of Poland,
   edited by Stephen Paul Mizwa.   New York: Macmillan,
   1941. p300-12
Joseph Conrad.   In Poland in world civilization, by Ro-
   man Dyboski, edited by Ludwik Krzyżanowski.   New
   York: J. M. Barrett Corp. [1950] p123-7
Kariera żeglarza.   In Joseph Conrad Korzeniowski, by
   Róża Jabłkowska.   Warsaw: Państwowe Zakłady Wy-
   dawnictwo Szokolynch, 1964. p263-74; same.   In
   Samotny geniusz.   W książce sto lat literatury angiel-
   skiej.   Warsaw: 1957
O zwierciadle morza Conrada.   Wiadomości Literackie
   14, no 713:4 Je 27 '37
Pierwiastki angielskie a pierwiastki polskie w umysło-
   wości Conrada.   (English and Polish elements in Con-
   rad's mentality) In Zagadnień kulturalno-literackich
   Wschodu i zachodu.   Prof. F. Baldensperger, Prof.
   G. Bertoni, Prof. J. Benesić, etc. , edited by Wacław
   Lednicki.   (Prace Polskiego Towarzystova dla Badań
   Europy Wschodniej i Bliskiego Wschodu... no. IV)
   Kraków: Gebethner i. Wolf, 1933/34. p199-209
   (Reviewed by Piotr Grzegorczyk in Ruch Literacki 7,
   no 8:253-4 Ag '32)
Spotkanie z Conradem.   Czas (Cracow) no 71, Mr 27 '32;
   same.   In Wspomnienia i studia o Conradzie, Wybrała

i opracowała Barbara Koćówna. [Warsaw:] Państwowy
Instytut Wydawniczy [1963] p103-9
(A meeting with Conrad)
Some aspects of contemporary England. Prague: Anglo-
American Club "Union" of Czecho-Slovakia, 1928
Sto lat literatury angielskiej. Warsaw: 1957
Z młodości Józefa Conrada. Czas no 296:25 '27; same.
In Wspomnienia i studia o Conradzie, wybrała i
opracowała Barbara Koćówna. [Warsaw:] Państwowy
Instytut Wydawniczy [1963] p35-42
Żeromski and Reymont. Slavonic Review 4, no 12:556
Mr '26; same. Poland 7, no 8:470-1 Ag '26
(A paragraph on Zeromski's relation with Conrad)
O "Zwierciadle morza." Młoda Rseczpospolita no 11,
1932
Żywioł morski w twórczości Józefa Conrada. Światopo-
gląd Morski no 3, 1932; same published separately:
Toruń: Wydawnictwa Instytutu Baltyckiego, 1932.
p[5]-25; same. In Światopogląd morski, edited by Józ-
ef Borowik. Toruń: 1934. p177-92
(The sea element in Conrad's work)
(Reviewed by Juljan Krzyżanowski in Ruch Literacki 7,
no 8:252-3 Ag '32) 528

Eagar, Hannah
Joseph Conrad. M. A. Thesis, Columbia Univ., 1918.
20p 529
Eagle, Solomon [pseud.]
See: Squire, (Sir) John Collings 530
Eames, R. P.
The depiction of national characteristics in the novels of
Joseph Conrad. M. A. Thesis, Wesleyan University,
1938 531
Eaton, Walter Prichard
Introduction to Conrad plays. In The Nature of a Crime,
by Joseph Conrad and Ford Madox Ford. (Memorial
Edition) Garden City, New York: Doubleday, Page,
1926. Volume XXII, p v-xi
(In this volume, Laughing Anne, One Day More, and
The Secret Agent follow The Nature of A Crime) 532
Eberhard, Florence Leon
A study of stage settings in the novels of Joseph Conrad.
M. A. Thesis, Ohio State University, 1925. 89p 533
Echeruo, W. J. C.
James Wait and The Nigger of the 'Narcissus. English
Studies in Africa 8:166-80 S '65 534

78   A Bibliography of Joseph Conrad

Eddleman, Ruth Ellie
The function of Marlow in Joseph Conrad's fiction.
M. A. Thesis, Univ. of Oklahoma, 1962. iii, 79f
(On "Youth," Lord Jim, Chance)   535
Edgar, Pelham
Joseph Conrad.   In The art of the novel from 1700 to the
present time. London: Macmillan, 1933. p184-95;
bibliography, p387-90   536
Edgren, C. Hobart
Of marble and mud; studies in spiritual values in fiction.
New York: Exposition Press [c1959] p78-90   536a
Editorial notes [Joseph Conrad] London Mercury 10:449-51
S '24   537
Edwards, Oliver
Conrad's women.   Times (London) S 20 '56 p13   538
Ehrentreich, Alfred
Verwendung von Leitmotiven bei Joseph Conrad. Neu-
philologische Monåtsschrift 10:403-6 N-D -39   539
Eigo-Seinen. 1924
(This magazine had a special number in memory of Con-
rad; in Japanese)   540
Ein model Joseph Conrads [by F. G.] Frankfurter Zeitung
nos 572-3, Ag '33   541
Einstein, Carl
Joseph Conrad.   Vossische Zeitung Unt. -Bl. no 260,
N '26   542
Ellis, Havelock
Mr. Conrad's world.   In The philosophy of conflict...
Boston: Houghton Mifflin, 1919. 2nd series, p246-56
A note on Conrad.   In Views and reviews, a selection
of uncollected articles, 1884-1932.   Boston: Houghton
Mifflin, 1932. 1st and 2nd series, p 116-20   543
Ellis, James N.
The short stories of Joseph Conrad. M. A. Thesis, Univ.
of Oklahoma, 1958. iii-iv, 109f   544
Ellsberg, Edward
Introduction. In Lord Jim, by Joseph Conrad. (Great Il-
lustrated Classics) New York: Dodd, Mead [1961]
p v-xii   545
Elphinstone, Petronella
Tuan Jim.   New Statesman 4:203-5 Ag 20 '32   546
Elvin, George
The Conrad memorial library; poem.   Lookout (NY)
25, no 6:12 Je '34   547
Emmet, Alida Chanler
Conrad; poem. In Psyche sleeps and other poems.
New York: Moffat Yard & co. , 1910. p99   548

The end of Conrad's Otago (editorial). Sun (NY) D 28 '37
                                                           548a
Enders, Anthony Talcott
    Aspects of structure in Conrad's Victory and Forster's
    A Passage to India. Honors Thesis, Harvard College,
    March 2, 1959. 42f; bibliography, f41-2   549
Endres, Fritz
    Joseph Conrad. Hamburg Fremdenblatt, Literarisches
    Rundschau no 313, 1928   550
Entwhistle, William J. and Gilbert, Eric
    The literature of England, A. D. 500-1942. London:
    Longmans, Green [1943] p217-18   551
Epron, Madeleine
    Joseph Conrad et la Pologne. Les Nouvelles Littéraires
    12, no 540:6 F 18 '33   552
Epstein, Jacob
    Conrad as a sitter. Daily Dispatch (Manchester) Ag 27
    '24 p6
    Joseph Conrad. In Epstein: an autobiography. New
    York: Dutton [1955] p73-7
    (An illustration of the bust of Conrad, 1924, faces
    p70)   553
    Epstein's bust of Conrad. Manchester Guardian Weekly 11,
    no 9: 189 Ag 29 '24   554
    Epstein's bust of Conrad on view. Sun (NY) N 5 '24
    (In the Tate Gallery, London)   554a
Erné, Nino
    Joseph Conrad und die Prosa der männlichen Einsamkeit.
    Geistige Welt 3:118-24 D '48   555
Ervine, St. John
    The novelist and the drama. Bookman (London) 66:8-13
    Ap '24   556
Eschbacher, Robert L.
    Lord Jim, classical rhetoric and the freshman dilemma.
    College English 25:22-5 O '63   557
Esenberg, K.
    Sprawa 'polkości' Konrada Korzeniowskiego (The problem
    of Conrad's Polish character). Kurier Poranny
    (Morning Courier) no 320, 1924   558
Estaunié, Edouard
    Hommage. La Nouvelle Revue Française 23:703 D 1 '24
    Le roman est-il en danger? Revue Hebdomadaire année
    34, no 7:132-50 F 14 '25   559
Estelrich, Juan
    José Conrad (1857-1924). El autor y su obra. Cuba
    Contemporánea (Havana) 38:244-73 Jl '25; same. Nos-
    otros (Buenos Aires) 50, año 19:289-316 Jl '25; same.

Estelrich, Juan (cont.)
  In Alma Rusa, by Joseph Conrad.   Translated by Juan
    Mateos de Diego.   Barcelona: Montaner y Simoñ
    [1925] Volume I, p[v]-xlv
  Joseph Conrad.   In Entre la vida i els llibres.   Barce-
    lona: Llibrería Catalonia, 1926. p275-314   560
[Ethel Barrymore on Conrad] Argonaut 55:404 D 12 '04   561
Evans, Benjamin Ifor
  A short history of English literature.   New York: Pen-
    guin Books [1940] p172-3   562
Evans, C. S.
  Joseph Conrad.   Music Teacher 14:541 Jl '22   563
Evans, J. M.
  A commentary and questionnaire on "Four Stories."
    (Joseph Conrad).   London: Pitman, (March) 1928. 32p
  A commentary and questionnaire on Typhoon.   (Joseph
    Conrad) London: Pitman, (March) 1928. 32p   564
Evans, Powys
  Modern portraits - XVII: Joseph Conrad.   London Mer-
    cury 7, no 38:119 D '22   565
Evans, Robert O.
  Conrad: a nautical image.   Modern Language Notes 72:
    98-9 F '57
  Conrad's underworld.   Modern Fiction Studies 2:56-62 My
    '56; same.   In The art of Joseph Conrad: a critical
    symposium edited by R. W. Stallman.   East Lansing,
    Michigan: Michigan State University Press, 1960. p171-
    81
    (Conrad made extensive use of Dante's Inferno in
    Heart of Darkness)
  Dramatization of Conra'ds Victory: and a new letter.
    Notes & Queries ns 8:108-10 Mr '61
    (Dramatization was by B. Macdonald Hastings.   The
    letter, dated July 19, 1916, is from Conrad to H. B.
    Irving)
  Further comment on The Heart of Darkness.   Modern
    Fiction Studies 3:358-60 Winter '59; same.   In The art
    of Joseph Conrad: a critical symposium edited by
    Robert Wooster Stallman.   East Lansing, Michigan:
    Michigan State University Press, 1960. p184-6   566
Exertions in the deep.   Time 50:107-8 S 29 '47; portrait
                                                      567
Fadiman, Clifton
  Introduction.   In The Pickwick Papers, by Charles
    Dickens.   New York: Simon & Schuster, 1949. p xliii
                                                      568
Fairley, Barker

Joseph Conrad, 1857-1924. Canadian Forum 5:19-20
  O '24
The new Conrad - and the old.   Canadian Bookman 2:26-
  9 Ja '20   569
Farber, Thomas David
  Illusion in Lord Jim... Honors Thesis, Harvard College,
  March 1, 1965. 51f   569a
Farmer, Norman Jr.
  Conrad's Heart of Darkness. Explicator 22, item 51,
  March 1964   570
The father of Joseph Conrad. Poland 7, no 7:414-15 Jl '26
                                                     571
Feaster, Jacob Henry
  The position of the adverb "only" in the works of Joseph
  Conrad. M. A. Thesis, Louisiana State University,
  1930   572
Feder, Lillian
  Marlow's descent into hell.   Nineteenth-Century Fiction
  9:280-92 Mr '55; same. In The art of Joseph Conrad:
  a critical symposium, edited by Robert Wooster Stall-
  man. East Lansing, Michigan: Michigan State Univ.
  Press, 1960. p162-70   573
Fehr, Bernhard
  Feuilleton. Joseph Conrad. Neue Zürcher Zeitung no
  1179: 1-2 Ag 8 '24
  Joseph Conrad. Beiblatt Zur Anglia 32, no 10:217-28
  O '21
  Joseph Conrad. In Die Englische Literatur des 19. und
  20. Jahrhunderts... Berlin: Akademische Verlags-
  gesellschaft Athenaion [1925] p402-7; portrait, p403
Von Englands geistigen beständen. Frauenfeld, 1944.
  p149-52   574
Feigenbaum, Lawrence H.
  Introduction to Typhoon. In Four complete English novels.
  New York: Globe Book Company, 1960.   575
Ferguson, Bessie Edna
  Joseph Conrad and his critics. M. A. Thesis, Univ. of
  Kansas, 1926. iii-vi, 175f   576
Ferguson, J. DeLancey
  Essay on Conrad's Suspense. Saturday Review of Litera-
  ture 2:315 N 21 '25
  The plot of Conrad's "The Duel." Modern Language Notes
  50: 385-90 Je '35
  (Suggests a possible source in Harper's Magazine,
  September, 1858, in "The Editor's Easy Chair" column)
                                                     577

Fernández, Ramón
L'art de Conrad. La Nouvelle Revue Française 23:730-7 D 1
'24; same. In Messages, translated from the French
by Montgomery Belgion. New York: Harcourt, Brace
[c1927] p137-51; same. (translated from the French by
Charles Owen) In The art of Joseph Conrad: a critical
symposium, edited by Robert Wooster Stallman. East
Lansing, Michigan: Michigan State University Press,
1960. p8-13
Balzac i Conrad. (translated into Polish by Maciej Zu-
rowski) Przegląd Humanistyczyny, 3 no 3:103-19 '59;
same. In Joseph Conrad Korzeniowski, by Róża Jab-
łkowska. Warsaw: Państwowe Zakłady Wydawnictwo
Szkolnych, 1964. p297-304
Lord Jim. La Nouvelle Revue Francaise 10, no 116,
May 1 '23   578
Ferrell, William R.
Some aspects of thematic development in five of Conrad's
novels: Heart of Darkness, Lord Jim, Nostromo,
Victory, and The Rover. Honors thesis, Swarthmore
College, 1954. 96p   579
Fichter, Robert Peter
Joseph Conrad's political novels. Harvard College honors
thesis, March 1, 1961. 42ff; bibliography f41-2
(Treats Nostromo, The Secret Agent, and Under Western
Eyes)   580
Filip, Tadeusz
Polskie przekłady utworów Conrada. Za i Przeciw no 9:
18 '58   581
F[ilochowski], W.
Nieporozumienie. Gazeta Warszawska no 223, 1926 582
Finger, Charles J.
Introduction. In The Inheritors, by Joseph Conrad and
Ford Madox Hueffer. (Memorial Edition) Garden City,
New York: Doubleday, Page, 1925. Volume I, p vii-x
(This volume also contains Almayer's Folly)   583
Finishing up Conrad. (Suspense) Sun (NY) Ap 11 '25 p12
                                                      584
First novels. Birmingham Post Ja 27 '25 p 3 (On Almayer's
Folly)   585
Fischer, S. (publishers)
Wer ist Joseph Conrad? Was sagen Europa und America
über ihn? [Berlin, S. Fischer, 1929] 8p   585a
Fisher, (Rev.) Ernest E.
Joseph Conrad as novelist. Holborn Review ns 20:497-
510 O '29   586
Fitzgerald, Louise Stephenson

A study of eight narrative devices in four novels by Joseph Conrad. M. A. Thesis, Univ. of Southern California, 1965. ii, 129f   586a
Fitzgerald, Ruth Kathleen
Joseph Conrad's supremacy in the field of the novel. M. A. Thesis, State College at Boston, 1948   587
Flamm, Dudley
The ambiguous Nazarene in Lord Jim. English Literature in Transition 11, no 1: 35-7 '68   587a
Fleischmann, Wolfgang Bernard
Conrad's Chance and Bergson's Laughter. Renascence 14:66-71 Winter '62   588
Fleishmann, Avrom Hirsch
Conrad's politics. Baltimore: Johns Hopkins press [c1967] vii-xv, 267p; portrait; bibliography, p253-8.
(Reviewed in Times Literary Supplement Jl 11 '68 p734)
Conrad's politics: community and anarchy in the fiction of Joseph Conrad. Ph. D. Thesis, Johns Hopkins University, 1963. 352f; bibl., f344-52
(Examines Nostromo, The Secret Agent, and Under Western Eyes)
The symbolic world of The Secret Agent. English Literary History 32:196-219 Je '65   589
Fleming, Emily Lenore
Mood effects in Conrad and Galsworthy. M. A. Thesis, Ohio State University, 1924. p7-21   590
Fletcher, James V.
Ethical symbolism in Conrad. College English 2:19-26 O '40   591
Folda, Olga
Joseph Conrad and Russia. M. A. Thesis, Univ. of Chicago, 1930 77p
(On Under Western Eyes)   592
Folejewski, Zbigniew
U kresu sił. Ze studiów nad techniką artystyczną Conrada. Roczniki Humanistyczne 6, no 6:127-35 '57   593
Follett, Helen Thomas and Follett, Wilson
Joseph Conrad. Atlantic Monthly 119:233-43 F '17; same. In Some modern novelists, appreciations and estimates. New York: Holt, 1918. p312-35
(Reviewed in London Mercury 2:243-4 Je '20)   594
Follett, Wilson
Joseph Conrad, 1907--. A humble apology. Bookman (NY) 67:640-7 Ag '28
Joseph Conrad: a salutation. New York Tribune Book News & Reviews Ap 29 '23 p19-20; portrait, p19

Follett, Wilson (cont.)
Joseph Conrad; a short study of his intellectual and emo-
tional attitude toward his work and of the chief charac-
teristics of his novels.   Garden City, New York:
Doubleday, Page (Privately printed) [c1915] [v]-x, 111p.
Reprinted: New York: Russell & Russell, 1966.
(Reviewed by H. L. Mencken in Smart Set 48: no 1:
305-6 Ja '16)
The modern novel... New York: Knopf, 1918. passim
                                                         595
Fonvielle, A. Rouquette de
Conrad et la Pologne.   Annales Politiques et Littéraires
88:527 My 15 '27   596
For future Conrads (editorial) New York Times Je 21 '45
p18   597
For readers of Conrad (editorial) New York Herald Tribune
S 10 '32 p8   598
Ford, Ford Madox (Ford Madox Hueffer)
Ancient lights and certain new reflections.   London:
Chapman and Hall, 1911
"C'est toi qui dors dans l'ombre..." Transatlantic Review
2, no 3:327-37; 4:454-65; 5:570-82; 6:689-700 O '24-
Ja '25
Conrad and the sea.   American Mercury 35:169-76 Je '35;
same.   London Mercury 32:223-31 Jl '35; same.   In
Portraits from life... Boston: Houghton Mifflin, 1937.
p57-69; same.   In Mightier than the sword... London:
Allen & Unwin [1938] p83-97; portrait facing p96
Decennial.   London Mercury 32:223-31 Jl '35
(Ten years have passed since Conrad's last book was
published in New York)
The English novel, from the earliest days to the death of
Joseph Conrad.   Philadelphia: Lippincott, 1929. p142-
9; same.   Bookman (NY) 69:77-8 Mr '29
Fragments from work in progress or about to appear.
Transatlantic Review 2, no 1:107-10 Jl '24
(Preface to The Nature of a Crime)
The Inheritors.   In Keating, George T.   A Conrad me-
morial library.   Garden City, New York: Doubleday,
Doran, 1929. p74-83
Introduction.   In The Sisters, by Joseph Conrad.   With an
introduction... New York: Crosby Gaige, 1928. p1-16
It was the nightingale.   Philadelphia & London: Lippincott,
1933. p308-11
(Sales of Conrad's manuscripts to Mr. Quinn)
Joseph Conrad.   English Review 10:68-83 D '11; same.
Public Opinion (London) 100:551 D 8 '11

Joseph Conrad. John O'London's Weekly 6, no 140:
323 D 10 '21

Joseph Conrad: a personal remembrance. London:
Duckworth [1924] 5-256p; portrait; Boston: Little,
Brown & Co., 1924. vii, 276 p excerpt. In Conrad.
A collection of critical essays, edited by Marvin Mud-
rick. (A Spectrum book) Englewood Cliffs, New Jer-
sey: Prentice-Hall [1966] p167-77. Reprinted: New
York: Octagon Books, 1965
(Reviewed in English Review 39:865-6 D '24; James
Milne in Graphic 100:1075 D 20 '24; G. C. T. in Ameri-
ca 32:378 Ja 31 '25; Pierre Denoyer in Ex Libris
(Paris) 2, no 8:240-1 My '25; Truth (London) 96:976
N 26 '24; J. F. in Bookman (NY) 61:83 Mr '25; Simon
Pure in Bookman (NY) 61:48-50 Mr '25; John O'Lon-
don's Weekly 12:321 N 29 '24; E. F. H. in Christian
Science Monitor D 6 '24 p11; L. D. Howland in Com-
monweal 1, no 24:666 Ap 22 '25; Publishers' Circular
& Booksellers' Record 122:483 Ap 25 '25; Wiadomości
Literackie 2, no 16:2 Ap 19 '25; Joseph Collins in
Bookman (NY) 61:173-6 Ap '25; same. In The doctor
looks at biography. New York: Doran [c1925] p120-5;
Overland Monthly 83, no 4:180 Ap '25; Contemporary
Review 127:128-9 Ja '25; E. F. Edgett in Boston Transcript D 13 '24 p 4; Current Opinion 78:177-8 F '25;
Christopher Morley in Saturday Review of Literature
1:415 D 27 '24; Times Literary Supplement N 13 '24
p727; corrected by Mrs. Jessie Conrad in Times Literary Supplement D 4 '24 p826; same. Bookman (NY)
61:252-3 Ap '25; Edward Garnett in Nation-Athenaeum
36:366, 368 D 6 '24; Thomas Moult in Yale Review ns
15:165-7 O '25; Robert Littell in New Republic 41:287
F 4 '25; Thomas Moult in Bookman (London) 67:174-6
D '24; Booklist 21:195 F '25; P. M. in Spectator 133:
989-90 D 20 '24; George Herbert Clarke in Sewanee
Review 33:253-5 Ap '25; Saturday Review 139:138-9 F
7 '25; Charles R. Walker in Independent 114:161 F 7
'25; H. I'A. Fausset in Manchester Guardian Weekly 11:
484 D 5 '24; Mark Van Doren in Nation (NY) 120:45 Ja
14 '25; Henry Louis Mencken in American Mercury 4:
505-7 Ap '25; Literary Review D 20 '24 p2; New Statesman 24: supplement xvi D 6 '24; New York Times D 7
'24 p3; L. Weitzenkorn in New York World D 7 '24 p
8e; Henry D.-Davray in Mercure de France année 38,
tome 193:487-9 Ja 15 '27; noted in John O'London's
Weekly 12:104 O 18 '24; Louis Cazamian in Revue
Anglo-Américaine 3:164-5 D '25; Westminster Gazette

Ford, Ford Madox (Ford Madox Hueffer) (cont.)
   F 21 '25 p4; noted in British Weekly 77:61 O 16 '24;
   New York Times Jl 30 '65 p23; Observer (London)
   N 9 '24 p5; Sidney Dark in Chicago Daily Tribune Ja 17
   '25 p9; Fanny Butcher in Chicago Daily Tribune F 2
   '25 p9)
Joseph Conrad and Ford Madox Ford. Bookman (NY) 68:
   216-18 O '28
Letter to the Editor. New York Herald Tribune Books F
   20 '27 p18; same. In Letters of Ford Madox Ford,
   edited by Richard M. Ludwig. Princeton: Princeton
   Univ. Press, 1965. p170-2
   (Discusses his collaboration with Conrad. The letter is
   dated February 15, 1927)
The letters of Ford Madox Ford, edited by Richard M.
   Ludwig. Princeton, New Jersey: Princeton Univ. press,
   1965. passim
The march of literature from Confucius to modern times.
   New York: Dial press, 1938. p835-45
Mr. Joseph Conrad and Anglo-Saxondom. English Review
   31:5-13, 107-9 Jl-Ag '20; same. Dial 69:52-60, 132-
   41, 239-46 Jl-Ag-S '20; same. In Thus to revisit:
   some reminiscences. London: Chapman and Hall, 1921.
   p79-101
La mort de Joseph Conrad. La Revue Européenne 4, no
   19:79-80 S 1 '24; same. Mercure de France 175:514-
   15 O 15 '24
[The Nature of a Crime] Transatlantic Review 1, no 1:98-
   9 Ja '24
On Conrad's vocabulary. Bookman (NY) 67:405-8 Je '28
Romance: an analysis. Transatlantic Review 1, no 2:
   84-9 F '24 ("Note" is on p84-5; analysis is on p85-9)
Techniques. Southern Review 1:20-35 Jl '35
Three Americans and a Pole. Scribner's Magazine 90:
   379-86 O '31
Tiger, tiger, being a commentary on Conrad's "The
   Sisters." Bookman (NY) 66:495-8 Ja '28
W. H. Hudson: some reminiscences. Little Review 7:
   4-7 My-Je '20 (Hudson discussed the "how" of writing
   with Conrad)
Working with Conrad. Yale Review ns 18:699-715 Je '29;
   same. In Return to yesterday. New York: Liveright,
   1932. p186-201
   (Discusses Ford's collaboration with Conrad, 1897-1909)
                                                        599
Ford, William J.
Lord Jim: Conrad's study in depth psychology. North-

western University Medical School Quarterly Bulletin
    24:64-9 Spring '50   600
Forst-Battaglia, Otto
    Um Joseph Conrads seele.   Frankfurter Zeitung no 40,
        Ja-F '28   601
Forster, Edward Morgan
    Joseph Conrad; a note.   In Abinger harvest.   New York:
        Harcourt, Brace [c1936] p136-41   602
Foulke, Robert Dana
    Conrad's sea world: the voyage fiction and the British
        Merchant Service, 1875-1895. Ph. D. Thesis, Univ.
        of Minnesota, 1961.   268p. Abstract in Dissertation Ab-
        stracts 22:1173 '61   603
Fox, R. M.
    Joseph Conrad: the supreme irony.   Irish Statesman 3,
        no 8:239-40 N 1 '24   604
Francillon, Robert
    Conrad, psychologue de l'imagination.   La Nouvelle Re-
        vue Française 23:724-9 D 1 '24   605
Francis, Kent Wheeler
    A study of animism in the writings of Joseph Conrad.
        M. A. Thesis, State Univ. of Iowa, 1930. 43p   606
Franzen, Erich
    Gegen die blinden mäuchte der zerstörung.   Frankfurter
        Zeitung Ag 24 '30 p20
    Über Joseph Conrad.   Die Neue Rundschau 45, heft 1:
        122-8 Ja '34   607
Franzero, C. M.
    Conrad vide il mare come un mostro divino. Il Tempo
        12:18 '58   608
Franzoni, Orfeo John
    Conrad's attitude towards the civilization of Spanish
        America. M. A. Thesis, Siena College, 1959. 69p
                                                     609
Fraser, G. S.
    Lord Jim: the romance of irony.   Critical Quarterly 8:
        231-41 Autumn '66
    The modern writer and his world.   London: Andre Deutsch,
        1955. p63-4 (On "Heart of Darkness")   610
Freeman, Dana Ward Jr.
    A study of Joseph Conrad as an explorer of the isolated
        mind.   M. A. Thesis, State College at Boston, 1955
                                                     611
Freeman, John
    Joseph Conrad. In The moderns. Essays in literary
        criticism. London: Scott, 1916. p243-64   612

Freeman, Rosemary
    Conrad's Nostromo: a source and its use.   Modern Fic-
        tion Studies 7:317-26 Winter '61-'62   613
Freislich, Richard
    Marlow's shadow side.   London Magazine 4:31-6 N '57
                                                      614
Freissler, Ernst Wolfgang von
    Conrad.   Neue Zürcher Zeitung no 253, F '28
    Joseph Conrad.   Atlantis heft 10:620 O '29
    Joseph Conrad in Deutschland.   Pologne Littéraire no 29
        '29; same.   Die Neue Rundschau 40, part 1:125-30
        Ja '29
        (Noted in Wiadomości Literackie 6, no 5:3 F 3 '29)
                                                      615
Frenkel, Mieczysław R.
    Kto zrobił z Conrada pisarza francuskiego?   (Who has
        made of Conrad a French writer?)   Odrodzenie (Ren-
        aissance) no 50, 1948   616
Freund, Philip
    Dream: Conrad.   In How to become a literary critic.
    New York: Beechhurst press, 1947. p110-24
    Introduction.   In Lord Jim, by Joseph Conrad.   New
        York: Collier books [1962] p9-26; bibliography, p347-
        8   617
Frewer, Louis B.
    The influence of Dickens.   Dickensian 28, no 221:40-1
        Winter '31-'32   618
Fricker, Robert
    Der moderne englische Roman.   Göttingen: 1958. p43-65
                                                      619
Friedman, Alan Howard
    Joseph Conrad.   In The turn of the novel.   Oxford: Ox-
        ford University press, 1966. p75-105.
        (Reviewed by Gerald Hoag in English Language Notes
        5, no 4:310-12 Je '68; Vereen M. Bell in South At-
        lantic Quarterly 66, no 4:619-20 Autumn '67)
    The turn of the novel: changes in the pattern of English
        fiction since 1890 in Hardy, Conrad, Forster, and
        Lawrence.   University of California at Berkeley, 1964.
        Ph. D. Thesis.   388p; abstract in Dissertation Abstracts
        25:6622 '65   620
Friedman, Joseph Herbert
    Joseph Conrad: the making of his reputation.   M. A.
        Thesis, Columbia University, 1947. 219p   621
Friedman, Norman
    Criticism and the novel: Hardy, Hemingway, Crane,
        Woolf, Conrad.   Antioch Review 18:343-70 Fall '58   622

"A friendly place." New York Times D 14 '26 p26
   (The proposed Seaman's Church Institute Memorial)
                                                          623
Frierson, William C.
   The English novel in transition, 1885-1940. Norman,
   Oklahoma: University of Oklahoma press, 1942.
   passim   624
Frisé, A.
   Joseph Conrad, Dichter des Meeres. Germania no 222,
   1932   625
Fry, Ruth Jerman
   A study of the collaboration of Joseph Conrad and Ford
   Madox Ford. Master's Thesis, Univ. of Texas, 1938.
   iii-iv, 86f   626
Fryde, Ludwik
   Realizm w twórczości Conrada. Pion no 52, 1935; same.
   In Wspomnienia i studia o Conradzie, ed. by Barbara
   Kocówna. Warsaw: Państwowy Instytut Wydawniczy
   [1963] p368-78   627
Frye, Northrop
   Anatomy of criticism. Princeton, New Jersey: Prince-
   ton University press, 1957. p39-40, 155, 237, 267
                                                          628
Fryer, Benjamin N. and Johnson, James
   Bruce Rogers and the figurehead of the Joseph Conrad.
   San Francisco: Windsor Press, 1938. 2-12p; 4 illus-
   trations; photographs
   (300 copies only)   629
Fryling, Jan
   The yield of the oceans. In Conrad żywy, edited by Wit
   Tarnawski. London: B. Świderski, 1957. p74-8   630
Fuchs, Carolyn
   Words, action, and the modern novel. Kerygma 4, no
   1:3-11 Winter '64   630a
The funeral of Joseph Conrad. New York Herald Tribune
   Ag 16 '24 p18   631
[Funeral picture of Joseph Conrad] Illustrated London News
   165:303 Ag 16'24   632
Furphy, A. A.
   The development of the technique of Conrad as an ironical
   novelist. Master's Thesis, University of Manchester,
   1953   633

G. , H.
   Conrad the realist and romanticist. Bookman's Journal
   10:199 S '24   634

Gałczyńska-Folkierska, Anna
O moralności Conradowskiej (Conrad's morality).   Wiatr
   od Morza no 1 '46   635
Gale, Bell
   Conrad and the romantic hero.   Ph. D.   Thesis, Yale Uni-
   versity, Nov. 1962.   274f; bibliography, f 268-274
   (Examines "Heart of Darkness," Lord Jim, Nostromo,
   Under Western Eyes, Chance, and Victory)   636
Gallaher, Elizabeth
   James and Conrad in France.   Ph. D.   Thesis, Radcliffe
   College, 1952   637
Galsworthy, John [John Sinjohn, pseud.]
   Forsytes, Pendyces and others.   London: William Heine-
   mann, 1935. p221, 226
   Introduction.   In Laughing Anne and One Day More: two
   plays by Joseph Conrad... London: John Castle, 1924.
   p5-15; same.   In The Nature of a Crime, by Joseph
   Conrad and Ford Madox Ford.   (Memorial Edition.
   Collected Works of Joseph Conrad)   Garden City, New
   York: Doubleday, Page, 1926.   Volume XXII, p v-xi
   ("Introduction" is dated "September, 1924")
   Introduction.   In Youth, A Narrative and Two Other Stor-
   ies, by Joseph Conrad.   (Memorial Edition) Garden
   City, New York: Doubleday, Page, 1925.   Volume VI,
   p vii-ix
   Jocelyn.   London: Duckworth & Co. , 1898. 309p
   (Dedication: "To Joseph Conrad This Book is Affec-
   tionately Dedicated by the Author")
   Joseph Conrad: a disquisition.   Fortnightly Review 89:
   627-33 Ap 1 '08; same.   Living Age 257:416-20 My 16
   '08
   A letter from John Galsworthy to Joseph Conrad. [London:
   First Edition Club, Curwen Press, 1926]   Text of
   letter, p[5-6]; Editor's note, p[3]
   (220 copies only)
   Letters from John Galsworthy, 1900-1932.   Edited and with
   an introduction by Edward Garnett.   London: Cape,
   1934.   passim; "Introduction," p5-16
   [Meeting with Conrad]   New York Daily Tribune O 27 '06
   p5 (A letter from Galsworthy to a friend which indi-
   cates that his first meeting with Conrad took place in
   March, 1893 on the sailing ship Torrens in Adelaide
   harbor)
   Nostromo.   In Keating, George T.   A Conrad memorial
   library.   Garden City, New York: Doubleday, Doran,
   1929. p138
   Preface to Conrad's plays.   In Castles in Spain, and

other screeds. New York: Scribner's, 1927. p173-84
(Prefaces to Conrad's One Day More, Laughing Anne,
and The Secret Agent)
Reminiscences of Conrad. La Nouvelle Revue Française
23:649-58 D 1 '24 (translated into French by André
Maurois); same. Die Literatur 27:194-201 D 5 '24
(translated into German by Max Meyerfeld); same.
Scribner's Magazine 77:3-10 Ja '25; same. (excerpt)
Observer (London) Ja 11 '25 p6; same. In Castles in
Spain, and other screeds. New York: Scribner's,
1927. p99-126; same. In Essays in liberal thought,
edited by William Henry Thomas and Stewart S. Mor-
gan. New York: Harcourt, Brace [c1928] p49-64; same.
Lesezirkel (Zürich) 14:77 '28-'29; same. In Candela-
bra... New York: Scribner's, 1933. p195-212; same.
Twórczość (Creative Work) Ja '47 p59-70
Six novelists in profile. In Candelabra... New York:
Scribner's, 1933. p 133-54; same. Castles in Spain...
New York: Scribner's, 1927. p201-35
Souvenirs sur Conrad.
See: Reminiscences of Conrad.
Two essays on Conrad, by John Galsworthy, with The
Story of a Remarkable Friendship, by Richard Curle.
Freelands: [Kentucky] Privately printed (Cincinnati,
Ebbert & Richardson, printers); 1930. 83p
(93 copies only); also issued in an edition of 25 copies
only.
Galsworthy, novelist and dramatist, dies at 65... New
York Herald Tribune F 1 '33 p13
(Mentions Conrad's meeting with Galsworthy)   638
Garczyński, Tadeusz
Conrad wśród rodziny (Conrad among his family).
Gazeta Ludowa (People's Gazette) no 322, 1946   639
Gard, Robert Royal
A study of Joseph Conrad's humanitarianism. Master's
Thesis, Univ. of Illinois, 1950. 73p   640
Gardiner, A. G.
Joseph Conrad. Daily News (London) Ag 4 '24; same.
(excerpt) Public Opinion (London) 126:128 Ag 8 '24
                                                    641
Gardner, Monica M.
Joseph Conrad as a Pole. Spectator 135:190-1 Ag 1
'25   642
Garland, Hamlin
My friendly contemporaries; a literary log. New York:
Macmillan, 1932. p489-502, 531-5   643

Garland, Herbert
  Joseph Conrad. Gypsy 1:67-70 My '15   644
Garner, Naomi
  Joseph Conrad's theory of narrative art. M. A. Thesis,
    Univ. of Colorado, 1939. Abstract in Colorado Uni-
    versity Bulletin 39, no 18:58 O '39   645
Garnett, Constance
  Constance Garnett to Joseph Conrad. [London: First
    Edition Club, Curwen Press, 1926] Text of letter,
    p[2-3]; Editor's note, p[1]
    (220 copies only)   646
Garnett, David
  The flowers of the forest (being volume 2 of The Golden
    Echo). London: Chatto & Windus, 1955. p248-9
  The golden echo. London: Chatto and Windus, 1953.
    p62-4 and passim   647
Garnett, Edward
  Conrad's place in literature. In Conrad's prefaces to
    his works... London: Dent [1937] p3-34
  The danger of idols. Saturday Review 140:505 O 31
    '25
  Four letters from Edward Garnett to Joseph Conrad.
    [London: First Edition Club, Curwen Press, 1926]
    Editor's note, p[1-3]; Letters, p[5-11]; [12]p
    (220 copies only)
  Introduction. In The Rover, by Joseph Conrad. (Me-
    morial Edition) Garden City, New York: Doubleday,
    Page, 1925. Volume XX, p vii-xii (Includes a letter
    from Conrad to Garnett, dated Dec. 4, 1923)
  Introduction. In Letters from John Galsworthy, 1900-
    1932. Edited... by Edward Garnett. London: Cape,
    1934. p5-16
  Introduction. In Letters from Joseph Conrad, 1895-1924.
    Edited with introduction and notes by Edward Garnett.
    London: The Nonesuch Press, 1928; Indianapolis: Bobbs-
    Merrill [c1928] p1-28
    (Reprinted in paperback by Bobbs-Merrill in August,
    1962)
  Joseph Conrad. I. Impressions and beginnings. Century
    Magazine 115:385-92 F '28
  Joseph Conrad. II. The long hard struggle for success.
    Century Magazine 115:593-600 Mr '28
  Mr. Joseph Conrad. Academy 55:82-3 O 15 '98; same.
    (enlarged and altered) In Friday nights: literary criti-
    cisms and appreciations. London: Jonathan Cape
    [1922]; New York: Knopf, 1922. 1st series, p83-101
  Reply to Gerald Gould. Saturday Review 140:505 O 31 '25

Tales of Unrest. In Keating, George T. A Conrad me-
morial library. Garden City, New York: Doubleday,
Doran, 1929. p50-6   648
Garrett, George
Conrad's The Nigger of the 'Narcissus.' Adelphi 12,
no 3:150-5 Je '36   649
Garruto, John Cajetan
Conrad's ideas on illusion and reality and their employ-
ment in Nostromo. M. A. Thesis, University of Vir-
ginia, 1952. 82f   650
Gaston, Paul Lee
Joseph Conrad's gospel of work. M. A. Thesis, Univer-
sity of Virginia, 1966. 48f   651
Gatch, Katherine H.
Conrad's Axel. Studies in Philology 48:98-106 Ja '51
(Parallels between Victory and the Axel of Villiers
de l'Isle-Adam)   652
Gausseron, B. H.
Le mouvement littéraire en Angleterre: les prosateurs.
Revue Encyclopédique 7, no 179:126 F 13 '97   653
Gazdzik, Barbara
"The Rescuer" manuscript. In Conrad żywy, edited by
Wit Tarnawski. London: B. Świderski, 1957. p169-
80   654
Gazzoni, Dario
The sea novels of Josef Conrad. Rome: Vatican
Polyglot Press [nd] 68p   655
Geddes, Gary
Clearing the jungle: the importance of work in Conrad.
Queen's Quarterly 73:559-72 Winter '66   656
Gee, John Archer
The final typescript of Book III of Conrad's Nostromo.
Yale University Library Gazette 16, no 4:80 Ap '42
657
Gee, John Archer and Sturm, Paul J.
Introduction. In Letters of Joseph Conrad to Marguerite
Poradowska, 1890-1920... New Haven: Yale Univer-
sity press, 1940. p[xiii]-xix   658
Gemme, Francis R.
Introduction. In Lord Jim, by Joseph Conrad. New
York: Airmont, 1966   659
The genius of Joseph Conrad (editorial). Christian Science
Monitor Ag 4 '24 p16   659a
George, Gerald A.
Conrad's "The Lagoon." Explicator 24, item 23, Nov.
'65   660

George Moore lets statement stand. New York Times Ap
22 '28 Section 3, p8
(Insists that "Conrad's works will be dead in a year") 661
Georgin, B.
Un conférence sur Joseph Conrad. Chronique des
Lettres Françaises 3:55-7 Ja-F '25 662
Gerhardi, William
Memoirs of a polyglot. New York: Knopf, 1931. p239-
40 663
Gerould, Gordon Hall
Explorers of the inner life. In The patterns of English
and American fiction. Boston: Little, Brown, 1942.
p447-55 664
Gerould, Katharine Fullerton
Stream of consciousness. Saturday Review of Literature
4:233-4 O 22 '27 665
Gers, José
Un capitaine au long cours: Joseph Conrad. In Le noir
Congolais vu par nos écrivains coloniaux... Bruxelles,
1953. p[209]-216; In Institute Royal Colonial Belge.
Section des Sciences Morales et Politiques. Memoire.
Collection i-8, tome xxxi, fasc. 2 666
Gets a Conrad letter. New York Times Jl 24 '38, Section 3,
p9
(The Seamen's Church Institute receives a letter Con-
rad wrote to the crew of the Tusitala) 667
Gettmann, Royal A. and Harkness, Bruce
Morality and psychology in "The Secret Sharer." In Con-
rad's Secret Sharer and the critics, edited by Bruce
Harkness. Belmont, California: Wadsworth [c1962]
p125-32 668
Gibbon, Perceval
Joseph Conrad: an appreciation. Bookman (London) 39:
177-9 supplement Ja '11; same. Sun (NY) Ja 21 '11
p8; same. Public Opinion (London) 99:80 Ja 27 '11
same. (excerpt) Literary Digest 42:207 F 4 '11
(Noted in New York Herald Ja 20 '12 p16) 669
Gide, André
Joseph Conrad. La Nouvelle Revue Française 23:659-62
D 1 '24; same published separately: Liege: Editions de
la Lampe d'Aladdin, 1927; same. In The art of Joseph
Conrad: a critical symposium, edited by Robert
Wooster Stallman. East Lansing: Michigan: Michigan
State Univ. Press, 1960. p3-5 (translated by Charles
Owen)
Joseph Conrad. In Autumn leaves. New York: Philo-

Gillon, Adam (cont.)
    Microfilm AC-1 no 8665
    The Jews in Joseph Conrad's fiction.   Chicago Jewish
        Forum 22:34-40 Fall '63
    Joseph Conrad in Poland.   Polish Review 4, nos 1-2:
        25-32 Winter-Spring '59; same.   In Joseph Conrad:
        centennial essays, edited by Ludwik Krzyżanowski.
        New York: Polish Institute of Arts & Sciences in
        America, 1960. p145-60
    The merchant of Esmeralda - Conrad's archetypal Jew.
        Polish Review (NY) 9, no 4:3-20 Autumn '64
    Some Polish motifs in the works of Joseph Conrad.
        Slavic & East European Journal 10:424-39 Winter '66
                                                            677
Gilmore, Nora E.
    Characterization in Joseph Conrad's novels.   Master's
        Thesis, West Texas State College, 1951. 148p   678
Gissing, George
    Letters of George Gissing to members of his family,
        edited by Algernon Gissing and Ellen Gissing.   London:
        Constable, 1927. p391
    Two letters from George Gissing to Joseph Conrad. [Lon-
        don: First Edition Club, Curwen Press, 1926] [7]p
        Editor's note, p[1]; Letters, p[3-7]
        (220 copies only)   679
Glaenzer, Richard Butler
    Joseph Conrad and others considered as "best sellers."
        New York Times Book Review Je 18 '16 p254
    Snap-shots of English authors.   Conrad.   Bookman (NY)
        45:346 Je '17   680
Glaser, Alice
    The critical reputation of Joseph Conrad.   Radcliffe Col-
        lege English Honors Thesis, 1950. 44f; bibliography,
        f41-4   681
Glasgow, Ellen
    Pages from the autobiography of Ellen Glasgow.   American
        Scholar 23:284-7 Summer '54; same.   The woman with-
        in.   New York: Harcourt, Brace, 1954. p200-4   682
Gleckner, Robert F.
    Conrad's "The Lagoon."   Explicator 16, item 33, March
        '58   683
Goa
    See: Gołubiew, Antoni   684
Goens, Mary B.
    The "mysterious and effective star:" the mythic world-
        view in Conrad's Victory.   Modern Fiction Studies 13,
        no 4:455-63 Winter '67-'68   684a

Gołubiew, Antoni [Goa]
Conradiana.   Tygodnik Powszechny 12, no 42:8 O 19 '58
Katolickoŝĉ Conrada.   Znak (Sign) no 6:484-511 S-O
'48
Nowele Conrada (Conrad's short stories).   Tygodnik
Powszechny (Universal Weekly) 9, no 5:1-2 F 15 '53
Poprawiam Kotta (I correct Kott).   Dziŝ i Jutro (Today
and Tomorrow) 1, no 3:5 D 9 '45
Rysunki Conrada.   Tygodnik Powszechny 11, no 48:5 D
8 '57 (Three drawings done by Conrad)
'Szeroki ŝwiat' i Conrad (The "wide world" and Conrad).
Tygodnik Powszechny no 22:7 Je 2 '46   692
Gomulicki, Wiktor
Polak czy Anglik?   (Pole or Englishman?) Życie i
Sztuka (Petersburg) no 1, 1905; same. Kraj (Homeland)
no 1, 1905   693
Gonski, Casimir
Joseph Conrad's works and how to read them.   Address
delivered at Marquette University.   Poland 7, no 6:
356-7, 378, 380 Je '26   694
Gonzalez, N. V. M.
Time as sovereign: a reading of Joseph Conrad's "Youth."
Literary Apprentice (University of the Philippines)
1954, p106-22   695
Goodwin, Cleon Walton
The function of imagination in the fiction of Joseph Con-
rad.   Honors Essay, Dept. of English, Univ. of N.
Carolina, 1965. 80f; bibl., f79-80   696
Gordan, John Dozier
An anniversary exhibition.   The Henry W. and Albert A.
Berg Collection 1940-1965.   Part II. Joseph Conrad.
The holograph and corrected typescript of "A Smile of
Fortune." Bulletin of the New York Public Library 69,
no 9:603 N '65
The Ghost at Brede Place.   New York Public Library
Bulletin 56:591-5 D '52
Joseph Conrad: his development as a novelist from ama-
teur to professional.   Ph. D. Thesis, Harvard Univer-
sity, February, 1939. 495f; "Works by Joseph Conrad,"
f[479]-481; bibliography, f484-95.   Abstract in Harvard
University, Summaries of Theses, 1939, p237-9
Joseph Conrad: the making of a novelist.   Cambridge,
Massachusetts: Harvard University Press, 1940. [vii]-
xiv, 430p; bibliography, p[311]-31; notes, p[333]-415;
portrait
(Reviewed by Joseph Warren Beach in Journal of English & Germanic Philology 40:446-8 '41; E. F. M. in

Christian Science Monitor Mr 8 '41 p11; F. Steegmuller
in New York Herald Tribune Books D 15 '40 p15;
Charles Kerby-Miller in Boston Transcript Book Section
Ja 18 '41 p1; Morton Dauwen Zabel in New Republic
103:873-4 D 23 '40; James McGovern in Commonweal 33:604-5 Ap 4 '41; noted in Book-of-the-Month
Club News Ja '41 p16; Harold N. Hillebrand in Accent
1, no 3:188-9 Spring '41)
Novels in manuscript. An exhibition from the Berg Collection. Part II. The Rover, by Joseph Conrad.
Bulletin of the New York Public Library 69, no 6:398
Je '65
The Rajah Brooke and Joseph Conrad. Studies in Philology 35:613-34 O '38
The Ranee Brooke and Joseph Conrad. Studies in Philology 37:130-2 Ja '40   697
Gordon, Alfred
A novel with some great scenes. Canadian Bookman 4,
no 4:119-20 Ap '22
(Compares Miss Pickthall with Conrad)   698
Gordon, W.
Joseph Conrad. Queen's Quarterly 32:264-75 Ja-F-Mr
'25   699
Górski, Kazimierz
Conrad. Gazeta Policji i Adm. Państ. nos 22-25,
1924
Conrad w Zakopanem (Conrad in Zakopane). Przegląd
Wołyński no 24, 1932; same. Gazeta Polska (Polish
Gazette) no 24, 1932   700
Górski, Konrad
Literatura a prady umysłowe. Warsaw: 1938. 314p 701
Gose, Elliott B., Jr.
Cruel devourer of the world's light: The Secret Agent.
Nineteenth-Century Fiction 15:39-51 Je '60
Pure exercise of imagination: archetypal symbolism in
Lord Jim. Publications of the Modern Language Association of America 79:137-47 Mr '64   702
The gossip shop [on Conrad's death] Bookman (NY) 60:247
O '24   703
Gossman, Ann M. and Whiting, George W.
The essential Jim. Nineteenth-Century Fiction 16, no 1:
75-80 Je '61   704
Gould, Gerald
The danger of idols. Saturday Review 140:471-2 O 24
'25 (Concerning Mr. Edward Garnett's criticism of
Conrad)
The English novel of today. London: John Castle, 1924.

Gould, Gerald (cont.)
    p193-4
    (Reviewed by Herbert Garland in Bookman's Journal &
    Print Collector 11: supplement p viii O '24)   705
Grabczak, E.
    Oriental vocabulary in Conrad and Orwell. Master's
    Thesis, University of Warsaw, 1962   706
Grabo, Carl Henry
    The art of the short story. New York: Scribner's
    [c1913] p146-7, 160-1, 259-60
    Conrad's management of the point of view. In The tech-
    nique of the novel. New York: Scribner's [c1928]
    p66-71 (On Chance)
    Conrad's The Rover and its structural method. In The
    technique of the novel. New York: Scribner's [c1928]
    p171-9   707
Grabowski, Zbigniew A.
    Co Conrad z Polski byƚ wywiózƚ (What did Conrad take
    out of Poland?) Kurier Poznański (Poznan Courier) no
    383, 1930; same. Lwówski Kurier Poranny (Lwów
    Morning Courier) no 379, 1930
    Conrad po trzydziestu latach. Wiadomości 12, no 50:2
    D 15 '57
    Dlaczego Conrad pisaƚ po angielsku? (Why did Conrad
    write in English?) Kurier Poznański (Poznań Courier)
    no 287, 1925
    Joseph Conrad after thirty years. In Conrad żywy, edited
    by Wit Tarnawski. London: B. Świderski, 1957.
    p134-40
    Joseph Conrad - under Polish eyes. Études Slaves et
    Est-Européennes 3:53-5 Spring '58
    Nowe spojrzenie na Conrada. Tygodnik Powszechny 11,
    no 48:4-5 D 8 '57
    O Polkość Josepha Conrada (Joseph Conrad's Polish char-
    acter). Illustrowany Kuryer Codzienny (Illustrated
    Daily Courier) no 69, 1929
    Ze studiów nad Josephem Conradem. Poznań: Skƚad
    Gƚówny: Księgarnia Gebethner i Wolffa, 1927. [7]-
    [142]p; notes, p[111]-139; same. (excerpt entitled:
    'Romantyzm Conrada") In Wspomnienia i studia o Con-
    radzie, edited by Barbara Kocówna. [Warsaw:] Pańs-
    twowy Instytut Wydawniczy [1963] p253-69
    (Reviewed by Z. Dębicki in Kurjer Warszawski no 274,
    1927; Monica Gardner in Slavonic Review 7, no 19,
    1927; W. Tarnawski in Sƚowo Pol. no 296, 1927)   708
Graebsch, Irene
    Joseph Conrad. Breslauer Zeitung no 140 Je-Jl '28   709

Graham, Robert Bantine Cunninghame
  See: Cunninghame Graham, Robert Bantine 710
Graham, Stephen
  "Dat ole davil sea." Saturday Review of Literature 1:90
    S 6 '24; same. In The death of yesterday. London:
    Benn [1930] p64-7 711
Ce grand gentilhomme anglais qui suivat la mer. Journal
    Littéraire Ag '34 (Noted in English Review 39:866 D
    '24) 711a
Graver, Lawrence S.
  Conrad's first story. Studies in Short Fiction (Newberry
    College) 2:164-9 Winter '65
    (On "The Black Mate")
  Conrad's "The Lagoon." Explicator 21, item 70, My '63
  Critical confusion and Conrad's "The End of the Tether."
    Modern Fiction Studies 9:390-3 Winter '63-'64
  The short stories of Joseph Conrad. Ph. D. Thesis,
    University of California, 1961. 372p
  "Typhoon:" a profusion of similes. College English 24:
    62-4 O '62 712
Gray, Hugh
  Conrad's political prophecies. Life & Letters Today 24:
    134-9 F '40 713
Graz, Albert G.
  Lord Jim, by Joseph Conrad, edited by Albert G. Graz.
    New York: Macmillan, 1963. 714
"The greatest of sea writers;" newspaper tributes to Joseph
    Conrad. Current Opinion 77:304, 313 S '24; portrait
    715
Green, A. Wigfall (and others)
  Complete college composition... New York: Crofts, 1945.
    2nd edition, p821-2 716
Green, Clarence Corleon
  The spirit of Joseph Conrad. M. A. Thesis, Univer-
    sity of Washington, 1924. 37f; bibliography, f35-7
    716a
Green, Jesse D.
  Diabolism, pessimism, and democracy: notes on Melville
    and Conrad. Modern Fiction Studies 5, no 3:287-305
    Autumn '62 717
Green-Armitage, Adrian
  The religion of Joseph Conrad. Tablet (London) D 7 '57
    p501-2 718
Greenberg, Evelyn Levow
  The friendship and literary collaboration between Joseph
    Conrad and Ford Madox Ford. M. A. Thesis, Univ.
    of Maryland, 1949. 95f; bibliography f93-5 719

Greenberg, Robert A.
    The presence of Mr. Wang.   Boston University Studies in
        English 4:129-37 Autumn '60   720
Greene, David Mason
    Critical biography. In Victory.   Chapter notes and criti-
        cism... New York: American RDM Corp. [1965] p5-21
                                                                 721
Greene, Graham
    The domestic background. In The lost childhood... Lon-
        don: Eyre & Spottiswoode, 1951. p100-1
    Remembering Mr. Jones. In The lost childhood... Lon-
        don: Eyre & Spottiswoode, 1951. p98-9   722
Greene, Marc T.
    The mystery of Conrad.   Poland 10:539-44, 561, 578,
        Ag '29   723
Greene, Maxine
    A return to heroic man.   Saturday Review (NY) 42:11
        Ag 22 '59
    Introduction. In The Nigger of the 'Narcissus,' by Joseph
        Conrad.   New York: Collier Books [1962] p7-13   724
Greenep, Francis M.
    Ze wspomnień o Conradzie.   Kurjer Warszawski no 269,
        1924   725
Greenwood, Thomas
    Joseph Conrad: Un centenaire littéraire.   Études Slaves
        et Est-Européennes 2, part 4:195-200 Winter '57-'58
                                                                 726
Grein, James Thomas
    The Secret Agent. In The new world of the theatre,
        1923-1924. London: Hopkinson, 1924. p1-3   727
Grenzow, Daisy Blossom
    Narrative method in four novels of Joseph Conrad. Mas-
        ter's Thesis, Ohio State University, 1931. 75p   728
[Grieg, J. Y. T.] John Carruthers [pseud.]
    Scheherazade, or the future of the English novel. New
        York: Dutton [c1928] p33-6   729
Griffiss, John McLeod
    Joseph Conrad's concept of the tragic and heroic figure.
        Honors Essay, University of North Carolina, 1962.
        96f   730
Griffith, Paul
    Joseph Conrad: Lord Jim.   Prepared for Barnes &
        Noble by Paul Griffith.   New York: Barnes & Noble
        [1967] 95p; bibliography, p94-5   731
Griffiths, J. G.
    Conrad's prose.   John O'London's Weekly 12:33 O 4 '24
                                                                 732

Grodzicki, Bogusław
Nad Conradem (Reflections on Conrad). Tygodnik
Powszechny (Universal Weekly) no 18:1-2 My 4 '52
733
Groom, Bernard
The novel. In A literary history of England. London:
Longmans, Green, 1929. p370-2   734
Gross, Harvey
Aschenbach and Kurtz, the cost of civilization. Centen-
nial Review 6:131-43 Spring '62   735
Gross, Seymour L.
Conrad and All the King's Men. Twentieth Century Litera-
ture 3:27-32 Ap '57
Conrad's revision of "Amy Foster." Notes & Queries ns
10:144-6 Ap '63
The devil in Samburan: Jones and Ricardo in Victory.
Nineteenth-Century Fiction 16, no 1:81-5 Je '61
A further note on the function of the frame in "Heart of
Darkness." Modern Fiction Studies 3:167-70 Summer
'57; same. In The art of Joseph Conrad: a critical
symposium, edited by Robert Wooster Stallman. East
Lansing, Michigan: Michigan State University Press,
1960. p181-4
Hamlet and Heyst again. Notes & Queries ns 6:87-8 Mr
'59   736
Grubiński, Wacław
Conrad na wielkim świecie. Wiadomości Literackie 1,
no 33:2 Ag 17 '24
Nierozumna szczodrobliwość. Kurjer Warszawski no 72,
1927
Walka o Conrada. Kurjer Warszawski no 204, 1928
Współczucie w literaturze. Kurjer Warszawski no 138,
1930   737
Gruyter, J. de
A master of English. English Studies 7:169-75 D '25
(Chiefly about Suspense)   738
Grzegorczyk, Piotr
Conrad i Zeromski. Ruch Literacki 2, no 5:159 My '27
Do problemu "zdrady" Conrada. Gazeta Warszawska no
247, 1932
Ostatni list Conrada. Ruch Literacki 2, no 7:207-8 S
'27 (Conrad's last letter, dated June 28, 1924)
Z dziejów J. Conrada-Korzeniowskiego w Polsce. Ruch
Literacki 2, no 5:136-8 My '27; same. In Joseph
Conrad Korzeniowski, by Róża Jabłkowska. Warsaw:
Państwowe Zakłady Wydawnictwo Szkolynch, 1964. p217-
20; same. In Wspomnienia i studia o Conradzie, edited

Grzegorczyk, Piotr (cont.)
　　by Barbara Kocówna.　Warsaw:　Państwowy Instytut
　　Wydawnicy [1963] p43-7　　　　　　　　　　739
Gschwind, Frank Henry
　　Joseph Conrad.　Neue Schweizer Rundschau 29:526-9
　　My '26　　　　　　　　　　　　　　　　　740
Guebels, L.
　　Conrad, marin d'eau douce.　Renaissance d'Occident
　　(Brussels) année 11, tome 31:253-88 D '29　741
Guedalla, Philip
　　Joseph Conrad - a master of ships and of story.　Vanity
　　Fair 20, no 5:64, 102 Jl '23
　　Men of letters.　London: Hodder & Stoughton, 1927.
　　p124-35
　　Under the knife. IV. - Mr. Joseph Conrad.　Illustrated
　　London News 161:240 Ag 12 '22; same.　In A gallery.
　　London: Constable, 1924.　p91-9　　　　　742
Guerard, Albert Joseph
　　Conrad the novelist.　Cambridge:　Harvard University
　　Press, 1958.　xiv, 322p.　Notes, p[307]-15.　Part re-
　　printed in:　Conrad.　A collection of critical essays,
　　edited by Marvin Mudrick.　Englewood Cliffs, New
　　Jersey:　Prentice-Hall, Inc. [1966] p17-36.　Reprinted:
　　Cambridge:　Harvard University Press, 1966
　　(Dated 1958 unless otherwise noted.　Reviewed by R. C.
　　Blackman in Christian Science Monitor S 11 p7; Book-
　　list 55:16 S 1; Edward Wagenknecht in Chicago Sunday
　　Tribune Ag 31 p2; Charles Mann, Jr. in Library Jour-
　　nal 83:2163-4 Ag; Marvin Mudrick in Virginia Quarterly
　　Review 34:630-3 Autumn; Dorothy Van Ghent in Yale
　　Review 48:153-5 Autumn; Adam Gillon in Dalhousie Re-
　　view 38:533-9 Winter '59; C. J. Rawson in Notes &
　　Queries ns 6:298-300 Jl-Ag '59; Richard Mayne in New
　　Statesman ns 57:264 F 21 '59; John Stedmond in Queen's
　　Quarterly 66:346-7 Summer '59; Pál Vámosi in Filo-
　　logiai Közlöny 9:287-90 '63; De Lancey Ferguson in
　　New York Herald Tribune Books Ag 17 p1, 8; David
　　Daiches in New York Times Book Review Ag 17 p 4,
　　18; C. L. Barber in Modern Language Review 55:275-6,
　　Ap '60; A. C. Kettle in Review of English Studies ns
　　12:100-2 '61; Idris Parry in Listener 61:769 Ap 30 '59;
　　David Daiches in Encounter 12:90-1 Ap '59; R. W.
　　Stallman in Sewanee Review 67:135-45 Winter '59;
　　Times Literary Supplement Ap 24 '59 p242; W. W. Rob-
　　son in London Magazine 6: 64-5 Je '59; M. C. Brad-
　　brook in Cambridge Review 80:539, 541 My 23 '59;
　　Leo Gurko in American Scholar 28:120)

Foreword. In Typhoon and other tales, by Joseph Conrad.
[New York:] New American Library [1963] p vii-xv
Introduction. In Joseph Conrad. Heart of Darkness,
    Almayer's Folly, The Lagoon. [New York: Dell
    c1960] p[7]-23
Introduction. In Heart of Darkness and The Secret
    Sharer, by Joseph Conrad. (Signet Books 834) New
    York: New American Library [c1950] p7-15
Introduction. In Nostromo, by Joseph Conrad. [New
    York: Dell Publishing Co. c1960] p[5]-20
Introduction. In An Outcast of the Islands, by Joseph
    Conrad. [New York: Dell Publishing Co. c1962] p[5]-
    21
Joseph Conrad. Direction (A Quarterly Magazine) 1:7-
    92 '47; bibliography, p89-92. same published separate-
    ly: [New York: New Directions, 1947] 92p; bibliogra-
    phy, p89-92. ($1.50)
    (Reviewed by B.V. Winebaum in New York Times Book
    Review Ja 11 '48 p29; Stanley Edgar Hyman in Accent
    8:187-91 Winter '48; Luigi Seravalli in Rivista di Let-
    terature Moderne ns 1:81-2 Jl '50)
The Nigger of the 'Narcissus.' Kenyon Review 19:205-32
    Spring '57; same. In The art of Joseph Conrad: a criti-
    cal symposium edited by Robert Wooster Stallman.
    East Lansing, Michigan: Michigan State University
    Press, 1960. p121-39
The voyages of Captain Korzeniowski. Reporter 16:42-4
    Mr 21 '57   743
Guetti, James Lawrence Jr.
    The failure of the imagination: a study of Melville,
    Conrad, and Faulkner. Ph.D. Thesis, Cornell Univer-
    sity, 1964. 240p; Abstract in Dissertation Abstracts
    25:4145-6 '65
    "The Heart of Darkness" and the failure of the imagina-
    tion. Sewanee Review 73:488-504 Summer '65
    "Heart of Darkness" and the failure of the imagination.
    [Ithaca, New York: Cornell University, 1963] (Guilford
    Prize Essays, 1963; 1st prize) 21f
    (At the Cornell University Library)
    "Heart of Darkness:" the failure of imagination. In The
    limits of metaphor. Ithaca, New York: Cornell Univer-
    sity press [1967] p46-68
    (This essay appeared in different form in Sewanee Re-
    view, 1965)
    (Reviewed by Robert S. Ryf in Nineteenth-Century Fic-
    tion 22, no 2:202-4 S '67)
    The rhetoric of Joseph Conrad. Amherst College Honors

Guetti, James Lawrence Jr. (cont.)
   Thesis, Amherst College press, 1960. 47p
   (Published by the Stinehour Press, Lunenberg, Ver-
      mont)   744
Guidi, Augusto
   Struttura e linguaggio di Nostromo. Convivium 35:289-
      306 '67   744a
Guiet, Pierre
   A dream and a fear: a study of Joseph Conrad. M. A.
      Thesis, Columbia University, 1950. 112p   745
Gullason, Thomas Arthur
   Conrad's "The Lagoon." Explicator 14, item 23, Ja '56
                                                              746
Gun, Ben [pseud.]
   See: Morley, Christopher   747
Gurko, Leo
   Conrad's first battleground. Almayer's Folly. University
      of Kansas City Review 25:189-94 Spring '59
   Death journey in The Nigger of the 'Narcissus." Nine-
      teenth-Century Fiction 15:301-11 Mr '61
   Joseph Conrad at the crossroads. University of Kansas
      City Review 25:97-100 D '58
   Joseph Conrad: giant in exile. New York: Macmillan;
      Galt, Ontario: Brett-Macmillan, 1962. 258p; bibliog-
      raphy, p[253]-254
      (Dated 1962 unless otherwise noted. Reviewed in Book-
      list 59:100 O 1; F. E. Faverty in Chicago Sunday Trib-
      une Ag 26 p4; J. D. Gordan in Christian Science Moni-
      tor S 20 p11; Kirkus 30:277 Mr 1; T. E. Boyle in Col-
      lege English 24:664 My '63; Frederick R. Karl in Se-
      wanee Review 71:680-3 Autumn '63; William Blackburn
      in South Atlantic Quarterly 62:444-5 Spring '63; Ian
      Watt in Victorian Studies 6:376-8 Je '63; R. D. Spector
      in New York Herald Tribune Books O 7 p10; J. R. Wil-
      lingham in Library Journal 87:1888 My 15; Douglas
      Hewitt in New Statesman 69:287 F 19 '65; Tony Tanner
      in Spectator no 7129:204 F 12 '65; Carlo Beuf in New
      York Times Book Review Jl 22 p5, 24; Lawrence
      Graver in Nineteenth-Century Fiction 17:293-5 D; New
      York Times Ag 30 p27)
   The Secret Agent: Conrad's vision of megalopolia.
      Modern Fiction Studies 4, no 4:307-18 Winter '58-'59
   The two lives of Joseph Conrad. New York: Crowell
      [1965] ix, 209p; bibliography, p198-202
      (Reviewed by Charlotte Jackson in Atlantic Monthly
      216:158 D '65; H. D. Leavitt in Book Week (Fall Chil-
      dren's issue) O 31 '65 p34; E. M. Guiney in Library

Journal 90:3804 S 15 '65; Carlo Beuf in New York
Times Book Review N 7 '65 part 2, p24)
Under Western Eyes: Conrad and the question of "Where
To?" College English 21:445-52 My '60   748
Gurko, Leo; Virgilia Peterson, and Lyman Bryson
Lord Jim. Invitation to Learning Reader 5, no 1:31-9
'55   749
Guthrie, William Bell
The technique of chronology in some novels of Joseph
Conrad. M. A. Thesis, University of Virginia, 1952.
96p   750
Gwynn, Stephen
The novels of Joseph Conrad. Edinburgh Review 231:
318-39 Ap '20   751

Hackett, Alice Payne
Fifty years of best sellers: 1895-1945. New York: R. R.
Bowker, 1945. p39-40
(Includes The Arrow of Gold)   752
Hackett, Francis
Back to Conrad. New Republic 135:20-1 Ag 6 '56   753
Haedens, Kleber
Un barbare scandinave... Paris-Matin Ap 2 '46   754
Hagan, John Jr.
The design of Conrad's The Secret Agent. English
Literary History 22:148-64 Je '55   755
Hagopian, John V.
Conrad's "Il Conde." Insight 2:62-9 '64
The pathos of "il Conde." Studies in Short Fiction 3:
31-8 Fall '65   756
Hahn, Willard Carl
Joseph Conrad: master mariner. Fair winds (NY) 2,
no 1:9-13 '40   757
Hainsworth, J. D.
An approach to Nostromo. The Use of English 10:181-6
Spring '59   758
Hale, Thomas
The element of avarice in the works of Joseph Conrad.
Master's Thesis, Univ. of Texas, 1943. iii-viii,
186f   759
Hall, James Norman
My Conrad. Atlantic Monthly 169:583-7 My '42
Tunnelled pages. In Under a thatched roof. New York:
Houghton Mifflin, 1942. p175-85   760
Hall, Leland
Joseph Conrad. In Columbia University course in litera-
ture. New York: Columbia University Press, 1929.

Hall, Leland (cont.)
    Volume 15, p345-56
    Joseph Conrad (1856-   ). In English literature during
        the last half-century, edited by John William Cunliffe.
        New York: Macmillan, 1919. p161-78; bibliography,
        p179; same. In Warner Library, Volume 7, p3956a-v
                                                            761
Halle, Louis J.
    Joseph Conrad: an enigma decoded. Saturday Review of
        Literature 31:7-8, 32 My 22 '48   762
Halverson, John and Ian Watt
    The original Nostromo: Conrad's source. Review of Eng-
        lish Studies ns 10:45-52 F '59   763
Hamalian, Leo and Edmond L. Volpe
    Ten modern short novels, edited by Leo Hamalian and Ed-
        mond L. Volpe. New York: G. P. Putnam's Sons [1958]
        p190-6 (On "Heart of Darkness")   764
Hamecher, Peter
    Joseph Conrad. Deutsche Allgemeine Zeitung no 430,
        1927   765
Hamer, Douglas
    Conrad: two biographical episodes. Review of English
        Studies ns 18, no 69:54-6 F '67
        (Conrad aboard the Tilkhurst)
    Conrad's Chance: a location. Notes & Queries 211:411-
        12 N '66   766
Hamerman, Marjorie Sandra
    A critical analysis of Joseph Conrad's Victory. M. A.
        Thesis, University of Washington, 1951. 82f   766a
Hamilton, Cosmo
    Joseph Conrad: blown sand and foam. In People worth
        talking about. New York: McBride, 1933. p41-9;
        caricature by Conrada Massaguer, p40   767
Hamilton, Elsie Catherine
    Selection and use of setting in the novels of Joseph Con-
        rad. M. A. Thesis, Univ. of Southern California at
        Los Angeles, 1929. iv, 65p   768
Hamilton, Margaret
    Joseph Conrad. Everyman 3, no 59:208 N 28 '13   769
Hammond, Percy
    Oddments and remainders. New York Tribune My 15 '23
        p10; My 28 '23 p10; My 31 '23 p8   770
Hancke, Kurt
    Die spätform des Europaischen Romans. Die Literatur
        40:517-20 My 16 '38   771
Hancox, P.
    The treatment of the theme of betrayal in the novels and

stories of Joseph Conrad. Master's Thesis, Univ. of
    Minnesota, 1938   772
Hanley, James
    Minority report. Fortnightly Review 159:419-22 Je '43
                                                            773
Hansen, Harry
    The first reader. New York World-Telegram My 25
    '34 p27; <u>same.</u> Lookout (NY) 25, no 6:1-2, 12 Je
    '34
    Mariner's haven. Daily News (Chicago) Ag 6 '24 p 16
    (An obituary)
    [Note on F. M. Ford's remark that Conrad drew inspira-
    tion from the maritime novels of Captain Marryat]
    Daily News (Chicago) F 4 '25 p16   774
Hanson, Paul Edward
    Character motivation in the novels of Joseph Conrad.
    Ph. D. Thesis, New York University, 1964. 214p;
    abstract in Dissertation Abstracts 26:3953 '66   775
Hardwick, Elizabeth
    Joseph Conrad. (Masters of world literature) London:
    Weidenfeld & Nicolson
    (Announced as "forthcoming" in Times Literary Supple-
    ment (London) Jl 25 '68 p 778)   775a
Hardy, John Edward
    "Heart of Darkness:" the Russian in motley. In Man in the
    modern novel. Seattle, Washington: Univ. of Washing-
    ton Press [c1964] p17-33
    (Reviewed by George S. Fayen, Jr. in Yale Review ns
    54:601 Je '65)   776
Harkness, Bruce
    Conrad on Galsworthy: the time scheme of <u>Fraternity.</u>
    Modern Fiction Studies 1, no 2:12-18 My '55
    The epigraph of Conrad's <u>Chance.</u> Nineteenth-Century
    Fiction 9, no 3:209-22 D '54
    The handling of time in the novels of Joseph Conrad.
    Ph. D. Thesis, University of Chicago, 1950. iii, 326p;
    bibliography, p320-26
    The secret of "The Secret Sharer" bared. College Eng-
    lish 27:55-61 O '65; rejoinder in College English 27:
    504-5 Mr '66   777
Harkness, Bruce (editor)
    Conrad's <u>Heart of Darkness</u> and the critics. San Fran-
    cisco: Wadsworth Publishing Co. , 1960. 176p; bibliog-
    raphy, p175-6
    (Reviewed by M. J. Bruccoli in Journal of English &
    Germanic Philology 60:185-6 '61; A. L. Soens in College
    English 22:68 O '60)

Harkness, Bruce (editor) (cont.)
  Conrad's Secret Sharer and the critics.   Belmont, Cali-
    fornia: Wadsworth Publishing Co.   [c1962] vii-xvii,
    170p; bibliography, p169-70; preface, p vii-ix; textual
    note, p151-61
    (Reviewed by James B. Meriwether in Journal of Eng-
      lish & Germanic Philology 64:594-5 Jl '65)   778
Harper, George Mills
  Conrad's knitters and Homer's cave of the nymphs.   Eng-
    lish Language Notes (University of Colorado) 1:53-7
    S '63   779
Harrington, David V. and Carol Estness
  Aesthetic criteria and Conrad's "The Tale." Discourse 7:
    437-45 Autumn '64   780
Harris, Joshua
  Writers of today.   V. Joseph Conrad.   T. P's Weekly 10:
    243 Ag 23 '07   781
Harris, Norman Townsend
  Conrad: short stories.   A critical commentary.   (Notes
    on chosen English texts) London: James Brodie [1941]
    56p   781a
Harris, Russell Lafferty
  The problem of character in Conrad.   An essay... in com-
    petition for the Meehan medal.   South Bend,   Univer-
    sity of Notre Dame, 1941. 37f   781b
Harrod, Lee V.
  The last Tories: the ideal of the "gentleman" in the works
    of Ford Madox Ford and Joseph Conrad.   M. A. Thesis,
    Pennsylvania State University, 1965. 55f; bibliography,
    f52-5   781c
Hart, Robert Edward
  Clartés anglaises - Joseph Conrad.   Le Radical (Port-
    Louis) Ap 25 '31   782
Hart-Davis, Rupert
  Hugh Walpole, a biography.   London: Macmillan, 1952.
    passim   783
Harman, (Captain) Howard
  I meet Joseph Conrad.   In The seas were mine.   New
    York: Dodd, Mead, 1935.   p78-84; an autograph of Con-
    rad's faces p80
    (Reviewed in John O'London's Weekly 35:899 S 26 '36)
  "Lord Jim" takes a wife.   In The seas were mine.   New
    York: Dodd, Mead, 1935.   p105-21   784
Harvey, David D.
  The collaboration of Ford Madox Ford and Joseph Conrad.
    Master's Thesis, Columbia University, 1958.   785
Hastings, Basil Macdonald

The Joseph Conrad I knew. In Ladies half-way and other
  essays. London: George C. Harrap [1927] p264-9
Victory. A play in three acts by Basil Macdonald Hastings. Founded on the novel of that name by Joseph
  Conrad. Produced at the Globe Theatre on Wednesday,
  March 26, 1919. 83 performances. End of run Fri-
  day, June 6, 1919. (Produced by Marie Löhr.) 116
  typed pages. Unpublished.
  (In 1964 a prompt copy of the play was in the Manu-
  script Dept. of Samuel French, Ltd., London. A type-
  script is in the New York Public Library)
  (Reviewed in Times (London) Mr 27 '19, p 15; Daily
  Express (London) Mr 27 '19; Daily Telegraph (London)
  Mr 27 '19; Sunday Times (London) Mr 30 '19; Observer
  (London) Mr 30 '19; Illustrated London News 159:498
  Ap 5 '19; Gilbert Cannon in Nation (London) 25, no 1:
  14 Ap 5 '19)   786
Haugh, Robert F.
  Conrad's Chance: progression d'effet. Modern Fiction
    Studies 1:9-15 F '55
  A critical study of Joseph Conrad. Ph. D. Thesis, Univer-
    sity of Michigan, 1952
  Death and consequences: Joseph Conrad's attitude toward
    fate. University of Kansas City Review 18:191-7
    Spring '52
  Joseph Conrad and revolution. College English 10:273-7
    F '49
  Joseph Conrad: discovery in design. Norman, Oklahoma:
    University of Oklahoma Press [1957] 173p; portrait
    (Reviewed by M. J. Friedman in Books Abroad 32:189
    Spring '58; M. C. Bradbrook in Review of English Stud-
    ies ns 10:209-11 '59; Nineteenth-Century Fiction 12:
    335 Mr '58; John Stedmond in Queen's Quarterly 66:347
    Summer '59)
  The structure of Lord Jim. College English 13:137-41
    D '51   787
Häusermann, Hans Walter
  Conrad's literary activity in Geneva. In The Genovese
    background... London: Routledge and Kegan Paul [1952]
    p199-213   788
Hausmann, Wolf
  Stilistische probleme in Joseph Conrad's Rescue. Ph. D.
    Thesis, Göttingen, 1952   789
Hawk, Affable (pseud.)
  [Joseph Conrad dies at the age of 66] New Statesman 23:
    523 Ag 9 '24   790

Hay, Eloise Knapp
Lord Jim from sketch to novel. Comparative Literature 12, no 4:289-309 Fall '60
The political novels of Joseph Conrad: a critical study. Chicago: University of Chicago press, 1963. vii-x, 350p; bibliography, p333-41. (Originally a Ph. D. Thesis, Radcliffe College, 1960) (Reviewed by C. J. Rawson in Notes & Queries ns 13: 433-4 N '66; Jan Librach in Polish Review 9, no 4:90-4 Autumn '64; Frederick P. W. McDowell in Philological Quarterly 46:113-24 Ja '67; Paul Goetsch in Die Neueren Sprachen 65, heft 2:95-7 '66; C. W. Mann, Jr. in Library Journal 88:3846-7 O 15 '63; Frederick R. Karl in Sewanee Review 71:680-3 Autumn '63; David Cowden in Modern Language Quarterly 25:227-8 Jl '64; Elisabeth Martell in Queen's Quarterly 71:138-9 Spring '64; W. S. Dowden in South Atlantic Quarterly 63:255 Spring '64; Times Literary Supplement Ja 9 '64 p28; Avrom Fleishman in Victorian Studies 7:404-5 Je '64; Lawrence Graver in Nineteenth-Century Fiction 18, no 3:302-5 D '63)   791
Heath, E. M.
Thirty paintings. London: Cape, 1935. p22 (portrait of Conrad)   792
Hedspeth, Robert N.
Conrad's use of time in Chance. Nineteenth-Century Fiction 21:283-9 '66   793
Heilman, Robert B.
Introduction. In Lord Jim, by Joseph Conrad. New York: Holt, Rinehart & Winston [1957] p v-xxxv; bibliography, p xxxi-xxxiii   794
Heimer, Jackson Wendell
The betrayer as intellectual: Conrad's Under Western Eyes. Polish Review 12, no 4:57-68 Autumn '67
Patterns of betrayal in the novels of Joseph Conrad. Ph. D. Thesis, Univ. of Cincinnati, 1963. 176p; abstract in Dissertation Abstracts 24:5408-9 '64
Betrayal, confession, attempted redemption, and punishment in Nostromo. Texas Studies in Language & Literature 8:561-79 Winter '67
Patterns of betrayal in the novels of Joseph Conrad. Ball State University Forum 8, no 3:30-9 '67   795
Heine, Herta
Joseph Conrad als dichter des meeres. Ph. D. Thesis, University of Vienna, 1932   796
Helsztyński, Stanisław
Joseph Conrad - człowiek i twórca (Joseph Conrad, the

man and the creative writer). Kwartolnik Neofilologiczny 5, nos 1-2: 39-60 '58; same. In Joseph Conrad Korzeniowski. Essays and Studies. Warsaw:
Państwowe Wydawnictwo Naukowe, 1958. p[39]-60
Historia literatury powszechnej. In Rocznik Literacki,
1961. [Warsaw:] Państwowy Instytut Wydawniczy [1962]
p215-16
Uroczystości Conradowskie. Polska Akademia Nauk.
Spraw. Wydz. Nauk. Spol. 4:66-73 '58   797

Hemingway, Ernest
[Death of Conrad] Transatlantic Review 2, no 3:341-2
O '24   798

Henkin, Leo J.
Darwinism in the English novel, 1860-1910. New York:
Corporate Press, 1940. p 256   799

Henriot, Émile
Un grand romancier anglais. Le Temps Ap 4 '22 p2
Des souvenirs de Joseph Conrad. Le Temps Ja 6 '25
p3; same. (excerpt) Chronique des Lettres Françaises
3:61-2 Ja-F '25   800

Henriquez Ureña, Max
La America de Joseph Conrad. Noverim (Havana) 2:7-21
N '58   801

Herget, Winfried
Untersuchungen zur Wirklichkeitsdarstellung im Frühwerk
Joseph Conrads (mit besonderer Berucksichtung des
Romanes Lord Jim). Ph. D. Thesis, Frankfurt am
Main, 1965. 289p; bibliography, p261-89   802

Herling-Grudziński, Gustaw
W oczach Conrada. Kultura (Paris) no 10:16-32 O '57
(In Conrad's eyes)   803

Hernandez, Jose M.
The philosophy of Joseph Conrad. Master's Thesis, University of Notre Dame, 1931. 55f; bibliography f51-5
                                                 804

Herndon, Richard James
The collaboration of Joseph Conrad with Ford Madox
Ford. Ph. D. Thesis, Stanford University, 1957. viii,
429f; Abstract in Dissertation Abstracts 21:3098 '61
The genesis of Conrad's "Amy Foster." Studies in Philol-
ogy 57:549-66 Jl '60   805

Herpin, Thérèse
Conrad et le vertige tropical. Le Jour O 21 '37   806

Herrland, Hanns
Englische romanciers: Joseph Conrad, H. G. Wells,
Hugh Walpole. Berliner Börsen Zeitung Kunst 175,
1930   807

Herrmann, Max
    Joseph Conrad. Neue Bücherschau 6:32-5 Ja '28   808
Hertz, Robert N.
    The scene of Mr. Verloc's murder in The Secret Agent:
    a study of Conrad's narrative and dramatic method.
    Personalist 43:214-25 Spring '62   809
Herzfeld, Margaret
    Die ethischen Grundbegriffe und Werte im Erzählwerk
    Joseph Conrads. Ph. D. Thesis, Univ. of Mainz, 1951.
    153p   810
Heufer, Kurt
    Joseph Conrads "Rettung." Berliner Tageblatt no 488,
    1931   811
Hewitt, Douglas
    Conrad: a reassessment. London: Bowes & Bowes
    [1952] vi-vii, 141p; "The works of Joseph Conrad,"
    p139-40
    (Reviewed in Times Literary Supplement My 30 '52
    p363; Peter Ure in Review of English Studies ns 4:193-4
    Ap '53; Madeleine L. Cazamian in Études Anglaises 6:
    167-9 My '53; William Blissett in University of Toronto
    Quarterly 23:90-2 O '53; Notes & Queries 197:505 N 8
    '52; V. S. Pritchett in New Statesman & Nation 43:560
    My 10 '52; George Herbert Clarke in Queen's Quarterly
    59:267-69 Summer '52; H. N. Maclean in Canadian
    Forum 32:93 Jl '52; Listener 48, no 1228:437 S 11
    '52)
    Joseph Conrad's hero: 'fidelity' or 'The choice of night-
    mares.' Cambridge Journal 2:684-91 Ag '49   812
Hicks, Granville
    Conrad after five years. New Republic 61:192-4 Ja 8
    '30; see also: Don Bregenzer in New Republic 61:277
    Ja 29 '30   813
Hicks, John H.
    Conrad's Almayer's Folly: structure, theme, and critics.
    Nineteenth-Century Fiction 19:17-31 Je '64   814
Hidaka, T.
    Reminiscences and travels in England, including a visit to
    Joseph Conrad. [Japan] 1924
    (In Japanese)   815
Higashida, C.
    The style and structure of Conrad's Victory. Anglica
    4:92-102 Ap '62
    (In Japanese, with an English summary)   816
Higenbotham, E. [Evelyn Wells, pseud.]
    The house of heavenly delight: a 4 act play. Based on
    Almayer's Folly by Joseph Conrad. Unpublished.

Copyrighted March 15, 1930   817
Hill, Enid
Nostromo: Conrad's political treatise. M. A. Thesis,
    University of Chicago, 1961. 77f   817a
Hill, Minnie L. D.
Some aspects of the philosophy of Joseph Conrad. Mas-
    ter's Thesis, University of Louisville, 1917   818
Hill, Ordelle Gehard
Hero-villain relationships in representative novels of Con-
    rad. Master's Thesis, Auburn University, 1959. vii,
    112f; bibliography, f109-12   819
Hillegass, Clifton K.
Lord Jim; notes... Lincoln, Nebraska: Cliff's Notes &
    Outlines [1960] 103p   819a
Hilles, Susan Ensign
Conrad's visual imagination. Radcliffe College Honors
    Essay in English & History, 1955. 72f; bibliography,
    f73-7   820
Hind, Charles Lewis
Joseph Conrad. In Authors and I. New York: Lane,
    1921. p61-4
    (Reviewed by James Milne in Graphic 103:672 Je 4 '21)
                                                             821
The history of Mr. Conrad's books. Times Literary Sup-
    plement Ag 30 '23 p570   822
Hoare, Dorothy Mackenzie
The tragic in Hardy and Conrad. In Some studies in the
    modern novel. Litchfield, Connecticut: Prospect
    press, 1940; London: Chatto and Windus, 1938. p113-
    32   823
Hodges, Robert Raymond
The death of Stefan Bobrowski: a Conrad discovery.
    Notes & Queries ns 9:109-10 Mr '62
The dual heritage of Joseph Conrad. The Hague: Mouton,
    1967. (Studies in English literature, Volume XXIX)
    [9]-229p; bibl., p226-9
    (Reviewed by John Espey in Nineteenth-Century Fiction
    22, no 3:311 D '67)
The four fathers of Lord Jim. University Review 31:103-
    10 D '64
Joseph Conrad's dual heritage. Ph. D. Thesis, Stanford
    University, 1961. iii, 304p; abstract in Dissertation Ab-
    stracts 24:1160-1 '63. For separate publication, see
    above: The Dual Heritage of Joseph Conrad.   824
Hoffman, Anastasia C.
Studies in the impressionistic novel, 1890-1914: James,
    Crane, Conrad, and Ford. Ph. D. Thesis, University

Hoffman, Anastasia C. (cont.)
　　of Wisconsin, 1952   825
Hoffman, Charles G.
　　Point of view in "The Secret Sharer." College English
　　　23:651-4 My '62
　　"We agreed that...": Ford's collaboration with Conrad.
　　　In Ford Madox Ford. New York: Twayne Publishers
　　　[c1967] p19-32   826
Hoffman, Frederick J.
　　The mortal no: death and the modern imagination.
　　　Princeton, New Jersey: Princeton University Press,
　　　1964. p50-7
　　　(On The Secret Agent)   827
Hoffman, Richard
　　Proportion and incident in Joseph Conrad and Arnold
　　　Bennett. Sewanee Review 32:79-92 Ja '24   828
Hoffman, Stanton de Voren
　　Comedy and form in the fiction of Joseph Conrad. Ph. D.
　　　Thesis, Pennsylvania State University, 1962. 332p;
　　　abstract in Dissertation Abstracts 23:3898-9 '63
　　Conrad's menagerie: animal imagery and theme. Buck-
　　　nell Review 12, no 3:59-71 D '64
　　The hole in the bottom of the pail: comedy and theme in
　　　"Heart of Darkness." Studies in Short Fiction 2:113-23
　　　Winter '65
　　Joseph Conrad's use of burlesque within the framework of
　　　moral allegory. Master's Thesis, Pennsylvania State
　　　Univ., 1957. 61p
　　Scenes of low comedy: the comic in Lord Jim. Ball State
　　　Teachers College Forum 5, no 2:19-27 Spring '64 829
Hogarth, Henry
　　The novels of Joseph Conrad. London Quarterly Review
　　　143:205-16 Ap '25   830
Hohoff, Curt
　　Über Joseph Conrad. Hochland 36, no 11:378-88 Ag '39
　　 831
Holder, Alfred
　　Beiträge zur ästhetik des Romans der ausgehenden Vik-
　　　torianischen und nach Viktorianischen Periode. Wur-
　　　temberg: G. Hauser Metzingen [1933] p33-45; Ph. D.
　　　Dissertation, Tübingen   832
Holder, Robert Conner
　　The idea of duty in Joseph Conrad's novels. Master's
　　　Thesis, Ohio State University, 1947   833
Holland, Michael
　　Conrad's favourite novel. Times Literary Supplement
　　　O 7 '55 p589 (Nostromo)   834

Holland, Norman N.
    Style as character: The Secret Agent. Modern Fiction
    Studies 12:221-31 Summer '66   835
Holliday, Robert Cortes
    Men and books and cities. New York: George H. Doran
    Co. [c1920] p169   836
Hollingsworth, Alan Merrill
    The destructive element: a study of Conrad's tragic vi-
    sion. Ph. D. Dissertation, University of California,
    1956. v, 257p
    Freud, Conrad, and the future of an illusion. Literature
    and Psychology 5:78-83 N '55   837
Hollingsworth, Joseph Keith
    The technique of Joseph Conrad, with particular reference
    to his handling of the point of view. Master's Thesis,
    Univ. of Chicago, 1931. 102p   838
Hollis, Christopher
    A study of George Orwell. London: Hollis & Carter,
    1956. p207 (Noted in Wiadomości 12, no 29:7 Jl 21
    '57)   838a
Holloway, Lowell Heckler
    The reading of Joseph Conrad. M. A. Thesis, Ohio State
    Univ., 1937. 76p; Abstract in Ohio State University
    Graduate School Abstracts of Masters' Theses 25:174-
    5 '38
    (Includes a table of books read by Conrad between
    1862-1924)   839
Holmes, Karen Sue
    Lord Jim, Conrad's alienated man. Descant 4:330-40
    Winter '60   840
Holt, Alfred and Co.
    The story of Lord Jim. Times Literary Supplement O
    11 '23 p670   841
Hommage à Joseph Conrad---(including reminiscences by
    John Galsworthy, André Gide, Paul Valéry, H. R.
    Lenormand, Georges Jean-Aubry, Richard Curle, Rob-
    ert B. Cunninghame Graham, and articles by Edouard
    Estaunie, A. Chevrillon, André Maurois, Edmond Ja-
    loux, J. Kessel, Robert Francillon, Ramón Fernández,
    and Albert Sangere; also unpublished letters) 15 plates
    and photographs
    La Nouvelle Revue Française 23:649-806 D 1 '24
    (Reviewed by Robert Littell in New Republic 41:287-8
    F 4 '25)   842
Hondequin, Ghislain
    The influence of Flaubert on Pater and Conrad. Ph. D.
    Thesis, Ghent University, 1950   843

Honoring marine authors.   Lookout (NY) 35, no 9:12-13
    S '44
    (A note on the Marine Authors' luncheon commemorat-
    ing the 20th anniversary of Conrad's death)   843a
Hood, Leslie Illingworth Jr.
    Conrad and the Orestes myth.   M. A. Thesis, Stanford
    Univ., 1950. 69f   844
Hopgood, Carolyn
    The uses of place in Conrad's Nostromo.   Senior Essay
    in English, Wells College, 1964. 42f   844a
Hopkinson, Tom
    The short stories.   London Magazine 4:36-41 N '57 845
Hopkins, R. Thurston
    Joseph Conrad: master mariner and novelist.   Books of
    the Month p iv, vi (about August 4, 1924)   846
Hopman, Frits
    Joseph Conrad. Engelsch romanschrijver.   De Amster-
    dammer Weekblad Ag 9 '14   847
Hoppe, A. J.
    Introduction.   In The Conrad reader, edited by A. J.
    Hoppe.   London: Phoenix House, 1946. p1-26; re-
    printed as: The Conrad companion... London: Phoenix
    House, 1947. p1-26
    Introduction.   In The Nigger of the 'Narcissus,' Typhoon,
    The Shadow-Line.   (Everyman's Library 980) London:
    Dent [1945] p vii-xii
    Joseph Conrad.   A biographical note.   In Almayer's
    Folly, and Tales of Unrest, by Joseph Conrad. (Col-
    lected Edition) London: Dent [1947] 3 unnumbered
    pages at end of volume   848
Horwill, Herbert W.
    London discusses Conrad and Wells.   New York Times
    Book Review O 11 '25 p10   849
Horzyca, Wilam
    Książka prawego człowieka.   Epoka no 22, 1927
    (Noted in Wiadomości Literackie 4, no 5:4 Ja 30 '27)
                                                          850
Hostowiec, Paweł
    Conrad's home country.   In Conrad żywy, edited by Wit
    Tarnawski.   London: B. Świderski, 1957. p87-91   851
Hough, Graham
    Chance and Joseph Conrad.   Listener 58:1063-5 D 26 '57;
        same.   In Image and experience... London: Duckworth
    [1960] p211-22
    (A centenary broadcast on the B. B. C. Third Pro-
    gramme)   852
Hourcade. Pierre

Hueffer, Ford Madox
    See: Ford, Ford Madox   866
Humbourg, Pierre and Neel, Philippe
    Un roman d' amour: Conrad et le navirs.   Les Nou-
       velles Littéraires 6, no 242:8 Je 4 '27   867
Huneker, James Gibbons
    The genius of Joseph Conrad.   North American Review
       200:270-9 Ag '14; same.   In Ivory apes and peacocks.
       New York: Scribner's, 1915. p1-21
       (Reviewed in Academy 89:234-5 D 20 '15)
    A letter from James Gibbons Huneker to Joseph Conrad.
       [London: First Edition Club, Curwen Press, 1926]
       [3]p; Editor's note, p[1]; Letter, p[3]
       (220 copies only)
    Letters of James Gibbons Huneker, edited by Josephine
       Huneker. New York: Scribner's, 1922. passim
    A visit to Joseph Conrad.   New York Times Magazine
       Section N 17 '12 p4 (portrait); same.   In [Doubleday,
       Page & Co.; Joseph Conrad. Garden City, New York: ?
       1913] p1; same.   In The Country Life Press... Garden
       City, New York: Doubleday Page, 1919. p99-100
    Will this author prove a second Conrad?   New York
       Times Magazine Ag 20 '16 p12
       (Refers to William McFee)
    With Joseph Conrad.   In Steeplejack.   New York: Scrib-
       ner's, 1920.   Volume II, p128-33, p233-4   868
Hunt, Kellogg W.
    Lord Jim and The Return of the Native: a contrast.
       English Journal 49:447-56 O '60   869
Hunt, Violet
    The flurried years.   London: Hurst and Blackett [1926]
       p26-8, 32-9, 51-4; portrait facing p32.   same pub-
       lished in America with title: I Have This To Say.
       New York: Boni & Liveright [1926]   869a
Hunter, Robert A.
    Conrad's use of Marlow in two novels and two tales.
       M.A. Thesis, Columbia University, 1953. 138p   870
Huntington, John Willard
    Joseph Conrad: analysis of a moral problem.   English
       Honors Thesis, Harvard University, March 1, 1962.
       31f
       (Discusses The Secret Agent, Nostromo, Victory &
       Under Western Eyes)   871
Huntsman-Trout, Pamela
    Nostromo - a study of the isolated integrity.   Radcliffe
       College Honors Thesis in English. 1952. 38f   872

Hutchinson, Vere
   A master of romance.   The life and work of Joseph Con-
      rad.   John O'London's Weekly 11:691 Ag 23 '24   873
Hutchison, Percy Adams
   Joseph Conrad, alchemist of the sea.   Literary Digest
      International Book Review 2:713-14 S '24; same.   In
      Essays in memory of Barrett Wendell by his assistants.
      Cambridge, Massachusetts: Harvard University Press,
      1926.   p291-9; same.   (excerpt) Literary Digest 82:
      48, 50 S 13 '24
Joseph Conrad, "master in sail for all oceans."   New
      York Times Book Review Ap 29 '23 p6
The Rescue screened.   New York Times Ja 13 '29
      Section 8 p8   874
Hynes, Samuel
   Two Rye revolutionists.   Sewanee Review 73:151-8 Winter
      '65 (Conrad and Ford Madox Ford)   875

Im Teil das Ganze (Joseph Conrad).   Frankfurter Zeitung no
      322, 1936 (by "M. M. R.")   876
In Memoriam Joseph Conrad, obiit August 3, 1924.   The
      Honour of Labor, an excerpt from [Conrad's] "The Fine
      Art."   Pittsburgh: American Institute of Graphic Arts,
      1924.   single sheet   877
The inspirations of Joseph Conrad: a literary journey in
      pictures.   Independent 113:189-92 S 27 '24 (map)   878
Iwaszkiewicz, Jarosław
   Conrad; poem.   Skamander (Warsaw) 2nd volume, 2nd
      year nos 5-6:133 F-Mr '21
   Conrad a Europa.   Wiadomości Literackie 2, no 5:3
      F 1 '25
   Jean-Aubry w Polsce.   Wiadomości Literackie 4, no 29:6
      Jl 17 '27
   Niebezpieczy prowokator.   Mniemany hr. Albert Potoki.
      (Przypuszczalny protopyt "Tajnego Agenta").   Illustro-
      wany Kurjer Codzienny no 356, 1928
   Rozmowa z pierwszym biografem Conrada co powiedział
      mi p. G. Jean-Aubry.   Wiadomości Literackie 2, no
      19:1 My 10 '25   879
Izzo, C.
   Le vie del mare.   Gazzetta del Popolo 7:18 '56   880

Jabłkowska, Róża
   Conrad w oczach nowszej krytyki angielskiej.   Kwartalnik
      Neofilologiczny 1:47-56 '57
   Joseph Conrad, 1857-1924.   Wrocław: Ossolinski National
      Institute, 1961.   [5]-406p; bibliography, p[389]-395.

Jabłkowska, Róża (cont.)
Ph. D. Thesis, University of Warsaw, 1961; portraits
Joseph Conrad Korzeniowski. Warsaw: Państwowe
Zakłady Wydawnictwo Szkolynch, 1964. [7]-408]p; portraits; illustrations. "Joseph Conrad o sztuce pisarkiej
i o sobie," p152-[199]; "Utwory Konrada w układzie
chronologicznym," p393-[404]; bibliographical references,
p[345]-[392]
(Reviewed by Stefan Zabierowski in Ruch Literacki 6, no
5:244-7 S-O '65; Ryszard Matuszewski in Rocznik
Literacki 1964. [Warsaw:] Państwowy Instytut Wydawn-
iczy [1965] p158-9; Peter Genzel in Zeitschrift für
Anglistik und Amerikanstik 12:425-7 '64)
Listy T. Bobrowskiego do Conrada. Kwartalnik Neofilologiczny no 2, 1956
Polska Conradystyka za Granica. Kwartalnik Neofilologicz-
ny 5 nos 1-2: 101-14 '58; same. In Joseph Conrad
Korzeniowski. Essays and studies. Warsaw: Państwowe
Wydawnictwo Naukowe, 1958. p[101]-114
Posłowie. In Józef Conrad, by Jessie Conrad, translated
by Wanda Nałęcz-Korzeniowska. Kraków: Wydawnictwo
Literackie [1959] p441-[459]
Posłowie. In Los, by Joseph Conrad (Chance) translated
by Wanda Tatarkiewiczowa. Warsaw: Państwowy Insty-
tut Wydawniczy, 1955. p451-[457]
Przypisy. In Józef Conrad, by Jessie Conrad, translated
by Wanda Nałęcz-Korzeniowska. Kraków: Wydawnictwo
Literackie [1959] p417-39
W rodzinie Josepha Conrada. Ziemia i Morze no 22:1, 3
'57; same. In Wspomnienia i studia o Conradzie,
edited by Barbara Kocówna. [Warsaw:] Państwowy
Państwowy Instytut Wydawniczy [1963] p132-46
Z angielskich i amerykanskich studiow nad Conradem.
Kwartalnik Neofilologiczny 5, nos 1-2:83-100 '58; same.
In Joseph Conrad Korzeniowski. Essays and studies.
Warsaw: Państwowe Wydawnictwo Naukowe, 1958.
p[83]-100   881
Jackson, Holbrook
The eighteen nineties: a review of art and ideas at the
close of the nineteenth century. London: Grant Richards,
1923. p274
Joseph Conrad. To-Day (London) 5, no 26:43-9 Ap '19
Literature and the adventurous life. Black & White 44:
90 O 21 '11
Pernicious literature. To-Day (London) 6, no 34:166
D '19   882
Jacob, Heinrich Eduard

Joseph Conrad. Berliner Tageblatt D 20 '26
Joseph Conrad. Madgeburgische Zeitung F 6 '27, no
    66   883
Jacobs, Robert Green
    Psychology, setting and impressionism in the major
    novels of Joseph Conrad. Ph. D. Thesis, University of
    Iowa, 1965. 462p; Abstract in Dissertation Abstracts
    26:6022 '66
    Comrade Ossipon's favorite saint: Lombroso and Conrad.
    Nineteenth-Century Fiction 23, no 1:74-84 Je '65   884
Jacyna, Felix M.
    Dlaczego Conrad pisał po angielsku? (Why did Conrad
    write in English?) Tygodnik Warszawski (Warsaw
    Weekly) no 9, 1946
    Do autora Godziny Śródziemnomorskiej. (To the author
    of The Mediterranean Hour) Dziś i Jutro (Today and
    Tomorrow) 2 no 5:5 F 3 '46 (Jan Parandowski on Con-
    rad's contribution to world culture)   885
Jahier, Piero
    L'uomo Conrad. Paragone 4, no 46:16-25 O '53; same.
    In Lo specchio del mare... Translated by Piero Jahier.
    Milan: Bompiani, 1954   886
Jak pisał Conrad? Wiadomości 9, no 1:4 Ja 3 '54   886a
Jakimiak, Z.
    Moja odpowiedź (My reply). Dziś i Jutro (Today and To-
    morrow) 5, nos 15-16:12 Ap 24 '49
    (His polemics with Jasienica)
    Obrana zaścianka (In defense of provincialism). Dziś i
    Jutro 5, no 9:8 Mr 6 '49   887
Jaloux, Edmond
    Joseph Conrad et le roman de'aventures anglais. La
    Nouvelle Revue Française 23:713-19 D 1 '24; same. In
    Figures étrangères. Paris: Librairie Plon, 1925.
    p202-10; same. Literarische Welt 2, no 47:4-5 N 19
    '26   888
James, Henry
    The letters of Henry James, selected and edited by Percy
    Lubbock. London: Macmillan, 1920. Volume I, p398,
    413
    The new novel. In The future of the novel, by Henry
    James, edited by Leon Edel. New York: Vintage paper-
    back, 1956. p279, 281
    Notes on novelists, with some other notes. New York:
    Scribner's, 1914. p345-55
    The selected letters of Henry James, edited and with an in-
    troduction by Leon Edel. New York: Farrar, Straus
    and Cudahy [1955] p157-8

James, Henry (cont.)
  (Reviewed in Wiadomości 12, no 43:5 O 27 '57)
  Three letters from Henry James to Joseph Conrad. [London: First Edition Club, Curwen Press, 1926] [8]p;
    editor's note, p[1-2]; letters, p[3-8]
    (220 copies only)
  Selected literary criticism, edited by Morris Shapira.
    New York: Horizon Press, 1964. p331-6   889
Jamison, Laura
  The ships in the stories of Joseph Conrad. Master's
    Thesis, Ohio State University, 1935. 100p   890
Janicki, Stanisław
  Conradiana. Wiadomości 4, no 186:4 O 23 '49   890a
Jankowski, Józef
  Conrad. Słowo nos 99-100 '24
  Przygoda marylska Conrada. Dzień Polski no 292, 1928. 891
Janssen, Joh.
  Joseph Conrad, van Pools Zeeman tot Engels romanschrijver. Katholiek Cultureel Tijdschrift 2:447-50
    Ag '46   892
Janta, Alexander
  A Conrad family heirloom at Harvard. Polish Review 2,
    no 4:41-64 Autumn '57; same. (entitled "Tuan Jim: a
    sketch") In Conrad żywy, edited by Wit Tarnawski.
    London: B. Świderski, 1957. p195-207; same. In
    Joseph Conrad: centennial essays, edited by Ludwik
    Krzyzanowski. New York: Polish Institute of Arts &
    Sciences in America, 1960. p85-110
    (The album at Harvard University contains 28 pages of
    manuscript of the first draft of Lord Jim)
  Conrad in Japan. Polish Review 5:64-7 Autumn '60;
    same. In Losy i ludzie... London: "Wiadomości" w
    Londynie Polski Instytut Naukowy w Ameryce, 1961.
    p335-9
  Conrad's place and rank in American letters. In Joseph
    Conrad: centennial essays, edited by Ludwik Krzyżanowski. New York: Polish Institute of Arts & Sciences
    in America, 1960. p11-26
  The first draft of Lord Jim and Conrad's Polish letters in
    American collections. In Conrad żywy, edited by Wit
    Tarnawski. London: B. Świderski, 1957. p208-28; 9
    facsimiles
  Introduction to Pisarze amerykańscy o Conradzie (Conrad
    and American literature). Wiadomości 13, no 35:1
    Ag 31 '58
  Józef Conrad Korzeniowski. In Losy i ludzie. Spotkania-przygody-studia, 1931-1960. London: "Wiadomosci" w

Jellenta, Cezary (cont.)
  Wiadomości Muszcne i Literackie (Lwow Musical &
  Literary News) no 11, 1929
  Szkice o Konradzie Korzeniowskim (Sketches of Conrad).
  Epoka nos 272-3, 277, 1929   901
Jenkins, Bridget McCormack
  A survey of criticism about Joseph Conrad's Victory,
  1952-1965. M. A. Thesis, Catholic Univ. of America,
  1966. 39f   902
Jesse, Fryniwyd Tennyson
  Joseph Conrad. In The post Victorians, with an introduc-
  tion by W. R. Inge. London: Nicholson & Watson, 1933.
  p119-28   903
Jézéquel, Roger
  Sentiment de la destinée chez Joseph Conrad. Biblio-
  thèque Universelle et Revue de Genève 2:111-23 S '28
                                                    904
Joerden, R.
  Sammelbesprechungen. Joseph Conrad. Bücherei und
  Bildungspflege 10, heft 4:271-9 '30
  (Includes reviews of 15 translations of Conrad's works)
                                                    905
John Quinn and Conrad. Public Ledger Literary Review
  (Philadelphia) S 7 '24 p11 (Refers to C. K. Shorter's
  comments in the Sphere)   906
Johnson, Bruce M.
  Conrad's "Falk:" manuscript and meaning. Modern Lan-
  guage Quarterly 26:267-84 Je '65
  Conrad's "Karain" and Lord Jim. Modern Language Quar-
  terly 24:13-20 Mr '63
  Joseph Conrad and Crane's The Red Badge of Courage.
  Papers of the Michigan Academy of Science, Arts, &
  Letters 48:649-55 '63   907
Johnson, Eunah
  Comparison of the descriptive powers of Conrad and Rus-
  kin. M. A. Thesis, Stetson Univ. 1926. 18f   908
Johnson, Fred Bates
  Notes on Conrad's finance. Indiana Quarterly for Book-
  men 3, no 1:27-30 Ja '47
  (Includes excerpts from 3 letters of Conrad to Pinker,
  J. B.)
  Joseph Conrad. Suspense. Papers of the Bibliographical
  Society of America 40:237-8 '46   909
Johnson, Gladys Marie
  Elements of moral conflict in Joseph Conrad. Master's
  Thesis, University of Iowa, 1960. 94p   910
Johnson, Richard P.

The ruinous dream: a study of guilt in Joseph Conrad's fiction. M. A. Thesis, University of Oregon, 1960. 77f; bibliography, f75-7   910a
Johnston, Patricia M.
Aspects of the treatment of time in some modern English novelists. Master's Thesis, McGill University, 1948
                                                              911
Johnstone, Will B.
"I do nothing but talk about myself," roars Joseph Conrad. Evening World (NY) My 2 '23 p23   911a
Jones, Bernard
Conrad the historian. Listener 73, no 1884:674 My 6 '65
                                                              911b
Jones, Harriette Cordelia
Dona Rita considered between the women of Conrad's early and late novels. M. A. Thesis, Ohio State University, 1930. 53p. Abstract in Ohio State University Graduate School, Abstracts of Master's Essays 3:64-5 '30 (Examines The Arrow of Gold, Lord Jim, Almayer's Folly, Suspense)   912
Jones, Howard Mumford
Introduction. In The Nigger of the 'Narcissus,' by Joseph Conrad... and illustrations by Millard Sheets. New York: Heritage press [1965] p vii-[xiv]   913
Jones, Lawrence Evelyn
An Edwardian youth. London: Macmillan, 1956. p112-13 (Noted in Wiadomości 12, no 29:7 Jl 21 '57)   913a
Jones, Sarah Ruth
Does Joseph Conrad present a fixed feminine type? Master's Thesis, Vanderbil University, 1926. 112f.   914
Joseph, Edward D.
Identity and Joseph Conrad. Psychoanalytic Quarterly 32, no 4:549-72 O '63   914a
Joseph Conrad
For pamphlets with this title, please see the name of the publisher, such as: J. M. Dent; Doubleday, Page; etc.
                                                              915
Joseph Conrad. Book Buyer 16:389 Je '98; Bookman (London) 20:173 S '01; Chronique des Lettres Françaises 1:267-70 Mr-Ap '23; Morning Post (London) Ag 4 '24 p6; same. (excerpt) Public Opinion (London) 126:128 Ag 8 '24; Manchester Guardian Ag 4 '24 p8; Nosotros 48: 513-14 D '24; Illustrated London News 165:280 Ag 9 '24; Outlook (London) 54:101 Ag 9 '24; New York Times Ag 5 '24 p16; Time & Tide 5, no 32:759 Ag 8 '24; British Weekly 76:403 Ag 7 '24; Times Literary Supplement Ag 14 '24 p493-4; Saturday Review 138:136 Ag 9 '24; Liter-

Joseph Conrad (cont.)
    ary Digest 82:27-8 Ag 23 '24; Independent 113:86-7
    Ag 16 '24; Bookman (NY) 37:594 Ag '13; World's Work
    (NY) 48:478 S '24; Literary News (NY) ns 23:156 My
    '02; Canadian Bookman 6, no 8:178 Ag '24; Travel 37,
    no 6:14 O '21; Truth (London) 96, no 2494:239 Ag 6
    '24; Manchester Guardian Weekly 11, no 6: 109, 116
    Ag 8 '24; Dial 77:269-70 S '24; World's Work (NY) 39:
    495 Mr '20; Sun (NY) Ag 4 '24 p10; Sun (NY) My 3 '23
    p20; New York Tribune Ap 22 '23; In The Americana
    annual... 1925... New York: Americana Corporation,
    1925. p185-6; In The New International Year Book...
    1900... New York: Dodd, Mead [c1901] p248-9; In
    The New International Year Book... for the year 1924.
    New York: Dodd, Mead, 1925. p178; Times Literary
    Supplement D 6'57 p739; World (NY) Ag 5 '24 p8;
    Tygodnik Powszechny 11, no 48:1 D 8 '57)   916
Joseph Conrad: a critical symposium. London Magazine 4:
    21-49 N '57 (Also see the December, 1957, number,
    p55)   917
Joseph Conrad. A great novelist to visit the United States.
    Time 1, no 6:15 Ap 7 '23   917a
Joseph Conrad: a new English writer of sea stories.
    Literary Digest 22, no 2:39-40 Ja 12 '01   918
Joseph Conrad: an unpublished diary. Blue Peter 5, no
    38:80 My '25   919
Joseph Conrad and Ford Madox Ford. Bookman (NY) 68:
    216-18 O '28   920
[Joseph Conrad and Russia] Literary World (Boston) 35:232
    Ag '04   921
Joseph Conrad, a Polish leader of English novelists. New
    York Sun Ja 31 '14   922
Joseph Conrad arrives; calls writing a grind. New York Eve-
    ning Post My 1 '23 p1-2   923
Joseph Conrad arrives in America. Publishers' Weekly 103:
    1383 My 5 '23   924
Joseph Conrad arrives in New York at the end of this month
    ... New York Tribune Magazine & Books Ap 22 '23
    (Part VI) p23   925
Joseph Conrad - artist of words. Bookseller & Stationer
    (Toronto) 40, no 9:43 S '24   926
Joseph Conrad, author, dies. San Francisco Examiner 121,
    no 36, editorial page, Ag 5 '24   926a
Joseph Conrad, author of Chance, unique in his literary
    methods. New York Herald Ja 20 '12 p22   927
[The Joseph Conrad Club] Poland 9, no 3:170-1 Mr '28;
    no 4:238 Ap '28   927a

Joseph Conrad confined to house by illness. Sun (NY) My
   3 '23 p21 (Conrad ill in the home of Frank N. Double-
   day at Oyster Bay, New York)   928
Joseph Conrad, Dichter der Männlichkeit. Christ und Welt
   (Stuttgart) 3, no 50:10 '50   929
Joseph Conrad died two years ago. Book Leaf (NY) Jl 21
   '26   930
Joseph Conrad dies suddenly. Sun (NY) Ag 4 '24 p13   930a
Joseph Conrad dies, writer of the sea. New York Times
   Ag 4 '24 p1, 4   931
Joseph Conrad et la France. Livres Choisis D '57 p1-2
                                                        932
Joseph Conrad et quelques écrivains français. Mercure de
   France (series moderne) 176:287 N 15 '24   933
Joseph Conrad; 1857-1924. In The literary tradition of Can-
   terbury from Chaucer to Conrad. Cambridge: Printed
   at the University press, 1930. p35-9; portrait, p34. 934
Joseph Conrad, famous writer of sea tales... New York
   Tribune My 6 '23 p1 of the Graphic Section; portrait
                                                        935
[Joseph Conrad granted a Ł100 pension out of the British
   Civil List] Nation (NY) 93:24 Jl 13 '11   936
Joseph Conrad: a great novelist to visit the United States.
   Time (NY) 1:15 Ap 7 '23   937
Joseph Conrad here for a visit. Sun (NY) My 1 '23 p9 938
Joseph Conrad indisposed, plans to take week's rest.
   Evening World (NY) My 3 '23 p27   938a
[Joseph Conrad is buried near Canterbury] Argonaut 96:8
   My 16 '25   939
Joseph Conrad is dead at 66... New York Herald & New
   York Tribune Ag 4 '24 p1, 3   940
Joseph Conrad is war bound. New York Times O 22 '14
   p5   941
Joseph Conrad. Jego sztuka. Wielkość i tajemnica.
   Wiadomości 12, no 47:3 N 24 '57   941a
Joseph Conrad Korzeniowski. Przegląd Warszawski rok 4,
   tom 3, no 36:399 S '24   942
Joseph Conrad Korzeniowski. Essays and studies. Kwartal-
   nik Neofilologiczny nos 1-2, 1958; same published:
   Warsaw: Państowe Wydawnictwo Naukowe, 1958. 115p
   (Contains articles by Baines, Bradbrook, Curle,
   Chwalewik, Helsztyński, Jabłowska, Tarnawski, and
   Vidan)
   (Reviewed by Zdzisław Najder in Twórczość no 10:165-
   8 '58)   943
...Joseph Conrad leaving [on the steamer Majestic] New
   York Times Je 2 '23 p14   944

Joseph Conrad makes first trip here on <u>Tuscania</u>. Evening
    World (NY) My 1 '23 p2   944a
[Joseph Conrad, master both of ships and English] New York
    Daily Tribune O 20 '06 p8   945
Joseph Conrad, master seaman and master writer. Mentor
    13:1 Mr '25 (Includes a portrait-sketch)   946
Joseph Conrad, master spinner of sea yarns... Sun (NY)
    My 4 '48 p 16 (Refers to his trip to New York in 1923,
    twenty-five years earlier; includes a sketch by May
    Mott-Smith)   947
[Joseph Conrad, master writer] Boston Evening Transcript
    Ag 4 '24 p2   948
The Joseph Conrad Memorial Library. Fair Winds (NY) 2,
    no 1:27-8 '40   949
Joseph Conrad, noted writer of sea tales, dies. Chicago
    Daily Tribune Ag 4 '24 p1
    (The Associated Press dispatch)   949a
Joseph Conrad peers toward Manhattan's towers. New York
    Tribune My 2 '23 p11   950
Joseph Conrad: a philosopher of the sea. Times (London)
    Ag 4 '24 p10; same. Publishers' Circular & Book-
    sellers' Record 121:199 Ag 9 '24   951
Joseph Conrad, rationalist. New York Tribune Magazine &
    Review O 26 '19 part VII p4; portrait, map, and fac-
    simile   952
Joseph Conrad, seaman and novelist. Outlook (NY) 137:562
    Ag 13 '24   953
Joseph Conrad tells why he chose English as a medium.
    New York Tribune My 23 '20 section VII p9; portrait
                                                              954
Joseph Conrad: the gift of tongues. Nation (NY) 116:561
    My 16 '23   955
Joseph Conrad to be guest of E. L. Adams. New York
    Tribune My 21 '23 p9   956
Joseph Conrad to visit in historic Berkshires. New York
    Tribune My 21 '23 p13   957
[Joseph Conrad will arrive in New York City at the end of
    the month] New York Tribune Ap 22 '23 p23   958
Joseph Conrad, writer of sea stories, is dead. Indianapolis
    News Ag 4 '24 p19   958a
Joseph Conrad writes no fiction stranger than his own life.
    Sun (NY) F 8 '13 p13   959
Joseph Conrads Beziehungen. Berliner Tageblatt no 35,
    1934 (by H. J. R.)   960
Joseph Conrad's first book. Westminster Gazette Ja 28 '14
    p4 (Indicates [erroneously] that Conrad was captain of
    the <u>Torrens</u> when Jacques read and approved of the ms.

Kane, Robert Joseph
   Some novels of Mr. Joseph Conrad. Master's Thesis,
      Ohio State University, 1922. 60p   977
A Kansas critic of Conrad. New York Times F 2 '16 p10
      (an editorial)   978
Kaplan, Harold J.
   Character as reality: Joseph Conrad. In The passive
      voice: an approach to modern fiction. Athens, Ohio:
      Ohio University press [c1966] p131-57   979
Karl, Frederick Robert
   Conrad's debt to Dickens. Notes & Queries 202:398-400
      S '57; see also p504
   Conrad's Stein: the destructive element. Twentieth Cen-
      tury Literature 3:163-9 Ja '58
   Conrad's waste land: moral anarchy in The Secret Agent.
      Four Quarters 9:29-36 Ja '60
   Joseph Conrad: a 'fin de siecle' novelist - a study in style
      and method. Literary Review 11:565-76 Summer '59
   Joseph Conrad: a modern Victorian (a study in novelistic
      technique). Ann Arbor, Michigan: University Micro-
      films [1957] Publication no. 21, 797. Ph. D. Thesis,
      Columbia University, 1957. 456p. Abstract in Disserta-
      tion Abstracts 17:1764 '57
   Joseph Conrad and Huckleberry Finn. Mark Twain Jour-
      nal 11:21-3 Summer '60
   Joseph Conrad's literary theory. Criticism 2:317-35 Fall
      '60
   A reader's guide to Joseph Conrad. New York: Noonday
      Press [1960] 308p; bibliography, p299-301
      (Reviewed in Times Literary Supplement O 21 '60 p678;
      Charles Kaplan in College English 23:167 N '61; Charles
      W. Mann Jr. in Library Journal 85:2594 Jl '60; Adam
      Gillon in Dalhousie Review 41, no 2:255-6 Summer '61)
   A reader's guide to the contemporary English novel.
      London: Thames & Hudson [1963] passim
   The rise and fall of Under Western Eyes. Nineteenth-
      Century Fiction 13:313-27 Mr '59
   The significance of the revisions in the early versions of
      Nostromo. Modern Fiction Studies 5:129-44 Summer '59
                                                              980
Karl, Frederick Robert and Magalaner, Marvin
   Joseph Conrad: life. In A reader's guide to great twenti-
      eth-century English novels. New York: Noonday press,
      1959. p42-6
   Joseph Conrad: works. In A reader's guide to great
      twentieth-century English novels. New York: Noonday
      press, 1959. p47-99   981

Karrakis
  Joseph Conrad at home in England. Poland 5, no 4:225-
    8, 247-8 Ap '24
  Wizyta u Conrada (A visit with Conrad). Naokoło Świata
    (Around the World) no 5, 1924   982
Kaufmann, Renate
  The typhoon and the butterfly: existentialist elements in
    Joseph Conrad. Radcliffe College Honors Thesis in
    English, 1949. 36f   983
Kay, Hubert Ames
  Joseph Conrad's creation of atmosphere. Master's Thesis,
    Columbia University, 1929. 36p   984
Kaye, Julian B.
  Conrad's Under Western Eyes and Mann's Doctor Faustus.
    Comparative Literature 9:60-65 Winter '57   985
Kazecka, M.
  Z pobytu Conrada w Polsce (From Conrad's stay in Po-
    land). Gazeta Lwowska nos 158-160, 1924   986
Keating, George T.
  Introduction. In A Set of Six, by Joseph Conrad. (Me-
    morial Edition) Garden City, New York: Doubleday,
    Page, 1925. Volume X, p vii-x   987
Keating, George T. (compiler)
  A Conrad memorial library: the collection of George T.
    Keating. Garden City, New York: Doubleday, Doran,
    1929. vii-xvi, 448p
    (501 copies only)
  Joseph Conrad, a record (a scrapbook of clippings, por-
    traits, proof sheets, etc.) Yale University Library
  Portraits of Conrad and others. 40 pieces.
    Yale University Library   988
Keating supplements Conrad gift to Yale. Adds author's
    manuscripts and letters to collection. New York Her-
    ald Tribune Ap 20 '38 p16   989
Keeffe, Daniel J.
  An analysis of Joseph Conrad's short stories. M. A.
    Thesis, Vanderbilt Univ., 1941. iii, 83f Abstract in Van-
    derbilt University, Abstracts of Thesis, 1942, p39   990
Keith, Priscilla
  Conrad's theme of self-discovery. Senior Essay in Eng-
    lish, Wells College, 1960. 40f   991
Kellett, Ernest Edward
  A note on Joseph Conrad. London Mercury 13:485-93
    Mr '26; same. In Reconsiderations; literary essays.
    New York: Macmillan, 1928. p243-61   992
Kennedy, Nellie Agnes
  Abnormal psychology in Joseph Conrad's characters. M. A.

Kennedy, Nellie Agnes (cont.)
     Thesis, University of Texas, 1940. iii-vi, 72f   993
Kenner, Hugh
     Conrad and Ford. In Gnomon; essays on contemporary
     literature. New York: McDowell, Obolensky, 1958.
     p162-70   994
Kerf, René
     Ethics versus aesthetics: a clue to the deterioration of
     Conrad's art. Revue des Langues Vivantes 31:240-9
     '65
     The Nigger of the 'Narcissus' and the manuscript version
          of The Rescue. English Studies 44:437-43 D '63
     Symbol hunting in Conradian land. Revue des Langues
          Vivantes 32:266-77 '66
     Typhoon and The Shadow Line. A re-examination. Revue
          des Langues Vivantes no 6:486-500 '61   995
Kessel, J.
     Conrad Slave. La Nouvelle Revue Française 23:720-3
     D 1 '24   996
Kettle, Arnold
     The greatness of Joseph Conrad. Modern Quarterly new
     series 3, no 3:63-81 Summer '48
     Joseph Conrad: Nostromo (1904). In An introduction to
     the English novel. Volume II. Henry James to the
     present day. London: Hutchinson's University Library,
     1953. p67-81 and passim
     (Reviewed in Times Literary Supplement O 23 '53
     p674)   997
Killam, C. Douglas
     Kurtz's country. Lock Haven Review (Lock Haven State
     College, Pennsylvania) no 7:31-42 '65   998
Kilroy, James F.
     Conrad's "Succès de Curiosité:" the dramatic version of
     The Secret Agent. English Literature in Transition 10,
     no 2:81-8 '67   999
Kimbrough, Robert (editor)
     Heart of Darkness. An authoritative text, backgrounds
     and sources, essays and criticism, edited by Robert
     Kimbrough. New York: W.W. Norton & Co., [c1963]
     v-viii, 231p; bibliography, p228-31   1000
Kimpel, Ben and T.C. Duncan Eaves
     The geography and history in Nostromo. Modern Philology
     56:45-54 Ag '58   1001
King, Carlyle
     Conrad for the classroom. English Journal 47:259-66
     My '58
     Introduction. In Three stories by Joseph Conrad, edited

by Carlyle King. New York: Macmillan, 1961. 247p
                                                          1002
Kinney, Arthur F.
    Jimmy Wait: Joseph Conrad's kaleidoscope. College Eng-
        lish 26:475-8 Mr '65   1003
Kinninmont, Kenneth
    A Conrad "Genesis." How he harks back to his youth in
        his novel The Arrow of Gold. Book Monthly 14:851-5
        N '19   1004
Kipling, Rudyard
    A letter from Rudyard Kipling to Joseph Conrad. [Lon-
        don: First Edition Club, Curwen Press, 1926] [6]p
        Editor's note, p[1]; Letter, p[3]
        (220 copies only)   1005
Kipling et Conrad. Mercure de France année 47, tome 266:
        218-19 F 15 '36   1006
Kirk, Carey Harris
    Conrad and the critic. M. A. Thesis, Univ. of Virginia,
        1967. 36f   1007
Kirschner, Paul
    Conrad and Maupassant. Review of English Literature
        (Leeds) 6, no 4:37-51 O '65
    Conrad and Maupassant: moral solitude and "A Smile of
        Fortune." Review of English Literature (Leeds) 7, no
        3:62-77 Jl '66
    Conrad and the film. Quarterly of Film, Radio and Tele-
        vision 11:343-53 Spring '57
    Conrad's strong man. Modern Fiction Studies 10:31-6
        Spring '64 (On "Gaspar Ruiz")
    Conrad: the psychologist as artist. (Biography and Criti-
        cism Series, no. 8) London: 1968
    Ford and Conrad. New York Times Book Review F 16
        '64 p33
    A study of Conrad's use of the principles of dramatic
        technique and construction in his fiction, with a com-
        ment on his three plays. Master's Thesis, University
        of London, 1956   1008
Kishler, Thomas C.
    Reality in "Heart of Darkness." College English 24:561-2
        Ap '63   1009
Kisielewski, Zygmunt
    J. Conrad, styl i człowiek (J. Conrad, style and personal-
        ity). Robotnik (Worker) no 238, 1924   1010
Kjw [pseud.]
    See: Wyka, Kazimierz   1011
Kleczkowski, Paul
    La vie intellectuelle: une traduction polonaise des oeuvres

Kleczkowski, Paul (cont.)
　de Joseph Conrad.　La Pologne (Paris) 4th année, no
　5:256-61 Mr 1 '23   1012
Kleczkowski, Stefan
　Polskość Conrada (Conrad's Polish character).　Illustro-
　wany Kuryer Codzienny (Illustrated Daily Courier) no
　18, 1928   1013
Klein, Barbara Jean
　Chaucer's Clerk's Tale, Conrad's Under Western Eyes,
　Stevens' Aesthetic Theory.　Master's Thesis, Pennsyl-
　vania State University, 1963.　72p   1014
Kleiner, Juliusz
　Oddźwięk ballady Mickiewiczowskiej w opowieści Conrada
　(Echoes of Mickiewicz's ballad in a tale by Conrad).
　Dziennik Literacki (Cracow) no 19, My 5 '49 p4
　(Refers to "Karain")
　Problematy improwizacji Konrada.　Lublin: Towarzystwo
　Naukowe Katolickiego Universytetu Lubelskiego, 1947.
　41p (Wykłady i Przemowienia, 21)   1015
Klemperer, Elizabeth Gallagher von
　The fiction of Henry James and Joseph Conrad in France:
　a study in penetration and reception.　Doctoral disserta-
　tion, Radcliffe College, March, 1958.　416ff; bibliogra-
　phy ff382-416; "French translations of Conrad's work,
　in periodicals" ff397-9; "in books," ff399-400   1016

Klingopulos, G. D.
　The criticism of novels.　The Use of English 3:85-90 Je
　'55
　Arthur Koestler.　Scrutiny 16, no 2:85-6 Je '49
　(Noted in Wiadomuści 4, nos 178-9:3 S 4 '49)
　[A comparison of Under Western Eyes with Darkness at
　Noon]   1017
Kliszczewski, H. Spirydion
　Conrad w moim domu rodzinnym (Conrad at my home).
　Wiadomości (News) 4, nos 176-177:4 Ag 21 '49   1018
Kloth, Friedrich
　Das Problem der Einsamkeit bei Conrad.　Ph. D. Thesis,
　Kiel University, 1952   1019
Klub Miłośników Conrada.　Wiadomości 4, nos 176-7:5 Ag
　21 '49   1020
Knight, Grant Cochran
　Joseph Conrad.　In The novel in English.　New York: R. R.
　Smith, 1931.　p305-13; bibliography, p375-6
　The greatest hero.　In Superlatives.　New York: Knopf,
　1925.　p169-87 (On The Rover)   1021
Knopf, Alfred A.

Joseph Conrad: a footnote to publishing history.   Atlantic
Monthly 201:63-7 F '58
Joseph Conrad.   The romance of his life and books.   In
Joseph Conrad.   [Garden City, New York: Doubleday,
Page, 1913] p3-19
(Noted in Bookman (NY) 38:352-4 D '13; Sun (NY) Ja
11 '14 p12)   1022
Knowlton, Edgar C.
An outline of world literature from Homer to the present
day.   New York: Nelson, 1937. p270-1   1023
Kobrzyński, Bolesław
Lord Jim; poem.   Wiadomości (London) 4, nos 176-7:1 Ag 21
'49   1024
Koc, Barbara
Conrad a Polska (Conrad and Poland).   Ph. D. Thesis,
University of Warsaw, 1962   1025
Koch, Ivan L.
Conrad's microcosm.   Master's Thesis, Univ. of Wyoming,
1962. 89p   1026
Kocmanová, Jessie
The revolt of the workers in the novels of Gissing, James,
and Conrad. Brno Studies in English 1:119-43 '59   1027
Kocówna, Barbara
Dwa listy Małgorzaty Poradowskiej do Józefa Korzeniow-
skiego.   Kwartalnik Neofilologiczny 6, no 4:329-31 '59
O Chance Conrada.   Kwartalnik Neofilologiczny 8:45-51
'61
Polkość Conrada.   [Kraków:] Ludowa Spółdzielnia Wydawni-
cza [1967] 5-264p; portraits and illustrations
Preface.   In Wspomnienia i studia o Conradzie, wybrała i
opracowała Barbara Kocówna.   Warsaw: Państwowy
Instytut Wydawniczy [1963] p5-[8]
Żywa tradycja Conradowska (The living Conrad tradition).
Przegląd Humanistyczny 5, no 1:165-78 '61   1028
Kocówna, Barbara (editor)
Wspomnienia i studia o Conradzie, wybrała i opracowała
Barbara Kocówna. [Warsaw] Państwowy Instytut Wyd-
awniczy [1963] 502p; preface, p5-[8]
(Reviewed by Edmund A. Bojarski in Books Abroad 39:
29-32 Winter '65; W. Chwalewik in Rocznik Literacki
1963, p277-8)   1029
Koeppen, Wolfgang
Joseph Conrad. Berliner Börs. Courant no 442, 1933
(Noted in Die Literatur 36 heft, 2:98-9 O 10 '33)
1030
Kohler, Dayton
Introduction.   In Lord Jim, by Joseph Conrad. (Perennial

138   A Bibliography of Joseph Conrad
library) New York: Harper, Row [c1965] p[xii]-xix 1031
Ko/aczkowski, Stefan
    Conrad po polsku. Wiadomości Literacki 5, no 238:2,
    Jl 22 '28
Józef Conrad (Korzeniowski). Przegląd Współczesny 4,
    no 33:45-66 Ja '25; 4, no 34:243-68 F '25; same. In
    Wspomnienia i studia o Conradzie, edited by Barbara
    Kocówna. Warsaw: Państwowy Instytut Wydawniczy
    [1963] p185-245; same. (excerpt) In Joseph Conrad
    Korzeniowski, by Róża Jab)/kowska. Warsaw: Państ-
    wowe Zak)/ady Wydawnictwo Szkolynch, 1964. p210-17
O decyzię zyciową Conrada. Wiadomości Literackie 4,
    no 52:1 D 25 '27   1032
Kolb, Jonathan Edward
    The Secret Agent and the change in Conrad. Harvard Col-
    lege Honors Thesis March 1, 1965. 33f   1033
Kolodziejczyk, J.
    The role of the description of nature in the narrative of
    Conrad's first three novels: Almayer's Folly, An Out-
    cast of the Islands, and The Nigger of the 'Narcissus.'
    Master's Thesis, Jagiellonian University, 1958   1034
Königsgarten, Hugo F.
    Die Qual des Dichters (Briefe von Conrad) Ebenda no
    128, 1933   1035
Korbut, G.
    Literatura polska od poczatków do wojny swiatowej. 2nd
    edition, Volumes II-IV. Warsaw: Sk)/ad G)/owny w Kasie
    Im. Mianowskiego, Pa)/ac Staszica, 1929-1931   1036
Korzeniowska, (Mrs.) Jessie Conrad
    See: Conrad, (Mrs.) Jessie (George)   1037
Korzeniowski, Apollo
    Dla milego grosza. Warsaw: Państwowy Instytut Wydawn-
    iczy, 1965. 157p   1038
Korzeniowski. He was not a literary man. Time 4, no 6:
    17 Ag 11 '24   1038a
Korzeniowski, Josef Teodor Konrad Na)/ęcz
    See Conrad, Joseph   1039
Korzeniowski, Józef (Conrad). S)/owo Pomorskie (Pomeranian
    Word) no 185, 1924   1040
Kosch, Teodor
    Memoria)/ Conrada (Korzeniowskiego) o sprawie polskiej w
    czasie weilkiej wojny (Conrad's memorandum on the Pol-
    ish cause during WW I). Czas (Time) no 89, Mr 31 '34
    Powrót Conrada do anglii (ze wspomnień o Conradzie).
    Tygodnik Powszechny no 30:600 '60   1041
Kossak, Jerzy
    Mauriac czy Conrad? In Humanizm skrępowany.

Warsaw: K i W, 1963.   1042
Kott, Jan
Conrad i Malraux. In Mitologia i realizm (Mythology and
realism). Warsaw: Czytelnik, 1946. p117-66
O laickim tragizmie (The lay tragic spirit). Twórczość
(Creative Work) 1, no 2:137-60 S '45   1043
Kovarna, Fr.
Conradova Nahoda. Rozhledy po Literaturě a Uměni 1:
119-20 N 2 '32   1044
Kowalkowski, Alfred
Pojęcie morskości u Conrada (The concept of the sea in
Conrad). Arkona nos 1-2, 1942   1045
Kowalska, Aniela
Conrad - moralista. Kultura i Społeczeństwo 3, no 2:147-
62 Ap-Je '59; same. In Joseph Conrad Korzeniowski,
by Róża Jabłkowska. [Warsaw:] Państwowe Zakłady
Wydawnictwo Szkolynch, 1964. p325-31
Conrad - poeta. Prace Polonistyczne (Wrocław) series
17:[165]-179 '61
Człowiek i morze w twórczości Conrada-Korzeniowskiego.
Prace Polonistyczne (Lódz) series 4:117-37, 1940-46
(Man and sea in Conrad's work)
W kręgu zagadnień rzemiosła pisarskiego Josepha Conrada.
Prace Polonistyczne (Lódz) series 7:247-65 '49; same.
In Joseph Conrad Korzeniowski, by Róża Jabłkowska.
[Warsaw] Państwowe Zakłady Wydawnictwo Szkolynch,
1964. p325-31
(Problems of Joseph Conrad's literary craftsmanship)
One of the shortest masterpieces of Joseph Conrad. The
problem of Conrad's autobiographical works. Bulletin
de la Société des Sciences et des Lettres de Lódź,
volume 11, no 5, 1960
Wśród bohaterów Conrada. Prace Polonistyczne series 19:
[185]-210 '63   1046
Koziarska, Aleksandra
Doda Conrad. Wiadomości 5, no 202:4 F 12 '50   1046a
Kozicki, Stanislaw
Wizyta u Conrada. Kierunki nos 14-15:15 '58   1047
Kozłowski, W. M.
Z literatury amerykańskiej. Przegląd Tygodniowy no 7,
1897   1048
Kramer, Dale
Marlow, myth, and structure in Lord Jim. Criticism 8:
263-79 Summer '66   1049
Kranendonk, A. G. van
Joseph Conrad. English Studies (Amsterdam) 2, no 7:1-
8 F '20

Kranendonk, A. G. van (cont.)
Joseph Conrad. De Stem 3:837-50, 883-900, 978-90
   O - D '23   1050
Kreemers, R.
Joseph Conrad. Boekzaal no 17:261-2 S 1'29   1051
Kreisel, Henry
Joseph Conrad and the dilemma of the uprooted man.
Tamarack Review issue 7:78-85 Spring '58   1052
Krewni Konrada Korzeniowskiego (Conrad's relatives).
Ziemia Pomorska (Pomeranian Land) no 354, 1946 1053
Kridl, Manfred
Lord Jim Conrada. Przegląd Współczesny no 81:113-125
   Ja '29; no 82:247-269 F '29; same. In Wspomnienia i
studia o Conradzie, edited by Barbara Kocówna [War-
saw:] Państwowy Instytut Wydawniczy [1963] p290-328;
same. In Joseph Conrad Korzeniowski, by Róża
Jabłkowska. Warsaw: Państwowe Zakłady Wydawnic-
two Szkolynch, 1964. p221-37   1054
Krieger, Murray
Afterword. In Lord Jim, by Joseph Conrad. [New York:]
New American Library [c1961] p309-17
Conrad's "Youth:" a naive opening to art and life. College
English 20:275-80 Mr '59
Joseph Conrad: action, inaction, and extremity. In The
tragic vision... New York: Holt, 1960. p154-94 1055
Krzyżanowski, Jerzy
Konrad czy Conrad (Konrad or Conrad). Dziś i Jutro
(Today and Tomorrow) no 28, 1953
Powrót Conrada (Conrad's return). Dziś i Jutro (Today
and Tomorrow) 11, no 24:4-5 Je 19 '55   1056
Krzyżanowski, Julian
O tragedii n Samburanie. Pion no 50, 1934; same. In
Wspomnienia i studia O Conradzie, edited by Barbara
Kocówna. [Warsaw:] Państwowy Instytut Wydawniczy
[1963] p333-7
U źródeł publicystyki Józefa Conrada (On the sources of
Conrad's political journalism). Ruch Literacki 7, no
8:243-8 Ag '32
Z głosów o Conradzie (Opinions on Conrad). Ziemia Lu-
belska (Lublin Region) no 22, 1928   1057
Krzyżanowski, Ludwik
Conrad. New York Times Book Review Ja 12 '58
(A letter to the editor)
Introduction. In Joseph Conrad: centennial essays, edited
by Ludwik Krzyżanowski. New York: Polish Institute
of Arts & Sciences in America, 1960. p7
Joseph Conrad. Bulletin of the Polish Institute of Arts &

Sciences in America, July, 1943, p942-4
Joseph Conrad: a bibliographical note. Polish Review 2,
nos 2-3:133-40 Spring-Summer '57
Joseph Conrad: some Polish documents. Polish Review
3, no 1:60-85 Winter-Spring '58; same. In Joseph
Conrad: centennial essays... New York: Polish Institute
of Arts & Sciences in America, 1960. p111-43
(Includes 5 hitherto-unpublished Conrad letters)
Joseph Conrad's "Prince Roman:" fact and fiction. Polish
Review 1, no 4:22-62 Autumn '56; same. In Joseph
Conrad: centennial essays... New York: Polish Insti-
tute of Arts & Sciences in America, 1960. p[29]-72
Kiedy Conrad poraz pierwszy widział morze i gdzie
chodził do szkoły? (When did Conrad first see the sea
and where did he attend school?) Wiadomości Literackie
(Literary News) 9, no 37:4 Ag 28 '32
Study of Joseph Conrad: Chapter IV. Washington: Photo-
duplication Service, Library of Congress, 1955. Micro-
film 2551, no 178 DR
Study of Joseph Conrad: introductory chapter. Washing-
ton: Photoduplication Service, Library of Congress,
1955. Microfilm 2551, no 177 DR
Tatrzański góral i artystyczana telewizja Conrada (Con-
rad's Tatra mountaineer and his artistic prescience).
Wiadomości Literackie (Literary News) 11, no 43:6 O
21 '34   1058
Krzyżanowski, Ludwik (editor)
Joseph Conrad: centennial essays, edited by Ludwik
Krzyżanowski. New York: Polish Institute of Arts and
Sciences in America, 1960. 174 p; bibliography, p163-
74; introduction, p7   1059
Kuczynski, A.
Portraits of the sailors in Joseph Conrad's novels. M. A.
Thesis, University of Warsaw, 1960   1060
Kuncewicz, Maria
Discovery of Patusan. In Conrad żywy, edited by Wit
Tarnawski. London: B. Świderski, 1957. p50-7 1061
Kunitz, Stanley J. (Editor)
Joseph Conrad, 1857-1924. In Authors to-day and yester-
day. New York: Wilson, 1933. p162-6; portrait, p164;
bibliography, p166   1062
Kunitz, Stanley J. and Howard Haycraft (editors)
Joseph Conrad. In Twentieth century authors. New York:
Wilson, 1942. p307-10; portrait, p307; bibliography,
p309-10   1063
Kureth, Sister Julia
The fatalism of Joseph Conrad and Thomas Hardy. M. A.

142 A Bibliography of Joseph Conrad

Kureth, Sister Julia (cont.)
Thesis, Duquesne University, 1935 1064
Kusenberg, K.
Roman des Verräters. Vossische Zeitung O 8 '33 p11,
no 41 1065
Kuyle, A.
Joseph Conrad. De Maasbode Mr 16 '26 1066
Kwieciński, Z. J.
Joseph Conrad. Astrea no 2:153-6 '24 1067
Łada, Gustaw
U źródeł polkości Conrada. Gazeta Warszawska no 265,
1932 1068
Lalou, René
Hommages à Joseph Conrad. La Revue Européenne 4,
no 24:65-6 F 1 '25
Joseph Conrad et le cosmopolitisme loyaliste. In Pano-
rama de la littérature anglaise contemporaine. Paris:
Kra [1926] p208-17
(Reviewed by Ludwig Karl in Literaturblatt für German-
ische und Romanische Philologie 51, nos 1-2:27-8 Ja-
F '30) 1069
Lambuth, David
Essay on Conrad's Suspense. Saturday Review of Litera-
ture 2:290-1 N 14 '25 1070
Lamont, William Hayes Fogg
A study of isolation in the life of Joseph Conrad. Ph. D.
Thesis, University of Pennsylvania, 1933 1071
Lanahan, William F. (Rev.)
The dramatization of the theme in Joseph Conrad's Under
Western Eyes. M. A. Thesis, Catholic Univ. of
America, 1962. 72f 1072
Land, Eugeniusz (also: Łann, Eugeniusz)
Roman ks. Sanguszko a Joseph Conrad Korzeniowski
(Prince Roman Sanguszko and Joseph Conrad). Przegląd
Warszawski (Warsaw Review) fasc. 47:140-5 '25 1073
Lane, Robert R.
Old books for new. The Secret Agent moving and convinc-
ing tale, which began Joseph Conrad's "second phase."
Newark Evening News Ag 26 '51 Section III p40 1074
Langford, H. D.
Studies in present-day fiction. Canadian Bookman 3, no
1:161-3 Je '21 1075
Łann, Eugeniusz (also: Land, Eugeniusz)
Joseph Conrad. In Izbrannych proizwiedienij. Moscow:
1924. same. (translated by Barbara Kocówna) Prze-
gląd Humanistyczny 6, no 5:53-70 '62; same. In Joseph

Conrad Korzeniowski, by Róża Jabłkowska. Warsaw: Państwowe Zakłady Wydawnictwo Szkolynch, 1964. p304-14   1076

Lapham, R. L.
Harmony and character in the novels and short stories of Joseph Conrad. M. A. Thesis, University of Oregon, 1926. 40f   1077

Larson, Charles R.
Come to the ship, Leggatt, honey. Atlantic Monthly 221: 111-12 Mr '68
(A student analysis of "The Secret-Sharer")   1077a

Laskowski, Irmina Teresa
Conrad's settings: a study of descriptive style. Ph. D. Thesis, Harvard University, 1963. ii, 172f   1078

Laskowsky, Henry Julius
Joseph Conrad: epistemology and the novel. Ph. D. Thesis, Syracuse University, 1967. iv, 178f   1078a

Las Vergnas, Raymond
Joseph Conrad. (Les Grands Écrivains Étrangers) Paris: Henri Didier, 1939. iv, 234p; bibliography, p[229]-231
(Reviewed by Joseph Warren Beach in Modern Language Notes 55:317 Ap '40)
Joseph Conrad, romancier de l'exil. Lyon, Paris: Emmanuel Vitte [1959] 9-164p; portrait
(Reviewed by J. D. in Revue Belge de Philologie et d'Histoire (Brussels) 1960, p636-7)   1079

Latcham, Ricardo A.
La obra novelesca de Joseph Conrad. Nosotros epoca 2, tomo 19, año 7:24-51 O '42   1080

The late Joseph Conrad. Publishers' Circular & Booksellers Record 121:238 Ag 16 '24   1081

The late Joseph Conrad. Dean of Canterbury's tribute. Morning Post (London) Ag 11 '24 p9   1082

The late Joseph Conrad: funeral at Canterbury. Morning Post (London) Ag 8 '24 p6   1083

The late Joseph Conrad: great master of English. Daily Telegraph (London) Ag 4 '24 p8   1084

The late Joseph Conrad. Polish Minister's tribute. Morning Post (London) Ag 5 '24 p9   1085

The late Joseph Conrad. Tributes from both sides of the Atlantic. Morning Post (London) Ag 6 '24 p9   1086

Late Mr. Joseph Conrad. Daily Telegraph (London) Ag 5 '24 p11; Daily Telegraph (London) Ag 7 '24 p10; Morning Post (London) Ag 7 '24 p6; Sphere 98:155 Ag 9 '24   1087

The late Mr. Joseph Conrad (signed "E. B. O.") Morning Post (London) Ag 4 '24 p4   1088

The late Mr. Joseph Conrad: a great novelist.   Morning
   Post (London) Ag 4 '24 p4   1089
Latorre, Mariano
  José Conrad.   Atenea (Santiago de Chile) 2:161-72 S
   30 '25   1090
Lawless, Ray McKinley
  Studies in the style of Joseph Conrad.   M. A. Thesis,
   Univ. of Chicago, 1924. 77f   1090a
Lawrence, David Herbert
  The letters of D. H. Lawrence, edited by Aldous Huxley.
   New York: Viking Press, 1932. p68, 72   1091
Lawrence, T. E.
  The letters of T. E. Lawrence, edited by David Garnett.
   London: 1938. p301-2   1091a
Leam, Harold Sherman
  Conrad and villainy: a study of the villains in his major
   novels. M. A. Thesis, Lehigh University, 1959.
   129p   1092
Leamon, Dorothy
  Joseph Conrad and Pierre Loti as interpreters of the sea.
   M. A. Thesis, Ohio State University, 1923. 45p   1093
Leavis, Frank Raymond
  Foreword. In Nostromo, by Joseph Conrad. [New York:]
   New American Library [c1960] p v-xi
  Joseph Conrad. (i) Minor works and Nostromo. In The
   great tradition. New York: George W. Stewart [1949];
   London: Chatto & Windus, 1949. p173-201 (Reprinted
   in New York: New York University press, 1963)
  Joseph Conrad. (ii) Victory, The Secret Agent, Under
   Western Eyes, and Chance. In The great tradition.
   New York: George W. Stewart [1949]; London: Chatto &
   Windus, 1949. p201-226
   (Reprinted: New York: New York University press,
   1963)
  Polish master of English prose.   Times (London) D 3 '57
   p11
  Revaluations (XIV): Joseph Conrad. Scrutiny 10:22-50,
   157-81 Je, O '41; same. In The great tradition. New
   York: George W. Stewart [1949]; London: Chatto &
   Windus, 1949. p173-226   1094
Leavis, Q. D.
  Fiction and the reading public.   London: Chatto & Windus,
   1932. p265-8
  Fleet Street and Pierian roses.   Scrutiny 2, no 4:388-91
   Mr '34
  Joseph Conrad.   Sewanee Review 66:179-200 Spring '58
                                                                1095

Le Bost, Barbara A.
    Study questions for Conrad's "Heart of Darkness." Exer-
        cise Exchange 7:3-7 O '59   1096
Lechoń, Jan
    [An untitled poem] Wiadomości Literackie 1, no 33:1
        Ag 17 '24; same. In Literatura Polski, edited by Man-
        fred Kridl. New York: Roy Publishers, 1945. p537-
        8; same. In Poezie zebrane, 1916-1953, by Jan
        Lechoń. London: 1954. p56, entitled: "Na Smierc
        Conrada" (On the Death of Conrad); same. In Conrad
        żywy, edited by Wit Tarnawski. London: B. Świderski,
        1957. p35; same. In Joseph Conrad Korzeniowski, by
        Róża Jabłkowska. Warsaw: Państwowe Zakłady Wy-
        dawnictwo Szkolynch, 1964. p342; same. Tygodnik
        Powszechny 12, no 42:8 O 19'58   1097
Lednicki, Wacław
    Poland and the world. New York: 1943. p32-3;
        reprinted from the Quarterly Bulletin (nos. 1-4) of the
        Polish Institute of Arts & Sciences in America   1098
Lee, Richard Eugene
    The political and social ideas of Joseph Conrad. Ph. D.
        Thesis, New York University, 1954. 308p; Abstract in
        Dissertation Abstracts 15:1073 '55
        (Deals with Romance, Nostromo, Under Western Eyes,
        and The Secret Agent)   1099
Lee, Robert Francis
    Conrad's colonialism. Ph. D. Thesis, Univ. of Minnesota,
        1962. 188p; Abstract in Dissertation Abstracts 24:1172
        '63   1100
    Joseph Conrad and the white man's burden. M. A. Thesis,
        Vanderbilt University, 1953. iv, 187f Abstract in
        Vanderbilt University Bulletin 53, no 2:40 S '53
Lee, Rupert
    Some British artists. Education Outlook & Educational
        Times 77:89 Mr '25 (Discusses Jacob Epstein's bust
        of Joseph Conrad)   1101
Leese, M. J.
    Joseph Conrad as a poetical novelist. M. A. Thesis, Univ.
        of Manchester, 1955   1102
Le Gallienne, Richard
    Introduction. In Romance, a novel by Joseph Conrad and
        Ford Madox Hueffer. (Memorial Edition) Garden City,
        New York: Doubleday, Page, 1925. Volume VII, p vii-
        ix   1103
Lehmann, John
    Foreword [to the Conrad number of the magazine] London
        Magazine 4:9, 11 N '57

Lehmann, John (cont.)
On re-reading The Rover. World Review 28:41-5 Je '51;
 same. In The open night. New York: Harcourt, Brace,
 1952. p54-62   1104
Leiter, Louis H.
Echo structures: Conrad's "The Secret Sharer." Twentieth Century Literature 5:159-75 Ja '60; same. In Ap-
 proaches to the short story, edited by Neil D. Isaacs
 and Louis H. Leiter. San Francisco: Chandler Pub-
 lishing Co. [1963] p185-208   1105
Lencznarowicz, Mieczysław
Dniom odchodzacym w zapomnienie (To the days passing
 into oblivion. "Heart of Darkness") Tygodnik Powszech-
 ny (Universal Weekly) no 16:4 Ag 30 '53   1106
Lenkowski, Stanisław
Jescze o Conradzie. Warszawianka no 49, 1924   1106a
Lenormand, H. -R.
Il y a quatre ans, en Corse avec Joseph Conrad, coureur
 de mer. Transatlantic Review 2, no 3:338-40 O '24
Met den zeevaarder Joseph Conrad op Corsica. Witte
 Mier 1:332-4 '24
Note sur un séjour de Conrad en Corse. La Nouvelle
 Revue Française 23:666-71 D 1 '24; same. In The art
 of Joseph Conrad: a critical symposium, edited by
 Robert Wooster Stallman. East Lansing, Michigan:
 Michigan State University, 1960. p5-8
Recontre avec Joseph Conrad. Gazette des Lettres 7:30-
 2 Mr 15 '51   1107
Lerner, Laurence
Conrad the historian. Listener 72:554-6 D 17 '64
The novelist as innovator: Conrad the historian. Lis-
 tener 73:554-6 Ap 15 '65
Joseph Conrad. In The novelist as innovator. London:
 1965. p78-92   1108
Leslie, Shane
The passing chapter. New York: Scribner's, 1934.
 p141   1109
Leszcza, Jan
[Poem to Conrad] In Conrad żywy, edited by Wit Tar-
 nawski. London: B. Świderski, 1957. p39-46   1110
Levin, Gerald Henry
An allusion to Tasso in Conrad's Chance. Nineteenth-
 Century Fiction 13:145-51 S '58
Conrad and the "atmosphere of authenticity;" an inquiry in-
 to the structure and meaning of Chance. Ann Arbor,
 Michigan: University Microfilms, 1957. Publication no.
 21327. Michigan University Library. Ph. D. Thesis,

University of Michigan, 1956. 197p; Abstract in Dissertation Abstracts 17:1340-1 '57
The scepticism of Marlow.   Twentieth Century Literature
    3:177-84 Ja '58   1111
Levine, George L.
The history of Conrad criticism.   Ph. D. Thesis, University of Minnesota (Minneapolis)   1112
Levine, Paul
Joseph Conrad's blackness.   South Atlantic Quarterly 63:
    198-206 Spring '64   1113
Levinson, André
Joseph Conrad est-il un écrivain français? polonais?
    Les Nouvelles Littéraires 7, no 301:8 Jl 21 '28; 7,
    no 302:8 Ag 4 '28
Croisières... Paris: Editions de "La Renaissance,"
    1927. p101-12   1114
Levinson, B. A.
A Conrad letter.   Times Literary Supplement Jl 25 '58
    p423   1115
Levy, Gail Susan
The remarkable hero: Joseph Conrad's moral ideal. M. A.
    Thesis, Tufts University, 1965.   84 f ("Heart of Darkness," Lord Jim, Under Western Eyes, Victory)   1116
Levy, Lora S.
Joseph Conrad's artistic treatment of women: an analysis.
    M. A. Thesis, University of Arizona, 1955. 116p   1117
Levy, Milton A.
Conrad's "The Lagoon."   Explicator 23, item 35, Dec.
    1964.   1118
Lewański, Juliusz
Józef Conrad Korzeniowski.   Trybuna Dolnoslaska (Lower
    Silesian Tribune) no 126, 1948   1119
Lewis, C. E. (editor)
Typhoon, by Joseph Conrad.   Edited by C. E. Lewis.
    (Special Canadian Edition) Toronto: Copp [1943] 134p
                                                           1119a
Lewis, Lawrence Bernard
Four character types in the fiction of Joseph Conrad.
    M. A. Thesis, Univ. of Missouri, 1955. 103p   1120
Lewis, Richard Warrington Baldwin
The current of Conrad's Victory.   In Twelve original essays on great English novels, edited by Charles Shapiro.   Detroit, Michigan: Wayne State University Press,
    1960. p203-31; same.   In Trials of the word... New
    Haven: Yale University press, 1965. p148-69   1121
Lewis, William Hall III
The hero of isolation in the novels of Joseph Conrad.

Lewis, William Hall III (cont.)
  Honors Thesis, Harvard College, March 1, 1961.   44ff
  (Examines Victory, Nostromo, Lord Jim, and Under
  Western Eyes)   1122
Lewis, Wilma Eleanor
  Joseph Conrad - his technique.   M. A.   Thesis, University
  of Washington, 1930.   59f; bibliography, f57-9   1122a
Library for sailors a Conrad memorial.   New York Times
  Jl 15 '25 p17   1123
Lichnerowicz, Jeanne
  Joseph Conrad.   Chronique des Lettres Françaises 3:
  [49]-55 Ja-F '25   1124
Lid, R. W.
  Return to yesterday.   In Ford Madox Ford: the essence
  of his art.   Berkeley and Los Angeles: University of
  California press, 1964.   p10-15   1125
Liebe zu einem element: Joseph Conrad.   Konigsburg Hart.
  Zeitung no 536, 1929   1126
Lifszycowa, Ernestyna
  Józef Korzeniowski jako powieściopisarz.   Ph. D.   Thesis,
  Univ. of Warsaw, 1925-6   1126a
Ligocki, Edward
  Conrad.   Kurier Poznański (Poznań Courier) no 181,
  1924
  Nieznany autograf Conrada.   Kurjer Poznański no 434,
  1927   1127
Lillard, Richard Gordon
  Irony: the integrant in the art and philosophy of Thomas
  Hardy and Joseph Conrad.   Master's Essay, Univ. of
  Montana, 1931.   167ff; same. (excerpt) Publications of
  the Modern Language Association of America 50:316-
  22 Mr '35   1128
Lindstrand, Gordon
  Joseph Conrad's Nostromo: the transmission of the text.
  Ph. D.   Thesis, Univ. of Illinois, 1967.   iii-v, 583f;
  bibliography, f379-88; appendixes follow   1128a
A link with Conrad.   Sea Breezes ns 8:250-3 S '49
  (With illustrations)   1129
Lipska, J.
  Women characters in Joseph Conrad's works.   M. A.
  Thesis, University of Warsaw, 1949   1130
Lisiewicz, Mieczysław
  On reading Apollo's letters.   In Conrad żywy, edited by
  Wit Tarnawski.   London: B. Świderski, 1957. p141-9
                                                          1131
Literary intelligence.   London Mercury 13:117 D '25 (On
  the Conrad Memorial Library)   1132

Littell, Robert
    Arriving with Joseph Conrad. New Republic 34:319 My
    16 '23; same. In Read America first. New York:
    Harcourt, Brace, 1926. p141-5
    Shadows of Conrad. New Republic 41:287-8 F 4 '25 1133
Littlehales, Frederick
    Cork fenders and collisions. Daily Express (London) Je
    11 '14 p4 (A letter in response to Conrad's "Protect
    the Ocean Liners")   1134
Lloyd, C. F.
    Joseph Conrad. Canadian Bookman 13:29-32 F '31   1135
Lockwood, Willard A.
    A folio of prints interpreting selected works of Joseph
    Conrad... B. A. Thesis, Wesleyan University, 1945.
    (30 copies only)   1135a
Lodge, David
    Conrad's Victory and The Tempest: an amplification.
    Modern Language Review 59:195-9 Ap '64   1136
Lohman, Mary Margaret
    A critical and historical survey of the stream of con-
    sciousness technique in contemporary fiction. M. A.
    Thesis, Columbia University, 1942. 82p   1137
Łomaczewska, Danuta B.
    Ojciec Conrada w Warszawie. Wiadomości 14, no 31:4
    Ag 2 '59   1137a
Long, Jerome A.
    Conrad's Nostromo: reception, theme, technique. M. A.
    Thesis, Loyola University, 1961   1138
Long, Robert Emmet
    The Great Gatsby and the tradition of Joseph Conrad.
    Texas Studies in Language & Literature 8:257-76 '66
    The Great Gatsby and the tradition of Joseph Conrad.
    Part II. Texas Studies in Language & Literature 8:
    407-22 '66   1139
Looking backward. Joseph Conrad. Evening Post (NY) Ap
    28 '23   1140
Lorch, Thomas M.
    The barrier between youth and maturity in the works of
    Joseph Conrad. Modern Fiction Studies 10:73-80
    Spring '64   1141
Lordi, R. J.
    The three emissaries of evil: their psychological rela-
    tionship in Conrad's Victory. College English 23:136-
    40 N '61   1142
Lorentzen, Renate
    Interpretation der Erzählung "Falk" von Joseph Conrad.
    (Die Entsprechung von Gehalt und Gestalt in J. Conrad's

Lorentzen, Renate (cont.)
    Erzählungen) Ph. D. Dissertation, Kiel University,
    1956. 149p   1143
Love, Evelyn S.
    The brutal gentlemen in Joseph Conrad's Victory, George
    Meredith's The Egoist, and Henry James' The Portrait
    of a Lady. Senior Essay in English, Wells College,
    1957. 33f   1144
Lovett, Robert Morss
    The realm of Conrad. Asia 23:325-7, 377-8 My '23   1145
Lovett, Robert Morss and Hughes, Helen Sard
    Joseph Conrad, (1857-1924). In The history of the novel
    in England. Boston: Houghton Mifflin [c1932] p401-11
    and passim; bibl. , p479   1146
Low, David
    [A caricature of Conrad] New Statesman volume 26, sup-
    plement, F 13 '26; Saturday Review of Literature 31:7
    My 22 '48; same. In Lions and lambs. New York:
    Harcourt, Brace [nd] p25
    (Done originally in Sept. 1923)   1147
Lowther, Frank H.
    Conrad after twenty years. London Quarterly & Holborn
    Review 169:145-52 Ap '44   1148
Łoziński, Jerzy
    Lord Jim i ksiądz Robak. Wiadomości (London) 4, nos
    176-7:3 Ag 21 '49   1149
Lubbock, Basil
    Cover picture. -- "Torrens." Blue Peter 9, no 85:166-9
    Ap '29; same. In Sail, the romance of the clipper
    ships. London: Blue Peter Publishing Co. [August,
    1929] Volume II, p81-7
    The "Loch Etive." In The Colonial clippers. Glasgow:
    James Brown & Son, 1921. p284-6; same. In Sail, the
    romance of the clipper ships. London: Blue Peter
    Publishing Co. [July, 1927] Volume I, p119-20
    (1000 copies only)
    The wonderful "Torrens." In The Colonial clippers. Glas-
    gow: James Brown & Son, 1921. p157-62   1150
Lucas, Edward Verrall
    Joseph Conrad, In Reading, writing, and remembering: a
    literary record. New York: Harper, 1934. p145-50;
    portrait facing p33
    E. V. Lucas to Joseph Conrad. [London: First Edition
    Club, Curwen Press, 1926] [3]p; p[1] has note concern-
    ing meeting of Lucas and Conrad
    (The letters are dated January 10, 1898 and October
    9 [1906]) (220 copies only)

Joseph Conrad: 1904-1924. In The Colvins and their
friends. New York: Scribner's, 1928. p302-11; por-
trait
Post-bag diversions... New York: Harper, 1934.
p1-2   1151
Luddy, Thomas Edmund
Two plays by Joseph Conrad: a matter of form. M. A.
Thesis, Boston College, 1965.   ii, 76f; bibliography,
f75-6
(On One Day More and To-Morrow)   1152
Ludwig, Jack Barry and Poirier, W. Richard
Instructor's manual to accompany "Stories: British and
American." Cambridge, Massachusetts: Houghton Miff-
lin, 1953. p20-4
(On "Heart of Darkness")   1153
Ludwig, Richard M.
The reputation of Ford Madox Ford. Publications of the
Modern Language Association of America 76:544-51
D '61   1154
Luecke, (Sister) Jane Marie
Conrad's secret and its agent. Modern Fiction Studies
10:37-48 Spring '64   1155
Lukacs, Georg
La signification presente du réalisme critique. Paris:
1960. p138   1156
Luma
Ein Meister Europäischer Prosa. Der Deutschen-Spiegel
(Berlin) 6, no 11:431-3 Mr 15 '29   1157
Lütken, Otto
Joseph Conrad in the Congo. London Mercury 22:40-3
My '30; replied to by Mrs. Jessie Conrad in London
Mercury 22:261-3 Jl '30; answered in London Mercury
22:350-1 Ag '30   1158
Lutoslawski, Wincenty
Emigracja zdolności (Emigration of talents). Kraj (Home-
land) (St. Petersburg) no 12, Mr 31 '99; no 14, 1899;
same. In Wspomnienia i studia o Conradzie, edited by
Barbara Kocówna. [Warsaw:] Państwowy Instytut
Wydawniczy [1963] p11-15
Iskierki Warszawskie. Warsaw: Nakładem Księgarni St.
Sadowskiego, 1911. p61-2, 104-5
Odwiedziny u Conrada (A visit with Conrad). Tygodnik
Wileśnki (Wilno Weekly) no 1, 1925
A visit to Conrad in 1897. Blue Peter 10:638-40 D '30
                                                           1159
Luzi, M.
Nota su Conrad. Giornale del Mattino 7:15 '56   1160

Lynd, Robert
    Joseph Conrad. New Statesman 1: literary supplement S
        20 '13 p iii-iv
    Mr. Conrad at home. New Statesman 16:674 Mr 12 '21;
        same. Living Age 309:221-4 Ap 23 '21; same. In
        Books and authors. New York: Putnam's, 1923. p196-
        205
    Mr. Joseph Conrad. In Old and new masters. New
        York: Scribner's, 1919. p212-23   1161
Lyngstad, Sverre
    Time in the modern British novel: Conrad, Woolf, Joyce,
        and Huxley. Ph. D. Thesis, New York University, 1960.
        630p. Abstract in Dissertation Abstracts 27:1374A-
        1375A '66   1162
Lynskey, Winifred
    Conrad's Nostromo. Explicator 13, item 6, October 1954.
    Partial analysis. In Reading modern fiction. New York:
        Scribner's [c1962] 3rd edition, p147-9
        (On Conrad's "The Secret Sharer")
    The role of the silver in Nostromo. Modern Fiction Stud-
        ies 1, no 1:16-21 F '55   1163

M., A. N.
    A bookman's notes: Joseph Conrad. Manchester Guardian
        Weekly 11, no 6:122 Ag 8 '24   1164
M., J.
    Conrad o Polsce. Rozmova z przed dziesięciu lat. (Con-
        rad about Poland. A conversation of ten years ago.)
        Wiadomości Literackie 1, no 6:1 F 10 '24
    Pisarj rejsów niepokojących Józef Konrad Korzeniowski
        (Writer of voyages of unrest.) Dziennik Powszechny
        no 345, 1946   1165
Maas, William
    The author of Chance is a novelist who "looks the whole
        world in the face." New York Herald Ja 19 '12 p5
                                                               1166
McAlmon, Robert
    [An estimate of Conrad's work] Transatlantic Review 2,
        no 3:343-4 O '24   1167
McAlpin, Edwin Augustus
    Lord Jim--the story of a guilty conscience. In Old and
        New books as life teachers. Garden City, New York:
        Doubleday, Doran, 1928. p50-65   1168
McCabe, Joseph (compiler)
    Joseph Conrad. In The biographical dictionary of modern
        rationalists. London: Watts, 1920. p178-9   1169

McCall, Dan
The meaning in darkness: a response to a psychoanalytic
study of Conrad.   College English 29, no 8:620-7 My
'68
(A response to an article by Frederic Crews)   1169a
McCann, Charles John
Conrad's "The Lagoon." Explicator 18, item 3, O '59
Lord Jim vs. the darkness: the saving power of human
involvement.   College English 27:240-3 D '65
Nature imagery in Conrad's novels.   Ph. D. Thesis, Yale
University, June, 1956.   215f; bibliography, f204-15
                                                   1170
McCann, Charles John and Victor Comerchero
Setting as a key to the structure and meaning of Nostromo.
Research Studies (Washington State University) 34:66-
84 Je '66   1171
McCann, (Captain) E. Armitage
My first ship and Joseph Conrad's last.   New York Trib-
une Magazine & Books Mr 9 '24 p9-11 (illustrated)
(On The Torrens)   1172
McCarthy, Desmond
Biography and reminiscence.   Listener 6, no 147:779 N
4 '31
(About a visit with Conrad at Kent)
Conrad.   In Portraits.   New York: Putnam [Nov. 1931]
Volume I, p68-78
Literary causerie: to a distant friend (VIII).   Empire
Review 40:291-9 S '24; same.   (translated by Betty
Colin) Europe (Revue Mensuelle) 6:470-9 D 15 '24   1173
McCarthy, Donald Clemens
Joseph Conrad.   M. A. Thesis, Trinity College (Hartford,
Conn.) 1918.   19f; bibliography f xviii-xix   1174
McClain, John
On the gang-plank.   American (NY) Ap 26 '36   1175
McClurg, Finas Avery
Joseph Conrad, mariner.   M. A. Thesis, East Texas
State College, 1942   1176
McConnell, Daniel J.
"The Heart of Darkness" in T. S. Eliot's "The Hollow
Men. " Texas Studies in Literature and Language 4:141-
53 Summer '62   1177
McConnell, Ruth
The theme of isolation in the work of Joseph Conrad.
M. A. Thesis, University of British Columbia, 1958.
162p   1178
McCorkle, Julia Norton
A study of stylistic departures from the conventional in

McCorkle, Julia Norton (cont.)
  twenty representative British and American novelists
  of the present day (1920-1924). M. A. Thesis, Univer-
  sity of Southern California, 1926. 237p   1179
McCormick, John
  Catastrophe and imagination... London: Longmans, Green,
  1957. p180
  (Conrad's influence on Ernest Hemingway)   1180
McCourt, Edward
  Joseph Conrad. Youth. Conrad's prose style. In Youth,
  a narrative, by Joseph Conrad. Toronto: Ryerson
  Press [c1958] p[3]-8   1181
McCullough, Bruce Welker
  The impressionistic novel. In Representative English
  novelists: Defoe to Conrad. New York: Harper, 1946.
  p336-48   1182
McCune, Samuel James
  A comparison between the style of Joseph Conrad and that
  of W. Somerset Maugham. M. A. Thesis, Louisiana
  State University, 1936   1183
MacDonald, Adrian
  English realism to a Canadian. Canadian Bookman 4,
  no 8:234-5 S '22   1184
MacDonald, Edward J.
  Joseph Conrad. Outlook (London) 54:128 Ag 16 '24 1185
McDonald, Evelyn
  David Copperfield and Lord Jim in the upper school...
  School (Toronto) 20:167-74, 265-9 O-N '31   1186
McDonald, Captain P. A.
  Conrad's "Otago." Sea Breezes ns 5:303 My '48
  Conrad's ships. Sea Breezes ns 15:158-68 Mr '53 (il-
  lustrated)   1187
McDowell, Frederick P. W.
  The most recent books on Joseph Conrad. Papers on
  Language & Literature (Journal of the Midwest Modern
  Language Association) 4, no 2:201-23 Spring '68
  (A review essay)   1187a
McFee, William
  The artist philosopher. In Lord Jim, by Joseph Conrad.
  Garden City, New York: Doubleday, Page, 1922. p vii-
  xviii; same. In Harbours of memory. Garden City,
  New York: Doubleday, Page, 1923. p278-92; same. In
  Youth and two other stories, by Joseph Conrad. (Edu-
  cational Edition) Garden City, New York: Doubleday,
  Page, 1925. p ix-xx
  Conrad after fourteen years. Yale University Library
  Gazette 13:3-15 Jl '38

Conrad's remark.   Sun (NY) N 24 '34
   (A letter to the editor)
Great tales of a great Victorian.   New York Times Book
   Review Ja 1 '22 p1, 22
Introduction.   In Almayer's Folly, by Joseph Conrad.
   (Memorial Edition) Garden City, New York: Doubleday,
   Page, 1925.   Volume I, p vii-ix
Introduction.   In A Conrad argosy... New York: Double-
   day, Doran, 1942. p vii-x
Introduction.   In Tales of land and sea by Joseph Con-
   rad... Garden City, New York: Hanover House [1953]
   p1-5
Joseph Conrad in a new edition.   In Swallowing the anchor.
   Garden City, New York: Doubleday, Page, 1925. p95-
   106
[Mrs. Conrad versus Ford Madox Ford]   Bookman (NY)
   61:500 Je '25
Reviewing books.   In Harbours of memory.   Garden City,
   New York: Doubleday, Page, 1921. p106-11
   (Concerning The Arrow of Gold)
Rolling home.   Saturday Review of Literature 1:89-90 S
   6 '24; same.   In Swallowing the anchor.   Garden City,
   New York: Doubleday, Page, 1925. p107-12
Romance.   In Keating, George T.   A Conrad memorial
   library.   Garden City, New York: Doubleday, Doran,
   1929. p120-7
The sea - and Conrad.   Bookman (NY) 53:102-8 Mr '21
                                                        1188
McGee, Mary Maddalena (Sister)
   An analysis of the voice structure of Conrad's Victory.
   M. A. Thesis, Catholic University of America, 1952.
   71f; bibl. , f70-1   1189
McGoldrick, Rita C.
   The coming of Joseph Conrad.   America 29:136-7 My 26
   '23   1190
Machen, Arthur
   Victory.   In Keating, George T.   A Conrad memorial li-
   brary.   Garden City, New York: Doubleday, Doran,
   1929. p245-9   1191
McIntyre, Allan O.
   Conrad on conscience and the passions.   University Re-
   view (Kansas City, Missouri) 31:69-74 O '64
   Conrad on the functions of the mind.   Modern Language
   Quarterly 25:187-97 Je '64
   Conrad on writing and critics.   Forum (Houston) 4, no
   5:37-42 Fall '64
   Joseph Conrad and the philosophy of illusion. Ph. D.

McIntyre, Allan O. (cont.)
>   Thesis, University of Texas, 1961.   172f.   Abstract
>   in Dissertation Abstracts 22:3649 '62   1192
McKay, Angus
>   The Arrow of Gold.   John O'London's Weekly 12:341,
>   343 N 29 '24   1193
Mackenzie, Compton
>   Joseph Conrad.   In Literature in my time.   London:
>   Rich and Cowan, 1933.   p168-74   1194
Mackenzie, Manfred
>   Fenimore Cooper and Conrad's Suspense.   Notes &
>   Queries ns 10:373-5 O '63   1195
McKie, George MacFarland
>   Studies in the Modern English novel.   (Univ. of North
>   Carolina Extension Bulletin, Volume III, no 10, Feb. 1,
>   1924) Chapel Hill, North Carolina: Univ. of No. Caro-
>   lina press, 1924.   p16-18   1196
McLaren, Jack
>   Books in the South Seas.   T. P.'s & Cassell's Weekly
>   4:448 Jl 25 '25   1197
McLauchlan, Juliet
>   The politics of Nostromo.   Essays in Criticism 17, no
>   3:398-406 Jl '67   1198
McLellan, R. S.
>   Knights of the sea.   Sea Breezes ns 2:73 Jl '46
>   (About Captain David W. Bone)   1199
Maclennan, D. A. C.
>   Conrad's vision.   English Studies in Africa 7:195-201
>   S '64
>   Freudian ideas in three tales by Joseph Conrad.   M. A.
>   Thesis, East Tennessee State University, 1956.   48p
>   1199a
Maclennan, Janet Fraser
>   The philosophy of Joseph Conrad.   M. A.   Thesis, Oberlin
>   College, 1928.   48p   1199b
McManus, C.
>   Mr. Conrad: a coincidence.   Athenaeum Je 5 '15 p509
>   1200
McPherson, Clarance Lowell
>   The narrative method of Joseph Conrad.   M. A.   Thesis,
>   Columbia University, 1925.   21p   1201
MacShane, Frank
>   Conrad collaboration.   In The life and work of Ford Madox
>   Ford.   New York: Horizon Press [1965] p36-54 and
>   passim
>   (Reviewed by John Fraser in Dalhousie Review 45, no
>   4:522-6 Winter '65-'66)

Conrad on Melville. American Literature 29:463-4
    Ja '58
Ford Madox Ford and his contemporaries: the techniques
    of the novel. English Fiction in Transition 4, no 1:2-
    11 '61   1202
Macy, John Albert
    Conrad: master on sea and land. Bookman (NY) 66:
    566-70 Ja '28
A Conrad miscellany. In The critical game. New York:
    Boni and Liveright [c1922] p121-32
Introduction. In Suspense, by Joseph Conrad. (Memorial
    Edition) Garden City, New York: Doubleday, Page,
    1925. Volume XXI, p v-vii
Joseph Conrad. Atlantic Monthly 98:697-702 N '06; same.
    Current Literature 42:58-9 Ja '07; same. In The criti-
    cal game. New York: Boni & Liveright [c1922] p105-
    20
The victorious Victorians. Bookman (NY) 67:547 Jl '28
                                                       1203
Madden, William A.
    The search for forgiveness in some nineteenth-century
    English novels. Comparative Literature Studies (Uni-
    versity of Maryland) 3:139-53 '66
    (Includes Lord Jim)   1204
Majestic leaves for Europe with record passenger list.
    Joseph Conrad returning home among more than 800 in
    cabins. New York Herald Je 3 '23 p14   1205
Majestic took 800 in her first cabin. Joseph Conrad, novel-
    ist of the sea, sails on big liner with praise for
    America. New York Times Je 3 '23 p5, Section I,
    Part 2   1206
Malbone, Raymond Gates
    "How to be:" Marlow's quest in Lord Jim. Twentieth Cen-
    tury Literature 10:172-80 Ja '65   1207
Malewska, Anna
    Jeszcze o heroiźmie (More on Conrad's heroism.) Tygod-
    nik Powszechny (Universal Weekly) no 15, 1945   1208
Malone, Andrew E.
    Joseph Conrad: 1857-1924. Studies (Dublin) 13:457-66
    S '24   1209
Malraux, Clara
    Lord Jim, le solitaire. Confluences, 3rd année, no 19:
    April-May, 1943, p448-50   1210
Mandl, Elly Vetö
    Die Frau bei Joseph Conrad. Budapest: Druckerei der
    Pester Lloyd-Gesellschaft, 1934. Abhandlung, Basel,
    1933. [5]-95p; bibliography, p[94]-95   1211

Manly, John Matthews and Rickert, Edith
    Contemporary British literature... New York: Harcourt,
        Brace, 1921. p42-5; bibliography, p43-5   1212
Mann, Charles William
    Dominant traits in Conrad's characters. M. A. Thesis,
        Pennsylvania State University, 1954. 95p   1213
Mann, Thomas
    Einleitung. In Der Geheimagent, roman von Joseph Con-
        rad. Mit einer einleitung... Translated by Ernst W.
        Freissler. Berlin: S. Fischer [c1926] [first 17
        pages, unnumbered]; same. In Die Forderung des
        Tages... Berlin: S. Fischer, 1930. p325-40; same.
        (translated into English by H. T. Lowe-Porter) In
        Past masters and other papers. New York: Knopf
        [c1933] p229-47; same. In Altes und neues. Frank-
        furt: Fischer, 1953. p493-506; same. In The art of
        Joseph Conrad: a critical symposium, edited by Rob-
        ert Wooster Stallman. East Lansing, Michigan:
        Michigan State University Press, 1960. p227-34
    Joseph Conrad i jego "Tajny Agent." (Translated into
        Polish by Wilam Horzyca) Wiadomości Literackie 4,
        no 11:2 Mr 13 '27   1214
Mansfield, Katherine
    Novels and novelists, edited by J. Middleton Murry.
        New York: Knopf, 1930. p60-4
        (On The Arrow of Gold)   1215
Mansion, J. E.
    Introduction. In The Idiots, by Joseph Conrad. (Bi-
        lingual series) London: Harrap; New York: Brentano's
        [1920] p4-8
        (In English and Spanish)   1216
Manuscript novels. Passing Show (London) Ag 25 '28 p3
    (A note that Mr. Keating has added to his collection of
        Conradiana all the original letters written by Conrad
        to his wife)   1217
[The manuscript of "The Sisters'] Bookman (NY) 66:vi, viii
    Ja '28   1218
Map [scenes of Conrad's stories] In Victory, an island tale,
    by Joseph Conrad. London: Methuen, 1915.   1219
A map illustrating the world of the novels and tales of
    Joseph Conrad. Bookman (NY) 41:128 Ap '15   1220
Marble, Annie Russell
    Joseph Conrad (1857-1924). In A study of the modern
        novel... New York: Appleton, 1928. p5-12; bibliogra-
        phy, p8-9   1221
Marcellini, Giovanni
    Presentazione di Joseph Conrad. Rassegna Italiana series

2, 19:571-4 '27   1222
Marcuse, Ludwig
Den Erzähler Joseph Conrad. Münchener Neue Nachrich-
ten Einkehr 43, June, 1927
Joseph Conrad. Germania, werk 10, Ap '27   1223
Marković, Vida
Đozef Konrad. Savremenik, Beograd 1958, I, 49-52
The emerging character. Northwest Review 8, no 1:80-
97 Summer '66 (On Lord Jim)   1224
Marquet, Jean
Sur les traces de Conrad. Mercure de France 272:444-7
D 1 '36   1225
Marrot, Harold Vincent
The life and letters of John Galsworthy. London &
Toronto: Heinemann [1935] passim   1226
Marsh, D. R. C.
Moral judgments in The Secret Agent. English Studies in
Africa 3:57-70 Mr '60   1227
Marshall, Margery Frances
The significant contributions of Arnold Bennett, John Gals-
worthy, and Joseph Conrad to the English novel.
M. Ed. Thesis, Teachers College of the City of Boston,
1926. xii, 60f; Conrad, f46-60   1228
Martin, Christopher William
Conrad as a delineator of human life. M. A. Thesis,
Catholic University of America, 1926. 35f; bibl., 9f
appended   1229
Martin, David Michael
The development of the idea of self-knowledge in Conrad's
early phase. M. A. Thesis, University of Rhode Island,
1959   1230
Martin, Dorothy
Two aspects of Conrad. Freeman 8:10-12 S 12 '23 1231
Martin, Ernest
Joseph Conrad, romancier de la mer. Les Langues
Modernes 42:233-48 My-Jl '48   1232
Martin, Sister M.
Conrad's "Typhoon." Explicator 18, item 57, June, 1960
Development of symbol: two exercises from Conrad's
"Heart of Darkness." Exercise Exchange 9:7-9 N '61
1233
Martin, W. R.
The captain of the Narcissus. English Studies in Africa
6:191-7 S '63
Allegory in Conrad's The Rover. English Studies in
Africa 10:186-94 S '67   1234

Maryskova, K.
　Personal experience and its literary expression in Joseph
　　Conrad's "Youth." 1961. Philologie I. Prague Studies
　　in English IX. Acta Universitatis Carolinae.　　1235
Masback, Frederic J.
　Conrad's Jonahs.　College English 22:328-33 F '61　　1236
Masefield tells of old sailing days.　New York Times N 4
　　'26 p11　　　　　　　　　　　　　　　　　　　　　1237
Maser, Frederick E.
　A collection of the books of Joseph Conrad.　Temple Uni-
　　versity Library Bulletin volume 2, no 2:[1]-21 My '57
　The philosophy of Joseph Conrad.　Hibbert Journal 56:
　　69-78 O '57　　　　　　　　　　　　　　　　　　　1238
Mason, John Edward
　Joseph Conrad.　Illustrated by C. R. Fisk.　(Makers of
　　literature, no. 3) Exeter:　A. Wheaton, 1938. 48p
　　　　　　　　　　　　　　　　　　　　　　　　　　　1239
Mason, Louise Marie
　Aspects of Joseph Conrad's art.　M. A. Thesis, Mills
　　College, 1935　　　　　　　　　　　　　　　　　　1240
Massey, B. W. A.
　Conrad i Melville jako piewcy morza.　Kurjer Poznański
　　no 598, 1931　　　　　　　　　　　　　　　　　　1240a
A master dies.　Independent 113:110-11 Ag 16 '24　　1241
A master makes mistakes [refers to a sentence in Conrad's
　　The Arrow of Gold] New York Times Ap 18 '19 p12
　　　　　　　　　　　　　　　　　　　　　　　　　　　1242
Matlaw, Ralph
　Dostoevsky and Conrad's political novels.　In American
　　contributions to the Fifth International Congress of
　　Slavists.　Sofia, Sept. 1963.　The Hague:　Mouton,
　　1963.　Volume II, p213-31　　　　　　　　　　　1242a
[Matysik, Stanisław] Mat., St.
　Jozef Conrad Korzeniowski.　Glos Demokratyczny (Demo-
　　cratic Voice) no 22, 1946　　　　　　　　　　　1243
Maud, Ralph
　The plain tale of "Heart of Darkness." Humanities Associ-
　　ation Bulletin 17, no 2:13-17 Autumn '66　　　1243a
Maurice, Furnley
　Old ships (To Joseph Conrad); poem.　Spectator 101:734-5
　　N 7 '08　　　　　　　　　　　　　　　　　　　　1244
Maurois, André
　Les écrivains anglais contemporains.　La Revue Hebdo-
　　madaire 31st année no 14:52-70; no 15:154-66 Ap 6,
　　13 '35
　Joseph Conrad.　In Magiciens et logiciens... Paris:
　　Éditions Grasset [c1935] p177-213; same.　In Prophets

and poets, translated by Hamish Miles. New York &
London: Harper, 1935. p175-211; portrait facing p182
(Reviewed by Geoffrey Hellman in New Republic 86:25
F 12 '36)
En marge des marées. La Nouvelle Revue Francaise
    23:708-12 D 1 '24   1245
Maxwell, J. C.
Conrad: a misdated letter. Notes & Queries 202:314-15
    Jl '57; see also 203:89
    (Refers to Conrad's letter to Spiridion Kliszczewski,
    in G. J. -Aubry's Joseph Conrad, Life and Letters,
    Volume I, p273-4)
Conrad and Turgenev: a minor source for Victory. Notes
    & Queries ns 10:372-3 O '63   1246
Maxwell, Perriton
A first meeting with Joseph Conrad. New York Herald &
    New York Tribune Magazine - Fiction - Books Ag 24
    '24 p1
Turning down Conrad. Sun (NY) D 4 '36 p32
    (As editor of Nash's Magazine (London) Maxwell had
    rejected Conrad's articles on the sinking of the Titanic.
    Includes one sentence from a Conrad letter to Max-
    well.)   1247
May, Nell Altizer
Conrad, Malraux, Lowry; the journey into the interior.
    M. A. Thesis, Emory University, 1962. 83f; bibliogra-
    phy, f82-3 (On Conrad's "Heart of Darkness")   1248
Mayne, Ethel Coburn
[Conrad's death] Transatlantic Review 2, no 3:345-7
    O '24   1249
Mayoux, Jean-Jacques
Joseph Conrad: l'enfer des consciences. Les Lettres
    Nouvelles no 57:222-36 F '58
Joseph Conrad: l'homme et sa liberté. Les Lettres
    Nouvelles no 56:15-34 Ja '58
Joseph Conrad (translated by Anna Iwaszkiewicz). Twór-
    czość 17, no 4:73-100 Ap '61   1250
Mazzotti, Giuliana
Sul 'metodo inversivo' di Joseph Conrad. Rivista di
    Letterature Moderne e Comparate 10:142-6 Ap-Je
    '57   1251
The meaning of Conrad. New Republic 39:341-2 Ag 20
    '24   1252
Medallion-portrait and panel in the Conrad Memorial Porch,
    Village Hall, Bishopsbourne, Kent, unveiled by R. B.
    Cunningham Grahame in October, 1927. The wood
    carved out of ship's teak by Miss Dora Clarke. Book-

Medallion-portrait (cont.)
    mark (London) 3, no 12: supplement, N '27; same.
    Schoolmaster & Woman Teacher's Chronicle 113, no
    973, new series, 1 F 2 '28   1253
Medanić, Lav
    [Conrad] Savremenik 27:829-40 '38   1253a
Mee, Arthur
    [An interview with Conrad] Western Mail (Cardiff)
    Ja 1 '97   1253b
Meeting Conrad at the ship. Literary Digest 77:27-8 My
    19 '23   1254
Mégroz, Rodolphe Louis
    Books and their authors. Joseph Conrad. Hindustan Re-
    view 48:256-7 Ap '25
    Conrad's craftsmanship. This Quarter (Paris) 4, no 1:
    130-40 Jl-S '31
    Joseph Conrad and Poland. Chambers's Journal series
    8, Volume 9:342-5 My '40
    Joseph Conrad before breakfast... T. P.'s & Cassell's
    Weekly 5:680 Mr 6 '26
    Joseph Conrad: man and artist. Bookman (London) 70:
    238-41 Ag '26
    Joseph Conrad's mind and method; a study of personality
    in art. London: Faber & Faber [1931] 7-269p; biblio-
    graphical list of Conrad's works, p249-56; Conradiana,
    p257-62
    .... New York: Russell & Russell,
    1964. 2nd edition; 5-269p
    (Reviewed in Spectator 147:579 O 31 '31; Saturday Re-
    view 152:819 D 26 '31; Times Literary Supplement N
    5 '31 p865; Geoffrey West in Bookman (London) 81:120
    N '31; noted in Publishers' Circular & Booksellers'
    Record 135:121 Ag 1 '31; R. Kreemers in Boekzaal
    no 21:333-4 N 1 '31)
    The personality of Joseph Conrad. Review of Reviews
    (London) 68:120-2 S '23
    A talk with Joseph Conrad and a criticism of his mind
    and method. London: Elkin Mathews, 1926. 9-95p
    (Reviewed in Times Literary Supplement N 11 '26 p801;
    Osbert Burdett, in London Mercury 15:437 F '27)
    Un entretien avec Joseph Conrad. Translated by Jeanne
    Bourret. Revue Hebdomadaire 8:416-37 Ag 27 '27
                                                       1255
Meixner, John A.
    Ford Madox Ford's novels: a critical study. Minneapolis,
    Minnesota: University of Minnesota press [c1962]
    p27-39   1256

Mélisson-Dubreil, Marie-Rose
   La personnalité de Joseph Conrad. Paris: Impr. de
   Maurice Lavergne, 1943. 7-392p; bibliography p381-7;
   Dissertation, University of Paris, 1943
   Le vocabulaire maritime de Joseph Conrad. Paris:
   Impr. de Maurice Lavergne, 1943. 3-214p; bibliogra-
   phy, p[205]-8   1257
Mellor, Ann P.
   Interpretations of evil in Gulliver's Travels, "Heart of
   Darkness," Lord of the Flies. Senior Essay in Eng-
   lish, Wells College, 1965. f16-29   1257a
Meloney, (Mrs.) William Brown)
   [Notes on Mr. and Mrs. Conrad] Delineator 101, no 1:11
   Ag '22   1258
Mencken, Henry Louis
   [Anything but novels [a review of Theodore Dreiser's A
   Traveler at Forty]] Smart Set 42, no 2:154 F '14
   Command, by William McFee. Smart Set 70, no 2:138-9
   F '23
   [A comparison of E. Bjorkman and Conrad] Smart Set 41,
   no 3:158 N '13
   Conrad. In Prejudices: fifth series. New York: Knopf
   [c1926] p34-41; same. In Selected prejudices. New
   York: Knopf, 1927. p37-45; same. In A Mencken
   chrestomathy. New York: Knopf, 1949. p518-22
   Conrad again. Smart Set 48:305-6 Ja '16; same. New
   Age ns 18:277 Ja 20 '16
   Conrad revisited. Smart Set 69, no 4:141-4 D '22; same.
   Paragone 11, no 124:76-81 Ap '60 (translated into
   Italian by Claudio Gorlier)
   [Conrad's method of presenting the story through a nar-
   rator-onlooker] Smart Set 60, no 3:139-40 N '19
   The further side of silence. Smart Set 51, no 1:268 Ja
   '17
   Joseph Conrad. Nation (NY) 119:179 Ag 20 '24
   Joseph Conrad. In A Book of prefaces. [opus 13] New
   York: Knopf [c1917] p11-64
   The Lost World, by A. Conan Doyle. Smart Set 39, no
   1:158 Ja '13   1259
   Mencken o Conradzie. Wiadomości 14, no 39:6 S 27 '59
                                                             1259a
Mendilow, Adam Abraham
   Time and the novel. London & New York: Peter Nevill
   [1952] passim Thesis, University of London   1260
Mentch, Bruce L.
   Conrad and the ironic spirit. M. A. Thesis, Trinity Col-
   lege (Hartford, Conn.), 1962. 67f; bibl., f64-7

Mentch, Bruce L. (cont.)
   (Treats The Secret Agent, Under Western Eyes, &
   "Heart of Darkness")   1261
Mérédac, Savinien
   Joseph Conrad chez nous.   Le Radical (Port-Louis)
   Ag 7 '31
   Joseph Conrad et nous.   L'Esor, Revue du Cercle Lit-
   téraire de Port Louis F 15 '31   1262
Meredith, Floyd
   Max Adeler.   New York Evening Post My 12 '23 p10
   (In Christopher Morley's column, "Bowling Green")
                                                            1263
Meredith, Mark
   Joseph Conrad.   Book News Monthly 34:431 Jl '17   1264
Merrick, Addison Hoyt
   Conrad and the true lie: the role of women in the politi-
   cal novels and Chance.   Ph. D. Thesis, Harvard Uni-
   versity, 1967.   155f   1265
Merrill, Flora
   Joseph Conrad's characters really lived... Sunday Eagle
   Magazine (of the Brooklyn Daily Eagle) Ag 24 '24 p8;
   portrait   1266
Merrix, Robert P.
   Joseph Conrad's portrait of Marlow.   M. A. Thesis, But-
   ler University, 1960.   73f (On "Youth," "Heart of Dark-
   ness," Lord Jim, Chance)   1266a
Messenger, William Edmund
   Historical background, sources and composition of Joseph
   Conrad's The Secret Agent, with a general interpreta-
   tion of the novel and its meaning.   M. A. Thesis,
   Cornell University, 1959. v, 104f   1267
Methods in fiction.   New York Times Book Review Ja 6 '18
   p4 (How Joseph Conrad wrote Lord Jim)   1268
Meyer, Bernard C.
   Conrad's duel.   Polish Review 8, no 3:46-60 Summer '63
   Death was the fate of his heroes.   Columbia University
   Forum 7, no 3:14-19 Summer '64
   Joseph Conrad: a psychoanalytic biography.   Princeton,
   New Jersey: Princeton University press, 1967. vii-
   [x], 396p; bibliography, p363-84; 9 drawings by Conrad
   and one photograph of him, between p326-7
   (Reviewed by Stanley Weintraub in Saturday Review 50,
   no 23:37-8 Je 10 '67; Calvin Bedient in Hudson Review
   20, no 3:526 Autumn '67; Edgar F. Harden in Victorian
   Studies 11, no 3:421-2 Mr '68; Edward Said in Journal
   of English & Germanic Philology 67, no 1:174-8 Ja
   '68)

Psychoanalytic studies of Joseph Conrad: I. The family
romance. Journal of the American Psychoanalytic
Association 12, no 1:32-58 Ja '64
Psychoanalytic studies of Joseph Conrad: II. Fetishism.
Journal of the American Psychoanalytic Association 12,
no 2:357-91 Ap '64   1269
Michael, George
The big five. London: Library of Fighting Poland [1944]
p18-23   1270
Michael, Marion Cicero
Joseph Conrad: a textual and literary study of four stor-
ies. Ph. D. Thesis, University of Georgia, 1963. vi,
129f; bibl., f119-129. Abstract in Dissertation Ab-
stracts 26:2756 '65
(Examines Almayer's Folly, The Nigger of the 'Narcis-
sus, "Heart of Darkness," and The Secret Agent) 1271
Michael, Nancy Carolyn
Demonic myth in Conrad's "Heart of Darkness." Master's
Thesis, University of Virginia, 1965. 27f   1272
Michałowicz, M.
Ambasador po śmierci (Ambassador after death). Kurier
Codzienny (Daily Courier) no 72, 1945   1273
Michel, Lois A.
The absurd predicament in Conrad's political novels.
College English 23:131-6 N '61   1274
Middleton, A. Safroni
See: Safroni-Middleton, A.   1275
Mille, Pierre
Why Conrad did not write in French. Les Nouvelles
Littéraires année 4:1 Ja 17 '25; same. Living Age
324:622-3 Mr 14 '25; same. (excerpt) Literary Digest
85:28-9 My 23 '25; noted in Wiadomości Literackie 2,
no 5:3 F 1 '25   1276
Miller, J. Hillis
The anonymous walkers. Nation (NY) 190, no 17:351-4
Ap 23 '60 (On The Secret Agent)
Joseph Conrad. I. The darkness. II. The Secret Agent.
In Poets of reality: six twentieth-century writers.
Cambridge, Massachusetts: Belknap Press of Harvard
University Press, 1965. p13-67
Some implications of form in Victorian fiction. Compara-
tive Literature Studies 3, no 2:109-18 '66   1277
Miller, James E. Jr.
The Nigger of the 'Narcissus': a re-examination. Publi-
cations of the Modern Language Association of America
66:911-18 D '51   1278

Miller, James E. Jr. and Bernice Slote
"Youth." In Notes for teaching The Dimensions of the
    Short Story... New York: Dodd, Mead, 1964. p17-18
                                                        1279
Miller, Jan Nepomucen
Klasow oblicze "Losu" Józefa Conrada.   Kamena nos 10,
    12:7, 9 '58
Słów kilka o Josephie Conradzie i o godności narodowej
    tu i tam (A few words about Joseph Conrad and about
    national dignity here and there). Kurier Polski no 232,
    1924   1280

Miller, Marjorie Eileen
Joseph Conrad's attitude toward women in his novels.
    B. A. Thesis, Univ. of Illinois, 1950. 54f   1281
Miller, Walter James
Reader's supplement. In Lord Jim. (Reader's enrich-
    ment series) New York: Washington Square Press
    [1966] [appendix of 54p]   1281a
Millett, Fred B.
Joseph Conrad. In Contemporary British literature...
    New York: Harcourt, Brace, 1935. p30-2, 177-8; bibli-
    ography, p178-83
Reading fiction. New York: Harper's, 1950. p175-7
    (On "The Lagoon")   1282
Mills, (Helen) Beatrice
Conrad's use of the people he knew as the basis of his
    characters, illustrated by his use of Dominic Cervoni.
    M. A. Thesis, Boston University, 1941. 113f   1283
Milne, James
A posthumous call for the writings of Joseph Conrad.
    Graphic 110:258 Ag 16 '24   1284
[Milner, (Mrs.) Florence (Cushman)]
[A scrapbook of Conrad items, publicity notices, etc.]
    At the Harvard University Library   1285
Miłosz, Czesław
Apollo Nałęcz Korzeniowski. Kultura (Paris) no 100:60-
    80 F '56
Conrad's political stereotype. In Conrad żywy, edited by
    Wit Tarnawski. London: B. Świderski, 1957. p92-9
Joseph Conrad in Polish eyes. Atlantic Monthly 200:219-
    28 N '57; same. In The art of Joseph Conrad: a criti-
    cal symposium, edited by Robert Wooster Stallman.
    East Lansing, Michigan: Michigan State University
    press, 1960. p35-45   1286
Mirande, R.
Joseph Conrad, curieux homme. Annales Politiques et

Littéraires 106:368-70 O 10 '35   1287
Mirrielees, Edith
    Those college writing courses.   Saturday Review of Litera-
        ture 17:4 Ja 15 '38   1288
Mr. Conrad and his interviewers.   Manchester Guardian
        Weekly 8, no 20:397 My 18 '23   1289
Mr. Conrad's collaboration.   Bookman (NY) 19:544 Ag
        '04   (With Hueffer on Romance.   Somewhat of a de-
        fense of Hueffer)   1290
Mr. Joseph Conrad.   Academy 55:82-3 O 15 '98; Bookman
        (London) 10:41 My '96; Book Monthly 12:287 F '15   1291
Mr. Joseph Conrad and Tales of Unrest.   Academy 56:66-7
        Ja 14 '99
        (Conrad receives an award of 50 guineas from The
        Academy)   1292
Mr. Joseph Conrad... is not English.   Literary News (NY)
        ns 23:156 My '02   1293
Mr. Joseph Conrad leaves £20,045.   Westminster Gazette
        N 17 '24 p7   1294a
[Mr. Joseph Conrad, the novelist] Daily Mail (London) '01;
Mr. Joseph Conrad leaves £20,000.   Observer (London) N 16
        '24 p7   1294
        same. NY Trib. Ill. Supplement Ag 25 '01 p11   1295
Mrs. Conrad, author's wife, dies in England.   New York
        Herald Tribune D 7 '36 p14   1296
Mrs. Conrad dies, widow of author.   New York Times D 7
        '36 p23 (She died on Conrad's birthday, Dec 6)   1297
Mrs. Joseph Conrad.   Widow of noted writer.   Daily News
        (NY) D 7 '36   1298
Mitchell, Sidney Hammond
    Conrad and his critics, 1895-1914.   Ph. D. Thesis, Uni-
        versity of Virginia, 1962.   355ff; bibliographies, ff321-
        53; abstract in Dissertation Abstracts 23:2917 '63
    Ideals and illusions in Conrad's short stories.   M. A.
        Thesis, University of Virginia, 1952.   78p   1299
Mitiguy, Arthur Andrew
    Joseph Conrad; romanticist.   B. A. Thesis, University of
        Notre Dame, 1928.   20p   1299a
Miyazaki, Koichi
    Conrad's novels.   Tokyo: Tarumishobo, 1962.   260p   1300
Mizener, Arthur
    Ford and Conrad.   New York Times Book Review F 16
        '64 p33   1301
Mleczko, Stanisław
    Ojczyzna Conrada (Conrad's native land).   Nowy Kurier
        Polski nos 207, 209, Ag 29, Ag 31 '36   1302

Mlynarska, Maria
Conrad's position among Polish people at home and abroad.
In Conrad żywy, edited by Wit Tarnawski. London:
B. Świderski, 1957. p262-6   1303
Moczulski, M. B.
Conrad's position among Polish people at home and abroad.
In Conrad żywy, edited by Wit Tarnawski. London:
B. Świderski, 1957. p272-5   1304
Moffat, Donald
On salt water. In The prejudices of Mr. Pennyfeather.
Boston: Little, Brown, 1938. p244-74   1305
Molski, Zbigniew
Conrad Korzeniowski w oczach Anglików (Conrad in Eng-
lish eyes). Odnowa (Renewal) no 31, 1946   1306
Monk, D. E.
A study of selected novels by James and Conrad as evi-
denced in their literary theory and exemplified in these
selected novels by each of them. M. A. Thesis, Uni-
versity of Manchester, 1959   1307
Monro, Charles Bedell
Description in Conrad. 53f. M. A. Thesis, University of
Pittsburgh, 1926   1308
Monroe, N. Elizabeth
The novel and society... Chapel Hill, North Carolina:
University of North Carolina Press, 1941. p169-70
1309
Monsarrat, Nicholas
Introduction. In Lord Jim, a tale by Joseph Conrad...
New York: Printed for members of the Limited Edi-
tions Club, 1959. pvii-[xi]
Introduction. In Lord Jim... New York: Heritage Press
[1960, c1959] p vii-[xi]   1310
Moore, Carlisle
Conrad and the novel as ordeal. Philological Quarterly
42:55-74 Ja '63   1311
Moore, Edward
A note on Mr. Conrad. New Statesman 13:590-2 S 13
'19; same. Current Opinion 67:320-1 D '19; same.
Living Age 304:101-4 Ja 10 '20; same. (excerpt) New
York Herald Tribune O 26 '19   1312
Moorthy, P. Rama
The Nigger of the 'Narcissus.' Literary Criticism (Uni-
versity of Mysore, India) 7, no 1:49-58 '65   1313
Moran, Bernice Amelia
The tragedy in the novels and stories of Joseph Conrad.
M. A. Thesis, Ohio State University, 1932. 125p   1314
More about Conrad. New York Evening Post Literary Re-

view Ag 30 '24 p8 (Signed "G. E. W. '") 1315
Moreines, Harvey
A 'new' novel. Joseph Conrad's "Heart of Darkness:" a
study of image and structure. M. A. Thesis, University of Maryland, 1962. 145f; bibliography f140-5 1316
Morel, Edmund Dene
King Leopold's rule in Africa. New York: Funk & Wagnalls, 1905. p117 (Conrad letter to a friend on the custom of cutting off hands of natives) 1317
Morey, Elizabeth Kind
A study of the themes of four English novels. M. A. Thesis, Columbia University, 1923. 145p 1318
Morey, John Hope
Joseph Conrad and Ford Madox Ford: a study in collaboration. Ph. D. Thesis, Cornell University, 1960. 322p; abstract in Dissertation Abstracts 21:1568 '60
Joseph Conrad and the milieu of man. M. A. Thesis, Cornell University, 1955. vi, 115f 1319
Morf, Gustav
Joseph Conrad - ein Schweizer? Neue Zürche Zeitung no 1209, 1929
The Polish heritage of Joseph Conrad. London: Sampson, Low, Marston & Co. [nd 1930] [iii-vi], 248p; bibliography, p241-3; portraits. Published in America: New York: Smith [1930]
(Reviewed in Times Literary Supplement Mr 27 '30 p268; Rodolphe L. Mégroz in Bookman (London) 78:56-7 Ap '30; Harry Hansen in Harper's Magazine F '31 advertising pages; Henry L. Mencken in American Mercury 23:251-3 Je '31; Richard Curle in Saturday Review of Literature 7:879 Je 6 '31; Charles Phillips in Commonweal 14:82-3 My 20 '31; W. Fischer in Literaturblatt für Germanische und Romanische Philologie 51:2429-31 '30; Alan R. Thompson in Bookman (NY) 72:657-9 F '31; R. L. Mégroz in Christian Science Monitor My 10 '30 p15; Cleveland Open Shelf D '31 p156; Eleuter in Wiadomości Literackie 7, no 22:2 Je 1 '30; Julian Krzyżanowski in Przegląd Współczesny rok 9, tome 33:314-17, no 97 My '30; W. Chwalewik in Slavonic Review 10, no 28:217-18 Je '31; W. Chwalewik in Ruch Literacki 7, no 8:250-2 Ag '32; A. Bronarski in Illustrowany Kurjer Codzienny no 179, 1930; Z. Dębicki in Kurjer Warszawska no 159, 1930; Ludwik Krzyżanowski in Czas, 1932; S. L. in Droga no 5, 1930)
Ueber den symbolismus in Conrads Werken. Psychologische Rundschau 2:356-61 Mr '31; same. Pologne Littéraire 5th année, no 54:1 Mr 15 '31; same. (trans-

Morf, Gustav (cont.)
    lated with the title: "Conrad and Cowardice") Living
      Age 340:571-6 Ag '31   1320
Morgan, Gerald
    Joseph Conrad and the sea. M. A. Thesis, University of
      Montreal, 1959. 106f
    Sea symbol and myth in the works of Joseph Conrad.
      Ph. D. Thesis, University of Montreal, 1962. 250f;
      bibliography f237-48   1320a
Morgan, Gerould
    Captain Korzeniowski's "Prince Roman:" nautical allusion
      in Conrad's patriotic tale. Études Slaves et Est-
      Européennes 4:49-57 Spring-Summer '59
    Conrad, Madach et Calderon. Études Slaves et Est-
      Européennes 6:196-209 Autumn-Winter '61
    Narcissus afloat. Humanities Association Bulletin
      (Canada) 15, no 2:45-57 Autumn '64   1321
Morgan, Joseph Theodore
    The philosophy of Joseph Conrad. M. A. Thesis, Ohio
      State University, 1931. 59p; abstract in Ohio State
      University Graduate School Abstracts of Masters' Es-
      says 5:102-3 '31   1322
Morley, Christopher Darlington [Ben Gun, pseud.]
    Ballade of books unbought. Life 77:902 Je 23 '21
    The Bowling Green. New York Evening Post My 24 '23
      p8
    The Bowling Green. The Master. New York Evening
      Post Ap 28 '23 p10
    Conrad and Stevenson. Catholic World 135:472-3 '32;
      same. In Ex libris carissimis. Philadelphia: Univer-
      sity of Pennsylvania Press, 1932. p41-4
    Conrad and the reporters. New York Evening Post My 3
      '23 p8; My 4 '23 p10; My 5 '23 p10; My 7 '23 p8; My
      10 '23 p8; same published separately: Garden City,
      New York: Doubleday, Page, 1923. 63p; portrait
      (815 copies only, presented to bookseller friends only
      ...from the author and the publishers)
    Escaped into print. In Ex libris carissimis. Philadel-
      phia: University of Pennsylvania press, 1932. p49-64
    The folder. Saturday Review of Literature 10:55 Ag 19
      '33
    Granules from an hour-glass. Saturday Review of Litera-
      ture 10:727 Je 2 '34
    Granules from an hour-glass. The longest parenthesis.
      Saturday Review of Literature 5:997 My 11 '29
      (On Chance)
    Introduction. In 'Twixt Land and Sea, by Joseph Conrad.

(Memorial Edition) Garden City, New York: Doubleday,
   Page, 1925. Volume XIII, p vii-xi
Inward Ho! Garden City, New York: Doubleday, Page,
   1923.
   (Dedicated: "To Joseph Conrad: A Novelist Who Un-
   derstands As Poets Do")
[Joseph Conrad, by an old shipmate]   Sydney Bulletin
   '27; same. In Internal revenue. Garden City, New
   York: Doubleday, Doran, 1933. p192-3
A new estimate of a great novelist. New York Times
   Book Review Ag 14 '49 p1, 15
The Nigger of the 'Narcissus.'   In Keating, George T.
   A Conrad memorial library. Garden City, New York:
   Doubleday, Doran, 1929. p28-31; same. In Internal
   revenue. Garden City, New York: Doubleday, Doran,
   1933. p196-9 (as the 5th part of "Temperamental
   writing")
A note on Conrad. Saturday Revuew of Literature 4:
   519 Ja 14 '28
Old books beat baseball. New York Evening Post
   Nov. 15 '23); same. (excerpt) Springfield Republican
   D 9 '23 p7 A
   (Discusses prices of Conrad's ms. sold at the Ander-
   son Galleries)
The ship "Tusitala."   New York Evening Post My 14 '23
   p8
The skipper. In Shandygaff... Garden City, New York:
   Doubleday, Doran [c1918] p238-45
Storms and calms. Saturday Review of Literature 1, no
   39:707 Ap 25 '25; same. In Essays. Garden City,
   New York: Doubleday, Doran, 1928. p1066-71; same.
   In The Romany stain. Garden City, New York:
   Doubleday, Page, 1926. p218-22; same. In Morley's
   variety... (Forum books) New York: World publishing
   co. [1944] p565-7
The strangest cruise. New York Evening Post Ap 26
   '23 p8
"Temperamental writing." In Internal revenue. Garden
   City, New York: Doubleday, Doran, 1933. p185-99
Two enthusiasms. Atlantic Monthly 149:403-6 Ap '32
   (Stevenson and Conrad)
A word about Joseph Conrad. Mentor 13:24-6 Mr '25
                                                     1323
Morley sets sail with Conrad relic. New York Times Ag
   20 '49 (The wheel of the Otago)   1323a
Morrell, (Lady) Ottoline
   Joseph Conrad: an impression. Nation (London) 35:666

Morrell, (Lady) Ottoline (cont.)
  Ag 30 '24
  Memoirs of Lady Ottoline Morrell, a study in friendship,
    1873-1915. Edited by Robert Gathorne-Hardy. New
    York: Knopf, 1964. p232-9   1324
Morris, [Lena] Antoinette
  Joseph Conrad: his literary inheritance. M. A. Thesis,
    Univ. of Texas, 1940. iii-vii, 81f   1325
Morris, Maurice
  To Joseph Conrad; poem. New York Herald My 3 '23
    p8; same. Book Leaf (NY) My 4 '23   1326
Morris, Robert
  Barron's simplified approach to Lord Jim; Joseph Conrad.
    Woodbury, New York: Barron's Educational Series
    [1966] [vii-x], 187p   1327
Morris, Robert L.
  The classical reference in Conrad's fiction. College Eng-
    lish 7:312-18 Mr '46
  Eliot's "Game of Chess" and Conrad's "The Return."
    Modern Language Notes 65:422-3 Je '50   1328
Morrison, R.
  Last of the Otago. Blackwood's Magazine 290:416-19
    N '61   1329
Mort de Joseph Conrad. Mercure de France (series
    moderne) 174:282-3 Ag 15 '24   1330
Moscrop, S. F.
  Introduction. In Four stories by Joseph Conrad, edited
    by S. F. Moscrop. London: Dent [1926] p7-16   1331
Moseley, Edwin M.
  Christ as tragic hero: Conrad's Lord Jim. In Pseudo-
    nyms of Christ in the modern novel: motifs and
    methods. Pittsburgh: University of Pittsburgh press,
    1963. p15-35   1332
Moser, Thomas Colborn
  Afterword. In An outcast of the islands, by Joseph Con-
    rad. [New York:] New American Library [c1964]
    p275-84
  Joseph Conrad: achievement and decline. Cambridge,
    Massachusetts: Harvard University Press, 1957. viii,
    227p. Reprinted with minor corrections: Hamden,
    Connecticut: Archon Books, 1966. Part reprinted in:
    Conrad. A collection of critical essays, edited by
    Marvin Mudrick. Englewood Cliffs, New Jersey:
    Prentice-Hall, Inc. [1966] p145-65
    (Dated 1957 unless otherwise noted. Reviewed by Ed-
    ward Wagenknecht in Chicago Sunday Tribune Jl 28 p2;
    Edward Wagenknecht in Christian Science Monitor Jl 18

p5; J. R. Willingham in Library Journal 82:1673 Je 15;
Bruce Harkness in Journal of English and Germanic
Philology 57:358-64 '58; John Bayley in National &
English Review 150:72-3 F '58; W. M. Blackburn in
South Atlantic Quarterly 57:141-2 Winter '57-'58;
noted in Nineteenth-Century Fiction 12:254 D; Pál
Vámosi in Filológiai Közlöny 9:287-90 '63; Times Literary Supplement N 29 p723; Jocelyn Baines in Spectator
199:583 N 1; Richard M. Ludwig in College English 19:
281 Mr '58; David Daiches in New York Times Book
Review Je 30 p5; Adam Gillon in Dalhousie Review
38, no 4:533-7 Winter '59; Wiadomości 12, no 51-2:
29 D 22-29 '57; Vernon Young in Southwest Review
43:80-1 Winter '58; Leo Gurko in American Scholar
27:128-30 Winter '57-'58; Madeleine M. Cazamian in
Études Anglaises 13:66-7 Ja-Mr '60; Charles Barber
in Modern Language Review 54:301-2 Ap '59; M. C.
Bradbrook in Review of English Studies ns 10:209-11
My '59; R. W. Stallman in Sewanee Review 67:135-45
Winter '59; New Yorker 33, no 29:154 S 7; Listener
59, no 1504:169 Ja 23 '58)
Joseph Conrad's surrender: some sources and character-
istics of the decline of his creative powers. Ph. D.
Thesis, Harvard University, May 1955. ix, 487f; list
of works cited, f406-8
Pleasure of creative surprise. Nation 190:386-8 Ap 30
'60
The 'Rescuer' manuscript: a key to Conrad's development
- and decline. Harvard Library Bulletin 10:325-55
Autumn '56
(Noted in Times Literary Supplement F 1 '57 p72) 1333
Moses, Elizabeth Petway
A study of character in the novels of Joseph Conrad.
M. A. Thesis, State College of Washington, 1939. 68p
1334
Moult, Thomas
Joseph Conrad. Bookman (London) 66:301-2, 304 S '24
Joseph Conrad. Quarterly Review 242:247-61 O '24
Joseph Conrad as playwright. Bookman's Journal & Print
Collector 7, no 15:65-6 D '22
The life and work of Joseph Conrad. Yale Review ns 14:
295-308 Ja '25; same. (excerpt) Christian Science
Monitor Ja 21 '25 p9 1335
Mouradian, Jacques
Conrad and Anatole France. Times Literary Supplement
O 30 '30 p890 (Suggests parallel passages in The Ar-
row of Gold and Anatole France's Le Lys Rouge) 1336

Moustafa, Sadik [now Sadik M. Balkan]
    Joseph Conrad. The man behind his art. Master's es-
    say, Lehigh University, 1937. ii, 84ff; bibliography,
    ff83-4   1337
Mowat, Angus McGill
    A critical study of the life, philosophy and art of Joseph
    Conrad. M. A. Thesis, Univ. of Saskatchewan, 1935
                                                              1338
Moynihan, William T.
    Conrad's "The End of the Tether:" a new reading. Modern
    Fiction Studies 4:173-7 Summer '58; same. In The
    art of Joseph Conrad: a critical symposium, edited
    by Robert Wooster Stallman. East Lansing, Michigan:
    Michigan State University press, 1960. p186-91   1339
Mroczkowski, Przemysław
    A glance back at the romantic Conrad: "The Lagoon."
    Polish Review 4, nos 1-2:15-23 Winter-Spring '59;
    same. In Joseph Conrad: centennial essays, edited
    by Ludwig Krzyżanowski. New York: Polish Institute
    of Arts and Sciences in America, 1960. p73-83; same.
    In Wspomnienia i studia o Conradzie, edited by Barbara
    Kócowna. Warsaw: Państwowy Instytut Wydawniczy
    [1963] p457-71
    The gnomic element in Conrad. Kwartalnik Neofilologiczny
    no 3: 193-209 '58; same. In Wspomnienia i studia o
    Conradzie, edited by Barbara Kócowna. Warsaw:
    Państwowy Instytut Wydawniczy [1963] p472-93
    Heart of Darkness revisited. Roczniki Humanistyczne 6,
    no 6:53-93 '57
    A Polish view of Joseph Conrad. Listener 58:979-80 D
    12 '57; portrait
    Tajemnica Lorda Jima. Kwartalnik Neofilologiczny 11,
    no 1:31-49 '64   1340
Mrs. Conrad refuses (editorial). New York Telegram Jl 13
    '25 (She will not permit Conrad's Suspense to be "com-
    pleted")   1340a
Muccigrosso, Robert M.
    Conrad's Lord Jim: teaching the first chapter. English
    Journal 55:1039-41 N '66   1341
Muddiman, Bernard
    The men of the nineties. London: Henry Danielson, 1920.
    passim   1342
Mudrick, Marvin
    The artist's conscience and The Nigger of the 'Narcissus.'
    Nineteenth-Century Fiction 11:288-97 Mr '57
    Conrad and the terms of modern criticism. Hudson Re-
    view 7:419-26 Autumn '54

Introduction. In Conrad. A collection of critical essays,
    edited by Marvin Mudrick. Englewood Cliffs, New
    Jersey: Prentice-Hall, Inc. [1966] p1-11
The originality of Conrad. Hudson Review 11:545-53
    Winter '58-'59; same. In Conrad. A collection of
    critical essays, edited by Marvin Mudrick. (A Spec-
    trum book) Englewood Cliffs, New Jersey: Prentice-
    Hall, Inc. [1966] p37-44
Communication: Mr. Stallman's remarks. Kenyon Re-
    view 19, no 3:483 Summer '57   1343
Mudrick, Marvin (editor)
    Conrad. A collection of critical essays, edited by Marvin
    Mudrick. (A Spectrum book) Englewood Cliffs, New
    Jersey: Prentice-Hall, Inc. [1966] 182p; bibliography,
    p181-2
    (Introduction by Marvin Mudrick, p1-11. Includes
    articles by M. Beerbohm, A. Guerard, Marvin Mud-
    rick, Stephen A. Reid, Douglas Hewitt, Paul L. Wiley,
    Daniel Curley, Jocelyn Baines, E. M. W. Tillyard, M.
    D. Zabel, Thomas Moser, and F. M. Ford)
    (Reviewed by Edgar F. Harden in Victorian Studies 11,
    no 3:421-2 Mr '68; Fred C. Thomson in Studies in
    Short Fiction 5, no 2:198-200 Winter '68)   1344
Muir, Edwin
    A note on Mr. Conrad. In Latitudes. New York:
    Huebsch, 1924. p47-56
    (Reviewed by Henry James Forman in New York Times
    Book Review Ag 31 '24 p11)   1345
Mukherjee, Sujit K.
    Conrad's Lord Jim. Explicator 23, item 42, Ja '65 1346
Müller, E.
    Joseph Conrad und der tragik des Westens. Literatur
    (Stuttgart) 40:161 D '37   1347
Muller, Herbert Joseph
    Joseph Conrad. In Modern fiction: a study of values.
    New York: Funk & Wagnalls, 1937. p244-61   1348
Munro, Neil
    Introduction. In The Nigger of the 'Narcissus,' by Joseph
    Conrad. (Memorial Edition) Garden City, New York:
    Doubleday, Page, 1925. Volume III p vii-x
    Joseph Conrad. In The Encyclopaedia Britannica. Lon-
    don: Encyclopaedia Britannica [c1937] 14th edition,
    volume 6, p278-9
    The Rescue. In Keating, George T. A Conrad memorial
    library. Garden City, New York: Doubleday, Doran,
    1929. p288-93   1349

Muntz, Herbert Eugene
    Conrad's use of autobiographical material in his short
        stories and novels. M. A. Thesis, Ohio State Univer-
        sity, 1930. 83p; abstract in Ohio State University
        Graduate School Abstracts of Masters' Essays 4:178-9
        '30   1350
Murdoch, Walter Logie Forbes
    The Balfour-Conrad question. Three tombstones. In
        Collected essays... London: Angus & Robertson, Ltd.,
        1938. p176-9, 573-5; 267-8; same. In 72 Essays: a
        selection. Sydney, Australia: Angus & Robertson,
        Ltd., 1947. p120-3   1351
Murphy, Daniel J.
    Conrad the novelist. M. A. Thesis, University College of
        Cork, 1949   1352
Murray, Phyllis Marjorie
    The English novel of the sea from Smollett to Conrad.
        M. A. Thesis, McGill University, 1927   1353
Myth of Conrad as Jew exploded by his letter. New York
        Herald Tribune N 7 '25
        (A letter of Conrad to Rabbi Louis Brown of Newark,
        New Jersey, dated c. 1918; see also New Republic 16:
        109 Ag 24 '18 for another Conrad letter on the same
        subject)   1354

Nagler, Herminia
    The call. In Conrad Żywy, edited by Wit Tarnawski.
        London: B. Świderski, 1957. p69-73   1355
Najder, Zdzisław
    Conrad. Twórczość (Creative Work) 11, no 10:143-55 O
        '55; same. In Nad Conradem, by Zdzisław Najder.
        [Warsaw:] Państwowy Instytut Wydawniczy [1965] p[11]-
        45   •
    Conrad a Dostojewski. Życie Literackie no 8, 1963; same.
        In Nad Conradem. [Warsaw:] Państwowy Instytut
        Wydawniczy [1965] p150-170
    Conrad i Bobrowski. Przegląd Humanistyczny 8, no 5:
        [13]-24 '64 (Combines Najder's "Polski lata Conrada"
        and "Conrad w Marsylli")
    Conrad in the Congo. Polish Perspectives 4, no 1:25-33
        Ja '61
    Conrad i teatr. Dialogu no 7, 1958; same. In Nad Con-
        radem. [Warsaw:] Państwowy Instytut Wydawniczy
        [1965] p[204]-212
    Conrad under Polish eyes. Polish Perspectives no 1:37-
        42 My '58   •
    Conrad w Marsylii. Życie Literackie no 40:298 '57 (also

p1-3); same. In Wspomnienia i studia o Conradzie,
edited by Barbara Kocówna. [Warsaw:] Państwowy
Instytut Wydawniczy [1963] p414-26; same. In Nad
Conradem. [Warsaw:] Państwowy Instytut Wydawniczy
[1965] p[46]-69
Conradiana Angielskie i Amerykańskie. Twórczość 13, no
12:182-3 D '57
Conrad's position among Polish people at home and abroad.
In Conrad żywy, edited by Wit Tarnawski. London:
B. Świderski, 1957. p258-61
Człowick-walka-ucieczka (Man-struggle-flight). Dziś i
Jutro (Today and Tomorrow) nos 39-40, 1950
Do kresu nocy. Nowa Kultura no 42:551 '60
Igrazki losu. Twórczość no 12, 1955; same. In Nad
Conradem. [Warsaw:] Państwowy Instytut Wydawniczy
[1965] p[171]-184
Introduction. In Conrad's Polish background. Letters to
and from Polish friends, edited by Zdzisław Najder and
translated by Halina Carroll. London & New York:
Oxford University Press, 1964. v-vii, 313p; Introduc-
tion, p1-31; bibliography, p307-8
Lord Jim. Nowiny Literackie in Wydawnicze no 18, 1957;
same. In Nad Conradem. [Warsaw:] Państwowy Instytut Wydawniczy [1965] p[99]-111
"Malajska trylogia" Conrada. Morze (The Sea) no 12,
1957; same. In Nad Conradem. [Warsaw:] Państwowy
Instytut Wydawniczy [1965] p70-98
Nad Conradem. [Warsaw:] Państwowy Instytut Wydawniczy [1965] 5-234p; preface, p[5]-9; bibliography and
notes, p[223]-234
(Reviewed by Edmund A. Bojarski in English Literature in Transition 9:169-71 '66; Stefan Zabierowski in
Ruch Literacki 7:95-8 Mr-Ap '66)
Nad Conradem (On Conrad). Tygodnik Powszechny (Uni-
versal Weekly) no 10, 1952; same. In Nad Conradem.
[Warsaw:] Państwowy Instytut Wydawniczy [1965]
p[11]-45
Na tropach Conrada. Tygodnik Powszechny 11, no 48:1,
4 D 8 '57; same. In Nad Conradem. [Warsaw:]
Państwowy Instytut Wydawniczy [1965] p[213]-222
O 'filozofii' Conrada. Przegląd Kulturalny no 49:3 D '57;
same. In Nad Conradem. [Warsaw:] Państwowy Insty-
tut Wydawniczy [1965] p[185]-203
Polityka w pismach Conrada. Nowa Kultura no 49:2 '57
Polskie lata Conrada (Conrad's Polish years). Twórczość
12, no 11:137-52 N '56; same. In Nad Conradem.
[Warsaw:] Państwowy Instytut Wydawniczy [1965]

Najder, Zdzisław (cont.)
  p[46]-69
Posłowie. In Wykolejeniec, by Joseph Conrad. [Warsaw:]
  Państwowy Instytut Wydawniczy [1956] p381-[391]
  Trzy pory życia (Three seasons of life). Twórczość 13,
  no 12:63-9 D '57; same. In Nad Conradem [Warsaw:]
  Państwowy Instytut Wydawniczy [1965] p[112]-127   1356
Najder, Zdzisław (editor)
  Conrad's Polish background. Letters to and from Polish
  friends, edited by Zdzisław Najder and translated by
  Halina Carroll. London & New York: Oxford Univer-
  sity press, 1964. v-vii, 313p; introduction, p1-31;
  bibliography, p307-8
  Nad Conradem. [Warsaw:] Państwowy Instytut Wydawn-
  iczy [1965] 5-234p   1357
Najder, Zdzisław and Lord David Cecil
  Joseph Conrad - a recorded discussion between Zdzisław
  Najder and Lord David Cecil. Gemini (London) Jan.
  1960, p3-9   1358
Nalepiński, Tadeusz
  Wspomnienia Conrada (Conrad's reminiscences). Kurier
  Warszawski no 84, Ap 24 '12   1359
Nałkowska, Zofia
  Widzenie bliskie i dalekie. Warsaw: Czyt., 1957. (On
  Dostoievski and Conrad)   1360
Napier, Edna Marwick
  Joseph Conrad's women. M. A. Thesis, Univ. of British
  Columbia, 1920. 65p   1361
Napier, James
  Conrad's praise of Joseph Hergesheimer. Notes &
  Queries ns 6:210 Je '59   1362
Napierski, Stefan
  Z uwag o Josephie Conradzie. Wiadomości Literackie 3,
  no 32:1 Ag 8 '26   1363
Nathan, George Jean
  Why are manuscripts rejected? Bookman (NY) 43:281
  My '16   1364
Navin, Thomas R. Jr.
  French idiom in Conrad. Hika (Kenyon College, Gambier,
  Ohio) 6, no 8:10-11 Je '39   1364a
Nelson, Harland S.
  Eden and Golgotha. Conrad's use of the Bible in The
  Nigger of the 'Narcissus.' Iowa English Yearbook no
  8:63-7 Fall '63   1365
Nelson, Kenneth G.
  Irony in Joseph Conrad's early novels. M. A. Thesis,
  Northern Illinois University, 1961   1366

Nelson, Mary Kristin
    Moby Dick and Lord Jim: a study in similarities. M. A.
        in Teaching Thesis, Brown University, 1962. iii, 91f;
        bibl., f90-1   1366a
Neri, Ferdinando
    La persona velata. In Saggi di letteratura: italiana,
        francese, inglese. Napoli: Loffredo [1936] p9-17 1367
Neufeldówna, Bronisława
    Conrad w Krakowie w rok 1914. Wiadomości Literackie
        1, no 33:4 Ag 17 '24   1368
Neuschäffer, Walter
    Dostojewskijs Einfluss auf den englischen Roman. Ang-
        listische Forschungen 81:1-102 '35   1369
Nevins, Allan
    The book column. Conrad's appeal. His art. Sun (NY)
        Ag 5 '24 p12   1369a
Nevinson, Henry Woodd
    Joseph Conrad, the English foreigner. New Leader (Lon-
        don) 8, no 6:8 Ag 8 '24   1370
The "New great figure." Book-Lover 4, no 20:384 S-O '03
    (From the New York American '03)   1371
New International Encyclopaedia. New York: Dodd, Mead,
    1914. volume 15, p773   1372
A new novelist on Dickens. Mr. Joseph Conrad's opinion of
    Dickens. Western Mail Ja 1 '97; same. Anglo-Welsh
    Review 15, no 36:61-2 Summer '66   1373
Newbolt, (Sir) Henry John
    Conrad and Trafalgar. In My world as in my time,
        memoirs, 1862-1932. London: Faber & Faber [1932]
        p300-12
        (Includes letters from Conrad, p304-5, 306-8, 311-12)
                                                               1374
Newhouse, Neville H.
    Literature in perspective. Joseph Conrad. London:
        Evans Brothers, Ltd., [1966] 5-143p   1375
Newman, Paul B.
    The drama of conscience and recognition in Lord Jim.
        Midwest Quarterly 6:351-66 Summer '65
    Joseph Conrad and the Ancient Mariner. Kansas Magazine
        1960, p79-83   1376
New writer. Joseph Conrad. Bookman (London) 20:173
    S '01   1377
New writers. Mr. Joseph Conrad. Bookman (London) 10:
    41 My '96   1378
Nield, Jonathan
    A guide to the best historical novels and tales. London:
        Elkin Mathews, 1929. p215, 222, 224, 249   1379

Niemiec o Conradzie. Wiadomości Literackie rok 4, no
266:3 F 3 '29 1380
Nieznany list do Jozefa Korzeniowskiego. Podaļa do druku
Barbara Kocówna. Kwartalnik Neofilologiczny no 1:
37-43 '59; same. Nowa Kultura no 26:1 '59 1381
The Nigger of the "Narcissus." New York Times Saturday
Review of Books & Art Mr 4 '99 1382
Niketas, George
The eastern spirit of resignation versus the western spirit
of action in Joseph Conrad's fiction. M. A. Thesis,
Univ. of South Carolina, 1961 1383
Noble, Edward
Conrad's last writing. New York Times S 14 '24 Section
II p6
Foreword. In Five letters by Joseph Conrad written to
Edward Noble in 1895... London: Privately printed
[by Strangeways] 1925. p[7]-9 1384
Nogueira, Hamilton
Linha de sombra; ensaio sôbre a obra de Joseph Conrad.
Rio de Janeiro: Gráfica Record Editôra, 1966. 13-180p;
portrait 1385
Nolan, John Arthur
A critical study of selected short stories of Joseph Con-
rad with reference to themes found in the novels.
M. A. Thesis, Canisius College, 1957. iii, 125f; bib-
liography, f120-5 1386
Nolen, JoAnn Thomas
The individual and the community in the world of Joseph
Conrad. M. A. Thesis, Johns Hopkins University, 1962.
86f 1387
Nordby, Jack S.
Joseph Conrad: the curse of facts. Honors Thesis,
Harvard Univ. 1964 1388
Noriega, Lawrence Karl
Fidelity and isolation in three Conrad novels. M. A.
Thesis, Univ. of Virginia, 1967. 32f (Examines Nos-
tromo, Under Western Eyes, Victory) 1389
Norman, (Rev.) Charles J.
Nostromo by Joseph Conrad: a study of atmosphere and
symbol. M. A. Thesis, Niagara University, 1968. iii-
vi, 82f; bibliography, f79-82 1389a
North, Douglas McKay
Joseph Conrad and the "facts." M. A. Thesis, Syracuse
University, 1965. 71f 1389b
Noskowski, Witold
Jak Conrad dâwaļ wskazówski rezyserskie (How Conrad
gave staging directions). Kurier Poznański (Poznań

Courier) no 112, 1931; same. Teatr no 5, 1931
   (The staging of Victory in Poland)   1390
Nostromo Joseph Conrada w 'Tygodniku Illustrowanym.'
   Tygodnik Illustrowany no 4:75 Ja 24 '25   1391
Notes on Conrad. Book Buyer ns 16:389-90 Je '98; Argo-
   naut 54:136 F 29 '04; Bookman (NY) 38:352-4 D '13;
   Przegląd Literacki no 11, 1896   1392
[Note on Conrad's life] Current Literature 30:222 F '01
                                                    1393
[Note on Conrad's shorter conversations] Notes & Queries
   149:200 S 19 '25   1394
[Note predicting psychological studies of Conrad] Review
   (NY) 2, no 56:604 Je 5 '20   1395
[Notes on Joseph Conrad] Public Opinion (London) 83:624 My
   15 '03; Bookman (NY) 38:352-4 D '13; Bookman (NY)
   57:587 Jl '23; Everybody's Magazine 53:94 O '25 1396
Notice concerning Captain J. C. Korzeniowski. Port-Louis
   Radical Je 16 '31   1397
A novelist among critics. New York World My 3 '23 p 10;
   same. Book Leaf (NY) My 4 '23   1398
The novelist as innovator. London: British Broadcasting
   Corp., 1965   1399
Novelist of sea life is dead. Daily News (Chicago) Ag 4
   '24 p5   1399a
Novels. Glasgow Evening News Ja 13 '98 p2
   (The Nigger of the 'Narcissus' is on the list of best
   novels of year)   1400
Nowaczyński, Adolf
   Jasnodwidz Conrad Korzeniowski (Clairvoyant Joseph Con-
   rad). Gazeta Warszawska no 133, 1929
   Joseph Conrad. (Praca z rok 1916). Sfinks no 94-5:
   82-105 '16; same. In Góry z piasku. szkice. Nak-
   ładem polskiego posterunku wydawniczego "Placówka."
   Warsaw: Nowy Świat 40-Rok, 1922. p238-78
   Kronica literacka. In Kalendarz Literacki (Warsaw) 1917,
   p55-104
   Natus est Conradus. Wiadomości Literackie rok 12, no
   617:1-2 S 15 '35
   Ojciec Conrada (Conrad's father). Skamander 43:482-
   93 O '35   1401
Nowakowski, Zygmunt
   Josephus obiit - natus est Conrad. Wiadomości no 108,
   1948   1402
Noyes, Alfred
   The accusing ghost of justice for Casement. London:
   Gollancz, 1957
   (Noted in Wiadomości 12, no 29:7 Jl 21 '57)   1402a

Oaklander, Lucille
  Political symbolism in the novels of Joseph Conrad.
    M. A. Thesis, Smith College, 1950. 98p   1403
Ober, Warren U.
  "Heart of Darkness;" "The Ancient Mariner" a hundred
    years later.   Dalhousie Review 45:333-7 Autumn '65
                                                   1404
Obituaries (dated 1924 unless otherwise noted)   New States-
    man 23:523 Ag 9; Criterion 3:1 O; Annual Register...
    for the Year 1924. London: Longmans, Green, 1925.
    p137-8; Die Literatur 27:56; La Temps Ag 5; Times
    (London) Ag 4 p10; same.   Publishers' Circular &
    Booksellers' Record 121:199 Ag 9; same. (excerpt) Pub-
    lic Opinion (London) 126:128 Ag 8; Pomorzanin no 102;
    Nowa Ziemia Lubelska no 226; Józef Brodzki in Pani nos
    8, 9; Bluszcz no 35; W. Dąbrowski in Rzeczpospolita
    nos 214, 217; Z. Dębicki in Kurjer Warszawski no 220
    and in Tygodnik Illustrowany no 34; R. Dyboski in
    Czas no 10; Dziennik Ludowy no 88; Dziennik Poznański
    no 188; W. Filochowski in Gazeta Warszawa no 229;
    Gazeta Lwowska no 180; Głos Narodu no 188; E. Li-
    gocki in Kurjer Poznański no 181 and in Goniec Krak.
    no 191; W. Zawistowski in Kurjer Polskim no 214;
    Rzeczpospolita no 229; Naprzód no 188   1405
O'Brien, Justin
  Camus and Conrad: an hypothesis.   Romanic Review 58:
    196-9 '67   1405a
O'Connor, Thomas Power
  How Joseph Conrad came into his own.   T. P.'s & Cas-
    sell's Weekly 2:583 Ag 23 '24
  Joseph Conrad.   The author of our next serial. T. P.'s
    Weekly 3:113 Ja 22 '04
  (Nostromo was serialized in T. P.'s Weekly)
  (Noted by William L. Alden in New York Times Satur-
    day Review of Books F 13 '04 p109)   1406
Odczycie o Conrada.   Gazeta Lwowska no 74, 1930   1407
Odden, Edmund S.
  The concept of the frailty of idealism in Conrad's works.
    M. A. Thesis, University of Arizona, 1962   1408
Odell, Maryann E.
  The theme of betrayal in Joseph Conrad's Nostromo.
    M. A. Thesis, Dominican College of San Rafael, 1958.
    61p   1409
O'Donovan, Peter
  British novels in America.   Daily Express (London) O 5
    '20 p4; same.   John O'London's Weekly 4:83 O 23 '20
                                                   1410

O'Flaherty, Liam
    Joseph Conrad. An appreciation. (Blue Moon Booklets,
      no. 1) London: Lahr [1930] 5-11p
'Twixt Land and Sea. In Keating, George T. A Conrad
    memorial library. Garden City, New York: Doubleday,
    Doran, 1929. p207-11   1411
O'Grady, Walter
    On plot in modern fiction: Hardy, James, and Conrad.
    Modern Fiction Studies 11, no 2:107-15 Summer '65
                                                   1412
O'Hanlon, Mary Kathleen (Sister)
    The theme of discipline and conflict in Conrad's Heart of
    Darkness. M. A. Thesis, Dominican College of San
    Rafael, 1960. 43p   1413
O'Hara, J. D.
    Unlearned lessons in "The Secret Sharer." College Eng-
    lish 26:444-50 Mr '65   1414
Okamura, Sonoko
    The orientalism of Joseph Conrad. M. A. Thesis, Smith
    College, 1942. 103f   1415
Okęcki, Stanisław
    Małżeństwo Józefa Conrada Korzeniowskiego (The mar-
    riage of Joseph Conrad). Twórczość (Creative work)
    no 1:124-8 S '47   1416
"Old Peyrol" as sketched by Conrad himself. Poland 7, no
    8: facing p469 Ag '26   1417
O'Leary, (Sister) Jeanine
    The function of city as setting in Dickens' Our Mutual
    Friend, Trollope's The Way We Live Now, James's
    The Princess Casamassima, and Conrad's The Secret
    Agent. Ph. D. Thesis, Notre Dame University, 1966.
    187p; p118-53; abstract in Dissertation Abstracts 26:
    6048-9 '66   1418
Oliver, H. J.
    A note on Joseph Conrad. Times Literary Supplement S
    6 '47 p451   1419
O'May, H.
    Wheel of the "Otago." Sea Breezes ns 3:208 Mr '47 1420
O'Neill, Mary Alphonsus (Sister)
    Religious imagery in Nostromo. M. A. Thesis, Catholic
    University of America, 1965. 43f; bibl., f43   1421
Onofrio, Lilia d'
    El hombre y el mar en la novela de José Conrad. In
    Nueve ensayos de critica literaria. Buenos Aires:
    Librería y Editorial "El Ateneo" [1942] p47-56   1422
Ordoñez, Elmer Alindogan
    The early development of Joseph Conrad: revisions and

184   A Bibliography of Joseph Conrad

Ordoñez, Elmer Alindogan (cont.)
  style.   Ph. D. Thesis, University of Wisconsin, 1963.
  520p; abstract in Dissertation Abstracts 23:4362 '63
                                                          1423
Orme, Daniel
  Au coeur d'un cyclone avec M. Richard Hughes.   Le
  Mois O '38 (Comparison between Hughes' In Hazard
  and Conrad's "Typhoon")   1424
Orvis, Mary
  The art of writing fiction.   New York: Prentice-Hall,
  1948. p83-5 (On Lord Jim)   1425
Orzeszkowa, Eliza
  Emigracja zdolności (Emigration of talents).   Kraj (Home-
  land) nos 12, 14 Ap 28 '99; same.   In Wspomienia i
  studia o Conradzie, edited by Barbara Kocówna.
  [Warsaw:] Państwowy Instytut Wydawniczy [1963] p16-
  30   1426
Osbourne, Maitland Le Roy
  Joseph Conrad - interpreter of the sea.   National Maga-
  zine (Boston) 52:31-2 Je '23; same.   Poland 5, no 2:
  87-9, 114, 116 F '24   1427
Ostaszewski, Janusz
  Jądro ciemności współczesnego świata ("The Heart of
  Darkness" of the contemporary world).   Dziśi Jutro no
  9, 1953   1428
Ostatni pobyt Conrada w Polsce.   Przegląd Wieczorny no
  181, 1924   1429
Ostrowski, Witold
  Podróż Conrada do jadra ciemności (Conrad's trip to the
  "Heart of Darkness").   Dziś i Jutro no 20, 1953
  Polak z załogi "Torrensa" (The Pole from the "Torrens").
  Dziś i Jutro 10, no 32:3-4 Ag 8 '54
  Problem Josepha Conrada.   Kultura i Społczenstwo 1, no
  4:48-80 O - D '57; same.   In O literaturze angielskiej.
  Warsaw: Pax, 1958. p292-6; same. (excerpt) In Joseph
  Conrad Korzeniowski, by Róża Jabłkowska.   Warsaw:
  Państwowe Zakłady Wydawnictwo Szkolynch, 1964.
  p320-4   1430
Otis, Julia
  Heroism and the human community: an approach to three
  novels by Joseph Conrad.   Radcliffe College Honors
  Thesis in History & Literature, 1958. 56f; bibl. , f52-6
  (On The Nigger of the 'Narcissus, ' Lord Jim, and
  Victory)   1431
Our awards for 1898: the "Crowned" books.   Academy 56:
  65 Ja 14 '99 (Conrad awarded 50 guineas for Tales of
  Unrest)   1432

Our literary snobs.   New York Tribune My 10 '23 p12
    (an editorial)   1433
Our three sea writers... Book Monthly 9:294 F '12
    (Conrad, Bullen, Patterson)   1434
Over, Mark [pseud.]
    [Conrad and McFee]   Outlook (London) 55:91 F 7 '25 1435
Overton, Cora M.
    The treatment of duty in the writings of Joseph Conrad.
    M. A. Thesis, State University of Iowa, 1928. 160p
                                                            1436
Overton, Grant
    In the kingdom of Conrad. In Authors of the day, studies
    in contemporary literature. New York: George H.
    Doran [1922] p 32-56; bibliograph, p53-6; same. Book-
    man (NY) 57:275-84 My '23, bibliography, p284; same.
    American nights' entertainment. New York: Appleton,
    1923. p64-90; bibliography, p87-90
    Joseph Conrad. Nostromo. In The philosophy of fiction.
    New York: Appleton, 1928. p161-84
    Lord Jim: do you remember it? Mentor 22:34-5 O '30
                                                            1437
Owen, Guy Jr.
    A note on Heart of Darkness. Nineteenth-Century Fiction
    12, no 2:168-9 S '57
    Conrad's "The Lagoon." Explicator 18, item 47, My '60
    Crane's "The Open Boat" and Conrad's Youth. Modern
    Language Notes 73:100-2 F '58   1438
Owen, Lyman B.
    Adventuring with Joseph Conrad. English Journal (High
    School Edition) 24:567-71 S '35
    (On studying Conrad's works)
    The Polish-French Joseph Conrad. M. A. Thesis, New
    York State College for Teachers, 1937   1439
Owens, R. J.
    Joseph Conrad: two books. Notes & Queries 203:260
    Je '58   1440

Packer, Pamelia Archer
    The character technique of the double in the fiction of
    R. L. Stevenson and Joseph Conrad... Master's Thesis,
    Duke Univ. , 1966. iii, 147f; bibl. , f144-7   1441
Page, R. Edison
    Recent English novels. Transatlantic Review 1, no 5:365
    My '24 (On The Rover)   1442
Pałęcki, Stanisław
    Etyka Conrada-Korzeniowskiego. Życie no 7:1-2 '50
    O katolickości Conrada. Życie no 8:4-5 '50   1443

Palffy, Eleanor
  Drunk on Conrad.   Fortnightly Review 132:534-8 O '29
                                                              1445
Palmer, Anita Rose
  A study of some memorable women characters in the
    novels of Joseph Conrad.   M. A.   Thesis, University of
    Texas, 1937. iii-xi, 110f   1446
Palmer, John Alfred
  Joseph Conrad's fiction.   Ph. D.   Thesis, Cornell Univer-
    sity, 1962.   468p; abstract in Dissertation Abstracts
    23:3383 '63   1447
Parandowski, Jan
  Joseph Conrad.   Tygodnik Powszechny (Universal Weekly)
    no 48, 1948
  Preface.   In Złota Strzała, by Joseph Conrad (The Arrow
    of Gold), translated by Aniela Zagórska and Jadwiga
    Korniłowiczova.   Krakow: Instytut Wydawniczy
    "Poziom," 1948. p7-[21]   1448
Parker, Robert Wilson
  The Slavic aspects of Joseph Conrad. M. A. Thesis,
    North Texas State University, 1955. 100f.   1449
Parker, W. M.
  The high seas bookshop.   John O'London's Weekly 11:60
    Ap 12 '24
  With Joseph Conrad on the high seas.   Blue Peter 13:
    221-3 My '33   1450
Parrill, Anna Sue
  The theme of revolution in the English novel from Dis-
    raeli to Conrad.   Ph. D. Thesis, University of Tennes-
    see, 1965. f199-241.   Abstract in Dissertation Abstracts
    26:4669 '66   1451
Parry, Albert and Goode, Gerald
  The literary sacrifice of Conrad's father.   Literary Digest
    International Book Review 3:607, 610 Ag '25   1452
Partington, Wilfred
  The correspondence of Joseph Conrad.   Bookman's Jour-
    nal and Print Collector 11, no 38:86 N '24
  Forging ahead...   New York: Putnam's [c1939] p207-16;
    bibliography, p291-2; same.   Thomas Wise in the
    original cloth.   London: Hale [c1946] p220-31; bibliog-
    raphy, p330-1
  Joseph Conrad behind the scenes: unpublished notes on
    his dramatisations.   Bookman's Journal 3rd series,
    15, no 4:179-84 '27
  The literature of travel.   Bookman's Journal 3rd series
    16, no 6: 342 '28   1453
Parton, Herwig

188   A Bibliography of Joseph Conrad

Pendlebury, B. J. (cont.)
   763-4 Je '27   1468
Pennell, Joseph
   The adventures of an illustrator... Boston: Little, Brown,
      1925. p236
      (Reviewed in New York Times Book Review D 27 '25
      p6)   1468a
Penton, Brian
   Note on the form of the novel. London Aphrodite no 6:
      437, 442-4 Jl '29   1469
[Peretiatkowicz, Hanna] Skarbek-Peretiatkowicz, Hanna
   Conrad w Indiach (Conrad in India). Skamander (Warsaw)
      p74-6 Ap '35
   Conradiana. Wiadomości 4, no 186:4 O 23 '49
   ...Dwie Godziny u Joseph Conrada. Wiadomości Liter-
      ackie 1, no 38:2 S 21 '24; same. Świat no 32, 1924.
      same. Voice of Poland (Glasgow) 24:12-13 N '43
   Powrót do Conrada (A return to Conrad). Wiadomości
      no 154, 1949
   Szlacheckie dziedzictwo Conrada (Conrad's Polish gentry
      heritage). Wiadomości nos 176-7:3 Ag 21 '49   1470
Perlowski, Jan
   O Conradzie i Kiplingu (On Conrad and Kipling). Prze-
      gląd Współczesny 16, no 180:16-39 Ap '37; same. In
      Wspomienia i studia o Conradzie, edited by Barbara
      Kocówna. Warsaw: Państwowy Instytut Wydawniczy
      [1963] p110-31   1471
Perry, Bliss
   Introduction. In Victory, by Joseph Conrad. (Memorial
      Edition) Garden City, New York: Doubleday, Page,
      1925. Volume XVI, p vii-x   1472
Perry, Frances Melville
   Joseph Conrad... In Story-writing: lessons from the
      masters. New York: Holt [c1926] p104-39   1473
Perry, Gwendolyn Gray
   Joseph Conrad and compostion. M. A. Thesis, Univ. of
      California, 1923   1474
Perry, John Oliver
   Action, vision, or voice: the moral dilemmas in Conrad's
      tale-telling. Modern Fiction Studies 10:3-14 Spring '64
                                                          1475
   Personalities and powers. Joseph Conrad. Time & Tide 4,
      no 11:287-9 Mr 16 '23   1476
   Personalities: Joseph Conrad. Academy 66:198 F 20 '04
                                                          1477
Peterkiewicz, Jerzy
   Patriotic irritability. Conrad and Poland: for the cen-

tenary. Twentieth Century 162:545-7 D '57   1478
Peters, Agnes Drummond
   The art of Joseph Conrad: his theory and practice.
   M. A. Thesis, Stanford University, 1928. 117f; bibli-
   ography f112-17   1479
Pettigrew, Elizabeth
   Ford Madox Ford and Joseph Conrad. M. A. Thesis,
   Vanderbilt Univ., 1941. 72f. Abstract in Vanderbilt
   University Abstracts of Theses, 1942, p41   1480
Pezet, Maurice J.
   A psychological study of Conrad's main characters in his
   major novels. Thesis for Diplome d'Études Superi-
   eures, Université de Caen, 1958. 109p   1481
Pfabe, Teresa
   Bertrand Russel o Conradzie. Kultura i Społeczeństwo 1,
   no 4:46-7 O-D '57   1482
Pfister, Kurt
   Joseph Conrads Selbstbildnis. Zu seinem 80. Geburtstag.
   Frankfurter Zeitung no 615-16, 1937-38   1483
Phelps, Gilbert
   Joseph Conrad. In The Russian novel in English fiction.
   London: Hutchinson's Universal Library, 1956. p125-
   32   1484
Phelps, William Lyon
   The advance of the English novel. Bookman (NY) 43:297-
   304 My '16; same. In The advance of the English
   novel. New York: Dodd, Mead, 1916. p192-217
   Conrad the writer. Springfield Republican O 22 '14 p3
   Introduction. In Under Western Eyes, by Joseph Conrad,
   with an introduction by William Lyon Phelps. (Me-
   morial Edition) Garden City, New York: Doubleday,
   Page, 1925. Volume XI, p vii-x   1484a
Phillips, A. W.
   II. The "Torrens" among the ice. Blue Peter 9, no 86:
   268-9 My '29   1485
Phillips, May H.
   Joseph Conrad: the depth of courage. M. A. Thesis,
   Columbia University, 1954. 86p   1486
Phillipson, John S.
   Conrad's pink toads: the working of the unconscious.
   Western Humanities Review 14:437-8 Autumn '60   1487
Photographs of Joseph Conrad. Fair Winds (NY) 1, no 1:15-
   18 Fall '37 (The ship of that name)   1488
A pictorial survey of the literary life of Joseph Conrad.
   Saturday Review of Literature 1:206-7 O 18 '24   1489
Piątkowski, Bolesław Pomian
   Proba wierności shipmastera Conrada. Wiadomości 5,

Piątkowski, Bolesław Pomian (cont.)
    no 2:1 Ja 8 '50; same. Nowa Kultura 13, no 37:6-7
    S 16 '62; same. In Wspomnienia i studia o Conradzie,
    edited by Barbara Kocówna. [Warsaw:] Państwowy
    Instytut Wydawniczy [1963] p76-82   1490
Pierrefeu, Jean de
    Un romancier d'aventures: Joseph Conrad. Journal des
    Debats 134, no 143:2 My 24 '22   1491
Pierwsza przygoda Conrada (by "R.R."). Dziennik Poznań-
    ski no 194, 1924; Kurjer Poranny no 228, 1924   1492
Pietrkiewicz, Jerzy
    The knotted cord. London, Heinemann, 1955
    (Noted in Wiadomości 10, no 50:4 D 11 '55)   1492a
Pilecki, Gerard A.
    Conrad's Victory. Explicator 23, item 26, N '64
    Conrad's Victory. Explicator 23, item 36, Ja '65   1493
Pinker, E. S.
    Conrad's letters. Times Literary Supplement N 27 '24
    p798 (A request for letters)   1494
Pizarze angielscy O Conradzie. Wiadomości (News) 4, nos
    176-7:6 Ag 21 '49   1495
Plan Conrad memorial for Seamen's Institute [in New York
    City] New York Herald Tribune Ap 25 '26 p3   1496
Plan Conrad memorials [in Bishopsbourne] New York Times
    Ap 25 '26 p18   1497
Plans for Conrad library. New York Times O 31 '26, Sec-
    tion 1, p26   1498
Platt, Rutherford Hayes Jr.
    How Conrad came to write. Mentor 13:20-3 Mr '25 1499
Platzer, Martin
    Abschied von Joseph Conrad. Weltstimmen 11:15-17
    '37   1500
Plomer, William
    At home. London: Cape, 1958. p93-4
    (Noted in Wiadomości 16, no 45:5 N 5 '61)
    Introduction. In Victory, by Joseph Conrad. (World's
    Classics 561) New York: Oxford University press,
    1957. p vii-xiii   1501
Płoszewski, Leon
    Smierc Conrada Korzeniowskiego. Przegląd Warszawski
    rok 4, tom 4, no 38:262-6 N '24   1502
A plot for Conrad. Literary Digest 88, no 6:73 F 13 '26
                                                          1503
Pocock, Guy Noel
    Contemporary writers. VI. Joseph Conrad. In Pen and
    ink... London: Dent, 1925. p220-5   1504
Podhorska-Okołów, Stefania

Pospisil, Robert (cont.)
    Queen's College, 1954. 144p   1520
A posthumous bust of Joseph Conrad, by Jacob Epstein.
    Vanity Fair 23, no 4:73 D '24   1520a
Potocki, Antoni
    Conrad Korzeniowski w literaturze angielskiej.   Kurjer
    Poranny no 42, 1927
    Joseph Conrad.   Nowy Przegląd Literatury i Sztuki (New
    Review of Literature & Art) tom 1, no 2:176-96 Jl
    '20
    Joseph Conrad. In Polska literatura wspolczesna.   War-
    saw: Gebethner and Wolff, 1911. Volume I
    Józef Konrad Korzeniowski.   Próba syntezy przeżyć i
    powołania (Joseph Conrad.   Attempt at a synthesis of
    his experience and vocation).   Przegląd Wspołczesny
    (Contemporary Review), 1, no 2:196-208 Je '22
    Le cas de Joseph Conrad.   Transatlantic Review 2, no
    3:348-50 O'24   1521
Potocki, Geoffrey
    Miss Aniele Zagórska.   Pologne Littéraire 9th année, nos
    94-95: 7 Jl 15 - Ag 15 '34 (An interview)   1522
Potter, Norris Whitfield, Jr.
    The critical theory and literary practice of Joseph Con-
    rad.   Ph. D. Thesis, Boston Univ. , 1944. 198f; bibl. ,
    f176-92   1523
Powell, John
    Conrad and casement hut mates in Africa.   New York Eve-
    ning Post My 11 '23 p16   1524
Powis, M. B.
    The individual and society in Conrad's novels.   M. A.
    Thesis, University of London, 1957   1525
Powys, John Cowper
    Chance. In Keating, George T.   A Conrad memorial li-
    brary. Garden City, New York: Doubleday, Doran,
    1929. p217-22
    Joseph Conrad. In Suspended judgments, essays and books
    and sensations. New York: Shaw, 1916. p335-64;
    same. In Essays on Joseph Conrad and Oscar Wilde.
    Girard, Kansas: Haldeman-Julius Co. [1923] p3-28
    (Reviewed in North American Review 218:572 O '23)
                                                         1526
Powys, Llewelyn
    Youth. In Keating, George T.   A Conrad memorial li-
    brary. Garden City, New York: Doubleday, Doran,
    1929. p88-93   1527

Powys, T. F.
  Lord Jim. In Keating, George T.   A Conrad memorial
    library. Garden City, New York: Doubleday, Doran,
    1929. p65-70   1528
Poznar, Walter Paul
  The two worlds of Joseph Conrad.   Ph. D. Thesis, Indi-
    ana University, 1957. 219p; abstract in Dissertation
    Abstracts 19:532 '58   1529
Pratt, Mary
  The French contacts of Joseph Conrad.   M. A. Thesis,
    Indiana University, 1928. 188p   1530
Prawdziwa historja Lorda Jima.   Wiadomości Literackie 5,
    no 28:2 Jl 8 '28   1531
Prędski, Artur
  W sprawie Conrada.   Wiadomości Literackie 5, no 12:1
    Mr 18 '28; also volume 5, no 19:2 My 6 '28 & 5, no
    22:4 My 27 '28   1532
Pressey, William Benfield
  Joseph Conrad.   In The new international year book... for
    the year 1924. Edited by Frank Moore Colby and
    Herbert Treadweel Wade.   New York: Dodd, Mead,
    1925. p178   1533
Preston, Hayter
  The tragedy of Stephen Crane.   T. P.'s & Cassell's Week-
    ly 2:799 O 11 '24   1534
Price, Arthur J.
  An appreciation of Joseph Conrad... with an introduction
    by David W. Oates... Newport, Monmouthshire: Joyce
    and Sons; London: Simpkin, Marshall [1931] 73p; por-
    trait   1535
Priestley, Joseph B.
  The English novel.   London: Benn [1927] p133-7
  Modern English novelists: Joseph Conrad.   English
    Journal 14:13-21 Ja '25   1536
Prieur, Francois
  Joseph Conrad et les pilotes de Marseille.   Le Petit
    Provençal My 15 '25   1537
Prilipp, Beda
  Joseph Conrad, der Dichter der Heimatlosen.   Hochland
    26, no 2:214-16 N '28   1538
Pritchett, Victor Sawdon
  Books in general.   New Statesman & Nation ns 23:78 Ja
    31 '42; New Statesman & Nation ns 40:72-3 Jl 15 '50
  Conrad.   In The living novel and later appreciations.
    New York: Random House [1964] p190-99

Pritchett, Victor Sawdon (cont.)
  Conrad. In The working novelist. London: Chatto &
    Windus [1965] p193-[201] (from the New Statesman)
  Current literature. Books in general. New Statesman
    & Nation ns 22:282 S 20 '41
  An emigré. In Books in general. New York: Harcourt,
    Brace, 1953. p216-22
  The exile. New Statesman 54:229 Ag 24 '57; see reply
    by William McFee in New Statesman 54:385 S 28 '57
  An exotic English novelist. Listener 36:480-1 O 10 '46
  Introduction... In Victory, an island tale. Joseph Conrad.
    London: Book Society [1952] p v-vii
  London letter. New York Times Book Review Ja 12 '58
    p22 (On the revival of interest in Conrad)
  A Pole in the far East. In The living novel and later
    appreciations. New York: Reynal & Hitchcock [1947]
    p143-8   1539
Profitt, Doris La Verne
  The novellas of Joseph Conrad: a study in craftsman-
    ship. M. A. Thesis, Stanford University, 1959. iii,
    78f   1540
Przelj, J.
  Dva angleška romana. Ljubljanski Zvon no 5, 1932
    (Compares Conrad's The Shadow-Line and Stevenson's
    Kidnapped)   1540a
Przybyszewski, Eugenjusz
  Lata dziecinne Conrad (The last years of Conrad). Wia-
    domości Literackie 1, no 33:4 Ag 17 '24   1541
Pugh, Edwin
  Joseph Conrad as I knew him. T. P.'s & Cassell's Week-
    ly 2:575 Ag 23 '24; same. (excerpt) Publishers' Circu-
    lar & Booksellers' Record 121:259 Ag 23 '24   1542
Purdy, Strother B.
  On the relevance of Conrad: Lord Jim over Sverdlovsk.
    Midwest Quarterly 9, no 1:43-51 Autumn '67   1542a
Pure, Simon [pseud.]
  See: Swinnerton, Frank Arthur   1543
Putnam, George Palmer
  Conrad in Cracow. Outlook (NY) 124:382-3 Mr 3 '20   1544
Puzon, (Mother) M. Bridget
  Joseph Conrad and his reviewers. M. A. Thesis, Boston
    College, 1963. 63f; bibl., f59-63   1545
Pyszhowski, Richard John
  Joseph Conrad Korzeniowski and his Polish heritage.
    M. A. Thesis, University of Ottawa, 1952. 103p   1546

Quick, D. E.
   The technique of Conrad in relation to the moral conduct
   of his characters.   M. A. Thesis, University of Wales,
   1953   1547
Quinn, John
   Joseph Conrad on Poland.   The new barbarism that she
   fights on behalf of us all.   New York Tribune Ap 5
   '20 p10
   (Quotations from a letter which Conrad wrote to
   Quinn)
   Letters in the Quinn Collection, Manuscript Room, New
   York Public Library
   (12 letters to Joseph Conrad; 45 from Conrad to John
   Quinn; 2 from Mrs. Conrad to John Quinn; 1 from
   Richard Curle to John Quinn)   1548
Quiz [pseud.]
   Mr. Joseph Conrad [a caricature] Saturday Review (Lon-
   don) 134:537 O 14 '22; same.   Current Opinion (NY)
   74:677 Je '23   1548a

Rabey, Hetty R.
   Joseph Conrad.   M. A. Thesis, Wittenberg College,
   1930   1549
Race, Herbert
   Joseph Conrad: The Rover.   (Notes on chosen English
   texts) London: James Brodie [1958] 56p
   Joseph Conrad: The Secret Agent.   (Notes on chosen
   English texts) London: James Brodie [1960] 71p 1550
Raczyński, Edward
   Spotkanie w poselstwie w Londynie (A meeting [with Con-
   rad] at the [Polish] Legation in London).   Wiadomości
   (News) nos 176-7: volume 4:4 Ag 21 '49   1551
Radley, Philippe Daniel
   The ineluctable modality of the divisible.   An essay on
   the use of doubles in Dostoevsky and Conrad.   Honors
   Thesis, Harvard College, 1956   1552
Rahv, Philip
   Introduction [to "Heart of Darkness," by Joseph Conrad]
   In Seven great British novels... [New York] Berkley
   Publishing Corporation [c1963] p12-13
   Fiction and the criticism of fiction.   Kenyon Review 18,
   no 2:285-95 Spring '56
   (On "The Secret Sharer")   1553
Raimond, Michel
   La crise du roman... [Paris:] Librairie José Corti,
   1966. p327-9   1553a

Raimondi, Giuseppe
    Capitano Conrad. In Giornale ossia taccuino (1925-1930).
        Firenze: Le Monnier, 1942. p73-8   1554
Rainalter, Erwin H.
    Drei englische dichter: London, Conrad, Galsworthy.
        Kölnische Volkszeitung, Lit. Bl. 186, 1929   1555
Rakower, Benito
    Hamlet and Lord Jim: two studies in literary adumbra-
        tion. D. Ed. Thesis, Harvard University, 1967. iii,
        116f; (Conrad, f56-91)   1556
Rakowska, Maria
    Józef Conrad. Biblioteka Warszawa (Warsaw Library)
        3:558-68 '08; same. In Wspomnienia i studia o Con-
        radzie, edited by Barbara Kocówna. Warsaw: Pań-
        stwowy Instytut Wydawniczy [1963] p149-62
    Zarys literatury angielskiej. Warsaw: 1910. Volume
        III   1557
Rakowska-Luniewska, Irena
    U Konrada Korzeniowskiego (At Conrad's home). Pion
        no 50, 1934   1558
Randall, John Herman
    Joseph Conrad - his outlook on life. Unity 96:281-6 Ja
        18 '26
    Joseph Conrad: his outlook on life. New York: The
        Community Church, Park Avenue and 34th Street
        [1924-1925] The Community Series, 1924-1925, No.
        VI. 24p   1559
Rang, Bernhard
    Joseph Conrad. Hefte für Büchereiwesen 12:277-87
        '28   1560
Raphael, Alice Pearl
    Joseph Conrad's Faust. In Goethe, the challenger. New
        York: Cape & Ballou [c1932] p39-83
        (The influence of Goethe on Conrad's Victory)   1561
Rapin, René
    Conrad's Nostromo. Explicator 13, item 50, June, 1955
    La français de Joseph Conrad. In Lettres de Joseph
        Conrad à Marguerite Poradowska. Edition critique,
        précédée d'une étude sur le français de Joseph Conrad
        [par] René Rapin. Genève: Droz, 1966. p15-53
    Introduction. In Lettres de Joseph Conrad à Marguerite
        Poradowska... Genève: Droz, 1966. p11-14
    Réalité et imagination dans l'oeuvre de Joseph Conrad.
        Lausanne: 1957   1562
Rascoe, Burton
    A bookman's day book. New York Tribune Magazine &
        Books My 6 '23 p26; My 13 '23 p31

A bookman's day book.   New York: Horace Liveright,
1929. p98, 101, 105, 111, 113, 115-16 (from the
New York Herald Tribune)
Contemporary reminiscences.   A remembered interview
with Conrad on the occasion of his first visit to
America.   Arts & Decoration 21, no 5:36, 63, 65 S
'24
Joseph Conrad comes to see us, not to chide or "uplift."
New York Tribune My 2 '23 p1, 6; same. Book Leaf
(NY) My 4 '23   1563
Raskin, Jonah
"Heart of Darkness:" the manuscript revisions.   Review
of English Studies ns 18, no 69:30-9 F '67
Imperialism: Conrad's "Heart of Darkness." Journal of
Contemporary History 2:113-31 Ap '67
Nostromo: the argument from revision.   Essays in
Criticism 18, no 2:183-92 Ap '68   1564
Rawson, C. J.
Conrad's Heart of Darkness.   Notes & Queries ns 6:110-
11 Mr '59   1565
Rea, Gardner
Joseph Conrad; poem.   Life 84:22 S 11 '24
The lesson.   Life 84:4 S 18 '24   1566
Read, Herbert
[The genius of Conrad] New Age ns 29:273 O 6 '21   1567
Reade, A. R.
The stranger in our gate.   In Main currents in modern
literature.   London: Ivor Nicholson and Watson,
1935. p117-29   1568
Ready, Marie E.
Joseph Conrad's women.   M. A. Thesis, University of
Wyoming, 1955. 131p   1569
Rébora, Piero
James, Conrad, Mansfield.   In Letteratura inglese del
Novecento.   Firenze: Edizioni Lingue estere, 1950.
p48-55   1570
Reck-Halleczewen, Friedrich
Für Joseph Conrad.   Deutsches Wollen (Berlin) no
131:2 '34
Joseph Conrad.   Berliner Tageblatt no 110, March
1938
Joseph Conrad als typus des heutigen Angelsachsen.
Tag, Unt. Rundschau no 4, Jan-Feb 1928   1571
A record task.   New York Times Literary Section My 16
'20 p254
(An editorial on the writing of The Rescue, including quo-
tations from a Conrad letter to one of his friends)   1572

Redfern, Percy
     Conrad.   Seafarer (London) no 37:7-8 Ja '43; portrait
                                                          1573
Reed, Dr. J. G.
     Ships and Conrad.   Sea Breezes ns 13:74 Ja '52
     Two Conrad incidents.   Sea Breezes ns 11:160 F '51   1574
Rees, Florence Helen
     Recent developments in narrative method... M. A. Thesis,
        Ohio State University, 1920. 66p
        (On Victory and Chance)   1575
Rees, Richard
     The unobscure Conrad.   In For love or money. Studies
        in personality and essence.   London: Secker & War-
        burg; 1960; Carbondale, Illinois: Southern Illinois
        University press, 1961. p124-9   1576
Reflections of the strenuous life on sea and plain [signed
        "Lector'] Booklovers Magazine 3:94 Ja '04   1577
Rehder, Jessie
     The story at work.   New York: Odyssey Press, 1963.
        p254-5
        (On "The Lagoon")   1578
Reid, Stephen A.
     The "Unspeakable Rites" in Heart of Darkness. Modern
        Fiction Studies 9, no 4:347-56 Winter '63-'64; same.
        In Conrad.   A collection of critical essays, edited by
        Marvin Mudrick.   (A Spectrum book) Englewood Cliffs,
        New Jersey: Prentice-Hall, Inc. [1966] p45-54   1579
Reilly, Joseph John
     The short stories of Joseph Conrad.   Catholic World
        109:163-75 My '19; same.   In Of books and men.
        New York: Messner, 1942. p79-92   1580
Reinecke, George F.
     Conrad's Victory: psychomachy, Christian symbols, and
        theme.   In Louisiana State University Studies: Humani-
        ties Series number 18.   Explorations of Literature,
        edited by R. D. Reck.   Baton Rouge, Louisiana: Louisi-
        ana State University Press, 1966. p70-80   1580a
The reporter's viewpoint [a letter by F. S. to Christopher
        Morley] New York Evening Post My 8 '23 p8   1581
Resch, H. T.
     Reue und Heimweh.   Der konterrevolutionär Joseph Con-
        rad.   Berliner Tageblatt no 428, 1932   1582
[The Rescue noted as Conrad's Malay romance soon to come
        out] Argonaut 42, no 1091:9 F 7 '99   1583
Resink, G. J.
     De Archipel voor Joseph Conrad.   In Overdruk Bijdragen
        Tot de Taal-Land-en Volkenkunde. Deel 115. 1959

Axel Heyst and the second king of the Cocos Islands.
English Studies 44:443-7 D '63
Conradiaanse interraciale vriendschappen.   Forum der
Letteren 6:35-47 F '65
De excentrieke Lord Jim.   De Gids 124, no 3:178-80
Mr '61
Jozef Korzeniowski's Voornaamste Lectuur betreffende
Indonesië.   Bijdragen tot de Taal-Land- en Volken-
kunde deel 117, no 2:209-37 '61
Marlow-Almayer-Havelaar.   De Gids 124, no 8:28-35
Ag '61
Samburan encantada.   English Studies 47:35-44 F '66
Stuurman Korzeniowski ontmoet Shawlman.   De Gids
124, no 9:107-12 S '61   1584
Retinger, Joseph Hieronim
Conrad and his contemporaries: souvenirs... Drawings
by Feliks Topolski.   London: Minerva Publishing Co.
[June 1941] [5]-156p; excerpt: Polish Review 3, no 4:
8-9 Ja 25 '43.   also: New York: Roy [1943] 5-183p;
end paper maps
(Reviewed by Benjamin Gilbert Brooks in Nineteenth
Century 130:345 D '41; Times Literary Supplement Jl
19 '41 p350; Edward Wagenknecht in New York Times
Book Review Ap 4 '43 p30; Time 41:80, 82 Mr 8 '43;
Booklist 39:332 Ap 15 '43; Nation (NY) 156:499 Ap 3
'43; G. F. Whicher in New York Herald Tribune Books
Je 20 '43 p5; New Yorker 19:67 F 27 '43; Edna Lerner
in Saturday Review of Literature 26:8 My 8 '43; Edith
S. Blessing in New Mexico Quarterly Review 14:237
Summer '44; Poland Fights 3, no 36:7-8 Ap 20 '43)
The dual nationality of Joseph Conrad.   In Conrad żywy,
edited by Wit Tarnawski.   London: B. Świderski,
1957.   p129-33
Moje wspomnienia o Conradzie; Conrad i jego otoczenie.
Wiadomości Literackie rok 11, no 571:3 O 28 '34
Moje wspomnienia o Conradzie; działność literacka Con-
rada.   Wiadomości Literackie rok 12, no 582:2 Ja
13 '35
Moje wspomnienia o Conradzie; literatura Angielska no
przełomie XIX i XX w.   Wiadomości Literackie rok 11,
no 564:3 S 9 '34
Moje wspomnienia o Conradzie; podróż do Polski.   Wia-
domości Literackie rok 11, no 576:3 N 2 '34
Moje wspomnienia o Conradzie; stosunek Conrada do
Polski.   Wiadomości Literackie rok 12, no 584:1
F 27 '35   1585

Retinger, (Mrs.) Otolia
   See: Zubrzycka, T.   1586
[Review of the movie adaptation of Lord Jim] Exceptional
   Photoplays 6:4 N '25   1587
Reynolds, Ann
   Prose-poetry in Joseph Conrad.   M. A. Thesis, Univ. of
   Texas, 1938. iv-vii, 144f   1588
Reynolds, Stephen
   Joseph Conrad and sea fiction.   Quarterly Review 217:
   159-80 Jl '12; same. Living Age 276:264-78 F 1 '13
                                                      1589
Rhys, Ernest
   An interview with Joseph Conrad.   Bookman (NY) 56:
   402-8 D '22
   A night with Joseph Conrad. In Everyman remembers.
   New York: Cosmopolitan Book Corporation, 1931.
   p291-301 London: Dent [1931] p259-68.   Portrait by
   Caffyn. p263   1590
Rice, Howard C. Jr.
   Additions to the Doubleday Collection: Kipling, T. E.
   Lawrence, Conrad.   Princeton University Library
   Chronicle 24:191-6 Spring '63   1591
Richard Curle starts quest for Conrad's old shipmates.
   World (NY) O 25 '25 Third Section, p 6M   1592
Richardson, (Captain) Leslie
   Conrad and the Riviera.   T. P.'s & Cassell's Weekly 5:
   341 D 19 '25   1593
Richmond, Ralph
   Conrad's preference.   New York Times My 19 '23
   p14   1594
Ridd, John Carl
   Conrad's Lingard novels: an index of change.   M. A.
   Thesis, University of Manitoba, 1955. 145p   1595
Ridley, Florence H.
   The ultimate meaning of "Heart of Darkness." Nineteenth-
   Century Fiction 18, no 1:43-53 Je '63   1596
Riesemann, Oskar von
   Joseph Conrad.   Europäische Review 5:359-63 Ag '29
                                                      1597
Riesenberg, Felix
   An appreciation of Last Essays. In Last Essays, by
   Joseph Conrad. (Memorial Edition) Garden City, New
   York: Doubleday, Page, 1926. Volume XXIII, p vii-x
   The Mirror of the Sea. In Keating, George T. A Con-
   rad memorial library. Garden City, New York:
   Doubleday, Doran, 1929. p151-3   1598

Rita, Sister
Introduction. In Lord Jim, by Joseph Conrad.   New
   York: Harper & Brothers, 1964   1599
Rivoallan, A.
L'alchimie de Conrad.   Bulletin de France-Grande-Bre-
   tagne année 13, no 96:5-10 My '30   1600
Robert, Wilma Anna
Joseph Conrad: the effect of his Polish birth and British
   citizenship upon his writings. M. A. Thesis, Univ. of
   Denver, 1959   1601
Roberts, Cecil
Joseph Conrad: a reminiscence. Bookman (NY) 61:536-
   42 Jl '25; same. Bookman (London) 69:95-9 N '25;
   same. Living Age 328:308-13 F 6 '26
[Letter indicating Conrad's personal preference for
   Nostromo] Times (London) D 10 '57 p11   1602
Roberts, Iris Siler
Nine women in the fiction of Joseph Conrad. M. A. Thesis,
   North Texas State University, 1961. iii, 117f   1603
Roberts, James L.
"Heart of Darkness" and "The Secret Sharer," a critical
   study. Lincoln, Nebraska: Cliff's Notes and Outlines
   [c1965] 72p   1603a
Roberts, John H.
A Conrad setting. Times Literary Supplement N 15 '47
   p591   1604
Robertson, John M.
The novels of Joseph Conrad. North American Review
   208:439-53 S '18   1605
Robinson, E. Arthur
Conrad's "The Secret Sharer." Explicator 18, item 28,
   Feb. 1960   1606
Robson, W. W.
The politics of solitude. London Magazine 4:26-31 N '57
   (On Under Western Eyes)   1607
Rockwood, Stanley W.
A comparative study of the works of Pierre Loti and
   Joseph Conrad. Ph. D. Thesis, Univ. of Wsiconsin,
   1929. 215p   1608
Rodes, Roberta M.
The eternal river: a study in Conrad and Melville.
   M. A. Thesis, Occidental College, 1958   1609
Roditi, Edouard
Trick perspectives. Virginia Quarterly Review 20: no
   4:547-9 Autumn '44   1610
Roehl, (Sister) Barbara Marie
Joseph Conrad; a study of his theory and techniques.

Roehl, (Sister) Barbara Marie (cont.)
    M. A. Thesis, St. Louis University, 1941. 123f; bibli-
       ography, f114-22   1610a
Rogalski, Aleksander
    Profile i preteksty. Warsaw: Pax, 1958.
    (Noted by Ryszard Matuszewski in Rocznik Literacki
       1958-60, p191)   1611
Rogers, B. J.
    The collaboration of Conrad and Ford Madox Ford.
       Ph. D. Thesis, Geneva University, 1952   1612
Rogers, Philip Edward
    Russia and the West: political point of view in Joseph
       Conrad's Under Western Eyes. M. A. Thesis, Cornell
       University, June, 1960. ii, 24f   1612a
Rogers, W. A.
    The Conrad interview [a letter dated May 4] New York
       Tribune My 8 '23 p10   1613
Rogowicz, Wacław
    Wspomnienie o księciu Romanie Sanguszce (A reminiscence
       of Prince Roman Sanguszko). Wiadomości Literackie
       2, no 36:1 S 6 '25   1614
Rolle, Michal
    In illo tempore... Szkice historyczyno-literackie.
       Brody: F. West, 1914. p43-53   1615
Romance: an analysis (by a "correspondent"). Transatlantic
    Review 1, no 2:84-9 F '24   1616
Romano, Alberto
    Esotismo. In Scritti letterari. Napoli: A. Guida, 1930.
       p121-4   1617
The romantic life of Joseph Conrad. In The Duel. A Mili-
    tary Tale, by Joseph Conrad. Garden City, New York:
    Garden City Publishing Co. 1923. p[119]   1618
Rooney, Lawrence Frederick
    A symbolic pattern in Conrad's early fiction. M. A.
    Thesis, Montana State University, 1950. 83p; abstract
    in Montana State University Graduate School Abstracts
    of Masters' Theses 1950-1951, p65-6   1619
Root, Edward Merrill
    Frank Harris. New York: Odyssey press, 1947. p136-7
    (Noted in New York Times My 13 '47 p23)   1620
Rops, Daniel Henry
    Conrad. D'Europe Jl 15 '24
    Joseph Conrad. In Carte d'Europe... Paris: Perrin,
    1928. p53-84   1621
Roques, K. R. von
    Joseph Conrad. Frankfurter Zeitung no 940, D '26 1622
Rosati, S.

Joseph Conrad. Il Mondo 7:27 '54   1623
Rose, Alan Manuel
    Joseph Conrad and the Eighteen-Nineties. Ph. D. Disser-
        tation, Columbia University, 1965. 187f.
        Abstract in
        Dissertation Abstracts 27: 485A '66   1624
Roselli, Alexander (Brother)
    The parodies of Max Beerbohm on Joseph Conrad and
        Henry James. M. A. Thesis, U. of Notre Dame,
        1964. 117f   1624a
Roseme, Diane
    The threefold interpretation of the "Heart of Darkness."
        M. A. Thesis, Sacramento State College, 1958.
        104p   1625
Rosenfield, Claire
    An archetypal analysis of Conrad's Nostromo. Texas
        Studies in Literature and Language 3:510-34 Winter
        '62
    Paradise of snakes: an archetypal analysis of Conrad's
        political novels. Chicago: University of Chicago press
        [c1967] vii-xi, 187p; bibliography, p177-82
        (Treats Nostromo, The Secret Agent, and Under West-
        ern Eyes)
    Paradise of snakes: archetypal patterns in two novels by
        Conrad. Ph. D. Thesis, Radcliffe College, 1960. 216f
        (Examines Nostromo and The Secret Agent)
    The shadow within. Daedalus 92:333 Spring '63
        (On "Heart of Darkness" and "The Secret Sharer") 1626
Ross, Betty
    New light on Conrad. Brentano's Book Chat 8, no 5:33-
        7 S-O '29   1627
Ross, Ernest Carson
    Joseph Conrad. In The development of the English sea
        novel from Defoe to Conrad. Ann Arbor, Michigan:
        Edwards Brothers [1926?] p83-97 (A Ph. D. Thesis,
        University of Virginia, 1924)   1628
Rothenstein, John
    Summer's lease: autobiography 1901-1938. New York:
        Holt, Rinehart & Winston [c1965] p43-4 (Includes a let-
        ter from Conrad to the author, dated August 28, 1917)
                                                        1629
Rothenstein, William
    Conrad and Hudson. In Men and memories: recollec-
        tions of William Rothenstein. London: Faber & Faber
        [1932] p38-44
    Genius at the turn of the century. Atlantic Monthly
        149:233-43 F '32 (Includes 4 letters from Joseph Con-
        rad)

Rothenstein, William (cont.)
    Introduction. In Notes on Life and Letters, by Joseph
        Conrad. (Memorial Edition) Garden City, New York:
        Doubleday, Page, 1925. Volume XIX, p v-vii
    Joseph Conrad. In The portrait drawings of William
        Rothenstein, 1889-1925. An iconography by John Roth-
        enstein... London: Chapman & Hall, 1926. Plate XLI
        (described as page 21, no 178, the property of the
        National Portrait Gallery, formerly owned by Mr.
        Charles Rutherson; the work was done in 1903). An-
        other drawing, not located, is on page 21, no. 179;
        two others, nos. 371 and 372, are described on page
        43
    Joseph Conrad. In Twenty-four portraits. With critical
        appreciations by various hands. London: Allen & Un-
        win [1920] [unpaged, but pp25-6] portrait, p[27]. This
        portrait was also used as a frontispiece to The Secret
        Agent. New York: Doubleday, Page, 1923.
    Two letters to Edmund Gosse, June 31 [sic] 1904. In
        The Keating Collection, Yale University Library   1629a
Roughead, William
    Conrad on crime: a note of admiration. Juridical Re-
        view 40:250-65 S 1 '28; same. In Malice domestic.
        Edinburgh: Green & Son, 1928. p263-78; portrait,
        facing p272   1630
Rouquette de Fonvielle, A.
    See: Fonvielle, A. Rouquette de   1631
Roussel, Royal
    The metaphysics of darkness: a study in the development
        of Conrad's fiction. Ph. D. Thesis, Johns Hopkins
        Univ., 1966. 353f; abstract in Dissertation Abstracts
        27:3469A '67   1632
Routh, Harold Victor
    Towards the twentieth century... New York: Macmillan,
        1937. p336-9   1633
Rowlands, Hobart Ernest
    Joseph Conrad and the Russian novelists. M. A. Thesis,
        Ohio State University, 1923. 63p
        (Studies Conrad's Under Western Eyes, The Secret
        Agent, Turgenev, Dostoievsky, and Tolstoi)   1634
Roy, Jaqueline Colette M. J.
    Joseph Conrad and France. M. A. Thesis, Univ. of Cin-
        cinnati, 1952. 116p   1635
Ruch, Gertrud
    Zeitverlauf und Erzählerstandpunkt in Joseph Conrads
        Romanen. Herrnstadt in Schlesien: Drache, 1926.
        60, v pages; bibliography, p[i]-v. Ph. D. Thesis,

University of Zürich 1636
Rudd, May
Conrad's power of developing scene and characterization.
M. A. Thesis, University of South Dakota, 1923. 168p
1637
Russell, Bertrand
Portraits from memory - V. Joseph Conrad. Listener
50:462-3 S 17 '53; same. In Portraits from memory
and other essays. London: Allen & Unwin; New York:
Simon & Schuster, 1956. p86-91; same. (translated
by Zdzisław Broncel) Wiadomości 9, no 7:1 F 14 '54
(Reviewed in Wiadomości 12, no 22:4 Je 2 '57) 1638
Ruthven, K. K.
The savage God: Conrad and Lawrence. Critical Quar-
terly 10, nos 1-2:39-54 Spring-Summer '68 1638a
Ryan, Alvan S.
Conrad's "The Secret Sharer." Insight 2:70-6 '64
Robert Penn Warren's Night Rider: the nihilism of the
isolated temperament. Modern Fiction Studies 7, no
4:338-46 Winter '61-'62
(Refers to The Nigger of the 'Narcissus') 1639
Ryan, John K.
Conrad's Catholicism questioned. America 31:14 Ap 19
'24; see also p479, Ag 30 '24 1640
Rychliński, Jerzy Bohdan
Ostatnia powieść Conrada. Wiadomości Literackie 1, no
33:3 Ag 17 '24 (The Rover) 1641
Ryf, Robert S.
Conrad's stage Victory. Modern Drama 7:148-60 S '64
(A history of the writing of the drama, with excerpts
from reviews and a summary of the play) 1642

S., T.
See: Skarszewski, Tadeusz Żuk 1643
S., Z.
See: Skarszewski, Tadeusz Żuk 1644
Sackville-West, Edward
The moment of silence. In Inclinations. London: Secker
& Warburg, 1949. p72-7 1645
Sadleir, Michael
Joseph Conrad. In The dictionary of national biography...
1922-1930. Edited by R. H. Weaver. London: Oxford
University Press, 1937. p205-10 1646
Saeki, Shôichi
Politics and ethics - Joseph Conrad. In Some points of
issue in the contemporary English and American
novels. 1956. p5-62 (In Japanese) 1647

Safroni-Middleton, A.
[Joseph Conrad] In Tropic shadows, memories of the
South Seas... London: Richards press, 1927. p35-60
1648
Said, Edward William
Conrad, Nostromo: record and reality. In Approaches
to the twentieth century novel, edited by John Untereck-
er. New York: Crowell, 1965. p108-52
Joseph Conrad and the fiction of autobiography. Cambridge, Massachusetts: Harvard University Press,
1966. [vii]-[xiv], 219p ("In its original form this
study was a doctoral dissertation done at Harvard University" in 1964)
(Reviewed by Tony Tanner in Spectator 217:845-6 D
30 '66; Choice 4:47 Mr '67; C.W. Mann, Jr. in Library Journal 92:116 Ja 1 '67; Stanley Weintraub in
Saturday Review 50: no 23:37-8 Je 10 '67; Douglas
Hewitt in Review of English Studies ns 19, no 74:233-
5 My '68; Edgar F. Harden in Victorian Studies 11,
no 3:421 Mr '68; Denis Donoghue in Nineteenth-Century
Fiction 22, no 2:199-202 S '67)
The letters and shorter fiction of Joseph Conrad. Ph.D.
Thesis, Harvard University, Feb. 1, 1964. ii, 320f;
bibl., f313-20
The letters of Joseph Conrad by Felix Bumbastus
[pseudonym]. Graduate School of Arts and Sciences,
5th year. Submitted for the Bowdoin Prize, Harvard
College, 1963. 37f; bibliography of Conrad's letters,
f34   1649
A sailor and a manuscript. Book Leaf (NY) N 23 '23 1650
Sakowski, Juliusz
One only lives once. In Conrad żywy, edited by Wit
Tarnawski. London: B. Świderski, 1957. p79-83
Joseph Conrad. In Asy i damy. Portrety z pamięci.
Paris: Księgarnia Polska w Paryżu, 1962   1651
[A sale of letters written by Joseph Conrad to Madame Pora-
dowska] Saturday Review of Literature 10:453 F 3
'34   1652
Salmon, Arthur L.
Joseph Conrad: an attempt at appreciation. Everyman 2,
no 41:461-2 Jl 25 '13
Russian Pole, British seaman, English novelist. Book
News Monthly 36:442-3 Ag '18   1653
Sanders, A. T.
Joseph Conrad Korzeniowski. Nautical Magazine 105,
no 6:567-8 Je '21   1654
Sanders, Charles

Conrad's "Heart of Darkness." Explicator 24, item 2,
    S '65   1655
Sandison, Alan
    Joseph Conrad: a window on to chaos. In The wheel of
    empire... London: Macmillan; New York: St. Martin's
    press, 1967. p120-48   1655a
Sapieha, Lew
    Istota polskości Conrada (The essence of Conrad's Polish
    character). Wiadomości (News) 4, no 183:3 O 2
    '49   1656
Sargent, George H.
    American notes. Joseph Conrad and the American news-
    paper interviewers. Bookman's Journal & Print Col-
    lector 8, no 22:125 Jl '23
    In Joseph Conrad's literary workshop. Boston Evening
    Transcript Book Section O 20 '23 part 6, p1-2; il-
    lustrated   1657
Sasse, Maria-Elisabeth
    Wesenmerkmale der Völker im Spiegel Werke Joseph
    Conrads. Ph. D. Thesis, Münster, 1951. 155p   1658
Saugère, Albert
    Quelques recherches dans la conscience des héros de
    Conrad. La Nouvelle Revue Française 23:738-42
    D 1 '24   1659
Saurat, Denis
    Conrad et la Provence. In Perspectives. Paris: Stock,
    1938. p229-33   1660
Saveson, J. E.
    Masterman as a source for Nostromo. Notes & Queries
    ns 10:368-70 O '63   1661
Sawamura, Torajiro
    Introduction. In The mirror of the sea, by Joseph Con-
    rad (abridged). (Kenkyusha New English texts) Tokyo:
    Kenkyusha [nd ? 1930?] p i-iii (In Japanese)
    Joseph Conrad: a biographical study. 1934. 134p
    (In Japanese)   1662
Sawyer, Arthur Edward
    Tragedy in the fiction of Joseph Conrad. Ph. D. Thesis,
    University of Toronto, 1960. 253f
    Joseph Conrad: a centenary review. Canadian Slavonic
    Papers 4:182-98 '59
    (Excerpts from three public lectures given Dec. 3-5,
    1957 at the University of British Columbia)   1663
Saxton, Eugene F.
    The romantic story of Joseph Conrad. In A set of six,
    by Joseph Conrad. Garden City, New York: Doubleday,
    Page, 1916. [4]p (appended); same. In The Country

Saxton, Eugene F. (cont.)
Life Press... Garden City, New York: Doubleday,
Page, 1919. p101-4; same. In The duel, a military
tale, by Joseph Conrad. Garden City, New York:
Garden City Publishing Company, 1923. p119; same.
In Joseph Conrad. Garden City, New York: Doubleday,
Page [nd] p[3-6]   1664
Sayre, Ira Clarke
Conrad's treatment of the short story. In The subjective
or expressionistic element in the short story. M. A.
Thesis, Ohio State University, 1931. p41-54
(On "Youth")   1665
Scheifley, William H.
Why Conrad wrote his fiction in English. Indianapolis
Star '25; same. In Impressions of postwar Europe.
Los Angeles, California: Wetzel Publishing Co.
[c1935] p277-80   1665a
Schelling, Felix Emmanuel
Joseph Conrad on life and letters. In Appraisements and
asperities as to some contemporary writers. Philadel-
phia: Lippincott, 1922. p62-6   1666
Schieszlová, Olga
Národnostni blondění Josefa Conrada. (Vicissitudes of
Joseph Conrad's national consciousness). Časopis Pro
Moderní Filologik (Prague) 22:338-48 '36   1667
Schirmer, Walter Franz
Joseph Conrad. In Der englische Roman der neuesten
Zeit. Heidelberg: Carl Winter, 1923. p23-30   1668
Schlecht, Elvine
Mensch und Welt in den Werken Joseph Conrads. Dis-
sertation, Wien, 1950. (Maschinenschrift)   1669
Schlefer, Richard Myer
The moral experience of Conrad's heroines. Honors
Thesis, Department of English, Harvard College,
March, 1962. 34f   1670
Schnack, Friedrich
Joseph Conrad, Kapitän-Schriftsteller. Hannoverscher
Kourier D 18 '26
Kapitän und Schriftsteller. Baden-Badener Bühnenblatt
7, no 14 Mr '27
Die Romane Josef Conrads. Der Kunstward und Kultur-
wart 40, no 12:398-400 S '27   1671
Schneider, Daniel J.
Symbolism in Conrad's Lord Jim: the total pattern.
Modern Fiction Studies 12:427-38 Winter '66-'67   1672
Scholes, Robert and Robert Kellogg
The nature of narrative. New York: Oxford University

Press, 1966. p260-1   1673
Schorer, Mark
    The story: a critical anthology. New York: Prentice-
    Hall, 1950. p243-6
    (On "Amy Foster")   1674
Schriftgiesser, Karl
    Joseph Conrad. The true apostle of romance. Boston
    Evening Transcript Book Section Ag 1 '25 p1   1675
Schultheiss, Thomas
    Conrad on stage censorship. American Notes & Queries
    5, no 8:117-18 Ap '67
    Lord Hamlet and Lord Jim. Polish Review 11, no 4:101-
    33 Autumn '66   1676
Schunk, Karl
    Der Zufall bei Joseph Conrad. Ph. D. Thesis, Univ. of
    Göttingen, 1942. 140p   1677
Schwab, Arnold T.
    Conrad's American speeches and his reading from Victory.
    Modern Philology 62:342-7 My '65
    Joseph Conrad's American friend: correspondence with
    James Huneker. Modern Philology 52:222-32 My '55
                                                       1678
Schwamborn, Heinrich
    Joseph Conrad, der Dichter des Abenteuers. Kölnische
    Zeitung no 152, July 1935
    Joseph Conrad: der Mann und das Werk. Die Neueren
    Sprachen neue folge 7, heft 5:233-42 '58   1679
Schwartz, Edward
    The destructive element. M. A. Thesis, Columbia Univer-
    sity, 1948. 66p   1680
Schwarz, Daniel Roger
    Joseph Conrad as a philosophic novelist: a criticism.
    B. A. Honors Thesis in English, Union College, 1965.
    65f   1680a
Schweikert, Harry Christian
    Joseph Conrad. (1857-1924). In Short stories, edited by
    H. C. Schweikert. New York: Harcourt, Brace [c1925]
    p372-3   1681
Schwertman, Mary P.
    Materialism and the individual in Conrad's Nostromo.
    M. A. Thesis, Columbia University, 1953. 114p   1682
Scott-James, Rolfe Arnold
    Above the battle. In Fifty years of English literature,
    1900-1950. London: Longmans, Green [1951] p54-74
    The new romance. In Modernism and romance. London:
    Lane, 1908. p229-35   1683

Scrimgeour, Cecil
  Jimmy Wait and the dance of death: Conrad's Nigger of
    the "Narcissus." Critical Quarterly 7:339-52 Winter
    '65   1684
Scrimgeour, Gary J.
  Against The Great Gatsby. Criticism 8:75-86 Winter '66
    (A comparison of this book with Conrad's Heart of
    Darkness)   1685
Sealey, Ethel M.
  Notes... In Youth: a narrative, by Joseph Conrad.
    Toronto: Copp Clark [192-] p49-61
    Typhoon. School (Toronto) 24:393-6 Ja '36   1686
Seamen's Institute opens Conrad Library Thursday. New
    York Herald Tribune My 20 '34 p11   1687
Seaver, Lillian Fitzgerald
  Some patterns of imagery in Joseph Conrad's Typhoon.
    M. A. Thesis, Dominican College of San Rafael, 1960.
    61p   1688
Secor, Robert Arnold
  Conrad and Hawthorne. M. A. Thesis, Brown University,
    1963. iv, 165f; bibl., f162-5
    (Examines "A Smile of Fortune," and Victory)   1689
The secret of Joseph Conrad's appeal. Current Opinion
    (NY) 74:677-9 Je '23   1690
Sée, Ida R.
  Joseph Conrad à Montpellier. Le Petit Méridional S 6
    '24   1691
Seek funds to complete Conrad memorial library. New York
    Herald Tribune My 22 '32   1692
Selle, Cäcilie
  Das Wesen der Schicksalsmacht nach dem Werk Joseph
    Conrads und ihre Bedeutung für seine Weltbetrachtung.
    Ph. D. Thesis, Univ. of Marburg, 1943. 163p   1693
Shand, John
  Some notes on Joseph Conrad. Criterion 3:61-4 O '24;
    same. In The art of Joseph Conrad: a critical sym-
    posium, edited by Robert Wooster Stallman. East Lan-
    sing, Michigan: Michigan State University Press, 1960.
    p13-19   1694
Shanks, Edward Buxton
  Mr. Joseph Conrad. London Mercury 9:502-11 Mr '24;
    same. In Second essays on literature. London:
    Collins [c1927] p23-40; same. In Essays for our day,
    edited by Louis Byron Shackelford and Florien Preston
    Gass. New York: Norton [c1931] p360-72
  [A new serial by Conrad: Chance] Dial 66:417-18 Ap
    19 '19   1695

Shannon, Homer S.
[Joseph Conrad's "The Sisters"]   Bookman (NY) 68:216-
    17 O '28   1696
Shapiro, Barbara
Modes of being: illusion and actuality in Joseph Conrad.
    Honors Essay, City College of New York, 1963. 52p
                                                               1697
Sharon, Adeline
Nationalism in the works of Joseph Conrad.   M. A. Thesis,
    State University of Iowa, 1934. 62p   1698
Shaw, Ann B.
Conradian elements in the novels of Robert Penn Warren.
    M. A. Thesis, University of Tennessee, 1961. 130f
    (Issued as a microcard)   1698a
Shaw, Roger
Ports of the Conrad country.   Golden Book 10:124 O
    '29   1699
Shaw, William Frederick
A study of self-portraiture and technique in the Marlow
    group in Joseph Conrad's fiction.   M. A. Thesis, Univ.
    of Texas, 1936. vi-[xx], 150f   1700
Shelton, (Mrs.) Evie La Grone
Joseph Conrad: a study of his creative imagination at
    work. M. A. Thesis, University of Texas, 1935. iii-
    xi, 235f
    (On Almayer's Folly, The Nigger of the 'Narcissus,'
    An Outcast of the Islands, The Rescue)   1701
Sherbo, Arthur
Conrad's Victory and Hamlet.   Notes & Queries 198:492-
    3 N '53   1702
Sherman, Ellen Burns
Joseph Conrad, poet.   New York Herald Tribune Books
    N 23 '24 Section 11, p11   1703
Sherman, Stuart
Introduction. In The Secret Agent, by Joseph Conrad.
    (Memorial Edition) Garden City, New York: Doubleday,
    Page, 1925. Volume IX, p vii-xv   1704
Sherrill, Rowland A.
Conrad's Lord Jim; Explicator 25, no 7, item 55, Mr
    '67   1705
Sherry, Norman
Conrad. (The Critical Heritage Series)   London: Rout-
    ledge & Kegan Paul (Announced in Times Literary
    Supplement Ja 18 '68 p52)
Conrad and the Bangkok Times.   Nineteenth-Century Fic-
    tion 20:255-66 D '65
Conrad and the S. S. Vidar.   Review of English Studies

Sherry, Norman (cont.)
  ns 14:157-63 My '63
  Conrad's Eastern port: the setting of the inquiry in
    Lord Jim. Review of English Literature (Leeds) 6,
    no 4:52-61 O '65
  Conrad's Eastern world. Cambridge: Cambridge Univ.
    press, 1966. [v]-[xii], 340p; portraits
    (Dated 1966 unless otherwise noted. Reviewed by C. W.
    Mann, Jr. in Library Journal 91:3434 Jl; Denis Dono-
    ghue in New Statesman 72:291 Ag 26; Times Literary
    Supplement N 3 p993; Ian Watt in Virginia Quarterly
    Review 42:644-9 Autumn; Tony Tanner in Spectator no
    7201:86 Jl 15; Stanley Weintraub in Saturday Review
    50, no 23:37-8 Je 10 '67; New York Times D 17 p31;
    W. J. Harvey in Notes & Queries 211:432-3 N; L.
    Graver in Nineteenth-Century Fiction 21:403-5 Mr '67;
    Quarterly Review 304:468 O; Jerry Allen in Times
    Literary Supplement Ag 5 p174; N. Sherry in S 16
    Times Literary Supplement p347; Jerry Allen in ibid.
    S 23 p378; A. H. Verkuyl in ibid. O 14 p481; A. von
    Marle in ibid. D 8 p1149; Michael Thorpe, Jerry
    Allen, & J. D. Gordan in Times Literary Supplement D
    15 p1175; W. K. Seymour in Contemporary Review 209:
    276 N; Philip Hobsbaum in Listener 76:430-1 S 22; C.
    T. Watts in Review of English Studies ns 19, no 73:
    92-4 F '68; Jerome Zuckerman in Books Abroad 42,
    no 1:129-30 Winter '68; noted by Edgar F. Harden in
    Victorian Studies 11, no 3:420 Mr '68)
  Conrad's Otago: a case of mistaken identity. Notes &
    Queries ns 10:370-2 O '63
  Conrad's source for Lord Jim. Modern Language Review
    59:545-57 O '64
  Correspondence. Review of English Studies ns 17:183-4
    My '66 (A rejoinder to the article by C. T. Watts)
  "Exact biography" and The Shadow-Line. Publications of
    the Modern Language Association of America 79:620-5
    D '64
  The Greenwich Bomb Outrage and The Secret Agent. Re-
    view of English Studies ns 18, no 72:412-428 N '67
  Lord Jim and "The Secret Sharer." Review of English
    Studies ns 16:378-92 N '65
  The pilgrim ship in Lord Jim: Conrad's two sources.
    Philological Quarterly 44:88-99 Ja '65
  Rajah Laut - a quest for Conrad's source. Modern Phi-
    lology 62:22-41 Ag '64   1706
Sherwin, Jane King
  The literary epiphany in some early fiction of Flaubert,

Sievert, William
Review notes and study guide to Conrad's Lord Jim,
Heart of Darkness, The Secret Sharer.   New York:
Monarch press [c1964] 100p   1715a
Sigaux, Gilbert
Sur une livre de Conrad.   Gazette des Lettres Ag 17
'46   1716
Sikes, Jimmie R.
Style and thought in Conrad's Lord Jim.   English Honors
Thesis, March 1, 1957, Harvard College. 39f   1717
Silberman, Donald
Conrad's method of composition in Lord Jim and Chance.
M. A.   Thesis, Cornell University, September, 1958.
78f   1717a
Simmons, J. L.
The dual morality in "The Secret Sharer."   Studies in
Short Fiction 2:209-20 Spring '65   1718
Simon, Irène
Joseph Conrad.   In Formes du Roman anglais de Dickens
à Joyce.   Liège: Faculté de Philosophie et Lettres,
1949.   p[258]-97 (Bibliothèque de la Faculté de
Philosophie et Lettres de l'Université de Liège.
Fasc. 118)   1719
Sims, George
Copies of Chance, dated "1913."   Book Collector 14, no
4:213-14 Winter '65   1720
Sinclair, Upton
Mammonart; an essay in economic interpretation.   Pasa-
dena, California: Published by the author, 1925.
p374   1721
Singleton, Emma Mildred
Joseph Conrad's personal philosophy of life.   M. A. Thesis,
Univ. of Southern California at Los Angeles, 1936.
iii, 143p   1722
Sinha, Dr. Murari Shri
The craft of Joseph Conrad as a novelist.   Ph. D. Thesis,
Lucknow University, 1943   1723
Sinjohn, John [pseud.]
See: Galsworthy, John   1724
Sister Estelle, S. P.
Thematic and formal function of Gentleman Brown. Notre
Dame English Journal 1:26-8 Spring '62   1725
Skarbek-Peretiatkowicz, Hanna
See: Peretiatkowicz, Hanna Skarbek   1726
[Skarszewski, Tadeusz Żuk] S. , T. ; also: S. , Z.
Amicus Plato.   Kraj nos 12, 14, 1899
Biblioteka Conrada.   Ruch Literacki nos 1-2, Ja-F '26

Conradiana.   Poland (NY) 7, no 8:469-71, 512 Ag '26;
   7, no 9:542-3, 573-4 S '26; 7, no 10:615-16, 637,
   640 O '26; 7, no 11:675-77, 700-2, 704 N '26; 8, no
   1:22-4, 45-8, 50 Ja '27; 8, no 8:471-2, 490 Ag '27
Conradiana.   (Kolekcje amerykańskie).   Ruch Literacki
   no 6:192 Je '27

Sklare, Arnold B.
   Joseph Conrad.   In The art of the novella.   New York:
   Macmillan, 1965.   p344-5
   (On "Heart of Darkness")   1728
Ślaski, B.
   O terminologię morską.   Warsaw: 1937   1729
Slater, Mary Margaret
   A structural study of Joseph Conrad.   M. A. Thesis,
   University of Toronto, 1934. 96p   1730
Sloane, Eugene Hulse
   Joseph Conrad and the classical ideal.   M. A. Thesis,
   Ohio State University, 1926. 85p   1731
Słonimski, Antoni
   Conrad i Wells.   Nowiny Literackie (Literary News) no
   24, 1948
   Dialog o miłośći ojczyzny między Josephem a Stefanem
   (Dialogue concerning love of country between Joseph
   [Conrad] and Stefan [Zeromski]); a poem.   Skamander
   rok 4, tome 4, vol. 28:15-21 Ap '23
   Na śmierć Conrada; poem.   Wiadomości Literackie 1, no
   33:2 Ag 17 '24; same.   (translated by Edward A. Sy-
   manski as "Death of Joseph Conrad")   In From the
   fourth province.   Florence: 1952. p76-7; same.   In
   Poezje 1916-1961.   Warsaw: 1961;   same.   In Joseph
   Conrad Korzeniowski, by Róża Jabłkowska.   Warsaw:
   Państwowe Zakłady Wydawnictwo Szkolynch, 1964.
   p343-[344]   1732
Small, Ray
   Joseph Conrad's use of superstition and tradition in nine
   of his novels.   M. A. Thesis, University of Texas,
   1941. iii-viii, 139f   1733
Smaridge, N. A.
   Master mariner: the adventurous life of Joseph Conrad.
   Illustrated by Charles Waterhouse.   (Hawthorn junior
   biographies) New York: Hawthorn Books [c1966] 174p;
   illustrations   1734
Smet, Joseph de
   Joseph Conrad.   Mercure de France 97:51-75 My 1 '12;
   same.   La Nouvelle Revue Française 7:1093-5 Je
   1 '12   1735

Smialkowa, A.
  Conrad's passion for the sea and ships.   M. A. Thesis,
    Univ. of Warsaw, 1950   1736
Smith, Annie Emma
  Dominant character traits of Conrad's men.   M. A. Thesis,
    George Peabody College for Teachers, 1936.   141p
                                                              1737
Smith, Arthur J. M.
  Joseph Conrad: Victory.   In Introduction to literature
    and the fine arts.   East Lansing, Michigan: Michigan
    State College Press, 1950.   p362-6; same.   In The
    laureate fraternity; an introduction to literature, edited
    by Adrian Jaffé and Herbert Weisinger.   Evanston,
    Illinois: Row, Peterson, 1960.   p267-70   1738
Smith, Curtis C.
  Conrad's Chance: a dialectical novel.   Thoth 6, no 2:
    16-24 Spring '65   1739
Smith, David R.
  Nostromo and the three sisters.   Studies in English Lit-
    erature, 1500-1900 (Rice University) 2:497-508 Autumn
    '62
  Conrad's manifesto: preface to a career.   The history
    of The Preface to The Nigger of the "Narcissus" with
    facsimiles of the manuscripts, edited with an essay
    by David R. Smith.   Philadelphia: Philip H. & A. S. W.
    Rosenbach Foundation, 1966.   [5]-78p
    (1100 copies only)
    "Acknowledgements," p[5]; "Foreword," p9-[14]; "Con-
    rad's manifesto; preface to a career." p47-[77].
    Woodcut portrait of Conrad by Leonard Baskin.   (Noted
    in Philadelphia Inquirer Jl 7 '68 Section 7 p7)   1740
Smith, J. Oates
  The existential comedy of Conrad's "Youth."   Renascence
    16:22-8 Fall '63   1741
Smith, Jack Edward
  The unity of Joseph Conrad's short story collections.
    Ph. D. Thesis, Univ. of Arkansas, 1967.   221p; abstract
    in Dissertation Abstracts 28:243A '67   1742
Smith, James Walter
  Joseph Conrad - master mariner and novelist.   Boston
    Evening Transcript My 12 '23   1743
Smith, John William
  A study of character relations in five novels of Joseph
    Conrad.   M. A. Thesis, University of Toronto, 1965.
    224f
    (Lord Jim, Nostromo, Under Western Eyes, Victory,
    The Shadow-Line)   1743a

Smock, George Edward
    Joseph Conrad's theory of the art of fiction.   M. A.
    Thesis, University of Chicago, 1928   1744
Smolka, Georg
    Joseph Conrad, der Dichter des Meeres.   Germania no
    117, 1937   1745
Snell, Frank M.
    Joseph Conrad: the truth of existence and fidelity to life.
    M. A. Thesis, Columbia University, 1950.   63p   1746
Sobol, Ken
    Review notes and study guide to Conrad's Victory, Nos-
    tromo, The Nigger of the "Narcissus," The Shadow-
    Line.   New York: Monarch [1964] 142p   1746a
Solomon, Barbara
    Conrad's Marlow as a narrator and a character.   M. A.
    Thesis, University of Kansas, 1960.   115f
    (On "Youth," "Heart of Darkness," and Lord Jim) 1747
Solomon, Eric
    Joseph Conrad, William Faulkner, and the Nobel Prize
    speech.   Notes & Queries ns 14:247-8 Jl '67
    Stephen Crane in England: a portrait of the artist.
    [Columbus:]   Ohio State University press [c1964] p91-
    118
    (On Ford and Conrad)   1748
Solomon, W. L.
    [Note on Conrad in Heywood Broun's column, "Books"]
    New York Tribune Je 7 '20 p10   1749
Somermier, Cornelia Eloise
    Idée Fixe as it manifests itself in certain of Conrad's
    characters.   M. S. Thesis, Kansas State Teachers Col-
    lege of Emporia, 1933   1750
Somerville, Peter F.
    Stephen Crane.   Outlook (London) 54:319 N 1 '24   1751
Spalding, Branch
    Conrad's evolved descriptive method.   M. A. Thesis, Uni-
    versity of Virginia, 1931.   63p   1752
Spector, Robert D.
    Irony as theme: Conrad's The Secret Agent.   Nineteenth-
    Century Fiction 13:69-71 Je '58   1753
Sper, Felix
    The cream of Conrad.   Poet Lore 38:422-5 Summer '27
                                                   1754
Spicer-Simson, Theodore
    Men of letters of the British Isles... New York: Rudge,
    1924.   p39-40   1755
Spinner, Kaspar
    Embracing the universe: some annotations to Joseph

Spinner, Kaspar (cont.)
  Conrad's Heart of Darkness.   English Studies 43:420-3
  O '62   1756
Spivack, Charlotte K.
  The journey to Hell: Satan, the shadow, and the self.
  Centennial Review 9, no 4:420-37 Fall '65
  (Includes references to "Heart of Darkness")   1756a
Spoerri-Müller, Ruth
  Joseph Conrad: das problem der Vereinsamung. Winter-
  thur: P. G. Keller, 1959. xii, 143p; bibliography,
  p v-x   1757
Squire, (Sir) John Collings [Solomon Eagle, pseud.]
  Joseph Conrad - Conrad's last book. Observer (London)
  Ag 10 '24; same. In Sunday mornings. London: Wil-
  liam Heinemann [1930] p260-9
  Mr. Conrad's masterpiece. Land & Water 69, no 2881:15
  Jl 26 '17; same. In Life and letters... London: Heine-
  mann, 1921; New York: Doran [c1921] p153-60
  (On Lord Jim)
  Other people's books. In Books in general. New York:
  Knopf, 1919. p185-6
  (On Almayer's Folly)   1758
Stackpole, Edouard A.
  Introduction. In Typhoon and other tales of the sea.
  (Great illustrated classics) New York: Dodd, Mead
  [c1963] p v-xi; portrait   1759
Stallman, Robert Wooster
  Conrad and The Great Gatsby. Twentieth Century Litera-
  ture 1:5-12 Ap '55; same. In The houses that James
  built... East Lansing, Michigan: Michigan State Uni-
  versity press, 1961. p150-8
  Conrad and "The Secret Sharer." Accent 9:131-43 Spring
  '49; same. In The art of modern fiction, edited by
  Ray Benedict West and R. W. Stallman. New York:
  Rinehart, 1949. p490-8; same. In The art of Joseph
  Conrad: a critical symposium, edited by Robert
  Wooster Stallman. East Lansing, Michigan: Michigan
  State University Press, 1960. p275-88
  Conrad criticism today. Sewanee Review 67:135-45
  Winter '59
  The creative reader. New York: Ronald press, 1954.
  p326-8
  (On "Amy Foster")
  Introduction. In The art of Joseph Conrad: a critical
  symposium, edited by Robert Wooster Stallman. East
  Lansing, Michigan: Michigan State University Press,
  1960. p[ix]-xxviii

Life, art, and "The Secret Sharer." In Forms of modern
fiction... edited by William Van O'Connor. Minneapolis, Minnesota: University of Minnesota Press, 1948.
p229-42
(Reviewed in Times Literary Supplement F 5 '49 p85)
The structure and symbolism of Conrad's Victory.
Western Review 13:146-57 Spring '49; same. In The
art of modern fiction, edited by Ray Benedict West
and Robert Wooster Stallman. New York: Rinehart,
1949. p607-20
Time and The Secret Agent. Texas Studies in Language
& Literature 1:101-22 Spring '59; same. In The art of
Joseph Conrad: a critical symposium, edited by Ro-
bert Wooster Stallman. East Lansing, Michigan:
Michigan State University Press, 1960. p234-54; same.
In The houses that James built... East Lansing, Michi-
gan State University Press, 1961. p111-30   1760
Stallman, Robert Wooster (editor)
The art of Joseph Conrad: a critical symposium, edited
by Robert Wooster Stallman. East Lansing, Michigan:
Michigan State University Press, 1960. xxix, 354p;
bibliography, p342; introduction, p[ix]-xxviii
(Reviewed by C. W. Mann, Jr. in Library Journal 85:
2172 Je 1 '60; W. Chalewik in Rocznik Literacki 1963
p277-8)   1761
Stanga, Carolyn Annette
Irony in Conrad's The Secret Agent. M. A. Thesis, Uni-
versity of Georgia, 1967. iii, 85f; bibl., f83-5   1762
Staniewski, Maurycy
Angielskość Conrada. Wiadomości Literackie 6, no 14:1
Ap 7 '29; same. In Wspomnienia i studia o Conradzie,
edited by Barbara Kocówna. Warsaw: Państwowy
Instytut Wydawniczy [1963] p48-60
Mixed loyalty Conrada. Wiadomości Literackie 6, no 25:
1 Je 23 '29   1763
Staral, Margarete
Die Behandlung des Meeres bei Joseph Conrad. Ph. D.
Thesis, University of Prague, 1943. 139p   1764
Stasko, Mary Lucentia, Sister
A first translation into English of The World of Conrad's
Novels and Tales by Jozef Ujejski and a consideration
of Ujejski's critique in the light of recent Conrad criti-
cism. M. A. Thesis, Canisius College, 1954. ii, 130f;
bibliography f128-30   1765
Stauffer, Ruth Mathilda
Joseph Conrad; his romantic-realism. Boston: Four Seas,
1922. [7]-122p

Stauffer, Ruth Mathilda (cont.)
    (Originally an M. A. Thesis, University of California, 1919. 139p)
    (Reviewed in Literary Review F 3 '23 p438; Henry Salpeter in Nation (NY) 116:670 Je 6 '23; Philip Littell in New Republic 34:301 My 9 '23; Theodore T. Stenberg in Sewanee Review 30:500-1 O '22; New York Times Book Review F 4 '23 p9; Catholic World 117: 417-18 Je '23; Dial 74:634 Je '23; Booklist 19:248 My '23; Henry D. -Davray in Mercure de France 165:821 Ag 1 '23; America 28:596 Ap 7 '23; noted in Pittsburgh Monthly Bulletin 28:300 Je '23; New York Times Book Review F 24 '23 p9)   1766

Stavrou, C. N.
    Conrad, Camus, and Sisyphus.   Audience 7:80-96 Winter '60   1767

Stawell, Florence Melian
    Conrad. In Essays and studies by members of the English Association. Oxford: Clarendon press, 1920.
    volume 6, p88-111
    (Reviewed in Boston Evening Transcript Ap 6 '21) 1768

Stegner, Wallace
    Variations on a theme by Conrad. Yale Review ns 39: 512-23 Mr '50   1769

Stein, Marion Louise
    Joseph Conrad's second novel: An Outcast of the Islands. M. A. Thesis, Univ. of North Carolina, 1967. 52f   1770

Stein, William Byashe
    Buddhism and "Heart of Darkness." Western Humanities Review 11:281-5 Summer '57
    Conrad's East: time, history, action, and Maya. Texas Studies in Language and Literature 7:265-83 Autumn '65
    Conrad's underworld. Modern Fiction Studies 2:235-7 Winter '56
    "The Heart of Darkness:" Bodhisattva Sceneria. Orient/ West 9: no 5:37-46 S-O '64
    The lotus posture and "The Heart of Darkness." Modern Fiction Studies 2:235-7 Winter '56-'57; same. In The art of Joseph Conrad: a critical symposium, edited by Robert Wooster Stallman. East Lansing, Michigan: Michigan State University Press, 1960. p179-81   1771

Steinmann, Martin Jr.
    The old novel and the new. In From Jane Austen to Joseph Conrad... edited by Robert C. Rathburn and Martin Steinmann, Jr. Minneapolis: University of Minnesota press [1958] p288-9, 294, 299, 301-2   1772

Stencel, Michelle M.
 A strain of pessimism in The Red Badge of Courage and
  Lord Jim. M. A. Thesis, Tulane University, 1966.
  36f; bibliography, f33-6   1773
Stephens, Rosemary
 Students, Mr. Conrad. English Journal 57, no 2:188-90
  F '68   1773a
Stepp, Nancy Terrell
 The ideal woman in the work of Joseph Conrad. M. A.
  Thesis, University of Virginia, 1962. 44p   1774
Stern, Anatol
 Droga do potęgi. Joseph Conrad, Jack London i Stefan
  Żeromski. Poeci morza i profesorowie energji
  narodowej. Wiadomości Literackie 1, no 2:1 Ja 13
  '24   1775
Sternberg, Sima
 Two aspects of the voyage: a critical study of Moby Dick
  and "Heart of Darkness." Honors Essay, City College
  of New York, 1957. 102p   1776
Stevens, Arthur W.
 George Orwell and contemporary British fiction of Burma:
  the problem of "place." Ph. D. Thesis, Univ. of Wash-
  ington, 1957. 163p; abstract in Dissertation Abstracts
  18:1799-1800 '58; p 121-33 are on Conrad's Victory.
                                                       1777
Stewart, John Innes Macintosh
 Joseph Conrad. In Eight modern writers. (Oxford His-
  tory of English Literature, volume 12) Oxford: Oxford
  University press, 1963. p184-222
 Joseph Conrad. New York: Dodd, Mead, 1968. 272p
 Joseph Conrad: a heart in exile. Times Educational
  Supplement 2138:621 My 11 '56; portrait   1778
Stewart, Powell and Bradshaw, Michael Jr. and others
 A goodly company. New York: American book company
  [c1934] p46-8, 184-5, 5-7, 273-4   1779
Stoessl, Otto
 Zwei Englische Erzähler. Zeitwende 3:268-74 S '27 1780
Stoińska, Celina
 Józef Conrad. Gazeta Warszawska no 99, Ap 10 '14 1781
Story, Mattison Low
 Joseph Conrad: autobiographical elements in his work.
  M. A. Thesis, University of Texas, 1938. iii-xi, 95f
                                                       1782
Straat, E.
 Joseph Conrad. Groene Amsterdammer Ja 15 '49 p8
                                                       1783

Straight, Michael
  Conrad - the hollow center. New Republic 142:15-17
    Ap 18 '60   1784
Strandberg, A. Edith
  Characterization in the novels of Joseph Conrad. M. A.
    Thesis, De Paul University, 1944. 105f   1785
Strandgaard, Henrik
  Joseph Conrad. In Fremmede digtere i det 20. århun-
    drede. Copenhagen: G. E. C. Gad, 1967. Volume I,
    p269-81   1786
Strawson, H.
  Joseph Conrad - master mariner and master novelist.
    London Quarterly Review 159:315-24 Jl '34   1787
Street, George Slythe
  About our fiction. Pall Mall Magazine 34:136-7 S '04;
    same. In Books and things... London: Duckworth,
    1905. p136-7   1788
Stresau, Hermann
  Joseph Conrad, der tragiker des westens. Berlin: Ver-
    lag die Runde [c1937] [11]-[203]p; Conrad's works,
    p[198]-200. Reissued: Hannover: Richard Beeck-Ver-
    lag [1947] 11-196p
    (Reviewed by E. T. Sehrt in Englische Studien 73, no
    3:410-11 '39; Karl Hugo Reichart in Anglia Beiblatt 49:
    210-12 Ap '38; Erich Müller in Die Literatur 40:161 N
    17 '37; Georg Smolka in Germania 28, Ja '38; W. E.
    Süskind in Die Literatur 40:247 D 7 '37; Horst Rüdiger
    in Geistige Arbeit 10:10-11 S 5 '38)
  Joseph Conrad. Tragische Figuren im Konflict mit der
    Wirklichkeit. Deutsche Universitäts-Zeitung 8, no 10:
    7-10 My 18 '53
  Der junge Joseph Conrad. Die Neue Rundschau 48, part
    1:354-79 Ap '37   1789
Strunsky, Simeon
  About books, more or less: Complex or complicated.
    New York Times Book Review Ag 17 '24 p4   1790
Stuart, John McH.
  London compares thriller of Willard's and Conrad's plays.
    Herald (NY) N 19 '22 (Conrad's Secret Agent on the
    London stage)   1790a
Stuckert, Frances Ann
  Conrad and Melville: the sea aspects of their works.
    M. A. Thesis, University of Texas, 1938. iii-xv,
    162f   1791
  The study table. Mr. Joseph Conrad. Everyman 13, no
    327:344-5 Ja 18 '19 (Signed "Bookworm")   1792
Sudler, Culbreth

Joseph Conrad comes to America.   New York Herald
    Books Ap 29 '23 p1-2   1792a
Sullivan, Sister Mary Petrus
    The descriptive style of Joseph Conrad.   Ph. D. Thesis,
    University of Notre Dame, 1964. 400p; abstract in
    Dissertation Abstracts 25:486-7 '64   1793
Süskind, Walter E.
    Arbeit und kunst.   Anmerkungen zu Joseph Conrad.
    Kölnische Zeitung nos 359-60:1 Jl 20 '39
Joseph Conrad.   Die Neue Rundschau 49, part 1:292-305
    Mr '38; 37, part 2:536-48 N '26
Die Seele des Kriegers.   Anmerkungen zu Joseph Conrad.
    Kölnische Zeitung nos 365-6:1-2 Jl 23 '38   1794
Suspense, by Joseph Conrad.   Bookmark (London) 1, no 2:
    13 Summer '25
    (A note on its imminent publication)   1794a
Sutherland, (Captain) John Georgeson
    At sea with Conrad.   Nautical Magazine 105, no 5:385-
    90 My '21
    At sea with Joseph Conrad... With a foreword by Joseph
    Conrad.   London: Richards, 1922. 7-150p; foreword,
    p9-10; portraits
    (1250 copies only)
    (Reviewed by L. B. in Freeman 6:358 D 20 '22; Herbert
    S. Gorman in New York Times Book Review O 1 '22
    p2, 24; Times Literary Supplement Jl 6 '22 p440;
    Spectator 129:214 Ag 12 '22; [Richard Curle in] Daily
    Mail (London) Je 28 '22 p7; John O'London's Weekly
    7:493 Jl 22 '22; Outlook (NY) 133:321 F 14 '23; Clement
    King Shorter in Sphere 95:364 D 22 '23; New York
    Herald O 29 '22; Bookman (NY) 56:511 D '22; Independ-
    ent 109:284 N 11 '22; New Statesman & Nation 19:546
    Ag 19 '22)   1795
Swarthout, Glendon F.
    The creative crisis.   Ph. D. Thesis, Michigan State Uni-
    versity, 1955. 349p; abstract in Dissertation Abstracts
    19:816 '58
    (Includes The Rescue)   1796
Swettenham, Frank
    The story of Lord Jim.   Times Literary Supplement S 6
    '23 p588; answered, Times Literary Supplement S 13
    '23 p604; rejoinder in Times Literary Supplement S 20
    '23 p620
    How Conrad wrote.   John O'London's Weekly 62:1021
    N 13 '53   1797
Świderska, P. Alina
    Sprawa polskości Conrada (The problem of Conrad's Polish

Świderska, P. Alina (cont.)

character). Sprawozdania z czynności i posiedzeń
Polskiej Akademii Umiejetności (Proceedings of the
Polish Academy of Science and Letters) 49: no 10:
521-2 '48   1798

Swinnerton, Frank Arthur

Authors I never met. London: Allen & Unwin, 1956.
p25-32

An estimate of Joseph Conrad... with a special comment
on The Rover. Vanity Fair 22, no 1:54, 100 Mr '24

From Henry James to Gissing. In Background with
chorus... New York: Farrar, Straus, 1956. p118-36
(Reviewed in Times Literary Supplement Jl 6 '56 p406)

Georgian literary scene. New York: Farrar, Straus
[1950] p123-31

Mr. Conrad. Bookman (NY) 60:196 O '24

Romance. Saturday Review of Literature 1:193-4 O 18
'24

Swinnerton: an autobiography. London: Hutchinson &
Co. [nd 1937?] passim

Travellers. [IV. Joseph Conrad] In The Georgian scene:
a literary panorama. New York: Farrar & Rinehart
[c1934] p146-67   1799

Symon, J. D.

[The late Joseph Conrad] Illustrated London News 165:
312 Ag 16 '24   1800

Symons, Arthur

Conrad. Forum 53:579-92 My '15; same. In Dramatis
personae. Indianapolis: Bobbs-Merrill [c1923] p1-23

Figures of several centuries. New York: Dutton, 1917.
(Dedicated to Joseph Conrad)

Joseph Conrad. Land & Water 70, no 2895:14-15 N 1
'17; same. Current Opinion 64:53 Ja '18

Joseph Conrad: a personal impression. Queen 155, no
4052:5 Ag 20 '24

Notes on Joseph Conrad; with some unpublished letters.
London: Myers and Co., 1925. [7]-38p; portrait.
There was another edition, with the same pagination,
limited to 250 copies only, signed by the author.
(Reviewed in Times Literary Supplement O 22 '25
p701; C. H. W. in Bookman (London) 69:224 Ja '26;
Truth (London) 98:863 N 4 '25; English Review 41:737
N '25)

Reviews. D'Annunzio in English. Saturday Review 85:
145-6 Ja 29 '98

A Set of Six. In Keating, George T. A Conrad memorial
library. Garden City, New York: Doubleday, Doran,

1929. p170-81   1801
Syroczyński, L.
    Sprzed 50 laty.   Lwów: 1914   1802
Szczepański, Jan Józef
    Conrad mojego pokolenia (Conrad and my generation).
    Życie Literackie no 307:3 D '57   1803
Szukalski, Szymanowski, Conrad.   Wiadomości 9, no 23:6
    Je 6 '54   1803a

T. , R.
    Notes on Joseph Conrad.   National Education (Wellington,
    N. Z.) 28:120 Ap '46   1804
Taborski, Roman
    Apollo Korzeniowski; ostatni dramatopisarz romantyczny.
    Wroclaw: Pan, 1957. 167p
    Przypominam Conrada (Drawing attention to Conrad).
    Kamena nos 3-4, 1955   1805
Taege, Allen Leslie
    Human relationships in the major novels of Joseph Conrad,
    1900-1911; a study of four novels... M. A. & Honors
    Thesis, University of Canterbury, 1961. 196p
    (Lord Jim; Nostromo; The Secret Agent; Under Western
    Eyes)   1806
Taggart, Michael
    Joseph Conrad: his vision of existence. M. A. Thesis,
    Colorado College, 1962. 61p   1807
Tajemnicze momenty pobytu J. Conrada w Marsylii. Kurjer
    Poranny no 1, 1929   1808
Talbot, Francis X.
    Conrad, seas and men.   America 31:452-3 Ag 23 '24 1809
Tank, Kurt Lothan
    Ein Fass ohne Boden. Joseph Conrad. Sonntagsblatt
    (Hamburg) 3, no 33:7 '50   1810
Tanner, Jimmie Eugene
    The chronology and the enigmatic end of Lord Jim.
    Nineteenth-Century Fiction 21:369-80 Mr '67
    The twentieth century impressionistic novel: Conrad and
    Faulkner. Ph. D. Thesis, Univ. of Oklahoma, 1964.
    iii-iv, 216f; abstract in Dissertation Abstracts 25:
    1927-8 '64   1811
Tanner, Tony
    Butterflies and beetles: Conrad's two truths. Chicago
    Review 16, i:123-40 Winter-Spring '63
    Conrad the great. Spectator 212:636 My 8 '64
    Conrad's Lord Jim. (Studies in English Literature, no
    12) London: Edward Arnold; Great Neck, New York:
    Barron's Educational Series [1963] 62p; bibliography,

Tanner, Tony (cont.)
p[60]
(Reviewed by W. J. Harvey in Modern Language Review 58:568-9 O '63; Mark Roberts in Essays in Criticism 13:408 O '63; Lucien A. Leclaire in Études Anglaises 20, no 2:201 Ap-Je '67)
Mountains and depths - an approach to nineteenth-century
dualism. Review of English Literature (Leeds) 3, no
4:51-61 O '62
Nightmare and complacency: Razumov and the Western
Eye. Critical Quarterly 4:197-214 Autumn '62   1812

Tarnawski, Wit M.
Conrad a Janko Góral (Conrad and Yanko Goorall). Wia-
domości Literackie 11, no 47:7 N 18 '34
Conrad a Polska (Conrad and Poland). Wiadomości 4,
nos 176-7:1 Ag 21 '49
Conrad przeciwko Sartre'owi (Conrad versus Sartre).
Tygodnik Powszechny no 45, 1947; same. In The pen
in exile, an anthology of exiled writers, edited by Paul
Tabori. [London:] International P. E. N. Club Centre,
1954. p215-18
Conrad's position among Polish people at home and abroad.
In Conrad żywy, edited by Wit Tarnawski. London: B.
Świderski, 1957. p267-72
O Conradzie. Myśl Polska (London) no 1:13-14 Mr '48
Dlaczego i kiedy Conrad zaczal pisac? (Why and when
Conrad began to write). Wiadomości 21, no 35-6:6
Ag 28 - S 4 '66
Echa Mickiewiczowski w twórczości Conrada (Echoes of
Mickiewicz in Conrad's works). In Mickiewicz żywy,
edited by Herminia Nagler. London: B. Świderski,
1955. p166-75
Georges Jean-Aubry i Conrad. Wiadomości 5, no 47:3
N 19 '50
Introduction. In Lord Jim, by Joseph Conrad, translated
by Aniela Zagórska. Jerusalem: Interim Treasury
Committee for the Polish Question, 1946. Volume I, p
v-xlvii
O artystcznej osobowości i formie Conrada. Kwartalnik
Neofilologiczny 5, nos 1-2:61-78 '58; same. In Joseph
Conrad Korzeniowski, Essays and Studies. Warsaw:
Państwowe Wydawnictwo Naukowe, 1958. p[61]-78; same.
In Joseph Conrad Korzeniowski, by Róża Jabłkowska.
Warsaw: Państwowe Zakłady Wydawnictwo Szkolynch,
1964. p281-97
O szerokie podejście do Conrada. Wiadomości 5, no

196:4 Ja 1 '50
Od tłumacza (by the translator). In W oczach zachodu
(Under Western Eyes) by Joseph Conrad, translated by
Wit Tarnawski. London: Veritas [1955] p7-11
"Powrót" Conrada. Wiadomości 13, no 1:2 Ja 5 '58
Przypowieść o Polaku. Życie no 1:2 '50
Tam, skąd Conrad odszedł (The place where Conrad
passed away). Wiadomości 3, nos 13-14:4 '48
An underestimated novel by Conrad. In Conrad żywy,
edited by Wit Tarnawski. London: B. Świderski,
1957. p181-92
(An Outcast of the Islands)
Uwagi o formie artystycznej Conrada. Kultura no 26:74-
86 D '49
W co Conrad wierzył? (What did Conrad believe in?)
Skamander N '30 p488-93
Zamiast przedmowy. In Conrad żywy, edited by Wit
Tarnawski. London: B. Świderski, 1957. p5-9
"Zwycięstwo" Conrada po polsku. Kurjer Poznany no 518,
1928   1813
Tarnawski, Wit (editor)
Conrad żywy, edited by Wit Tarnawski. London: B.
Świderski, 1957. 304p; portrait by K. Gorski
("The Living Conrad." Contains essays; the text is in
Polish, with an English summary on pages 279-300)
(Reviewed by Feliks Fornalczyk in Tygodnik Morski
nos 24-5:8 '58; Zdzisław Najder in Twórczość 14, no
2:200-1 F '58; Joseph Swastek in Polish American Stud-
ies 14, nos 1-2:60-1 Ja-Je '57; Stefania Zahorska in
Wiadomości 13, no 11:3 Mr 16 '58)
The living Conrad. An English summary of the Polish
text [of Conrad Zywy] London: B. Świderski, 1957.
24p   1814
Taylor, Edith C.
Joseph Conrad. M. A. Thesis, Washington State College,
1923. 52p   1815
Taylor, Gordon Overton
Guilt and self-redemption in Conrad's Under Western Eyes
and Dostoievsky's Crime and Punishment: a compara-
tive character study of Razumov and Raskolnikov.
Honors Thesis, Harvard College, March 1, 1960. 45f
                                                        1816
Taylor, Harry H.
The imagination of disaster. M. A. Thesis, Columbia
University, 1954. 83p   1817
Taylor, Ouita Winona
Social and political conservatism in Joseph Conrad's fic-

Taylor, Ouita Winona (cont.)
   tion.   M. A.   Thesis, North Texas State College, 1951.
   iii, 74f   1818
Taylor, Robert H.
   Authors at work, an address delivered by Robert H. Tay-
   lor... New York: The Grolier Club, 1957. p48; plate
   60
   (A facsimile of Tuan Jim, one page, and the Preface
   to The Nigger of the 'Narcissus')   1819
Taylor, S. H. N.
   Conrad's ships.   Sea Breezes ns 15:438 Je '53   1820
Taylor, W. D.
   The novels of Joseph Conrad.   Queen's Quarterly 28:
   15-31 Jl-S '20   1821
Teare, Richard Wallace
   Joseph Conrad's Dombey and Son.   An essay in literary
   transformation.   Senior Honors Thesis, Harvard Col-
   lege, September, 1958. 39f
   (A comparison of Chance with Dickens' Dombey and
   Son)   1822
Teincey, Jean
   Le roman américain et Le Négre du "Narcisse." Revue
   Britannique 75th année, 3:194-215 Je '99   1823
Teitel, Nathan R.
   Introduction.   In An Outcast of the Islands, by Joseph
   Conrad.   New York: Airmont Publishing Co., Inc.
   [c1966] p3-6   1824
Temple, Phillips
   Fatalism of Joseph Conrad.   America 68:213-14 N 28
   '42   1825
Terlecki, Tymon
   Conrad and Polish culture.   In Conrad żywy, edited by
   Wit Tarnawski.   London: B. Świderski, 1957. p100-
   13   1826
Tetauer, Frank
   Svět Josepha Conrad.   Rozhledy po Literatuře a Umeňi
   3:91-3 O 15 '34   1827
Thale, Jerome
   Marlow's quest.   University of Toronto Quarterly 24:351-
   8 Jl '55; same.   In The art of Joseph Conrad: a criti-
   cal symposium, edited by Robert Wooster Stallman.
   East Lansing, Michigan: Michigan State University
   Press, 1960. p154-61; same.   In Joseph Conrad's
   Heart of Darkness: backgrounds and criticisms, edited
   by Leonard F. Dean.   Englewood Cliffs, New Jersey:
   Prentice-Hall [c1960] p159-66
   The narrator as hero.   Twentieth Century Literature

3:69-73 Jl '57   1828
Theimer, Helen Agnes Prentice
    Conrad and impressionism.   Ph. D. Thesis, Stanford Uni-
        versity, 1962. iv, 214f.   Abstract in Dissertation Ab-
        stracts 23:1024 '62   1829
Thiess, Frank
    Vom Abenteurerroman: über Conrad und London.   Neue
        Deutsche Rundschau 38, part 2:537-47 N '27   1830
Thomas, Edward
    Joseph Conrad.   T. P. 's Weekly 23:273 F 27 '14   1831
Thompson, Alan Reynolds
    Farewell to Achilles.   Bookman (NY) 70:468 Ja '30
    The humanism of Joseph Conrad.   Sewanee Review 37:
        204-20 Ap-Je '29   1832
Thompson, (Sir) Ivan
    Introduction.   In Lord Jim, by Joseph Conrad.   (New
        Classics Series)   London: W. W. Norton & Co. [1957]
        p13-19. "Joseph Conrad," by "J. A. T.," p7-9   1833
Thomson, David S.
    The subjective novel: Joseph Conrad and André Gide.
        Master's Thesis, Columbia Univ., 1951. 103p   1834
Tick, Stanley
    Conrad's "Heart of Darkness."   Explicator 21, item 67,
        April '63
    (On snake symbolism)
    The gods of Nostromo.   Modern Fiction Studies 10:15-26
        Spring '64   1835
Tillyard, Eustace Mandeville Wetenhall
    Conrad's Nostromo.   In The epic strain in the English
        novel.   Fairlawn, New Jersey: Essential Books, 1958.
        p126-67, 199-203
    The Secret Agent reconsidered.   Essays in Criticism 11:
        309-18 Jl '61; same.   In Essays, literary and educa-
        tional.   New York: Barnes & Noble, 1962. p144-53;
        same.   In Conrad.   A collection of critical essays,
        edited by Marvin Mudrick.   (A Spectrum Book) Engle-
        wood Cliffs, New Jersey: Prentice-Hall, Inc. [1966]
        p103-10   1836
Tindall, William York
    Apology for Marlow.   In From Jane Austen to Joseph Con-
        rad, edited by Robert C. Rathburn and Martin Stein-
        mann, Jr.   Minneapolis, Minnesota: University of
        Minnesota press, 1958. p274-85
    Forces in modern British literature.   New York: Knopf,
        1947. p63-111; 283-317
    The literary symbol.   New York: Columbia University
        press, 1955. p86-91

Tindall, William York (cont.)
> The symbolic novel. A. D. 52 volume 3:56-68 Winter
> '52   1837

Tipton, Margaret Ethel
> Joseph Conrad's artistic use of silence. M. A. Thesis,
> Ohio State University, 1923. 20p
> (On Almayer's Folly, An Outcast of the Islands,
> Victory, The Rescue)   1838

Tittle, Walter
> The Conrad who sat for me. Outlook (NY) 140:333-5,
> 361-2 Jl 1, 8 '25
> Mrs. Conrad was not eclipsed by her husband. New
> York Times Book Review My 17 '25 p2
> Portrait of Conrad, inscribed: "For Mrs. Conrad, with
> happy recollections." In Joseph Conrad, a Record [a
> scrapbook of clippings, portraits, etc.] compiled by
> George T. Keating. Yale University Library. Keat-
> ing Collection no 271
> Portraits in pencil and pen. Century 106:53-61 My '23;
> Century 108:641-5 S '24; same. Strand Magazine 67:
> 546-50 Je '24; same. Poland 5, no 9:141-4, 188-9,
> 192, 194 S '24
> (Noted in Globe (NY) My 3 '23 p18)
> Spotkania z Conradem. Wiadomości 9, no 32:1 Ag 8 '54
> (translated by Tymon Terlecki) (Meetings with Con-
> rad)   1839

Titus, Edward K. Jr.
> Write and burn, Conrad advises Yale aspirants. World
> (NY) My 20 '23 Second News Section p1, 3   1840

Tkaczecki, B.
> Polish themes in Conrad's works. M. A. Thesis, Univ.
> of Warsaw, 1961   1841

To discuss Conrad. Philadelphia Record O 12 '24 (litera-
> ture page)
> (A meeting of the Society of Arts and Letters)   1842

Toliver, Harold E.
> Conrad's Arrow of Gold and pastoral tradition. Modern
> Fiction Studies 8:148-58 Summer '62   1843

Tolley, A. T.
> Conrad's 'favorite' story. Studies in Short Fiction (New-
> berry College) 3:314-20 Spring '66
> ("An Outpost of Progress")   1844

Tomlinson, Henry Major
> Below London Bridge. New York & London: Harper,
> 1935. (Includes a note that Conrad referred to the
> New South Dock, London, in his The Mirror of the Sea)
> [Conrad is dead] In Gifts of fortune... New York &

London: Harper, 1926. p132-8
Joseph Conrad. Saturday Review of Literature 4:191-2
O 15 '27
Jungle life in literature. T. P. 's & Cassell's Weekly 7:
200 D 4 '26
(On Conrad's Congo)
On the Chesil Bank. In The face of the earth... London:
Duckworth [1950] p91-6
(Noted by John K. M. McCaffery in Publishers' Weekly
160:2145 D 1 '51)
The prelude: Almayer's Folly. In Keating, George T.
A Conrad memorial library. Garden City, New York:
Doubleday, Doran, 1929. p3-7   1845
Tomlinson, Maggie
Conrad's integrity: Nostromo, Typhoon, The Shadow-
Line. Melbourne Critical Review (University of Mel-
bourne) 4, no 5:40-53 '61   1846
Tonquédec, Joseph de
Le message de Conrad. Études. Revue Catholique
(Paris) 208:69-77 Jl 5 '31   1847
Tooker, L. Frank
The joys and tribulations of an editor... New York: Cen-
tury co. [c1924] p65, 180, 185-6, 234-6, 285; same.
(excerpt) Christian Science Monitor O 15 '24 p11   1848
Torchiana, Donald
The Nigger of the 'Narcissus:' myth, mirror and me-
tropolis. Wascana Review 2, no 2:29-41 '67   1848a
Tove, A.
Constance Garnett, translator and propagandist of Russian
literature. Russkaja Literatura no 4:193-9 '58   1848b
Toye, Francis
Truly thankful? A sequel to an Autobiography. London:
Barker, 1957. 192p
(Noted in Wiadomości 12, no 29:7 Jl 21 '57)   1848c
Tretiak, Andrzej
A note on Joseph Conrad. Revue Anglo-Américaine 12:
46-7 O '34 (Musset's "La Table du Nuit" and A Set of
Six)
Z powodu "Lorda Jima." Pion D 15 '34   1849
A tribute to a great seafarer. [Outline for the Conrad me-
morial Library. Courtesy of Mr. Cesare, the New
York Times, and Arthur H. Harlow and Co. New
York: Seamen's Church Institute of New York, 19 ?]
[5] pages; portrait on cover   1850
Tribute to Joseph Conrad. New York World O 24 '24 p13
(The Dean of Canterbury's words)   1851

A tribute to Mr. Hazeltine by Sealaw. A letter to Christo-
  pher Morley. New York Evening Post My 2 '23 p8
  (Comments on Mr. Hazeltine's review of Lord Jim in
  the Sunday Sun)   1852
Tributes to Joseph Conrad. Living Age 322:613-14 S 20
  '24   1853
Triller, A.
  Joseph Conrad (Korzeniowski) in polnischer sicht. Zeit-
    schrift für Slavische Philologie 32:46-60 '65   1854
Trilling, Lionel
  On the modern element in modern literature. Partisan
    Review 28:25-6 Ja-F '61; same. In Varieties of
    literary experience... ed. by Stanley Burnshaw. [New
    York:] New York University press, 1962. p423-4
                                                      1854a
Tschiffely, A. F.
  Don Roberto; being the account of the life and works of
    R. B. Cunninghame Graham, 1852-1936. London:
    William Heinemann [1937] p324-32
    (Includes letters from Conrad to R. B. Cunninghame
    Graham)   1855
Tuong-Buu-Khanh, M.
  Conrad et l'Orient. Ph. D. Thesis, University of Paris,
    1952   1856
Turnbull, Isabel
  Joseph Conrad as a novelist of subjective adventure.
    M. A. Thesis, University of Manitoba, 1919. 160p 1857
Turner, Lionel Harold
  Conrad's craftsmanship. M. A. Thesis, University of
    Western Australia, 1943.
  The genius of Joseph Conrad. A study of the neurotic
    emotions that stimulated his imagination. Ph. D.
    Thesis, University of Southern California at Los Ange-
    les, 1949. 452p; bibliography, f435-52; abstract in Ab-
    stracts, University of Southern California, 1950, p59-
    61   1858
Turner, Michael
  Conrad and T. J. Wise. Book Collector 15:350-1 '66 1859
Turno, Witold
  See: Wit M. Tarnawski   1860
Tuschwitz, K.
  Joseph Conrad. Schule der Freiheit 2:45 '34-'35   1861
O tytuł powieści Conrada. Wiadomości Literackie 4, no
    27:2 Jl 3 '27
    (On the title of The Arrow of Gold)   1862

Ujejski, Józef
    Conrad i świat (Conrad and the world). Skamander (War-
        saw) no 65:596-612 D '35; same. In Wspomnienia i
        studia o Conradzie, edited by Barbara Kocówna. War-
        saw: Państwowy Instytut Wydawniczy [1963] p338-67
    Conrad i świat jego powieści. Przegląd Humanistyczny
        2, no 1:125-38 Ja-F '58
    Conrad i sztuka. Pion no 52, 1935; same. In Joseph
        Conrad Korzeniowski, by Róza Jabłkowska. Warsaw:
        Państwowe Zakłady Wydawnictwo Szkolynch, 1964.
        p238-50
    Konserwatyzm Conrada. Wiadomości Literackie 12, no
        625:2 N 10 '35
    O Konradzie Korzeniowskim... Warsaw: Dom Książki
        Polskiej, 1936. 7-[301]p; portrait; bibliographical foot-
        notes; same translated: Joseph Conrad... traduit du
        polonais par Pierre Duméril. Preface de Z. L. -Za-
        leski. Paris: Société Française d'Editions Littéraires
        et Techniques [c1939] [5]-300p (Collection polonaise);
        portrait
        (Reviewed by M. J. Toporowski in Wiadomości Liter-
        ackie 14, no 690:4 Ja 24 '37
    Romantycy. Warsaw: Państwowy Wydawniczy Naukowe,
        1963
        (On Conrad and Zeromski)   1863
Umiastowski, Roman
    Ludzie głębin... In Pamietnikow i dokumentów wybraý i
        zestawił. Warsaw: 1929. 325p   1864
Unbekannte Conrad-Illustrationen [von] Hans Peters - Lübeck,
    J. C. Schmitz - Berlin [signed "G. K. S."] Philobiblon
    (Vienna) 10, heft 3:118-26 '38
    (Text by G. K. S., p118; illustrations by Peters, p119-
        22; by Schmitz, p123-6)   1865
Unger, Leonard
    La Forgue, Conrad, and T. S. Eliot. In The man in the
        name: essays on the experience of poetry. London:
        Oxford University press, 1957; Minneapolis: University
        of Minnesota press, 1956. p190-242   1866
An unusual modern. America 29:111 My 19 '23   1867
Unwin, Garton Herbert
    Structural studies in modern fiction. M. A. Thesis, Uni-
        versity of Toronto, 1928. 85p   1868
T. Fisher Unwin, London
    Joseph Conrad. London: T. Fisher Unwin [nd ? 1923-4?]
        16 pages, 2 portraits
        (Contents: Joseph Conrad. A pen portrait, by James
        Huneker, p3 (from the Country Life Press, by courtesy

T. Fisher Unwin, London (cont.)
    of Doubleday, Page & Co.); Almayer's Folly, p4-8;
    same.   T. P. O'Connor in Weekly Sun Je 9 '95 p1-2;
    An Outcast of the Islands, p9-11; same.   Saturday Re-
    view 81:509-10 My 16 '96; Tales of Unrest, p12-14;
    same.   Literary Gazette Je 20 '98 p2-3; The Arrow of
    Gold, p15-16; same.   Public Opinion (London) 116:157-
    8 Ag 15 '19)
    [A letter about being Joseph Conrad's first publisher]
    Publishers' Circular & Bookseller's Record 121:199
    Ag 9 '24   1869
Urbanowicz, Halina
    The sea in Conrad's fiction.   M. A. Thesis, Catholic Uni-
    versity of Lublin, 1956   1870
Ure, Peter
    Character and imagination in Conrad.   Cambridge Journal
    3:727-40 S '50   1871
Ureña, Max Henriquez
    See: Henriquez Ureña, Max   1871a
Ursell, Geoffrey
    Conrad and the "Riversdale." Times Literary Supplement
    (London) Jl 11 '68 p733-4; same.   Times (London) Jl
    11 '68 p1   1871b
Utility novels.   Times Literary Supplement Ap 22 '44
    p199   1872

Valéry, Paul
    Sujet d'une conversation avec Conrad.   La Nouvelle Re-
    vue Française 23:663-5 D '24   1873
Valjean, Pierre
    Échos de partout.   Semaine Littéraire année 32, no 1599:
    405-6 Ag 23 '24
    Échos de partout.   Semaine Littéraire année 30, no 1500:
    488-9 S 30 '22   1874
Vámosi, Pál
    Joseph Conrad éz as imperializmus (Joseph Conrad and
    imperialism).   Filológiai Közlöny 7:316-26 D '61 1875
Van Baaren, Betty Bishop
    Character and background in Conrad.   Doctoral Disserta-
    tion, University of Wisconsin, 1958. vii, 303p; ab-
    stract in Dissertation Abstracts 19:1392 '58   1876
Vančura, Zdeněk
    The Negro in the white man's ship: a critical triptych.
    Prague Studies in English 8:73-97 '59
    (On The Nigger of the "Narcissus")   1877
Van Doren, Carl and Van Doren, Mark
    American and British literature since 1890.   New York:

Century [c1925] p177-81; revised and enlarged edition,
published in 1940, p201-6   1878
Van Ghent, Dorothy
Introduction. In Nostromo, by Joseph Conrad.   New York:
Holt, Rinehart & Winston [1961] p vii-xxv
On Lord Jim. In The English novel. Form and function.
New York: Rinehart and Co. [c1953] p229-44; prob-
lems for study and discussion, p440-54   1879
Van Kranendonk, A. G.
See: Kranendonk, A. G. van   1880
Van Slooten, Henry
The reception of the writings of Joseph Conrad in England
and the United States from 1895 through 1915. Ph. D.
Thesis, University of California at Los Angeles, 1957.
309p; Abstract in University of So. California Ab-
stracts of Dissertations... 1957. p103-5   1881
Vast reading room for sailors will be named for Joseph
Conrad. New York Herald Tribune O 7 '25 p15   1882
Verdoner, Josefine
A study of the structure, imagery, and symbolism in
Conrad's Victory. M. A. Thesis, University of North
Carolina, 1957. iv, 74f   1883
Verena, Hedy
Joseph Conrad, der Dichter des Meeres. Neue Freie
Presse (Wien) no 21543:22-4 Ag 31 '24   1884
De verteller op het dek. Groene Amsterdammer My 8
'48 p7   1885
Vestdijk, S.
Eenige proefjes zout water. Criterium (Amsterdam)
3 no 1:48-60 Ja-F '42   1886
Veth, Cornelis
Joseph Conrad. Socialistische Gids 9:844-7 O '24   1887
Vetö-Mandl, Elly
See: Mandl, Elly Vetö   1888
[Victory. An obituary] Literary Review of the New York
Evening Post Ag 9 '24 p945   1889
[Victory dramatized, staged in Poland] Wiadomości Liter-
ackie 7, no 11:5 O 12 '30   1889a
Vidan, Ivo
Bilješke o političkom Romanu. Naše Teme (Zagreb) 6:
910-17 '63
(On Nostromo)
Conrad in Yugoslavia. Kwartalnik Neofilologiczny 5,
nos 1-2:79-81 '58; same. In Joseph Conrad Korzeniow-
ski. Essays and studies. Warsaw: Państwowe Wy-
dawnictwo Naukowe, 1958. p[79]-81
Conradov Lord Jim. Ogled o Strukturi. Filologija

Vidan, Ivo   (cont.)
   (Zagreb) 3:175-99 '62
   [The moral theme of Lord Jim]   Narodni list (Zagreb)
     Ag '51
   One source of Conrad's Nostromo.   Review of English
     Studies 7:287-93 Jl '56
     (Suggests G. F. Masterman's Seven Eventful Years in
     Paraguay)
   Perspective of Nostromo.   Studia Romanica et Anglica
     Zagrabiensia nos 13-14:43-54 Jl-D '62
   Politički roman vremena (Konradov Nostromo).   Život
     (Sarajevo) 11, no 9:695-712 '62
   The Princess Casamassima between Balzac and Conrad.
     Studia Romanica et Anglica Zagrabiensia nos 21-22:
     259-76 '66
   Rehearsal for Nostromo: Conrad's share in Romance.
     Studia Romanica et Anglica Zagrabiensia no 12:9-16
     D '61
   Some aspects of structure in the works of Conrad.
     Kwartalnik Neofilologiczny 5:19-28 '58; same.   In
     Joseph Conrad Korzeniowski.   Essays and studies.
     Warsaw: Państwowe Wydawnictwo Naukowe, 1958.
     p[19]-28; same.   (translated by Zdzisław Najder)
     Twórczość 14, no 7:105-15 Jl '58   1890
Villard, Leonie
   A Conrad heroine in real life.   T. P. 's & Cassell's
     Weekly 5:476 Ja 23 '26; same.   Living Age 328:637-9
     Mr 20 '26
   (The background of Suspense)
   Joseph Conrad et les mémorialistes.   (À propos de Sus-
     pense).   Revue Anglo-Américaine 3:313-21 Ap '26 1891
Villiers, Alan
   Conrad and the Riversdale.   Times Literary Supplement
     (London) Jl 18 '68 p753
   Cruise of the Conrad: a journal of a voyage round the
     world, undertaken and carried out in the ship Joseph
     Conrad... New York: Scribner's, 1937. vii-xv, 387p
     (Reviewed in Times Literary Supplement Ag 28 '37
     p17; Spectator 159:656 O 15 '37)   1892
Vincenz, Stanisław
   Conrad - convention or conviction?   In Conrad żywy,
     edited by Wit Tarnawski.   London: B. Swiderski,
     1957. p114-28   1893
Vines, Sherard
   100 years of English literature, 1830-1940.   London:
     Duckworth, 1950. p247-8   1894
Visiak, Edward Harold [pseud.] [Edward Harold Physick]

Creative memory. Notes & Queries 177:292-3 O 21
   '39
Joseph Conrad. Notes & Queries 177:349, 402-3 N
   11, D 2 '39
Joseph Conrad. The evolution of love.   Notes &
   Queries 177:473-4 D 30 '39
The long short story. Times Literary Supplement Ap
   22, 29 '44 p199, 211
The mirror of Conrad. London: Werner Laurie [1955];
   New York: Philosophical Library [1956] 255p; por-
   traits and illustrations; bibliography, p245-9
   (Reviewed by Walter Magnes Teller in New York Times
   Book Review N 25 '56 p24; Times Literary Supplement
   S 23 '55 p558; Arnold T. Schwab in Nineteenth-Century
   Fiction 11:235-7 D '56; Thomas Moser in Modern Lan-
   guage Notes 72:297-300 Ap '57; Joseph W. Krutch in
   Saturday Review of Literature 40:12 F 9 '57; Bruce
   Harkness in Journal of English & Germanic Philology
   56:507-9 '57; New York Times O 11 '56 p37; Joseph L.
   Blotner in College English 20:54-5 O '58)
The spiritual fall: a note on Joseph Conrad's philosophy.
   Notes & Queries 177:114-16, 402-3, 473-4 Ag 12, D 2,
   30 '39; Notes & Queries 178:25-6 Ja 13 '40
   (Some of these articles are listed above separately.)
                                                      1895
Vogel, Zdzisɬawa
   Konrad Korzeniowski. Poradnik Bibliotekarza rok 10,
   no 5, 1958   1896
Voisins, Gilbert de
   Joseph Conrad. Revue de Paris tome 2:5-16 Mr 1 '18
   (An account of Conrad's works)   1897
Vorse, M. H.
   A writer who knows the sea. Critic 43:280 S '03 1898
Vowinckel, Ernst
   Der englische Roman der neuesten Zeit und Gegenwart:
   Stilformen und Entwicklungslinien. Berlin: F. A.
   Herbig, 1926. p195-200   1899

Waddell, Helen
   Mass-penny. New Statesman 12:375-6 F 1 '19   1900
Wagenknecht, Edward
   "Pessimism" in Hardy and Conrad. College English
   3:546-54 Mr '42
   Values and Joseph Conrad. In Cavalcade of the English
   novel from Elizabeth to George VI. New York: Holt
   [c1943] p423-40; bibliography, p611-13   1901

Wagner, Geoffrey
John Bull's other empire. Modern Age 8, no 3:284-90
    Summer '64   1901a
Wagner, Marianne
Der Dichter Joseph Conrad. Der Vorstoss 1, no 49:
    1942 '31   1902
Wain, John
The test of manliness. London Magazine 4:23-6 N
    '57   1903
Walbridge, Earle
Literary characters drawn from life... New York:
    Wilson, 1936. p29, 150
    (Refers to The Secret Agent, "The Sisters," and
    Suspense)   1904
Walbrook, H. M.
Joseph Conrad and the theatre. Daily Telegraph (London)
    Ag 8 '24 p4   1905
Walcutt, Charles C.
Interpreting the symbol. College English 14:452-4
    My '53
    (On "The Secret Sharer")   1906
Waliszewski, Kazimierz
Un cas de naturalisation littéraire: Joseph Conrad.
    Revue des Revues 47:734-48 D 15 '03
Listy Józefa Conrada-Korzeniowskiego. Uwagi. Ruch
    Literacki no 6, volume 2:174-80 Je 27; same. In
    Joseph Conrad Korzeniowski, by Róża Jabłkowska.
    Warsaw: Państwowe Zakłady Wydawnictwo Szkolynch,
    1964. p187-92
    (Eight letters of Conrad)
Polski powieściopisarz w angielskiej literaturze (A Polish
    novelist in English literature). Kraj (Homeland) Jan-
    Feb 1904, nos 3, 4, 5, 7   1907
Walker, Helen
The Rover: a study of Joseph Conrad. M. A. Thesis,
    Birmingham-Southern College, 1931   1908
Walker, Rosemary E.
Joseph Conrad's "Il Conde:" a study of ironic method.
    M. A. Thesis, Catholic University of America [1964]
    36f; bibliography, f37-8   1909
Waller, David Allan
Joseph Conrad and the romantic imagination. Honors
    Thesis, Harvard College, March, 1964. 43f
    (Treats "The Secret Sharer," Typhoon, and Lord Jim)
                                                   1910
Walpole, Hugh S.
Introduction. In Chance, by Joseph Conrad. (Memorial

Edition) Garden City, New York: Doubleday, Page,
1925. Volume XIV, p vii-xii
Joseph Conrad. (Writers of the Day) London: Nisbet;
   New York: Holt [1916] 5-127p; "A Short Bibliography of
   Joseph Conrad's Principal Writings," p121-2; "American
   Bibliography," p123-4; portrait.
   A new, revised edition was issued in 1924.
   (Reviewed in Booklist 13:121 D '16;   Edith Borie in
   New Republic 9: supplement p4-5 N 18 '16; noted in
   To-Day ns 1:252 Je 24 '16; John O'London's Weekly 1:
   359 Je 28 '19; H. G. in Bookman's Journal & Print Col-
   lector 10:199 S '24; H. L. Mencken in Smart Set 50,
   no 2:138-9 O '16; America 16, no 1:20 O 14 '16)
Note, dated January 26, 1927 (Laid into a volume of The
   Secret Agent) In the Keating Conrad Collection, Yale
   University Library
The Secret Agent. In Keating, George T.   A Conrad me-
   morial library. Garden City, New York: Doubleday,
   Doran, 1929. p159-64   1911
Walpole says seaman started Conrad career.   Herald (NY)
   N 7 '22   1911a
Walpole, V.
   Conrad's method: some formal aspects. (Annals of the Uni-
   versity of Stellenbosch) Kaapstad: Stellenbosch en
   Bloemfontein, 1930. Beperk, Capetown: Nasionale Pers,
   1930. Volume VIII, Section B, No 1 (January, 1930).
   20p
   (On Chance and Lord Jim)   1912
Walsh, James J.
   Literature and twaddle. America 17:381 Jl 21 '17   1913
Walton, James Hackett
   The backgrounds of The Secret Agent: a biographical and
   critical study. Ph. D. Thesis, Northwestern University,
   1966
   Conrad and The Secret Agent... Polish Review 12, no 3:
   28-42 Summer '67
   Conrad and naturalism: The Secret Agent. Texas Studies
   in Literature and Language 9:289-301 Summer '67
   Mr. X's 'little joke:' the design of Conrad's "The In-
   former." Studies in Short Fiction 4:322-33 '67   1913a
Wang, Joan Parsons
   Joseph Conrad, proto-existentialist: a comparative study
   of Conrad, Camus, and Sartre. Ph. D. Thesis, Indiana
   University, 1964. 284p; abstract in Dissertation Ab-
   stracts 26:1051-2 '65   1914
Ward, Alfred Charles
   Epilogue. In English literature. Modern -1450-1939, by

Ward, Alfred Charles (cont.)
   G. H. Mair. (Home University Library) New York:
      Oxford University press [1944] 2nd ed, p220-1
   Introduction. In The Secret Agent, by Joseph Conrad.
      (Heritage of Literature Series, no 32) London: Long-
      mans, Green, 1958. p xxi-xxvii
   Joseph Conrad. In Twentieth-century literature... New
      York: Longmans, Green, 1940. 7th edition, p42-52
   Joseph Conrad: Typhoon. In Aspects of the modern short
      story: English and American. New York: Dial Press,
      1925. p145-57; portrait
      (Reviewed in Bookman's Journal & Print Collector 11,
      no 41:211 F '25; A. N. M. in Manchester Guardian Week-
      ly 11, no 18:377 O 31 '24)   1915
Ward, Christopher
   Robinson Crusoe. By J-s-ph C-nr-d. Literary Review
      of the New York Evening Post O 20 '23 p 149; same.
      In Twisted tales. New York: Holt, 1924. p151-62
      (A parody indicating what Conrad might have done with
      the story of Robinson Crusoe)   1916
Ward, Laura A.
   The sea in English fiction from 1918-1930. Ph.D. Thesis,
      University of Pennsylvania. 169p; bibliography, p162-9
                                                              1917
Warger, Howard Nicholas
   The unity of Conrad's Nostromo: irony as vision and in-
      strument. Ph.D. Thesis, Fordham University, 1965.
      175f; abstract in Dissertation Abstracts 26:3931 '66
                                                              1918
Warner, John Riley
   The ethics of Joseph Conrad. Ph.D. Thesis, University
      of Colorado, 1955. 208p; abstract in Dissertation Ab-
      stracts 16:1458 '56   1919
Warner, Oliver
   Introduction. In An Outcast of the Islands and Almayer's
      Folly, by Joseph Conrad. (New Collins Classics) Lon-
      don: Collins, 1955. p11-15; bibliography, p383-4
   Joseph Conrad. (Bibliographical Series of Supplements to
      the British Book News) London: Published for the Brit-
      ish Council and the National Book League by Longmans,
      Green & Co. [1950] 7-39p; portrait. A second edition
      was published in 1964.
      (Contents: "Joseph Conrad, An Appreciation," p7-32;
      "Joseph Conrad, A Select Bibliography," p33-8; "Index
      of Short Stories," p39)
   Joseph Conrad. In British writers and their work No. 10.
      Lincoln, Nebraska: University of Nebraska Press

[c1966] p[43]-80
(A reprint, with but slight changes, of the volume published in London in 1950 and in 1964)
Joseph Conrad.   (Men and Books) London & New York:
Longmans, Green [1951] vii-xii, 196p; bibliography,
p183-9
(Reviewed by Harvey Curtis Webster in New York
Times Book Review F 17 '52 p14; Times Literary Supplement D 28 '51 p832; Contemporary Review 181:190-
1 Mr '52; Nineteenth-Century Fiction 7:149 S '52; F. C.
Danchin in Études Anglaises 5:262 Ag '52)
The sea writer.   London Magazine 4:21-3 N '57   1920
Warren, Robert Penn
Nostromo.   Sewanee Review 59:363-91 Summer '51; same.
In Nostromo, by Joseph Conrad.   New York: Modern
Library [c1951] p vii-xxxix; xl-xli; same.   In Joseph
Conrad: a critical symposium, edited by Robert Wooster Stallman.   East Lansing, Michigan: Michigan State
University press, 1960.   p209-27; same.   In Selected
essays.   New York: Random House, 1958.   p31-58
                                                            1921
Warschausky, Sidney
The ego and darkness: a study of the early works of
Joseph Conrad.   M. A. Thesis, Columbia University,
1949.   120p   1922
Wasiolek, Edward
Yanko Goorall, a note on name symbolism in Conrad's
"Amy Foster."   Modern Language Notes 71:418-19 Je
'56   1923
Wassermann, Jakob
Joseph Conrad's Schattenlinie.   In Lebensdienst... Leipzig:
Grethlein & Co. [c1928] p270-8; same.   In Bekenntnisse
und Begegnungen... Zürich: Carl Posen Verlag, 1950.
p73-9   1924
Wasserstrom, William
Joseph Conrad.   In The modern short novel... New York:
Holt, Rinehart & Winston [c1965] p195-6 (On The
Shadow-Line)   1925
Watson, Wallace Steadman
Joseph Conrad's debts to the French.   Ph. D. Thesis,
Indiana Univ. , 1966.   370p; abstract in Dissertation Abstracts 27:3473A-3474A '67
(Discusses Conrad's debt to Flaubert and De Mauspassant)   1926
Watt, Ian P.
Conrad criticism and The Nigger of the 'Narcissus.'
Nineteenth-Century Fiction 12, no 4:257-83 Mr '58

Watt, Ian P. (cont.)
Joseph Conrad: alienation and commitment. In The English mind... edited by Hugh Sykes Davies and George Watson. London: Cambridge University press, 1964. p257-78
Story and idea in Conrad's The Shadow-Line. Critical Quarterly 2:133-48 Summer '60; same. (revised) In Modern British fiction: essays in criticism, edited by Mark Schorer. New York: Oxford University Press, 1961. p119-36   1927

Watts, C. T.
Joseph Conrad and the Ranee of Sarawak. Review of English Studies ns 15:404-7 N '64
Joseph Conrad, Dr. Macintyre, and "The Inheritors." Notes & Queries ns 14:245-7 Jl '67
Joseph Conrad, R. B. Cunninghame Graham, and the Tourmaline. Notes & Queries ns 12:262-5 Jl '65
(Prints two unpublished letters from Conrad to Graham)
A minor source for Nostromo. Review of English Studies ns 16:182-4 My '65
Stepniak and Under Western Eyes. Notes & Queries ns 13:410-11 '66   1928

Watts, Richard Jr.
Mr. Conrad still eludes the screen. New York Herald Tribune Ja 20 '29, Section VII, p3
(An unfavorable review of the film, The Rescue)   1929

Waugh, Arthur
Mr. Joseph Conrad and the discipline of fear. In Tradition and change; studies in contemporary literature. New York: Dutton, 1919. p276-84   1930

Weber, David C.
Conrad's Lord Jim. Colby Library Quarterly series 2, no 16:266-9 N '50   1931

Weber, (Rev.) George L.
The problem of self-knowledge and self-identity in four works of Joseph Conrad. M. A. Thesis, University of Notre Dame, 1956. 59f
(On Nigger of the "Narcissus," Lord Jim, "Heart of Darkness," "The Secret Sharer")   1932

Webster, H. T.
Conrad's changes in narrative conception in the manuscripts of Typhoon and Other Stories and Victory. Publications of the Modern Language Association of America 64:953-62 D '49
Conrad's Falk. Explicator 7, item 56, Je '49
Joseph Conrad: a reinterpretation of five novels. College English 7:125-34 D '45   1933

Wedgwood, C. V.
  Conradiana. Wiadomości 4, no 181:4 S 18 '49   1933a
Weeks, Edward A.
  Introduction. In Joseph Conrad. Three short novels.
    New York: Bantam books [1960] p vii-xvi
    (Heart of Darkness, Youth, Typhoon)
  Joseph Conrad. Introduction. In Great short novels, an
    anthology. New York: Literary Guild of America
    [c1941] p283-6
    (On "The End of the Tether")   1934
Weeks, N. Wendell
  Christian faith of the characters in the fiction of Joseph
    Conrad and its relation to the author's personal phi-
    losophy. M. A. Thesis, New York State College for
    Teachers, 1938   1935
Weiand, Hermann Joseph
  Conrad's "Typhoon." Insight 2:49-58 '64
  The story as a creative medium in the work of Joseph
    Conrad. Ph. D. Thesis, Univ. of Edinburgh, 1959
                                                      1936
Weingart, Seymour Leonard
  The form and meaning of the impressionist novel. Ph. D.
    Thesis, University of California, Davis, 1965. 195p;
    abstract in Dissertation Abstracts 26:1656-7 '65 1937
Weintraub, Wiktor
  Alexander Fredro and his anti-romantic memoirs. Ameri-
    can Slavic & East European Review 12, no 4:535-48
    D '53
    (Discusses A Personal Record)   1938
Weiss, Ernst
  Conrad. In Das Unverlierbare. Berlin: E. Rowohlt
    [1928] p121-31
  Joseph Conrad. Das Tagebuch (Berlin) 8, no 10:387-90
    Mr 5 '27   1939
Weitzenkorn, Louis
  Conrad, in light and shadow, talks of Crane and Hardy
    and the paleness of words. World (NY) Je 3 '23 Sec-
    ond News Section, p 1S, 3S (Report of an interview
    with Conrad)   1939a
Welker, Robert L. and Herschel Gower
  The sense of fiction, edited by Robert L. Welker and
    Herschel Gower. Englewood Cliffs, New Jersey:
    Prentice-Hall [c1966] p193-6
    (On "Youth")   1940
Wellek, René
  Joseph Conrad. English Post (Prague) 1:15-16, 119-21,
    137-8 '33

Wellek, René (cont.)
　　Joseph Conrad. Rozhledy po Literatuře a Uměni (Prague)
　　　1:80-2 Jl 22 '32　　　　　　　　　　　　　　　1941
Welles, Evelyn [pseud.]
　　See: Higenbotham, Evelyn　　　　　　　　　　　1942
Wellisz, Leopold
　　Echa ankiety Conradowskiej w Ameryce. Wiadomości
　　　5, no 239:4 O 29 '50　　　　　　　　　　　　1942a
Wells, Catherine
　　A note on Mr. Bullen's Literature of the Sea. Readers'
　　　Review 1:19 Mr '08　　　　　　　　　　　　　1943
Wells, Herbert George
　　The book of 1906 which has interested me most. Book-
　　　man (London) 31:163 Ja '07
　　　(The Mirror of the Sea)
　　Experiment in autobiography, discoveries and conclusions
　　　of a very ordinary brain (since 1866). New York:
　　　Macmillan, 1934. p525-35
　　The sleeper awakes. (The Works of H. G. Wells. At-
　　　lantic Edition) New York: Scribner's, 1924. Volume
　　　II, p328
　　　(Mentions "Heart of Darkness" as a tale which will
　　　survive till the 22nd century)
　　Two letters from H. G. Wells to Joseph Conrad. [London:
　　　Printed for the First Edition Club, Curwen Press,
　　　1926] Letters, p[3-6]
　　　(220 copies only)　　　　　　　　　　　　　　1944
Welsh, A.
　　The allegory of truth in English fiction. Victorian Stud-
　　　ies 9:22-4 S '65
　　　(On "Heart of Darkness")　　　　　　　　　　1945
Weltmann, Lutz
　　Versuch über Joseph Conrad. Chronik der Menschheit 6,
　　　nos 70-71, 1931; same. (excerpt) Die Literatur 34:
　　　38-9 S 5 '31　　　　　　　　　　　　　　　　1946
Wertheim, W. F.
　　Joseph Conrad. Vrije Kunstenaar O 11 '46　　　1947
Werumeus Buning, J. W. F.
　　Joseph Conrad. Witte Mier 1:328-32 '24　　　1948
Węsławska, Emilia
　　Przedmowa do Lorda Jima w przekładzie z. 1904 rok.
　　　In Wspomnienia i studia o Conradzie, edited by Barbara
　　　Kocówna. Warsaw: Państwowy Instytut Wydawniczy
　　　[1963] p31-4; same. Warsaw, Biblioteka Dzieł Wyboro-
　　　wych, Druk Józefa Sikorskiego, 1904.　　　　1949
Wesolowski, Florence
　　Illusion and reality in the theme and structure of Conrad's

Chance. M. A. Thesis, University of Detroit, 1963.
88p   1950
Wesselhoeft, Edward Charles
    The sea and the sailor in fiction. In Pennsylvania, Uni-
    versity of. University Lectures 1915/16. University
    lectures delivered by members of the faculty in the
    free public lecture course, 1915-16. Philadelphia,
    Pennsylvania: University of Pennsylvania, 1916.
    Volume 3, p192-225   1950a
West, Herbert Faulkner
    Joseph Conrad's funeral. Saturday Review of Literature
    1:96 S 6 '24
    A little more light on Joseph Conrad. American Book
    Collector 18, no 3:27-8 N '67
    (W. H. Chesson, as reader for T. Fisher Unwin, read
    Conrad's Almayer's Folly in manuscript and encouraged
    him to publish it.)   1951
West, Paul
    The modern novel. London: Hutchinson's University Li-
    brary [1963] passim   1952
West, Ray Benedict and Robert Wooster Stallman
    "The Secret Sharer." Analysis. In The art of modern
    fiction. New York: Rinehart, 1949. p490-8   1953
West, Rebecca
    The court and the castle: some treatments of a recur-
    rent theme. New Haven: Yale University press, 1957.
    p209-12   1954
Wethered, Herbert Newton
    Conrad. In The Curious art of autobiography... New
    York: Philosophical Library [1956] p218-29   1955
Weygandt, Cornelius
    The art of Joseph Conrad. In Schelling anniversary pa-
    pers, by his former students. New York: Century,
    1923. p319-41
    The pageant of Joseph Conrad. In A century of the Eng-
    lish novel. New York: Century [c1925] p369-79   1956
Wharton, Edith
    The writing of fiction; constructing a novel. Scribner's
    Magazine 77:612 Je '25   1957
The wheel of the Otago. Times (London) Ag 29 '49 (illus-
    tration on p10)   1957a
Whelan, Robert
    Joseph Conrad and the romantic feeling of reality. M. A.
    Thesis, Niagara University, 1957. vii, 133f; plus an
    abstract.   1958
Where the scenes of Joseph Conrad's tales are laid. Chi-
    cago Sunday Times Ap 18 '15 part 8 p 6 (A map, with

Where the scenes... (cont.)
  21 notes in the key)   1958a
Whiteford, Robert Naylor
  Motives in English fiction.   New York: Putnam, 1918.
    p352-3   1959
Whitehead, Lee Melvin
  Alma renamed Lena in Conrad's Victory.   English Lan-
    guage Notes (University of Colorado) 3:55-7 S '65
  Joseph Conrad and the vision of tragedy.   Ph. D. Thesis,
    Univ. of Wisconsin, 1965.   354p; abstract in Disserta-
    tion Abstracts 28:1091A '67   1960
Whiteley, Thomas Saunders
  The technique of Joseph Conrad's fiction as revealed in
    the Pantai group of his novels.   M. A. Thesis, Univ.
    of Texas, 1940.   143f
    (On Almayer's Folly, An Outcast of the Islands, and
    The Rescue)   1961
Whiting, George Wesley
  Conrad's revision of "The Lighthouse" in Nostromo.
    Publications of the Modern Language Association of
    America 52:1183-90 D '37
    (Refers to Part III, Chapters 1-7 of Nostromo)
  Conrad's revision of Lord Jim.   English Journal (College
    Edition) 23:824-32 D '34
  Conrad's revisions of six of his short stories.   Publica-
    tions of the Modern Language Association of America
    48:552-7 Je '33
    ("An Outpost of Progress," "The Lagoon," "Karain,"
    "Youth," "Heart of Darkness," and "The End of the
    Tether")   1962
Whitlock, Brand
  Introduction.   In An Outcast of the Islands, by Joseph
    Conrad.   (Memorial Edition) Garden City, New York:
    Doubleday, Page, 1925.   Volume II, p vii-x   1963
Whittemore, Reed
  The fascination of the abomination - Wells, Shaw, Ford,
    Conrad.   In The fascination of the abomination...
    New York: Macmillan, 1963.   p129-66   1964
Whyte, Frederic
  Some novelists of the 'nineties.   In William Heinemann:
    a memoir.   London: Cape [1928] p125-51   1965
Wiadomości Literackie Conradowi.   Wiadomości 4, nos
    176-7:5 Ag 21 '49   1966
Widmer, Kingsley
  Conrad's Pyrrhic 'Victory.'   Twentieth Century Litera-
    ture 5, no 3:123-30 O '59   1967
Widow saves Conrad's book.   Sun (NY) Ap 7 '25

(Suspense will not be "completed.") 1967a
Wiegler, Paul
  Geschichte der Weltliteratur. Berlin: Ullstein [c1932]
    p402 1968
Wiendlocka, Maria
  The perennial and the exotic in Conrad's presentation of
    the coloured people. M. A. Thesis, Catholic University
    of Lublin, 1955 1969
Wierzyński, Kazimierz
  Wielka cisza Conrada. Wiadomości Literackie 1, no
    33:2 Ag 17 '24 1970
Wilcock, Edith
  Joseph Conrad, theory and practice. Senior Essay in
    English, Wells College, 1960. 43f 1971
Wilcox, Stewart C.
  Conrad's 'complicated presentations' of symbolic imagery
    in "Heart of Darkness." Philological Quarterly 39:1-
    17 Ja '60 1972
Wild, Friedrich
  Die Englische Literatur der Gegenwart seit 1870, Drama
    und Roman. Wiesbaden: Dioskuren-Verlag, 1928.
    p254-67 and passim 1973
Wilding, Michael
  The politics of Nostromo. Essays In Criticism (Oxford)
    16:441-56 O '66 1974
Wiley, Paul Luzon
  Conrad's measure of man. Madison, Wisconsin: Univer-
    sity of Wisconsin Press, 1954. 227p; bibliography,
    p217-20; part reprinted In Conrad. A collection of
    critical essays, edited by Marvin Mudrick. Englewood
    Cliffs, New Jersey: Prentice-Hall, Inc. [1966] p63-
    73. Reprinted: New York: Gordian Press, 1966.
    (Reviewed by Walter F. Wright in Nineteenth-Century
    Fiction 9, no 2:155-6 S '54; Notes & Queries 199:320-
    1 Jl '54; E. A. Bloom in Saturday Review of Literature
    37:22 N 13 '54; M. L. Cazamian in Etudes Anglaises
    8:81-2 Ja-Mr '55; Vernon Young in Southwest Review
    39, no 3: xii-xiv, 273 Summer '54) 1975
Wilhelm, Frederick Oscar
  The place of memory in Joseph Conrad's novels. M. A.
    Thesis, Wesleyan University, 1944 1976
Wilkening, Vjera
  Die Erzählsituation der Ich-Form in Werke Joseph Con-
    rads... Ph. D. Thesis, University of Berlin, 1960.
    93p 1977
William McFee lectures at Yale's Conrad display. New York
  Herald Tribune Ap 21 '38 p17 1978

Williams, Eluned
    Joseph Conrad: a study in the spiritual values of his
       work.   Master's Thesis, Pennsylvania State College,
       1931. 47p   1979
Williams, Eric
    The Arrow of Gold.   John O'London's Weekly 12:502 D
       27 '24   1980
Williams, George Walton
    Conrad's "The Lagoon." Explicator 23, item 1, S '64
    Conrad's "The Lagoon." Explicator 23, item 51, Mr '65
    The turn of the tide in "Heart of Darkness." Modern
       Fiction Studies 9:171-3 Summer '63   1981
Williams, Harold
    Joseph Conrad, 1857-1924. In Modern English writers...
       London: Sidgwick & Jackson, 1925. p405-11
    Outlines of modern English literature, 1890-1914. London:
       Sidgwick & Jackson, 1920. p246-9   1982
Williams, Michael
    Joseph Conrad.   America 14:113-14 N 13 '15   1983
Williams, Porter Jr.
    The brand of Cain in "The Secret Sharer." Modern
       Fiction Studies 10:27-30 Spring '64
    The matter of conscience in Conrad's "The Secret
       Sharer." Publications of the Modern Language Associa-
       tion of America 79:626-30 D '64
    Story and frame in Conrad's "The Tale." Studies in Short
       Fiction 5, no 2:179-85 Winter '68   1984
Williamson, Claude Charles H.
    Joseph Conrad: sailor and novelist. In Writers of
       three centuries, 1789-1914. London: Richards, 1920.
       p391-7   1985
Wills, John Howard
    Adam, Axel, and "Il Conde." Modern Fiction Studies 1,
       no 1:22-5 F '55; same. In The art of Joseph Conrad:
       a critical symposium, edited by Robert Wooster Stall-
       man. East Lansing, Michigan: Michigan State Univer-
       sity press, 1960. p254-9
    Conrad's organic artistry. Ph.D. Thesis, Washington
       University, 1961. 164p; abstract in Dissertation Ab-
       stracts 22:4356 '62
    Conrad's "The Secret Sharer." University of Kansas City
       Review 28:115-26 D '61
    Conrad's "Typhoon:" a triumph of organic art. North Da-
       kota Quarterly 30:62-70 Summer '62
    A neglected masterpiece: Conrad's Youth. Texas Studies
       in Literature and Language 4:591-601 Spring '63   1986
Willson, Constance Gertrude

Joseph Conrad. M. Ed. Thesis, State College at Boston,
    1932. ix, 82f.
    (Formerly Teachers College of the City of Boston)
                                                          1987
Wilson, Angus
    Evil in the English novel.   Kenyon Review 29, no 2:167-
    94 Mr '67
    (Includes references to "Heart of Darkness")   1987a
Wilson, Arthur Herman
    The complete narratives of Joseph Conrad. Susquehanna
    University Studies 4:229-62 My '51
    The great theme in Conrad. Susquehanna University
    Studies 5:51-84 My '53
    Joseph Conrad's children of Pan. Susquehanna Univer-
    sity Studies 2, no 1:246-8 Mr '41   1988
Wilson, Edmund
    Axel's castle.   New York & London: Scribner's, 1931.
    p193   1989
Wimsatt, W. K.
    The verbal icon: studies in the meaning of poetry.
    Lexington: University of Kentucky press, 1954.
    p196-7   1990
Winter, John L.
    A Conrad letter.   Notes & Queries ns 13:94 Mr '66
    (Conrad's letter to a friend supporting his case re-
    garding labor and administrative conditions in the
    Belgian Congo)
    Conrad's San Tomé.   Notes & Queries 211:412-13 N
    '66   1991
Winter, L. B.
    Nor they understand.   Brisbane: Jacaranda press, 1966.
    Appendix 2, p157-73
    (Identifies the river inn in Chance as the old Tilbury
    Hotel)   1992
Winter, Thelma Vera Payne
    The malevolent shadow: a study of Conrad's problems of
    evil as demonstrated in "Heart of Darkness," Victory,
    Nostromo, and Lord Jim. M. A. Thesis, University
    of Oregon, 1961. ii, 86f; bibliography f81-6   1992a
Wirpsza, Witold
    Smuga cienia.   Nowa Kultura no 49 '57; same.   In
    Wspomienia i studia o Conradzie, edited by Barbara
    Kocówna. [Warsaw:] Państwowy Instytut Wydawniczy
    [1963] p70-5   1993
Wisehart, M. K.
    Joseph Conrad described by Jo Davidson.   Sun (NY) Mr
    2 '19   1993a

Wister, Owen
    Introduction. In Typhoon and Other Stories, by Joseph
        Conrad. (Memorial Edition) Garden City, New York:
        Doubleday, Page, 1925. Volume V, p vii-viii   1994
Wit, Augusta de
    Chance. Nieuwe Rotterdamsche Courant Mr 5 '16   1995
Witt, Dorothy
    The epic strain in Joseph Conrad. M. A. Thesis, N.
        Texas State Univ. 1968. iii, 70f   1995a
Wittmeyer, Herman Fredrick
    The spirit of man in the writings of Joseph Conrad.
        M. A. Thesis, Univ. of North Carolina, 1939. vii,
        85f; bibl., f83-5   1996
Wizyta u Conrada. Naokoło Świata no 5:73-82 '24   1997
Wohlfarth, Paul
    Der Gattenmord in "Der Geheimagent" von Joseph Conrad.
        Monatsschrift für Kriminalpsychologie und Strafrechts-
        reform 26:523-31 F '36
    Joseph Conrad. C. V. Zeitung 15, no 2, Beiblatt 3:1
        Ja 9 '36
    Joseph Conrad als Geschichtserzähler. Schweizer Rund-
        schau 60 Heft 16/17: 978-84 Jl-Ag '61
    Joseph Conrad and Germany. German Life & Letters ns
        16:81-7 Ja '63
    Joseph Conrad und die Rahmenerzählung. Die Literatur
        36:507-10 My 7 '34
    Der kranke Joseph Conrad. Sudhoff's Archiv 41:68 '57
    [Letter about the Conrad Symposium] London Magazine
        4, no 12:55 D '57
    Die verbrecherische Persönlichkeit bei Dostojewskij und
        Joseph Conrad. Monatsschrift für Kriminalpsychologie
        und Strafrechtsreform 26:349-57 S '35
    War Joseph Conrad ein englischer Dichter? Germano-
        slavica 4:143-51 '36   1998
Wojtowicz, Zdzisław
    Conrad-London. Prawda no 7, 1927
    (Cites parallel passages in the two authors)   1999
Wolfe, Peter
    Conrad's The Mirror of the Sea: an assessment. Mc-
        Neese Review (McNeese State College, Lake Charles,
        Louisiana) 15:36-45 '64   2000
Wollnick, Ludvig
    Joseph Conrad. En kritisk studie. Edda. Nordisk
        Tidssckrift for Litteraturforskning 34, heft 2:183-218;
        heft 3:307-26 '34   2001
Wolpers, Theodore
    Formen Mythisierenden Erzählens in der Modernen Prosa:

Joseph Conrad im Vergleich mit Joyce, Lawrence und
Faulkner. In Lebenden Antike: Symposium für Rudolf
Sühnel. 1967. p397-422   2001a
Wolski, Stefan
Słowo o Józefie Conradzie-Korzeniowskim-pizarzu. (A
word on Conrad the writer). Zdrój (Spring) 1947,
no 4   2002
Wood, Miriam Hathaway
A source of Conrad's Suspense. Modern Language Notes
50:390-4 Je '35
(Memoris of the Comtesse de Boigne)   2003
Wood, William Parker Jr.
The evolution of the concept of innocence in four short
stories of Joseph Conrad. Honors Thesis, Harvard
College, March 15, 1954. 50f   2004
Woodruff, Neal Jr.
The structure of Conrad's fiction. Ph. D. Thesis, Yale
University, November, 1954. 370f; bibl. , f345-70
(Examines Typhoon, Lord Jim, "Heart of Darkness,"
and Nostromo)   2005
Woolf, Leonard Sidney
Joseph Conrad. Nation (London) 35:595 Ag 9 '24; same.
In Essays... New York: Harcourt, Brace [1927] p57-
71   2006
Woolf, (Mrs.) Virginia Stephen
[Essay on Conrad] Translated by Käthe Rosenberg in
Fischer Almanach Jahr. 48:94-102 '34; same. Ber-
liner Hefte für Geistiges Leben 4:70-5 Jl '49
Joseph Conrad. Times Literary Supplement Ag 14 '24
p493-4
Joseph Conrad. In The common reader. New York:
Harcourt, Brace [c1925] p309-18; London: Hogarth,
1925. p282-91
(Reviewed by George B. Dutton in Atlantic Bookshelf
O '25)
Mr. Bennett and Mrs. Brown. London: Hogarth press,
1924. p11
Mr. Conrad: a conversation. Nation & Athenaeum
(London) 33:681-2 S 1 '23; same. In The captain's
death bed... New York: Harcourt, Brace, 1950.
p76-81
(Reviewed in Times Literary Supplement My 26 '50
p319)
Mr. Conrad's crisis. Times Literary Supplement Mr
14 '18 p126; same. Times Literary Supplement Mr
14 '68 p275
A writer's diary, by Virginia Woolf. Edited by Leonard

A writer's diary (cont.)
  Woolf. London: Hogarth, 1953. p25-6   2007
The work of Joseph Conrad. San Francisco Examiner
  121, no 36, editorial page, Ag 5 '24   2007a
Woroniecki, Edward
  Conrad a Polska (Conrad and Poland). Wiadomości
  Literackie 4, no 19:1 My 8 '27   2008
Worth, George J.
  Conrad's debt to Maupassant in the Preface to The Nigger
  of the 'Narcissus.' Journal of English and Germanic
  Philology 54:700-4 O '55   2009
Worth its weight in gold. Facsimile 1st page of manuscript
  of Joseph Conrad's Victory... Public Ledger (Phila.)
  D 1 '23 p17; photograph   2010
Wright, Edgar
  Joseph Conrad: his expressed views about technique and
    the principles underlying them, with a study of their
    relevance to certain novels. Master's Thesis, Univer-
    sity of London, March, 1955. 344f; bibl., f333-44
                                                2011
Wright, Elizabeth Cox
  The defining function of vocabulary in Conrad's "The
    River." South Atlantic Quarterly 59:265-77 Spring
    '60   2012
Wright, Walter Francis
  Critical discussion of Joseph Conrad's novels. Ph.D.
    Thesis, University of Nebraska, 1948
  How Conrad tells a story. Prairie Schooner 21:290-5
    Fall '47
  Introduction. In Lord Jim, by Joseph Conrad. (College
    edition) New York: Harper & Brothers, 1958
  Introduction: Conrad's critical perspectives. In Joseph
    Conrad on fiction, edited by Walter F. Wright.
    (Regents Critics Series) Lincoln, Nebraska: University
    of Nebraska Press [1964] p ix-xiv
  Joseph Conrad's critical views. Research Studies of the
    State College of Washington 12:155-75 S '44
  Romance and tragedy in Joseph Conrad. Lincoln, Ne-
    braska: University of Nebraska press, 1949. [iii-iv],
    217p; bibliography, p215-16
    (Reviewed by L. Davidson in Modern Language Notes
    66:198-200 Mr '51; Madeleine L. Cazamian in Études
    Anglaises 6:169 My '53; Booklist 45:389-90 Jl 15 '49;
    United States Quarterly Booklist 5:452 D '49; Albert J.
    Guerard in Western Review 14:151-3 Winter '50)
  The truth of my own sensations. Modern Fiction Studies
    1, no 1:26-9 F '55   2013

Wright, Walter F. (editor)
Joseph Conrad on fiction, edited by Walter F. Wright.
(Regents Critics Series) Lincoln, Nebraska: University
of Nebraska press [c1964] xv, 236p
(Letters and essays by Conrad)
(Reviewed by Sverre Lyngstad in Books Abroad 39:349
Summer '65; Elliott Gose in College English 26:491-2
Mr '65; Samuel Hynes in Sewanee Review 73:151-8
Winter '65; Edgar F. Harden in Victorian Studies 11,
no 3:420-1 Mr '68)   2014
Wrote of the seas he had sailed and told their secrets...
Boston Evening Transcript Ag 4 '24 p2   2015
Wspominki literackie. Conrad o Polsce. Rozmova z przed
dzięsieciu lat. Wiadomości Literackie 1, no 6:1 F
10 '24
(Signed "J. M.")   2016
Wüscher, Albert
Schau und Veranschaulichung der Aussenwelt bei Joseph
Conrad... Theyngen: Augustin, 1934. 7-100p; Ab-
handlung, Zürich, 1934. Bibliography, p[8]-11   2017
Wyka, Kazimierz [Kjw pseud.]
Joseph Conrad. In Inter arma. Krakow, 1946. p122
O polskość Conrada (Conrad's Polish character). Tygod-
nik Powszechny (Universal Weekly) no 5, 1948   2018
Wyzewa, Teodor de
Un conteur anglais: M. Joseph Conrad. Revue des
Deux Mondes 6th periode, tome 20:935-46 Ap 15 '14
(Examines Chance, A Set of Six, and Under Western
Eyes)   2019

Yale receives Conrad works of G. T. Keating. New York
Herald Tribune Ja 17 '38 p9   2020
Yates, Norris W.
Social comment in The Nigger of the 'Narcissus.' Publi-
cations of the Modern Language Association of America
79:183-5 Mr '64   2021
Yelton, Donald Charles
Symbol and metaphor in Conrad's fiction. Ph. D. Thesis,
Columbia University, 1962. 487p; abstract in Disserta-
tion Abstracts 24:752-3 '63
Mimesis and metaphor, an inquiry into the genesis and
scope of Conrad's symbolic imagery. The Hague:
Mouton, 1967 [1968] 336p; bibliography, p[323]-329
(Studies in English Literature, volume 39)
(Based upon his thesis done at Columbia University,
1962)   2022

Young, Barbara
    Joseph Conrad; poem.   New York Times Ag 15 '24 p12
                                                                  2023
Young, Filson
    [The death of Conrad]   New York Times Book Review
        Ag '24 p 48   2023a
Young, Vernon
    Joseph Conrad: outline for a reconsideration.   Hudson
        Review 2:5-19 Spring '49
    Joseph Conrad. II: Lingard's folly: the lost subject.
        Kenyon Review 15:522-39 Autumn '53; same. In The
        art of Joseph Conrad: a critical symposium, edited
        by Robert Wooster Stallman.   East Lansing, Michigan:
        Michigan State University press, 1960. p96-108
    Trial by water.   Joseph Conrad's The Nigger of the
        'Narcissus.'   Accent 12:67-81 Spring '52; same. In
        The art of Joseph Conrad: a critical symposium,
        edited by Robert Wooster Stallman.   East Lansing,
        Michigan: Michigan State University Press, 1960.
        p108-20   2024
Young, W. J.
    Conrad against himself.   Critical Review (University of
        Melbourne) no 11 '68   2024a
Young Boswell interviews Joseph Conrad.   New York Tribune
        My 31 '23 p11   2025

Zabel, Morton Dauwen
    A Conrad chronology.   In The portable Conrad.   New
        York: Viking press, 1947. p50-3
    Conrad in his age.   New Republic 107:644-5 N 16 '42;
        same.   In Craft and character in modern fiction.
        New York: Viking press, 1957. p202-27
        (Reviewed by Horace Gregory in New York Times
        Book Review Jl 21 '57 p10)
    Conrad: Nel Mezzo del Cammin.   New Republic 103:
        873-4 D 23 '40
    Conrad: The Secret Sharer.   New Republic 104:567-8,
        570-4 Ap 21 '41
    East and the sea.   In Craft and character in modern fic-
        tion.   New York: Viking press, 1957. p168-86
    Editor's introduction.   In The portable Conrad.   New
        York: Viking press, 1947. p1-47
    Introduction.   In The Nigger of the 'Narcissus,' a tale
        of the sea by Joseph Conrad.   (Harper's Modern Clas-
        sics) New York: Harper & Brothers [c1951] p vii-
        xxxi
    Introduction.   In Lord Jim, by Joseph Conrad.   (River-

side Editions B23) Boston: Houghton Mifflin Co.
[c1958] p v-xxxvii
Introduction. In The mirror of the sea, and A personal
record, by Joseph Conrad. (Anchor books) Garden
City, New York: Doubleday, 1960. p[ix]-xlix
Introduction. In Shadow-Line and two other tales:
Typhoon and The Secret Sharer, edited and with an
introduction by M. D. Zabel. (Anchor Books) Garden
City, New York: Doubleday, 1959. p[1]-27
Introduction. In Tales of the East. Garden City, New
York: Doubleday, 1961. (Anchor Books) p[9]-39
Introduction. In Tales of the East and West... Edited
and with an introduction by M. D. Zabel. Garden City,
New York: Hanover House [1958] p[ix]-xxx
Introduction. In Tales of heroes and history, by Joseph
Conrad. Garden City, New York: Doubleday, 1960.
(Anchor Books A228) p[vii]-xlv; bibliographical note,
p xlvii-xlviii
Introduction. In Under western eyes, by Joseph Conrad.
[New York: New Directions Books, James Laughlin,
1951] (New Classics Series) p[xi]-xxxvi
Introduction. In Under western eyes, by Joseph Conrad.
(Winchester Classics series) London: Nelson, 1956
Introduction. In Under western eyes, by Joseph Conrad.
(Anchor Books) Garden City, New York: Doubleday
[1963] p[ix]-lviii; same. In Conrad. A collection of
critical essays, edited by Marvin Mudrick. (A Spec-
trum Book) Englewood Cliffs, New Jersey: Prentice-
Hall [1966] p111-44
Introduction. In Youth, a narrative and two other stories:
Heart of Darkness, The End of the Tether, by Joseph
Conrad. (Anchor Books) Garden City, New York:
Doubleday [1959] p[1]-25
Joseph Conrad: chance and recognition. Sewanee Review
53:1-22 Winter '45; same. Origenes (Havana) año 2,
no 11:27-41 O '46; same. In Critiques and essays on
modern fiction, 1920-1951, edited by John Watson Ald-
ridge. New York: Ronald, 1952. p270-85; same. In
Craft and character in modern fiction. New York:
Viking Press, 1957. p147-67
Threat to the west. In Craft and character in modern
fiction. New York: Viking press, 1957. p187-207
2026

Zagórska, Aniela
Conrad. In Wielka Encycklopedia Powszechna. Warsaw:
Państwowe Wydawnictwo Naukowe [1963] Volume 2,
p594-5

Zagórska, Aniela (cont.)
Conrad a literatura polska (Conrad and Polish literature).
Wiadomości Literackie 1, no 33:4 Ag 17 '24
Conrad a Polska (Conrad and Poland). Wiadomości
Literackie 1, no 36:4 S 7 '24
Conrad's visit to Poland. Poland 7, no 9:545-7, 574-8,
580, 582 S '26
Kilka wspomnień o Conradzie (A few reminiscences of
Conrad). Wiadomości Literackie 6, no 51:3 D 22 '29;
same. In Wspomnienia i studia o Conradzie, edited
by Barbara Kocówna. Warsaw: Państwowy Instytut
Wydawniczy [1963] p89-102
Souvenirs sur Conrad. La Messager Polonaise (Warsaw)
. nos 10, 11, 13, 1928
Żeromski a Conrad (Żeromski and Conrad). Wiadomości
Literackie 2, no 51:8 D 20 '25   2027
Zagórska, Karola
Pod dachem Konrada Korzeniowskego (Under Konrad Kor-
zeniowski's roof). Kultura nos 2-3, Ja 10-17 '32
                                                     2028
Zawodziński, K. W.
Jeszcze o motywy decyzji życiowej Conrada. Z nadmiaru
czy niedostatku miłości do ojczyzny? Wiadomości
Literackie 5, no 16:1 Ap 15 '28; see also: 5, no 17:4
Ap 22 '28
Nieuwzględnione motywy decyzji życiowej Conrada. Wia-
domości Literackie 4, no 39:1 S 25 '27
Pierwszy czar Conrada (The first spell of Conrad).
Skamander (Warsaw) Ja-Mr '38, p8-19
Wyjaśnienie do artykułu o decyzji Conrada. Wiadomości
Literackie 5, no 22:4 My 27 '28   2029
Zelie, John Sheridan
An evening with Joseph Conrad. Christian Century 42:
251-3 F 19 '25
Joseph Conrad: the man, by Elbridge L. Adams. A
burial in Kent, by John Sheridan Zelie, together with
some bibliographical notes. New York: Rudge, 1925.
72p
(Contents: Joseph Conrad, the man, p3-38; A burial
in Kent, p41-52, reprinted from the Christian Century
41:1363-4 O 23 '24; bibliographical notes, p55-72)
(485 copies, of which 450 were for sale)
(Reviewed in Saturday Review of Literature 2:89 Ag
29 '25; New York Times Book Review Ag 9 '25 p13)
                                                     2030
Zellar, Leonard Eugene
Conrad's use of extra-narrative devices to extend time.

Ph. D. Thesis, University of Illinois, 1958. 238p;
abstract in Dissertation Abstracts 19:1075 '58
(On Nostromo, Under Western Eyes, and The Nigger
of the "Narcissus")
Joseph Conrad, 1898-1904: a study of his philosophy and
technique. M. A. Thesis, University of Denver, 1953
                  2031
Zerbini Rosa
 Vita e arte in Conrad. Acme 19:269-80 '66 2031a
Żeromski, Stefan
 Autor Rodak. Naokolo Świata no 10:6-11 '25; same. In
 Elegie. Warsaw: Wyd. W. Borowy, 1928. p141-8
 Joseph Conrad. Wiadomości Literackie 1, no 33:1 Ag
 17 '24; same. In Joseph Conrad Korzeniowski, by
 Róża Jabłkowska. Warsaw: Państwowe Zakłady Wy-
 dawnictwo Szkolynch, 1964. p200-10; same. In Elegie,
 by Stefan Zeromski. Warsaw: W. Borowy, 1928.
 p127-40
 Joseph Conrad. Nineteenth Century 101:406-16 Mr '27
 [Preface to] Szalenstwo Almayera, by Joseph Conrad,
 translated by Aniela Zagórska. Warsaw: Dom
 Książki Polskiej Spótka, 1928. p vii-xxxi; same. In
 Elegie. Warsaw: Wyd. W. Borowy, 1928. p321-48;
 same. In Wspomnienia i studia o Conradzie, edited by
 Barbara Kocówna. Warsaw: Państwowy Instytut
 Wydawniczy [1963] p163-84   2032
Zieliński, Stanisława
 Wycieczki balonem. 1964.
 (Noted in Rocznik Literacki 1964, p179)   2033
Znamierowski, Czesław
 Wspomnienié o Conradzie. Głos Prawdy no 125, 1927
                 2034
Żona Conrada o swoim mężu. Polska Zbrojna no 316, 1929
 (translated by Hanna Skarbek [Peretiatkowicz]) (from
 the Sunday Express)   2035
Zrębowicz, Roman
 Conrad a literatura polska. Wiadomości Literackie 1,
 no 33:4 Ag 17 '24
 Conrad a proza angielska. Wiadomości Literackie 1,
 no 33:3 Ag 17 '24   2036
Zubrzycka, T. [pseud.] [Mrs. Otolia Retinger]
 Syn dwu ojczyzn. Ze wspomnień o Józefie Conradzie-
 Korzeniowskim. (Son of two fatherlands: some
 reminiscences of Joseph Conrad) Iskry nos 8-10,
 1931   2037
Zuckerman, Jerome Stanley
 Contrapuntal structure in Conrad's Chance. Modern Fic-

Zuckerman, Jerome Stanley (cont.)
    tion Studies 10:49-54 Spring '64
"A Smile of Fortune:" Conrad's interesting failure.
    Studies in Short Fiction (Newberry College) 1:99-102
    Winter '64
    The theme of rule in Joseph Conrad.   Ph. D.   Thesis,
    University of Wisconsin, 1963.   264p; abstract in Dis-
    sertation Abstracts 23:4367 '63   2038
Żuk-Skarszewski, Tadeusz
    See: Skarszewski, Tadeusz Żuk   2039
Zwinge, Mildred Christiane
    A study of Joseph Conrad.   M. A.   Thesis, Columbia Uni-
    versity, 1924. 56p   2040
Zwycięstwo Conrada.   Wiadomości Literackie rok 7,   no
    354:5 S 12 '30   2041
Życie i dzieła Conrada.   Tygodnik Powszechny 11,   no
    48:5 D 8 '57   2041a
Życie literackie w. Anglji.   W step Conrad do książki
    kucharskiej jego zony... Wiadomości Literackie 1,
    no 19:3 My 11 '24   2042
Zywina, Josef
    [Poem to Conrad] In Conrad żywy, edited by Wit Tar-
    nawski.   London: B. Świderski, 1957. p47-9   2043
Żywioł Conrada i Dostojewskiego.   Tygodnik Illustrowany
    no 24, 1931

Works Written by Joseph Conrad
Arranged Alphabetically, With Reviews

Admiralty paper. See: The unlighted coast.   2045
Almayer's folly, a story of an Eastern river. London:
T. Fisher Unwin, 1895. 272p
Completed by May 22, 1894   Original manuscript,
315 quarto pages, is at The Philip H. & A. S. W. Rosen-
bach Foundation. Only Chapter IX is lacking.
Published on April 29, 1895. Various estimates have
been made as to the number of copies in the first edi-
tion, ranging from 1000 copies (W. M. Mackay in
Bookman's Journal); to 1, 100 (Joseph Conrad's letter
of May 2, 1895 to Madame Poradowska); to 1, 500 (Mr.
A. D. Marks, formerly of T. Fisher Unwin); to 2, 000
(T. J. Wise, p5); to 3, 000 (Richard Curle sale, item
21) Price, 6 shillings)
.... New York: Macmillan & Company, 1895. 276p
(Published about May 3, 1895.   650 copies. $1. 25)
(Dated 1895 unless otherwise noted.   Reviewed in
Sketch 11:314 S 4; Publishers' Circular 62:474 My 4;
same. Book News 13:446 Je; Critic (NY) 28:335 My
9; Athenaeum 1:671 My 25; James Ashcroft Noble in
Academy 47:502 Je 15; James MacArthur in Bookman
(NY) 2:40-1 Ag-S; same.   Literary News ns 16:268-9
S; Independent 72:1277 Je 6 '12; Saturday Review (Lon-
don) 79:797 Je 15; Spectator 75:530 O 19; Literary
World (Boston) 26:155 My 18; Annie Logan in Nation
(NY) 61:278 O 17; Book Buyer ns 12:353 Jl; National
Observer 14:513-14 14:513-14 S 14; Speaker 11:722-3
Je 29; World (London) no 1089:31 My 15; Guardian 50:
1001 Jl 3; Christian World (London) 39:510 Je 27;
Bookselling 1:139 My; New York Times My 12 p31;
Arthur Waugh in Critic (NY) 26:349, 481 My 11, Je
29; Bookman (London) 8:176 S; British Weekly 18:86
My 30; Black & White 9:680 My 18; Literary World
(London) ns 51:505 My 31; Atlantic Monthly 76:420 S;
William Morton Payne in Dial 19:92-3 Ag 16; T. P.
O'Connor in Weekly Sun Je 9 p1-2; Birmingham Post
c. My - Je; [Henry Norman in] Daily Chronicle (London)

Almayer's folly (cont.)
My 11 p3, Manchester Courier My 15 p3; Scotsman Ap
29 p3; Glasgow Evening News My 14 p2; noted in
Westminster Gazette Ap 23 p8; noted in Sunday Times
(London) Ap 21 p2; Realm My 10 p966; Woman My 29
p7; Daily News (London) Ap 25 p6)   2046
Alphonse Daudet. Outlook (London) 1:294-5 Ap 9 '98 (entitled: "Views and reviews à propos of Alphonse
Daudet"); same published separately: London: Printed
for the author by Richard Clay and Sons, Ltd. , 1920.
5-11p
[Actually printed for T. J. Wise]
(25 copies only) (Light brown covers)
Later included in: Notes on Life and Letters   2047
Amy Foster. Illustrated London News 119:915-16, 965-6,
1007-8 D 14, 21, 28 '01 (illustrated by Gunning King);
same. Poland 5, no 6:367-70, 397-400; no 7:9-12,
59-61, 64, 66; no 8:81-4, 120, 122-5, 128 Je-Ag '24
(Completed on June 18, 1901. Was originally entitled
"The Husband")
The original manuscript is at the Yale University Li-
brary: 100 folio pages, in pencil.
Later included in: Typhoon and Other Stories, and in
Falk, Amy Foster, To-morrow   2048
An anarchist. Harper's Magazine 113:406-16 Ag '06 (il-
lustrated by Thornton Oakley)
Composed by November, 1905. The manuscript is 70
pages quarto.
Later included in: A Set of Six   2049
Anatole France. Speaker ns 10:359-61 Jl 16 '04; same pub-
lished: London: Printed for Joseph Conrad, Orlestone
by Richard Clay & Sons, Ltd. , 1919. 5-17p
(25 copies only) (Dark red covers)
[Actually printed for T. J. Wise]
Later included in: Notes on Life and Letters (en-
titled: "Anatole France I 'Crainquebille' ")   2050
Anatole France, "L'ile des Pingouins." English Review 1:
188-90 D '08; same published separately: London:
Printed for the author by Richard Clay and Sons, Ltd. ,
1920. 5-10p
(25 copies only) (Light green covers)
[Actually printed for T. J. Wise]
Later included in: Notes on Life and Letters (en-
titled: "Anatole France II 'L'ile des Pingouins' ")
                                                     2051
The aristocrat. See: Prince Roman   .   2052
The arrow of gold; a story between two notes. Garden City,

New York: Doubleday, Page & Co., 1919. vi, 385p
(Published April 12. 15,000 copies. $1.50 in cloth;
$2 leather)
.... London: T. Fisher Unwin, Ltd. [1919] x, 336p
(Published August 6. 20,000 copies. 8 shillings)
Composed by June 14, 1918. Was also entitled:
"The Laugh" and "Rita Lastaola, A Tale."
The typescript is at the Yale University Library
(Serially in Lloyd's Magazine 31:110-18, 209-17,
290-9, 360-9, 435-44, 511-18, 583-92, 659-66, 731-9,
812-20, 875-81; 32:51-8, 172-8, 246-52, 318-24 D
'18 - F '20 (illustrated by Herbert Pizer).
(Dated 1919 unless otherwise noted.) Reviewed in
Chicago Daily News before My 24; same. Boston Eve-
ning Transcript My 24 part 3 p11; Argonaut 84:313
My 17; D. S. Meldrum in Book Monthly 14:697-700 S;
Sidney Colvin in Daily Telegraph (London) Ag 24 p3;
same. Living Age 302:792-5 S 27; Sidney Colvin in
Observer Ag 24 p3; Review of Reviews (NY) 59:670
Je; W. L. Courtney in Daily Telegraph (London) Ag 15
p4, Ag 29 p4; James Douglas in Star (London) Ag 8
p2; Scotsman Ag 7 p2; World (London) Ag 23 p22;
Birmingham Post Ag 12 p5; A. N. M. in Manchester
Guardian Ag 6 p5; Westminster Gazette Ag 9 p9;
James Thorp in Sunday Times (London) Ag 10 p5;
Glasgow Evening News Ag 21, S 11 p2; Edwin Francis
Edgett in Boston Evening Transcript Ap 19 part 3 p8;
Philip Littell in New Republic 19:56 My 10; Louis Gillet in Revue des Deux Mondes 6th période, volume 53:
676-85 O 1; Booklist 15:313 My; Katherine Mansfield
in Athenaeum 2:720 Ag 8; same. In Novels and novelists... New York: Knopf, 1930. p60-4; Canadian Bookman 1:69 Jl; Public Opinion (London) 116:157-8 Ag 15;
Times Literary Supplement Ag 7 p422; Independent 99:
264 Ag 23; Pem in John O'London's Weekly 1:570 Ag
23; Spectator 123:410 S 27; Nation (London) 25:680,
682 S 6; Katharine Fullerton Gerould in Bookman (NY)
49:368-70 My; New York Times Review of Books Ap
13 p189-90; Nation (NY) 108:951 Je 14; Outlook (NY)
122:122 My 21; Frederic Taber Cooper in Publishers'
Weekly 95:1129 Ap 19; Saturday Review (London) 128:
179 Ag 23; H. W. Boynton in Review (NY) 1:61-2 My
31; Annual Register... for the year 1919. London:
Longmans, Green, 1920. p42-3 (Literature); New
Statesman 13:497 Ag 16; Morning Post (London) Ag 6
p3; Hamilton Fyfe in Daily Mail (London) Ag 6 p8;
Robert Lynd in Daily News (London) Ag 6 p6; Holbrook

The arrow of gold... (cont.)
    Jackson in New Nation Ag; J.D. Beresford in Every-
    man 14:425-6 Ag 9; Bookman (NY) 49:640 Jl; Bookman
    (London) 57:27 O; Outlook (London) 44:180 Ag 16;
    Peter Bell in Land & Water no 2990:40 Ag 28; Lennox
    Robinson in Irish Statesman 2:134-5 F 7 '20; Desmond
    B. O'Brien in Truth (London) 86:301-2 Ag 13; Literary
    Digest 63, no 2:67 O 11; E.B. Osborn in Illustrated
    London News 155:282 Ag 23; Joseph Hergesheimer in
    Sun (NY) Books & the Book World Ap 13, section 7 p1;
    English Review 29:287 S; James Milne in Graphic 100:
    232 Ag 16; America 21:80 Ap 26; Punch 157:199 Ag 27;
    L. Leonhard in Das Literarische Echo 22, no 22:1383
    Ag 15 '20; Henry D. Davray in Mercure de France
    (series moderne) 136:793-4 D 15; Wisconsin Library
    Bulletin 15:143 My; H.J.M. in Nation (London) 25:563
    Ag 9; Evening Sun (NY) Ap 19 p9; World (NY) Ap 13
    Editorial Section p5E; Thomas Seccombe in Daily
    Chronicle (London) Ag 12 p4; noted in Publishers' Week-
    ly 95:1013 Ap 12; Evening Standard Ag 28 p11; Public
    Ledger (Philadelphia) Ap 26 '19 p14; North American
    (Philadelphia) Ap 19 p14; W. E. Süskind in Literatur
    35:413-14 Ap '33; H. L. Mencken in Smart Set 59: no
    4:141-2 Ag; Willis Fletcher Johnson in Tribune (NY)
    Ap 12 p13; noted in advance in Chicago Daily Tribune
    Ap 19 p12; Fanny Butcher in Chicago Daily Tribune
    Ap 20 part 7 p7)   2053
L'art et la morale de Conrad éclairés par quelques cita-
    tions [extracts]   La Nouvelle Revue Française 23:743-
    9 D '24   2054
The art of fiction.   New Review 17:628-31 D '97; same.
    Harper's Weekly 49:690 My 13 '05; same. (excerpt)
    Literary Digest 30, no 21:776-7 My 27 '05; same pub-
    lished separately: Hythe and Cheriton: Printed by J.
    Lovick, 1902. 7p (100 copies only, of which about 40
    were accidentally destroyed); same.   Garden City, New
    York: Doubleday, Page & Co., 1914. [vii]-xiii p;
    same.   Lebanon, Pennsylvania: 1927. 7p
    The Preface to The Nigger of the 'Narcissus.' The
    manuscript of this preface, 10 pages, is at The Philip
    H. & A. S. W. Rosenbach Foundation.   2055
The ascending effort.   See: Can poetry flourish in a scien-
    tific age?   2056
Autocracy and war.   Fortnightly Review 84:1-21 Jl 1 '05;
    same.   North American Review 181:33-55 Jl '05; same
    published separately: London: Printed for private
    circulation (for Thomas J. Wise), [Feb.] 1919. 5-65p

(25 copies only) (Gray covers)
Completed by March, 1905.   The typescript of 45 pages
is in the Lena R. Arents Rare Book Room, Syracuse
University
    Later included in: Notes on Life and Letters   2057
Because of the dollars.   Metropolitan Magazine 40:19-21,
57-61 S '14 (entitled: "Laughing Anne," and illustrated
by Frederic Dorr Steele); same.   Golden Book 2:581-
96 N '25.   The manuscript of 62 pages is at The
Philip H. & A. S. W. Rosenbach Foundation.
Completed by December, 1913. Another manuscript is at
the Lilly Library, Indiana University.   The first 42
pages are typed, with revisions, plus 20 pages in Con-
rad's handwriting.
    Later included in: Within the Tides
    For dramatization, please see: Laughing Anne   2058
Big Brierly.   See: Lord Jim.   A tale   2059
The black mate.   London Magazine 20:121-35 Ap '08 (illustrated by A. Mason); same published separately:
Printed for the author (by the Dunedin Press, Ltd.,
Edinburgh), For Private Distribution Only, February,
1922. 5-74p
(50 copies only) (Green cloth)
[Actually printed for T. J. Wise]
Completed in 1908.   Of the story, Conrad wrote: 'I
have a notion that it was first written sometime in the
late eighties and retouched later."
    Later included in: Tales of Hearsay   2060
Books.   Speaker ns 12:369-70 Jl 15 '05; same.   Living Age
246:500-3 Ag 19 '05; same published separately:
London: Printed for the author by Richard Clay & Sons,
Ltd., 1920. 5-15p
(25 copies only) (Bluish-green cover)
[Actually printed for T. J. Wise]
    Later included in: Notes on Life and Letters   2061
The books of my childhood.   IX (A letter written by Joseph
Conrad).   T. P. 's Weekly 1:271 Ja 9 '03   2062
The brute; tale of a bloodthirsty brig.   Daily Chronicle
(London) D 5 '06 (Christmas number); same.   Mc-
Clure's Magazine 30:72-85 N '07 (subtitled: "A piece
of invective" and illustrated by E. L. Blumenschein);
same.   In Great short stories of detection, mystery,
and horror, edited by Dorothy L. Sayers.   London:
Gollancz, 1928. p914-33; same.   Golden Book 14:334-
47 N '31; same.   New York Tribune My 1 '21 part
VII p4, 6
(Composed in the summer of 1905) Original manu-

The brute (cont.)
   script is 52 pages folio, at Baker Library, Dartmouth
   College.
   Later included in: A Set of Six (entitled: "The
   Brute") 2063
Can poetry flourish in a scientific age? (A review of
   George Bourne's The Ascending Effort) Daily Mail
   (London) Jl 30 '10 p8
   Later included in: Notes on Life and Letters (en-
   titled: "The Ascending Effort") 2064
The censor of plays. See: The censorship of plays 2065
The censorship of plays (a letter to the editor). Daily Mail
   (London) O 12 '07 p4; same. New York Tribune Ja
   23 '23; same. Times (London) Ag 13 '09 p4
   Later included in: Notes on Life and Letters (en-
   titled: "The Censor of Plays; an Appreciation") 2066
Certain aspects of the admirable inquiry into the loss of the
   Titanic. See: Some aspects of the admirable inquiry
   into the loss of the Titanic 2067
Chance, An Episodic Tale, With Comments. See: Chance:
   A Tale in Two Parts
Chance; a tale in two parts. London: Methuen & Co.,
   Ltd., [1913] vii, 406p 2068
   (Composed between June 3, 1911 and March 25, 1912)
   Original manuscript is 1252 pages quarto, of which 35
   pages are in the handwriting of Mrs. Jessie Conrad.
   Published September 18, 1913 (first edition, first
   issue)
..........London: Methuen & Co., Ltd., 1914. vii, 406p
   Published January 15, 1914. 3000 copies. 6 shillings
   (first edition, second issue)
..........Garden City, New York: Doubleday, Page and
   Co., 1914 (copyright 1913). viii, 468p
   Published March 26, 1914. $1.35
   (There was also an American copyright issue of
   Chance, published October 7, 1913, of which approxi-
   mately 150 copies were printed)
   Serially in the New York Herald, Magazine Section,
   January 21 to June 30, 1912, entitled: "Chance, An
   Episodic Tale, With Comments," illustrated by L. A.
   Shafer.
   (Dated 1914 unless otherwise noted. Reviewed by
   James Huneker in North American Review 200:270-9
   Ag; Everyman 3, no 69:572 F 6; Spectator 112:101-2
   Ja 17; Richard Curle in Bookman (London) 45:265 F;
   Academy 86:145-6 Ja 31; Athenaeum 1:88-9 Ja 17;
   Booklist 10:369 My; Richard Curle in English Review

16:443-5 F; Clement King Shorter in Sphere 56:176 F
7; Atlantic Monthly 114:530 O; Frederic Taber Cooper
in Bookman (NY) 39:323-4 My; Literary Digest 48:
1119 My 9; Saturday Review (London) 117:117-18 Ja
24; Outlook (NY) 107:45-6 My 2; H. C. Shelley in Boston Evening Transcript Ja 31 part 3, p9; Edwin Francis Edgett in Boston Evening Transcript Mr 21 part 3,
p8; Independent 78:173 Ap 27; Helen Bullis in New
York Times Review of Books Mr 22 p129-30; Frederic
Taber Cooper in Publishers' Weekly 85:1335-6 Ap 18;
Review of Reviews (NY) 49:373-4 Mr; Times Literary
Supplement Ja 15 p21-2; Nation (London) 14:720, 722
Ja 24; N. H. W. in T. P.'s Weekly 23:426 Ap 3; Cur-
rent Opinion (NY) 56:375 My; Outlook (London) 33:427
Mr 28; Mary Austin in Harper's Weekly 58, no 2995:
20 My 16; Desmond B. O'Brien in Truth (London) 75:
206-7 Ja 28; noted in Argonaut 74:281 Ap 25; noted in
Dial 54:252 Mr 16; Sketch 85: pages j and l Mr 25;
Sidney Colvin in Observer (London) Ja 18 p5; same.
Public Opinion (London) 105:109 Ja 23; Literary World
(London) ns 80:46 F 5; Punch 146:79 Ja 28; World
(London) Ja 27 p156; H. L. Mencken in Smart Set 42:
155-7 Mr; C. D. Morley in Book News Monthly 32:
384-5 Ap; Springfield Republican Ap 16 p5; noted in
Publishers' Weekly 85:1110 Mr 28; noted in New York
Tribune Ja 31 p8; H. W. Boynton in Nation (NY) 98:
396-7 Ap 9; Jeanette L. Gilder in McClure's Magazine
43:208 Ag; Sun (NY) Ja 31 p9; noted in Book Monthly
11:345 F; D. S. Meldrum in Daily Chronicle (London)
Ja 15 p4; W. L. Courtney in Daily Telegraph (London)
Ja 21 p15; Morning Post (London) Ja 19 p2; Robert
Lynd in Daily News (London) Ja 15 p4; Daily Mail
(London) Ja 16 p3; Scotsman Ja 26 p2; Standard (London) Ja 16 p10; Birmingham Post Ja 28 p4; C. E. M.
in Manchester Guardian Ja 15 p6; Westminster Gazette
Ja 17 p15; Sunday Times (London) Ja 18 p4; Glasgow
Evening News F 5 p10; Evening Standard (London) Ja
15 p9; New York Tribune Ap 4 p11; J. W. D. in
America 11, no 6:138-9 My 23; K. Arns in Gral 21:
327 '27; M. Behler-Hagen in Schöne Literatur 29:29-
30 Ja '28; Valéry Larbaud in Nouvelle Revue Française 11, no 63:527-9 Mr 1 '14; same. In Ce vice
impuni... Paris: Messein, 1925. p271-5; H. M. Tomlinson in Star (London) Ja 19; noted in New York
Times Book Review Je 14 p274)   2069
The character of the foe. See: Gales of wind   2070

The character of the sea. Appleton's Booklovers Magazine
7, no 1:28-32 Ja '06 (illustrated by W. J. Aylward)
Later included in: The Mirror of the Sea (section
XXXVI, as the second part of "Initiation")   2071
The children of the sea; a tale of the forecastle. New
York: Dodd, Mead and Co., 1897. iv, 217p
(Published November 30. 1000 copies. $1.25)
For this American edition, the title was changed from
The Nigger of the 'Narcissus' to The Children of the
Sea "in deference to American prejudices."
For reviews, please see the English title, The Nigger
of the 'Narcissus'   2072
Christmas day at sea. Daily Mail (London) D 24 '23 p4;
same. Delineator 103:10 D '23 (illustrated by Jacob
Riegel, Jr.); same. Country Life (NY) 55:72-3 D '28
Later included in: Last Essays   2073
A clipper ship I knew. Collier's Weekly 72, no 17:8 O
27 '23 (illustrated by John Richard Flanagan); same.
Blue Peter ns 3, no 19:251-4 O '23; same published
separately: [London:] Twenty copies privately
printed by F. A. Hook, October, 1923.
[Printed by Riddle, Smith & Duffus] 6p (20 copies
only); same. In Sail, the romance of the clipper ships.
London: Blue Peter Publishing Co. [1929] Volume II,
p87-90
Later included in: Last Essays (entitled: "The Torrens:
A Personal Tribute")   2074
Cobwebs and gossamer. See: The tallness of the spars
                                                    2075
The commanding officer. See: The tale   2076
A comment on Hugh Walpole, by Joseph Conrad. In Hugh
Walpole; appreciations, by Joseph Conrad, Arnold Ben-
nett, Joseph Hergesheimer, together with notes and
comments on the novels of Hugh Walpole by Grant
Overton. New York: George H. Doran [1923 ?] p1
                                                    2077
Communication. Transatlantic Review 1, no 1:98-9 Ja '24
                                                    2078
The complete short stories of Joseph Conrad. London:
Hutchinson & Co. [1933] vii, 9-1007p
(Issued in October. 8 shillings, 6 pence)   2078a
Il Conde. Cassell's Magazine 46:243-53 Ag '08 (illustrated
by Cyrus Cuneo); same. Hampton's Magazine 22:
236-44 F '09 (illustrated by G. W. Peters); same.
Canadian Magazine 41:595-604 O '13; same. Golden
Book 13:43-9 My '31; same. Il Conte... with other
stories by famous American authors, edited by Charles

Donald Fox.   (Renard's Famous Authors Series)
New York: Renard, 1925. p1-18; same. Great stories of all nations, edited by Maxim Lieber and Blanche
Colton Williams. New York: Brentano's, 1927. p391-
403
(Composed by late 1907) The manuscript is 56 pages
quarto. This story is sometimes called "Il Conte"
Later included in: A Set of Six   2079
Confidence. "The British Merchant Marine has been chal-
lenged in its supremacy before." Daily Mail (London)
Je 30 '19 (Golden Peace Number) p3; same published
separately (entitled "Confidence.") London: Printed for
the Author by Richard Clay and Sons, Ltd. , 1920. 5-
13p
(25 copies only) (Light tan covers)
[Actually printed for T. J. Wise]
Later included in: Notes on Life and Letters (en-
titled: "Confidence")   2080
The Congo Diary. See: Joseph Conrad's Diary.   2081
A Conrad argosy. With an introduction by William McFee.
With woodcuts by Hans Alexander Mueller. New York:
Doubleday, Doran, 1942. v-x, 713p "Introduction,"
p vii-x; bibliography, p711-13
(Issued in August. $5.)
(Reviewed by Morton Dauwen Zabel in New Republic
107:644-5 N 16 '42; Edward Larocque Tinker in New
York Times Book Review D 27 '42 p10; Marshall
Bragdon in Springfield Republican O 3 '42 p6; noted in
New York Times Book Review Ag 23 '42 p10; noted by
Samuel David Newberry and Bruce Gentry in Pub-
lishers' Weekly 142:858 S 5 '42; Sun (NY) S 1 '42)
                                                   2082
The Conrad companion, arranged and introduced by A. J.
Hoppé. London: Phoenix House, 1947. 343p. "Intro-
duction," p1-26; "A Conrad bibliography," p26-7;
"Some critical and biographical writings about Conrad,"
p27
(Originally published in 1946 as The Conrad Reader)
                                                   2083
Conrad memories. Printed for Mentor readers with Mr.
Conrad's special consent. Mentor 13:3-11 Mr '25
                                                   2084
The Conrad reader, arranged and introduced by A. J.
Hoppé. London: Phoenix House, 1946. [i-ii], 343p
(Reviewed by H. M. Tomlinson in Observer (London)
D 8 '46 p3; Sunday Times (London) D 1 '46; Daily
Herald (London) D 16 '46; Yorkshire Post D 13 '46 p3;

The Conrad reader (cont.)
    Books of the Month D '46; Liverpool Echo D 27 '46)
                                                    2085
Conrad to a friend: 150 selected letters from Joseph Con-
    rad to Richard Curle, edited with an introduction and
    notes by Richard Curle.   Garden City, New York:
    Doubleday, Doran, 1928. [v]-x, 192p.   "Introduction,"
    p vii-x
    (Issued about October 27. $2.50)
.... New York: Crosby Gaige, 1928. 151p.
    Portrait.   "Preface," p[iii]-[v]
    (850 copies on all-rag paper; 9 copies on green paper)
    Entitled: Letters.   Joseph Conrad to Richard Curle.
    Edited with an introduction and notes by Richard
    Curle.
.... London: Sampson, Low, Marston and Co. , 1928.
    vii-xi, 242p.   "Introduction," p vii-xi
    (Issued in October.   10 shillings, 6 pence)
    Published also with the title: Letters of Joseph Con-
    rad to Richard Curle
    (Reviewed in Spectator 142:88 Ja 19 '29; New States-
    man 32:329-30 D 15 '28; New Statesman 32:290 D 8
    '28; Wilbur Cross in Yale Review ns 18:583 Mr '29;
    Percy Hutchison in New York Times Book Review N
    4 '28 p2, 10; Harry Hansen in New York World O 28
    '28 Editorial Section p8E; William McFee in New York
    Herald Tribune Books N 4 '28 p4; Mary Ellen Chase
    in Commonweal 9:295 Ja 9 '29; noted in Publishers'
    Weekly 114:1798 O 27 '28)   2086
Conrad's Diary.   See: Joseph Conrad's Diary   2087
Conrad's Polish background; letters to and from Polish
    friends, edited by Zdzisław Najder and translated by
    Halina Carroll.   London: Oxford University Press,
    1963.   v-vii, 313p; introduction, p1-31; bibliography,
    p307-8
    (Reviewed by Richard Curle in Contemporary Review
    205:552 O '64; Tony Tanner in Spectator 212:636 My
    8 '64; Times Literary Supplement Je 4 '64 p488; C. A.
    Bojarski in English Studies in Africa 8:81-9 Mr '65;
    M. C. Bradbrook in Modern Language Review 60:267-8
    Ap '65; Douglas Hewitt in Review of English Studies ns
    16:326-8 Ag '65; Maria Kuncewicz in Slavic Review
    24:349-50 Je '65; Norman Sherry in Notes & Queries
    ns 13:109-10 Mr '66; V. S. Pritchett in New Statesman
    67:846 My 29 '64; Frederick P. W. McDowell in Philo-
    logical Quarterly 46:109-13 Ja '67; Edmund A. Bojar-
    ski in English Literature in Transition 7, no. 4:234-8

'64 & in Polish American Studies 22, no 2:119-26
Jl-D '65; Andrew Busza in Slavonic & East European
Review 44, no 102:209-11 Ja '66)   2088
Conrad's prefaces to his works. With an introductory essay
by Edward Garnett and a biographical note on his
father by David Garnett. London: J. M. Dent [1937]
[v-x], 218p; "Biographical note," p [v]-viii; "Conrad's
place in literature," p3-34; "A chronological list of
the published works of Joseph Conrad," p213-18
(Issued August 26. 1500 copies. 7 shillings, 6 pence)
(Reviewed by Edwin Muir in London Mercury 37:354
Je '38; Times Literary Supplement S 4 '37 p637;
Graham Greene in Spectator 159:469-70 S 17 '37;
Henry Major Tomlinson in New Statesman & Nation ns
14:537-8 O 9 '37; Tablet 170:353 S 11 '37; G. K.'s
Weekly 26:52 S 23 '37; René Galland in Etudes Ang-
laises 2 no 1:58-9 '38)   2089
Conrad's private letters. See: Joseph Conrad's letters to
his wife   2090
Il Conte. See: Il Conde   2091
Cookery. See: Joseph Conrad (Prefacer)   2092
The crime of partition. See: Poland, the crime of
partition   2093
The death of Lord Jim. (A selection from Lord Jim:
part of Chapter 45). Golden Book 18:202-7 S '33
                                                     2094
The Dover patrol: a tribute. See: Heroes of the straits
                                                     2095
The duel. A military story. Pall Mall Magazine 41:65-77,
193-204, 320-32, 480-9, 614-21 Ja-My '08 (illustrated
by W. Russell Flint); same. (entitled: "The Point of
Honor") Forum 40:89-102, 142-62, 229-44, 348-68 Jl-
O '08; same published separately: The Duel. A Mili-
tary Tale. (Famous Authors Series, no 32) Garden
City, New York: Garden City Publishing Co., Inc.,
1923. 118p; same edition published in boards in 1924;
same. In Twelve short novels, selected by Thomas
B. Costain. Garden City, New York: Doubleday &
Co., 1961. p173-234
Identical in content with The Point of Honor: A Mili-
tary Tale, published in New York by the McClure
Company in 1908.
Composed by April, 1907
Later included in: A Set of Six (entitled: "The Duel:
A Military Tale")   2096
Eighteen unpublished letters from Joseph Conrad to John
Galsworthy, edited by Maria Danilewicz. In Conrad

Eighteen unpublished letters... (cont.)
    żywy, edited by Wit Tarnawski. London: B. Świder-
    ski, 1957. p299-57 (with English and Polish texts and
    two facsimiles); same published as: Listy do Johna
    Galsworthy 'ego... same. (excerpt) In Joseph Conrad
    Korzeniowski, by Róża Jabłkowska. Warsaw: Państ-
    wowe Zakłady Wydawnictwo Szkolynch, 1964. p175-81
                                                        2097
Emblems of hope. See: "Up anchor."   2098
The end of the tether. Blackwood's Magazine 172:1-20,
    202-18, 395-408, 520-37, 685-702, 794-814 Jl-D '02;
    same. In Great short novels. An anthology by Ed-
    ward Weeks. New York: Literary Guild of America
    [c1941] p287-396
    Completed by October, 1903. Original manuscript is
    146 pages quarto.
    Later included in: Youth: A Narrative and Two Other
    Stories   2099
L'enigme de Joseph Conrad. See: Letter from Conrad
    (dated December 19, 1885)   2100
The enterprise of writing a book. Forum 74:308-10 Ag '25;
    same. T. P. 's & Cassell's Weekly 4:475, 494 Ag 1
    '25 (entitled: "Joseph Conrad as Critic"); same. Living
    Age 326:514-17 S 5 '25
    Composed on March 2, 1904
    Later included in: Last Essays (entitled: "A Glance at
    Two Books," a review of John Galsworthy's The Is-
    land Pharisees and of W. H. Hudson's Green Mansions)
                                                        2101
Facsimile of a letter (to Ford Madox Ford). Transatlantic
    Review 2, no 3:326 O '24   2102
The faithful river. See: London river   2103
Falk, Amy Foster, To-morrow. Three stories. New
    York: McClure Phillips & Co., 1903. vi, 271p
    (Issued about September 25. $1.50)
    (Published in England as Typhoon and Other Stories,
    1903. In America, Typhoon was published separately
    in 1902.)
    "Falk" was composed in May, 1901; the manuscript,
    247 pages folio, is at the Yale University Library.
    (Dated in 1903 unless otherwise noted. Reviewed by
    Frederic Taber Cooper in Bookman (NY) 18:309-12 N;
    New York Times Saturday Review of Books & Art O
    24 p756; New York Tribune Illustrated Supplement S
    27 p11; Literary World (Boston) 34:308 N; Review of
    Reviews (NY) 28:756 D; Public Opinion (NY) 35:472 O
    8; Herbert Copeland in Reader 2:622-3 N; Book Buyer

27:471 D; Current Literature 36:115 Ja '04; Argonaut
53:supplement N 9 p318; Sun (NY) S 26 p6-7; noted in
Literary News (NY) ns 24:343 N; noted in Publishers'
Weekly 64, no 22:126 N 28)   2104
A familiar preface. In Modern essays, edited by Christo-
pher Morley. New York: Harcourt, Brace [1921]
p81-93
(The Preface to A Personal Record, first issued in
1912)   2105
The famous stories of Joseph Conrad. Garden City, New
York: Doubleday, Doran, 1938. 403p
(Contains: The Nigger of the "Narcissus," Youth, The
Lagoon, The Shadow-Line, and Il Conde)   2106
The "Fine Art." Pall Mall Magazine 35, no 144:439-46 Ap
'05 (illustrated by David B. Waters); same. Book-
lovers Magazine (Philadelphia) 5, no 5:[647]-653 My
'05 (with one illustration, and entitled: "Sailing as a
fine art. The philosophy of yachting seamanship.")
Later included in: The Mirror of the Sea (sections
VII-IX, entitled: "The Fine Art")   2107
The first and last of Conrad. London: Benn, 1929. 1014p
(Contains: Almayer's Folly, An Outcast of the Islands,
The Arrow of Gold, and The Rover)
(Issued in July. About 10,000 copies. 7 shillings, 6
pence)
(Reviewed by Mary Agnes Hamilton in Time & Tide
10:1094-5 S 13 '29; Scotsman Ag 8 '29 p2; Gerald
Gould in Observer (London) Ag 4 '29 p6)   2108
The first news. Reveille (London) no 1:16-19 Ag'18; same
published separately: London: Privately printed by
Clement Shorter (by Eyre and Spottiswoode), August,
1918. 5-11p
(25 copies only, on hand-made paper) (Gray covers)
Later included in: Notes on Life and Letters (en-
titled: "First News")   2109
The first thing I remember. By the Prime Minister and
many other famous men and women. John O'London's
Weekly 6, no 140:301-2 D 10 '21   2110
Five letters by Joseph Conrad written to Edward Noble in
1895. With a foreword by Edward Noble. London:
Privately printed (by Strangeways, Printers), 1925.
[7]-21p. "Foreword," p[7]-9
(100 copies only, numbered and signed by Edward
Noble)   2111
Five prefaces. London Mercury 3:493-509 Mr '21; same.
(excerpt) La Nouvelle Revue Francaise 23:804-5 D
'24

Five prefaces (cont.)
(Prefaces to Victory, Chance, The Secret Agent, The
Shadow-Line, 'Twixt Land and Sea written for the Sun
Dial Edition in New York and the Collected Edition in
London)
(Reviewed in John O'London's Weekly 4:804 Ap 2 '21;
Valéry Larbaud in Revue de France année 1, tome 2:
423-8 My 15 '21)   2112
Flight. See: Never any more   2113
Four stories by Joseph Conrad, edited by S. F. Moscrop.
(The Kings treasuries of literature, no 129) London:
Dent [1926] 7-256p; bibliography, p251-2. "Introduc-
tion," p7-16; "Questions and exercises," p253-6; por-
trait; "Author's note," p19-20
(Contains: The Secret-Sharer, The Partner, The Inn
of the Two Witches, Freya of the Seven Isles)   2114
Fragments from work in progress or about to appear.
Transatlantic Review 2, no 1:106-10 Jl '24
(The "Preface" to The Nature of a Crime: pages 106-
7 by Joseph Conrad; pages 107-10 by Ford Madox
Hueffer)   2115
Freya of the seven isles.   Metropolitan Magazine (NY) 35:
20-9, 51-4 Ap '12 (illustrated by Clifford W. Ashley);
same. London Magazine 28:649-84 Jl '12 (illustra-
tion by Gilbert Holiday, p650) (and a dedication to
Captain C. M. Harris); same. Golden Book 12:17-26,
105-13, 120, 124, 127-9; no 70:84-92, 94, 105-9 Ag
- O '30 (illustrated by John Alan Maxwell)
(Original manuscript is 224 pages quarto)
(Written between December 26, 1910 and February 28,
1911)
Later included in: 'Twixt Land and Sea   2116
A friendly place. See: A friendly place for sailors   2117
A friendly place for sailors.   Daily Mail (London) D 10
'12 p 8
(The manuscript of 6 leaves is in the Smith College
Library Rare Book Room)
Later included in: Notes on Life and Letters (en-
titled: "A Friendly Place")   2118
The future of Constantinople [a letter]. Times (London) N
7 '12 p5
Later included in: Last Essays   2119
Gales of wind. Pall Mall Magazine 35:363-8 Mr '05 (il-
lustrated by David B. Waters); same. Reader 5:
534-8 Ap '05
Later included in: The Mirror of the Sea (sections
XXII-XXIV, entitled: "The character of the foe") 2120

Gaspar Ruiz. The story of a guerilla chief. Pall Mall
   Magazine 38:81-9, 231-40, 375-83, 497-504 Jl-O '06
   (illustrated by Cyrus Cuneo); same. Saturday Evening
   Post 179, no 4:3-5, 23; no 5:10-11, 19; no 6:7-9, 22;
   no 7:10-11, 21-2 Jl 28 - Ag 18 '06 (illustrated by
   P. V. E. Ivory)
   Composed in November, 1905
   Later included in: A Set of Six and in Youth and
   Gaspar Ruiz   2121
Geography and some explorers. Preface to Countries of
   the World no 1:xviii-xxviii F '24 (entitled: "The romance of travel"); same. National Geographic Magazine 45:239-74 Mr '24 (with 16 full-page illustrations);
   same published separately: London: Privately printed
   by Strangeways and Sons, January, 1924. ii, [3]-40p
   (30 copies only, numbered and signed by Joseph Conrad)
   Later included in: Last Essays
   (Reviewed in New York Times Mr 30 '24 Section 2
   p6)   2122
A glance at two books. See: The enterprise of writing a
   book   2123
The grip of the land. See: Stranded.   2124
Guy de Maupassant. See: Conrad, Joseph (Prefacer) 2125
A happy wanderer. Daily Mail (London) Jl 23 '10 p8
   (A review of C. Bogue Luffman's Quiet Days in
   Spain)
   Later included in: Notes on Life and Letters   2126
Harbour story. See: A Smile of Fortune.   2127
The heart of darkness. Blackwood's Magazine 165:193-
   220, 479-502, 634-57 F-Ap '99; same. Living Age
   225:665-72, 750-5, 812-21; 226:21-7, 90-7, 153-7,
   221-8, 284-94 Je 16 - Ag 4 '00; same. Golden Book
   17:1-17, 176-92, 272-87, 370-83 Ja-Ap '33
   (The manuscript is at the Yale University Library.
   Several pages in typescript are in the Henry W. and
   Albert A. Berg Collection, New York Public Library)
   Composed in January-February, 1899
   Later included in: Youth: A Narrative and Two Other
   Stories (entitled: "Heart of Darkness")
   (Reviewed in New York Times Saturday Review of
   Books & Art My 6 '99 p304; noted by W. L. Alden in
   New York Times Saturday Review of Books & Art Mr
   11 '99 p160)   2128
Henry James; an appreciation. North American Review 180:
   102-8 Ja '05; same. (excerpt) Literary Digest 30:198-
   9 F 11 '05; same. North American Review 203:585-91

Henry James; an appreciation (cont.)
Ap '16; same published separately: London: Printed
for private circulation (for Thomas J. Wise), [Feb.]
1919. 5-20p
(25 copies only) (pink covers); same. (excerpt) In
The question of Henry James, edited by F. W. Dupee.
London: Allan Wingate [1947] p62-3
(Completed by October, 1904)
Later included in: Notes on Life and Letters   2129
Her captivity. Blackwood's Magazine 178:325-33 S '05
Later included in: The Mirror of the Sea (sections
XXXIII-XXXIV, entitled: "In Captivity")   2130
Heroes of the straits. Dover Patrol Memorial. Mr. Joseph
Conrad's Tribute. Times (London) Jl 27 '21 p11-12;
same published separately: Canterbury: Printed for
private circulation by H. J. Goulden, Limited, 1922.
(Entitled: "The Dover Patrol: A Tribute") iv, 14p
(75 copies only) (pale blue covers) (This pamphlet
exists in two states, one without, one with, a separate
title-page; of the two, the one without the title-page is
the earlier printing.)
Later included in: Last Essays (entitled: "The Dover
Patrol")   2131
The heroic age. Standard (London) O 21 '05 p13; same. In
The Queen's gift book... London: Hodder & Stoughton
[1915] p35-40 (with a painting by C. M. Padday and il-
lustrations by J. H. Hartley)
Later included in: The Mirror of the Sea (sections
XLVI-XLIX)
(Reviewed in T. P.'s Weekly 26:634 D 25 '15; A.St.
John Adcock in Everyman 7, no 166:168-9 D 17 '15)
                                                  2132
His war book. See: Joseph Conrad (Prefacer). The Red
Badge of Courage, by Stephen Crane, With a Preface
by Joseph Conrad   2133
The husband. See: Amy Foster   2134
The idiots. Savoy Magazine no 6:11-30 O '96; same.
Modern American and British short stories, edited by
Leonard Brown. New York: Harcourt, Brace, 1929.
p148-77; same. Modern short stories, edited by
Leonard Brown. New York: Harcourt, Brace [c1937]
enlarged edition, p148-77
(Composed in May, 1896)
Later included in: Tales of Unrest   2135
In captivity. See: Her captivity   2136
The Indispensable Conrad. See: The portable Conrad 2136a
The informer. Harper's Magazine 114:131-42 D '06 (illus-

trated by Wolcott Hitchcock)
(Composed in December, 1905). The manuscript of
76 pages is at The Philip H. & A. S. W. Rosenbach
Foundation.
Later included in: A Set of Six   2137
"The Inheritors" - a letter from Joseph Conrad. New York
Times Saturday Review of Books and Art Ag 24 '01
p603
(Noted in Academy 61:185 S 7 '01)
[The letter, dated August 2, 1901, refers to The In-
heritors as "an experiment in collaboration."]   2138
Initiation. Blackwood's Magazine 179:1-14 Ja '06
Later included in: The Mirror of the Sea (sections
XXXV-XXXVI, entitled: "Initiation")
The manuscript of 55 pages is at The Philip H. &
A. S. W. Rosenbach Foundation.   2139
The inn of the two witches; a find. Pall Mall Magazine 51:
335-52 Mr '13 (illustrated by Maurice Greiffenhagen);
same. Metropolitan Magazine (NY) 38:24-7, 48-9 My
'13 (illustrated by H. J. Mowat); same. Everybody's
Magazine 53:104-16, 182 O '25 (illustrated by Stockton
Mulford); same. World Review 1:261-2, 280-1; 2:6-7
F 1-15 '26; same. Golden Book 5:765-77 Je '27;
same. Short stories, edited by Harry Christian Schwei-
kert. New York: Harcourt, Brace, 1939. enlarged
edition, p425-51
(Composed early in 1912) The manuscript of 75 pages
is at The Philip H. & A. S. W. Rosenbach Foundation.
Later included in: Within the Tides   2140
The intimate letters of Joseph Conrad to John Galsworthy,
H. G. Wells, and Arnold Bennett. World's Work (NY)
53:16-24, 181-90, 331-40, 445-54 N '26 - F '27; same.
World Today (London) 49:30-8, 134-43, 217-26, 319-28
D '26 - Mr '27; same. (excerpt) Wiadomości Liter-
ackie 4, no 8:2 F 20 '27; same. Polska Zachodnia no
55, 1927
(Noted in Boston Evening Transcript N 27 '26)   2141
Jak Joseph Conrad borykał się z życiem? Illustrowany Kur-
jer Codzienny no 111, 1932
(Includes a letter from Conrad to William Rothenstein
dated September 3, 1904)   2141a
John Galsworthy. An appreciation. See: A middle class
family   2142
Joseph Conrad as critic. See: The enterprise of writing
a book   2143
Joseph Conrad on fiction, edited by Walter F. Wright.
(Regents Critics Series) Lincoln, Nebraska: University

Joseph Conrad on fiction... (cont.)
of Nebraska Press [1964] xv, 236p.   "Introduction:
Conrad's critical perspectives," p ix-xiv
(Reviewed by Samuel Hynes in Sewanee Review 73:151
Winter '65; Elliott Gose in College English 26:491
Mr '65)   2144
Joseph Conrad on Poland [part of a letter from Joseph Con-
rad to Joseph Quinn]   New York Tribune Ap 5 '20
p10   2145
Joseph Conrad on Stephen Crane.   Ysleta, Texas: Edwin B.
Hill, 1932. [4]p.   "Note," by Vincent Starrett, p[2];
letter by Conrad, p[3]
(A letter from Conrad to Peter F. Somerville, then
editor of The Englishman.   The letter is undated, but
it was received by Mr. Somerville shortly after the
publication, in December, 1919, of Conrad's article on
Crane in the London Mercury.)
(31 copies only, privately printed July 27, 1932; none
for sale)   2146
Joseph Conrad on the art of writing.   See: The art of
fiction   2147
Joseph Conrad's diary (hitherto unpublished) of his journey
up the valley of the Congo in 1890.   With an introduction and notes by Richard Curle.   Blue Peter 5, no
43:319-25 O '25 ("Introduction," p319-21); same.   Yale
Review ns 15:254-66 Ja '26 ("Introduction," p254-9);
same published separately: London: Privately printed
(by Strangeways), January, 1926. [5]-35p.   "Introduction," p[5]-13
(100 copies only)
Later included in: Last Essays (entitled: "The Congo
Diary")
(Noted in New York Times D 5 '25 p22; noted by
Frederick M. Hopkins in Saturday Review of Litera-
ture 2:439 D 19 '25)   2148
Joseph Conrad's first novel.   Westminster Gazette F 3 '14
p4 (a letter from Conrad denying, as stated in the
Westminster Gazette, January 28, 1914 p4, that he
was Captain of the Torrens when the manuscript of
Almayer's Folly was read; he was chief mate)   2149
Joseph Conrad's intimate letters.   See: The intimate
letters of Joseph Conrad   2150
Joseph Conrad's last writing.   See: Legends   2151
Joseph Conrad's letters to his wife.   London: Privately
printed (by Neill and Company, Edinburgh, produced
by the Bookman's Journal), 1927. 7-131p.   "Preface"
by Jessie Conrad Korzeniowska, p7-8; same. (excerpt)

World's Work 53:331-40, 445-54 Ja-F '27 (entitled:
"Conrad's private letters")
(Issued in October. 220 copies, numbered and signed
by Jessie Conrad. 42 shillings)   2152
Karain: a memory. Blackwood's Magazine 162:630-56 N
'97; same. Living Age 215:796-806, 852-64 D 18-25
'97
(Composed by April 14, 1897)
Later included in: Tales of Unrest
(Noted in Saturday Review (London) 84:503-4 N 6 '97)
2153
Kipling, Rudyard - a criticism on his poems. Outlook
(London) 1, no 9:258 Ap 2 '98
(A hitherto unattributed writing by Conrad, unsigned,
which defends Kipling against criticism in the Edin-
burgh Review. Conrad described the article as "a
chatter about Kipling provoked by a silly criticism."
The title is found in the index of Outlook.)   2154
The lagoon. Cornhill Magazine 3rd series, volume 2:59-
71 Ja '97; same. Golden Book 4:467-73 O '26
(Composed in 1896, perhaps in August)
Later included in: Tales of Unrest   2155
Landfalls and departures. Pall Mall Magazine 35:104-9 Ja
'05 (illustrated by David B. Waters); same. Reader
5:278-83 F '05
Later included in: The Mirror of the Sea (sections
I-III)   2156
Last essays. London and Toronto: J. M. Dent & Sons,
Ltd., 1926. v-xvii, 253p. "Introduction," by Richard
Curle, p vii-xvii
(Issued March 3. 7, 200 copies. 7 shillings, 6 pence)
.... with an introduction by Richard Curle. Garden
City, New York: Doubleday, Page, 1926. v-xiv, 171p.
"Introduction," p[vii-xiv]
(Issued March 26. $2)
(Dated 1926 unless otherwise noted. Reviewed in
Times Literary Supplement Mr 4 p159; Dudley Carew
in London Mercury 14:440 Ag; Herbert Read in Nation
& Athenaeum 39:20 Ap 3; Lawrence S. Morris in New
Republic 46:383 My 12; Booklist 22:409 Jl; Louis Kron-
enberger in New York Herald Tribune Books My 23
p16; Karl Schriftgiesser in Boston Evening Transcript
Book Section Ap 10 p1; Mary Childs in Literary Digest
International Book Review 4:590 Ag; Grace Willard in
Literary Review My 1 p5; Living Age 329:555 Je 5;
Nation (NY) 123:381-2 O 13; New Statesman 27:84-5
My 1; Percy A. Hutchison in New York Times Book

Last essays (cont.)
Review Mr 28 p3, 14; Spectator 136:765-6 Ap 24;
Milton Waldman in New York World Ap 11 Metropolitan Section p6; Ethel Parton in Outlook (NY) 142:654
Ap 28; St. Louis 24:248 S; Springfield Republican My
16 p7; Capt. Felix Riesenberg in Saturday Review of
Literature 2:736 Ap 24; Wilbur L. Cross in Yale Review ns 16:161-3 O; Punch 170:362 Mr 21; René Rapin
in Bibliothèque Universelle et Revue de Genève part 2,
p677-8 N; Grenville Vernon in Commonweal 4:194 Je
23; A. S. W. in Manchester Guardian Weekly 14:215 Mr
12; Will Cuppy in Bookman (NY) 63:598 Jl; [Richard
Curle ? in] Daily Mail (London) Mr 3 p14; A. E. S in
Cambridge Review 47:389 My 7; R. Ellis Roberts in
Bookman (London) 70:173 Je; Irish Statesman 5, no 3:
78-9 Mr 27; John Shand in New Criterion 4:782-5 O;
A. C. in T. P. 's & Cassell's Weekly ns 5, no 128:833
Ap 3; Henry-D. Davray in Mercure de France année
38, tome 193:489-90 Ja 15 '27; Mary Agnes Hamilton
in Time & Tide 7:308-9 Mr 26; John O'London's Weekly 14:987 Mr 27; Robert Lynd in Daily News (London)
Mr 5 p4; Publishers' Circular & Booksellers' Record
124:559 My 1; Canadian Forum 6:280-1 Je; B. J. Circle
in Bookman's Journal 14:97 Jl; A. K. in English Re-
view 42:714-15 My; James Milne in Graphic 113:526
Mr 20; Francis X. Talbot in America 35:93-4 My 8;
Wiadomości Literackie 3, no 26:3 Je 27; noted in Pub-
lishers' Circular & Booksellers' Record 124:235 Mr 6;
noted in McNaught's Monthly 5, no 6:186 Je; noted in
Saturday Review (London) 141:301 Mr 6; Morning Post
(London) Mr 3 p13; Daily Chronicle (London) Mr 4 p2;
Arthur Waugh in Daily Telegraph (London) Mr 16 p15;
Star (London) Mr 4 p4; H. M. Tomlinson in Observer
(London) Mr 14 p6; A. S. W. in Manchester Guardian
Mr 3 p7; P. B. in Westminster Gazette Mr 10 p6;
H. C. Minchin in Sunday Times (London) Mr 14 p9;
noted in Glasgow Evening News Mr 11 p2; J. F. Muir-
head in Landmark My; Van Wyck Brooks in Sun (NY)
Ap 10 p9; Sidney Dark in Chicago Daily Tribune Mr
27 p16; British Weekly Ap 29 p104)   2157
The laugh
[A manuscript in the Keating Collection at the Yale
University Library, being all that was written of The
Arrow of Gold in the form originally planned by the
author, Joseph Conrad. 1917. The title, "The Laugh,"
is stricken out and "The Arrow of Gold" is written be-
low it on the next line.]   2158

Laughing Anne. See also: Because of the dollars 2158a
Laughing Anne. A play, by Joseph Conrad. (The Vine
Books, no. 4) London: Morland press, September,
1923. 9-66p
(200 copies only, signed by the author, issued to the
Subscribers of Bookman's Journal, London. 63 shil-
lings.)
Adaptation, first written Dec. 15, 1920, of the story
"Because of the Dollars" 2159
Laughing Anne and One Day More; two plays by Joseph Con-
rad. With an introduction by John Galsworthy. Lon-
don: John Castle, 1924. 5-127p. "Introduction,"
p5-15
(Issued about October 21. 6 shillings)
Adaptations of Conrad's stories "Because of the Dol-
lars" and "To-morrow" respectively
.... Garden City, New York: Doubleday, Page,
1925. xvii, 124p
(Issued May 8. $2)
(Dated 1924 unless otherwise noted. Reviewed by E. A.
Baughan in Daily News (London) O 25 p6; K. K. in
Standard (London) O 18 p3; Saturday Review 138:450 N
1; Times Literary Supplement N 6 p705; Richard Ald-
ington in Nation & Athenaeum 36:272, 274 N 15; noted
[by Richard Curle ?] in Daily Mail (London) O 22 p14;
Hugh I'A. Fausset in Bookman (London) 67:194 D;
Walter Prichard Eaton in Saturday Review of Litera-
ture 2:42 Ag 15; John Hyde Preston in Literary Digest
International Book Review 3:808 N '25; Booklist 22:22
O '25; Percy A. Hutchison in New York Times Book
Review My 10 '25 p3; John Galsworthy in New York
Herald Tribune Books My 3 '25 p1-2; A. N. M. in Man-
chester Guardian Weekly 11, no 17:353 O 24; Clement
King Shorter in Sphere 99:188 N 15; Archibald Y.
Campbell in London Mercury 11:324 Ja '25; Morning
Post (London) O 20 p7; A. N. M. in Manchester Guardian O 23 p7; noted in Publishers' Weekly 107:1582 My
9 '25; noted in Glasgow Evening News O 23 p2; noted
in Evening Standard (London) O 18 p3; Lennox Robinson in Observer (London) N 9 p11) 2160
Legends. Joseph Conrad's last article. Daily Mail (London)
Ag 15 '24 p8 (with a prefatory note by Richard Curle
and a facsimile of "The Last Written Page" of the manuscript); same. New York Times Magazine Section S
7 '24 p1-2 (entitled: "Joseph Conrad's last writing")
same. (excerpt). Publishers' Circular & Booksellers'
Record 121:257, 259 Ag 23 '24; same. (first six para-

Legends (cont.)
    graphs) Bookmark (London) 2, no 5:2-3 Spring '26
    Later included in: <u>Last Essays</u> 2161
The lesson of the collision. (A monograph upon the loss
    of the "Empress of Ireland.") Illustrated London News
    144:944 Je 6 '14; <u>same.</u> Globe (London) Je 13 '14 p5;
    same published separately: London: Printed for
    Joseph Conrad, Orlestone by Richard Clay and Sons,
    Ltd., 1919. 5-15p
    (25 copies only) (blue covers)
    [Actually printed for T. J. Wise]
    The original manuscript of 4 pages was listed in
    Maggs Brothers Catalogue no 449, 1924, page 89,
    item 120.
    Later included in: <u>Notes on Life and Letters</u> (as the
    first part of "Protection of Ocean Liners") 2162
A letter from Conrad. Bulletin (Sydney, Australia) Mr 23
    '16 (The Red Page)
    (Conrad identifies his "Frenchman without hands," whom
    he knew in December, 1878, a reference to Conrad's
    story, "Because of the Dollars") 2163
Letter from Conrad [from Calcutta, December 19, 1885, to
    a Polish friend] New Statesman & Nation ns 9:813 Je
    1 '35; <u>same.</u> L'Européen O 30 '29 2164
Letter [to the editor] H. R. H. Princess Louise Sailors' Rest
    Hut, Granton Monthly Magazine, Aug. 1918; Oswes-
    trian, Dec. 1922 2165
Una lettera inedita a Carlo Placci (con una nota di Carlo
    Angeleri) Paragone vol 8, fasc. 88:55-8 Ap '57
    (fac. of letter, dated 26 Oct 1911, is given bet.
    pages 58 and 59) 2166
Letters from Joseph Conrad, 1895-1924. Edited with an
    introduction and notes by Edward Garnett. Indianapol-
    is: Bobbs-Merrill [c1928] 313p.
    "Introduction," p1-28; portrait. Excerpt in Joseph Con-
    rad Korzeniowski, by Róża Jabłkowska. Warsaw:
    Państwowe Zakłady Wydawnictwo Szkolynch, 1964.
    p157-74
    (Issued about April 1. $3.50)
.... Bloomsbury (London): Mark of Nonesuch Press
    (Printed in Great Britain by R. and R. Clark, Ltd.,
    Edinburgh) 1928. xxxiii, 334p; 2 portraits
    (Issued in June. 925 copies only. 25 shillings)
    (Dated 1928 unless otherwise noted. Reviewed in
    Times Literary Supplement Je 28 p483; Richard Church
    in Spectator 141:23-4 Jl 7; Barrington Gates in Nation
    & Athenaeum 43:464 Jl 7; James Norman Hall in At-

lantic Monthly Bookshelf 142:12, 14 Ag; Gilbert Seldes
in Dial 85:249-53 S; Robert Littell in Bookman (NY)
67:xxii-xxiii Jl; Wilbur L. Cross in Yale Review ns
18:583 Spring '29; Booklist 24:399 Jl; William McFee
in New York Herald Tribune Books Ap 1 p1-2; K. S. in
Boston Evening Transcript (Book Section) Je 2 p1;
C. M. in Catholic World 128:247 N; Christian Century
45:980 Ag 9; G. W. Harris in New York Evening Post
Ag 7 p12; New York Times Book Review Mr 25 p5,
18; Mary Ellen Chase in Commonweal 8, no 8:230,
232 Je 27; Springfield Republican Ag 29 p7; noted in
Pittsburgh. Carnegie Library. Among Our Books 33:
342 Je; A. N. M. in Manchester Guardian Weekly 18, no
26:512 Je 29; America 39:526 S 8)   2167
Letters. Joseph Conrad to Richard Curle... See: Conrad
    to a friend...   2168
Letters of Joseph Conrad to Marguerite Poradowska, 1890-
    1920; translated from the French and edited with an
    introduction, notes, and appendices by John Archer
    Gee and Paul J. Sturm. New Haven: Yale University
    Press, 1940. [v-xxv], 147p. "Preface," p[v]-vii;
    "Introduction," p[xiii]-xix; bibliography, p[141]-143;
    portrait
    (Issued about the 16th of November. $2.75)
.... London: Oxford University Press, 1941. 174p.
    (Issued in April-June. 12 shillings, 6 pence)
    (Reviewed by Charles Kerby-Miller in Boston Tran-
    script (Book Section) Ja 18 '41 p1; M. D. Zabel in New
    Republic 103:873-4 D 23 '40; Christian Century 57:
    1451 N 20 '40; Francis Steegmuller in New York Herald
    Tribune Books F 2 '41 p12; Joseph B. Harrison in
    Modern Language Quarterly 3:147-8 Mr '42; William
    McFee in Yale Review ns 30:606-8 My '41; J. F.
    Murphy in America 64:641 Mr 15 '41; John D. Gordan
    in Modern Language Notes 57:233-4 Mr '42; Francis
    W. Knickerbocker in Sewanee Review 50:287-8 Ap-Je
    '42; noted in College English 2:411 Ja '41; Harold N.
    Hillebrand in Accent 1, no 3:188-9 Spring '41)   2169
The letters of Joseph Conrad to Stephen and Cora Crane,
    edited by Carl Bohnenberger and Norman Mitchell
    Hill. Bookman (NY) 69:225-35, 367-74 My-Je '29
                                                      2170
Letters to William Blackwood and David S. Meldrum, edited
    by William Blackburn. Durham, North Carolina: Duke
    University Press, 1958. [v]-xxxvii, 209p
    (Letters from Joseph Conrad to the publisher, William
    Blackwood, and to this company's literary advisor)

Letters to Wm. Blackwood... (cont.)
(Dated 1959 unless otherwise noted. Reviewed by Kenneth Millar in San Francisco Chronicle Ap 19 p24; Times Literary Supplement Ap 24 p242; Jocelyn Baines in Book Collector 8:440, 443 Winter and in College English 21:111 N; New Statesman 58:369-70 S 19; Albert J. Guerard in American Scholar 28:244, 246 Spring; G. D. Klingopulos in Spectator 203:85 Jl 17; M. D. Zabel in New York Times Book Review F 8 p4; Jerzy R. Krzyżanowski in Twórczość no 6:183-4; Harry T. Moore in New York Times Book Review N 30 '58 p62; Reginald L. Cook in American Oxonian 46:155-6 Jl; C. L. Barber in Modern Language Review 55:275-6 Ap '60; Thomas Moser in Modern Language Notes 75: 363-6 Ap '60; M. L. Cazamian in Études Anglaises 14, no 1:75 Ja-Mr '61; Denis Donoghue in New Statesman 72:291 Ag '66; New York Times N 30 '58 Section VII p62; C. W. Mann, Jr. in Library Journal 83:3138 N 1 '58; New Yorker 35:67 Ag 1; Z. A. Grabowski in Time & Tide 40, no 45:1222 N 7 '59)   2171
Letters to William Rothenstein, 1903-1921. Manuscripts in the Harvard College Library   2172
Lettres de Joseph Conrad à Marguerite Poradowska. Edition critique, précédée d'une étude sur le français de Joseph Conrad [par] René Rapin. Genève: Droz, 1966. 230p (Lausanne. Université Faculte des Lettres. Publications, 17) "Introduction," p11-14; "Le francais de Joseph Conrad," p15-53
(Contains 110 letters)   2173
Lettres françaises de Joseph Conrad. La Nouvelle Revue Française 23:750-8 D 1 '24
(Six letters, 1 to Joseph de Smet, 2 to André Gide, 1 to Philippe Neel, 2 to Georges Jean-Aubry)   2174
Lettres françaises de Joseph Conrad, avec une introduction et des notes de Georges Jean-Aubry. Paris: Gallimard [c1929] [7]-210p.
"Introduction," p[7]-23
(Reviewed by René Rapin in Bibliothèque Universelle et Revue de Genève 2:656 N '30; Dominique Braga in Europe 34:280 O 1 '30)   2175
The life beyond. Daily Mail (London) Jl 16 '10 p8
(A review of Jasper B. Hunt's Existence After Death Implied By Science)
Later included in: Notes on Life and Letters   2176
List Conrada do Stefana Żeromskiego. Naokoʄo Świata no 10: 5-6 '25
(A letter from Conrad to Zeromski)   2178

List Conrada w sprawie Polski w roku 1916. Poda∤ do
druku, komentarzem i przypisami opatrzy∤ Bogus∤aw
Leśnodorski. Twórczość 13, no 2:47-53 D '57
(A letter from Conrad to J. H. Retinger, August 21,
1916)   2179
Listy Conrada. Wiadomości Literackie rok 4, no 164:2
F 20 '27
(Letters of Conrad)   2180
Listy Conrada. G∤os Prawdy no 114, 1926
(Six letters from Conrad to Bruno Winawer)   2181
Listy... do Bertranda Russella. Edited by Zdzis∤aw Najder.
Życie Literackie no 11:3-4 '58   2182
Listy do Johna Galsworthy'ego. Edited by Maria Danilewicz.
London: B. Świderski, 1957. 3-31p
(Reprinted from Conrad Żywy, edited by Wit Tarnawski.
The English translation is entitled: "Eighteen Unpub-
lished Letters from Joseph Conrad to John Gals-
worthy.")   2183
Listy do rodziny. Droga no 6, 1928   2184
Listy J. Conrada-Korzeniowskiego do sióstr Anieli i Karoli
Zagórskich. (Translated by Halina Carroll) Twórczość
rok 19, no 12:45-57 D '63
(Nineteen letters from Conrad to Aniela and Karole
Zagórska edited by Zdzis∤aw Najder)   2185
London River: the great artery of England. World's Work
(London) 5:19-32 D '04 (illustrated with photographs);
same. Metropolitan Magazine 21, no 5:[563]-571 F '05
(illustrated from the "Thames Series" of etchings by
James McNeill Whistler); same. London Magazine 16:
481-8 Jl '06 (illustrated by Edgar Wilson); same. pub-
lished separately: London: Privately printed by Clem-
ent Shorter (by Eyre & Spottiswoode), April, 1919.
(entitled: "London's River") 5-19p
(25 copies only) (Red covers)
Later included in: The Mirror of the Sea (sections
XXX-XXXII, entitled: "The Faithful River")   2186
London's River. See: London River   2187
Lord Jim. A tale. Edinburgh and London: William Black-
wood & Sons, 1900. [viii], 451p
(Published October 9. 2893 copies. 6 shillings)
Completed on July 16, 1900 (Conrad's letter, July 28,
1900, to R. B. Cunninghame Graham in the Baker Li-
brary, Dartmouth College).
The manuscript is in the Harvard University Library
.... A romance. New York: Doubleday, McClure &
Co., 1900. 392p
(Published October 31. $1. 50)

Lord Jim. A tale (cont.)
(Serially in Blackwood's Magazine, 166:441-59, 644-57,
807-28; 167:60-73, 234-46, 406-19, 511-26, 666-87,
803-17; 168:88-106, 251-63, 358-83, 547-72, 688-710
O '99 - N '00; same.   (excerpt) Golden Book 17:1-17,
176-92, 272-87, 370-83; 18:202-7 Ja-Ap, S '33; same.
(excerpt from Chapter VI) Living Age 229:331-4 My 4
'01)
(Dated 1900 unless otherwise noted. Reviewed in
Publishers' Circular 73:469 N 3; Outlook (London) 6:
604 D 8; Academy 59:443 N 10; Athenaeum 2:576 N 3;
Bookman (NY) 13:187 Ap '01; W. L. Alden in New York
Times Saturday Review of Books & Art N 10, D 1,
p770, 836, 839; L. R. F. O. in Speaker ns 3:215-16 N
24; Spectator 85:753 N 24; Public Opinion (London) 78:
656, 658 N 23; Current Literature 30:222 F '01; Outlook (NY) 66:711 N 17; Rassegna Italiana 49:211-12 Mr
'39; H. -D. Davray in Mercure de France 38:262 Ap 1
'01; Review of Reviews (NY) 22:762 D; A. Schade Van
Westrum in Book Buyer 22:63 F '01; J. B. P. in Critic
(NY) 38:437-8 My '01; Bookman (London) 19:61 F '01;
New York Daily Tribune N 3 p10; Criterion (NY) ns 2:
43 Je '01; O. O. in Sketch 32:142 N 14; A. H. in Literature 7:409 N 24; Literature 7:488 D 15; Literary
World (London) ns 62:402 N 23; Monthly Review 2:10-
11 Mr '01; Guardian 56:189 F 6 '01; Illustrated London
News 118:48 Ja 12 '01; British Weekly 29:180 N 29;
Graphic 62:946 D 22; noted in Boston Evening Tran-
script D 5 p21; noted in Nation (NY) 114:698 Je 7 '22;
noted in Publishers' Weekly 58:1267 N 10; L. Leon-
hard in Das Literarische Echo 20, no 9:539-40 F 1
'18; noted in Pall Mall Gazette 71, no 11078:1 O 1;
Pall Mall Gazette 71, no 11134:4 D 5; Daily Chronicle
(London) O 29 p3; Daily Telegraph (London) N 7 p11;
Morning Post (London) D 26 p7; Daily News (London)
D 14 p 6; Daily Mail (London) O 26 p3; Scotsman O 22
p2; noted in Standard (London) D 31 p2; Manchester
Guardian O 29 p7; noted in Westminster Gazette O 16
p10; Glasgow Evening News O 18 p2, N 1 p2; noted in
Sunday Times (London) O 14 p2; World (London) O 10
p30; Times Literary Supplement Jl 26 '17 p355)   2188
The loss of the "Dalgonar." London Mercury 5:187 D '21
(A letter by Conrad)
Later included in: Last Essays   2189
Marriage. (A fragment of an unpublished manuscript, con-
sisting of 3 folio pages in Conrad's handwriting, in the
Yale University Library)   2190

Memorandum on the scheme for fitting out a sailing ship...
(Written in 1919 for the Holt Steamship Company)
    Later included in: Last Essays   2191
A middle class family. Outlook (London) 17:449-50 Mr 31
'06; same. (excerpt) Bookmark (London) 2, no 5:3-4
Spring '26; same published separately: Canterbury:
Printed for private circulation by H. J. Goulden, Lim-
ited, 1922. iv, 13p (entitled: "John Galsworthy. An
appreciation.")
(This pamphlet exists in two states, one without, one
with a separate title-page. Of the two, the one lack-
ing a title-page is the earlier printing.)
(A review of John Galsworthy's The Man of Property)
(75 copies only) (Green covers)
Later included in: Last Essays (entitled: "John Gals-
worthy")   2192
The mirror of the sea: memories and impressions. Lon-
don: Methuen & Co. [1906] viii, 306p
(Published October 4. 1500 copies. 6 shillings)
..........New York: Harper & Brothers, 1906. 328p
(Published October 4. 3000 copies. $1.50)
Completed by April, 1906
(Contains: Landfalls and Departures; Emblems of
Hope; The Fine Art; Cobwebs and Gossamer; The
Weight of the Burden; Overdue and Missing; The Grip
of the Land; The Character of the Foe; Rulers of
East and West; The Faithful River; In Captivity; Ini-
tiation; The Nursery of the Craft; The "Tremolino;"
The Heroic Age)
For serialization, please see entries under these titles.
(Dated 1906 unless otherwise noted. Reviewed in Cur-
rent Literature 42:58-9 Ja '07; H.-D. Davray in Mer-
cure de France 69:755-6 O 16 '07; Saturday Review
102:777-8 D 22; Academy 71:393-4 O 20; Athenaeum
2:513 O 27; Spectator 97:888-9 D 1; Morning Post
(London) O 22 p2; Literary Digest 33:685 N 10; Times
Literary Supplement O 12 p344-5; Nation (NY) 83:374
N 1; New York Times Saturday Review of Books N 10
p734; Outlook (NY) 84:678-9 N 17; Booklist 2:236 D;
Outlook (London) 18:480-1 O 13; Book News Monthly
25:259 D; Christian Register 85, no 49:1362 D 6;
J. B. Kerfoot in Life (NY) 48:634 N 29; Pall Mall Ga-
zette 83, no 12991:4 N 27; Shipbuilding & Shipping
Record (London) 42:364 O 19 '33; noted in Publishers'
Weekly 70:1085 O 20; noted in Argonaut 59, no 1553:
309 D 15; Sun (NY) O 20 p9; J. E. Patterson in Daily
Chronicle (London) O 17 p4; R. A. Scott-James in Daily

The mirror of the sea (cont.)
    News (London) O 10 p4; Daily Mail (London) O 16 p2;
    Standard (London) O 18 p9; World (London) N 13
    p973; F. G. Bettany in Sunday Times (London) D 23 p2;
    Birmingham Post O 5 p4; Manchester Guardian O 16
    p5; Glasgow Evening News O 25, N 1 p4; Evening
    Standard N 1 p5; noted in Scotsman O 4 p2; noted in
    Westminster Gazette O 4 p10)   2193
Missing. The passing of a ship at sea. Daily Mail
    (London) Mr 8 '04 p4
    Later included in: The Mirror of the Sea (section
    XVI of "Overdue and Missing")   2194
Mr. Conrad and the Warspite. Times (London) Mr 1 '24
    p8   2195
Mr. Conrad is not a Jew. New Republic 16:109 Ag 24
    '18
    (A letter by Conrad)   2196
Mr. Joseph Conrad replies. Globe (London) Je 13 '14 p5
    (A letter from Conrad to the editor, referring to
    Conrad's article in the Illustrated London News and
    replying to Mr. Tom Moore)   2197
My best story and why I think so. Grand Magazine 3:87
    Mr '06
    (Refers to "An Outpost of Progress")
    The manuscript is 4 pages quarto.   2198
My English! Book Monthly 14:928 D '19
    (Five paragraphs extracted from Conrad's A Personal
    Record)   2199
My hotel in mid-Atlantic. Modern ocean luxury - a con-
    trast with sailing-ship days. Evening News (London)
    My 15 '23 p4
    (Written by Conrad on board the Tuscania on its way
    across the Atlantic Ocean in April, 1923) Original
    manuscript is 7 folio sheets.
    Later included in: Last Essays (entitled: "Ocean
    Travel")   2200
My "Lord Jim." Bookman (NY) 46:539-40 Ja '18
    (Conrad's rejoinder to objections which had been raised
    against his use of the character Marlow and an account
    of the real-life Lord Jim. Later this statement was
    included as the preface to the Sun Dial Edition of Lord
    Jim, published by Doubleday, Page and Company)
    (Noted in the Evening Post (NY) D 28 '17 p8)   2201
My return to Cracow. Poland in war-time. Daily News &
    Leader (London) Ap 9 '15 p4; same. Boston Evening
    Transcript Ap 17 '15 part 3 p4-5; same published
    separately: London: Printed for private circulation

(for Thomas James Wise, [April] 1919. 5-23p (en-
titled: "My return to Cracow")
(25 copies only) (Dark red covers); <u>same.</u> <u>In</u> The
book of the homeless, edited by Edith <u>Wharton.</u> New
York: Scribner's, 1916. p90-7
Later included in: <u>Notes on Life and Letters</u> (section IV of "Poland Revisited")   2202
Never again... See: Never any more...   2203
Never any more: a first and last flying experience.
Fledgling volume 1, no 1:17-18 Je '17
(The flight took place in September, 1916. Conrad
wrote the article in 1917 for this "Monthly Journal of
the No. 2 Royal Flying Corps Cadet Wing," edited by
Basil Macdonald Hastings at one of the R. F. C. train-
ing stations on the southern coast of England. The
cover page is headed: "Joseph Conrad On His Flying
Experience.")
The manuscript of 5 pages was in a Red Cross Sale,
April 22, 1918, and was then sold to B. F. Stevens for
Ł 35, 14s.
Later included in: <u>Notes on Life and Letters</u> (entitled:
"Flight")   2204
A new book by Joseph Conrad. Garden City: Doubleday,
Page, 1918. 17p, 124 leaves
(The "Dummy" for the novel, <u>The Arrow of Gold;</u> the
author had not yet decided upon a title for the work)
A copy is at the New York Public Library.
Pages 15-17 include a letter from Joseph Conrad to
Mr. Everitt, dated Feb. 18, 1918, with the appended
statement: "Contents of letter are not for publicity
in daily or weekly press, but for use of Messrs.
Doubleday, Page and Co.'s travellers."   2205
Nieznane dwa listy. Conrada. Tęcza no 18, 1929   2206
Nieznany list Conrada do Jozefa Korzeniowskiego, edited
by Barbara Kocówna. Kwartalnik Neofilologiczny
1:37-43 '59   2207
Nieznany list Konrada Korzeniowskiego. Illustrowany
Kurjer Codzienny no 101, 1931   2208
Nieznany listy... Tygodnik Powszechny 13, no 13:4 Mr 29
'59
(Letters from Conrad to Stanisław Zajączkowski edited
by Albertyna Cichocka, and from Conrad to Gustaw
Sobotkiewicz edited by Maria Korniłowiczówna)   2209
Nieznane listy J. Conrada-Korzeniowskiego. Ruch Liter-
acki 2, no 5:138-43 My '27
(Five letters from Conrad to M. B. Tyszkowej, three
to Aniela Zagórska, and one to M. Jasieńskiego) 2210

The Nigger of the "Narcissus." A Tale of the Forecastle,
by Joseph Conrad. London: William Heinemann,
1897. 120p
(Printed July 29, 1897. 7 copies only, printed for
purposes of copyright. Copies are in the British
Museum, Bodleian Library, Cambridge University Li-
brary, National Library in Edinburgh, and the Yale
University Library)
.... A Tale of the Sea. London: William Heinemann,
1898 [actually 1897] vi, 259p
(Issued December 2, 1897. 1500 copies. 6 shillings)
Written between June, 1896 and February 19, 1897.
The manuscript of 194 pages is at The Philip H. &
A. S. W. Rosenbach Foundation.
Published in America with the title: The Children of
the Sea: A Tale of the Forecastle. In the 1914 Double-
day, Page edition, published in New York, Conrad
provided an introductory note entitled "To My Readers
in America." The manuscript of this note, 3 pages
long, is at The Philip H. & A. S. W. Rosenbach
Foundation.
Serially in New Review 17:125-50, 241-64, 361-81,
485-510, 605-28 Ag-D '97; "Author's Note," p628-31;
excerpt in: Country Life in America 66, no 4:74-5
Ag '34
For separate appearances of the Preface, see: "The
art of fiction" and David R. Smith's edition, called
"Conrad's Manifesto."
Dedicated: "To Edward Garnett / This Tale / About
My Friends / of the Sea"
(Dated 1898 unless otherwise noted. Reviewed in
Pall Mall Magazine 14:425, 428-9 Mr; Standard (Lon-
don) D 24 '97 p6; Star (London) D 16 '97 p1; H. -D.
Davray in Mercure de France 131:265-6 Jl 1 '99;
noted by W. J. in Sunday Times (London) D 19 '97 p2;
Morning Leader (London) D 3 '97 p9; Glasgow Evening
News Ja 13 p2; Glasgow Herald D 9 '97 p10; Irish Independent D 18 '97; Literary World (Boston) 29:187 Je
11; Academy 53:fiction supplement 1-2 Ja 1; Academy
53:163 F 5; George Middleton in Bookman (NY) 39:
563-5 Jl '14; Annie Logan & H. Collins in Nation (NY)
67:54 Jl 21; New York Times Saturday Review of
Books & Art My 21 p344; New York Tribune Illustrated Supplement Ap 3 p17; Arthur T. Quiller-Couch
in Pall Mall Magazine 14:428-9 Mr; Speaker 17:83-4
Ja 15; Literature 2:354 Mr 26; Spectator 79:940 D 25
'97; Harold Frederic in Saturday Review (London) 85:

211 F 12; Bookman (London) 13:131 Ja; Christian
World (London) 42:13 Ja 27; T. R. Sullivan in Book
Buyer ns 16:350-1 My; Bookman (NY) 8:91 O; Liverpool Daily Courier D 30 '97 p6; Christian Intelli-
gencer 69:442 Jl 6; Illustrated London News 112:50
Ja 8; James Payn in Illustrated London News 112:172
F 5; Frederic Taber Cooper in Bookman (NY) 18:310-
11 N '03; Outlook (NY) 58:929 Ap 9; Publishers'
Circular 67:690 D 11 '97; Country Life (London) 2:
744-5 Ja 1; Bookman (NY) 7:3 Mr; Publishers' Weekly
53:605 Ap 2; Literary World (London) ns 57:78-9 Ja
28; O. O. in Sketch 20:474 Ja 12; Guardian 53:166 F 2;
William Morton Payne in Dial 25:78 Ag 1; British
Weekly 23, no 594:439 Mr 17; noted in Boston Evening
Transcript Ap 16 p18; News Agent D 11 '97 p544;
Army & Navy Gazette F 26 p195; Birmingham Daily
Gazette D 27 '97 p8; Books & News Gazette D 11 '97;
Bradford Observer Ja 3; Manchester Courier D 22 '97
p3; Court Journal D 11 '97 p2086, 2088; Daily Chronicle (London) D 22 '97 p3; Daily News (London) Ja 7
p6; W. L. Courtney in Daily Telegraph (London) D 8
'97 p4; Pearson's Weekly Ja 15 supplement, p2; noted
in Literary News (NY) ns 19:152 My; Pall Mall Gazette 65, no 10214:11 D 20 '97; A. Eichler in Anglia
Beiblatt 41:281-2 S '30; Glasgow Evening News D 16
'97 p2; Scotsman D 6 '97 p3; Daily Mail (London) D 7
'97 p3; World (London) Ja 12 p31; Manchester Guardian
D 21 '97 p4; noted in Westminster Gazette D 2 '97 p4;
William L. Alden in New York Times F 5 p91 & Mr
26 p197 & Ag 6 p520; Arthur Symons in Saturday Review 85:145-6 Ja 29; Stephen Crane in Bookman (NY)
7:22-4 Mr; World (London) D 15 '97 p42)   2211
The North Sea on the eve of war.   See: Poland revisited.
The North Sea on the eve of war   2212
Nostromo: a tale of the seaboard.   London: Harper &
Brothers, 1904. viii, 480p
(Issued October 14. 2000 copies, plus 1000 more for
the Colonial market. 6 shillings)
..........New York: Harper & Brothers, 1904. [iii-v,]
631p
(Issued November 23. 3000 copies. $1. 50)
Dedicated: "To John Galsworthy"
Composed by August 30, 1904.   The manuscript of 763
pages (not altogether complete) is at The Philip H. &
A. S. W. Rosenbach Foundation.
Serially in T. P. 's Weekly 3:133-8, 173-6, 205-7,
237-40, 269-71, 305-7, 337-40, 369-71, 401-3, 433-5,

Nostromo: a tale of the seaboard... (cont.)
　465-7, 497-9, 529-31, 561-3, 593-5, 625-7, 657-8,
　689-90, 721-2, 753-4, 785-6, 817-18; 4:5-6, 37-8,
　69-70, 101-2, 133-4, 165-6, 197-8, 229-30, 261-3,
　293-5, 325-7, 357-9, 389-91, 420-4, 453-7, Ja 29 -
　O 7 '04
　(Dated 1904 unless otherwise noted. Reviewed by
　Edwin Francis Edgett in Boston Evening Transcript
　D 14; noted by M. F. M. in Literary World (Boston) 35,
　no 10:298-9 O; Graphic 70:644 N 12; Athenaeum 2:619
　N 5; Frederic Taber Cooper in Bookman (NY) 20:217-
　19 N; William Morton Payne in Dial 38:126 F 16 '05;
　Booklist 1:19 Ja-F '05; O. H. Dunbar in Critic (NY)
　46:377-8 Ap '05; Independent 58:557-8 Mr 9 '95; Reader
　Magazine 5:618-19 Ap '05; Mary Moss in Atlantic
　Monthly 97:45-7 Ja '06; William L. Alden in New York
　Times Saturday Review of Books O 29 p735; Spectator
　93:800-1 N 19; Times Literary Supplement O 21 p320;
　Outlook (NY) 78:994 D 17; Frederic Taber Cooper in
　World's Work (NY) 9:5654 D; Alice Duer Miller in
　Book Buyer ns 29:447-8 D; Outlook (London) 14:389 O
　29; Bookman (London) 27:221 F '05; William L. Alden
　in New York Times Saturday Review of Books & Art
　D 31 p944; R. W. L. in Black & White 28, no 718:668
　N 5; Edward Garnett in Speaker ns 11:138-9 N 12;
　Argonaut 56:76 Ja 30 '05; J. B. Kerfoot in Life (NY)
　45:258 Mr 2 '05; New York Tribune Illustrated Supple-
　ment D 11 p10; Illustrated London News 125:774 N 26;
　C. D. O. Barrie in British Weekly 37:129 N 10; Chris-
　tian Register 83, no 50:1387 D 15; noted in Review of
　Reviews (London) 30:539 N 1; noted in Publishers'
　Weekly 66:1162, 1591 N 12, D 10; noted in Boston Eve-
　ning Transcript D 7 p21; noted in Literary News (NY)
　ns 25:189 D; L. Leonhard in Das Literarische Echo 20,
　no 23: 1436-7 S 1 '18; noted in Pall Mall Gazette 79,
　no 12340:9 O 22; K. Arns in Gral 22:465 '28; Sun (NY)
　D 10 p7; Henry-D. Davray in Mercure de France 193:
　490-1 Ja-F '27; Daily Chronicle (London) O 26 p3;
　Daily Telegraph (London) N 9 p4; Morning Post (Lon-
　don) O 26 p4; Daily News (London) D 28 p5; Daily Mail
　(London) N 7 p4; Scotsman N 1 p7; Standard (London)
　D 2 p 3; World (London) D 20 p1078; Birmingham Post
　N 18 p4; Manchester Guardian N 2 p5; noted in West-
　minster Gazette O 17 p10; Book News 23:429 Ja '05;
　Henry D.-Davray in Mercure de France 54:300-1 Mr
　1 '05)　　　　　　　　　　　　　　　　　　　　　　2213
A note on the Polish problem. See: The Polish question　2214

Notes by Joseph Conrad, written in a set of his first editions in the possession of Richard Curle with an intro-
duction and explanatory comments. With a preface by
Jessie Conrad. London: Privately printed (by Strange-
ways, Printers), 1925. [5]-41p. "Preface," p[5]-7;
"Introduction," p[9]-13
(100 copies only)   2215
Notes on life and letters. London: J. M. Dent & Sons, Ltd.,
1921. v-xii, 3-354p. "Author's note," p v-ix
(Published March 25. 9350 copies. 9 shillings)
.... London: [Privately printed by] J. M. Dent & Sons,
Ltd., 1921. xii, 354p. "Author's note," p v-ix
(Printed before February 21. 33 copies only "on
rather larger paper before the ordinary edition")
(Light green cloth binding)
.... Garden City, New York: Doubleday, Page & Co.,
1921. 3-262p. "Author's note," p v-viii
(Published April 22. $1.90)
(Dated 1921 unless otherwise noted. Reviewed by Ed-
mund Lester Pearson in Weekly Review (NY) 4:363 Ap
20; Weekly Review (NY) 5:217 S 3; George Herbert
Clarke in Sewanee Review 30:108 Ja '22; Robert Calvin
Whitford in South Atlantic Quarterly 21:189-90 Ap '22;
Booklist 17:291 My-Je; Dial 71:374 S; G. S. in Bookman
(London) 60:33-4 Ap; E. B. Osborn in Illustrated Lon-
don News 158:332 Mr 12; E. S. in London Mercury 4:
99-100 My; English Review 32:379 Ap; Newark Evening
News Ap 30 p8; Edwin Francis Edgett in Boston Evening Transcript Ap 30 part 4 p5; J. S. K. in America
25:381 Ag 6; noted in Public Opinion (London) 119:306
Ap 1; noted in Life 77:964 Je 30; John Macy in Liter-
ary Review of New York Evening Post Je 4 p3; Ben
Ray Redman in Nation (NY) 112:921 Je 29; Nation &
Athenaeum 28:881-2 Mr 19; Louise Maunsell Field in
New York Times Book Review My 8 p10; Outlook (NY)
128:297 Je 15; Spectator 126:624-5 My 14; Time Liter-
ary Supplement Mr 3 p141; Springfield Republican Ag 2
p6; Joseph I. Cheskis in All's Well 1:207 Ag; Philip
Littell in New Republic 27:25 Je 1; E. G. in Manchester
Guardian Weekly 4:214 Mr 18; Robert Lynd in New
Statesman 16:674-5 Mr 12; same. Living Age 309:
221-4 Ap 23; same. In Books and authors. London:
Putnam, 1923. p196-205; Bookman's Journal & Print
Collector 3:354 Mr 11; Outlook (London) 47:277 Mr 26;
Mary Agnes Hamilton in Time & Tide 2, no 9:214-15
Mr 4; New York Herald Magazine & Books My 1 section
7 p12; Current Opinion 70:819-21 Je; Saturday Review

Notes on life and letters (cont.)
(London) 131:337-8 Ap 23; To-Day (London) 8, no 45:
121 Mr; Grace Phelps in New York Tribune My 8 '21
part VII p8; noted in Bookman (NY) 53:66 Mr; noted in
John O'London's Weekly 4:745, 772 Mr 19, 26; noted
in Publishers' Weekly 99:1324 Ap 30; Catholic World
114:100 O; Arthur Waugh in Daily Telegraph (London)
Mr 4 p15; Morning Post (London) Mr 4 p4; Star (London) Mr 1 p3; Scotsman F 28 p2; J. C. Squire in Observer (London) F 27 p4; Manchester Guardian Mr 15
p5; S. M. Ellis in Sunday Times (London) F 27 p7;
Glasgow Evening News Mr 3 p2; H. L. Mencken in
Smart Set 65, no 3:142 Jl; Philadelphia Record My 1
p12; Daily News (London) Ap 16 p6; E. H. B. in Canadian Forum 1, no 8:248, 250 My; Westminster Ga-
zette Mr 12 p9; Robert Lynd in Manchester Guardian
Mr 3 p4)   2216
Notes on my books. Garden City, New York: Doubleday,
Page, 1921. vi, 3-178p
(Issued March 4. 250 copies, numbered and auto-
graphed by Joseph Conrad. $10)
.... London: William Heinemann, 1921. vi, 3-178p
(Issued May 19. 250 copies for England, numbered and
autographed by Joseph Conrad)
(Published also as prefatory material in collected edi-
tions of Joseph Conrad's works)
(Reviewed by William McFee in World's Work 38:181-6
Jl '21; same. Bookman (NY) 53:102-8 Ap '21; Georges
Jean-Aubry in Fortnightly Review 115:782-90 My 1 '21;
noted in Evening Post (NY) Book Review Je 19 '20 p3)
                                                        2217
Notices to mariners. Manchester Guardian Weekly 7, no
23:453 D 4 '22; same. Manchester Guardian, Supple-
ment D 4 '22 p iii; same. (entitled: "Outside Litera-
ture") Bookman (NY) 56:680-2 F '23
Later included in: Last Essays (entitled: "Outside
Literature")
(Noted in New York Times D 24 '22 p4)   2218
An observer in Malay. Academy 53:441-2 Ap 23 '98; same
published separately: London: Printed for the author
for private circulation only by Richard Clay & Sons,
Ltd. , 1920. 5-9p
(25 copies only) (Dark red covers)
[Actually printed for T. J. Wise]
Later included in: Notes on Life and Letters (entitled:
"An Observer in Malaya." A review of Hugh Clifford's
Studies in Brown Humanity)   2219

Ocean travel. See: My Hotel in Mid-Atlantic 2220

On the North Sea outrage. Times (London) O 26 '04 p 10;
same. (excerpt) Times Weekly Edition Supplement
(London) O 28 '04 p2
(A letter to the editor) 2220a

One day more; a play in one act. English Review 15:16-35
Ag '13; same. Smart Set 42, no 2:125-41 F '14;
same published separately: London: Privately printed
[by Eyre & Spottiswoode] by Clement Shorter, [February 26] 1917. ii, 56p (25 copies only); same. In
The Smart Set anthology, edited by Burton Rascoe and
Groff Conklin. New York: Reynal & Hitchcock [c1934]
p311-40
.... [London: Beaumont Press, January 31, 1919.]
[5]-48p
(24 copies, 4 not for sale, on Japanese vellum, signed
by the author, nos. 1-24; and 250 copies on hand-made
paper, nos. 25-274. Prices: 42 shillings; and 12
shillings 6 pence respectively)
(Reviewed by John V. A. Weaver in Daily News (Chicago) My 21 '19 p12)
.... Garden City, New York: Doubleday, Page, 1920.
3-68p
(377 copies only)
The manuscript is 60p. The typescript of the play,
titled "To-Morrow," is 41 pages long and is at The
Philip H. & A. S. W. Rosenbach Foundation. This version is that which was played by the Stage Society in
London in 1905.
(A dramatization of Conrad's story, "To-morrow."
Performed at the Théâtre de l'Oeuvre, Paris, in 1904;
in the Court Theatre, London, June 26-27, 1905, by
the Stage Society, and produced by Sir Sidney Colvin.)
(Reviewed by Charles Whibley in Outlook (London) 15:
943 Jl 1 '05; New York Tribune Mr 27 '21 part VII
p7; noted by A. W. Schüddekopf in Das Literarische
Echo 15, no 24:1720 S 15 '13)
Later included in: Laughing Anne and One Day More
2221

An outcast of the islands. London: T. Fisher Unwin,
1896. vi, 3-391p (Published March 4. 3000 copies.
6 shillings)
.... (Appleton's Town & Country Library, no. 198)
New York: D. Appleton & Co., 1896. 335p
(Published about August 15. 50¢, paper; $1, cloth)
Completed by September 14, 1895. Originally entitled: "Two Vagabonds. A Tale of the Islands."

An outcast of the islands (cont.)
   The manuscript of 516 quarto pages is at The Philip
   W. & A. S. W. Rosenbach Foundation.

   (Dated 1896 unless otherwise noted.   Reviewed in
   Sketch 13:330 Mr 18; Publishers' Circular 64:375 Ap
   4; Sketch 14:62 My 6; Academy 49:525 Je 27; Athenae-
   um 2:91 Jl 18; Bookman (NY) 4:166 O; Herbert G.
   Wells in Saturday Review (London) 81:509-10 My 16;
   Bookselling 2:205-6 Ap; Christian World 40:510 Je 25;
   Annie Logan in Nation (NY) 64:287 Ap 15 '97; New
   York Times S 23 p10; Richard Henry Stoddard in Mail
   & Express (NY) Ag 28 p5; noted in Mail & Express
   (NY) S 5 p14; same.   Literary News (NY) ns 17:307
   O; Tablet 87:560 Ap 25; Neuphilologisches Centralblatt
   11:174 Je '97; Speaker 13:376 Ap 4; Spectator 76:778
   My 30; James Payn in Illustrated London News 108:
   418 Ap 4; Book Buyer ns 13:537-8 O; Citizen (London)
   My 2 p5; Daily Chronicle (London) Mr 16 p3; Daily
   Telegraph (London) My 15 p4; Daily Record (Glasgow)
   My 2 p2; Guardian 51:906 Je 10; National Observer 15:
   680 Ap 18; World (London) no 1135:31 Ap 1; Black &
   White 11, no 274:566 My 2; noted in Publishers' Week-
   ly 50:231 Ag 15; Bradford Observer My 22; Aberdeen
   Daily Free Press Mr 30 p3; Dundee Advertiser Mr 9
   p2; Literary World (London) 53:384 Ap 24; Educational
   Times Ap 1 p219-20; Yorkshire Post Ap 22 p3; Daily
   News (London) Ap 4 p6; Land & Water no 79:551 O 3;
   Leeds Mercury Mr 25 p3; Morning Post (London) Ap
   18 p4; Pall Mall Gazette 62:9 Ap 17; Liverpool Mercury
   Ap 22 p7; Manchester Guardian My 19 p5; Scotsman
   Mr 16 p3; Western Daily Press My 25 p7; North Brit-
   ish Daily Mail Mr 23 p2; Court Circular Ap 25 p426;
   Dublin Freeman's Journal Mr 27 p2; Star (London) Ap
   23 p1; Review of Reviews (London) 14:186 Ag; Home
   News (London) Ap 10 p14; Newcastle Chronicle Ap 10
   p4-5; Review of Reviews (NY) 14:369-70 S; Sub Rosa in
   Gentlewoman 12:556 My 2; Glasgow Herald Mr 19 p10;
   Westminster Gazette Mr 9 p8; T. P. in Weekly Sun
   (London) My 10 p1; Whitehall Review Mr 28 p11; Acad-
   emy 51:77-8 Ja 16 '97; noted in Bookman (London) 9:
   177 Mr; Glasgow Evening News S 26 '07 p4; News
   Agent Ap 11 p58; World (NY) Ja '97)   2222
An outpost of progress.   Cosmopolis 6:609-20; 7:1-15 Je-Jl
   '97; same.   In The ladysmith treasury, edited by
   James Eveleigh Nash.   London: Sands & Co., 1900.
   p[25]-64

Composed by July 22, 1896. The manuscript is at
Yale University Library, 36 folio sheets.
Later included in: Tales of Unrest   2223
Outside literature. See: Notices to mariners   2224
Overdue. Daily Mail (London) N 16 '04 p4
    Later included in: The Mirror of the Sea (sections
    XVIII-XIX of "Overdue and Missing")   2225
Overdue and missing. See: Overdue. Also see:
    Missing   2226
'Palman Qui Neurit Ferat. See: The heroic age   2226a
The partner. Harper's Magazine 123:850-65 N '11 (il-
    lustrated by Anton Otto Fischer)
    Composed by December, 1910. The manuscript of
    84 pages is at The Philip H. & A. S. W. Rosenbach
    Foundation.
    Later included in: Within the Tides   2227
A personal record. New York: Harper & Brothers, 1912.
    [220]p
    (Published January 19. 2500 copies. $1.25)
    In England until 1916 this volume was issued with the
    title: Some Reminiscences. For serialization, please
    see this title.
    .... London: Thomas Nelson [1916] 285p
    (Published in October, 1916. 1 shilling, 3 pence)
    The first English edition with this title. After 1916
    the title Some Reminiscences is not used.
    Dated 1912 unless otherwise noted.
    (Reviewed in the New York Daily Tribune Ja 20 p8;
    Book News Monthly 30:685 My; Frederic Taber Cooper
    in Bookman (NY) 35:61-71 Mr; Perceval Gibbon in
    Bookman (London) 42:26-7 Ap; Nation (NY) 94:238-9
    Mr 7 by H. W. Boynton; Spectator 109:60-1 Jl 13;
    Booklist 8:297 Mr; Athenaeum 1:124 F3; Catholic
    World 95:254-6 My; Dial 52:172 Mr 1; Independent 72:
    678 Mr 28; North American Review 195:569-70 Ap;
    New York Times Book Review F 18 p77-8; Nation
    (London) 10:857-8 F 24; Richard Curle in Manchester
    Guardian F 2 p4; John O'London's Weekly 2:171 N 22
    '19; T. P.'s Weekly 19:457 Ap 12; English Review 11:
    158 Ap; Outlook (London) 29:253 F 17; Times Literary
    Supplement (London) Ja 25 p34; Current Literature 52:
    471-2 Ap; Desmond B. O'Brien in Truth (London) 71:
    662 Mr 13; Sketch 77:150 F 7; New Age ns 26:194 Ja
    22; Canadian Magazine 39:289-90 Jl; New York Daily
    Tribune Ja 27 p8; Public Opinion (London) 101:205 Mr
    1; Newark Evening News no 8806:26 Mr 9; Edwin
    Francis Edgett in Boston Evening Transcript F 3 part

A personal record (cont.)
> 3, p4; noted in Book Monthly 15:62-3 Ja '20; noted in Publishers' Weekly 81:306 Ja 27; noted in Argonaut 70:74, 138 F 3, Mr 2; noted by A. W. Schüddekopf in Das Literarische Echo 14, no 12:852 Mr 15; Punch 142:108 F 7; noted in Athenaeum no 4672:1210 N 14; Sun (NY) Ja 27 p8; W. H. Chesson in Daily Chronicle (London) Ja 29 p6; Evening Sun (NY) Before F 11; W. L. Courtney in Daily Telegraph (London) Ja 31 p6; Andrew Lang in Morning Post (London) F 22 p2; Daily News (London) Ja 26 p3; Daily Mail (London) F 9 p8; Scotsman F 22 p2; Standard (London) F 6 p5; Observer Ja 28 p5; World (London) F 13 p244; Birmingham Post F 2 p4; Westminster Gazette F 3 p4; Sunday Times (London) Ja 28 p 7; Glasgow Evening News F 8 p10; Evening Standard F 2 p5; Athenaeum N 14 '19 p 1210; H. L. Mencken in Smart Set 38, no 2:149-50 O; J. H. Retinger in Museion rok 2, no 6:105-6 Je; Star (London) Ja 31 p2)   2228

The planter of Malata.   Metropolitan Magazine (NY) 40, no 2:25-7 46-50 52-3; no 3:32-4 48-55 Je-Jl '14 (Illustrated by Frederic Dorr Steele); same.   Empire Magazine '14
> (Completed by Dec. 1913) The manuscript, 182p, is in the Henry W. and Albert A. Berg Collection, New York Public Library.
> Later included in: Within the Tides   2229

The point of honor; a military tale.   Illustrations by Dan Sayre Groesbeck. New York: McClure Co. 1908. 182p
> (4 illustrations in color)
> (Published about October 2. $1.25)
> Identical in content with "The Duel"
> Later included in: A Set of Six (entitled: "The Duel. A Military Tale")
> Dated 1908 unless otherwise noted
> (Reviewed in Independent 65:1066 N 5; Nation (NY) 87:364 O 15; William Morton Payne in Dial 46:263 Ap 16 '09; World To-day (Chicago) 15:1188 N; New York Times Book Review O 24 p624; Book News Monthly (Phila.) 27:216 N; P. N. Beringer in Overland Monthly 2nd series, 52:582 D; New York Daily Tribune O 18 part II, p7; noted in Booklist 4:301 D; noted in Publishers' Weekly 74:987-8 O 10; noted by Sidney G. P. Coryn in Argonaut 63:297 N 7; noted in New York Daily Tribune O 4 part II, p6; noted in Boston Evening Transcript D 2 p27; Sun (NY) O 3 p7; Philadelphia Press O 8 (Sporting & Automobile Section) p10; H. L.

Mencken in Smart Set 26, no 4:153-5 D; Philadelphia
Record O 18 p3)   2230
Poland: the crime of partition. Fortnightly Review 111:
657-69 My 1 '19; same. (illustrated by W. T. Benda)
Collier's Weekly 63, no 24:9-10, 38, 40, 42 Je 14
'19; same. Slavonic nations of yesterday and today...
edited by Millivay S. Stanoyevich. (The handbook se-
ries) New York: H. W. Wilson, 1925. p216-22
Later included in: Notes on Life and Letters (en-
titled: "The Crime of Partition")   2231
Poland revisited. See: The Shock of War Through Germany
to Cracow; To Poland in War-time; Poland revisited.
The North Sea on the eve of war; and My return to
Cracow. Poland in war-time   2232
Poland revisited. The North Sea on the eve of war. Daily
News & Leader (London) Ap 6 '15 p4; same. Boston
Evening Transcript Ap 10 '15 part 3, p4; same. The
book of the homeless, edited by Edith Wharton. New
York: Scribner's, 1916. p83-9; same published sepa-
rately: London: Printed for private circulation only
(for Thomas James Wise) [April] 1919. 5-20p
(25 copies) (entitled "The North Sea on the Eve of
War")
The manuscript is at the Yale University Library
(Dark red covers)
Later included in: Notes on Life and Letters (entitled: "Poland Revisited," part III)   2233
The Polish question; a note on the joint protectorate of the
western powers and Russia. London: Privately printed
by Clement Shorter [by Eyre and Spottiswoode] March
1919. 5-[14]p
(25 copies only, on hand-made paper) (Red covers)
Originally written in 1916. The manuscript of 14
pages is at The Philip H. & A. S. W. Rosenbach Foundation.
This is probably the article Conrad referred to in his
letter of August 20, 1916, to Richard Curle: "I too
have dipped my fingers in diplomacy by writing a
memorandum on the peace settlement which got into
the Foreign Office. The official I interviewed later
said as I was leaving, 'Well I never thought I would
have this sort of conversation with the author of The
Nigger of the 'Narcissus'...' "
Later included in: Notes on Life and Letters: (entitled: "A Note on the Polish Problem")   2234
The portable Conrad. Edited, and with an introduction and
notes, by Morton Dauwen Zabel. New York: Viking

The portable Conrad (cont.)
   Press, 1947. v-vi, 760p. "Editor's introduction,"
   p1-47; "A Conrad chronology," p50-3; "Editor's note,"
   p56-7, 112-14, 290-1, 456-8, 606-8, 702-4; "Bibliographical note," p758-60. Published in New York by
   The Book Society in 1947 as "The Indispensable Conrad. "
   (Reviewed by Albert Guerard in Nation (NY) 166:21-2
   Ja 3 '48; John Farrelly in New Republic 117:31-2 O
   27 '47; Wilson Follett in New York Times Book Re-
   view O 19 '47 p5; New Yorker 23:110 O 4 '47; Queen's
   Quarterly 54:538-40 Winter '47-'48; William Hogan in
   San Francisco Chronicle N 16 '47 p16; Ben Ray Red-
   man in Saturday Review of Literature (NY) 30:30 N 15
   '47; Time 50:107-8 S 29 '47; William McFee in New
   York Sun S 30 '47 p19; Arthur Steslicki in Polish
   American Studies 4, nos 3-4:121-3 Jl-D '47; William
   G. Wing in New York Herald Tribune Ag 22 '63 p19)
                                                       2235
The potato story. See: A smile of fortune   2236
Preface. In The shorter tales of Joseph Conrad. Garden
   City, New York: Doubleday, Page, 1924. p v-xii.
   The typescript of 10 pages, corrected in ink, is at the
   Baker Library, Dartmouth College.
   Later included in: Last Essays (entitled: "Preface
   to The Shorter Tales of Joseph Conrad")   2237
Preface to The Nigger of the 'Narcissus. ' See: The art
   of fiction   2238
Preface to A Personal Record. See: A familiar preface
                                                       2239
Prefaces to The Collected Edition of the Works of Joseph
   Conrad. See: Notes on My Books   2240
Prince Roman. Oxford and Cambridge Review no 16:201-26
   O '11; same. Metropolitan Magazine 35:19-22, 56, 58
   Ja '12 (entitled: "The Aristocrat" and illustrated by
   Frederick Gardner); same published separately: Lon-
   don: Printed for the author by Richard Clay and Sons,
   Ltd. , 1920. 5-42p
   (25 copies only) (Yellow covers)
   [Actually printed for T. J. Wise)
   Composed early in 1911 or late December, 1910)
   Later included in: Tales of Hearsay   2241
Private letters of Joseph Conrad. Reveal the tragedy of the
   great author's life. How he climbed up from obscurity
   to world fame along a pathway of woe. New York
   American October 3 '26, March of Events Section, p1-
   2; Oct. 10 '26, March of Events Section, p3-4; Oct. 17

'26, March of Events Section, p3-4; Oct. 24 '26,
March of Events Section, p4; Oct. 31 '26, March of
Events Section, p3-4
(Conrad's letters to his wife, to his publishers, and
to his intimate friends, published by the Hearst news-
papers for the first time. Letters to Edward Garnett,
J. de Smet, E. L. Sanderson, Mrs. Sanderson, John
Galsworthy, J. B. Pinker, Mrs. Galsworthy, to rela-
tives, and to publishers.)   2242
Protect the ocean liners. Would a fender have saved the
Empress of Ireland? Daily Express (London) Je 10
'14 p4
[A letter dated June 8 to the editor in answer to let-
ters which had responded to Conrad's article in the
Illustrated London News, "The lesson of the collision"]
Later included in: Notes on Life and Letters (as the
second part of "Protection of Ocean Liners")   2243
Protection of ocean liners. See: The lesson of the colli-
sion. Also see: Protect the ocean liners.   2244
Proust as creator. In Marcel Proust, an English tribute by
Joseph Conrad, Arnold Bennett, etc., collected by
Charles Kenneth Scott-Moncrieff. London: Chatto &
Windus, 1923. p126-8
(Published in November. 6 shillings. A large paper
edition, limited to 150 numbered copies only, was is-
sued in December at 12 shillings, 6 pence)
(Reviewed in Argonaut 94:105 F 16 '24)   2245
The red ensign. "The Times" broadsheets. [London war-
time] A single sheet. (an extract from the last pages
of A Personal Record. See: The Richard Curle Con-
rad Collection. The American Art Association, New
York, April 28, 1927, Sale, Item 82)   2246
The rescue. A romance of the shallows, by Joseph Conrad.
Garden City, New York: Doubleday, Page, 1920. viii,
404p
(Published May 21. 25,000 copies. $2)
.... London & Toronto: Printed for private circulation (by J. M. Dent & Sons, Ltd.) 1920. 408p
(Issued on June 4, 1920. 40 copies only, specially
printed and issued before the first regularly published
English edition to certain newspapers and booksellers
for review purposes. The text differs from that of
the first published edition, and there is no sub-title,
the book being called simply The Rescue.)
.... A romance of the shallows, by Joseph Conrad.
London & Toronto: J. M. Dent & Sons, Ltd., 1920.
416p

The rescue (cont.)

(Published June 24. 23, 750 copies. 9 shillings)
(Serially in Land & Water no 2960:18-19, 22-7; 2961:
22-6; 2962:20-3; 2963:20-3; 2964:20-3; 2965:22-5;
2966:20-2; 2967:20-3; 2968:20-3; 2969:28-30; 2970:23-6;
2971:22-6; 2972:19-24; 2973:23-7; 2974:22-6; 2975:25-
30; 2976:31-6; 2977:33-6; 2978:36-40, 42; 2979:33-7;
2980:34-8; 2981:33-6, 38; 2982:36-8, 40, 42; 2983:36-8,
40, 42; 2984:33-6, 38; 2985:33-6, 38; 2986:35-8 Ja 30 -
Jl '19; illustrated by Maurice Greiffenhagen, Dudley
Hardy, H. L. Bacon, and Christopher Clark; same.

Romance (NY) 1, no 1:4-30; no 2:157-84; no 3:68-96;
no 4:73-102; no 5:96-127; no 6:57-82 N '19 - Ap '20;
2, no 1:145-69 My '20
Completed by May 25, 1919

(Dated 1920 unless otherwise noted. Reviewed by
A. S. W. in Manchester Guardian Weekly 3:10 Jl 2;
Katherine Mansfield in Athenaeum 2:15 Jl 2; same. In
Novels and novelists. New York: Knopf, 1930. p222-
6; Spectator 125:52-3 Jl 10; Philip Littell in New Re-
public 23:128 Je 23; H. W. Boynton in Weekly Review
(NY) 2:629 Je 16; Nation (London) 27:503-4 Jl 17; Ed-
win Francis Edgett in Boston Evening Transcript My
26 part 3 p4; Truth (London) 88:87-8 Jl 14; To-Day
(London) 7, no 42:230-1 Ag; D. Willoughby in Outlook
(London) 46:14 Jl 3; W. Douglas Newton in Sketch 110:
428 Jl 21; A. E. C. in Studies (Dublin) 10:146-8 Mr '21;
G. H. C. in Sewanee Review 28:597-9 O-D; Morning
Post (London) Je 25 p4; Observer (London) Je 27 p5;
W. L. Courtney in Daily Telegraph (London) Je 25 p16;
same. Public Opinion (London) 118:13-14 Jl 2; H. C. R.
in Sunday Times (London) Je 27 p7; same. Public
Opinion (London) 118:13 Jl 2; Newark Evening News My
26 p8; R. Ellis Roberts in Daily News (London) Je 25
p6; Westminster Gazette Je 25 p8; James Milne in
Graphic 102:66 Jl 10; W. D. in America 23:233 Je 26;
Catholic World 112:394-5 D; Gilbert Seldes in Dial 69:
191-6 Ag; C. M. R. in Freeman 1:454 Jl 21; Nation (NY)
110:804-5 Je 12; Louise Maunsell Field in New York
Times Book Review My 23 p263-4; Outlook (NY) 125:
280 Je 9; Weekly Review 2:604 Je 5; Times Literary
Supplement (London) Jl 1 p419; Wisconsin Library Bulletin 16:193 N; Annual Register... for the year 1920.
London: Longmans, Green, 1921. p34 (Literature);
Richard Curle in New Statesman 15:368-9 Jl 3; Wilson

Follett in Evening Post Book Review My 29, p1, 13;
Canadian Bookman 2:96 D; noted in British Book News
no 125:76 Ja '51; F. Arens in Der Gral 30:228 '35-'36;
Canadian Forum 1:56 N; Sidney Dark in John O'London's
Weekly 3:353 Jl 3; New York Times Book Review My
30 p290; Current Opinion 69:270 Ag; Rose Macaulay in
Time & Tide 1, no 9:188 Jl 9; noted in Bookman (NY)
52:54 S; noted in Booklist 16:346 Jl; Review (NY) 2:604
Je 5; Heywood Broun in New York Tribune Je 4 p10;
E. B. Osborn in Illustrated London News 157:108 Jl 17;
London Mercury 2:497-8 Ag; B. E. G. in Philadelphia
Sunday Press My 30 p11; R. E. Roberts in Bookman
(London) 58:160-2 Ag; Argonaut 86:373 Je 12; Punch
159:39 Jl 14; Hindustan Review 48:125 O; noted in New
York Tribune My 23 Section VII p9; New Age ns 28:
no 12:143 Ja 20 '21; World (NY) My 30 Editorial Sec-
tion p4E; Daily Chronicle (London) Je 27 p7; Star (Lon-
don) Jl 6 p4; Scotsman Je 28 p2; Birmingham Post Je
29 p4; Manchester Guardian Je 25 p5; Glasgow Eve-
ning News Ag 5 p2; Evening Standard Je 25 p11; H. L.
Mencken in Smart Set 62, no 4:138-9 Ag; Public
Ledger (Philadelphia) Je 12 p15; Les Langues Modernes
34:396 Je-Jl '36; Daily Mail (London) Je 26 p8; Standard (London) Je 25 p11; Fanny Butcher in Chicago
Sunday Tribune My 30 part 1 p7; Elia W. Peattie in
Chicago Daily Tribune Je 12 p13; Henry J. Smith in
Daily News (Chicago) My 26, p12)   2247

The return. The manuscript, 113 quarto pages, is in the
Henry W. and Albert A. Berg Collection, New York
Public Library.
(Dated September 24, 1897) The manuscript was once
in the possession of Dr. A. S. W. Rosenbach (Book-
man's Journal & Print Collector 9, no 28:137-8 Ja '24)
Later included in: Tales of Unrest   2248
Rita Lastaola, A Tale. See: The Arrow of Gold   2248a
The romance of travel. See: Geography and some
explorers   2249
The rover. Garden City, New York: Doubleday, Page,
1923. 371p
(Published November 30. A limited de luxe edition of
377 copies on large paper, signed by the author. $25)
.... Garden City, New York: Doubleday, Page, 1923.
286p
(Published December 1. $2)
.... London: T. Fisher Unwin, 1923. 317p
(Published December 3. 7 shillings, 6 pence)
Completed in June, 1922

The rover (cont.)
(Serially, illustrated by Mead Schaeffer, in Pictorial
Review 24, no 12:5-9, 96-104; 25, no 1:5-9, 99-100,
102, 126, 128-40; 2:5-9, 24, 26, 28, 30, 32, 36, 38,
40; 3:14-17, 20, 22, 24-5, 27-8, 30, 32, 35 S - D
'23)
(Dated 1923 unless otherwise noted. Reviewed by Isabel Patterson in New York Herald Tribune Books D 2
p17-18; L. Cazamian in Revue Anglo-Américaine 3:
164 D '25; W. L. Courtney in Daily Telegraph (London)
D 14 p13; I. B. in Manchester Guardian Weekly 9:459
D 7; Percy A. Hutchison in Literary Digest International Book Review 2:31, 67 D; Robert Herrick in
Literary Review 4, no 17:387 D 22; Edwin Francis
Edgett in Boston Evening Transcript Book Section D 8
p4; same. In Current reviews, edited by Lewis W.
Smith. New York: Holt [C1926] p162-6; H. I. Brock
in New York Times Book Review D 2 p6, 22; Times
Literary Supplement (London) D 6 p849; Leonard Woolf
in Nation-Athenaeum 34:377 D 8; Saturday Review 136:
626, 628 D 8; Raymond Mortimer in New Statesman
22:306 D 15; Booklist 20:175 F '24; Greensboro (North
Carolina) Daily News D 30 p10; Philip Littell in New
Republic 37:124 D 26; R. D. Townsend in Outlook (NY)
136:69-70 Ja 9 '24; George Herbert Clarke in Sewanee
Review 32:499-502 O '24; Gilbert Seldes in Dial 76:
541-3 Je '24; J. B. Priestley in London Mercury 9:
319-20 Ja '24; William McFee in Atlantic Monthly Bookshelf 133:10 F '24; Christopher Morley in Bookman
(NY) 58:658-60 F '24; Nation (NY) 118:538 My 7 '24;
C. Lewis Hind in International Interpreter 2:1273 Ja 5
'24; Life & Letters (London) 1:126-8 Ja '24; Martin
Armstrong in Spectator 131:960-1 D 15; Richard Curle
in Daily Mail (London) D 3 p8; Annual Register... for
the year 1923. London: Longmans, Green, 1924. p47
(Literature); John O'London's Weekly 10:418 D 15;
J. C. Squire in Observer (London) D 9 p4; Evening
Standard D 1 p3; Morning Post (London) D 3 p7; same.
(excerpt) Public Opinion (London) 124:570 D7; Independent 111:144 S 29; New York World before D 8;
Henry L. Mencken in American Mercury 1:252-3 F
'24; Richard Curle in Blue Peter ns 3: no 22:434 Ja
'24; Louis Weitzenkorn in World (NY) D 9 Editorial
Section p6E; same. Current Opinion (NY) 76:37-8 Ja
'24; Walther Preusler in Zeitschrift für Französichen
und Englischen Unterricht 24:465 '25; A. M. in T. P. 's
& Cassell's Weekly ns 1:313 D 15; Richard Ellis Rob-

erts in Bookman (London) 65:218 Ja '24; J. S. in Irish
Statesman 1, no 15:470, 472 D 22; Basil Bunting in
Transatlantic Review 2, no 1:132-4 Ag '24; H. C. Har-
wood in Outlook (London) 52:428 D 8; Kathleen M.
Bowker in Canadian Bookman 6, no 1:11 Ja '24; Truth
(London) 94:1028 D 12; Sketch 124:590, 592 D 19;
Clement King Shorter in Sphere 95:364 D 22; O. T.
Baker in Forum 71:122-3 Ja '24; Canadian Forum 4:
117-18 Ja '24; J. L. B. in Canadian Bookman 6, no 2:
40 F '24; Times (London) D 3 p15; same. (excerpt)
Public Opinion (London) 124:570 D 7; Thomas L. Mas-
son in World's Work (NY) 47:221 D; Georges Jean-
Aubry in Revue de Paris 5:447-9 S-O '24; James Milne
in Graphic 108:820 D 1; America 30:288 Ja 5 '24;
Punch 165:599 D 19; Frederick F. Van de Water in New
York Tribune D 4 p16; Sun (NY) D 5 p28; Emil Breiter
in Wiadomości Literackie 2, no 65:3 Mr 29 '25; noted
in T. P. 's & Cassell's Weekly ns 1, no 5:176 N 24;
R. Ellis Roberts in Daily News (London) D 3 p9; Horace Thorogood in Star (London) D 7 p4; Scotsman D 3
p2; Manchester Guardian D 3 p5; Westminster Gazette
D 4 p4; Sunday Times (London) D 16 p8; Glasgow Eve-
ning News D 6 p2; Public Ledger (Philadelphia) D 1
p16; K. K. in Standard (London) D 1 p3; Filson Young
in New York Times Book Review D 16 p4; noted in
Mainly About Books ns 16, no 4:267 Autumn; Mainly
About Books ns 17:13-14 Winter '23-'24; Bruno Wina-
wer in Wiadomości Literackie 1, no 11:2 Mr 16 '24;
Daily Chronicle (London) D 13 p4; Fanny Butcher in
Chicago Daily Tribune D 1 p10; John Gunther in Daily
News (Chicago) D 5 p15; E. F. H. in Christian Science
Monitor Ja 5 '24 p13; National Newsagent D 8 p8)
                                                              2250

The rulers of east and west. (Part I) Pall Mall Magazine
    35:580-7 My '05 (illustrated by David B. Waters);
    same (with an additional opening sentence) Reader 10:
    301-6 Ag '07
    Later included in: The Mirror of the Sea (sections
    XXV-XXVII, entitled: "Rulers of East and West")
                                                              2251

The rulers of east and west. (Part II) Pall Mall Magazine
    35:718-23 Je '05 (illustrated by David B. Waters);
    same. Putnam's Monthly 5:19-23 O '08
    Later included in: The Mirror of the Sea (Sections
    XXVIII-XXIX, entitled: "Rulers of East and West")
                                                              2252

Sagesse de Conrad.   Edited by Georges Jean-Aubry.   [Paris:]
    Gallimard [1947] 142p
    (Reviewed in Times Literary Supplement (London) N
    29 '47, p614, 645)   2253
Sailing as a fine art.   See: The "Fine Art"   2253a
The sea of adventure.   Some chapters in autobiography.
    See: The 'Tremolino'   2254
Sea tales: Youth, Typhoon, The Shadow-Line.   New York:
    Doubleday, Doran, 1930.   3-42; 102; vii-x, 3-133p
    (Each story is separately paginated)
    (Published Sept. 12. 89¢)
.... New York: Doubleday, Doran, 1937.
    (Noted in Booklist 27:110-11 N '30)   2255
The secret agent, a simple tale.   London: Methuen &
    Co., 1907. vi, 442p
    (Published September 10. 2500 copies. 6 shillings)
.... New York: Harper & Brothers, 1907. 372p
    (Published September 12. 4000 copies. $1.50)
Begun in February and finished by September, 1906.
The manuscript of 637 pages is at The Philip H. &
A. S. W. Rosenbach Foundation.
(Serially in Ridgway's Weekly (NY) 1, no 1:12-15, 63;
no 2:49-52; no 3:21-4, 63-4; no 4:50-4, 63-4; no 5:21-
4, 61; no 6:21-4, 61; no 7:49-52, 61-4; 8:41-8; 9:41-8;
10:41-6; 11:41-7 O 6 - D 15 '06, illustrated by Henry
Raleigh)
(Dated 1907 unless otherwise noted.   Reviewed by Ed-
ward Garnett in Nation (London) 1:1096 S 28; Country
Life 22:403-5 S 21; Sketch 60:96 O 30; Glasgow Eve-
ning News O 3 p5; Evening Standard S 12 p5; Stewart
Edward White in Bookman (NY) 26:531-2 Ja '08; Frederic Taber Cooper in Bookman (NY) 26:669-70 F '08;
Current Literature 44:223-4 F '08; Independent 64:105-
6 Ja 9 '08; Outlook (London) 20:652 N 16; New York
Daily Tribune S 14 '07 p5; S. Squire Spriggs in Academy 74:413-15 F 1 '08; Athenaeum 2:361-2 S 28;
William Morton Payne in Dial 43:252 O 16; Time Literary Supplement S 20 p285; Desmond MacCarthy in
Albany Review 2:229-34 N; Literary World (London) ns
73:435 O 15; Review of Reviews (NY) 37:126-7 Ja '08;
Henry-D. Davray in Mercure de France (series moderne) 71:350 Ja 16 '08; Nation (NY) 85:285 S 26; New
York Times Saturday Review of Books & Art S 21
p562; Outlook (NY) 87:309 O 12; Putnam's Monthly 3:
370 D; Spectator 99:400-1 S 21; Book News Monthly 26:
226-7 N; T. P.'s Weekly 10:425-6 O 4; Edinburgh Review 207:458-9 Ap '08; Public Opinion (London) 92, no

2404:497-8 O 18; Truth (London) 62:817 O 2; Sidney
G. P. Coryn in Argonaut 61:249 O 19; Clement King
Shorter in Sphere 31:142 N 16; World To-Day (Chicago)
13:1283 D; J. B. Kerfoot in Life (NY) 50:464 O 17;
Boston Evening Transcript O 9 p18; noted in Boston
Evening Transcript S 18 p19; noted in Review of Re-
views (London) 36:539 N; noted in Publishers' Weekly
72:585 S 14; noted in Publishers' Weekly 72:650 S 21;
Sun (NY) O 3 p6-7; Philadelphia Press O 13 Editorial
Section p5; Daily Chronicle (London) S 13 p3 by W. H.
Chesson; Morning Post (London) S 19 p2; R. A. Scott-
James in Daily News (London)S 12 p3; Daily Mail
(London) S 14 p2; James Douglas in Star (London) O 5
p1; Scotsman S 16 p2; Observer S 15 p8; Birmingham
Post S 13 p8; Manchester Guardian S 12 p5 by A. N. M. ;
Westminster Gazette O 5 p11; Lloyd Williams in Week-
ly Sun S 21 p2; F. G. Bettany in Sunday Times (London)
O 20 p2; noted in Standard S 12 p8; Public Ledger
(Philadelphia) O 19 p10; World (London) S 17 '489)
                                                           2256
The secret agent. Drama in four acts. Canterbury:
Printed for the author by H. J. Goulden, Limited, 1921.
iii, 69p
(52 copies only)
Completed in March, 1920 as a four act play.   2257
The secret agent; a drama in three acts. London: Privately printed for subscribers only by T. Werner Laurie,
1923. vi, 185p; portrait
(Published in May. 1000 numbered and signed copies
only. 63 shillings)
Performed for the first time on November 3, 1922, at
the Ambassador's Theatre, London; it lasted one week,
10 performances.
(Reviewed in Times Literary Supplement (London) Je 8
'23 p429; Desmond MacCarthy in New Statesman 20:
174-5 N 11 '22; Simon Pure (Frank A. Swinnerton in
Bookman (NY) 56:739-40 F '23; Clement King Shorter
in Sphere 99:188 N 15 '24; Illustrated London News
161:784 N 11 '22; 161:864 N 25 '22; Nation & Athenaeum 32:262 N 11 '22; Herman Ould in English Review
35:526-31 D '22; noted by C. L. Hinds in International
Interpreter 1:1106 D 2 '22; Daily News (London) O 25
'24 p6)   2258
The secret-sharer; an episode from the sea. Harper's Magazine 121:349-59, 530-41 Ag-S '10 (illustrated by W. J.
Aylward)
Composed in November-December 1909. The manu-

The secret-sharer (cont.)
script is 126 pages quarto.
Later included in: 'Twixt Land and Sea (entitled:
"The Secret Sharer; An Episode from the Coast") 2259
A set of six. London: Methuen and Co. [1908] viii, 310p
(Published August 6. 2500 copies. 6 shillings)
.... Garden City, New York: Doubleday, Page, 1915.
x, 356p
(Published January 15. $1.50)
Contents: Gaspar Ruiz; The Informer; The Brute; An
Anarchist; The Duel; Il Conde.
For serialization, please see the individual stories.
Later dedicated: "To Miss M. H. M. Capes"
(Reviewed in Athenaeum 2:237 Ag 29 '08; Outlook (Lon-
don) 22:246 Ag 22 '08; Independent 65:1066 N 5 '08;
Nation (NY) 87:364 O 15 '08; New York Times O 24
'08 p616; Review of Reviews (London) 38:291 S '08;
Spectator 101:237 Ag 15 '08; Edward Thomas in Book-
man (London) 35:39 O '08; same. Public Opinion (Lon-
don) 94:501 O 23 '08; Booklist 11:315 Mr '15; Edwin
Francis Edgett in Boston Evening Transcript Ja 23 '15
Part 3, p6; Catholic World 100:825 Mr '15; Nation
(NY) 100:199 F 18 '15; New York Times Review of
Books Ja 31 '15 p38; Fremont Rider in Publishers'
Weekly 87:480 F 13 '15; Springfield Republican Ap 1
'15 p5; Wisconsin Library Bulletin 11:89 Mr '15; Times
Literary Supplement (London) Ag 13 '08 p261; Arnold
Bennett (Jacob Tonson) in New Age ns 3:412 S 19 '08;
[Edward Garnett] in Nation (London) 3:746, 748 Ag 22
'08; Times (London) before Ag 22 '08; noted in Daily
News (London) Jl 17 '08 p3; Anderson Graham in
Country Life (London) 24, no 606:234-5 Ag 15 '08;
Morning Post (London) Ag 20 '08 p2; T. P.'s Weekly
12:226 Ag 28 '08; Robert Lynd in Black & White 36:260
Ag 29 '08; Sketch 63:232 Ag 26 '08; Literary World
(London) ns 74:377 S 15 '08; New York Tribune Ja 16
'15 p10; W. D. in America 12:418 F 6 '15; Henry -D.
Davray in Mercure de France (Series Moderne) 75:348-
9 S 16 '08; noted in Publishers' Weekly 87:276 Ja 23
'15; Robert Lynd in Daily News (London) Ag 10 '08 p3;
T. De Wyzewa in Revue des Deux Mondes 6th periode
20:935-46 Ap '14; Sun (NY) Ja 16 '15 p9; World (NY)
Ja 23 '15 p7; Daily Chronicle (London) S 14 '08 p3;
W. L. Courtney in Daily Telegraph (London) Ag 12 '08
p4; Daily Mail (London) Ag 15 '08 p8; James Douglas
in Star Ag 15 '08 p1; Scotsman Ag 10 '08 p2; Observer
Ag 16 '08 p4; Manchester Guardian Ag 19 '08 p5; West-

minster Gazette Ag 22 '08 p4; Sunday Times (London)
S 6 '08 p2; Glasgow Evening News S 24 '08 p5; Biblio-
theque Universelle et Revue de Genéve 2:796 D '27 by
Emmanuel Buenzod; W. E. Süsskind in Magdeburgische
Zeitung D 28 '32; Book News Monthly 27:216 N '08;
William Morton Payne in Dial 46:263 Ap 16 '09; Henry-
D. Davray in Mercure de France 75:346 Ja 16 '09;
noted in Standard Ag 7 '08 p8; World S 23 '08 p540;
Birmingham Post Ag 14 '08 p4; Evening Standard Ag
27 '08 p4; H. L. Mencken in Smart Set 45, no 4:432-3
Ap '15; Booklist 4:301 D '08; Elia W. Peattie in Chi-
cago Daily Tribune Ja 23 p10)   2260
The shadow-line. London & Toronto: J. M. Dent and Sons,
Ltd. ; Paris: J. M. Dent et Fils [1917] vi, 227p
(Published March 19. 5000 copies. 5 shillings)
[The first edition was exhausted by March 23, 1917]
.... Garden City, New York: Doubleday, Page, 1917.
197p
(Published April 27. $1. 35)
(Serially in Metropolitan Magazine (NY) 44, no 4:25-7,
39-42; no 5:26-8, 30-32 S-O '16 (illustrated by Anton
Otto Fischer); same. English Review 23:197-220 295-
309 392-410 485-96; 24:6-21 104-11 199-208 S '16 -
Mr '17)
Completed on December 15, 1915
The manuscript is at the Yale University Library
Later dedicated: "To Borys and All Others Who Like
Himself Have Crossed in Early Youth the Shadow-Line
of Their Generation With Love"
(Dated 1917 unless otherwise noted. Reviewed by L.
Leonhard in Das Literarische Echo 19, no 19:1208-9
Jl 1; W. A. L. B. in Bookman (London) 52:98 Je; Eugénie
M. Fryer in Book News Monthly 35:422 Jl; Booklist
13:402 Je; Athenaeum 1:253 My; H. W. Boynton in Book-
man (NY) 45:536-7 Jl; Edwin Francis Edgett in Boston
Evening Transcript My 5 part 3 p6; John Macy in Dial
62:442-3 My 17; Independent 90:437 Je 2; Literary Di-
gest 55:36 O 27; Nation (NY) 104:760-1 Je 28; H. W.
Boynton in Nation (NY) 105:600 N 29; Current Opinion
62:424 Je; Q. K. in New Republic 11:194-5 Je 16; New
York Times Review of Books Ap 22 p157; North American Review 205:949-50 Je; Outlook (NY) 116:116 My 16;
Review of Reviews (NY) 55:663 Je; Saturday Review
(London) 123:281-2 Mr 24; Spectator 118:391-2 Mr 31;
Springfield Republican My 27 p19; Times Literary Supplement (London) Mr 23, p138; Nation (London) 20:828,
830 Mr 24; Annual Register... for the year 1917. Lon-

The shadow-line (cont.)
don: Longmans, Green, 1918. p113-14; Gerald Gould
in New Statesman 8:618 Mr 31; Arthur Waugh in Outlook (London) 39:301-2 Mr 31; same. In Tradition and
change... London: Chapman & Hall, 1919. p276-84;
Sir Sidney Colvin in Observer (London) Mr 23 p4;
James Douglas in Star (London) My 25 p2; Lucian Old-
ershaw in Land & Water 68, no 2863:16 Mr 22; Truth
(London) 81:493 Mr 28; Publishers' Circular 106:351
Ap 14; Clement King Shorter in Sphere 69:42 Ap 14;
Public Opinion (London) 111:279 Mr 23; J.B. Kerfoot
in Life 69:997 Je 7; W.D. in America 17:145 My 19;
Henry -D. Davray in Mercure de France (Series Moderne) 121:340-1 My 16; noted in Publishers' Weekly
91:1464, 1620 My 5, 19; Daily Chronicle (London) Mr
23 p2; Thomas Seccombe in Daily Telegraph (London)
Mr 21 p3; Times (London) before Mr 23; Sun (NY) My
5 p6; World (NY) My 13 (Editorial Section) p4; Morning Post (London)Mr 26 p4; Robert Lynd in Daily News
(London) Mr 19 p2; Daily Mail (London) Mr 27 p4;
Scotsman Mr 22 p2; World (London) Mr 20 p274; Birmingham Post Mr 28 p3; Manchester Guardian Mr 19
p3; Westminster Gazette Mr 24 p3; Sunday Times (London) Ap 1 p4; noted in Evening Standard Mr 16 p4;
Augusta de Wit in Nieuwe Rotterdamsche Courant Ag
11; Public Ledger (Philadelphia) My 12 p14; Philadelphia Record Je 9 p10; Standard (London) Mr 20 p4; A.
Eichler in Beiblatt zur Anglia 41, no 5:149-50 My '30;
Elia W. Peattie in Chicago Daily Tribune My 12 p7)
2261
The shock of war. Through Germany to Cracow. Daily
News & Leader (London) Mr 29 '15 p4; same. Boston
Evening Transcript Ap 3 '15 part 3 p4; same. In The
book of the homeless, edited by Edith Wharton. New
York: Scribner's, 1916. p71-6; same published sepa-
rately: London: Printed for private circulation for
Thomas James Wise, [April] 1919. 5-17p
(25 copies only)
Later included in: Notes on Life and Letters (as part
I of "Poland Revisited") 2262
The shorter tales of Joseph Conrad. Garden City, New
York: Doubleday, Page, 1924. v-xii, 452p Preface,
p v-xii
(Published October 30. $5)
Contents: Youth; The Secret Sharer; The Brute; To-
morrow; Typhoon; Because of the Dollars; The Partner;

Falk
(The Preface which Conrad wrote for this volume was
later included in: Last Essays entitled: "Preface to
The Shorter Tales of Joseph Conrad")
(Reviewed in Saturday Review of Literature 1:384 D
13 '24; Edwin Francis Edgett in Boston Evening Transcript N 5 '24 part 2, p7; Kenneth Fuessle in Literary
Digest International Book Review 3:98-9 Ja '25; Mark
Van Doren in Nation (NY) 120:45 Ja 14 '25; Robert Littell in New Republic 41:288 F 4 '25; Henry L. Mencken
in American Mercury 4:505-7 Ap '25; J. F. in Bookman (NY) 61:83 Mr '25; noted in Booklist 21:233 Mr
'25; noted in Publishers' Weekly 106:1652 N 15 '24;
noted in McNaught's Monthly 3, no 1:26 Ja '25; noted
in New York Herald Tribune Books (Section 11)N 9 '24
p18; noted in Century Magazine 109:432 Ja '25)   2263
The silence of the sea. Daily Mail (London) S 18 '09; same.
    Notes & Queries ns, no 8:292-4 Ag '68   2263a
The sisters. Bookman (NY) 66:481-95 Ja '28; same published separately: With an introduction by Ford Madox
Ford. New York: Crosby, Gaige, 1928. 70p. "Intro-
duction," p1-16 (926 copies on handmade paper; 9 copies
on green paper. Distributed in the United States by
Random House)   2264
Six lettres inédites de Conrad, edited by P. Meykiechel
[Six letters, in French, from Joseph Conrad to Emilie
Briquel] Les Nouvelles Littéraires 42, no 1927:7 Ag
6 '64
(The letters are dated June 10, July 14, August 26,
October 1, November 14, and December 29, all 1895)
                                                   2265
A sketch of Joseph Conrad's life. Written by himself in
1900. Portland, Maine: Privately printed for the
friends of Marguerite and Howard Eric by the South-
worth-Anthoesen press, 1939. 4 leaves; 7p
(75 copies only) excerpt. The Historic Edward Gar-
nett Conrad-Hudson Collection. New York: American
Art Association, 1928. p12   2266
A smile of fortune. London Magazine 25:801-36 F '11 (il-
lustrated by S. Spurrier, facing p695)
The manuscript of 140p is in the Henry W. and Albert
A. Berg Collection, New York Public Library
Composed between May 18 and September 2, 1910
Later included in: 'Twixt Land and Sea
Also called "The potato story." Also subtitled, in the
first American edition, "Harbour Story"   2267
Some aspects of the admirable inquiry. English Review 11:

Some aspects of the admirable inquiry (cont.)
581-95 Jl '12; same published separately, entitled:
Some Aspects of the Admirable Inquiry into the Loss
of the Titanic. London: Printed for private circula-
tion only [for Thomas James Wise] [March] 1919. 5-
42p
(25 copies only) (Blue covers)
The manuscript of 44 quarto pages is entitled: "Some
Aspects of the English Titanic Inquiry" and is dated
April 14, 1912
Later included in: Notes on Life and Letters (entitled:
"Certain Aspects of the Admirable Inquiry into the Loss
of the Titanic")   2268
Some aspects of the English Titanic inquiry. See: Some
aspects of the admirable inquiry   2269
Some reflections on the loss of the Titanic. See: Some re-
flexions, seamanlike and otherwise, on the loss of the
Titanic   2270
Some reflexions, seamanlike and otherwise, on the loss of
the Titanic. English Review 11:304-15 My '12; same
published separately: London: Printed for private
circulation only [for Thomas James Wise] [March]
1919. 5-34p
(25 copies only) (Dark blue covers)
Later included in: Notes on Life and Letters (entitled:
"Some Reflections on the Loss of the Titanic")
(Noted in Daily Telegraph (London) My 2 '12 p4) 2271
Some reminiscences. New York: Paul R. Reynolds, 1908.
20p
(A reprint of the English Review, December, 1908 in-
stallment of Some Reminiscences)
(Probably 6 copies only. See: Yale University Li-
brary Gazette 13:35-7 Jl '38)
.... London: Eveleigh Nash, 1912. 237p
(Published in January, about the 23rd. 1000 copies.
5 shillings)
A privately printed edition, perhaps of 3 or 4 copies
only, was issued in October, 1911. See: Book Prices
Current, Volume XLI, London, 1927, p233-4
Published in the United States under the title: A Per-
sonal Record. In 1916 the volume was issued in Eng-
land as A Personal Record, after which time the name
Some Reminiscences was abandoned.
(Serially in English Review 1:36-51, 234-47, 432-46,
650-64; 2:59-69, 231-45, 500-7 D '08 - Je '09; same.
(excerpt) Sun (NY) F 3 '12 p9)
Composed by Autumn, 1908

For reviews, please see: A Personal Record   2272
Stephen Crane: a note without dates. London Mercury 1:
192-3 D '19; same. Bookman (NY) 50:529-31 F '20;
excerpt. Current Opinion 68:537-8 Ap '20
Later included in: Notes on Life and Letters   2273
Stephen Crane: A Preface to Thomas Beer's Stephen Crane.
See: Joseph Conrad (Prefacer)   2274
The story of an indomitable captain. See: Tradition   2275
Stranded. Daily Mail (London) D 2 '04 p6
Later included in: The Mirror of the Sea (sections
XX-XXI, entitled: "The Grip of the Land")   2276
Suspense: A Napoleonic novel. With an introduction by
Richard Curle. Garden City, New York: Doubleday,
Page, 1925. v-vii, 274p "Introduction," p v-vii
(Published July 3. De luxe limited edition, consisting
of only 377 copies, signed by the editor, was issued
at $15.)

(Published September 15. $2)
.... London & Toronto: J. M. Dent & Sons, Ltd.,
1925. v-ix, 303p "Introduction," pages v-vii
(Published September 16. 21,000 copies. 7 shillings,
6 pence)
An unfinished novel.
(Serially in Saturday Review of Literature (NY) 1:856-9
876-9 893-5 910-13 929-31; 2:8-11, 25-7, 44-7, 64-7,
83-5, 104-5, 122-3, Je 27 - S 12 '25)
Dated 1925 unless otherwise noted:
(Reviewed in Wiadomości Literackie 2, no 73:2 My 24
'25; America 34:94 N 7; J. C. Squire in Observer
(London) S 20 p4; same. In Sunday Mornings. London:
Wm. Heinemann [1930] p270-9; H. C. Harwood in Out-
look (London) 56:204 S 26; Times Literary Supplement
(London) S 17 p597; Saturday Review (London) 140:373
O 3; C. Henry Warren in Bookman (London) 69:27-8 O;
Milton Waldman in London Mercury 13:97-8 N; P. C.
Kennedy in New Statesman 25:665-6 S 26; Spectator
135:613-14 O 10; Outlook (NY) 141:243 O 14; Booklist
22:72 N; Herschel Brickell in Bookman (NY) 62:337-8
N; Karl Schriftgiesser in Boston Evening Transcript S
19 Book Section p5; Cleveland Open Shelf N p106;
Leonard Woolf in Nation-Athenaeum 38:18 O 3; Henry
-D. Davray in Mercure de France (Series Moderne)
année 38, tome 193:490 Ja 15 '27; Louis Gillet in Revue des Deux Mondes 7th periòde, année 95, volume
30:931-42 D 15; William McFee in Literary Digest International Book Review 3:705-6 O; same. Literary

Suspense: a Napoleonic novel (cont.)
Digest 87:46, 48 O 10; Sinclair Lewis in Literary Review S 19 p1-2; Nation (NY) 121:738 D 23; Robert Littell in New Republic 44:263 O 28; Percy A. Hutchison
in New York Times Book Review S 13 p3; Joseph Aynard in Journal des Debats 33, part 2:121-2 Jl 16 '26;
Albert Guerard in New York Herald Tribune Books N
29 p4; A. N. M. in Manchester Guardian Weekly 13:232
S 18; [Richard Curle] in Daily Mail (London) S 16 p13;
excerpt. Notes & Queries 149:200 S 19; Times (London) S 16 p10; Oliver Scribe in T. P. 's & Cassell's
Weekly 4:786 O 10; Hugh Walpole in John O'London's
Weekly 14:35 O 3; Mary Agnes Hamilton in Time &
Tide 6:936 S 25; noted in John O'London's Weekly 13:
758 S 12; noted by Simon Pure [Frank A. Swinnerton]
in Bookman (NY) 61:189, 703 Ap '25, F '26; noted in
New York Times S 16 p27; noted in Publishers' Weekly
108:815 S 12; Alan Kemp in Sketch 132:46 O 7; Isabel
M. Patterson in McNaught's Monthly 4, no 5:155-6 N;
Richard Church in New Age ns 37:270-1 O 8; Adelphi
3, no 6:456 N; Canadian Forum 6:86 D; Clement King
Shorter in Sphere 103:157 O 31; Edward Garnett in
Weekly Westminster O 10 p614; same. Sphere 103:157
O 31; Public Opinion (London) 128:302 S 25; D. S. Mel-
drum in Morning Post (London) S 16 p6; same. Public
Opinion (London) 128:302 S 25; C. E. B. in Illustrated
London News 167:624 O 3; James Milne in Graphic 112:
512 S 26; Horace Thorogood in Star (London) S 16 p4;
D. W. in Evening Standard (London) S 24 p3; Birming-
ham Post S 22 p4; Daily Telegraph (London) S 22 p15;
Country Life (London) 58:465 S 26; J. B. Priestley in
Daily News (London) S 16 p4; Ralph Straus in Sunday
Times (London) S 20 p9; World (NY) S 18; P. R. Sanftle-
ben in Zeitschrift für Französichen und Englischen Unt-
erricht 27:156-7; William McFee in Sun (NY) S 19 p16;
Milton Waldman in World (NY) O 25 Third Section p 6M;
Daily Chronicle (London) S 16 p9 & S 17 p5; Scotsman
S 21 p2; Manchester Guardian S 16 p7; Westminster Ga-
zette S 16 p4; Glasgow Evening News S 17 p2; Evening
Standard S 24 p3; Sydney Williams in Philadelphia In-
quirer O 3 p22; Henry G. Hart in Philadelphia Record
S 26 p7; Public Ledger (Philadelphia) S 19 p15; F. B.
in Chicago Daily Tribune S 26 p19; E. F. H. in Christian
Science Monitor O 10 p7; Ellen Russe in Boekzaal 1925
p363-4)   2277
The tale. Strand Magazine 54:345-53 O '17 (illustrated by
C. M. Padday); same. (entitled: "The Commanding Of-

ficer") Metropolitan Magazine 47:24-6, 45, 50 F '18
(illustrated by Boardman Robinson); published separate-
ly: London: Privately printed for Clement Shorter
[Eyre and Spottiswoode] March, 1919. 5-34p
(25 copies only on handmade paper) (Light red covers);
same. Golden Book 5:37-44 Ja '27
Composed early in 1916
Later included in: Tales of Hearsay   2278
Tales of hearsay. With a preface by R. B. Cunninghame
Graham. London: T. Fisher Unwin [1925] 7-288p
"Preface," p7-28
(Published January 23. 7 shillings, 6 pence)
.... Garden City, New York: Doubleday, Page, 1925.
vii-xv, 120p "Preface," p vii-xv
(Published January 23. $1. 50)
Contents: The Warrior's Soul; Prince Roman; The
Tale; and The Black Mate
(For serialization, please see individual titles)
Dated 1925 unless otherwise noted:
(Reviewed in Saturday Review (London) 139:138-9 F 7;
Times Literary Supplement Ja 29 p70; Edward Garnett
in New Republic 42:189-90 Ap 8; Spectator 134:206 F
7; Milton Waldman in London Mercury 11:543-4 Mr;
Booklist 21:274 Ap; Cleveland Open Shelf Jl p84; Dial
79:350 O; Percy A. Hutchison in Literary Digest Inter-
national Book Review 3:429, 439 My; Grace Willard in
Literary Review of the New York Evening Post Mr 21
p3; Edward Garnett in Nation-Athenaeum 36:718 F 21;
William Rose Benét in Saturday Review of Literature
1:594 Mr 14; Spectator 134:121 Ja 24; Sewanee Review
33:510 O-D; A. S. W. in Manchester Guardian Weekly
12:98 Ja 30; Dilys Powell in T. P. 's & Cassell's Week-
ly 3:817 Mr 21; John O'London's Weekly 12:775 F 21;
S. L. M. in Irish Statesman 3, no 21:668-9 Ja 31;
Richard Curle in Blue Peter 4:522-3 F; America 32:
500 Mr 7; Sketch 129:319-20 F 18 '25; Publishers'
Circular 122:615 My 9; Arthur Waugh in Daily Tele-
graph (London) Ja 23 p13; Canadian Forum 5:279 Je;
Clement King Shorter in Sphere 100:152 F 7; L. P.
Hartley in Bookman (London) 67:314-15 Mr; H. W. B. in
Canadian Bookman 7, no 3:47 Mr; James Milne in
Graphic 111:254 F 14; Punch 168:112 Ja 28; J. C.
Squire in Observer (London) Ja 25 p4; noted in Times
Literary Supplement (London) My 3 '28 p339; noted in
Bookman (NY) 61:512 Je; noted in Publishers' Weekly
107:375 Ja 31; Standard (London) Ja 25 p7; Wiadomości
Literackie 2, no 9:3 Mr 1; noted in Truth (London) 97,

Tales of hearsay (cont.)
    no 2522:264 F 11; noted in McNaught's Monthly 3, no
    3:96 Mr; Scotsman F 2 p2; Daily Mail (London) Ja 22
    p12; noted by James Milne in Graphic 111:136 Ja 24;
    William McFee in Sun (NY) Ja 31 p7; J. M. Bullock in
    Daily Dispatch (Manchester) Ja 23 p12; Morning Post
    (London) Ja 23 p10; Gerald Bullett in Daily News (Lon-
    don) Ja 23 p9; Horace Thorogood in Star (London) Ja
    23 p4; Birmingham Post Ja 27 p3; Manchester Guardi-
    an Ja 23 p7; Westminster Gazette F 21 p4; Glasgow
    Evening News Ja 22 p2; Evening Standard Ja 23 p7;
    Philadelphia Record F 15 p12; noted in America 32:
    500 Mr 7; noted in Spectator 134:121 Ja 24; O. Glöde
    in Zeitschrift für Französichen und Englischen Unter-
    richt 26:239 '27; W. E. Süskind in Literatur 40:754 S
    '38; H. L. Mencken in American Mercury 4:507 Ap;
    Fanny Butcher in Chicago Daily Tribune F 7 p9;
    Christian Science Monitor F 14 p8; Albert Steenhof-
    Smulders in Boekzaal 1925 p147; Harry Hansen in
    Daily News (Chicago) F 11 p16; National Newsagent Ja
    17 p8; Daily Graphic (London) Ja 23 p13)   2279
Tales of land and sea.   Introduction by William McFee. Il-
    lustrated by Richard M. Powers.   Garden City, New
    York: Hanover House [1953] 695p; "introduction,"
    p1-5
    (Contents: Youth; Heart of Darkness; The Nigger of
    the 'Narcissus;' Il Conde; Gaspar Ruiz; The Brute;
    Typhoon; The Secret Sharer; Freya of the Seven Isles;
    The Duel; The End of the Tether; The Shadow-Line)
    (Noted by Harvey Breit in New York Times Book Re-
    view N 8 '53 p45)   2280
Tales of the East and West.   Edited and with an introduc-
    tion by Morton D. Zabel.   Garden City, New York:
    Hanover House [1958] 544p.   "Introduction," p ix-xxx
    (Contents: Almayer's Folly; Karain; The Planter of
    Malata; An Outpost of Progress; Falk; Prince Roman;
    The Warrior's Soul; Amy Foster; The Secret Agent)
                                                      2281
Tales of the sea.   Outlook (London) 1 no 18:560-1 Je 4 '98
    (entitled: "Views and Reviews.   Tales of the Sea.");
    same published separately: London: Printed for
    Joseph Conrad, Orlestone, by Richard Clay & Sons,
    Ltd. , 1919. 5-10p
    (25 copies only) (Light green covers)
    [Actually printed for T. J. Wise]
    Later included in: Notes on Life and Letters   2282
Tales of unrest.   New York: Charles Scribner's Sons,

1898. 3-348p
(Published March 26.   About 1250 copies. $1. 25)
. . . . London: T. Fisher Unwin, 1898. viii, 297p
(Published April 4.   3000 copies. 6 shillings)
Contents: Karain: A Memory; The Idiots; An Outpost
of Progress; The Return; The Lagoon
Later dedicated: "To Adolf P. Krieger for the Sake of
Old Days"
Dated 1898 unless otherwise noted.
(Reviewed in Academy 53: supplement 417-18 Ap 16;
Academy 56:66-7 Ja 14 '99; William L. Alden in New
York Times F 11 '99 p96; Outlook (London) 1:372 Ap
23; Athenaeum 1:564 Ap 30; Annie Logan and H. Col-
lins in Nation (NY) 67:54 Jl 21; T. R. Sullivan in Book
Buyer ns 16:351-2 My; Literary World (London) ns 57:
534 Je 10; Cosmopolis 11:412 Ag; Critic (NY) 32:328
My 14; Outlook (NY) 58:979 Ap 16; Literature 2:507-8
Ap 30; Spectator 81:219 Ag 13; Literary World (Boston)
29:204 Je 25; Henry Wysham Lanier in American
Monthly Review of Reviews (NY) 18:729 D; World (Lon-
don) no 1245:33-4 My 11; Henry -D. Davray in Mercure
de France (Series Moderne) 38:262-3 '01; Public Opini-
on (NY) 24:665-6 My 26 '98; Chautauquan 27:428 Jl;
Citizen 4:87 Je; Publishers' Circular 68:490 Ap 30;
New York Tribune Illustrated Supplement Ap 3 p17;
Literary Gazette Je 20 p2-3; noted in Daily Evening
Telegraph (Philadelphia) Ap 9 p7; same. Book News
16:574 My; Black & White 15, no 377:570 Ap 23; Des-
mond B. O'Brien in Truth (London) 43:1262-3 My 19;
Daily Telegraph (London) Ap 9 p8; noted in Argonaut
42, no 1101:9 Ap 18; American (Philadelphia) 28:255
Ap 16; Independent 50, no 2580:629 My 12; noted in
Literary Review (Boston) 3, no 2:30 Mr '99; noted in
Publishers' Weekly 53:485, 501 Mr 12; William Morton
Payne in Dial 25:78 Ag 1; Boston Evening Transcript
Ap 30 p18; Daily Mail (London) Ap 12 p3; Scotsman
Ap 7 p7; Manchester Guardian Ap 26 p11; Westminster
Gazette My 4 p3; noted in Glasgow Evening News Ap 2
p2; New York Times F 19 p128; Harold Frederic in
Saturday Review 85:211 F 12; Newsagent (London) Ap
2 p98)   2283
The tallness of the spars.   Harper's Weekly 49, part 1:
840-2 Je 10 '05 (illustrated by H. J. Peck)
Later included in: The Mirror of the Sea (sections
x-xii, entitled: "Cobwebs and Gossamer")   2284
Three Conrad novels.   Dial 69:619-30 D '20
Published later as prefaces in the Sun-Dial Collected

Three Conrad novels (cont.)
 Edition of Conrad's novels, An Outcast of the Islands,
 Lord Jim, and Nostromo.   2285
Three plays. Laughing Anne, One Day More, and The
 Secret Agent. London: Methuen, 1934. v, 184p
 (Published in October, 5 shillings)
 (Reviewed by H. I'A. Fausset in London Mercury 31:
 292 Ja '35; Quarterly Review 264:185 Ja '35; F. C.
 Danchin in Revue Anglo-Américaine 12:355-6 Ap '35)
                   2286
To-morrow. Pall Mall Magazine 27:533-47 Ag '02 (illus-
 trated by A. S. Hartrick)
 Composed by January 16, 1902. The manuscript is 81
 pages quarto.
 Later included in: Typhoon and Other Stories and in
 Falk, Amy Foster, To-morrow. Three Stories
 For dramatization, please see: One Day More 2287
To my brethren of the pen. Privately printed, 1927.
 4 leaves (Issued April 15. 150 copies only)
 (A letter from Conrad to Mr. William R. Kane) 2288
To Poland in war-time. A journey into the East. Daily
 News (London) Mr 31 '15 p4; same. Boston Evening
 Transcript Ap 3 '15 part 3 p4; same. In The book of
 the homeless, edited by Edith Wharton. New York:
 Scribner's, 1916. p76-83; same published separately:
 London: Printed for private circulation (for Thomas
 James Wise), [April] 1919. (entitled: "To Poland in
 war-time. A journey into the East") 5-20 p
 (25 copies only) (Dark red covers)
 Later included in: Notes on Life and Letters (as section II of "Poland Revisited")   2289
The Torrens. A personal tribute. See: A clipper ship I
 knew   2290
Tradition. Daily Mail (London) Mr 8 '18 p2; last part reprinted (entitled: "The story of an indomitable captain") Current History 8:292 My '18; whole published
 separately: London: Printed for private circulation
 only (for Thomas James Wise) [Feb] 1919. [5]-19p
 (25 copies only) (Brown covers)
 Later included in: Notes on Life and Letters 2291
Travel. See: Joseph Conrad (Prefacer). Into the East;
 Notes on Burma and Malaya, by Richard Curle. With
 a Preface by Joseph Conrad.   2292
The "Tremolino." Tribune (London) Ja 22 '06 p4; Ja 23 '06
 p4; Ja 24 '06 p4; Ja 25 '06 p4 (entitled: "The sea of
 adventure. Some chapters in autobiography"); same
 published separately: (illustrated by Edward A. Wilson)

New York: Philip C. Duschnes, 1942. 59p (This edition was planned by Bruce Rogers, limited to 1000 copies signed by the artist); same. In The Conrad companion, arranged and introduced by A. J. Hoppé. London: Phoenix House, 1947. p263-84 Later included in: The Mirror of the Sea (sections xl-xlv) (Reviewed by Edward Larocque Tinker in New York Times Book Review O 11 '42; noted in Publishers' Weekly 141:2015 My 30 '42)   2293

Turgenev. See: Joseph Conrad (Prefacer). Turgenev, A Study by Edward Garnett, with a Foreword by Joseph Conrad.   2294

'Twixt land and sea; tales. London: J. M. Dent and Sons, Ltd., 1912. viii, 264p
(Published October 14. 3600 copies. 6 shillings)
.... New York: Hodder & Stoughton, George H. Doran Co. [c1912] 287p
(Published December 3. $1.25)
(Contents: A Smile of Fortune; The Secret Sharer; Freya of the Seven Isles)
For serialization, please see individual titles.
Dedicated: "To Captain C. M. Harris Late Master and Owner of the Araby Maid: Archipelago Trader in Memory of Those Old Days of Adventure"
(Dated 1912 unless otherwise noted. Reviewed in Sketch 80:xiv N 6; New York Tribune F 8 '13 p12; Springfield Republican F 20 '13 p5; Argonaut 72:201 Mr 29 '13; Spectator 109:815-16 N 16; Athenaeum 2:446 O 19; Chicago Evening Post Je 27 '13 p8; Booklist 9:298 Mr '13; Frederic Taber Cooper in Bookman (NY) 37: 85 Mr '13; Richard Curle in English Review 12:668-9 N; Richard Curle in Everyman 1, no 11:338 D 24; E. W. in Bookman (London) 43:187 D; Edwin Francis Edgett in Boston Evening Transcript Ja 29 '13 p22; Independent 74:538-9 Mr 6 '13; H. W. Boynton in Nation (NY) 96:360-1 Ap 10 '13; Warrington Dawson in New York Times Review of Books F 2 '13 p51; Outlook (NY) 103:596 Mr 15 '13; Review of Reviews (NY) 47:762-3 Je '13; Saturday Review 114:492-3 O 19; Nation (London) 12:187-8 O 26; Current Opinion (NY) 54:57-8 Ja '13; Times Literary Supplement (London) O 17 p443; Mary Alden Hopkins in Publishers' Weekly 83:563 F 15 '13; Outlook (London) 30:599 N 2; Canadian Magazine 41:319 Jl '13; Gardner W. Wood in McClure's Magazine 41: 212 My '13; Public Opinion (London) 102:587 N 29; Illustrated London News 141:950 D 28; Newark Evening

'Twixt land and sea; tales (cont.)
News Mr 15 '13 p26; America 8:571 Mr 22 '13; Punch
143:483-4 D 11; Julie Sotteck in Zeitschrift für Franz-
ösichen und Englischen Unterricht 13:180 '14; Daily
Chronicle (London) O 15 p4; Daily Telegraph (London)
O 16 p16; Morning Post O 14 p2; Robert Lynd in Daily
News (London) O 14 p8; Scotsman O 17 p3; Standard
O 25 p7; Observer O 20 p5; Manchester Guardian O 16
p7; Westminster Gazette O 19 p4; Glasgow Evening
News N 14, D 12 p2; Evening Standard O 18 p11; noted
by A. W. Schüddekopf in Das Literatur 15, no 6:416 D
15; noted in T. P. 's Weekly 20:606 N 8; noted by Henry-
D. Davray in Mercure de France (series moderne) 101:
208 Ja 1 '13; noted in Nation (London) 13:562 Jl 12 '13;
noted in Book Monthly 10:123 N; noted in Sun (NY) Ja
25 '13 p10, F 1 '13 p11; Book News Monthly 31:600
Ap '13; Critic (NY) 54, no 1:57-8 Ja 13; World (London) O 15 p585) 2295
[Two letters of Joseph Conrad] Sphere 103:157 O 31 '25
(Letters from Conrad to Mr. Clement Shorter and to
Mr . Gils) 2296
Two tales of the Congo. Foreword by S. A. With copper
engravings by Dolf Rieser. London: Folio Society
[1952]; New York: Philip Duschnes [1953] 166p.
"Foreword," p[7]-8
Contents: An Outpost of Progress; Heart of Dark-
ness) 2297
Two Vagabonds. A tale of the Islands. See: An Outcast
of the Islands 2298
Typhoon. Illustrated by Maurice Greiffenhagen. New York:
G. P. Putnam's Sons, 1902. vi, 205p
(Published September 4. $1)
Completed by January 11, 1901
(For reviews, please see next entry) 2299
Typhoon and other stories. London: William Heinemann,
1903. vi, 304p
(Published about April 22. 3000 copies, of which 1500
were issued as a "Colonial Edition." 6 shillings)
(Typhoon was serialized in Pall Mall Magazine 26:91-
108, 214-29, 408-20 Ja-Mr '02 (illustrated by Maurice
Greiffenhagen); same. Critic (NY) 40:168-75, 269-78,
363-71, 459-69 F - My '02)
(Contents: Typhoon; Amy Foster; Falk; and To-
morrow)
The manuscript of "Typhoon" is 191 quarto and folio
pages. In America, the three stories other than "Typhoon" were published in 1903 with the title: Falk,

Amy Foster, To-morrow.
Dedicated: "To R. B. Cunninghame Graham"
(Dated 1903 unless otherwise noted. Reviewed in New
York Tribune S 27 p11; Harper's Weekly 46:1412-13
O 4 '02; Neue Bücher (Bonn) 5:103-4 '28; Frank Jewett
Mather, Jr. in Forum 34:400-2 Ja; Athenaeum 1:558-9
My 2; Academy 64:463-4 My 9; New York Times Satur-
day Review of Books & Art S 20 '02 p626 & O 24 '03
p756; New York Tribune Illustrated Supplement S 14
'02 p12; Academy 64:414 Ap 25; Public Opinion (NY)
33:377 S 18 '02; Eleanor M. Hoyt in Book Buyer 25:
256 O '02; Desmond B. O'Brien in Truth (London) 53:
1449 My 28; Sketch 42:63 Ap 29; Independent 54, no
2814:2658 N 6 '02; J. B. Kerfoot in Life (NY) 40:302
O 9 '02; Outlook (NY) 72:231 S 27 '02; Illustrated
London News 122:708 My 9; Graphic 67:624, 626 My 9;
Outlook (NY) 72:800 D 6 '02; Munsey's Magazine 28:
602-3 Ja; Spectator 90:823-4 My 23; Argonaut 51:201
S 29 '02; same. Argonaut 51: supplement 319 N 10 '02;
Literary World (London) ns 67:476-7 My 22; Nation
(NY) 75:330-1 O 23 '02; Speaker ns 8:238-9 Je 6; C. N.
in Reader 1:101-2 N '02; Outlook (London) 11:360 My
2; Times Literary Supplement (London) Ap 24 p128-9;
New York Tribune S 14 '02 p12; same. Literary News
(NY) ns 23:293 O '02; T. P.'s Weekly 1:859 My 15;
Saturday Review 95:656 My 23; Clement King Shorter in
Sphere 13:132 My 9; Daily Telegraph (London) My 30
p10; Scotsman My 4 p3; Standard (London) Je 6 p4;
World (London) My 19 p850; Birmingham Post Ap 24
p4; Glasgow Evening News Ap 30 p2; noted in West-
minster Gazette Ap 22 p12; Henry L. Mencken in Smart
Set 42, no 3:154-5 Mr '14; K. Arns in Graal 22:465
'28; Jörn Oven in Schöne Literatur 29:89 F '28; A. T.
Quiller-Couch in Bookman (London) 24:108-9 Je; Jean
Vaudai in Nouvelle Revue Française 45:779-80 N '35;
Morning Post (London) Ap 22 p3; Daily Chronicle
(London) Ap 22 p3; Daily News (London) Ap 22 p8;
Daily Mail (London) Ap 22 p4; Manchester Guardian Ap
23 p10; Today (London) My 6 p54)   2299a
Under western eyes. London: Methuen & Co., Ltd. [1911]
     vi, 377p
     (Published October 5. 3000 copies. 6 shillings)
.... New York: Harper & Brothers, 1911. 377p
     (Published October 19. 4000 copies. $1.25)
     (Original title was "Razumov") Manuscript is 1351 pages
quarto.
Completed by January 22, 1910, perhaps as early as

Under western eyes (cont.)
late December 1909
(Serially in North American Review 192:855-74; 193:
147-60 303-20 464-80 622-40 782-800 935-54; 194:161-
76 317-36 475-96 638-56 D '10 - O '11; same. English Review 7:130-65 321-44 507-29 671-99; 8:74-100
275-303 444-63 640-59; 9:86-102 305-19 449-76 D '10 -
O '11)
The manuscript is at the Yale University Library
All dated 1911 unless otherwise noted:
(Reviewed in Book News Monthly 30:346 Ja '12; H. L.
Mencken in Smart Set 36:153-7 Ja '12; A. W. Schüddekopf in Das Literarische Echo 14, no 4:270 N 15;
Punch 141:326 N 1; Newark Evening News D 30 p22;
Henry -D. Davray in Mercure de France (series moderne) 95:205 Ja 1 '12; Booklist 8:172-3 D; Athenaeum
2:483-4 O 21; Frederic Taber Cooper in Bookman (NY)
34:440-2 D; New York Times Review of Books D 10
p818; North American Review 194:935-6 D; Saturday
Review 112:495 O 14; Nation (NY) 94:60 Ja 18 '12;
Independent 72:311 F 8; Academy 81:699-700 D 2; Current Literature 52:236-7 F '12; Edward Garnett in Nation (London) 10:140-2 O 21; Perceval Gibbon in Bookman (London) 41:94-5 N; Morning Post (London) O 12
p3; Richard Curle in Manchester Guardian O 11 p5;
William Morton Payne in Dial 52:134 F 16 '12; Times
Literary Supplement O 12 p385; T. P.'s Weekly 18:566
N 3; Outlook (London) 28:546 O 21; Truth (London) 70:
supplement ii D 6; Pall Mall Gazette O 11 p5; Sketch
76: page f O 25; Publishers' Circular & Booksellers'
Record 95:870 D 9; Clement King Shorter in Sphere 47:
supplement xvi N 11; Catholic World 94:535-6 Ja '12;
Overland Monthly 2d series, 59:290 Mr '12; J. B. Kerfoot in Life 59:396 F 22 '12; New York Daily Tribune
O 28 p8; Illustrated London News 139:1064 D 16; noted
in Review of Reviews (NY) 45:126 Ja '12; noted in Publishers' Weekly 80:1755-6 O 28; noted in Truth (London) 70:788 O 4; noted in Argonaut 69:282 O 28; noted
in Book Monthly 9:125 N; New Age ns 9:615 O 26;
George Cram Cook in Chicago Evening Post Mr 24, section 6, p1; Sun (NY) N 4 p9; W. H. Chesson in Daily
Chronicle (London) O 13 p6; W. L. Courtney in Daily
Telegraph (London) O 25 p4; R. A. Scott-James in Daily
News (London) O 13 p3; Daily Mail (London) O 13 p8;
James Douglas in Star O 16 p 2; Scotsman O 16 p2;
Standard O 20 p5; Westminster Gazette O 14 p12; Sunday Times (London) O 15 p7; Glasgow Evening News N

9 p8; noted in Observer O 8 p5; noted in World (London) O 3 p521; noted in Spectator 105:1033 D 10 '10)
Evening Standard O 12 p5; Graal 28:183 '33; W. E. Süskind in Literatur 36:172-3 D '33; T. de Wyzewa in Revue des Deux Mondes 6th periôde, 20:935-46 Ap '14; Eugene Schmahl in Widerstand 8:339 N '33)   2300
The unlighted coast. A lost article by Conrad. Zeppelin "strafing." Times (London) Ag 18 '25 p13-14; same published separately (entitled: "Admiralty Paper") New York: Privately printed for Jerome Kern, Christmas, 1925. 16p
(93 copies only) The manuscript is 30 pages.
Composed in January, 1917
Later included in: Last Essays (entitled: "The unlighted coast")   2301
"Up anchor." Pall Mall Magazine 35:183-8 F '05 (illustrated by David B. Waters); same. Reader 5:428-32 Mr '05
Later included in: The Mirror of the Sea (sections iv-vi, entitled: "Emblems of hope")   2302
Victory: an island tale. Garden City, New York: Doubleday, Page & Co., 1915. vi, 462p
(Published c. March 27. 10,000 copies. $1.50)
.... London: Methuen & Co., Ltd., [1915] viii, 415p
(Published September 24. 8,000 copies. 6 shillings)
Completed on May 29, 1914. The manuscript is 1139 pages folio.
Dedicated: "To Perceval and Maisie Gibbon"
(Serially in Munsey's Magazine 54:112-240 F '15; same. Star (London) Ag 24 - N 9 '15 (with illustrations by J. F. H.)
Dated 1915 unless otherwise noted
(Reviewed in Spectator 115:450 O 2; Academy 89:203-4 O 16; Nation (London) 18:25-6 O 2; Current Opinion (NY) 58:351 My; Grace Isabel Colbron in Bookman (NY) 41:322-3 My; Richard Curle in Fortnightly Review ns 98:670-8 O 1; Edith Borie in New Republic 2:supplement part II:6-7 Ap 17; Nation (NY) 100:416-17 Ap 15; Booklist 11:411 My; Athenaeum 2:208 S 25; Atlantic Monthly 116:511 O; Edwin Francis Edgett in Boston Evening Transcript Mr 24 p24; William Morton Payne in Dial 58:383-4 My 13; Literary Digest 50:885 Ap 17; New York Times Review of Books Mr 28 p109-10; Outlook (NY) 110:44 My 5; Robert Lynd in Publishers' Weekly 87:924 Mr 20; Review of Reviews (NY) 51:761 Je; Saturday Review 120:298-9 S 25; Springfield Republican My 13 p5; Western Mail Jl 22; Annual Register for the year 1915. London: Longmans, Green, 1916.

Victory: an island tale (cont.)
p108 (literature); W. A. F. in Bookman (London) 49:21
O; Holbrook Jackson in T. P. 's Weekly   S '15; Times
Literary Supplement (London) S 30 p330; Truth (London) 78:515-16 S 29; Sketch 92:xiv N 10; Publishers'
Circular 103:608 D 11; Clement King Shorter in Sphere
63:50 O 9; Literary World (London) ns 81:152 O 7;
Gerald Gould in New Statesman 5:622 O 2; Land &
Water no 2787:19 O 2; Scotsman S 27 p2; same. Public Opinion (London) 108:334 O 1; New York Tribune Mr
27 p10; J. H. F. in America 13:75-6 My 1; Argonaut
76:304 My 8; Henry -D. Davray in Mercure de France
(series moderne) 112:724 D 1; Sidney Colvin in Observer (London) S 26 p3; Sun (NY) Mr 27 p9; D. S. Meldrum in Daily Chronicle (London) S 25 p4; W. L.
Courtney in Daily Telegraph (London) S 24 & D 29, p4
& p10; Morning Post (London) O 4 p2; Robert Lynd in
Daily News (London) S 24 p6; Standard S 24 p3; World
(London) O 12 p365; Birmingham Post O 8 p4; Manchester Guardian S 24 p5; Walter de la Mare in Westminster Gazette O 2 p3; F. G. Bettany in Sunday Times
(London) S 26 p5; Glasgow Evening News O 7 p8 & O
14 p8; Evening Standard S 24 p5; noted in Publishers'
Weekly 87:976 Mr 27; noted in Book Monthly (London)
12:287 F; H. L. Mencken in Smart Set 45, no 4:430-2
Ap; Stefan Kołaczkowski in Wiadomości Literackie 4,
no 205:3 D 4 '27; K. Arns in Graal 22:465 '28; Elis
W. Peattie in Chicago Daily Tribune My 1 p10; Globe
(NY) before April 3; New Witness S 23 p505)   2303
Views and reviews à propos of Alphonse Daudet.   See:
Alphonse Daudet   2304
The warrior's soul.   Land & Water 68, no 2864:29-30, 32,
35-6, 38-9 Mr 29 '17 (illustrated by Dudley Hardy);
same. Golden Book: 18:525-38 D '33 (subtitled: "A
debt to love is repaid on the battlefield"); same pub-
lished separately: London: Printed for the author for
private circulation by Richard Clay & Sons, Ltd. ,
1920. 5-40p
(25 copies only) (Green covers)
[Actually printed for T. J. Wise]
Composed by early 1916
Later included in: Tales of Hearsay   2305
The weight of her burden.   Harper's Weekly 49:880-2 Je
17 '05
Later included in: The Mirror of the Sea (sections
xiii-xv, entitled: "The Weight of the Burden")   2306
The weight of the burden. See: The weight of

her burden   2307
"Well done!" Daily Chronicle (London) Ag 22 '18 p2; Ag
    23 '18 p2; Ag 24 '18 p2; same. Living Age 299:166-
    73 O 19 '18; same published separately: London:
    Privately printed by Clement Shorter [by Eyre and
    Spottiswoode] September, 1918. 5-[20]p
    (25 copies only, on hand-made paper)
    (excerpt in Current Opinion (NY) 65:326 N '18)
    Later included in: Notes on Life and Letters   2308
Werkbriefe. Aus dem englischen Übertragen von Erich
    Franzen. Die Neue Rundschau 46, part 1:149-59,
    312-24 F-Mr '35   2309
Why I wrote "The Arrow of Gold." New York Herald & New
    York Tribune Magazine - Fiction - Books My 4 '24
    (Sections 10-11) p24   2310
Wisdom and beauty from Conrad, selected and arranged by
    M. Harriet M. Capes. London: Andrew Melrose, 1915.
    5-158p
    (Brown cloth binding, with gold lettering on the spine)
.... New York: Doubleday, Page [1922] 9-143p
    "Prefatory note" by "A. M." p5-6
    (Dark blue binding with orange spine label)
.... London: Andrew Melrose [1922] 9-143p
    "Prefatory note" by "A. M." p5-6
    (Published in November. 6 shillings)
    (Light blue binding, with dark blue spine; gold letter-
    ing on spine)
    (Reviewed by Richard Curle in Times Literary Supple-
    ment (London) Mr 1 '23 p138; noted in Times Literary
    Supplement (London) N 9 '22 p730; noted in Daily
    Chronicle (London) D 20 '15 p4; noted in Scotsman D
    20 '15 p2; NY Times Book Review Ap 29 '23 p20)
                                                   2311
Within the tides: tales. London & Toronto: J. M. Dent &
    Sons, Ltd., 1915. viii, 280p
    (Published February 24. 3,500 copies. 6 shillings)
.... Garden City, New York: Doubleday, Page, 1916.
    300p
    (Published January 15. $1.25)
    Contents: The Planter of Malata; The Partner; The
    Inn of the Two Witches; Because of the Dollars
    Dedicated: "To Mr. and Mrs. Ralph Wedgwood This
    Sheaf of Care-Free Ante-Bellum Pages in Gratitude for
    their Charming Hospitality in the Last Month of Peace."
    Dated 1915 unless otherwise noted:
    (Reviewed by W. L. Courtney in Daily Telegraph (Lon-
    don) Mr 3 p4; Outlook (NY) 112:unpaged F 23 '16;

Within the tides... (cont.)
F. G. B. in Bookman (London) 48:52-3 My; Spectator
114:338-9 Mr 6; Athenaeum 1:211 Mr 6; Edwin Francis
Edgett in Boston Evening Transcript Ja 22 '16 part
three p6; Cleveland Open Shelf Ap '16 p33; Edward E.
Hale in Dial 60:216 Mr 2 '16; Independent 86:73-4 Ap
10 '16; Nation (NY) 102:164 F 10 '16; New York Times
Book Review Ja 16 '16 p17, 22; Robert Lynd in Publishers' Weekly 89:642 F 19 '16; Review of Reviews
(NY) 53:377 Mr '16; Saturday Review 119:311-12 Mr
20; Springfield Republican F 20 '16 p15; Nation (London)
16:758, 760 Mr 13; Annual Register... for the year
1915. London: Longmans, Green, 1916. p104-5 (Literature); Times Literary Supplement (London) Mr 4 p
74; Morning Post (London) Mr 8 p2; World (London)
Ap 6 p581; Holbrook Jackson in T. P. 's Weekly 20:2
Mr 13; Publishers' Circular 102:343-4 Ap 17; Clement
King Shorter in Sphere 61:50 Ap 10; Gerald Gould in
New Statesman 4:538 Mr 6; Public Opinion (London)
107:224 F 26; R. A. Scott-James in Land & Water 65,
no 2762:40 Ap 17; New York Tribune F 5 '16 p9;
Times (London) before Mr 12 '15; J. K. Prothero in
Everyman 5, no 127:381-2 Mr 19; J. B. Kerfoot in Life
67:354 F 24 '16; Argonaut 78:136 F 26 '16; noted in
Booklist 12:288 Mr '16; W. D. in America 14:403 F 5
'16; Sun (NY) Ja 23 '16 p6; noted in World (NY) Ja 22
'16 p10; Robert Lynd in Daily News (London) Mr 9 p7;
Scotsman Mr 8 p3; Standard (London) Mr 5 p3; Observer F 28 p4; Birmingham Post Mr 5 p4; Manchester
Guardian Mr 4 p5; F. G. Bettany in Sunday Times (London) Mr 7 p5; Glasgow Evening News Ap 15 p8; Evening Standard Mr 1 p7; noted in Daily Chronicle (London) F 24 p4; H. L. Mencken in Smart Set 48, no 4:
156 Ap '16; Public Ledger (Philadelphia) Ja 29 '16 p13;
Kurt Wittig in Englische Studien 73 heft 1:120-2 N '38;
W. E. Süskind in Literatur 40:247 Ja '38; Magdeburgh-
ische Zeitung Ja 21 '38; Westminster Gazette F 22 p3)
                                                    2312
The works of Joseph Conrad. (Canterbury Edition) New
York: Doubleday, Page & Co. for William H. Wise
and Co. , 1928. 26 volumes ($31)   2313
The works of Joseph Conrad. (Collected Edition) London:
J. M. Dent and Sons, Ltd. , 1925. 21 volumes: 7 shil-
lings, 6 pence each
.... Garden City, New York: Doubleday, 1925. 2314
The works of Joseph Conrad. (Concord Edition) Garden
City, New York: Doubleday, Page, 1924. 24 volumes

for $60 (or $2.50 each volume)
(Reviewed by Lee Wilson Dodd in Saturday Review of
Literature 1:27 Ag 9 '24; William McFee in Sun (NY)
Ap 5 '24)   2315
The works of Joseph Conrad. (Deep Sea Edition) Garden
City, New York: Doubleday, Page, 1914. 24 volumes;
($60) in sea blue leather; in cloth, $1.90 per volume
2316
The works of Joseph Conrad. (De Luxe Edition) London:
Dent, 1923.
(Reviewed by Clement King Shorter in Sphere 95:xxiv
D 8 '23)   2317
The works of Joseph Conrad. (Kent Edition) Garden City,
New York: Doubleday, Page & Co., 1926. 26 volumes
(In cloth, $35; in leather, $60)   2318
The works of Joseph Conrad. (Inclusive Edition) Garden
City, New York: Doubleday, Page & Co., 1925. 24
volumes ($35)   2319
The works of Joseph Conrad. (Malay Edition) Garden City,
New York: Doubleday, Page & Co., 1927. 10 volumes
$13.85
.... 1928-9. 25 volumes   2320
The works of Joseph Conrad. (Medallion Edition) London:
Gresham Publishing Co., 1925-7. 22 volumes (Blue
cloth, gilt edges)
(December. 10 shillings, 6 pence per volume)
(Reviewed in John O'London's Weekly 14:697 F 6 '26;
R. H. P. Curle in Daily Mail (London) D 28 '25 p6)
2321
The works of Joseph Conrad. (Memorial Edition) Garden
City, New York: Doubleday, Page & Co., 1925-6.
23 volumes. ($175.50)
("This edition is limited to 499 numbered sets and ten
sets for presentation." Ninety-nine were signed by
Mr. Conrad before his death; the other 400 are large
paper copies.)   2322
The works of Joseph Conrad. (Pocket edition) London:
Methuen, 1924. 6 volumes (3 shillings, 6 pence each)
(Reviewed in Daily Chronicle (London) D 11 '24 p7)
2322a
The works of Joseph Conrad. (Sun-Dial Edition) Garden
City, New York: Doubleday, Page & Co., 1920-1928.
24 volumes
(A limited edition published for Gabriel Wells; edition
limited to 735 copies. The first volume of each set
is signed by the author. $175.25)
(Reviewed by William McFee in New York Times Book

The works of Joseph Conrad. (Sun-Dial Ed.) (cont.)
Review & Magazine 27:1, 22 Ja 1 '22; same. In
Swallowing the anchor. Garden City, New York:
Doubleday, Page, 1925, p85-94; E. F. Edgett in Boston
Evening Transcript D 17 '21; New York Times Book
Review & Magazine Ja 2 '21 p25)   2323
The works of Joseph Conrad. London: William Heinemann,
1921-7. 20 volumes
(Limited to 780 sets)   2324
The works of Joseph Conrad. (Personal edition) Garden
City, New York: Doubleday, Page, 1924. 10 volumes
($19)   2325
The works of Joseph Conrad. (Uniform Edition) London:
J. M. Dent & Sons, Ltd., 1923-1938. 22 volumes
(10 shillings, 6 pence each volume)
(Reviewed in New York Tribune Mr 14 '24 p8; noted in
Times Literary Supplement Mr 13 '24 p162)   2326
Youth: a narrative and two other stories. Edinburgh &
London: William Blackwood & Sons, 1902 [viii] 375p
(Published November 13. 3,150 copies. 6 shillings)
.... New York: McClure, Phillips & Co., 1903. 381p
(Published about February 8. $1.50)
Contents: Youth: A Narrative; Heart of Darkness; and,
The End of the Tether.
Youth was composed in May-June, 1898, and completed
by June 3. The manuscript is 43 pages quarto. Heart
of Darkness was composed in January-February, 1899.
The End of the Tether was composed in October, 1902.
Youth appeared serially in Blackwood's Magazine 164:
309-30 S '98; same. Outlook (NY) 60:326-41 O 1 '98;
same. Golden Book 8:652-66 N '28
For serialization of Heart of Darkness and The End of
the Tether please see individual entries.
Preface was reprinted in Bookman (NY) 47:31-2 Mr '18
Dated 1903 unless otherwise noted:
(Reviewed in Public Opinion (NY) 34:346-7 Mr 12; by
Henry -D. Davray in Mercure de France (series mod-
erne) 45:830-1; George Jean Nathan in Bookman (NY)
43:281 My '16; A. J. Dawson in Athenaeum 2:824 D 20
'02; same. Literary News (NY) ns 24:106-7 Ap; Wil-
liam L. Alden in New York Times Saturday Review of
Books & Art D 13 '02 p898; New York Times Saturday
Review of Books & Art Ap 4 p224; William L. Alden in
New York Times Saturday Review of Books & Art Je 17
'99 p388; New York Times Saturday Review of Books
& Art My 6 '99 p304; William L. Alden in New York
Times Saturday Review of Books & Art Mr 3 '00 p138;

Review of Reviews (NY) 27:629-30 My; Independent 55, part 2:801-2 Ap 2; Academy 63:552 N 22 '02; Edward Garnett in Academy 63:606-7 D 6 '02; Argonaut 52:231 Ap 13; Hugh Clifford in Spectator 89:827-8 N 29 '02; same. Living Age 236:120-3 Ja 10; Literary World (Boston) 34:121 My; Literary World (London) ns 67:55 Ja 16; J. Stewart Doubleday in Reader 1:561-2 My; same. Saturday Review of Literature 4:519 Ja 14 '28; Frederic Taber Cooper in Bookman (NY) 18:311 N; Times Literary Supplement D 12 '02 p372; Illustrated London News 121:990 D 27 '02; M. H. Vorse in Critic (NY) 43:280 S; Annie Logan in Nation (NY) 76:478 Je 11; T. P.'s Weekly 1:73 N 28 '02; New York Tribune Illustrated Supplement S 18 '98 p12; New York Tribune Illustrated Supplement Mr 8 p11; T. P.'s Weekly 1:73 N 28; noted in Evening Telegram (NY) F 14 p10; Manchester Guardian D 10 '02 p3; Desmond B. O'Brien in Truth (London) 53:231-2 Ja 22; O. O. in Sketch 40: 262 D 3 '02; Clement King Shorter in Sphere 12:20 Ja 3; Literary Digest 26, no 15:547 Ap 11; Monthly Review 11:21-2 Ap; Graphic 67:28 Ja 3; noted by Wallace Rice in World To-Day (Chicago) 5:862 Jl; noted in Outlook (London) 10:480 N 22 '02; noted in Literary News (NY) 25, no 6:82 Je '04; noted in Literary World (Boston) 35:231 Ag '04; noted in Boston Evening Transcript Mr 11 p17; Philadelphia Press F 28 p10; New York Telegram before Mr 7 '03; John Masefield in Speaker ns 7:442 Ja 31; Sun (NY) Mr 14 p8; Daily Chronicle (London) D 20 '02 p3; Daily Telegraph (London) N 26 '02 p6; Daily News (London) D 9 '02 p8; Daily Mail (London) N 25 '02 p2; Glasgow Evening News N 27 '02 p2; notcd in Morning Post N 19 '02 p4; noted in Standard N 19 '02 p4; noted in Observer N 23 '02 p8; noted in Westminster Gazette N 19 '02 p12; Book News 21: 557-8 Ap; Literary News (NY) 24:106-7 Ap; H. L. Mencken in Smart Set 40, no 3:159-60 Jl '13; K. Arns in Graal 21:327 '27; Mally Behler-Hagen in Schöne Literatur 29:29-30 Ja '28; P. Sire in Cahiers du Sud 19:476-9 Jl '32; Leonardo Kociemski in Italia che Scrive 12:18 Ja '29)   2327

Youth and Gaspar Ruiz. New York: Dutton; London: J. M. Dent & Sons, Ltd., [1920] 192p; bibliography, p175-6   2328

Conrad, Joseph and Hueffer, Ford Madox (Ford) The inheritors; an extravagant story. New York: McClure, Phillips & Co., 1901. vi, 324p (Pub. about June 8. $1.50)
. . . . London: William Heinemann, 1901. iv, 324p

The inheritors (cont.)
(Published June 26. 1500 copies. 6 shillings)
Completed by March, 1900
(Dated 1901 unless otherwise noted. Reviewed in
Academy 61:93 Ag 3; Athenaeum 2:151-2 Ag 3; Spec-
tator 87:61 Jl 13; New York Times Saturday Review of
Books & Art Jl 13 p499; Book Buyer 23:137 S; Critic
(NY) 39:277 S; Current Literature 31:118 Jl; Saturday
Review 92:403-4 S 28; Times (London) S 3 p9; Daily
Telegraph (London) Jl 19 p9; L. R. F. O. in Speaker ns
4:424-5 Jl 13; Literature 9:164 Ag 17; Argonaut 49:
297 N 4; Independent 53, no 2761:2597 O 3; J. B. Ker-
foot in Life (NY) 38:226-7 S 19; Literary World (Lon-
don) ns 64:174 S 13; Outlook (NY) 68:459 Je 22; Illustrated London News 119:172 Ag 3; Graphic 64:192 Ag
10; noted in Academy 60:554 Je 29; noted in Publishers'
Weekly 59:1365 Je 8; Daily Chronicle (London) Jl 11
p3; Daily News (London) Jl 24 p8; Daily Mail (London)
Jl 4 p3; Scotsman Jl 4 p2; Standard (London) Ag 16
p2; Manchester Guardian Jl 10 p4; noted in Westminster
Gazette Je 25 p12; Glasgow Evening News Ag 15 p2;
Outlook (London) 7:700 Je 29)   2329
The nature of a crime.   London: Duckworth & Co. [1924]
5-119p
Preface by Joseph Conrad, dated "June 1924, " p5-7;
Preface by Ford Madox Hueffer, p8-13; text, p15-103.
Appendix, "A Note on Romance," p105-19
(Published September 26. 9025 copies. 5 shillings)
.... Garden City, New York: Doubleday, Page, 1924.
xv, 108p
Prefaces, p v-xv: by Conrad, p v-viii; by Ford
Madox Hueffer, p ix-xv; text p1-94.   Appendix, "A
Note on Romance," p95-108.
(Published September 26. $2. 50)
(Serially, under the pseudonym of Baron Ignatz von
Aschendorf, in English Review 2:70-8, 279-301 Ap-My
'09; same.   Transatlantic Review 1, no 1:15-36; no
2:15-35 Ja-F '24.   Preface in Transatlantic Review 2,
no 1:106-7 Ag '24)
(Dated 1924 unless otherwise noted.   Reviewed by For-
rest Reid in Nation-Athenaeum 36:58, 60 O 11; Times
Literary Supplement O 2 p610; John Hyde Preston in
Literary Digest International Book Review 3:137-8 Ja
'25; Herbert J. Seligmann in Literary Review of the
New York Evening Post S 27 p4; John Franklin in New
Statesman 24:82 O 25; F. Vinci Roman in New York
World (Editorial Section) O 12 p8e; Spectator 133:472,

474 O 4; Gerald Gould in Saturday Review 138:578 D 6;
Booklist 21:197 F '25; Robert Littell in New Republic
41:287-8 F 4 '25; Manchester Guardian Weekly 11:292
O 3; Thomas Moult in Bookman (London) 67:117-18 N;
Richard Curle in Daily Mail (London) S 30 p13; Christian Science Monitor N 22 p8; H. C. Harwood in Outlook (London) 54:250 O 4; Mary Agnes Hamilton in
Time & Tide 5, no 42:1004 O 17; Gerald Gould in
Bookman's Journal & Print Collector 11:81 N; English
Review 39:729-30 N; Argonaut 94:105 F 16; noted in
Booklist 24:172 Ja '28; noted by J. F. in Bookman (NY)
61:83 Mr '25; noted by James Milne in Graphic 110:
598 O 11; noted in Publishers' Weekly 106:1225 O 4;
noted in Publishers' Circular & Booksellers' Record
121:238 Ag 16; noted in British Weekly 76:357, 451 Jl
17, Ag 21; noted in New York Herald Tribune Books
(Section 11) S 28 p14; noted in Observer (London) Ag 17
p4; Allan Nevins in Sun (NY) S 27 p6; W. L. Courtney
in Daily Telegraph (London) S 26 p15; Daily News (London) O 10 p9; Scotsman O 13 p2; Birmingham Post O
7 p6; noted in Morning Post (London) S 26 p11; noted
in Sunday Times (London) Ag 17 p5; Manchester Guardian S 26 p8; Star (London) S 29; Fanny Butcher in Chicago Daily Tribune O 25 p9)   2330
The nature of a crime, by Joseph Conrad and Ford Madox
Ford. Laughing Anne and One Day More (Two Plays)
With an Introduction to Laughing Anne by John Galsworthy. The Secret Agent. Drama in Four Acts by
Joseph Conrad. Garden City, New York: Doubleday,
Page, 1926. (Separate pagination for each work:) v-ix,
49p; Prefaces: p v-vi (by Conrad); vi-ix (by Ford);
Appendix, "A Note on Romance," p51-9; v-xi, 34, 35p;
"Introduction," by John Galsworthy, p v-xi, 129p 2331
Romance; a novel. London: Smith, Elder & Co., 1903.
    viii, 463p
(Published about October 23. 3000 copies. 6 shillings)
.... illustrated by Charles Raymond Macauley. New
    York: McClure, Phillips & Co., 1904. [iii]-[vii] [3]-
    428p
(Published in March. $1. 50)
Completed by July, 1902
Dedicated: "To Elsie and Jessie"
Dated 1903 unless otherwise noted:
(Reviewed in Outlook (NY) 77:424-5 Je 18 '04; William
Morton Payne in Dial 37:37 Jl 16 '04; Athenaeum 2:610
N 7; Academy 65:469 O 31; Bookman (NY) 19:544 Ag
'04; New York Times Saturday Review of Books & Art

Romance; a novel (cont.)

My 14 '04 p325; Spectator 92:21-2 Ja 2 '04; Annie Logan in Nation (NY) 79:120-1 Ag 11 '04; Outlook (London) 12:402 N 7; John Masefield in Speaker ns 9:149-50 N 14; T. P. 's Weekly 3:10 Ja 1 '04; Current Literature 37:282 S '04; Desmond B. O'Brien in Truth (London) 54:1672 D 17; Saturday Review 97:209 F 13 '04; Argonaut 54:424 Je 27 '04; Literary Digest 29, no 4: 119-20 Jl 23 '04; Illustrated London News 123:688 N 7; Public Opinion (London) 84:592 N 6; Edwin Francis Edgett in Boston Evening Transcript D 14 '04 p22; Times Literary Supplement (London) O 30 p312; Times Literary Supplement (London) O 23 p307; Pilot 8:516 N 21; Munsey's Magazine 32:600 Ja '05; Daily News (London) O 30 p5; Daily Mail (London) O 28 p2; World (London) O 27 p697; Birmingham Post N 13 p4; Manchester Guardian O 28 p4; Glasgow Evening News D 31 p2; noted in Daily Chronicle (London) O 21 p7; noted in Daily Telegraph (London) O 21 p12; noted in Morning Post (London) O 21 p2; noted in Scotsman O 22 p2; noted in Standard O 21 p2; noted in Westminster Gazette O 22 p12; noted in Outlook (London) 12:340 O 24; noted in Publishers' Weekly 65:1211 My 7 '04; noted in Literary World (Boston) 35:117, 120 Ap '04; noted in Literary World (Boston) 35:178 Je '04; noted in Book Buyer ns 28:216-17 Ap '04; Outlook (London) 12:340 O 24; Sketch 44:95 N 4; Book News 22:1137-8 Jl '04 by H. T. P. ; Henry -D. Davray in Mercure de France 49: 267-8 Ja 1 '04)   2332

Prefatory Material Written by Joseph Conrad

CONRAD, JOSEPH (Prefacer)

Beer, Thomas
Stephen Crane; a study in American letters, by Thomas
Beer. With an introduction by Joseph Conrad. New
York: Knopf, 1923. "Introduction," pages 1-33; same.
In Hanna Crane and the Mauve Decade. New York:
Knopf, 1941. p211-34
Later included in: Last Essays (entitled: "Stephen
Crane")
(Reviewed in Observer (London) S 7 '24 p5; J. D. Cole-
man in Outlook (London) 54:300-1 O 18 '24; Edmund
Candler in Time & Tide 5:1084-5 N 7 '24; A. N. M. in
Manchester Guardian Weekly 11, no 13:270 S 26 '24;
Henry L. Mencken in Dial 76:73-4 Ja '24; Thomas
Craven in Freeman 8:475-7 Ja 23 '24; Charles R.
Walker in Atlantic Monthly Bookshelf 133:11 Mr '24;
Punch 168:168 F 11 '25; noted by Thomas L. Masson
in World's Work (NY) 47:450 F '24; noted by Burton
Rascoe in New York Tribune Magazine & Books Je 3
'23 p22; Wiadomości Literackie 1, nos 40-42:3 O 19
'24)   2333
Conrad, (Mrs.) Jessie (George)
Simple cooking precepts for a little house, by Jessie
Conrad, with preface by Joseph Conrad; preface published separately, together with title-page; London:
Printed for private circulation only, 1921. 6p (100
copies only, numbered by Joseph Conrad); same. Delineator 101, no 1:11 Ag '22; same. In A handbook of
cookery for a small house, by Jessie Conrad, with a
preface by Joseph Conrad. London: William Heinemann, Ltd. [Feb. 1923] "Preface," p v-viii; Garden
City, New York: Doubleday, Page & Co., 1923.
"Preface," p v-viii; same. In Home cookery, by Jessie Conrad; preface by Joseph Conrad. London: Jarrolds [1936] "Preface," p v-viii (with a one-paragraph
postscript by Mrs. Conrad on p viii)
Later included in: Last Essays (entitled: "Cookery")
(Reviewed in Bookman (NY) 53:66 Mr '21; Edmund
Lester Pearson in Independent 110, no 3839: 231 Mr
31 '23; Times Literary Supplement Ap 19 '23 p272;

Conrad, (Mrs.) Jessie (George) (cont.)
    Laura B. Everett in Bookman (NY) 57:688 Jl '23;
    Hindustan Review 46:512-13 Jl '23; Wilfred G. Parting-
    ton in Bookman's Journal & Print Collector 8, no 20:
    48 My '23; Times Literary Supplement Ap 4 '36 p301;
    New York Herald Book Section Mr 4 '23 p9)
    [A letter by L. M. Hallowes, November 29, 1921, indi-
    cates that this preface was published separately for
    those who wished to have everything written by Joseph
    Conrad but who might not want a cookery book. The
    preface was written "10 or 12 years ago," the letter
    indicates, as the result of a half-jocular suggestion
    that Mrs. Conrad should write a book on cooking.]
                                                           2334
Crane, Stephen
    The red badge of courage, by Stephen Crane, with a
    preface by Joseph Conrad. London: Heinemann [1925]
    p v-xii; same. In Novelists on novelists, an anthology
    edited by Louis Kronenberger. (Anchor Books A 293)
    Garden City, New York: Doubleday & Co. , Inc. , 1962.
    p259-63
    Later included in : Last Essays (entitled: "His War
    Book")
    The first draft of Conrad's preface from the manu-
    script - a typescript heavily corrected by Conrad - is
    in 7 pages at the Baker Library, Dartmouth College.
    (Noted in Public Opinion (London) 127:399 Ap 24 '25)
                                                           2335
Curle, Richard
    Into the East; notes on Burma and Malaya, by Richard
    Curle. With a preface by Joseph Conrad. Blue Peter
    S-O '22; same. published separately: Edinburgh:
    Privately printed by R. and R. Clarke for Richard
    Curle, December, 1922. xxi p (entitled: "Travel. A
    Preface to Into the East: Notes on Burma and Malaya,
    by Richard Curle")
    (20 copies only); same. London: Macmillan, 1923
    (dated August 1, 1922). p ix-xxv (125 copies on large
    paper, printed March, 1923)
    Later included in: Last Essays (entitled: "Travel")
    (Reviewed in Blue Peter 3:77 My '23 by C. L. R. ; noted
    in Hindustan Review 47:234 Ja '24)   2336
Dawson, (Major) Alec John
    Britain's life-boats; the story of a century of heroic ser-
    vice, by Major Alec John Dawson with a foreword by
    Joseph Conrad. London: Hodder and Stoughton, 1923.
    p v   2337

Dawson, [Francis] Warrington
  Adventure in the night, by [Francis] Warrington Dawson,
  with a foreword by Joseph Conrad. London: T.
  Fisher Unwin [1924] p[7]
  (Includes a note by Conrad, signed, in facsimile)
  The book is dedicated "To My Friend Joseph Conrad"
                                                    2338
Garnett, Edward
  Turgenev, a study by Edward Garnett, with a foreword
  by Joseph Conrad. London: W. Collins Sons & Co.
  [c1917] "Foreword," p v-x
  Later included in: Notes on Life and Letters (en-
  titled: "Turgenev")
  The typescript of the Foreword, 6 pages quarto, is at
  the Baker Library, Dartmouth College
  (Reviewed in English Review 25:573 D '17)   2339
Kinkead, A. S.
  Landscapes of Corsica and Ireland, by A. S. Kinkead, with
  foreword by Joseph Conrad. [London: United Arts
  Gallery, 1921, Nov. -Dec.] 2 p
  The manuscript and typescript are at the Yale University Library   2340
Maupassant, Guy de
  Yvette and other stories by Guy de Maupassant. Translated by A. G. [Mrs. John Galsworthy] With a preface
  by Joseph Conrad. London: Duckworth & Co., 1904.
  p v-xvi; same. Yvette, a novelette, and ten other
  stories, translated from the French of Guy de Maupassant by Mrs. John Galsworthy, with an introduction by
  Joseph Conrad. New York: Knopf, 1919. 5-13p;
  same. Mademoiselle Fifi, by Guy de Maupassant,
  translated by Mrs. John Galsworthy, with a preface by
  Joseph Conrad. Boston: Four Seas Co. [1919] p7-14;
  same published separately: London: Printed [for
  Thomas J. Wise] for private circulation, [April] 1919.
  5-18p (entitled: "Guy de Maupassant")
  (25 copies only) (Green covers)
  Conrad wrote: "The preface was written at the request
  of Mrs. Galsworthy"
  Later included in: Notes on Life and Letters (entitled:
  "Guy de Maupassant")
  (Reviewed in T. P.'s Weekly 4:234 Ag 19 '04; Outlook
  (London) 14:362 O 22 '04; Literary World (London) ns
  70:301-2 O 21 '04; noted in T. P.'s Weekly 26:82 Jl
  24 '15)   2341
Sutherland, John Georgeson
  At sea with Joseph Conrad, by J. G. Sutherland. With a

Sutherland, John Georgeson (cont.)
    foreword by Joseph Conrad.   London: Richards, 1922.
    7-150p "Foreword," p9-10
    (1250 copies only)   2342
Walpole, Hugh
    A Hugh Walpole anthology.   Selected by the author with a
    note by Joseph Conrad.   (The Kings Treasuries of
    Literature) London: J. M. Dent [1922] "Introductory
    note by Joseph Conrad," p7-8   2343

Conrad, Joseph (Translator)

Winawer, Bruno
    The Book of Job; a satirical comedy by Bruno Winawer.
    Translated [from the Polish] by Joseph Conrad.   Lon-
    don: J. M. Dent & Sons [1931] v-xvi, 143p. "Introduc-
    tion," p v-viii; "Letter from Joseph Conrad to Mr.
    Winawer," p ix-xii; same. Pologne Littéraire (War-
    saw) 5, no 53:2-5 F 15 '31 (The "Introduction" and the
    "Letter" are both on p2); same. Bookmark (London) 7,
    no 27:10-11 Autumn '31   2344

Translations of Joseph Conrad's Works
(Some With Reviews)

ALMAYER'S FOLLY

La Folie-Almayer. Translated by Geneviève Séligmann-Lui.
Paris: La Nouvelle Revue Française, 1919. 7-[185]p
(Reviewed by André Bellesort in Revue Politique et
Littéraire: Revue Bleue 58:599-603 O 2 '20) 2345
.... Translated by Georges Jean-Aubry. Lausanne:
La Guilde du Livre, 1954. 212p 2346
La Folie Malaise. Translated by René Lécuyer. Paris:
Éditions Cosmopolites [c1930] [7]-249p 2347
Shigyono Shel Almayer. Translated by Ester Kaspi. Tel-
Aviv: Am Oved, 1961. 208p 2347a
Almayers Wahn. Translated by Elsie McCalman. Berlin:
S. Fischer [c1935] [9]-234p
(Reviewed by W. E. Süskind in Die Literatur 37:511-12
Je 13 '35) 2348
Perdição. Contos de inquietude. Translated by Virginia
Lefèvre. S. Paulo: Boa Leitura, 1964. 381p 2348a
Fantazja Almayera. Warsaw: Gronowski, 1923. xxxii, 211p
(Reviewed by M. Dąbrowska in Bluszcz 1923 p35; K.
Górski in Gaz. Administr. 1924 p24; Z. Grabowski in
Akademik 1923 p12; Kurjer Poznański 1929 p52; Cz.
Jankowski in Słowo 1924 p99; Z. Kisielewski in Robot-
nik 1:29 '23; Przegląd Warszawska 1923 p18; A. Sied-
lecki in Rzeczpolita 1:26 '23; A. Skwarczyński in Droga
1923 p1; A. Zagórska in Kurjer Polski 3:1 '23) 2349
.... Translated by Aniela Zagórska. Warsaw: Tow.
Wydawnicze "Ignis" [c1924] xxxvi, 211p 2350
Hanul lui Almayer. Translated by Jul. Giurgea. Bucharest:
Tip Cartea de Aur. 1939. 318p 2350a
Szaleństwo Almayera. Translated by Aniela Zagórska.
Warsaw: Dom Książki Polskiej Spółka, 1928. [5]-[221]
p; preface by Stefan Żeromski, p vii-xxxi
(Noted in Literatura Piękna, 1928. Warsaw: 1930.
p217) 2351
La locura de Almáyer. Translated by Rafael Marquina.
Barcelona: Montaner y Simón [c1925] 267p 2352
Félvér. Translated by J. De Gruyter. [Budapest] Genius
Kiadás [nd] 2353

ALMAYER'S FOLLY (cont.)
Félvér. Translated by Dezsö Kiss. Budapest: Tolnai,
1937. 285p   2353a
Almeyeruv blud. Translated by Josef Elgart. Praha:
Topič, 1919. 5-247p   2354
Almayers dårskab. Translated by Peter Holm. Copen-
hagen: John Martin, 1916. 256p   2355
Almayerovo Sialenstvo. Translated by Elena Chmelová.
Bratislava: Slov. Spisovatel, 1960. 259p   2355a
Almayers dårskag. Translated by Greta Akeshielm. Stock-
holm: Lindquist, 1955. 219p   2356
Almayers' dwaasheid. Translated by M. E. Bunge. Amster-
dam: C. Hafkamp, 1947. 222p   2357
Almayers gaest. Translated by Peter Holm and C. T. Mel-
dal. Copenhagen: John Martin, 1919. 2 volumes:
[7]-191p; [7]-175p   2358
Orang Blanda... Translated by Felix van Zijll. Baarn:
Ned. Uitgeverij, 1941. 260p   2359
Almayers Traum... Translated by Benvenuto Hauptmann.
Zürich: W. Classen, 1949. 228p   2360
La follia di Almayer. Translated by Lorenzo Gigli. Milan:
Modernissima, 1926. 316p   2361
La follia d'Almayer. Translated by Mario Benzi. Milan:
A. Barion, 1930. [7]-380p (Includes: "The End of
the Tether," "Youth.")   2362
.... Translated by Giovanni Fletzer. [Milan:] Bompi-
ani, 1956. 7-492p   2362a
Almayers dårskap. Translated by Sigurd Hoel. Oslo:
Nasjonalforlaget, 1931. 216p   2363
.... Translated by Vera and Stig Dahlstedt. Stock-
holm: Tidens Bokklubb [1961] 5-191p   2363a
La locura de Almáyer. Translated by Rafael Marquina.
Buenos Aires: Editorial Losada [1938] 201p   2364
Almayerova Ludnica. Zagre: Naklada Zaklade Tiskare
Narodnih Novina. 196p. "Joseph Conrad," p[5]-11
                                                     2364a
Almayer's Folly, translated into Japanese by Mamoru
Osawa. 1940   2365
.... Translated into Celtic by Seosamh MacGrianna.
1926. [5]-285p   2366
A szigetek szamuzottje. Translated by Pogány Kázmér.
Budapest: Pantheon Irodalmi Intezet rt. Kiadasa
[nd]   2366a

"Alphonse Daudet"

Alphonse Daudet. Translated by Aniela Zagórska.

1925.   2367

"Amy Foster"

Amy Foster. Translated by Elise Eckert. Stuttgart: J.
    Engelhorn [1936] 77p
    (Reviewed by Elisabeth Hackbarth in Die Bücherei 3,
    heft 12:639 D '36)   2368
Amy Foster. Translated by Aniela Zagórska. Wiadomości
    Literackie 8, no 48:2-6 N 29 '31; same published:
    Warsaw: Biblioteka Polska, 1938. 43p (Noted by W.
    Chwalewik in Rocznik Literacki 1937, p128-9)   2369
Amy Foster. Translated by Georges Jean-Aubry. Revue
    de Paris 39, no 1:138-71 Ja 1 '32   2370
Janko Góral. Translated by Maria Bunikiewiczowa. Lwów:
    P. Skargi, 1914. 52p   2371
Mensen en de Zee. Translated by C. Buddingh. Antwerp:
    Het Spectrum, 1953. 260p (Contains: Amy Foster,
    The End of the Tether, The Secret Sharer, The Brute,
    and The Black Mate)   2372

"An Anarchist"

Anarchista. Translated by Tadeusz Pużjanowski. Przegląd
    Warszawski rok 3, tome 1, no 18:360-79 Mr '23
                                                         2373

THE ARROW OF GOLD

Der goldene Pfeil. Translated by Elsie McCalman. Berlin:
    S. Fischer [1932] [9]-440p
    (Reviewed by W. E. Süskind in Die Literatur 35:413-14
    Ap '33)   2374
.... Translated by Walter Schürenberg. [Frankfurt
    am Main:] S. Fischer, 1966. 7-389p   2374a
Az Arany Nyíl. Translated by Szinnai Tivadar. [Budapest]
    Genius Kiadás [192-?] 317p   2375
La flecha de oro... Translated by Marco-Aurelio Galindo.
    Barcelona: Montaner y Simon [1935] 2 volumes: 270p,
    339p   2376
La flèche d'or; roman. Translated by Georges Jean-Aubry.
    Revue des Deux Mondes 7th periòde, 34:548-77, 778-
    806; 35:91-127, 338-74 Ag 1 - S 15 '26; same pub-
    lished: Paris: Gallimard, 1928. [ix]-xii, 362p.
    Preface by Georges Jean-Aubry, p[ix]-xii   2377
Gulpilen. Translated by E. Brusewitz. Stockholm: Albert
    Bonniers [1920] 419p   2378

THE ARROW OF GOLD (cont.)
Den Gyldne Pil. Translated by Knud Poulsen. Kφbenhavn:
  Martin, 1925. 368p   2379
A flexa de ouro. Translated by Marques Rebello. Pôrto
  Alegre: Globo, 1941. 307p   2380
Zɫota strzaɫa... Translated by Aniela Zagórska and Jadwiga
  Korniɫowiczowa. Kraków: Instytut Wydawniczy
  "Poziom," 1948. 366p
  Preface by Jan Parandowski, p7 -[21]; portrait
  (Noted in Literatura Piękna, 1958. Warsaw: 1960.
  p218; reviewed by Wiktor Weintraub in Wiadomoŝci 4,
  nos 176-7:3 Ag 21 '49)   2381
La freccia d'oro. Translated by Franca Violani Cancogni.
  [Torino:] Einaudi, 1951. 7-496p. Note, p7-10   2382
.... Il salvataggio. Translated by Luigi Biagi.
  Milan: Bompiani, 1958. 7-679p. (Also contains:
  The Rescue)   2382a
Lo strale d'oro. Translated by A. Paronelli. Milan:
  Delta, 1929. 369p   2383
Zlatý ŝíp. Translated by E. A. Saudek. Praha: Melan-
  trich, 1934. 335p   2384

"Autocracy and War"

Autokratyzm a wojna. Translated by Teresa Sapieżyna.
  Wiadomoŝci Literackie 10, no 509:1-2 S 3 '33   2385

"Because of the Dollars"

Z powodu dolarów. Translated by Teresa Tatarkiewicz.
  1928   2386

"The Black Mate"

L'Officier noir. Translated by Georges Jean-Aubry. Revue
  de Paris 40, no 3:348-79 My 15 '33   2387
Czarny sternik. Translated by R. Zbrzeżny. Dookoɫa
  Świata nos 5-7:17-18; no 8:17-18 '55   2388

"Books"

Książki. Translated by Bogusɫaw Grodzicki. 1957   2389

"The Brute"

Das Biest, und andere Erzählungen. Translated by Ernst
  Wolfgang Günter [Ernst W. Freissler] Munich: Albert

Langen [1912] 136p
(Contains: The Brute, The Secret Agent, and The
Anarchist)
(Reviewed by Karl Hans Strobl in Das Literarische
Echo 15, no 20:1411 Jl 15 '15)   2390
Bestia.   Translated by Wilam Horzyca.   1924   2391

"The Censor of Plays"

Cenzor teatralny.   Wiadomości Literackie 5, no 48:1 N
25 '28   2392

CHANCE

Spiel des Zufalls.   Translated by Ernst W. Freissler.
Berlin: S. Fischer [c1926] [9]-495p   2393
Destino.   Translated by Margherita Guidacci.   [Milan:]
Bompiani, 1961. 5-503p.   Translator's note, p497-
503   2393a
Chance... Translated by J. de Gruyter with an introduction
by Frits Hopman.   Amsterdam: Uitgevers-Maat-
schappij, "Elsevier," 1923. xii, 437p.   "Joseph Con-
rad," by Frits Hopman, p[vii]-xii   2394
Fortune... Translated by Philippe Neel.   Introduction by
Georges Jean-Aubry.   Paris: Gallimard [1949] xii,
399p.   "Introduction" by G. Jean-Aubry, p[vii]-xii
(Reviewed by René Lalou in Les Nouvelles Littéraires
12 no 570:3 S 16 '33; Georges Clarete in L'Ami du
Peuple S 19 '33; Robert Kemp in Les Nouvelles Lit-
téraires 12 no 574:1 O 14 '33; Jacques Chabannes in
Notre Temps S 29 '33; Marcel Brion in Cahiers du
Sud année 20, no 157:30-1 D '33)   2395
Los.   Translated by Barbara Beaupré.   Czas nos 177-298,
1921; no 1, 1922   2396
Los.   Translated by Wanda Tatarkiewiczowa.   Warsaw:
Państwowy Instytut Wydawniczy, 1955. 457p; "Pos-
łowie" by Róża Jabłkowska, p451-[457]
(Noted by Grzegorz Sinko in Rocznik Literacki 1955,
p427; reviewed by Zdzisław Najder in Twórczość 11,
no 12:158-61 D '55)   2397
La figlia des Galeotto.   Translated by Mario Benzi. Milan:
Barion, 1934. 363p   2398
Náhoda.   Translated by René Wellek and E. A. Saudek.
Praha: Melantrich, 1932. 471p   2399
Ett tärningskast... Translated by E. Brusewitz.   Stockholm:
Bonnier, 1919. 2 volumes: 285p; 219p   2400
Tilfaeldet.   Translated by Knud Poulsen.   Copenhagen:

CHANCE (cont.)
John Martin, 1931. 470p   2401

"Il Conte"

Il Conte.   Translated by Leon Piwiński.   Przegląd Warsz-
awski rok 2, tome 4, no 14:217-32 N '22   2402
Il Conte.   Translated by Philippe Neel.   Les Nouvelles
Littéraires 3, no 115:5 D 27 '24   2403

"Confidence"

Confiance.   Translated by Georges Jean-Aubry in Cahiers du
Sud année 27, no 221:[73]-79 F '40   2404

"Cookery"

Wstęp Conrada do książki kucharskiej jego żony.   Wiadomości
Literackie 1, no 33:3 '24   2405

"The Crime of Partition"

Zbrodnia rozbiorów.   Translated by Czesław Miłosz.
1948   2406

"The Duel"

Das Duell... Translated by Ernest Wolfgang Günter [Ernst
W. Freissler]. Munich: A. Langen [1914] 270p
(Contains: The Duel, Gaspar Ruiz, Il Conte)
(Reviewed by Walter Hoerich in Zeitschrift für Bücher-
freunde. Beiblatt 6, heft 4:187-8 Jl '14)   2407
The Duel.   Kursk: Kn. izd. 1956. 110p   2407a
Le duel.   Translated by Philippe Neel.   Revue de Paris 30,
no 5:810-31; no 6:87-123, 363-90 O 15 - N 15 '23
                                                           2408
Pojedynek.   Translated by Wilam Horzyca.   Warsaw: Biblio-
teka Polska, 1937. 81p
(Noted by Witold Chwalewik in Rocznik Literacki 1937
p127)   2409
The Duel.   Translated by M. M. Ljubimowa.   Moscow:
"Krasnyj Proletarij," 1926. 157p   2410

"The End of the Tether"

El cabo de la cuerda.   Translated by Marco-Aurelio Galindo.
Barcelona: Montaner y Simón [1932] [7]-304p   2411

Fino all'estremo. Translated by Giovanni Marcellini.
Milan: Corticelli, 1928. 265p
(Reviewed by Leonard Kociemski in L'Italia Che
Scrive 12, no 1:18 Ja '29)   2412
U kresu si*y*. Translated by Aniela Zagórska. Warsaw:
Biblioteka Polska, 1939. 186p. Preface by Georges
Jean-Aubry, p5-10
(Noted by Andrzej Tretiak in Rocznik Literacki 1938
p125-7)   2412a
Le Vidar. Translated by Gabrielle d'Harcourt. Paris:
Nouvelle Revue Française   2413
Au bout du rouleau. Translated by Gabrielle d'Harcourt.
Introduction by Georges Jean-Aubry. Paris: Nouvelle
Revue Française, 1931. 251p. "Introduction," p[7]-14
(Reviewed by P. Sire in Cahiers du Sud 9:476-9 Jl
'32; La Nouvelle Revue Française 37:827 N '31) 2413a
Jusqu'au bout de la chaine. Translated by Mlle. Gabrielle
d'Harcourt. Revue Hebdomadaire année 33, tome 2:
453-472 F 23 '24; année 33, tome 3:54-72, 175-92,
333-54, 445-56, 576-94 Mr 1 - 29 '24; année 33, tome
4:80-102 Ap 5 '24   2414
Dohráno. Translated by Ivan Schulz. Praha: Ústřed.
Tiskové Družstvo, 1920. 160p   2415
Verhalen van de zee. Amsterdam: Arbeiderspers, 1941.
453p
(Contains also: The Nigger of the 'Narcissus,' and
Typhoon)   2415a

"Falk"

Falk, suivi de Amy Foster, pour Demain. Translated and
with an introduction by Georges Jean-Aubry. Revue de
Paris 37, no 6:505-25, 870-93; 38, no 1:102-21, 340-
62 D 1 '30 - Ja 15 '31; same published: Paris: Gallimard [1934] [17]-252p. "Introduction," p[9]-15
(Reviewed by Jean Vaudal in Nouvelle Revue Française
45:779-80 N 1 '35)   2416
Falk, Amy Foster, Tomorrow. Translated by Aniela Zagórska. Rzym: Polska Y. M. C. A. , 1946. 3-229p
                                          2417
Falk: wspomnienie, Amy Foster, Jutro. With an introduction by Stefan Zeromski. Translated by Aniela Zagórska. Warsaw: Dom Książki Polskiej, 1932. vii-
xii, 199p (Contains: Falk; Reminiscences; Amy Foster;
To-morrow)
(Reviewed by Emil Breiter in Wiadomości Literackie
9, no 14:3 Ap 3 '32; K. Czachowski in Kultura

"Falk" (cont.)
    no 2, 1932)   2418
Sonderbare Käuze.   Drei Novellen.   Translated by Elise
Eckert.   Stuttgart: Engelhorns, 1928. 283p.   (Contains:
Falk, Amy Foster, To-morrow)
(Reviewed by Karl Arns in Der Gral 23, heft 8:718
My '29)   2419

            "Freya of the Seven Isles"

Freya von den sieben Inseln.   Translated by Elsie McCal-
man.   Berlin: S. Fischer [1929] [9]-152p
(Reviewed by Karl Arns in Der Gral 24, heft 3:283
D '29; Ernst Weiss in Berliner Börs.   Courant no 193,
1929)   2420
Frejja semi ostrovov.   Translated by A. V. Krivcova.
Moscow: Goslitizdat, 1935. 515p   2420a
Freja z siedmiu wysp.   Translated by Aniela Zagórska.
[Rome] War Relief Services, National Catholic Welfare
Conference, 1946. 5-124p   2421
Frejja z semi ostroviv.   Translated by E. Ja. Homenko.
Kiev: Molod'. 1960. 93p   2421a
I fjärran farvatten.   Translated by Harald Jernström.
Stockholm: Bonnier, 1914. 296p   2422
Freja sa sedam ostrva.   Njegov kraj.   Translated by Albin
Vilhar & Luka Semenović.   Sarajeva: Svjetlost,
1960. 279p   2422a
Freya fra de syv Øer.   Translated by C. Th. Meldal.
Copenhagen: John Martin, 1919. [5]-221p.   (Contains:
Freya of the Seven Isles, A Smile of Fortune, The
Secret-Sharer)   2423
Freya fra de syv Øer.   Translated by Thorvald Thorgersen.
Oslo: Gyldendal Norsk forlag, 1933. 264p. (Contains:
Freya of the Seven Isles, A Smile of Fortune, The
Secret-Sharer)   2424
Freya, la de las siete islas.   Translated by R. Vázquez
Zamora.   Barcelona: Destino, 1944. 297p. (Contains:
Freya of the Seven Isles, A Smile of Fortune, The
Secret-Sharer)   2425

                "Gaspar Ruiz"

Gaspar Ruiz, El Delator, La Bestia, Un Anarquista, El
Duelo, El Conde.   Barcelona: Montaner y Simoń
[c1928] (The first story is translated by D. Gonzalo
Guasp; "La Bestia" by D. José Torroba; the rest are
done by Ramón D. Perés)   2426

Gaspar Ruiz. Translated by Wilam Horzyca. Warsaw:
Dom Książki Polskiej, 1936. 77p. (Also contains:
The Duel)
(Noted by Władysław Tarnawski in Nowa Książka 4,
no 3:150 '37; noted by W. Chwalewik in Rocznik Lit-
eracki 1937, p127-8) 2427
Gaspar Ruiz. Translated by A. Lerer. Warsaw: Nakł.
A. Ryba, 1928. 83p 2428
Gaspar Ruiz. Translated by Ernst W. Freissler. Atlantis
heft 10:621-8; 11:681-91; 12:741-9 O - D '29; same
published: Berlin: S. Fischer, 1934. 110p
(Reviewed by W. E. Süskind in Die Literatur 37:219-20
D 13 '34) 2429
Gaspar Ruiz a jiné povídky. Translated by Aloys Skoumal.
Praha: SNDK, 1957. 154p 2429a
Gaspar Ruiz. Translated by Philippe Neel. Revue de
l'Amérique Latine année 2, volume 4:300-13 Ap 1 '23;
5:32-45, 118-28, 214-26 My 1 - Jl 1 '23; same pub-
lished: Paris: Nouvelle Revue Française, 1927. [7]-
320p
(Reviewed by Pierre Humbourg in Les Nouvelles Lit-
téraires 6:13 S 24 '27) 2430
Gaspar Ruiz. Milan: Alpes, 1930. 365p 2431

"Geography and Some Explorers"

Geografia i niektórzy jej twórcy. Translated by Józef
Brodzki. Naokoło Świata no 1:25-48 '24 2432
Geography and some explorers. Translated by Georges
Jean-Aubry. Le Magazine d'Aujourd'hui Ap 10 '35 p7
2432a

"The Heart of Darkness"

Das Herz der Finsternis. Translated by Ernst W. Freissler.
Berlin: S. Fischer [c1926] [5]-134p; same. Berlin:
Afbau-Verlag, 1958. 145p
(Reviewed by Klaus Udo Szudra in Zeitschrift für
Anglistik und Amerikanstik 6:312-15 '58) 2433
Mørkets hjerte. Translated by C. Th. Meldal & Inger
Budtz-Jørgensen. København: Aschehoug, 1956. 134p
2433a
Cuore de tenebra. Translated by A. C. Rossi. Milan:
Bottega di Poesia [c1924] 256p
(Reviewed by Corrado Pavolini in L'Italia Che Scrive
8, no 6:120 Je '25) 2434
Eo'dum eui sog. Translated by Ra Yeongyun. Seoul:
Sin'yang'sa, 1959. 185p 2434a

"The Heart of Darkness" (cont.)
El corazón de las tinieblas.   Translated by Julia Rodríguez
Danilewsky.   Barcelona: Montaner y Simón [c1931]
[7]-205p   2435
Mörkrets hjärta.   Translated by Margaretha Odelberg.
Stockholm: Biblioteksförl.   1960.   121p   2435a
Coeur di ténèbres.   Translated by André Ruyters.   La
Nouvelle Revue Française 23:759-804; 24:35-72, 172-
209 D 1 '24 - F 1 '25   2436
Srdce temnôt.   Translated by Jozef Svrcek.   Bratislava:
Smena, 1960.   47p   2436a
Jądro ciemności.   Translated by Aniela Zagórska.   Warsaw:
Świat, 1930   2437
Pimeduse süda.   Translated by L. Anvelt.   Tallin: Gaz. -
zurn. izd. 1963.   112p   2437a
Cuore di tenebra.   Translated by Stanis La Bruna.   Milan:
Universale Economica, 1954.   xii, 124p   2438
Opowieści wybrane.   Translated by Aniela Zagórska and
Anna Niklewicz.   Warsaw: Pax, 1952.   250p
(Contains also: An Outpost of Progress, Amy Foster,
The Partner)   2439
Yami no oku.   Translated by Nakano Yoshio.   Tokyo:
Iwanami Shoten, 1958.   174p   2440
Srce tami i dvojnik.   Translated by Marijan Despalatovic.
Zagreb: Znanje, 1960.   224p
(Contains also: The Secret Sharer)   2440a

"The Idiots"

The Idiots, by Joseph Conrad.   London: Harrap; New York:
Brentano's [1920] Bilingual series, edited by J. E.
Mansion.   (French translation by M. Coppin; German,
by Henry B. Cotterill; Italian, by Hilda Campioni;
Spanish by José Plá; Russian, by Anna H. Meonoff)
                                   2441
Die Blödsinnigen.   Translated by Erich Wötzel.   Leipzig:
Rohmkopfs Englische Reihe [nd]   2442
Les Idiots.   Translated by Geneviève Séligmann-Lui.   La
Grande Revue 75:324-47 S 25 '12   2443
Idioci.   Translated by Helena Gay.   1925   2444

"The Informer"

Szpieg.   Translated by Wilam Horzyca.   Naród.   O - n '20
                                   2445

"Initiation"

Initiation. Translated by Georges Jean-Aubry. Correspondant 295:102-17 Ap 10 '24; <u>same</u>. (revised) Gazette
des Lettres Ag 17 '46   2446

"The Inn of the Two Witches"

Gospoda pod dwiema wiedźmami. Translated by Teresa
Tatarkiewicz. Z Całego Świata no 4:15-60 '25   2447
La locanda delle streghe e altri racconti. Translated by
Giovanni Marcellini. Milan: Universale Economica,
1952. 142p
(Contains also: The Planter of Malata, To-morrow)
                                                  2448
A estalagem das duas bruxas. Translated by José Marinho.
Lisboa: 1941. 66p   2448a

"Karain"

Karain. Translated by Henry -D. Davray. Mercure de
France 64:245-69, 390-409 N 15 - D 1 '06   2449
.... Translated by Henry Borjane. La Revue Hebdo-
madaire 31st année, no 14:71-97; no 15:167-93 Ap 6
- 13 '35   2450
.... Russki Vestnik (Russian Messenger) 1898   2451
.... Translated by Bronisław Zieliński. 1961   2452

"The Lagoon"

Laguna. Translated by Aniela Zagórska. 1925   2453
.... Translated by Bolesław Wieniawa-Długoszowski.
Wiadomości Literackie 2, no 1:4 Ja 4 '25   2454
Ragûn... Translated by Shôichi Saeki and Yoshiro Masuda.
Tokyo: Eiho-sha, 1956. 192p
(Includes: Outpost of Progress, Amy Foster, and
Gaspar Ruiz)   2455
The Lagoon. Ljubljanski Zvon, 1927   2455a
Povŕdky z tropů z anglictiny. Translated by Karel Wein-
furter. Král. Vinohrady, F. Jiroušek. 115p 2455b

LAST ESSAYS

Last Essays. Translated into French.
(Reviewed by H.-D. Davray in Mercure de France 193:
485-91 Ja 15 '25)   2456

"Letters"

Epistolario. Translated by Alessandro Serpieri. Milan: Bompiani, 1966. 398p. "Introduction," by Serpieri, p5-31; bibliography, p386.
(Conrad letters drawn from eight different volumes) 2456a

"Letters to Friends"

Briefe an Freunde. Translated by Leo Klein. Neue Rundschau 38, no 6:621-37 Je '27
(Contains 5 letters to Edward Garnett, 1 to E. L. Sanderson, 1 to R. B. Cunninghame Graham, 1 to H. G. Wells, 1 to Mrs. E. L. Sanderson, 3 to John Galsworthy, and 1 to George T. Keating) 2457

LORD JIM

Historja Miłosna. Translated by Aniela Zagórska. Wiadomości Literackie 9, no 39:2-6 S 11 '32; same. Kultura nos 19, 21, 1932
(A fragment drawn from Lord Jim) 2458
Lord Jim. Translated by Aniela Zagórska. Warsaw: Państwowy Instytut Wydawniczy, 1949. 2 volumes: 5-267p; 5-197p
(Reviewed by Z. Najder in Życie Literackie no 37:1, 6 '62; Pomian Piatkowski in Nowa Kultura no 37:6-7 '62; noted in Literatura Piękna, 1956. Warsaw: 1958. p173-4; noted in Literature Piękna, 1962. Warsaw: 1963. p175) 2459
Lord Jim. Translated by Fukizawa Tadashi. Tokyo: Shinchôsha, 1965. 2 vols. 2459a
Lord Jim. Translated by Ono Kyôichi. Tokyo: Yashio Shuppasha, 1965. 398p 2459b
Lord Jim. Translated by Emilja Węsławska. Warsaw: Bibljoteki Dzieł Wyborowych, 1904. 2 volumes: 159p; 157p
(Reviewed in Nowa Reforma 1905, p57; M. Komornicka in Chimera 9:33-4 '05) 2460
Lord Jim. Translated by Cenĕk Syrový. Praha: Melantrich, 1933. 441p
(Reviewed by J. Šnobr in Rozhledy 2:72 Jl 1 '33) 2461
Lord Jim. Translated by Magda Hajkova. Praha: MF, 1959. 301p 2461a
Lord Jim. Translated by Hedwig Lachmann and Ernst W. Freissler. Berlin: S. Fischer [1927] [9]-438p 2462

Lord Jim. Translated by Fritz Lorch. [Berlin:] S.
  Fischer, 1964. 7-461p   2463
Lord Jim. Translated by Philippe Neel. Paris: Nouvelle
  Revue Française, 1922. 7-356p
  (Reviewed by Ramón Fernández in La Nouvelle Revue
  Française 20:841-3 My 1 '23; noted in Bookman (NY)
  57:581 Jl '23)   2464
Lord Jim. Translated by Ramón D. Perés. Barcelona:
  Montaner y Simón [c1927] 2 volumes   2465
Lorde Jim. Translated by Mário Quintana. Pôrto Alegre:
  Globo, 1940. 388p   2466
Lord Jim. Translated by Corrado e Marcella Pavolini.
  Milan: Bompiani, 1949. 5-514p. "L'arte di Conrad,"
  by Ramón Fernández, p5-12; "Lord Jim," by Ramón
  Fernández, p13-15   2467
Prżok za bort. Translated by Eugenjusz Łann. Moscow:
  "Krasnyj Proletarij," 1926. 404p   2468
Lordas Dzimas. Translated by Z. Naujokaitis. Vil'njus:
  Goslitizdat. 1960. 419p   2468a
Lordi Jim. Translated by O. Kostiainen. Porvoo: Werner
  Söderström, 1930. 436p   2469
Lord Jim. Translated by Ivan Krčméry. Bratislava:
  SVKL, 1963. 276p   2469a
Lord Jim. Translated by Tin Ujević. Zagreb: Zora, 1951.
  392p   2470
Lord Jim. Translated by Ticu Archip. Bucuresti: Editura
  Pentru Literatură Universală, 1964. 528p   2470a
Lord Jim. Translated by Vera and Stig Dahlstedt. Stock-
  holm: Forum, 1955. 325p   2471
Lord Jim. Translated by Bice Pareto Magliano. Milan:
  Corticelli, 1927. 403p
  (Reviewed by Corrado Pavolini in L'Italia Che Scrive
  10, no 8:183 Ag '27)   2472
Lord Jim. Translated by Alfredo Pitta. Milan: Sonzogno,
  1938. 373p   2472a
Lord Jim. Translated by Alessandro Gallone. [Milan:]
  Rizzoli [1951] 2 volumes: 430p. Note, p5-[7]   2473
Lord Jim. Translated by Renato Prinzhofer. Milan:
  Mursia, 1965. 318p   2473a
Lord Jim. Translated by Sigurd Hoel. Oslo: Gyldendal
  Norsk Vorlag, 1932. [5]-498p   2474
Lord Jim. Translated by Nuri Eren. Istanbul: Millî
  Eğitim Basimevi, 1946. 2 volumes: 250p; 253p   2475
Lord Jim; Nostromo. Translated by Hedwig Lachmann and
  E. W. Freissler. Frankfurt a. M. : G. B. Fischer,
  1953. 733p   2476

LORD JIM (cont.)

Lord Jim. Translated by Jerzy Andrzejewski. 1956   2477
Lord Jim. Translated by Cármen Gonzales. [Portugal:]
Publicações Europa-América, 1965. [5]-387p; note by
F. Namora, p[5-6]   2477a

THE MIRROR OF THE SEA

Spiegel der See. Translated by Görge Spervogel. Berlin:
S. Fischer, 1939. 262p
(Reviewed by W. E. Süskind in Der Literatur 41:695-6
Jl 16 '39)   2478
Der Obersteuermann. Translated by Görge Spervogel. Die
Neue Rundschau 50, heft 3:258-64 Mr '39
(Part of Section XIV and all of Section XV of The
Mirror of the Sea)   2479
Zerkalo morej. Translated by M. E. Abkina. Moscow:
Geografgiz. 1958. 174p   2479a
Le miroir de la mer. Translated by Joseph De Smet and
Georges Jean-Aubry. Correspondant 290:266-90 Ja
25 '23   2480
Zwierciadło morza. Translated by Aniela Zagórska. War-
saw: Dom Książki Polskiej Spółka Akcyjna, 1935;
same. Pion no 31, 1934
(Reviewed by Witold Chwalewik in Rocznik Literacki
1935 p121-7)   2481
Le miroir de la mer. Translated by Georges Jean-Aubry.
Revue de Paris année 53, no 3:[56]-65 Mr '46 (a
part only).   2482
Le miroir de la mer. Translated by Georges Jean-Aubry.
Paris: Gallimard [1946] [9]-226p. "Introduction" by
Jean-Aubry, p[9]-17
(Reviewed by Emmanuel Buenzod in Gazette de Lau-
sanne S 21 '46; Gabriel Picabia in Paru Mr '47 p84;
Robert Kanters in Gazette de Lettres S 6 '46 p4-5)
   2483
Havets spegel. Translated by Gunnar Barklund. Stockholm:
Rabén & Sjögren, 1966. 7-199p   2483a
Havets spejl. Translated by Tom Smidth. Copenhagen:
Martin, 1929. 222p   2484
Rei Ha-Yam. Translated by Shimeon Sandbank, Mordekhay
Avi-Shaul, Yehuda Dalman. Merhavya: Sifriyat
Poalim, 1961. 338p   2484a
Dusza Przeciwnika. Translated by St. Olgierd. Morze no
10, 1925   2485
Lo specchio del mare. Translated by Piero Janier. Milan:
Bompiani, 1954. 736p

(Contains: The Mirror of the Sea, A Personal Record, 'Twixt Land and Sea). "L'umo Conrad," by Jahier, p5-15
(Reviewed by Roberto Vivarelli in Il Ponte 10, no 9: 1536-8 S '54)   2486

THE NIGGER OF THE "NARCISSUS"

Le nègre du 'Narcisse.' Translated by Robert d'Humières. Le Correspondant ns 200:771-98, 922-50, 1141-79 Ag 25 - S 25 '09; ns 201:165-84 O 10 '09; same published: Paris: Mercure de France, 1910. 266p; same. Paris: La Nouvelle Revue Française, 1924. [v]-xii, 266p
(Reviewed by Francis Gerard in La Revue Européenne 4, no 21:77 N 1 '24; Revue Hebdomadaire 33:372 O 18 '24)   2487
Negeren paa "Narcissus." Translated by A. Halling. Copenhagen: Martin, 1917. 192p   2488
Blámaöur um borö... Reykjavík: Sjómannaútgáfan, 1949. 223p   2488a
Il negro del "Narciso." Translated by Umberto Pittola. Milan: Corticelli, 1926. 253p   2489
Il negro del Narciso. Translated by Maria Gallone. [Milan:] Rizzoli [1960] 5-224p; note, p5-11   2489a
.... Translated by Mario C. Guidotti. [Milan:] Bompiani, 1955. (Together with: Typhoon, Amy Foster, Falk, and To-morrow, translated by Giorgio Zampa) 5-530p. "Lettura del Typhoon" by Piero Bigongiari, p5-14
(Reviewed by Francesco Bruno in L'Italia Che Scrive 38, no 11:234 N '55)   2490
.... Translated by Edgardo Baldi. Milan: Sonzogno [1930] 9-312p   2491
.... Translated by Renato Prinzhofer. Milan: Mursia, 1965. 256p   2491a
"Narkissoksen" neekeri. Translated by Jussi Tervaskanto. Porvoo: Werner Söderström, 1933. 198p   2492
Il negro del "Narciso." Translated by Alda Politzer. Milan: Mondadori, 1950. 151p   2492a
Der Nigger vom "Narzissus." Translated by E. W. Günter [Ernst W. Freissler]. Munich: Albert Langen [1912] 234p
(Reviewed by Ernst Weiss in Berliner Börs. Courant no 267, June, 1927; R. Joerden in Bücherei und Bildungspflege 9, heft 2:175 '29)   2493

THE NIGGER OF THE "NARCISSUS" (cont.)
The Nigger of the "Narcissus." Translated into Greek.
   [Athens: nd] 205p   2493a
Murzyn z załogi "Narcyza." Translated by Jan Lemański.
   Nowy Przegląd Literatury i Sztuki 1, no 2:149-75;
   no 3:277-300; 2, no 4:3-18; no 5:131-63; no 6:263-79
   Jl - D '20; 1, nos 1-3:197-282 Ja-Mr '21; same pub-
   lished: Warsaw: Dom Książki Polskiej, 1928. 217p
   (Reviewed by W. Chwalewik in Gazeta Warszawska
   1928 p287; K. Górski in Gazeta Administracji i Pol.
   Pań. 1924 p22-3; Z. Kisielewski in Robotnik 7:24 '23;
   S. Kołaczkowski in Droga 1928 p61; W. Noskowski in
   Kurjer Poznański 1928 p506)   2494
. . . . Translated by Bronisław Zieliński. [Warsaw:]
   Państwowy Instytut Wydawniczy [1961] 5-204p
   (Noted by Róża Jabłkowska in Rocznik Literacki 1961
   p304-5)   2495
El negro del "Narcissus." Translated by Ricardo Baeza.
   Barcelona: Montaner y Simón [1932] [9]-278p   2496
. . . . México: Novaro, 1956. 192p   2496a
Negeren paa "Narcissus." Translated by Sigurd Hoel. Oslo:
   Gyldendal Norsk Forlag, 1928. 200p   2497
Negern på "Narcissus." Translated by Louis Renner.
   Stockholm: Forum, 1948. 273p (Contains also: Ty-
   phoon)   2497a
Stormen. Translated by Teresia Eurén. Stockholm: Alhén,
   1937. 271p   2498
De Neger van de "Narcissus." Translated by W. J. Roldanus,
   Jr. Amsterdam: Arbeiderspers, 1962. 5-171p
   (Reviewed in Boekzaal 1925. p235)   2498a
A "Narcissus" négere. Translated by Pál Vámosi. Buda-
   pest: Európa Könyvkiado, 1960. [7]-357p (Contains
   also: Youth, Heart of Darkness)   2499
Niegr s "Narcissa." Translated by W. A. Azowa. Lenin-
   grad: Kniga, 1925. 216p   2500
Crnac sa "Narcisa." Srce tame. Translated by Nada Čurčija-
   Prodanović. Beograd: Nolit, 1957. 272p   2500a
The Nigger of the "Narcissus." Translated into the Celtic
   by Seosamh MacGrianna. Baile Atha Cliath: 1933.
   [5]-217p   2501

NOSTROMO

Nostromo. Translated by Marka Wołosowa. Leningrad:
   "Wremja," 1928. 369p   2502
Nostromo. Translated by Ernst Wolfgang Freissler. Berlin:
   S. Fischer [c1927] [11]-617p

(Reviewed by Karl Arns in Der Gral 22, heft 7:465
Ap '28)   2503
Nostromo. Translated by Svetislav Predič. Beograd:
Prosveta, 1961. 496p   2503a
Nostromo. Translated by Joseph De Smet. La Temps
(Paris) [cMid-1913-14 ?]   2504
Nostromo. Translated by Philippe Neel. Le Quotidien May
1 - Oct. 13, 1924; same published: Paris: La Nou-
velle Revue Française, 1926. 2 volumes
(Reviewed by Henry -D. Davray in Mercure de France
année 38, tome 193:491 Ja 15 '27; La Grande Revue
122:167-8 N '26; A. Brule in Revue Anglo-Américaine
10:459 Je '33; H. Daniel-Rops in Revue Nouvelle Mr
'27 p59; René Lalou in Revue Européenne 4th année,
volume 8, no 45:66 N 1 '26)   2505
Nostromo. Translated by Stanisław Wyrzykowski. Tygodnik Illustrowany 1925; same published: Warsaw: Dom
Książki Polskiej, 1928. 2 volumes: 350p; 288p
(Reviewed by R. Blüth in Głos Prawdy no 289, 1929
and in Polska Zbroj. no 47, 1929; K. Czachowski in
Czas no 94, 1929; M. Dąbrowska in Wiadomości Literackie 6, no 24:3 Je 16 '29; Kurjer Poznański no 36,
1929)   2506
Nostromo. Translated by Gastone Rossi. Milan: Sonzogno
[1952] [9]-379p   2506a
Nostromo. Translated by Juan Mateos de Diego. Barce-
lona: Montaner y Simón [c1926] 2 volumes: [5]-295p;
[5]-244p   2507
Nostromo. Translated by Vittorio Caselli. Milan: Alpes,
1928. 361p   2508
Nostromo. Translated by Ettore Camesasca. [Milan:]
Rizzoli [1954] 502p   2509
Nostromo. Translated by Giovanni Fletzer. Milan: Bompi-
ani, 1956. 484p
(Reviewed by Francesco Bruno in L'Italia Che Scrive
40, no 9:167 S '57)   2509a
Nostromo. Translated by Jadwiga Korniłowicz. Warsaw:
Państwowy Instytut Wydawniczy [1959] 7-619p
(Reviewed by M. Korniłowicz in Tygodnik Powszechny
no 13:4 '59; M. Dąbrowska in Nowa Kultura no 1:3
'60; S. Treugutt in Przegląd Kulturalny no 39:5 '59;
noted in Literatura Piękna 1959. Warsaw: 1960. p205)
                                                     2510
Nostromo. Translated by Božo Vodušek. Ljubljana: Can-
karjeva Založba, 1958. 492p   2510a
Veřný Nostromo. Translated by Aloys Skoumal. Praha: Melantrich, 1935. 469p   2511

NOSTROMO (cont.)
Nostromo.   Translated by Cevat Şakir Karaagacligil.   Istan-
    bul: Millî Eğitim Basimevi, 1946.   2 volumes: 227p;
    240p   2512
Nostromo.   Translated by Sten Söderberg.   Stockholm:
    Saxon & Lindström, [1960] 396p   2512a

NOTES ON LIFE AND LETTERS

Appunti di vita e di letteratura.   Translated by Piero Jahier
    and Maj-lis-Rissler Stoneman.   Introduction by Edward
    Garnett, p5-23.   [Milan:] Bompiani, 1950.   5-363p.
    Note by P. Jahier, p349-63   2513

"The Nursery of the Craft"

Le berceau du métier.   Translated by Georges Jean-Aubry.
    Le Correspondant 290:266-90 Ja 25 '23 (part of The
    Mirror of The Sea)   2514

"One Day More"

Encore un jour, pièce en une acte.   Translated by Georges
    Jean-Aubry.   Les Oeuvres Libres ns no 31:[289]-318
    D '48   2515
Un giorno ancora.   Anne la ridente.   L'agente segreto.
    (Plays) Translated by Marcella Bonsanti.   [Milan:]
    Bompiani, 1965.   308p   2515a
Jutro.   Translated by Florian Sobieniowski.   1928   2516
Jutro.   Translated by Zbigniew Herbert.   1958   2517

AN OUTCAST OF THE ISLANDS

Un vagabundo de las islas.   Translated by Antonio Guardiola.
    Barcelona: Montaner y Simón [c1931] 2 volumes:
    [7]-307p; [7]-221p   2518
Een banneling van de eilanden.   Translated by Clara Eggink.
    Amsterdam: J. M. Meulenhoff, 1951.   268p   2519
En fredlös på öarna.   Translated by Håken Norlén.   Stock-
    holm: Folket i bilds forlag, 1950.   298p   2520
Der verdammte der inseln.   Translated by Elsie McCalman.
    Berlin: S. Fischer, 1934.   400p
    (Reviewed by W. E. Süskind in Die Literatur 37:219-20
    D 13 '34)   2521
..........Translated by G. Danehl.   [Frankfurt am Main:]
    Fischer, 1964.   591p (Contains also: Almayer's
    Folly)   2522

Il reietto dell isole.   Translated by G. D'Arese.   Torino:
Slavia, 1932.   2 volumes: [7]-264p; [9]-238p; preface,
p[7]-13 of the first volume
(Reviewed by Enrico Caprile in L'Italia Che Scrive 16,
no 1:22 Ja '33)   2523
Un paria des Iles.   Translated by Georges Jean-Aubry.
Le Jour April 12 - May 25, 1937; same published:
Paris: Gallimard, 1937. [9]-318p
(Reviewed by Joë Bousquet in Cahiers du Sud 24:677-8
N '37; François Porché in L'Epoque N 1 '37; G. Cha-
rensol in Les Nouvelles Littéraires no 819:5 Je 25
'38; A. Digeon in Études Anglaises 2:199 Summer '38;
Pierre Lorson in Études (Revue Catholique) 234:144 Ja
5 '38)   2524
Bunka hatsuru tokoro.   Translated by Tadae Fukizawa.
Tokyo: Kodokawa shoten, 1953. 2 volumes   2525
. . . . Translated by Akira Honda.   Tokyo: Hayakawa
shobô, 1953. 367p   2526
Banita.   Translated by Wili Zyndram-Kościałkowska.
Kwrier Litewski (Wilno) nos 147-58, 160-3, 165-9,
172-5, 177-8, 180-4, 186, 189-92, 194-8, 201-4, 207-
10, 212-16, 218-20, 223, 225-8, 231-3, 237-8, 240,
243, 1913; same published: Lwów: Kuriera Lwowski-
ego, 1913. 326p
(Reviewed in Czas 1919, p123)   2527
Wygnaniec.   Translated by Maria Gąsiorowska.   Tygodnik
Mód i Powieści (Weekly Magazine of Fashion and Fic-
tion) (Warsaw) nos 1-26, Ja - Je '97
(The first translation of any of Conrad's works) 2528
Wykolejeniec.   Translated by Aniela Zagórska.   Warsaw:
Dom Książki Polskiej, 1936.   2 volumes: vii-[xii],
164p; 7-218p
(Reviewed by Władysław Tarnawski in Nowa Książka 3,
no 4:224 '36; noted by Witold Chwalewik in Rocznik
Literacki 1936 p112-13; noted in Literatura Piękna
1956. Warsaw: 1958. p174; noted in Literatura
Piękna 1964. Warsaw: 1966. p202-3; T. S. in Stolica
39:7 '64)   2529
. . . . Warsaw: Państwowy Instytut Wydawniczy [1956]
380p; "posłowie" by Zdzisław Najder, p381-[91]   2530

"An Outpost of Progress"

Awanpost ciwilizacii.   Translated by A. W. Kiwcowoj.   Mos-
cow: 1927. 96p   2531
Un avant-poste de la civilisation.   Translated by G. -D.
Périer.   Bruxelles: Renaissance d'Occident,

"An Outpost of Progress" (cont.)
1925. 55p   2532
Un avant-poste du progrès.   Translated by Georges Jean-
   Aubry.   Revue Hebdomadaire 6:[131]-162 Je 14 '30
                                                 2533
.... Translated by Henry Borjane.   Revue Bleue:
   Politique et Littéraire 73:617-30 S 21 '35   2534
Placówka postępu.   Translated by Aniela Zagórska.   Robot-
   nik nos 187-8, 190-5 1925   2535
Izgnanik sa ostrva.   Translated by Zivojin Simić.   Beo-
   grad: Nolit. 1962. 299p   2535a

A PERSONAL RECORD
See: SOME REMINISCENCES

"The Partner"

L'Associé.   Translated by Georges Jean-Aubry.   Revue de
   Genève 1:[88]-113 Jl '20   2536
Wspólnik.   Translated by Teresa Tatarkiewiczowa.
   Świat 1927   2537

"The Planter of Malata"

Il piantatore di Malata.   Translated by Gilberto Altichieri.
   Milan: Muggiani [1944] 159p   2538
.... Translated by Vittorio Caselli.   Milan: Maia,
   1929. (with two other stories) 250p   2539
Le planteur de Malata.   Translated by Georges Jean-Aubry.
   Correspondant année 92, tome 278:1073-1105 Mr 25
   '20; année 92, tome 279:[35]-67 Ap 10 '20.   Note,
   p[1070]-1072   2540
Plantator.   Translated by Teresa Tatarkiewiczowa.
   Bluszcz, 1927; same. published: Rzym: K. Breiter,
   1946. 83p   2541
Planteren paa Malata.   Translated by Tom Smidth.   Copenhagen: Martin, 1926. [5]-218p (With three other
   stories)   2542

"Poland Revisited"

Conrad v Krakowie w rok 1914.   Translated by Bronisława
   Neufeldówna.   Wiadomoś∶i Literackie 1, no 33:4 Ag
   17 '24   2543
Retour en Pologne.   Translated by Georges Jean-Aubry.
   La Revue de France année 16, tome 2:418-35, 611-30
   Ap 1, 15 '36   2544

Translations   355

"Prince Roman"

Książe Roman.   Translated by Teresa L. Sapieżyna.
Wiadomości Literackie 3, no 18:3-4 My 2 '26; same
published: Warsaw: Dom Książki Polskiej, 1935. 38p
(Reviewed by Witold Chwalewik in Rocznik Literacki
1936 p112-13)   2545
.... Translated by Janusz Jasieńczyk and Witold Turno
[i. e., Wit Tarnawski] Jerusalem: Gazeta Polska,
1945. 23p   2546
Un héros polonais de Conrad: "Le Prince Roman." Translated by Georges Jean-Aubry. Maestricht: A. A. M.
Stols [1933] Translation, p 7-[36]   2547

"Proust as Creator"

Conrad o Prouscie. Wiadomości Literackie 4, no 48:2 N
7 '27   2547a

THE RESCUE

Die rettung. Translated by Elsie McCalman. Berlin: S.
Fischer [1931] [9]-511p
(Reviewed by Kurt Schrey in Die Neue Literatur 32,
heft 12:599-600 D '31; Werner Schickert in Die Litera-
tur 34, heft 10:580 Jl '32)   2548
.... Translated by Hermann Stresau. Berlin: S.
Fischer [1965] 7-501p   2549
Spas.   Translated by Tanasije Mladenović. Beograd:
Biblioteka Minerva, 1964. 9-432p   2549a
Wybawienie. Translated by Aniela Zagórska. Głos Prawdy
nos 335-360, 1928; nos 1-171, 1929   2550
Ocalenie. Translated by Aniela Zagórska. Warsaw: Dom
Książki Polskiej Spółka Akcyjna, 1929. 2 volumes:
vii-xi, 217p; 7-289p
(5250 numbered copies)
(Reviewed by E. Breiter in Wiadomości Literackie 6,
no 49:1 D 8 '29; K. Czachowski in Tygodnik Illustrowany no 35, 1929; S. Furmanik in Polska Zbrojna no
288, 1929; J. Kaden-Bandrowski in Głos Prawdy no
313, 1929; A. Madej in Głos Lit. no 20, 1929; J.
Piotrowiczowa in Słowo nos 283-4, 1929; S. Podhorska
in Bluszcz no 36, 1929; L. Pomirowski in Kurjer
Poranny no 273, 1929; A. Tretiak in Pamiętnik Warszawski no 3, 1929; Wł. Tarnawski in Kurjer Poznan-

THE RESCUE (cont.)
ski no 24 '30; noted in Literatura Piękna 1957. Warsaw: 1958. p201) 2551
El rescate. Translated by Marco-Aurelio Galindo. Barcelona: Montaner y Simón [c1932] 2 volumes: 348p;
444p 2552
Únik. Translated by Timotheus Vodička. Praha: Melantrich, 1936. 455p 2553
Denstore redning. Translated by Knud Poulsen. Copenhagen: John Martin, 1921. 2 volumes: 240p; 192p
2554
La rescousse. Translated by Georges Jean-Aubry. Mercure de France 264:96-126, 348-61, 531-56; 265:92-
126, 297-344, 537-80; 266:86-131, 315-43, 530-76;
267:85-119 N 15 '35 - Ap 1 '36; same published:
Paris: Gallimard [1936] [9]-400p; introduction p[9]-14
(Reviewed by Louis Bonnerot in Études Anglaises 1:
176 Mr '37; Thérèse Herpin in Le Jour S 23 '36;
noted in Nouvelles Littéraires Ag 1 '36; François
Porché in Echo de Paris Ag 13 '36 p6) 2555

"The Return"

Powrót. Translated by Maria Bunikiewicz. Gazeta Wiecz-
orna (Lwów) Je-Jl '14 2556
.... Translated by Helena Gay. 1925 2557

THE ROVER

Korsarz. Translated by Jerzy Bohdan Rychliński. Warsaw: Wacława Czarski & Sons, 1925. 274p
(Reviewed by Emil Breiter in Wiadomości Literackie
2, no 13:3 Mr 29 '25; L. André in Echo Tygodnik no
31, 1929; M. Dąbrowska in Wiadomości Literackie no
28, 1926; S. Kołaczkowski in Tygodnik Wileński no 8,
1925; B. Winawer in Wiadomości Literackie no 11,
1924; R. Zrębowicz in Rzeczpolita no 69, 1925; J.
Jedrzejewicz in Droga no 4, 1925; noted in Literatura
Piękna 1958. Warsaw: 1960. p216-17; noted in Literatura Piękna 1963. Warsaw: 1965. p182; reviewed
by Z. Najder in Życie Literackie no 8:6-7 '63) 2558
Le frère-de-la-côte. Translated by Georges Jean-Aubry.
Revue de Paris année 2:93-143, 399-438 Mr 1, Mr 15
'27; 1:26-45, 348-86, 638-67, 894-915 Ja 1, 15, F 1,
15 '27; same published: Paris: Gallimard [1928] 10th
edition. [9]-317p
(Reviewed by Louis Cazamian in Revue Anglo-Améri-

caine 3:164-5 D '25; Vient de Paraitre My '24 p264)
                                                   2559
El hermano de la costa. Translated by J. G. de Luares.
Barcelona: Destino, 1943. 257p   2560
L'avventurièro. Translated by Camillo Pellizzi. Milan:
Bompiani, 1950. 366p   2561
Der Freibeuter. Translated by Elsie McCalman. Berlin:
S. Fischer, 1930. 322p
(Reviewed by Mally Behler-Hagen in Die Schöne Lit-
eratur 31, heft 9:437 S '30)   2562
Pirát. Praha: Melantrich, 1932   2563
Fribytaren. Translated by Ernst Lundquist. Uppsala:
Lindblad, 1924. 314p   2564
Fribytteren. Translated by Knud Poulsen. Copenhagen:
John Martin, 1924. [5]-304p   2565

THE SECRET AGENT

L'agent secret... Translated by Henry -D. Davray. Paris:
Mercure de France & Librairie Gallimard, 1912.
[7]-446p
(Reviewed by Madeleine Cazamian in Revue Critique
des Livres Nouveaux 7th année, 2nd series, no 10:
208 D 15 '12; L. D. in Dietsche Warande en Belfort
nos 7-8:553 Jl-Ag '37)   2565a
Provokatören. Translated by G. A. J. Stockholm: Hierta,
1910. 332p   2566
Tajny agent. Translated by Maria Gasiorowska. Warsaw:
G. Centnerszwer, 1902. 2 volumes: 137p; 151p 2567
.... Translated by Aniela Zagórska. Warsaw: Dom
Ksiazki Polskiej, 1939. 360p   2568
Der Geheimagent. Translated by Ernst W. Freissler.
With an introduction by Thomas Mann. Berlin: S.
Fischer [c1926] [9]-382p.
(The introduction is on 17 unnumbered pages at the
beginning of the volume)
(Reviewed by Mally Behler-Hagen in Die Schöne Lit-
eratur 29, heft 1:29-30 Ja '28; noted in Zeitschrift
für Bücherfreunde 18:285-6 N-D '26)   2569
.... Translated by G. Danehl. [Berlin:] S. Fischer,
1963. 7-332p   2570
Prowokator. Translated by Dr. Felicya Nossig. Lwów:
Nakładem "Ludowego Towarzystwa Wydawniczego,"
1920. 185p; illustrated   2571
.... Translated by M. Lubimowa. Moscow: Krasnyj
Proletarij, 1927. 64p   2572
El huésped secreto. Translated by Mariano Latorre.

THE SECRET AGENT (cont.)
Atenea 2:3-25, 135-60 Ag 31, S 30 '25   2573
Den hemmelige agent.   Translated by Louis V. Kohl.
Copenhagen: John Martin, 1917. 288p   2574
Anarkistit.   Translated by Kristiina Kivivjori.   Helsinki:
Otava, 1961. 284p   2574a
L'agente segreto.   Translated by Gastone Rossi.   Milan:
Sonzogno, 1928. 314p   2575
.... Translated by Lela Jahn.   Milan: Valsecchi,
1946. 327p   2576
.... Translated by Carlo Emilio Gadda. [Milan:]
Bompiani, 1953. 7-396p.   Preface by Thomas Mann
(Translated by Gabriella Bemporad) p7-18   2577
.... Translated by Bruno Maffi.   Milan: Rizzoli,
1953. 263p   2578
El agente secreto.   Translated by Marco-Aurelio Galindo.
Barcelona: Montaner y Simón [1935] [9]-337p   2579
The Secret Agent [in Russian]   Vestnik Evropy 1908   2580
Tajny agent [the play]   Translated by Bruno Winawer.
1923
(Reviewed by A. Gruszecka in Przegląd Warszawski
no 23, 1923; Czas 1923 p71)
[The play had its premiere at the Bagatela Theatre in
Krakow on March 26, 1923]   2581

"The Secret-Sharer"

Ukryty sojusznik.   Translated by Jerzy Bohdan Rychliński.
Rome: Polish Dom Wydawniczy, 1946. 62p   2582
Der heimliche Teilhaber.   Translated by Maria von
Schweinitz.   Ebenhausen bei München: Langewiesche-
Brandt, 1955. 101p   2582a
L'hote secret.   Translated by Georges Jean-Aubry. Revue
de France 4:[559]-581, [777]-802 Ag 1, 15 '24 2583
Il passeggero clandestino.   In Romanzo E Racconti, anno
1, no 4:3-58 '66   2583a

"Selected Tales"

Opowieśc wybrane.   Warsaw: Pax, 1952. 3-250p. Preface
by Antoni Gołubiew. (Contains: The Partner, translated by Anna Niklewicz; Heart of Darkness, Outpost
of Progress, and Amy Foster, translated by Aniela
Zagórska)   2584
Wybór nowel.   Wrocław: Zakład Naradowy im. Ossolińs-
kich-Wydawnictwo, 1957. 316p.   Introduction by Stefan
Zabłocki, p5-55.

(Contains: Because of the Dollars, The Inn of the
Two Witches, translated by Teresa Tatarkiewicz;
Freya of the Seven Isles, Youth, Amy Foster, translated
by Aniela Zagórska; and Prince Roman, translated by
Teresa Sapieżyna) (Noted in Literatura Piekna 1957.
Warsaw, 1958. p202)   2585
Zagle znikaja z oceanow.   Gydnia: Wydawnictwo Morskie,
1965. 64p   (Excerpts about sailing)   2585a
Tutti i racconti e i romanzi brevi.   Milan: Mursia, 1967.
xlviii, 1243p
(Reviewed by Augusto Guidi in L'Italia Che Scrive 50,
no 12:195-6 D '67)   2585b

A SET OF SIX

Sześć opowieści.   Translated by Wilam Horzyca, Leon Pi-
wiński, Tadeusz Pużjanowski.   Warsaw: Towarzystwa
Wydawnicze "Ignis," [1924] 9-310p
(Contains: Gaspar Ruiz, The Informer, The Brute,
and The Duel, translated by Horzyca; Il Conte, trans-
lated by Piwiński; and The Anarchist, translated by
Pużjanowski)
(Reviewed by K. Górski in Gaz. Administr. 1924 p25;
Z. Kisielewski in Robotnik 1:20 '24; noted in Litera-
tura Piękna, 1958.   Warsaw: 1960. p217-18)   2586
Staerke sind og vilde skaebner.   Translated by Tom Smidth.
Kφbenhaven: Martin, 1927. [7]-311p   2587
Un gruppo di sei.   Translated by Giovanni Fletzer. [Milan:]
Bompiani, 1964. 5-376p; note, p371-6
(Reviewed by Paolo Padovani in L'Italia Che Scrive 47,
nos 11-12:199 N-D '64)   2587a

THE SHADOW-LINE

La línea de sombra.   Translated by Ricardo Baeza.   Barce-
lona: Montaner y Simón [c1931] [7]-209p; note by
Baeza, p[7]-11   2588
La linea d'ombra.   Translated by Mario Benzi.   Milan:
Bietti, 1929. 240p   2589
.... Translated by Maria Jesi.   [Torino:] Einaudi,
1947. xi, 101p.   Preface by Cesare Pavese, p ix-xi
                                                              2590
.... Translated by Francesco Arcangeli.   Milan:
Bompiani, 1963. 7-374p; preface by Arcangeli, p7-29;
note on the text by Piero Bigongiari, p371-4
(Contains also: Within the Tides, translated by Gil-
berto Altichieri and G. D'Arese)   2590a

THE SHADOW-LINE (cont.)
Dodssejleren. Translated by Knud Poulsen. København:
Martin, 1922. [5]-174p   2591
Pojas sjene. Translated by Branko Brusar. Zagreb:
Zora, 1963. 167p   2591a
Die Schattenlinie. Translated by Elsie McCalman. With
an introduction by Jakob Wassermann. Berlin: S.
Fischer [1926] [9]-182p
("Vorwort" is on first nine unnumbered pages)   2592
.... Translated by Elsie McCalman. Berlin: S.
Fischer 1961. 7-154p. "Nachwort," by Rudolf Sühnel,
p155-60; bibliography, p161-2   2592a
A linha de sombra. Translated by Moura Brás. Pórto:
Libraria Civilização, 1945. 339p   2592b
De Schaduwgrens. Translated by M. J. Bennindijk-Paauw.
Amsterdam: L. J. Veen; Antwerp: Het Kompas, 1947.
209p   2593
Hranice stĭnu. ᵕ Translated by Luba & Rudolf Pellarovi.
Praha: Čs. spisovatel, 1957. 139p   2593a
Smuga cienia. Translated by Jadwiga Sienkiewicz. Warsaw:
E. Wende i-ska (Ignis) [c1926] 165p
(Reviewed by M. Dąbrowska in Głos Prawdy no 94,
1926; Echo Tygodnik no 5, 1930; Gazeta Warszawska
no 61, 1930; A. Madej in Współczesnośc Literackie
1930; J. Herbst in Trybuna Literacka no 25:3 '58;
noted in Literatura Piękna, 1962. Warsaw: 1963.
p176)   2594
La ligne d'ombre. Translated by Hélène and Henri Hoppenot. Revue de Paris année 36, no 5:721-47; no 6:79-
116, 307-58 O 15 - N 15 '29; same published: Paris:
Nouvelle Revue Française [1929] [7]-237p. "Introduction," by Georges Jean-Aubry, p[7]-35
(Reviewed by Nicolas Segur in La Revue Mondiale 31st
année, volume 196:88-9 Mr 1 '30; Marcel Brion in
Cahiers du Sud année 17, no 120:233 Ap '30)   2595
Eodumeui sog. Translated by Bong-Sun Lee and Yeong-
Gyun La. Seoul: Jeongeumsa, 1965. 402p   2595a

"The Sisters"

Siostry. Translated by Aleksandra Poleska and Wit Tarnawski. Wiadomości 4, nos 176-7:2 Ag 21 '49   2595b

"A Smile of Fortune"

Un sourire de la fortune. Translated by Georges Jean-
Aubry. Revue de Paris année 36, no 1:33-53, 348-71,

659-92 Ja 1 - F 1 '29 2596
Ha-mazzal sihek li. Translated by M. Ben-Eliezer. Tel-
Aviv: Chief Educational Officer, Ministry of Defense,
1965. 129p 2596a
Ein Lächeln des Glücks. Translated by Elsie McCalman.
Berlin: Wegweiser [1930] 136p 2597
Uśmiech szczęścia. Translated by Jan Lemański. Rome:
Polski Dom Wydawniczy, 1946. 124p 2598

SOME REMINISCENCES or A PERSONAL RECORD

Lebenserinnerungen. Translated by Elsie McCalman. Ber-
lin: S. Fischer, 1928. [9]-218p; (excerpt). Die Neue
Rundschau 39 no 2:263-81 '28
(Reviewed by Karl Arns in Literarische Handweiser 66,
heft 1:43 O'29; W. E. Süskind in Die Literatur 35:681-
2 Ag 9 '33; Die Neue Rundschau 39, no 9:263-81 '28;
Zeitschrift für Französichen und Englischen Unterricht
28, heft 3:230 '29; Erich Franzen in Die Literarische
Welt 4, no 48:7-8 N 30 '28) 2599
Ze wspomnień. Translated by Aniela Zagórska. Warsaw:
Dom Książki Polskiej, 1934. 175p (Noted by Witold Chwal-
ewik in Rocznik Literacki 1934, p137-8; Jan Parandowski
in Nowa Książka 1, no 4:171-2 '34; noted in Literatura
Piękna, 1965. Warsaw: 1967. p215; Maria Szpakowska
in Współczesność no 2:10 '66) 2600
Les souvenirs. Translated by Georges Jean-Aubry. Corre-
spondant 296:579-603, 916-44; 297:33-60, 196-221 Ag
25, S 25, O 25 '24; same published: Paris: Nouvelle
Revue Française [c1934] 266p
(Reviewed by René Lalou in Revue Européenne 3rd année, 6, no 31:78-9 S 1 '25) 2601
Über mich selbst. Einige erinnerungen. Translated by G.
Danehl. [Frankfurt am Main:] S. Fischer, 1965.
5-173p 2601a

"Stories"

Noveller. Translated by Peter Magnus. Oslo: Gyldendal,
1951. 343p 2602

SUSPENSE

Spannung. Translated by Elsie McCalman. Berlin: S.
Fischer, 1936. 322p. "Nachwort," by Georges Jean-
Aubry (translated from the French by M. M. R.),
p[306]-322
(Reviewed by W. E. Süskind in Die Literatur 38, heft
9:436-7 Je '36; Georges Jean-Aubry in Die Neue

SUSPENSE (cont.)
Rundschau 47, heft 3:325-35 Mr '36; M. M. R. in
Frankfurter Zeitung Je 26 '36) 2603
L'acquila ferita. Translated by Mario Benzi. Milan:
Bietti, 1929. 237p 2604
Suspense... with an introduction by Richard Curle. Leip-
zig: B. Tauchnitz, 1925. (No. 4705) 286p 2605
Oczekiwanie. Translated by Jerzy Bohdan Rychliński.
Warsaw: Państwowy Instytut Wydawniczy, 1960.
292p 2606
Angoisse. Translated with an introduction and notes by
Georges Jean-Aubry. Paris: Gallimard [c1956] [7]-
353p; preface, p[7]-22; appendix, p[339]-353 2607
Incertezza. Translated by Giovanni Fletzer. Milan: Bom-
piani, 1962. 7-358p. Article on Conrad by Jean-
Jacques Mayoux, p7-57; note, p353-8
(Reviewed by Paolo Padovani in L'Italia Che Scrive 46,
no 5:86 My '63) 2607a

TALES OF HEARSAY

Opowieści zasłyszane. Translated by Teresa X. Sapieżyna
and Stanisław Wyrzykowski. Warsaw: Dom Książki
Polskiej, 1928. xv, 149p. With a preface by R. B.
Cunninghame Graham.
(Reviewed by Stefan Kołaczkowski in Wiadomości 5,
no 30:3 Jl 22 '28) 2608
Opowieści zasłyszane i Sześć opowieści. Translated by
Teresa X. Sapieżyna and Stanisław Wyrzykowski.
Warsaw: Biblioteka Polska, 1938. (Tales of Hearsay
and A Set of Six)
(Reviewed by Hanna Wierzbica in Przegląd Powszechny
55, tom 220:231-2 N '38) 2609
Contos que ouvi contar. Translated by Barão de Villalva.
Pôrto: Livraria Civilização [1945] [7]-302p 2609a
Geschichten von Hörensagen. Translated by Richard Krau-
shaar and Hans Reisiger. With a preface by R. B.
Cunninghame Graham. Berlin: S. Fischer, 1938.
192p
(Reviewed by W. E. Süskind in Die Literatur 40:754
S '38) 2610
Derniers contes suivis de Notes sur les lettres. Trans-
lated by Georges Jean-Aubry. Paris: Gallimard
[c1941] 204p. "Introduction," by G. Jean-Aubry,
p[1]-8
(Contains also Part I of Conrad's Notes on Life and
Letters) 2611

Racconti ascoltati.   Ultimi saggi.   Translated by Margherita
Guidacci.   With an introduction by Ernest A.   Baker and
Edward Morgan Forster.   Milan: Bompiani, 1963.   374p
(Contains also: Last Essays)
(Reviewed by Vincenzo de Tomasso in L'Italia Che
Scrive 47, no 7:111 Jl '64)   2611a

TALES OF UNREST

Opowieści niepokojące.   Translated by Helena Gay and Aniela
Zagórska.   Warsaw: W.   Czarski & Sons, 1925.   iii-
vii, 205p
(Reviewed by Stefan Kołaczkowski in Wiadomości Liter-
ackie 2, no 46:5 N 15 '25; M. Dąbrowska in Tygodnik
Illustrowany no 34, 1925)   2612
Racconti inquieti.   Translated by Charis Cortese de Bosis.
Milan: Alpes, 1930.   255p   2613
Geschichten der Unrast...   Translated by Fritz Lorch.
[Frankfurt am Main:]   S.   Fischer, 1963.   7-514p (Con-
tains also: A Set of Six)   2614
Cuentos de inquietud.   Translated by Marco-Aurelio Galindo
and C. de Rivas Cherif.   Barcelona: Montaner y
Simón [c1928] 199p   2615
Hvileløse historier.   Translated by A. Halling.   Copenhagen:
V. Pio, 1904.   298p   2616
Basta civilizácie.   Translated by Viktor Krupa.   Bratislava:
Mladé Letá, 1964.   236p   2616a
Histoires inquiètes.   Translated by Georges Jean-Aubry.
Paris: Gallimard, 1932.   279p
(Reviewed by Jean Grenier in Nouvelles Revue Fran-
çaise 39:781-2 N '32)   2617
Fredlösa historier.   Translated by Karin Hirn.   Stockholm:
Wahlström & Widstrand, 1903.   viii, 292p
(According to Conrad, this was the first volume of his
works translated.)   2618

"Three Plays"

Teatro...   Translated by Marcella Bonsanti.   Milan: Bompiani, 1965.   5-305p.   With an introduction by Bonsanti,
p5-19   2618a

"To-morrow"

Pour demain.   Translated by Georges Jean-Aubry.   Europe
26, no 104: [465]-502 Ag 15 '31   2619
Jutro.   Translated by Aniela Zagórska.   Wiadomości Literackie
8, no 14:4-5 Ap 5 '31   2620

364   A Bibliography of Joseph Conrad

"To-morrow" (cont.)
.........Translated by Zbigniew Herbert.   Dialog 3, no 7:
[5]-18 Jl '58   2621
Menschen am Strande.   Translated by Elise Eckert and
George Goyert.   Stuttgart: Reclam, 1953. 95p (Con-
tains: To-morrow, Amy Foster)   2622
Mañana.   Translated by Ramón de Perés.   Barcelona: GP,
1958. 128p   2622a
Demain, pièce en 1 acte.   Translated by P. H. Raymond-
Duval. [1909 ?]
(Reviewed by R. De Bury in Mercure de France (series
moderne) 79:349-50 My 15 '09)   2623
Jutro.   Translated by Florian Sobieniowski.   Droga nos 1-2,
Ja - F '28
(A play in one act.)   2624

"The Tremolino"

Der Untergang der 'Tremolino. '   Translated by Ernst W.
von Freissler.   Die Neue Rundschau 41, part 1:799-
821 Je '30   2625
Die "Tremolino."   Translated by Görge Spervogel.   Munich:
Piper, 1954. 61p   2626
Karain och andra berättelser.   Translated by Vera & Stig
Dahlstedt.   Stockholm: Forum, 1954. 197p (Contains:
The Tremolino, Karain, An Outpost of Progress, The
Secret-Sharer)   2627
Le 'Tremolino. '   Translated by Georges Jean-Aubry.   Le
Correspondant 290:266-90 Ja 25 '23   2627a
"Tremolino."   Translated by Aniela Zagórska.   Wiadomości
Literackie 12, no 586:2-3 F 10 '35   2628

'TWIXT LAND AND SEA

Entre terre et mer.   Translated by Georges Jean-Aubry.
Paris: Gallimard, 1929. [9]-284p
(Reviewed by Ramón Fernández in La Nouvelle Revue
Française 33:571-2 O '29; Marcel Thiebaut in La Revue
de Paris année 36, no 18:475-7 S 15 '29)   2629
Między lądem a morzem.   Translated by Jan Lemański,
Jerzy Bohdan Rychliński, and Aniela Zagórska.   War-
saw: Towaryzstwa Wydawniczego "Ignis, " [c1924] ix,
267p
(Reviewed by E. Breiter in Wiadomości Literackie
1924 p33; Janusz Jędrzejewicz in Droga 1924 p8; Z.
Kisielewski in Robotnik 1924 p239; S. Zieliński in Nowe
Książki no 11:664-7 '62)   2630

Racconti di mare e di costa. Translated by Piero Jahier.
Torino: G. Einaudi, 1946. xx, 233p. Note on Conrad
by Jahier, p ix-xv   2631

TYPHOON

Tajfun. Translated by A. Halling and Peter Holm. Køben-
havn & Kristiania: Martin, 1918. 237p   2632
.... Hanower: Polski Związek Wychodźctwa Rzym,
1945. 40p   2633
.... Translated by Jerzy Bohdan Rychliński. Warsaw:
Tow. Księg. Polskich na Kresach [c1926] 128p
(Reviewed by A. Słonimski in Wiadomości Literackie
3, no 8:5 F 21 '26)   2634
Tajfun i inne opowiadania. Translated by J. B. Rychliński
and A. Zagórska. Warsaw: Panstwowy Instytut Wy-
dawniczy, 1957. 305p (Contains: Typhoon, Amy
Foster, Falk, To-morrow)
(Noted by Zdzisław Najder in Rocznik Literacki 1957
p324; noted in Literatura Piękna 1957. Warsaw:
1958. p201-2)   2635
Taifū. Translated by Ikusaburô Miyake. Tokyo: Shinchô-
sha, 1951. 127p   2636
Tuphónas; Phalf. All. Tertakēs. Athens: G. Papademe-
trios, 1952   2637
Un Tifón. Amata Fóster. Falk. Mañana. Translated by
Ramón D. Perés. Barcelona: Montaner y Simón
[c1929] 298p   2638
.... Translated by Federico López Cruz. Buenos
Aires: Siglo Veinte, 1945. 155p   2639
Typhoon. Translated by Joseph De Smet. Progrès Maga-
zine 1911   2640
Typhon. Translated by André Gide. Revue de Paris 25,
no 2:17-59, 334-381 Mr 1 - 15 '18; same published:
Paris: Nouvelle Revue Française [1918] [9]-200p.
(300 copies only); same. Paris: Gallimard [c1923]
[9]-224p   2641
Taifun. Translated by Harald Jernström. Stockholm:
Bonnier, 1918. 167p   2642
.... Translated by Nordahl Grieg. Oslo: Gyldendal
Norsk Forlag, 1930. [5]-146p   2643
.... Translated by Elise Eckert. Stuttgart: J.
Engelhorns Nachfolge, 1927. 152p
(Reviewed by Jörn Oven in Die Schöne Literatur 29,
heft 2:89 F '28; R. Joerden in Bücherei und Bildungs-
pflege 9, heft 2:175 '29)   2644
Taifun. Translated by Sonja Burkhard. Aarau: Sauer-

TYPHOON (cont.)
länder, 1956. 104p   2644a
Taifuns. Translated by Andrejs Johansons. Stockholm:
   Parnass, 1950. 109p   2645
Typhoon and other stories. Translated by Neményi Imre
   and Gaál Andor. [Budapest:] Pantheon Kiadás [nd]
   7-272p   2645a
De Typhoon. Translated by W. L. Leclercq. Antwerp:
   Wereldbibliotheek, 1951. 117p
   (Reviewed by Annie Solomons in Leven en Werken 8:
   [113]-18 F 29 '51)   2646
Taifun. Translated by Ana Popescu. Bucurest: ESPLA,
   1959. 112p   2646a
Taifun und andere Erzählungen. Translated by Elise Eck-
   ert. Zürich: Manesse-Verlag [1948] 331p
   (Contains: Amy Foster, Typhoon, To-morrow)   2647
Typhon. Translated by Angelos Terzakis. Athens:
   Galaxias, 1961. 190p   2647a
Tajfun; U scru tame. Translated by Branko Brusar. Zag-
   reb: Mladost, 1952. 140p (Contains: Typhoon, Heart
   of Darkness)   2648
.... Mladost. Translated by Aleksander Vidaković.
   Beograd: Rad, 1959. 136p (Contains: Typhoon,
   Youth)   2648a
Il tifone e altri romanzi. Translated by A. Politzer. Milan:
   Mondadori, 1949. 1252p (Contains: Typhoon and other
   stories)   2649
Tajfun, Mladost. Translated by Branko Pendovski. Skopje:
   Kočo Racin, 1963. 139p   2649a
Tifone. Translated by Tito Diambra. Milan: Monreale,
   1926. 138p   2650
.... Translated by Eliana Trinchero. Milan: Rizzoli
   [1950] 2nd edition, 107p. Note, p5-7   2651
Pyörremyrsky. Translated by Jorma Etto. Hameenlinna:
   A. A. Karisto, 1961. 5-115p. Note, p5-9   2651a
Tufão. Translated by Queiroz Lima. Pôrto Alegre: Globo,
   1943. 283p   2652
Typhoon. Translated into Japanese by Ikusaburô Miyake.
   1951.   2653
Typhoon. Translated into Celtic by Seosamh MacGrianna.
   1935. [7]-186p (Contains: Typhoon and Amy Foster)
                                                           2654

UNDER WESTERN EYES

W oczach zachodu. Translated by Helena Janina Pajzderska.
   Świat (Warsaw) nos 1-43, 1917; same published: Warsaw: E. Wende i Ska [1925] 404p; preface by Stefan

Żeromski
(Reviewed by Emil Breiter in Wiadomości Literackie
2, no 23:3 Je 7 '25; K. Górski in Gazeta Administracji i Pol. Pań. 1925; noted by Witold Chwalewik in
Rocznik Literacki 1934 p138-40)   2655
.... Translated by Wit Tarnawski. London: Veritas
[1955] 7-288p. Introductory remarks, p7-11   2656
Mit den augen des westens. Translated by Ernst Wolfgang
Günter [i. e., Ernst W. Freissler] Munich: A. Langen
[c1913] xv, 519p
(Reviewed by Rudolf Pechel in Das Literarische Echo
16, no 20:1435-6 Jl 15 '14; Hochland 31, no 3:286 D
'33; Der Gral 28:183 '33-'34; H. Stresau in Der Bü-
cherei 1, heft 5:247-8 My '34)   2657
.... Translated by G. Danehl. [Frankfurt am Main:]
S. Fischer, 1967. [7]-429p   2658
Sous les yeux d'occident. Translated by Philippe Neel.
Paris: Gallimard, 1920. 9-310p
(Reviewed by Paul Morand in Nouvelle Revue Française
16:495-7 Ap 1 '21)   2659
Sotto gli occhi dell'Occidente. Translated by Aldo Traverso.
Milan: Corticelli, 1928. 395p
(Reviewed by Leonard Kociemski in L'Italia Che Scrive
11, no 12:320 D '28)   2660
Očima západu. Translated by Josef Čihula. Praha: Laich-
ter, 1919. 435p   2661
Ruslands skygge. Translated by Jesper Ewald. Copen-
hagen: Martin, 1918. 286p   2662
Alma rusa. Translated by Juan Mateos de Diego. Introduc-
tion by Juan Estelrich. Barcelona: Montaner y Simón
[1925] 2 volumes: [v]-xlvi, 256p; [5]-248p. "José
Conrad," by Estelrich, Volume I, p[v]-xlvi   2663
Prowokator. Translated by Felicja Nossig. Lwów: Ludowe
Tow. Wydawnicze, 1920. 185p   2664

"The Unlighted Coast"

Polowanie na Zeppelina. Translated by W. D. Warszawianka
no 228, 1925   2665

VICTORY

Zwycięstwo. Translated by Aniela Zagórska. Lwów: Wydawnictwo Zakładu Nar. Imienia Ossolińskich, 1927.
2 volumes: xxi, 205p; 285p
(Reviewed by Stefan Kołaczkowski in Wiadomości Literackie 4, no 49:3 D 4 '27; R. Blüth in Polska Zbrojna

VICTORY (cont.)

    no 64, 1928; K. Czachowski in Czas no 20, 1928; M.
Dąbrowska in Świat Książek no 1, 1928; J. Gamska in
Słowo Pol. no 342, 1927; L. Pomirowski in Głos
Prawdy no 319, 1927; Wł. Tarnawski in Kurjer Poz-
nański no 518, 1927) 2666
Seger. Translated by Elin Palmgren. Stockholm: Bohlin,
1916. 444p 2667
.... Translated by Vera & Stig Dahlstedt. Stockholm:
Forum, 1952. 326p 2668
Sieg. Translated by Elsie McCalman. Berlin: S. Fischer
[1927] [9]-462p 2669
.... Translated by Walter Schürenberg. [Berlin:]
S. Fischer, 1963. 9-447p 2670
Victoria. Translated by Ramón D. Perés. Barcelona:
Montaner y Simón [1930] 2 volumes: [5]-255p; [5]-
357p 2671
Une victoire. Translated by Isabelle Rivière and Philippe
Neel. Le Temps Ap 4 - Je 11 '22; same published:
Paris: Nouvelle Revue Française [c1923] 2 volumes:
7-210p; 7-227p
(Reviewed by André Maurois in La Nouvelle Revue
Française 22:252-3 F '24; Charles Bastide in Revue
Critique d'Histoire et de Littérature ns 91:160 Ap 1
'24; Edmond Jaloux in Les Nouvelles Littéraires 2, no
60:6 D 8 '23) 2672
Nizzahon. Translated by Ester Kaspi. Tel-Aviv: "Am.
Oved." 1963. 229p 2672a
El solitario de Samburán. Translated by Carmen Gallardo
de Mesa. Mexico City: Lemuria, 1941. 189p 2673
Vitória. Translated by Leonel Vallandro. Pôrto Alegre:
Globo, 1942. 376p 2674
Overwinning. Translated by M. Blijstra van der Meulen.
Amsterdam: De Arbeiderspers, 1947. 380p 2675
Sejr. Translated by Knud Poulsen. Copenhagen: John Mar-
tin, 1920. 2 volumes: 176p; 354p 2676
Vítězství. Translated by Milada Nováková. Praha: Melant-
rich, 1929. 359p 2677
Vittoria. Translated by Gastone Rossi. Milan: Sonzogno
[1932] [11]-377p 2678
.... Translated by Enzo Giachino. Torino: Einaudi
[c1952] xvi, 5-362p; preface, p vii-xii
(Reviewed by Carola Ferrari in L'Italia Che Scrive 35,
no 10:179 O '52) 2678a
.... Translated by Gino Cornali. Milan: Speroni,
1946. 360p 2679
.... Translated by Francesco Pellizzi. Milan: Bompi-

ani, 1964. 5-449p
(Reviewed by Vincenzo de Tomasso in L'Italia Che
Scrive 48, no 4:270 Ap '65)   2679a
Seier.   Translated by Peter Magnus.   Oslo: Gyldendal,
1953. 325p   2680
Zwycięstwo.   W inscenizacji by Leon Schiller.   (A drama-
tization of the novel, produced at the Teatru Miejskiego
in Lwow, 1930)
(Reviewed by M. Piszczkowski in Lwowska Kurjer
Poranny no 266 '30; Gazeta Lwowska no 203 '30; W.
Moraczewski in Gazeta Lwowska no 217 '30; Słowo Pol.
nos 241-2 '30; A. Ćwikowski in Dzien. Lud. no 202
'30; H. Hescheles in Chwila no 4111 '30; T. Terlecki
in Słowo Pol. no 251, 1930; J. Jedlicz in Lwowskie
Wiadomości Muz. i Lit. no 10 '30)   2681

"The Warrior's Soul"

L'âme d'un guerrier.   Translated by Georges Jean-Aubry.
Revue de Paris 29, part 6:82-104 N 1 '22   2682
Dusza przeciwnika.   Translated by Józef Brodzki.   Wia-
domości Literackie 1, no 33:2 Ag 17 '24   2682a
Dusza wojownika.   Translated by Stanisław Wyrzykowski.
Gazeta Administracji i Pol. Pań. no 1, 1926   2683

"The Weight of the Burden"

Der Obersteuermann.   Translated by Görge Spervogel.   Neue
Rundschau 50, part 1:258-64 Mr '39   2684

WITHIN THE TIDES

Wśród prądów.   Translated by Teresa Tatarkiewicz.   War-
saw: Dom Książki Polskiej, 1928. 229p
(Reviewed by Stefan Kołaczkowski in Wiadomości Liter-
ackie 5, no 30:3 Jl 22 '28; K. Czachowski in Czas no
109 '28; Droga no 4 '28; E. Jędrkiewicz in Gazeta
Lwowska no 127 '28; J. Jodłowski in Głos Literackie
no 12 '28; J. Parandowski in Słowo Pol. no 158 '28;
A. Zagórska in Przegląd Powszechny no 534 '28)
                                                2685
En marge des marées.   Translated by Georges Jean-Aubry.
Paris: Nouvelle Revue Française, 1921. 2nd edition.
[7]-175p
(Reviewed in Times Literary Supplement Jl 6 '22 p442;
Benjamin Crémieux in Nouvelles Revue Française 19:
108-9 Jl 1 '22)   2686

WITHIN THE TIDES (cont.)
Entre mareas: El Colono de Malata; Por causa de los
dólares. Translated by Juan Guixé. Barcelona: Mon-
taner y Simón [c1931] [7]-200p (Contains also: The
Planter of Malata, Because of the Dollars) 2687
Zwischen Ebbe und Flut. Translated by Elsie McCalman.
Berlin: S. Fischer, 1937. 280p
(Reviewed by Richard Gerlach in Die Buchbesprechung
2: 104-5 Ap '38; W. E. Süskind in Die Literatur 40:
247 D 7 '37) 2688

YOUTH

Jugend, drei erzählungen. Translated by Ernst W. Freiss-
ler. Berlin: S. Fischer [1926] [3]-362p (Contains:
Youth, The Heart of Darkness, The End of the Tether)
(Reviewed by Karl Arns in Der Gral 21, heft 5:237-8
F '27) 2689
Jugend. Translated by Richard Mummendey. Frankfurt am
Main: Sauerländer, 1955. 64p 2689a
Conradova "Nahoda." Rozhledy Po Literatuře a Uměni 1:
119-20 N 2 '32 2690
Seishun. Translated by Nishijirô Tanaka. Tokyo: Shinchô-
Sha, 1951. 88p 2691
.... Translated by Miyanish Hoitsu. Tokyo: Kadoka-
wa Shoten, 1965 2691a
Youth and other stories. Translated into Japanese by
Shinzaburo Miyajima. 1929 2692
Juventud... Translated by Vicente Vera. Barcelona:
Montaner y Simón [c1931] [9]-181p (Contains: Youth,
translated by Vera; The Inn of the Two Witches and
"Un Socio" translated by Juan Guixé) 2693
Jeunesse. Translated by Marthe Duproix. Semaine Littér-
aire 29th année, no 1430:251-5; no 1431:268-72; no
1432:[275]-279 My 28 - Je 11 '21 2694
.... Translated by Georges Jean-Aubry. Revue de
Paris 32, no 9:89-107; no 10:339-57 My 1- 15 '25
2694a
Jeunesse suivi du Coeur des Ténèbres. Translated by
Georges Jean-Aubry and André Ruyters. Paris: Nou-
velle Revue Française, 1925. [7]-255p (Contains:
Youth, Heart of Darkness)
(Reviewed in Revue Hebdomadaire 12:117-18 D 5 '25;
Gabriel d'Aubarède in Cahiers du Sud année 12, no 75:
69-70 Ja '26; René Lalou in Revue Européenne 3rd
année, no 35, volume 6:67 Ja 1 '26; La Grande Revue
125:521 Ja '28) 2695

Młodość. Translated by Aniela Zagórska. Droga 1930,
p1-30   2696
Młodość. Jądro Ciemności. Translated by Aniela Za-
górska. Warsaw: Dom Książki Polskiej Spótka,
1930. 206p (Contains: Youth, Heart of Darkness)
(Reviewed in Droga no 1, 1930; K. Czachowski in
Czas no 254 '30; W. Horzyca in Gazeta Pol. no 311
'30 and Słowo Pol. nos 252-255 '31; K. Nitsch in
Język Polski 15, no 5 '30; A. Zahorska in Przegląd
Powszechny no 560 '30)   2697
Pozar na "Judei." Translated by Aniela Zagórska. Rome:
Polski Dom Wydawniczy, 1947. 52p   2698
Mladost. Translated by Griša Koritnik. Ljubljana:
Slovenski Knjiž ni Zavod, 1952. 158p   2699
. . . . Translated by Milenko Jovanović. Beograd:
Prosveta, 1948. 50p   2699a
. . . . Translated by Liuben Sečanov. Sofia: Nar.
Kniga, 1948. 52p   2700
. . . . Translated by Tin Ujević. Zagreb: "Zora,"
1950. 64p   2701
Ungdom. Translated by Sigurd Hoel. Oslo: Glydendal
Norsk Forlag, 1929. 3-195p   2702
. . . . Translated by C. T. Meldal. Copenhagen:
Martin, 1921. 174p   2703
Jeugd. Translated by A. Van der Vet. Antwerp: Wereld-
bibliotheek, Van Ditmar, 1952. 39p   2704
Jugend. Translated by Ernst W. Freissler. Leipzig:
Insel-Verlag, 1961. 62p   2705
Gioventù e altri due racconti. Translated by Piero Jahier
and Maj-Lis-Rissler Stoneman. Milan: Bompiani,
1949. 11-405p. Note by Jahier, p11-24; John Gals-
worthy's "Remembranze su Conrad," p25-41 (from his
Castles in Spain, p99-126). (Contains: Youth, Heart
of Darkness, The End of the Tether)   2706
Qiṣṣat al-Shabāb wa qalb al-Zulumāt. Al-Qāhirah: Dār
al-Kitab al-Misri, 1959. 259p   2706a
Mlodość i inne opowiadania. Translated by Aniela Zagórska.
Warsaw: Państwowy Instytut Wydawniczy, 1957. 381p
(Contains: Youth and Two Other Stories)
(Noted in Literatura Piękna 1957. Warsaw: 1958, p201;
Tygodnik Powszechny no 48:5 '57; M. C. Bradbrook in
Przegląd Kulturalny no 48:1, 3 '57; M. Dąbrowska in
Nowa Kultura no 49:3 '57; J. Iwaskiewicz in Życie
Literackie no 49:3 '57; Z. Broncel in Nowa Kultura no
1:3, 6-7 '58)   2707
Öregek és fiatalok. Budapest: Pantheon [nd] 7-272p
(Contains: Youth, The End of the Tether, and

YOUTH (cont.)
Amy Foster)   2708
Mocidade e outros contos.   Translated by Moura Brás.
Pórto: Livraria Civilização [1945] [19]-356p   2708a
Meistererzählungen.   Translated by Ernst W.
Elsie McCalman.   Zürich: Manesse-Verlag Conzett &
Huber [nd]   With afterword by Fritz Güttinger, p397-
412 (Contains: Youth, Heart of Darkness, Freya of
the Seven Isles)   2709

CONRAD, JOSEPH And HUEFFER, FORD MADOX

THE INHERITORS

Spadkobiercy.   Translated by Henryk Krzeczkowski.   Warsaw: Państwowy Instytut Wydawniczy, 1959.
244p
(Reviewed by Róża Jabłkowska in Nowe Książki no 1:
18-21 '60; noted in Literatura Piękna 1959. Warsaw:
1960.   p205-6)   2710
Gli eredi.   Translated by Claudio Gorlier and Luciano
Gallino.   Milan: Bompiani, 1966.   7-324p; introduction by Gorlier, p7-17   (Contains also: The Nature of
a Crime)   2710a

ROMANCE

Romanzo.   Translated by Vittorio Caselli.   Milano: Alpes,
1928.   432p   2711
L'aventure.   Translated by Marc Chadbourne.   Paris: Kra
[1926] [9]-451p
(Reviewed by J. D. in Les Nouvelles Littéraires 6, no
223:3 Ja 22 '27; Revue Nouvelle Ag-S '27 p80-1; Émile
Dermenghem in Europe 15, no 57:121-3 S 15 '27)
2712
Het Kapersnest.   Translated by Caspar Hendriks.   Tilburg:
Het Nederlandsche Boekhuis, 1927.   400p
(Reviewed by Kees Van Hoek in Boekzaal der Geheele
Wereld N 15 '27 p349-51; F. C. in Groot Nederland 26:
332-3 Mr '28)   2713
Przygoda.   Translated by Agnieszka Glinczanka.   Warsaw:
Państwowy Instytut Wydawniczy, 1960.   608p   2714
Avventura romantica.   Translated by Claudio Gorlier and
Luciano Gallino.   [Milan:]   Bompiani, 1964.   5-589p;
introduction by Gorlier, p5-23; note of the translators,
p587-9

Bibliographical Materials

Adams, Elbridge L.
Bibliographical notes. In Joseph Conrad: the man. A
  burial in Kent, by John Sheridan Zelie, together with
  some bibliographical notes. New York: Rudge, 1925.
  p55-72   2714a
American Art Association, Inc., New York
The Edward Garnett collection of inscribed books and
  autograph material by Joseph Conrad and W. H. Hudson... New York: American Art Association, 1928.
  74p
  "Foreword," by Richard Curle, p. 1.   Collection to be
  sold April 24 and April 25 [1928]   On the cover: "The
  Historic Edward Garnett Conrad-Hudson Collection"
  (Reviewed in New York Times Book Review Ap 22 '28
  p24)
Fine series of Conrad first editions, numbers 444 to 470
  inclusive. In The Charles Meeker Kozlay collection
  of Bret Harte... to which are added Mr. Kozlay's collection of first editions of modern authors, Conrad,
  etc.   To be sold March 18, 1926.   New York: American Art Association, Inc., 1926. unpaged
First editions, inscribed copies, and autograph letters of
  Joseph Conrad... New York: American Art Association, Nov. 21-23, 1938.   "Important series of Conrad
  first and autograph material," numbers 92-131, pages
  13-20
First editions of esteemed nineteenth century authors
  mainly in original bindings... To be sold April 1,
  1926.   New York: American Art Association, 1926.
  numbers 94-7
Important first editions, manuscripts and letters... mainly from English sources.   New York: American Art
  Association, 1928.
First editions of English and American authors.   The library of Ralph Samuel.   New York: American Art
  Association, Anderson Galleries, Inc., 1935. p6-8
The splendid Rudyard Kipling collection, formed by the
  late Arthur H. Scribner...   An extensive collection of

373

American Art Association, Inc. , (cont.)
  books. . . collected by the late Isabel Whitney Sage. . .
  First editions, autograph letters, and manuscripts by
  famous modern authors, selections from the libraries
  of Mrs. Florence E. Ramsay (and others). . . Public
  Sale April 22 and April 23. . . N. Y. : American Art Asso-
  ciation, Anderson Galleries, Inc. 1936. p34-7   2715
American collectors get many Conrad manuscripts. Herald
  Tribune (NY) Mr 14 '25
  (Sale at Hodgson's, London, on March 13, 1925)
                                                       2715a
Anderson Galleries, New York
  . . . Joseph Conrad: a fine series of unpublished letters to
  his publisher, T. Fisher Unwin. . . New York: Ander-
  son Galleries, 1927.
A remarkable group of Conrad first editions with special
  autograph inscriptions, signed (collected by Mr. Harry
  Glemby. . . sold. . . at. . . the Anderson Galleries. . .)
  New York: Anderson Galleries, 1926.   2716
Aubry, Georges Jean-
  Bibliography. In Joseph Conrad: life and letters. . .
  Garden City, New York: Doubleday, Page, 1927.
  Volume II, p351-61   2717
Babb, James T. (compiler)
  A check list of additions to a Conrad Memorial Library:
  1929-1938. Yale University Library Gazette 13:30-40
  Jl '38
  (Reviewed by Philip Brooks in New York Times Book
  Review Jl 24 '38 p19)   2718
Baker, Ernest Albert
  The history of the English novel. . . Yesterday. London:
  Witherby [1939] Volume X, p394-5   2719
Batho, Edith and Dobrée, Bonamy
  Bibliography. In The Victorians and after, 1830-1914.
  (Introductions to English and American literature. . .
  Volume IV) New York: McBride [c1938] p315   2720
Bennewitz, Hildegard
  Die charaktere in den romanen Joseph Conrads. (Greifs-
  walder Beiträge zur Literatur-und-Stilforschung, II)
  Griefswald: Dallmayer, 1933. iii-v; 70p; bibliography
  p67-70   2721
Bibliographies of modern authors. Joseph Conrad. London
  Mercury 2:476-477 Ag '20   2722
The bibliography of Joseph Conrad. Bookman's Journal 3rd
  series, 15, no 3:163-4 '27   2723
Bojarski, Edmund A. and Bojarski, Henry T.
  Joseph Conrad, a bibliography of masters' theses and

doctoral dissertations. (Occasional contributions, no
157) Lexington, Kentucky: Libraries of the University of Kentucky, 1964. 33p   2724
Books in the sale rooms. Bookman's Journal 12, no 47:
207 Ag '25   2725
Books in the sale rooms. High prices for Conrad manuscripts and books from his library. Bookman's Jour-
nal 12, no 43:30-1 Ap '25   2726
Books in the sale rooms. The Richard Curle Conrad Collection. Bookman's Journal 3rd series 15, no 2:106,
109-10, 113 '27   2727
Brown, Robert
Conrad by chance. Coronet 3:95-8 Ja '38; same. Lit-
erary Digest 125:15 F 5 '38   2728
Buyer of Conrad letters. New York Times D 20 '33 p19
(Mr. Alvin J. Scheuer)   2729
Cannon, Carl L.
Modern Literature. John Quinn. In American book col-
lectors and collecting. New York: Wilson, 1941.
p229-30   2730
Colby, Elbridge
A sample of bibliographical method. Bibliographical So-
ciety of America. Papers 16:[118]-136, 146 '23
                                                     2731
The collecting of first editions. Bookman's Journal & Print
Collector 10:216 S '24   2732
Colvin, (Sir) Sidney
Joseph Conrad, a splendid series of letters from 1904 to
1924. In ... Letters to the Colvins mainly about
Stevenson and Keats with a few others, sold by order
of E. V. Lucas... To be sold Monday afternoon and
evening May 7th... New York: Anderson Galleries,
1928. p18-47. Sale no 2267.
(Includes excerpts from many of the letters)   2733
A complete set of 26 pamphlets by Joseph Conrad, privately
printed by the author, Clement Shorter and T. J. Wise,
each limited to 25 copies, sold for Ł145 at Sotheby's
.....Saturday Review of Literature 2:123 S 12 '25
                                                     2734
Conrad, (Mrs.) Jessie (George)
The romance of first editions. Poland 8:662-4 N '27
(Includes a letter from J. S. Simpson to Joseph Conrad,
p664)   2735
Conrad after 100 years: books now in print. Saturday
Review 40:13 F 9 '57   2736
Conrad books offered. New York Times Ja 26 '36
(A part of the Elbridge L. Adams Collection at the

Conrad books offered (cont.)
  American Art Association Anderson Galleries, New
    York)   2736a
Conrad collection is sold for $10,000.   New York Times
    Mr 15 '25 p6
    (Conrad's books sold by his widow)   2737
Conrad first editions.   Publishers' Circular & Booksellers'
    Record 121:324 S 13 '24   2738
Conrad, Huxley, and Machen.   Bookman's Journal 13, no
    54:236 Mr '26   2739
Conrad mss. sale brings highest price ever paid for auto-
    graph work of living author.   Book Leaf (NY) N 23 '23
    (The ms. of Victory sold for $8,100)   2740
Conrad manuscripts.   Notes on sales.   Times Literary
    Supplement N 22 '23 p796   2741
The Conrad Mss.   Bookman's Journal & Print Collector 9,
    no 27:114-15 D '23   2742
Conrad ms. brings $2,200.   New York Times Ap 25 '28 p19
    (The typescript of Under Western Eyes is sold to
    Gabriel Wells)   2743
Conrad manuscript on Titanic brings $485 here.   New York
    Herald Tribune O 28 '24 p15
    (A sale at the Anderson Galleries)   2744
Conrad printed privately.   John O'London's Weekly 5:49
    Ap 16 '21   2745
A "Conrad" sale.   Publisher's Circular & Booksellers'
    Record 122:295 Mr 7 '25   2746
Conrad's book and mss.   Times Literary Supplement F 26
    '25 p144   2747
The Conrad sale.   Publishers' Circular & Booksellers'
    Record 122:363-4 Mr 21 '25   2748
Conrad's "Chance."   The real first edition and the "fakes."
    Bookman's Journal & Print Collector 3, no 57:77
    N 26 '20   2749
[Conrad's notebooks]   Newark Evening News no 13,019:5-x
    N 7 '25   2750
Coventry Public Libraries
    Some famous writers, IV.   Joseph Conrad novelist and
    seaman.   A bibliography of books and articles by and
    about Joseph Conrad in the Coventry Public Libraries.
    Coventry: Published by the Public Libraries Commit-
    tee [1924/?] 8p; portrait.   same.   Readers' Bulletin
    2, no 5: S-O '24
    (Reviewed by Clement King Shorter in Sphere 98:282
    S 6 '24)   2751
Curle, Richard Henry Parnell
    The bibliography of Chance.   Bookman's Journal

5:141 Ja '22

Early Conrad first editions. By an occasional con-
tributor. Bookman's Journal & Print Collector 4:189-
90 Jl 15 '21

The first U. S. Edition of Chance. Bookman's Journal 5,
no 5:175 F '22

A handlist of the various books, pamphlets, prefaces,
notes, articles, reviews and letters written about
Joseph Conrad by Richard Curle, 1911-1931. Compiled with an introduction and annotations by Richard
Curle. Brookville, Pennsylvania, 1932. 23p
(250 copies only)

List of Conrad's published books. In Joseph Conrad: a
study. Garden City, New York: Doubleday, Page,
1914. p237-8

New discoveries in the bibliography of Chance. By "A
Conrad collector." Bookman's Journal 5:81-2 D '21

Notes by Joseph Conrad, written in a set of his first editions in the possession of Richard Curle, with an introduction and explanatory comments. With a preface
by Jessie Conrad. London: Privately printed (by
Strangeways, printers) 1925. 41p
(100 copies only)

The Richard Curle Conrad collection. With thirty facsimile reproductions of autograph inscriptions and
manuscript pages throughout the text. New York:
American Art Association, Inc., [1927] [78]p; portrait
(Reviewed in Bookman's Journal series 3, volume 15,
no 2:106, 109-10, 112 '27; Times Literary Supplement
My 12 '27 p340; New York Times Ap 29 '27 p9; New
York Times Ap 30 '27 p18) 2752

Curle collection of Conrad is sold. New York Times Ap
29 '27 p9
(American Art Galleries sale of April 28) 2753

Currie, Barton
Fishers of books. Boston: Little, Brown, 1931. p32-6,
146, 148-9
(Photographs of original manuscripts of Victory and of
Typhoon facing p148) 2754

Cutler, Bradley D. and Stiles, Villa
Joseph Conrad, 1857-1924. In Modern British authors.
Their first editions. London: Allen & Unwin [1930]
p23-8
(300 copies for Great Britain and 1050 copies for
America only) 2755

Doubleday, Page & Co. , New York
Bibliography. In Joseph Conrad. Garden City: Double-
day, Page [1913?] p19-23
Books by Joseph Conrad. In Joseph Conrad. [Garden
City, New York: Doubleday, Page, nd] p[21]
Joseph Conrad: a bibliography. In Joseph Conrad.
Including an approach to his writings, a biographical
sketch, a brief survey of his works, and a bibliogra-
phy. Garden City, New York: Doubleday, Page
[c1926] p[57-60]
(Lists first editions)
A short bibliography of Joseph Conrad's works. In
Joseph Conrad, a sketch, with a bibliography, illus-
trated with many drawings by Edward A. Wilson.
Garden City, New York: Doubleday, Page [c1924]
p40-5   2756
Dougan, Elsie Caroline
Bibliography. Joseph Conrad. [1931] Manuscript at the
Drexel Institute of Technology Library, Philadelphia.
11f   2756a
Early Conrad first editions. Bookman's Journal 4:189-90
Jl 15 '21   2756b
[Early issue of the first edition of The Nigger of the
'Narcissus.'] Bookman's Journal & Print Collector 9,
no 25:30 O '23   2757
Edgar, Pelham
Bibliography. In The art of the novel from 1700 to the
present time. New York: Macmillan, 1933. p387-90
                                                       2758
Eno, Sara Wooster
Joseph Conrad. A contribution toward a bibliography.
Bulletin of Bibliography 9:137-9 Ap '17   2759
Evans, Henry Herman (compiler)
A guide to rare books. San Francisco, California:
Porpoise Book Shop, 1948. p20
(Refers to The Nigger of the 'Narcissus' and Chance)
                                                       2760
Fabes, Gilbert H.
Joseph Conrad. In Modern first editions: points and
values. London: W. & G. Foyle [1929] p6-10
(750 copies only)
Joseph Conrad. In Modern first editions: points and
values. London: W. & G. Foyle [1932] 3rd series,
p13-14
(750 copies only)   2761
The first edition of Conrad's Chance. Bookman's Journal
& Print Collector 3:109-10 D 10 '20

(Several correspondents, including Thomas James
     Wise) 2762
The first issue of Chance. Bookman's Journal 3rd series,
     volume 16, no 6:352-3 '28 2763
Flynn, William J.
     Conrad on the frontier. Publishers' Weekly 108:1727-
     8 N 21 '15 2764
Garnett, Edward
     A chronological list of the published works of Joseph Con-
     rad. In Conrad's prefaces to his works. With an in-
     troductory essay by Edward Garnett and a biographical
     note on his father by David Garnett. London: Dent
     [1937] p[213]-18 2765
Gee, John Archer
     The Conrad Memorial Library of Mr. George T. Keating.
     Yale University Library Gazette 13:16-28 Jl '38
          2766
Gee, John Archer and Sturm, Paul J.
     Bibliography. In Letters of Joseph Conrad to Marguerite
     Poradowska, 1890-1920... New Haven: Yale Univer-
     sity Press, 1940. p[141]-3 2767
Gordan, John Dozier
     General bibliography. In Joseph Conrad: the making of
     a novelist. Cambridge, Massachusetts: Harvard Uni-
     versity Press, 1940. p[311]-31; ['Notes'] p[333]-415
          2768
Grzegorczyk, Piotr
     Bibljografja Joseph Conrad w Polsce. Ruch Literacki
     7, no 8:255-6, no 9:276-84 Ag-S '32; same published:
     Warsaw: J. Rajskiego, 1933. 14p
     Bibljoteka Conrada. Ruch Literacki 2, no 5:159 My '27
          2769
Haslam, G. E. (editor)
     Wise after the event. A catalogue... Manchester: Li-
     braries Committee, 1964. p33-4
     (Lists 16 Conrad titles which were privately printed)
          2769a
High prices for Conrad Mss. and books from his library.
     Bookman's Journal 12, no 43:30-2 Ap '25 2770
High prices for Hardy's The Dynasts and a Conrad Ms.
     Bookman's Journal & Print Collector 9, no 28:145-6
     Ja '24 2771
Hill, Robert W. and Lewis M. Stark
     The Edward S. Harkness collection. New York Public
     Library Bulletin 54:585-94 D '50 2772
Hodgson, S.
     Higher prices for Conrad first editions. Publishers'

Hodgson, S. (cont.)
Circular & Booksellers' Record 113:476-7 O 16 '20
2773
Hodgson & Co., Booksellers, London.
A catalogue of books, manuscripts, and corrected type-
scripts from the library of the late Joseph Conrad,
sold by order of Mrs. Conrad and the executors...
which will be sold at auction by Messrs. Hodgson &
Co... on Friday, March 13th, 1925... London: Hodg-
son & Co., 1925. 19p; "Preface," by Richard Curle
(Noted in Times Literary Supplement F 26 '25 p144;
Mark Over in Outlook (London) 55:159 Mr 7 '25; Bos-
ton Evening Transcript My 18 '25 pt 3, p5; noted in
New York Herald Tribune Mr 14 '25 p7; New York
Times Book Review Mr 1 '25 p24)   2774
Hopkins, Frederick M.
Curle sale of Conradiana. Publishers' Weekly 111:2186-
8 Je 4 '27   2775
The J. B. Pinker collection of Conradiana. Bookman's
Journal & Print Collector 11, no 40:190-1 Ja '25
2775a
Joerden, R.
Joseph Conrad. Bücherei und Bildungspflege 10:271-9
'30   2775b
Joseph Conrad Mss. Bookman's Journal & Print Collector
9, no 27: 105, 114-15 D '23   2776
Joseph Conrad's library. Publishers' Circular & Book-
sellers' Record 122:305 Mr 7 '25   2777
Keating, George T.
A Conrad memorial library: the collection of George T.
Keating. Garden City, New York: Doubleday, Doran,
1929. vii-xvi, 448p; portrait
(501 copies only)
(Reviewed by Richard Curle in Saturday Review of
Literature 6:343 N 2 '29 and in Daily Telegraph
(London) N 6 '29 p12)   2778
Korbut, Gabrjel
Literatura polska od poczatków do wojny swiatowej. War-
saw: Im. Mianowskiego, 1929-1931. Volume IV,
1864-1914, p314-16   2778a
Korzeniowska, Jessie Conrad
See: Conrad, (Mrs.) Jessie (George)   2779
Krzyżanowski, Ludwik
Joseph Conrad. A bibliographical note. In Joseph Con-
rad: centennial essays, edited by Ludwik Krzyżanow-
ski. New York: Polish Institute of Arts and Sciences
in America, 1960. p163-74

A tentative selected bibliography for a study of the Polish
antecedents of Joseph Conrad. [Washington, District
of Columbia: Photoduplication Service, Library of
Congress, 1955] xiii, 114p   2780
Kunitz, Stanley J. and Haycraft, Howard (editors)
  Joseph Conrad. In Twentieth century authors. New
  York: Wilson, 1942. p309-10   2781
Latcham, Ricardo
  La obra novelesca de Joseph Conrad. Nosotros epoca 2,
  tomo 19, año 7, no 79:51-2 O '42   2782
Lohf, Kenneth A. and Sheehy, Eugene P.
  Joseph Conrad at mid-century, editions and studies, 1895-
  1955. Minneapolis, Minnesota: University of Minne-
  sota Press [c1957] vii-xiii, 114p
  (Reviewed by Joseph Swastek in Polish American Studies 14, nos 1-2:59-60 Ja-Je '57; Wiadomości 12, no
  51-2:29 D 22-29 '57)   2783
London. The Polish Library.
  Catalogue of an exhibition organized by the Polish Library
  at the request of the Union of Polish Writers abroad to
  commemorate Mr. John Conrad's lecture at the General Sikorski Historical Institute on the 30th of October,
  1956. Compiled by Janina Zabielska. London: The
  Polish Library, 5 Princes Gardens, S.W. 7, 1956.
  24p   2784
Long ms. by Conrad brings $2400 at sale. New York Times
  Mr 12 '36 p17
  (The manuscript of Under Western Eyes)   2785
Mackay, W. MacDonald
  The bibliography of Joseph Conrad. Bookman's Journal
  3rd series volume 15, no 3:163-4 '27
  (Answered by Mr. T. J. Wise, pages 226-7)   2786
Manuscript collecting [by "The Collector"] Bookman (London)
  78:311 Ag '30   2787
Mégroz, Rodolphe Louis
  Bibliographical list of Conrad's works. In Joseph Con-
  rad's mind and method; a study of personality in art.
  London: Faber & Faber [1931] p249-56
  Conradiana. In Joseph Conrad's mind and method; a
  study of personality in art. London: Faber & Faber
  [1931] p257-62   2788
Millett, Fred B.
  Contemporary British literature: a critical survey and
  232 author-bibliographies... New York: Harcourt,
  Brace, 1935. 3rd revised and enlarged edition, p178-
  83   2789

More frauds of the book forger. Conrad's A Set of Six...
    Bookman's Journal 3:177 Ja 7 '21   2790
North, Ernest Dressel
    Youth: A Narrative and Two Other Stories. In Famous
    fiction. A catalogue of one hundred first editions.
    New York: North, December, 1928. number 22
                                                            2791
Notes on rare books. New York Times Book Review Jl
    24 '38 p19
    (The opening of the Conrad Memorial Library of
    George T. Keating)   2792
100 Conrad letters sold. New York Times D 19 '33 p19
    (The letters of Joseph Conrad to Madame Poradowska)
                                                            2793
Overton, Grant
    In the kingdom of Conrad (and bibliography). Bookman
    (NY) 57:284 My '23; same. In Authors of the day...
    New York: George H. Doran [1922] p53-6; same. In
    American nights entertainment. New York: Appleton,
    1923. p87-90   2794
Partington, Wilfred
    [Notes on Life and Letters] Bookman's Journal & Print
    Collector 7, no 13:25 O '22
    Privately printed books, pamphlets, etc., issued by
    Thomas James Wise. In Forging ahead... New York:
    Putnam's [c1939] p291-2; same. In Thomas J. Wise
    in the original cloth... London: Robert Hale [c1946]
    p330-1   2795
Passing remarks. John O'London's Weekly 4:558 F 5 '21
                                                            2796
Quinn, John
    Complete catalogue of the library of John Quinn, sold by
    auction in five parts (with printed prices)... New
    York: Anderson Galleries, 1924. 2 volumes
    ...The library of John Quinn. Part One. (A-C) The
    manuscripts and books of Joseph Conrad which will be
    sold Tuesday evening, November 13, at 8:15. New
    York: Anderson Galleries, 1923. 50p
    (At Head of Title: Sale Number 1768.)
    (Noted in Manchester Quarterly Ag 7 '24 p5)   2797
Randall, David
    Copies of Conrad's Chance, dated '1913.' Book Collector
    15, no 1:68 Spring '66   2797a
Rare Conradiana. Bookman's Journal & Print Collector 11,
    no 39:129 D '24 (J. B. Pinker's Collection)   2798
Rare Conrad items. Book Leaf (NY) My 4 '27   2799
Rare autographs up for sale at auction; 104 Conrad letters.

New York Herald Tribune Ap 29 '28 (The letters of
Joseph Conrad to Sir Sidney Colvin, sold at Anderson
Galleries, New York, May 7, 1928)   2800
A record Nigger. Bookman's Journal 3rd series 16, no 6:
354-5 '28   2801
Rosenbach, (Dr.) A. S. W.
Books and bidders... Boston: Little, Brown, 1927.
p143-5 (Photographs of the original manuscripts of
Victory and Lord Jim)   2802
Rosenbach Company, Philadelphia and New York
The sea; books and manuscripts... Philadelphia and New
York: Rosenbach Co., 1938. p40-1   2803
Sadleir, Michael
Joseph Conrad (1857-1924). In The dictionary of national
biography... 1922-1930. Edited by R. H. Weaver.
London: Oxford University press [1937] p209-10 2804
A sale of Conrad letters (including 105 letters from Conrad
to Madame Poradowska) Saturday Review of Literature
10:453 F 3 '34   2805
[Sale of two Conrad volumes at Hodgson's sale, Oct. 21-23,
1925] Bookman's Journal 13: no 50:77 N '25 2806
Sanger, Vincent
Bibliographies of younger reputations. IV -- Joseph Con-
rad (Korzeniowski). Bookman (NY) 35:70-1 Mr '12
                                            2807
Sargent, George H.
American notes. Bookman's Journal & Print Collector
10:12 Ap '24
(On the Quinn Sale at the Anderson Galleries, New
York)
Conrad manuscripts in America. Bookman's Journal &
Print Collector 9, no 28:137-9 Ja '24 (illustration,
facing p137)   2808
Sawyer, Charles J. and Darton, Frederick J. Harvey
English books, 1475-1900; a signpost for collectors.
Westminster: Charles J. Sawyer, 1927. volume II,
p363-5   2809
Schwartz, (Dr.) Jacob
Joseph Conrad. In 1100 obscure points... The bibliogra-
phies of 25 English and 21 American authors... Lon-
don: Ulysses bookshop [1931] p15-17; facsimile of title-
page of The Nigger of the 'Narcissus,' first edition,
facing p iv
(1st edition of 666 numbered copies only)   2810
Shorter, Clement King
[Prices of manuscripts sold at the Anderson Galleries]
Sphere 95:364 D 22 '23   2811

Sim, George
    Copies of Conrad's Chance, dated '1913.' Book Collector
        15, no 2:213-14 Summer '66   2811a
Some Wise Conrads. The Month At Goodspeed's Jan. 1943,
        p100-2, volume 14, no 4
        (Lists 10 privately printed Conrad pamphlets)   2812
Sotheby, Wilkinson & Hodge, London
    A collection of the writings of Joseph Conrad (The major-
        ity inscribed by the author.) The Property of the late
        James B. Pinker, Esquire... In Catalogue of Valuable
        Printed Books... London. To be sold Dec. 15-17,
        1924.
        Pages 73-79, items 620-677   2813
Stark, Lewis M. & Robert W. Hill
    The bequest of Mary Stillman Harkness. New York Pub-
        lic Library Bulletin 55:213-24 My '51   2814
Stauffer, Ruth Mathilda
    Joseph Conrad; his romantic-realism. Boston: Four
        Seas, 1922. [7]-122p
    "Bibliographies," p91; "Conrad's Works," p92-101;
        "Criticisms of Conrad," p102-8; "Book Reviews," p109-
        15; "Miscellaneous," p116-17;   "Romanticism and Real-
        ism," p118-22   2815
Thomson, J. C.
    The "how" and "why" of cancel pages. Bookman's Journal
        & Print Collector 3:209 Ja 21 '21   2816
Thurston, Jarvis et. al.
    Short fiction criticism. Denver: Alan Swallow, 1960.
        p33-9, 2334   2817
    Title-page note in the handwriting of Joseph Conrad on the
        manuscript of "One Day More."... Bookman's Journal
        & Print Collector 13, no 54:225 Mr '26   2818
Todd, William Burton
    A handlist of Thomas J. Wise. In Thomas J. Wise.
        Centenary studies, edited by William B. Todd. Austin,
        Texas: Univ. of Texas Press, 1959. p89   2818a
Turner, Michael L.
    Conrad and T. J. Wise. Book Collector 15, no 3:350-1
        Autumn '66
        (Gives list of pamphlets privately printed for T. J.
        Wise, ms. sold to him, with the prices paid)   2818b
Union Art Galleries, Inc. , New York
    ...Important first editions, autographs and manuscripts,
        press books and bindings, an unusual series of in-
        scribed Conrad items... from the collection of Mr. G. I.
        Lehman... Public auction sale, Wednesday & Thursday
        evenings, May 23 & 24, 1934, at 8 o'clock. New York:

Union Art Galleries, Inc., 1934. Sale no 27.
(Includes 5 unpublished letters from Conrad to Perce-
val Gibbon; p.18-25)   2819
Van Patten, Nathan
An index to bibliographies and bibliographical contribu-
tions relating to the work of American and British
authors, 1923-1932. Stanford University, California:
Stanford University Press, 1934. p54-5   2820
Wagenknecht, Edward
Cavalcade of the English novel from Elizabeth to George
VI. New York: Holt [c1943] p611-13   2821
Walpole, Hugh
American bibliography. A short bibliography of Joseph
Conrad's principal writings. In Joseph Conrad. New
York: Holt [1916] p121-2, 123-4   2822
Warner, Oliver
Joseph Conrad, a select bibliography. In Joseph Conrad.
London: Published for the British Council and the Na-
tional Book League by Longmans, Green [1950] p33-8
Select bibliography. In Joseph Conrad. (Men and books)
London: Longmans, Green & Co. [1951] p183-9
                                                   2823
Williams, I.A.
Modern first editions. Observer (London) Ja 16 '21 p5
                                                   2824
Winterich, John T.
Collector's choice. New York: Greenberg [c1928] p61-2,
101-3, 131-2, 158-60   2825
Wise, Thomas James
The Ashley Library... London: Printed for private cir-
culation only, 1922. Volume I, p231-59. London:
1926. Vol. VIII, p115-33
The bibliography of Conrad. Bookman's Journal 3rd
series 15, no 4:226-7 '27
(An answer to W. Mackay)
A bibliography of the writings of Joseph Conrad (1895-
1920). London: Printed for private circulation only by
Richard Clay & Sons, Ltd., 1920. [vii]-xv, 107p
(150 copies only)
(Reviewed by Edmund Gosse in Sunday Times Ja 2 '21
p6)
A bibliography of the writings of Joseph Conrad (1895-
1921). London: Printed for private circulation only by
Richard Clay & Sons, Ltd., 1921. [vii]-xv, 125p;
frontispiece portrait. 2nd edition, revised and enlarged.
(170 copies only). Reprinted in 1964 by Dawson's of
Pall Mall

Wise, Thomas James (cont.)
(Reviewed by Edmund Gosse in Sunday Times (London)
Ja 2 '21 p6)
A Conrad library. A catalogue of printed books, manu-
scripts and autograph letters by Joseph Conrad... col-
lected by Thomas James Wise. London: Printed for
private circulation only, (by the Dunedin Press, Edin-
burgh) 1928. vii-xvii, 66p.
"Introduction," by Richard Curle, p[v]-xvii
(180 copies only on antique paper)
Conrad's first editions. Bookman's Journal & Print Col-
lector 3:160 D 31 '20
Mr. Wise and A Set of Six. Bookman's Journal & Print
Collector 3:177 Ja 7 '21   2826
Wright, Elizabeth and Hendrick, George (editors)
Bibliography. Studies in Short Fiction 2:392-3 Summer
'65
Bibliography. Studies in Short Fiction 3, no 4:483
Summer '66   2827
Zabel, Morton Dauwen
Bibliographical note. In The portable Conrad. New York:
Viking press, 1947. p758-60   2828
Zabielska, Janina
See: London. The Polish Library.   2829

Joseph Conrad
Photographs, Portraits, Drawings,
Sketches, Caricatures in Periodicals

Academy 55:82 O 15 '98; 67:59 Jl 23 '04   2830
Argonaut 72:250 Ap 19 '13   2831
Art and Archaeology 20:19 Jl '25 (Walter Tittle)   2832
Arts and Decoration 16:277 F '22 (William Rothenstein);
    21, no 5:36 S '24   2833
Annales Politique et Littéraire 106:369 O 10 '35   2834
Atlantic Bookshelf Ap '26   2835
Book Buyer 16:390 Je '98   2836
Book Leaf (NY) My 4 '23; N 23 '23   2837
Book Monthly 14:674 S '19 (photo by Malcolm Arbuth-
    not)   2837a
Book News Monthly 27:423 F '08   2838
Bookman (London) 10:41 My '96 (photo by Emberson & Sons);
    19:161 F '01; 20:173 S '01; 39:177 and facing p172 Ja
    '11; 40:207 Ag '11 (by Max Beerbohm); 45:265 F '14;
    49:86 D '15; 57:27 O '19 (Laurence Stone); 58:161 Ag
    '20 (Will Cadby photo); 65:237 F '24; 66:9 Ap '24; 66:
    303 S '24 (Will Cadby); 67: facing p164 supplement D
    '24 (in color by Walter Tittle); 68:facing p17 Ap '25
    (bust by Jacob Epstein); 69:95, 97 N '25; 70:238-9 Ag
    '26; 73:250 Ja '28; 75:8 O '28; 78:311 Ag '30   2839
Bookman (NY) 3:397 Jl '98; 35:65 Mr '12; 37:595 Ag '13
    (Will Rothenstein); 41:470 Jl '15; 42:637 F '16; 45:637
    Ag '17 (Jo Davidson); 46:658 F '18; 57:587 Jl '23; 60:
    247 O '24 (sketch by Dwight Taylor); 66:facing p481 Ja
    '28 (Amero)   2840
Bookmark (London) 2, no 5:2 Spring '26; 3, no 10:16 Je '27;
    1, no 2:13 Summer '25   2841
Blue Peter 5:318, 325 O '25; 10:306, 349 Je-Jl '30; 11, no
    110:253 My '31; ns 3, no 19:250 O '23   2842
Bookseller & Stationer (Toronto) 39, no 12:44 D '23; 40,
    no 9:43 S '24   2843
Boston Evening Transcript Ap 3 '15 part 3 p4 (Will Cadby);
    Ja 22 '16 part 3 p6; My 5 '17 part 3 p6; Ap 19 '19
    part 3 p8; My 26 '20 part 3 p4; Ap 6 '21 (drawing by
    Lilleso from a photo); Ap 30 '21 part 4 p5; Dec 17 '21

Boston Evening Transcript (cont.)
(Will Rothenstein); My 2 '23 p5; My 12 '23 (Walter
Tittle); O 20 '23 Book section part 6 p1-2; D 8 '23
Book section p4 (Oscar Césare); N 5 '24 part 2 p7;
Ap 25 '25 Book section p2; Ag 1 '25 Book section part
6 p1 (drawing by Krieg Hoff); S 19 '25 Book section
p5 (portrait by Bertrand Zadig); S 17 '27 Book section
p4   2844
Brentano's Book Chat 8, no 5:33 S-O '29 (caricature) 2845
Boekzaal p350, 1927; no 17:261 S 1 '29; no 21:333 N 1
'31   2846
Canadian Bookman 3, no 1:facing p1 Je '21; 13:29 F '31
                                                      2847
Century Magazine 106:55 My '23; 108:643 S '24   2848
Chicago Daily Tribune D 1 '23 p10; F 7 '25 p9; S 26 '25
(by T. & R. Annan & Sons); Mr 27 '26 p16 (Bertrand
Zadig); F 7 '15 part 8 p4; Je 12 '20 p13; D 1 '23 p10;
Ag 4 '24 p1   2848a
Christian Science Monitor S 19 '25 p7 (Bertrand Zadig)
                                                      2848b
Columbia University Forum 5, no 1:29-35 Winter '62   2849
Courier (London) 24, no 2:63 F '55 (Walter Tittle)   2849a
Critic (NY) 42:396 My '03   2850
Current Literature 52:470 Ap '12   2851
Current Opinion (NY) 56:374 My '14; 58:351 My '15; 67:321
D '19; 70:821 Je '21 (Malcolm Arbuthnot); 72:239 F
'22 (William Rothenstein); 73:478 O '22; 74:677 Je '23
(Quiz); 74:686 Je '23; 77:304, 313 S '24   2852
Daily Mail (London) Mr 8 '18 p2; Ap 7 '22 p8; D 24 '23 p4;
Ag 15 '24 p8   2853
Daily News (Chicago) My 26 '20 p12 (Lilleso); Ag 4 '24 p5
                                                      2853a
Daily News & Leader (London) Mr 29 '15 p4   2854
Daily Sketch (London) O 27 '22 p10-11   2855
Delineator 101, no 1:11 Ag '22; 103:10 D '23   2856
Dziś i Jutro 10, no 32:3 Ag 8 '54; 11, no 24:4 Je 19 '55
                                                      2856a
English Review 9:facing p476 O '11 (William Rothenstein)
                                                      2857
Evening News (London) My 15 '23 p4   2858
Evening Sun (NY) Ap 19 '19 p9   2859
Evening World (NY) My 2 '23 p23 (Will B. Johnstone) 2859a
Everybody's Magazine 53:94 O '25   2860
Everyman 3, no 59:201 N 28 '13 (W. H. Caffyn); ns 1, no
2:26 N '53   2861
Graphic 100:232 Ag 16 '19; 102:66 Jl 10 '20; 108:922 D 15
'23; 110:198 Ag 9 '24; 110:728 N 1 '24   2862

Harper's Weekly 49:59, 690 Ja 14, My 13 '05   2863
Illustrated London News 131:410 S 21 '07; 133:342 S 5 '08;
    139:686 O 28 '11; 157:108 Jl 17 '20; 161:240 Ag 12 '22;
    165:280 Ag 9 '24; 165:441 S 6 '24 (Will Cadby)   2864
Independent 65:1066 N 5 '08; 113:108 Ag 16 '24   2865
Indianapolis News Ag 4 '24 p19   2865a
John O'London's Weekly 1:621 S 6 '19; 2:171 N 22 '19;
    3:437 Jl 24 '20; 3:353 Jl 3 '20; 4:798 Ap 2 '21; 6:
    supplement D 10 '21 (R. G. Mathews); 7:493 Jl 22 '22;
    8:853 Mr 17 '23; 10:418 D 15 '23; 11:60, 561, 691,
    813, 850 Ap 12, Jl 19, Ag 23, S 20, S 27 '24; 12:321,
    502 N 29, D 27 '24; 12:775 F 1 '25; 13:758 S 12 '25;
    14:35 O 3 '25; 14:697 F 6 '26; 15:285 My 22 '26; 15:
    768 S 25 '26; 33:590 Jl 27 '35; 34:121 O 19 '35   2866
Juridical Review 40:facing p250 S 1 '28   2867
Land and Water no 2957: inside front cover Ja 9 '19; no
    2959: inside front cover Ja 23 '19   2868
Les Nouvelles Littéraires 3, no 115:5 D 27 '24; 6, no 242:
    8 Je 4 '27; 7, no 301:8 Jl 21 '28; S 16 '33; no 819:5
    Je 25 '38; 42, no 1927:7 Ag 6 '64; 8, no 368:1 N 2
    '29   2869
Listener 36:480 O 10 '46 (etching by Walter Tittle); 32,
    no 811:102 Jl 27 '44 (Percy Anderson); 72:554 D 17
    '64   2870
Literary Digest 26, no 15:547 Ap 11 '03; 29, no 1:12 Jl 2
    '04; 29, no 4:119 Jl 23 '04; 42:207 F 4 '11; 77, no
    7:27 My 19 '23; 80, no 11:46 Mr 15 '24; 82:27, 29, 48
    Ag 23, S 13 '24 (Keystone View Company)   2871
Literary Digest International Book Review 2:31, 67 D '23
    (photo by T. & R. Annan & Sons, Glasgow); 3:705
    O '25   2872
Literary Review of the New York Evening Post Ap 28 '23
    p645 (caricature); Krieghoff in Ag 9 '24 p946; S 19
    '25 p1   2873
Living Age 335:132-3 O '28   2874
London Magazine 25:802 F '11   2875
London Mercury 7:119 D '22; 32:330a Ag '35 (E. M. Heath)
                                                      2876
Lookout (NY) 18, no 9:15 S '27; 25, no 1:1 Ja '34   2877
Mainly About Books ns 17: no 1:1 Winter '23-'24 (photos
    by G. C. Beresford)   2878
Manchester Guardian Weekly 7, no 23:453 D 8 '22; 11, no
    6:124 Ag 8 '24   2879
Mentor 11:53 Jl '23; 12, no 4:45 My '24; 13, no 2:front
    cover, 1 (May Mott Smith); 2-3, 5, 7, 9, 11-12, 20,
    24, 26 (bust by Jacob Epstein); Mr '25; 13, no 11:56
    D '25   2880

Naokoƚo Świata no 5:73-4 '24   2881
National Magazine 52:31 Je '23   2882
Newark Evening News no 12, 631:4 Ag 4 '24   2883
Manchester Guardian Ag 4 '24 p8 (photo by Alvin L. Co-
    burn); Ag 6 '24 p5 (portrait first done in 1923 by
    Muirhead Bone)   2884
New Statesman 20:supplement F 13 '26 (caricature by
    Low)   2885
New York American O 10 '26 March of Events Section p3;
    O 17 '26 March of Events Section p3; O 24 '26 March
    of Events section p4; O 31 '26 March of Events Sec-
    tion p3; O 3 '26 editorial section p1   2886
New York Evening Post Saturday Graphic Section IV My 12
    '23 p4   2887
Newsweek 49:94 F 4 '57   2888
New York Herald My 2 '23 p24   2889
New York Herald Books Ap 29 '23 (photo by Malcolm
    Arbuthnot)   2889a
New York Herald Tribune Books O 4 '25 p20; N 21 '26 p6;
    O 2 '27 p11; Ap 1 '28 p2; S 30 '28 p1 (Walter Tittle)
                                                 2890
New York Herald & New York Tribune Magazine-Fiction-
    Books Ag 24 '24 Sections 10-11 p1   2891
New York Herald Tribune Magazine & Books N 25 '23 p28
                                                 2892
New York Herald & New York Tribune Ag 4 '24 p1   2893
New York Herald Tribune N 13 '27 Section III p2; My 13
    '34 Section VI p8   2894
New York Herald Tribune Magazine Ag 24 '30 p1   2895
New York Times Ag 4 '24 p1   2896
New York Times Book Review My 30 '20 p290; My 8 '21
    p10; Ja 1 '22 p1; O 1 '22 p2; Ap 29 '23 p6; Je 10
    '23 p1; Ag 26 '23 p9 (Oscar Césare); D 16 '23 p32;
    Ag 10 '24 p1; Ag 31 '24 p11; My 10 '25 p3; Ag 9 '25
    p13; D 7 '24 p3; Mr 28 '26 p3; S 18 '27 p1; Je 16 '35
    p11; S 29 '35 p4; S 13 '42 p30; Ap 4 '43 p30; Ja 11
    '48 p29; Ag 14 '49 p1 (Jacob Epstein); D 1 '57 p7
                                                 2897
New York Times Magazine My 13 '23; N 30 '24 p16 2898
New York Tribune My 2 '23 p11; My 6 '23 Graphic Section
    p1; Mr 27 '15 p10; My 17 '19 p8   2899
New York Tribune Book News & Reviews Ap 29 '23 p19,
    21   2900
New York Tribune Magazine & Review O 26 '19 Part VII
    p4   2901
New York World Ap 13 '19 editorial section p5E; D 9 '23
    editorial section p 6E; O 25 '25 third section p6M;

Je 3 '23 Second News Section p 1S (Walter Tittle)
                                                        2902
North American (Philadelphia) Ap 19 '19 p14   2903
La Nouvelle Revue Française 23:I-II D '24   2904
Nowa Kultura 10, no 21:1 My 24 '59   2904a
Observer (London) N 8 '25 p5   2905
Outlook (NY) (Jo Davidson) 124:382 Mr 3 '20; (Jo Davidson)
    125:280 Je 9 '20; 133:709, 884 Ap 18, (P. & A. Photo)
    My 16 '23; 137:562 Ag 13 '24 (Keystone Photo); 139:
    138 Ja 28 '25   2906
Overland Monthly 83, no 4:180 Ap '25   2907
Philadelphia Inquirer O 3 '25 p22   2908
Philadelphia Record My 12 '17 p14; My 1 '21 p12   2909
Pictorial Review 24, no 12:17 S '23   2910
Poland 5, no 2:87 F '24; no 4:226 Ap '24; no 7:74 Jl '24;
    8:138 Ag '24; 9:141, 143-4, 202 S '24 (Walter Tittle);
    6, no 1:66 Ja '25; no 2:130 F '25; 3:202 Mr '25; 5:
    322 My '25; 8:497, 513 Ag '25; 7, no 8:469 Ag '26;
    no 9:542, 544, 575, 577 S '26; no 10:615 O '26; 8, no
    1:49 Ja '27; 2:113 F '27; 3:171 Mr '27   2911
Pologne Littéraire 1, no 3:1 D 15 '26; 5, no 54:1 Mr 15
    '31; 9, nos 94-95:7 Jl 15-Ag 15 '34   2912
Popular Boating (NY) 7, no 3:138 Mr '60   2912a
Public Ledger (Philadelphia) Ja 29 '16 p13; My 12 '17 p14;
    D 1 '23 p16; S 19 '25 p15   2913
Public Opinion (NY) 35:472 O 8 '03   2914
Publishers' Circular & Booksellers' Record 119:785 D 15
    '23; 122:1 Ja 3 '25   2915
Publishers' Weekly 85:1336 Ap 18 '14; 91:1343 Ap 21 '17;
    99:948 Mr 19 '21; 103:1383 My 5 '23; 106:500 Ag 9
    '24   2916
Queen 5, no 4052:5 Ag 20 '24   2917
Reclams Universum (Leipzig) 43, no 52:1353 S 22 '27
                                                        2918
Review of Reviews (NY) 27:630 My '03; 45:557 My '12;
    51:761 Je '15   2919
Saturday Evening Post 197:12-13 S 13 '24   2920
Saturday Review (London) 134:537 O 14 '22 (Quiz)   2920a
Saturday Review of Literature (NY) 1:27 Ag 9 '24; 1:197 O
    18 '24 (C. Moorepark); 1:206 O 18 '24; 1:385 D 13
    '24; 4:193 O 15 '27; 17:3 Ja 15 '38; 31:7 My 22 '48
    (David Low); 33:10 Ap 22 '50; 40, no 6: front page
    and p12-13 F 9 '57   2921
Scholastic 29, no 11:24 D 5 '36   2922
Schoolmaster & Woman Teachers' Chronicle ns 113, no
    973:1 F 2 '28   2923
Seafarer (London) no 37:7-8 Ja '43   2924

Semaine Littéraire année 29, no 1432:275 Je 11 '21; année
30, no 1500:489 S 30 '22; année 32, no 1599:405 Ag
23 '24 2925
Sketch 14:62 My 6 '96; 77:150 F 7 '12; 125:275 F 6 '24
2926
Sphere 13:132 My 9 '03; 31:142 N 16 '07; 56:176 F 7 '14;
69:42 Ap 14 '17; 78:275 S 20 '19; 98:155, 276 Ag 9,
S 6 '24; 100:13, 87 Ja 3, 24 '25; 103:157 O 31 '25
2927
Strand Magazine (London) 50:576 N '15; 67:547 Je '24; 68:
343 O '24 2928
Sun (NY) F 3 '12 p9; Ja 31 '14 p9; Ja 16 '15 p9; Ap 13 '19
Books & The Book World, Section 7 p1; Ja 31 '25 p7;
Ag 4 '24 p13; Mr 2 '19 (bust by Jo Davidson); Ap 10
'26 p9 (Onorio Ruotolo); Ap 5 '24; My 4 '48 p 16 (May
Mott Smith) 2929
T. P.'s Weekly Mr 13 '15 2930
T. P.'s & Cassell's Weekly 1:176, 289, 474, 511 N 24, D
15 '23; Ja 19, 26 '24; 2:facing p67 My 10 '24; 2:576,
668 Ag 23, S 13 '24; 4:786 O 10 '25; ns 5:680, 833
Mr 6, Ag 3 '26; ns 8:271 Je 25 '27 2931
Theatre Arts 34:32 S '50 2932
Time 1, no 6: cover page Ap 7 '23 (Gordon Stevenson)
41:80 Mr 8 '43; 50:107-8 S 29 '47 2933
Times (London) Ag 4 '24 p12 2934
Time & Tide, 4, no 11:287 Mr 16 '23 2935
To-day (London) 5, no 26: facing p41 Ap '19 (Wilton
Williams) 2936
Transatlantic Review 2:facing p 104 Jl '24 (Jacob Epstein)
2937
Travel 37, no 6:14 O '21 2938
Tygodnik Illustrowany 55, no 16:308 Ap 18 '14 2939
Tygodnik Powszechny 9, no 21:6 O 4 '53; 11, no 48:1 D 8
'57; 12, no 42:8 O 19 '58 (Walter Tittle); 13, no
13:4 Mr 29 '59 2939a
Vanity Fair 22, no 1:54 Mr '24; 23, no 4:73 D '24 (Jacob
Epstein) 2939b
Weekly Dispatch O 23 '27 p19 2940
Weekly Westminster O 17 '25 (Muirhead Bone) 2941
Wiadomości 4, no 176-7:1 Ag 21 '49; 4, no 176-7:4 Ag 21
'49 (David Low); 9, no 7:1 F 14 '54 (Percy Anderson);
9, no 32:1 Ag 8 '54 (Walter Tittle); 11, no 43:2 O 21
'56; 12, no 51-2:9 D 22-29 '57; 13, no 11:3 Mr 16 '58
(Walter Tittle) 2941a
Wiadomości Literackie
1, no 2:1 Ja 13 '24; no 11:2 Mr 16 '24; no 19:3, 6 My
11 '24; no 21:6 My 25 '24; no 33:1, 6 Ag 17 '24; no

34:3 Ag 24 '24; no 38:2 S 21 '24 (caricature by Sava);
no 43:10 O 26 '24; no 45: 1 N 9 '24 (caricature by
Oscar Césare)
2, no 5:3 F 1 '25 (Jacob Epstein); no 11:2 Mr 15 '25
(Walter Tittle); no 13:3 Mr 29 '25 (caricature); no
16:2 Ap 19 '25; no 21:2 My 24 '25; no 23:3 Je 7 '25
(caricature); no 27:2 Jl 5 '25; no 46:5 N 15 '25 (Muirhead Bone); no 50:2 D 13 '25
3, no 8:5 F 21 '26; no 26:3 Je 27 '26; nos 28-9:1 Jl 8
'26
4, no 8:2 F 20 '27; no 14:3 Ap 3 '27 (William Rothenstein); no 26:4 Je 27 '27; no 27:2 Jl 3 '27; no 39:1 S
25 '27; no 49:3 D 4 '27 (Oscar J. W. Hansen); no 49:4
D 4 '27
5, no 12:1 Mr 18 '28; no 30:3 Jl 22 '28; no 48:1 N 25 '28
6, no 14:1 Ap 7 '29; no 24:3 Je 16 '29; no 49:1 D 8 '29;
no 51:3 D 22 '29
7, no 22:2 Je 1 '30
8, no 2:2 Ja 11 '31   2942
World Review 1:263 F 1 '26   2943
World Today (London) 49:320-1 324-6 Mr '27   2944
World's Work (London) 5:18 D '04   2945
World's Work (NY) 39:495 Mr '20; 42:189 Je '21; 46:114 Je
'23; (Walter Tittle) 47:121 D '23; 48:477 S '24 (Muirhead Bone); 53:2, 331-3, 446-7, 450-3 N '26, Ja-F
'27; 55:411 F '28 (Jacob Epstein)   2946

Motion Picture Films
Made From Conrad's Works

"Gaspar Ruiz."
"The Strong Man," a screenplay which Joseph Conrad in
1920 adapted from his short story, "Gaspar Ruiz."
The work is unpublished and has not been filmed.
2947
Laughing Anne. 1954
(Reviewed by Kate Cameron in Daily News (NY) My 8
'54 p18) 2948
Lord Jim. From the novel by Joseph Conrad. Directed
by Victor Fleming. A Paramount Picture. 1925
(Reviewed in Exceptional Photoplays 6:4 N '25) 2949
Lord Jim. Written and directed by Richard Brooks. A
Columbia-Keep Films Co-production, released by
Columbia Pictures. 1965
(Reviewed by Rose Pelswick in New York Journal-
American F 26 '65 p21; Judith Crist in New York
Herald Tribune F 26 '65; Bosley Crowther in New
York Times F 28 '65) 2950
Nostromo.
"The Silver Treasure." A film made by Fox Film
Corporation, derived from Joseph Conrad's Nostromo.
1926 2951
An Outcast of the Islands. London Films. 1951
(Reviewed by Alton Cook in World-Telegram and Sun
(NY) My 16 '52 p18; Doré Silverman in Coming
Events in Britain Ja '52 p24-5) 2952
The Rescue. Samuel Goldwyn. 1929
(Reviewed by Mordaunt Hall in New York Times Ja 14
'29 p20, Ja 20 '29 Section 8 p7; William McFee in
New York Times Ja 27 '29 Section 9 p8) 2953
Romance.
"The Road to Romance." Metro-Goldwyn-Mayer. 1927
2954
The Secret Agent.
"The Woman Alone." Gaumont British Picture Corpora-
tion. 1936 2955

The Secret Agent.
  "I Married a Murderer." (after 1936)   2956
"The Secret-Sharer."
  "Face to Face." Theasquare Productions. Released
    through RKO Radio Pictures. 1952   2957
Under Western Eyes.
  "Razumov." Productions André Daven, Paris. 1937.
    Released in the United States through Brandon Films,
    1938. (In French)   2958
Victory. Paramount-Artcraft. 1919   2959
Victory. Produced in England, November, 1920.
    (Conrad had nothing to do with this production) 2960
Victory.
  "Dangerous Paradise." Paramount. 1930   2961
Victory. Paramount. 1941
    Screen play by John L. Balderston   2962

Index
(Numbers refer to entries)

Atteridge, A. Hilliard 40
Attorp, Gösta 41
Aubry, Georges Jean- 43, 171,
429, 842, 879, 899, 900,
1077, 1246, 1813, 2174-5,
2217, 2250, 2253, 2346,
2370, 2377, 2387, 2395,
2404, 2412a, 2413a,
2416, 2432a, 2480, 2482-3,
2514-15, 2524, 2533,
2536, 2540, 2544, 2547,
2555, 2559, 2583, 2595-6,
2601, 2603, 2607, 2611,
2617, 2619, 2627a, 2629,
2682, 2686, 2694a, 2695,
2717
Auernheimer, Raoul 44
Austen, Jane 1837
Austin, Hugh P. 45
Austin, Mary 46, 2069
Avi-Shaul, Mordekhay 2484a
Aylward, W. J. 2071, 2259
Aynard, Joseph 47, 2277
Azowa, W. A. 2500

Baasner, Peter 50
Babb, James T. 51, 2718
Bacewicz, Wanda 51a
Bache, William B. 52
Bachrach, A. G. H. 53
Bacon, H. L. 2247
Bacon, Josephine D. 54a
Bączkowska, Irena 53a
Baeza, Ricardo 2496, 2588
Bagg, D. B. 54
Baily, John 430a
Baines, Jocelyn 42b, 55, 943,
1333, 1344, 2171
Baker, Carlos 42b
Baker, Cynthia P. 56
Baker, Ernest A. 57, 2611a,
2719
Baker Library, Dartmouth
College 115a, 430, 2064,
2188, 2237, 2335, 2339
Baldensperger, F. 528
Balderston, John L. 58a,
2962

Baldi, Edgardo 2491
Balfour, Lord 1351
Baliński, Ignacy 58b
Balkan, Sadik M. 1337
Ballard, E. G. 59
Balzac, Honoré de 578, 1890
Bancroft, William W. 60
Bantock, Geoffrey H. 61
Baranowicki, Antoni 61a
Barber, Charles L. 743,
1333, 2171
Barklund, Gunnar 2483a
Barrie, C. D. O. 2213
Barrymore, Ethel 561
Barth, Emil 62
Barthlome, Mary 62a
Bartlett, Paul 63
Bartoszewicz, Kazimierz 64
Baskett, S. S. 65
Baskin, Leonard 1740
Bass, Eben 66
Bastide, Charles 2672
Bataille, Georges 67
Bates, Herbert E. 68, 417
Batho, Edith 69, 2720
Battin, Joan 70
Baughan, E. A. 2160
Baum, Paul F. 71
Bayley, John 72, 1333
Bayne, C. Lambert 73
Beach, Joseph W. 74, 697,
1079
Beachcroft, T. O. 75
Beaupré, Barbara 2396
Bebee, M. 75a
Becker, May L. 76
Becker, Robert J. 77
Beckwith, E. C. 60
Bedient, Calvin 1269
Beebe, Maurice 78
Beer, Thomas 79, 2274, 2333
Beerbohm, Max 80, 1344,
2839
Begun, Jean E. 81
Behler-Hagen, Mally 2069,
2327, 2562, 2569
Beker, Miroslav 82
Belden, Albert D. 83

398

Brooks, Benjamin G. 1585
Brooks, John 310a
Brooks, Philip 2718
Brooks, Richard 2950
Brooks, Van Wyck 154, 185, 310a, 430b
Brotman, Jordan L. 186
Broun, Heywood 1749, 2247
Brown, Allen B. 148
Brown, Bob 187
Brown, Dorothy S. 188
Brown, Douglas 189
Brown, E. K. 190
Brown, Emerson L. 191
Brown, Leonard S. 192, 2135
Brown, (Rabbi) Louis 1354
Browne, Alex F. 193
Browning, Robert 409, 483
Brownrigg, (Rear Admiral) Douglas 194
Bruccoli, Matthew J. 195, 778
Bruecher, Werner 196
Bruffee, Kenneth A. 197
Brule, A. 2505
Bruno, Francesco 2490, 2509a
Brusar, Branko 2591a, 2648
Brusewitz, E. 2378, 2400
Bryson, Lyman 749, 1456, 1457
Brzeska, W. 198
Brzezinski, Roman 199
Brzozowski, Stanisław 200
Buck, Jule R. 201
Buckler, William E. 202
Buddhism 1771
Buddingh, C. 2372
Budrecki, Lech 203
Budtz-Jørgensen, Inger 2433a
Budziak, Lydia M. 204
Buenzod, Emmanuel 2260, 2483
Bullen, Frank T. 1434, 1943
Bullett, Gerard W. 205, 2279
Bullis, Helen 2069

Bullock, J. M. 2279
Bunge, M. E. 2357
Bunikiewicz, Maria 2371, 2556
Bunting, Basil 2250
Burdett, Osbert 305, 1255
Burgess, C. F. 206
Burgess, O. N. 207
Burkhard, Sonja 2644a
Burkhardt, Johanna 208
Burkhart, Charles 209
Burner, Jarvis 210
Burnshaw, Stanley 1854a
Burrell, Angus 170
Burrough, (Captain) 766
Burt, H. T. 211
Burt, Struthers 212
Burton, D. L. 213
Busja, Andrzej 215, 2088
Butcher, Fanny 215a, 599
Butler, Lillian 216
Butler, Samuel 483
Buus, Barbara 215b

C., C. 217
Cadby, Carine 217
Cadby, Will 218, 2839, 2844, 2862, 2864
Cadot, Raoul 219
Caffyn, W. H. 1590, 2861
Cagle, William R. 220
Cambon, Glauco 221
Cambridge University Library 2211
Camesasca, Ettore 2509
Camerino, A. 222
Cameron, Kate 2948
Campbell, Archibald Y. 2160
Campbell, Malcolm 223
Campioni, Hilda 2441
Camus, Albert 677, 140ɔa, 1767, 1914
Canario, John W. 224
Canby, Henry S. 225
Cancogni, Franca V. 2382
Candee, Marjorie D. 226
Cândido, Antônio 227
Candler, Edmund 2333

405

411

Doyle, A. Conan 1259
Dreiser, Theodore 1259
Drew, Elizabeth A. 516
Drinkwater, John 517
Droz, Juliette 518
Drucker, Rebecca 518a
Drzewiecki, Jerzy 519
Dudley, Edward J. 520
Dudzinski, Bolesław 521
Duffin, Henry C. 522
Duggan, (Sister) Mary R. 523
Duke, T. Arch. 524
Duméril, Pierre 1863
Dunbar, O. H. 2213
Duncan-Jones, E. E. 525
Dunn, Frederick D. 526
Dupee, F. W. 2129
Duproix, Marthe 2694
Dürr, Jan 527
Dutton, George B. 2007
Duvignaud, Jean 527a
Dyboski, Roman 528, 1405

Eagar, Hannah 529
Eagle, Solomon [pseud.] 530, 1758
Eames, R. P. 531
Eaton, Walter P. 532, 2160
Eaves, T. C. Duncan 1001
Eberhard, Florence L. 533
Eberhardt, Konrad 42c
Echeron, W. J. C. 534
Eckert, Elise 2368, 2419, 2622, 2644
Eddleman, Ruth E. 535
Edel, Leon 889
Edgar, Pelham 536, 2758
Edgett, Edwin F. 299, 2053, 2069, 2213, 2216, 2228, 2247, 2250, 2260, 2261, 2263, 2295, 2303, 2312, 2323, 2332
Edgren, C. Hobart 536a
Edwards, Oliver 538
Eggink, Clara 2519
Ehrentreich, Alfred 539

Eichler, A. 2211, 2261
Eigo-Seinen 540
Einstein, Carl 542
Elektor 12
Eleuter 1320
Elgart, Josef 2354
Eliot, T. S. 483, 1179, 1328, 1866
Ellis, Havelock 543
Ellis, James N. 544
Ellis, S. M. 2216
Ellison, Ralph 310a
Ellmann, R. 54
Ellsberg, Edward 545
Elphinstone, Petronella 546
Elvin, George 547
Emberson and Sons 2839
Emmet, Alida 548
Enders, Anthony T. 549
Endres, Fritz 550
Eno, Sara W. 2759
Enright, D. J. 863
Entwhistle, William J. 551
Epron, Madeleine 552
Epstein, Jacob 553, 554, 554a, 1101, 1520a, 2839, 2880, 2897, 2937, 2939a, 2942, 2946
Eren, Nuri 2475
Eric, Howard 2266
Eric, Marguerite 2266
Erne, Nino 555
Ervine, St. John 556
Eschbacher, Robert L. 557
Esenberg, K. 558
Espey, John 215, 824
Estaunie, Edouard 559, 842
Estelrich, Juan 560, 2663
Estness, Carol 780
Etto, Jorma 2651a
Eurén, Teresia 2498
Evans, Benjamin I. 305, 381, 417, 562
Evans, C. S. 563
Evans, H. Herman 2760
Evans, J. M. 564
Evans, Powys 565

Forster, Edward M. (cont.)
602, 620, 2611a
Foulke, Robert D. 603
Fox, Charles D. 2079
Fox, R. M. 604
France, Anatole 1336
Francillon, Robert 605, 842
Francis, Kent W. 606
Franklin, John 2330
Franzen, Erich 607, 2309,
2599
Franzero, C. M. 608
Franzoni, Orfeo J. 609
Fraser, G. S. 610
Fraser, John 1202
Frederic, Harold 2211, 2283
Fredro, Alexander 142, 1938
Freeman, Dana W. 611
Freeman, John 612
Freeman, Rosemary 613
Freislich, Richard 614
Freissler, Ernst W. von 615,
1214, 2390, 2393, 2407,
2429, 2433, 2476, 2493,
2503, 2569, 2625, 2657,
2689, 2705, 2709
French, Samuel, Ltd. 786
Frenkel, Mieczysław R. 616
Freud, Sigmund 837, 1176
Freund, Philip 617
Frewer, Louis B. 618
Fricker, Robert 619
Friedman, Alan H. 620
Friedman, Joseph H. 621
Friedman, M. J. 787
Friedman, Norman 622
Frierson, William C. 624
Frisé, A. 625
Fry, Ruth J. 626
Fryde, L. 627
Frye, Northrop 628
Fryer, Benjamin N. 629
Fryer, Eugénie M. 2261
Fryling, Jan 630
Fuchs, Carolyn 630a
Fuchsówny, Joli 305, 306
Fuessle, Kenneth 2263

Füger, Wilhelm 686
Fukizawa, Tadae 2525
Furmanik, S. 2551
Furphy, A. A. 633
Fyfe, Hamilton 2053

Gadda, Carlo E. 2577
Gałczyńska-Folkierska, Anna
635
Gale, Bell 636
Galindo, Marco-Aurelio 2376,
2411, 2552, 2579, 2615
Gaál, Andor 2645a
Gallaher, Elizabeth 637
Galland, René 2089
Gallino, Luciano 2710a, 2714a
Gallone, Alessandro 2473
Gallone, Maria 2489a
Galsworthy, John 43, 303,
428, 430, 590, 638, 842,
1228, 1555, 1724, 2097,
2101, 2141, 2142, 2160,
2192, 2242, 2331, 2457,
2706
Galsworthy, (Mrs.) John
2242, 2341
Gamska, J. 2666
Garczyński, Tadeusz 639
Gard, Robert R. 640
Gardiner, A. G. 641
Gardner, Frederick 2241
Gardner, Monica M. 642
Garland, Hamlin 643
Garland, Herbert 644, 705
Garner, Naomi 645
Garnett, Constance 43, 646,
1848c
Garnett, David 305, 647,
1091a, 2089, 2765
Garnett, Edward 42a, 43, 68,
305, 417, 429, 599, 638,
648, 705, 2089, 2166,
2211, 2213, 2242, 2256,
2260, 2266, 2277, 2279,
2294, 2300, 2327, 2339,
2457, 2513, 2715, 2765
Garrett, George 649

Górski, Kazimierz 700,
2349, 2494, 2586, 2655
Górski, Konrad 701
Gose, Elliott 702, 2014, 2144
Gosse, Edmund 1629a, 2826
Gossmann, Ann M. 704
Gottlieb, Hans J. 42b
Gould, Gerald 648, 705, 2108,
2261, 2303, 2312, 2330
Gower, Herschel 1940
Goyert, George 2622
Grabczak, E. 706
Grabo, Carl H. 707
Grabowski, Zbigniew A. 708,
2171, 2349
Graebsch, Irene 709
Graham, Anderson 2260
Graham, Robert B. C. 710
Graham, Stephen 711
Graver, Lawrence S. 712,
748, 791, 1706
Graves, Robert 381
Gray, Hugh 713
Graz, Albert G. 714
Green, A. Wigfall 716
Green-Armitage, Adrian 718
Green, Clarence C. 716a
Green, Jesse D. 717
Greenberg, Evelyn L. 719
Greenberg, Robert A. 720
Greene, David M. 721
Greene, Graham 305, 381,
722, 2089
Greene, Marc T. 723
Greene, Maxine 724
Greenep, Francis M. 725
Greenwood, Thomas 726
Gregory, Horace 2026
Greiffenhagen, Maurice
2140, 2247, 2299
Grein, James T. 727
Grenier, Jean 2617
Grenzow, Daisy B. 728
Grieg, J. Y. T. 729
Grieg, Nordahl 2643
Griffiss, John McLeod 730
Griffith, Paul 731

Griffiths, J. G. 732
Grodzicki, Bogusław 733,
2389
Groesbeck, Dan S. 2230
Groom, Bernard 734
Gross, Harvey 735
Gross, Seymour 168, 736
Grubiński, Wacław 737
Gruszecka, A. 2581
Grzegorczyk, Piotr 528, 739,
2769
Gschwind, Frank H. 740
Guardiola, Antonio 2518
Guebels, L. 741
Guedalla, Philip 742
Guerard, Albert J. 42b, 54,
310a, 743, 1344, 2013,
2171, 2235, 2277
Guetti, James L. 744
Guidacci, Margherita 2393a,
2611a
Guidi, Augusto 744a, 2585b
Guidotti, Mario C. 2490
Guiet, Pierre 745
Guiney, E. M. 748
Guixé, Juan 2687, 2693
Gullason, Thomas A. 746
Gun, Ben [pseud.] 747,
1323
Günter, Ernst Wolfgang
See: Freissler, Ernst W.
Gurko, Leo 54, 743, 748-9,
1333
Guthrie, William B. 750
Güttinger, Fritz 2709
Guze, Joanna 305
Gwynn, Frederick L. 23
Gwynn, Stephen 751

Hackbarth, Elisabeth 2368
Hackett, Alice P. 752
Hackett, Francis 753
Haedens, Kleber 754
Hagen, John 755
Hagopian, John 756
Hahn, Willard C. 757
Hainsworth, J. D. 758

Hajkova, Magda 2461a
Hale, Edward E. 2312
Hale, Thomas 759
Hall, James N. 760, 2166
Hall, Leland 761
Hall, Mordaunt 2593
Halle, Louis J. 762
Halling, A. 2488, 2616, 2632
Hallowes, L. M. 2334
Halman, C. Hugh 744
Halverson, John 763
Hamalian, Leo 764
Hamecher, Peter 765
Hamer, Douglas 766
Hamerman, Marjorie S. 766a
Hamilton, Cosmo 767
Hamilton, Elsie C. 768
Hamilton, Margaret 769
Hamilton, Mary A. 2108,
  2157, 2216, 2277, 2330
Hammond, Percy 116, 770
Hancke, Kurt 771
Hancox, P. 772
Hanley, James 773
Hansen, Harry 42a, 774,
  1320, 2086
Hansen, Oscar J. W. 2942
Hanson, Paul E. 775
Harden, Edgar F. 1269,
  1344, 1649, 1706, 2014
Hardwick, Elizabeth 775a
Hardy, Dudley 2247, 2305
Hardy, John E. 776
Hardy, Thomas 10, 68, 620,
  622, 823, 869, 1128, 1412,
  1901, 1939a, 2772
Harkness, Bruce 428, 431,
  668, 777-8, 1333, 1895
Harkness, Edward S. 2772
Harkness, Mary S. 2814
Harlow, Arthur H. 1850
Harman, (Captain) Howard
  784
Harper, George M. 779
Harrington, David V. 780
Harris, (Captain) C. M. 2116,
  2295

Harris, Frank 1620
Harris, G. W. 2166
Harris, Joshua 781
Harris, Mark 310a
Harris, Norman T. 781a
Harris, Russell L. 781b
Harrison, Joseph B. 2168
Harrod, Lee V. 781c
Hart, Henry G. 2277
Hart, Robert E. 782
Hart-Davis, Rupert 783
Harte, Bret 2715
Hartley, J. H. 2132
Hartley, L. P. 2279
Hartrick, A. S. 2288
Harvard University Library
  2188
Harvey, David D. 785
Harvey, W. J. 1706, 1812
Harwood, H. C. 2250, 2277,
  2330
Haslam, G. E. 2769a
Hastings, Basil Macdonald
  566, 786, 2204
Haugh, Robert F. 310a, 787
Hauptmann, Benvenuto 2360
Häusermann, Hans W. 788
Hausmann, Wolf 789
Hawk, Affable [pseud.] 790
Hawthorne, Nathaniel 1689
Hay, Eloise K. 791
Haycraft, Howard 1063, 2781
Hazeltine 1852
Heath, E. M. 792, 2876
Hedspeth, Robert N. 793
Heilman, Robert B. 794
Heimer, Jackson W. 795
Hein, Herta 796
Hellman, Geoffrey 1245
Helsztyński, Stanisław 797,
  943
Hemingway, Ernest 157, 622,
  798, 1181a
Hendrick, George 2827
Hendriks, Caspar 2713
Henkin, Leo J. 799
Henriot, Émile 800

423

Hoppenot, Hélène 2595
Hoppenot, Henry 2595
Horwill, Herbert W. 849
Horzyca, Wilam 850, 2391,
2409, 2427, 2586, 2697
Hostowiec, Paweł 851
Hough, Graham 852
Hourcade, Pierre 853
Housley, Robert W. 854
Howard, Gertrude G. 860
Howard, Hubert C. 861
Howe, Irving 863
Howland, L. D. 599
Howlett, Theodor J. 864
Hoyt, Eleanor M. 2299a
Hrynkiewicz-Moczulski,
Mariusz 306, 864a
Huber, Thomas 864b
Hudson, W. H. 302, 429, 599,
1629a, 2101, 2715
Hudspeth, Robert N. 865
Hueffer, Ford M. 303, 599,
825, 855, 866, 1290
Hughes, Helen S. 1146
Hughes, M. Richard 1424
Humbourg, Pierre 867, 2430
Huneker, James G. 43, 509,
868, 1678, 1869, 2069
Huneker, Josephine 868
Hunt, Jasper B. 2176
Hunt, Kellogg W. 23, 869
Hunt, Violet 690, 869a
Hunter, Robert A. 870
Huntington, John W. 871
Huntsman-Trout, Pamela 872
Hurst, Fannie 310a
Hutchinson, Vere 873
Hutchison, Percy A. 42a,
305, 430c, 874, 2086,
2157, 2160, 2250, 2277,
2279
Huxley, Aldous 381, 1091,
1161
Hyman, Stanley E. 743
Hynes, Samuel 875, 2014,
2144
Inge, W. R. 903

Irving, H. B. 566
Isaacs, Neil D. 1105
Ivory, P. V. E. 2121
Iwaskiewicz, Anna 1250
Iwaszkiewicz, Jarosław 42c,
879, 2707
Izzo, C. 880
Jabłkowska, Róża 25, 142,
305, 442, 528, 578, 739,
881, 943, 1032, 1046,
1054, 1076, 1097, 1430,
1732, 1813, 1863, 1907,
2032, 2097, 2166, 2397,
2495, 2710
Jackson, Charlotte 748
Jackson, Holbrook 430b,
882, 2053, 2303, 2312
Jacob, Heinrich E. 883
Jacobs, Robert G. 884
Jacyna, Felix M. 885
Jaffé, Adrian 1738
Jahier, Piero 886, 2486,
2513, 2631, 2706
Jahn, Lela 2576
Jakimiak, Z. 887
Jaloux, Edmond 842, 888,
2672
James, Henry 43, 75, 190,
825, 889, 1016, 1027,
1144, 1307, 1412, 1418,
1570, 1799, 1890
Jamison, Laura 890
Janicki, Stanisław 890a
Jankowski, C. 2349
Jankowski, Józef 891
Janssen, J. 892
Janta-Połczynski, Aleksander
894
Janta, Alexander 893
Janusz, Herlaine 895
Jasieńczyk, Janusz 896, 2546
Jasienica, Paweł 897
Jasiénskiego, M. 2210
Jasiński, Zbigniew 897a
Jaworski, Roman 898, 1405
Jean-Aubry, Georges 899

Kinkead, A. S. 2340
Kinney, Arthur F. 1003
Kinninmont, Kenneth 1004
Kipling, Rudyard 43, 131,
   303, 450, 1005, 1006,
   1471, 1591, 2154, 2715
Kirk, Carey H. 1007
Kirschner, Paul 1008
Kishler, Thomas C. 158,
   1009
Kisielewski, Zygmunt 1010,
   2349, 2494, 2586, 2630
Kiss, Dezsö 2353a
Kivivjori, Kristiina 2574a
Kiwcowoj, A. W. 2531
Kjw [pseud.] 1011, 2018
Kleczkowski, Paul 1012
Kleczkowski, Stefan 1013
Klein, Barbara J. 1014
Klein, Leo 2457
Kleiner, Juliusz 1015
Klemperer, Elizabeth G. von
   1016
Klingopulos, G. D. 54, 1017,
   2171
Kliszczewski, H. Spirydion
   1018, 1246
Kloth, Friedrich 1019
Klub Miłośników Conrada 1020
Knickerbocker, Francis W.
   2168
Knight, Grant C. 1021
Knopf, Alfred A. 509, 1022

Knowlton, Edgar C. 1023
Kobrzyński, Bolesław 1024
Koc, Barbara 1025
Koch, Ivan L. 1026
Kociemski, Leonard 2327,
   2412, 2660
Kocmanová, Jessie 1027
Koćówna, Barbara 120, 142,
   261, 439, 442, 528, 627,
   708, 739, 881, 1028, 1029,
   1032, 1054, 1059, 1076,
   1159, 1340, 1356, 1426,
   1471, 1490, 1557, 1763,

1863, 1949, 1993, 2027,
   2032, 2207
Koeppen, Wolfgang 1030
Koestler, Arthur 1017
Kohl, Louis V. 2574
Kohler, Dayton 1031
Kołaczkowski, Stefan 1032,
   2494, 2558, 2608, 2612,
   2666, 2685
Kolb, Jonathan E. 1033
Kolodziejczyk, J. 1034
Komornicka, M. 2460
Königsgarten, Hugo F. 1035
Korbut, Gabrjel 1036, 2778a
Korniłowicz, Jadwiga 238,
   1448, 2510
Korniłowicz, Maria 42, 2209,
   2510
Korzeniowska, (Mrs.) Jessie
   Conrad 1037
Korzeniowski, Apollo N.
   1038, 1286, 1805
Korzeniowski, Joseph 1039
Kosch, Teodor 1041
Kossak, Jerzy 1042
Kostiainen, O. 2469
Kott, Jan 246, 442, 692,
   1043
Kovarna, F. 1044
Kowalkowski, Alfred 1045
Kowalska, Aniela 1046
Koziarska, Aleksandra 1046a
Kozicki, Stanisław 1047
Kozlay, Charles M. 2715
Kozłowski, W. M. 1048
Kramer, Dale 1049
Kranendonk, A. G. van 1050,
   1880
Kraushaar, Richard 2610
Krčméry, Ivan 2649a
Kreemers, R. 1051, 1255
Kreisel, Henry 1052
Kridl, Manfred 460, 1054,
   1097
Krieger, Adolf P. 2283
Krieger, Murray 1055

1570, 2053, 2247
Mansion, J. E. 244, 1216
Marble, Annie R. 1221
Marcellini, Giovanni 1222,
   2412
Marcuse, Ludwig 1223
Mare, Walter de la 2303
Marinho, José 2448a
Markey, Gene 509
Marković, Vida 1224
Marks, A. D. 2046
Marquet, Jean 1225
Marquina, Rafael 2352, 2364
Marriott, James W. 175
Marrot, Harold V. 1226
Marryat, (Capt.) Frederick 774
Marsh, D. R. C. 1227
Marshall, Margery F. 1228
Martell, Elizabeth 791
Martin, Christopher W. 1229
Martin, David M. 1230
Martin, Dorothy 1231
Martin, Ernest 1232
Martin, (Sister) M. 1233
Martin, W. R. 1235
Maryskova, K. 1234
Masback, Frederic J. 1236
Masefield, John 862, 1237,
   1454, 2327, 2332
Maser, Frederick E. 1238
Mason, John E. 1239
Mason, Louise M. 1240
Massaguer, Conrada 767
Massey, B. W. A. 1240a
Masson, Thomas L. 2250,
   2333
Masterman, G. F. 1661, 1890
Masuda, Yoshiro 2454a, 2455
Mat., St. 1243
Mather, Frank J. Jr. 2299a
Mathew, Ralph 1242a
Mathews, R. G. 2866
Matuszewski, Ryszard 442,
   881, 1611
Matysik, Stanisław 1243
Maud, Ralph 1243a
Maugham, Somerset 1183

Maupassant, Guy de 1008,
   1926, 2009, 2125, 2341
Maurice, Furnley 1244
Maurice, André 430c, 638,
   842, 1245
Maurois, André 2672
Maxwell, John A. 2116
Maxwell, J. C. 1246
Maxwell, Perriton 1247
May, Nell A. 1248
Mayne, Ethel C. 1249
Mayne, Richard 743
Mayoux, Jean-Jacques 1250
Mazzotti, Giuliana 1251
Medanić, Lav 1253a
Mee, Arthur 1253b
Mégroz, Rodolphe L. 42a,
   381, 1255, 1320, 2788
Meixner, John A. 1256
Meldal, C. T. 2358, 2423,
   2433a, 2703
Meldrum, David S. 114, 2053,
   2069, 2171, 2277, 2303
Mélisson-Dubreil, Marie-Rose
   1257
Mellor, Ann P. 1257a
Meloney, (Mrs.) William B.
   1258
Melville, Herman 12a, 221,
   225, 717, 744, 1202, 1240a,
   1366a, 1609, 1776, 1791
Mencken, Henry L. 42a, 305,
   430b, 595, 599, 1259, 1259a,
   1911, 2053, 2069, 2216,
   2228, 2230, 2247, 2250,
   2260, 2263, 2279, 2299a,
   2300, 2303, 2312, 2327,
   2333
Mendilow, Adam A. 1260
Mentch, Bruce L. 1261
Meonoff, Anna H. 2441
Mérédac, Savinien 1262
Meredith, Floyd 1263
Meredith, George 1144
Meredith, Mark 1264
Meriwether, James B. 778
Merrick, Addison H. 1265

Moses, Elizabeth P. 1334
Moss, Mary 2213
Moult, Thomas 599, 1335, 2330
Mouradian, Jacques 1336
Moustafa, Sadik 1337
Mowat, Angus McGill 1338
Mowat, H. J. 2140
Moynihan, William T. 1339
Mroczkowski, Przemysław 1340
Muccigrosso, Robert M. 1341
Muddiman, Bernard 1342
Mudrick, Marvin 12, 54, 80, 430a, 431, 599, 743, 1333, 1343-4, 1579, 1836, 1975, 2026
Muir, Edwin 516, 1345, 2089
Muirhead, J. F. 2157
Mukherjee, Sujit K. 1346
Mulford, Stockton 2140
Müller, Erich 1347, 1789
Mueller, Hans A. 2082
Muller, Herbert J. 60, 1348
Mummendey, Richard 2689a
Munro, Neil 1349
Muntz, Herbert E. 1350
Murdoch, Walter L. F. 1351
Murphy, Daniel J. 1352
Murphy, J. F. 2168
Murray, Phyllis M. 1353
Murry, J. Middleton 1215
Musset, Alfred de 1849

Nagler, Herminia 1355, 1813
Nairne, Campbell 417
Najder, Zdzisław 23, 303, 943, 1356-8, 1814, 1890, 2088, 2182, 2185, 2459, 2530, 2558, 2635
Nakano, Yoshio 2438a
Nałęcz-Korzeniowska, Wanda 305, 881
Nalepiński, Tadeusz 1359
Nałkowska, Zofia 1360
Namora, Fernando 2477a
Napier, Edna M. 1361

Napier, James 1362
Napierski, Stefan 1363
Nash, James E. 2223
Nathan, George J. 1364, 2327
Nathan, Robert 310a
National Library, Edinburgh 2211
Naujokaitis, Z. 2468a
Navin, Thomas R. Jr. 1364a
Neel, Philippe 867, 2174, 2395, 2403, 2408, 2430, 2464, 2505, 2659, 2672
Nelson, Harland S. 1365
Nelson, Kenneth G. 1366
Nelson, Mary K. 1366a
Neményi, Imre 1402a
Neri, Ferdinando 1367
Neufeldówna, Bronisława 1368, 2543
Neuschäffer, Walter 1369
Nevins, Allan 2330
Nevinson, Henry W. 1370
Newberry, Samuel D. 2082
Newbolt, (Sir) Henry J. 1374
Newhouse, Neville H. 1375
Newman, Paul B. 1376
Newton, W. Douglas 2247
New York Public Library 212
Nield, Jonathan 1379
Niketas, George 1383
Niklewicz, Anna 2439, 2584
Nitsch, K. 2697
Noble, Edward 1384, 2111
Noble, James A. 2046
Nogueira, Hamilton 1385
Nolan, John A. 1386
Nolen, Jo Ann T. 1387
Nordby, Jack S. 1388
Noriega, Lawrence K. 1389
Norlen, Håken 2520
Norman, (Rev.) Charles J. 1389a
North, Douglas McKay 1389b
North, Ernest D. 2791
Norton, Sybil 405
Noskowski, Witold 1390, 2494
Nossig, (Dr.) Felicya 2571, 2664

2173, 2175
Rascoe, Burton 509, 1563, 2221, 2333
Raskin, Jonah 1564
Rathbone, Irene 381
Rathburn, Robert C. 1772, 1837
Rawson, C. J. 743, 791, 1565
Raymond-Duval, P. H. 2623
Rea, Gardner 1566
Read, Herbert 381, 1567, 2157
Reade, A. R. 1568
Ready, Marie E. 1569
Rebello, Marques 2380
Rébora, Piero 1570
Reck, R. D. 1580a
Reck-Halleczewen, Friedrich 1571
Redfern, Percy 1573
Redman, Ben Ray 251, 2216, 2235
Reed, (Dr.) J. G. 1574
Rees, Florence H. 1575
Rees, Richard 54, 1576
Rehder, Jessie 1578
Reichart, Karl H. 1789
Reid, Forrest 2330
Reid, Stephen A. 1344, 1579
Reilly, Joseph J. 152, 1580
Reinecke, George F. 1580a
Reisiger, Hans 2610
Renner, Louis 2497a
Resch, H. T. 1582
Resink, G. J. 1584
Retinger, Joseph H. 1585, 2179, 2228
Retinger, (Mrs.) Otolia 1586, 2037
Reymont, Ladislas 528
Reynolds, Ann 1588
Reynolds, Stephen 1589
Rheault, Charles A. Jr. 195
Rhys, Ernest 1590
Rice, Howard C. 1591
Rice, Wallace 2327
Richardson, (Captain) Leslie 1593

Richardson, Samuel 151
Richmond, Ralph 1594
Rickert, Edith 1212
Ridd, John C. 1595
Rider, Fremont 2260
Ridley, Florence H. 1596
Riegel, Jacob Jr. 2073
Riesemann, Oskar Von 1597
Riesenberg, (Captain) Felix 1598, 2157
Rieser, Dolf 2297
Rita, Sister 1599
Rivière, Isabelle 430, 2672
Rivoallan, A. 1600
Robert, Wilma A. 1601
Roberts, Cecil 1602
Roberts, Iris S. 1603
Roberts, James L. 1603a
Roberts, John H. 1604
Roberts, Mark 1812
Roberts, R. Ellis 2157, 2247, 2250
Robertson, John M. 1605
Robinson, Boardman 2278
Robinson, E. Arthur 1606
Robinson, Lennox 2053
Robson, W. W. 54, 743, 1607
Roche, Alphonse V. 476
Rockwood, Stanley 1608
Rodes, Roberta M. 1609
Roditi, Edouard 1610
Roehl, (Sister) 1610a
Rogalski, Aleksander 1611
Rogers, Bruce 27a, 629, 2194, 2293
Rogers, B. J. 1612
Rogers, Philip E. 1612a
Rogers, W. A. 1613
Roldanus, W. J. A. Jr. 2415a, 2498a
Rolle, Michal 1615
Rolo, Charles J. 42b
Roman, F. Vinci 2330
Romano, Alberto 1617
Rooney, Lawrence F. 1619
Root, Edward M. 1620

Sayers, Dorothy L. 2064
Sayre, Ira C. 1665
Saxton, E. F. 509, 1664
Schaeffer, Mead 2250
Schelling, Felix E. 1666, 1956
Scheuer, Alwin J. 2729
Schickert, Werner 2548
Schieszlová, Olga 1667
Schiller, Leon 2681
Schirmer, Walter F. 84, 1668
Schlecht, Elvine 1669
Schlefer, Richard M. 1670
Schmahl, Eugene 2300
Schmitz, J. C. 1865
Schnack, Friedrich 1671
Schneider, Daniel J. 1672
Scholes, Robert 1673
Schorer, Mark 1674, 1927
Schrey, Kurt 2548
Schriftgiesser, Karl 42a, 1675
Schüddekopf, A. W. 2221, 2228, 2295, 2300
Schultheiss, Thomas 1676
Schulz, Ivan 2415
Schunk, Karl 1677
Schürenberg, W. 2374a, 2670
Schwab, Arnold T. 1678, 1895
Schwamborn, Heinrich 1679
Schwartz, Edward 1680
Schwartz, (Dr.) Jacob 2810
Schwarz, Daniel R. 1680a
Schweikert, Harry C. 1681, 2140
Schwertman, Mary P. 1682
Scott-James, R. A. 1683, 2193, 2256, 2300, 2312
Scott-Moncrieff, Charles K. 2245
Scribe, Oliver 2277
Scribner, Arthur H. 2715
Scrimgeour, Cecil 1684
Scrimgeour, Gary J. 1685
Sea 12, 38, 117, 135, 180, 219, 258, 286, 293, 295,
306, 331, 364, 401, 403, 421, 450, 475, 499, 528, 599, 603, 608, 630, 655, 711, 711a, 856, 951, 986, 1045-6, 1058, 1093, 1126, 1188, 1197, 1199, 1232, 1237, 1245, 1422, 1450, 1507, 1577, 1589, 1628, 1709, 1729, 1736, 1745, 1775, 1791, 1795, 1809, 1870, 1898, 1917, 1943, 2015, 2026, 2212, 2254, 2282
Sealaw [pseud.] 1852
Sealey, Ethel 1686
Seaman's Church Institute 343, 358, 623, 667, 1123, 1496, 1687, 1850, 1882
Seaver, Lillian F. 1688
Sebba, Helen 42
Sečanov, Liuben 2700
Seccombe, Thomas 2053, 2261
Secor, Robert A. 1689
Sée, Ida R. 1691
Segel, H. B. 215
Segur, Nicolas 2595
Sehrt, E. T. 1789
Seldes, Gilbert 2166, 2247, 2250
Seligmann, Herbert J. 2330
Séligmann-Lui, Geneviève 2345, 2443
Selle, Cäcilie 1693
Semenović, Luka 2422a
Seravalli, Luigi 743
Serpieri, Alessandro 2456a
Sewall, Richard B. 1711
Seymour, W. K. 1706
Shackelford, Louis B. 1695
Shafer, L. A. 2069
Shakespeare, William 93, 1136, 1556, 1676, 1702
Shand, John 42a, 1694, 2157
Shanks, Edward B. 42a, 1695
Shannon, Homer S. 1696
Shapira, Morris 889

Sobol, Ken 1746a
Sobotkiewicz, Gustaw 2209
Soderberg, Sten 2512a
Soens, A. L. 778
Solomon, Barbara 1747
Solomon, Eric 1748
Solomon, W. L. 1749
Solomons, Annie 2646
Somerier, Cornelia E. 1750
Somerville, Peter F. 1751,
2146
Sotheby, Wilkinson & Hodge,
London 2813
Sotteck, Julie 2295
Spalding, Branch 1752
Speaight, Robert 381
Spector, Robert D. 23, 748,
1753
Sper, Felix 1754
Spervogel, Görge 2478-9,
2626, 2684
Spicer-Simson, Theodore
1755
Spinner, Kaspar 1756
Spivak, Charlotte K. 1756a
Spoerri-Müller, Ruth 1757
Spriggs, S. Squire 2256
Spurrier, S. 2267
Squire, (Sir) John C. 42b,
530, 1758, 2216, 2250,
2277, 2279
Stackpole, Edouard A. 1759
Stallman, Robert W. 415,
566, 573, 578, 670, 736,
743, 1107, 1214, 1286,
1333, 1339, 1343, 1694,
1760-1, 1771, 1828, 1921,
1953, 1986, 2024
Stanga, Carolyn A. 1762
Staniewski, Maurycy 1763
Stanoyevich, Millivay S. 2231
Staral, Margarete 1764
Stark, Freya 381
Stark, Lewis M. 2772, 2814
Starrett, Vincent 2146
Stasko, (Sister) Mary L. 1765
Stauffer, Ruth M. 1766, 2815

Stavrou, C. N. 1767
Stawell, Florence M. 1768
Stedmond, John 743, 787
Steegmuller, Francis 697,
2168
Steele, Frederic D. 2058,
2229
Stegner, Wallace 1769
Stein, Marion L. 1770
Stein, William B. 1771
Steinbeck, John 310a
Steinmann, Martin 1772, 1837
Stenberg, T. 1766
Stencel, Michelle M. 1773
Stephens, Rosemary 1773a
Stepp, Nancy T. 1774
Stern, Anatol 1775
Sternberg, Sima 1776
Steslicki, Arthur 2235
Stevens, Arthur W. 1777
Stevens, B. F. 2204
Stevenson, Gordon 2933
Stevenson, Robert L. 261,
317, 1323, 1441, 1540a
Stewart, John I. M.
1778
Stewart, Powell 1779
Stillman, Clara G. 305
Stoddard, Richard H. 2222
Stoessl, Otto 1780
Stoińska, Celina 1781
Stone, Laurence 2839
Stoneman, Maj-Lis-Rissler
2513, 2706
Stonier, G. W. 305
Story, Mattison L. 1782
Stowarzyszenie, W. 42c
Straat, E. 1783
Straight, Michael 54, 1784
Strandberg, A. Edith 1785
Strandgaard, Henrik 1786
Straus, Ralph 2277
Strawson, H. 1787
Streatfeild, Noel 381
Street, George S. 1788
Stresau, Hermann 1789, 2549,
2657

6, 270-1, 274, 278, 281, 284, 296, 298, 302a, 399, 403, 409-10, 413-14a, 420, 424, 432, 440, 446, 452, 458-9, 461-2, 469, 472, 478-9, 487, 490, 492, 496, 498, 512, 520, 523, 526, 529, 531, 533, 535, 544, 549, 569a, 572, 576, 579-80, 586a, 587, 589-90, 592, 603, 606, 609, 611, 620-1, 626, 633, 636-7, 640, 645, 650-1, 673-4, 677-8, 681, 688, 691, 696-7, 706, 712, 716a, 719, 728, 730, 744-5, 750, 759, 768, 772, 775, 777, 785, 787, 789, 791, 795-6, 802, 804-5, 810, 818-20, 824-5, 829, 832-3, 837-9, 843-4, 861, 864, 864a, 870-1, 872, 881, 884, 890, 902, 908, 910-12, 914, 970, 972, 976-7, 980, 983-4, 990-1, 993, 1007-8, 1014, 1016, 1019, 1025-6, 1033-4, 1052, 1060, 1064, 1071-2, 1077, 1078, 1078a, 1092-3, 1099, 1100, 1102, 1111-12, 1116-17, 1120, 1122, 1122a, 1126a, 1128, 1130, 1135a, 1137-8, 1143-4, 1152, 1161, 1170, 1174, 1176-8, 1180-1, 1183, 1189, 1192, 1201, 1213, 1228-30, 1240, 1248, 1257, 1260-1, 1265, 1267, 1270, 1272, 1283, 1299, 1307-8, 1314, 1316, 1318-19, 1320a, 1322, 1325, 1333-4, 1337-8, 1350, 1352-3, 1361, 1366, 1366a, 1383, 1386, 1387-9, 1403, 1408-9, 1413, 1415, 1418, 1421, 1423, 1431, 1436, 1439, 1441, 1446-7, 1449, 1451, 1454, 1458, 1462, 1464, 1465, 1467, 1474, 1479-81, 1486, 1520, 1523, 1525, 1529, 1530, 1540, 1545, 1546-7, 1549, 1552, 1556, 1569, 1575, 1588, 1595, 1601, 1603, 1608-9, 1612, 1612a, 1619, 1624-6, 1628, 1632, 1634, 1635-7, 1649, 1657, 1663, 1665, 1669-70, 1677, 1680, 1680a, 1682, 1688-9, 1693, 1697-8, 1700-1, 1707, 1717, 1717a, 1722-3, 1730, 1731, 1733, 1736-7, 1742, 1743a, 1744, 1746-7, 1750, 1752, 1762, 1764, 1765-6, 1770, 1773-4, 1776-7, 1782, 1785, 1791, 1793, 1796, 1806-7, 1811, 1815-18, 1822, 1829, 1838, 1841, 1856-8, 1868, 1870, 1876, 1881, 1883, 1908-10, 1914, 1917-19, 1922, 1926, 1932, 1935-7, 1950, 1958, 1960-1, 1969, 1971, 1976, 1977, 1979, 1986-7, 1992a, 1996, 2004-5, 2011, 2013, 2022, 2031, 2038, 2040

Thiébaut, Marcel 42, 2629
Thiess, Frank 1830
Thomas, Edward 1831, 2260
Thomas, Jean 305
Thomas, William H. 638
Thompson, Alan R. 422, 1320, 1832
Thompson, (Sir) Ivan 1833
Thomson, David S. 1834
Thomson, Fred C. 1344
Thomson, J. C. 2816
Thorgersen, Thorvald 2424
Thorogood, Horace 2250, 2277, 2279
Thorp, James 2053
Thorpe, Michael 1706
Thurston, Jarvis 2817
Tick, Stanley 1835
Tillyard, Eustace M. W. 1344, 1836

Weintraub, Wiktor 1938, 2381
Weisinger, Herbert 1738
Weiss, Ernst 1939, 2420, 2493
Weitzenkorn, Louis 599, 1939a, 2250
Welker, Robert L. 1940
Wellek, René 1941, 2349
Welles, Evelyn 1942
Wellisz, Leopold 1942a
Wells, Catherine 1943
Wells, Evelyn 817
Wells, Gabriel 2323, 2743
Wells, Herbert G. 43, 185a, 303, 807, 849, 1732, 1944, 1963, 2141, 2222, 2457
Welsh, A. 1945
Weltmann, Lutz 1946
Wendell, Barrett 874
Wertheim, W. F. 1947
Werumeus Buning, J. W. F. 1948
Wescott, Glenway 310a
Węsławska, Emilja 1949, 2460
Wesolowski, Florence 1950
Wesselhoeft, Edward C. 1950a
West, A. 54
West, Geoffrey 1255
West, H. F. 1951
West, Paul 1952
West, Ray B. 1760, 1953
West, Rebecca 1954
Wethered, Herbert N. 1955
Weygandt, Cornelius 1956
Wharton, (Mrs.) Edith 1957, 2202, 2233, 2262, 2289
Whelan, Robert 1958
Whibley, Charles 2221
Whicher, G. F. 1585
Whistler, James McNeill 2186
White, Stewart E. 2256
Whiteford, Robert N. 1959
Whitehead, Lee M. 1960
Whiteley, Thomas S. 1961

Whiteford, Robert N. 1959
Whitehead, Lee M. 1960
Whiteley, Thomas S. 1961
Whitford, Robert C. 2216
Whiting, George W. 704, 1962
Whitlock, Brand 1963
Whitman, Walt 409
Whittemore, Reed 1964
Whittier, H. S. 677
Whyte, Frederic 1965
Wibberley, Leonard 12, 430a
Wickenden, Dan 310a
Widmer, Kingsley 1967
Wieniawa-Długoszowski, Bolesław 2454
Wierzbica, Hanna 2609
Wiegler, Paul 1968
Wiendlocka, Maria 1969
Wierzyński, Kazimierz 1405, 1970
Wilcock, Edith 1971
Wilcox, Stewart C. 1972
Wild, Friedrich 1973
Wilde, Oscar 1526
Wilder, Thornton 310a
Wilding, Michael 1974
Wiley, Paul L. 1344, 1975
Wilhelm, Frederick O. 1976
Wilhelmi, J. 305
Wilkening, Vjera 1977
Willard, Grace 305, 2157, 2279
Williams, Blanche C. 2079
Williams, Eluned 1979
Williams, Eric 1980
Williams, George W. 1981
Williams, Harold 1982
Williams, I. A. 2824
Williams, Lloyd 2256
Williams, Michael 1983
Williams, Porter 1984
Williams, Sydney 2277
Williams, Wilton 2936
Williamson, Claude C. 1985
Willingham, J. R. 748, 1333
Willoughby, D. 2247

Wills, John H. 1986
Willson, Constance G. 1987
Wilson, Angus 1987a
Wilson, Arthur H. 1988
Wilson, Edgar 2186
Wilson, Edmund 1989
Wilson, Edward A. 509,
2293, 2756
Wimsatt, W. K. 1990
Winawer, Bruno 2181, 2250,
2344, 2558, 2581
Winebaum, B. V. 743
Wing, William G. 2235
Winter, Calvin 430b
Winter, John L. 1991
Winter, L. B. 1992
Winter, Thelma V. P. 1992a
Winterich, John T. 2825
Wirpsza, Witold 1993
Wise, Thomas James 16,
354, 430, 1859, 2046,
2047, 2050-1, 2057, 2060-
1, 2080, 2129, 2162, 2219,
2229, 2233, 2241, 2262,
2268, 2271, 2290, 2292,
2305, 2341, 2734, 2762,
2769a, 2786, 2795, 2812,
2818a, 2818b, 2826
Wisehart, M. K. 1993a
Wister, Owen 1994
Wit, Augusta de 1995
Witt, Dorothy 1995a
Wittig, Kurt 2312
Wittmeyer, Herman F. 1996
Wohlfarth, Paul 1998
Wojdowski, Bogdan 42c
Wojtowicz, Zdzisław 1999
Wolfe, Peter 2000
Wollnick, Ludvig 2001
Wołosowa, Marka 2502
Wolpers, Theodore 2001a
Wolski, Stefan 2002
Wood, Gardner W. 2295
Wood, Miriam H. 2003
Wood, William P. 2004
Woodruff, Neal 310a, 2005
Woolcott, Alexander 80

Woolf, Leonard S. 2006-7,
2250, 2277
Woolf, Virginia S. 81, 622,
1161, 2007
Woroniecki, Edward 2008
Worth, George J. 2009
Wötzel, Erich 2442
Wouk, Herman 310a
Wright, Edgar 2011
Wright, Elizabeth 2827
Wright, Elizabeth C. 2012
Wright, Walter F. 23, 1975,
2013, 2014, 2144
Wright, Willard H. 2221
Wüscher, Albert 2017
Wyka, Kazimierz 1011, 2018
Wyrzykowski, Stanisław 2506,
2608-9, 2683
Wyzewa, Teodor de 2019,
2260, 2300

Yale University Library 323,
2020, 2048, 2053, 2104,
2128, 2158, 2191, 2211,
2223, 2233, 2261, 2300,
2340
Yates, Norris W. 2021
Yelton, Donald C. 2022
Yeongyun, Ra 2434a
Yoshio, Nakano 2440
Young, Barbara 2023
Young, Filson 2023a, 2250
Young, Francis B. 130
Young, Vernon 1333, 1975,
2024
Young, W. J. 2024a

Zabel, Morton D. 12, 305, 310a,
430a, 697, 1344, 2026,
2082, 2168, 2171, 2235,
2281, 2828
Zabielska, Janina 2784, 2829
Zabierowski, Stefan 881,
1356
Zabłocki, Stefan 2585
Zadig, Bertrand 2844, 2848a,
2848b

448

WITHDRAWN